AF616361

THE SACRED BOOKS OF THE EAST

Translated by

VARIOUS ORIENTAL SCHOLARS

Edited by

F. MAX MÜLLER

Vol. 46

SACRED BOOKS OF THE EAST

(50 VOLUMES)

Series Editor : *F. Max-Müller*

ISBN: 978-81-208-0101-1 (Set) Rs. 15000 (Each Vol. Rs. 350)

These volumes of the Sacred Books of the East series include translations of all the most important works of the seven non-Christian religions that have exercised a profound influence on the civilisations of the continent of Asia. The Vedic Brahmanic system claims 21 volumes, Buddhism 10, and Jainism 2; 8 volumes comprise Sacred Books of the Parsis; 2 volumes represent Islam; and 6 the two main indigenous systems of China. Translated by twenty leading authorities in their respective fields, the volumes have been edited by the late F. Max Müller. The inception, publication and the compilation of these books cover almost 34 years.

I. BUDDHISM

Vol. 49: Buddhist Mahayana Texts (2 Parts)
Vol. 11: Buddhist Suttas
Vol. 10: The Dhammapada and Sutta Nipata
Vols. 35 & 36: The Questions of King Milinda (2 Parts)
Vol. 21: The Saddharma Pundarika or the Lotus of the True Law
Vols. 13, 17 & 20: Vinaya Texts (3 Parts)

II. CHINESE

Vol. 19: The Fo-Sho-Hing-Tsan-King
Vols. 3, 16, 27, 28, 39 & 40: The Sacred Books of China (6 Parts)

III. A GENERAL INDEX

Vol. 50: A General Index to the Names and Subject-matter of the Sacred Books of the East

IV. ISLAM

Vols. 6 & 9: The Qur'an (2 Parts)

V. JAINISM

Vols. 22 & 45: The Jaina Sutras (2 Parts)

VI. PARSIS

Vols. 5, 18, 24, 37 & 47: Pahlavi Texts (5 Parts)
Vols. 4, 23 & 31: The Zend-Avesta (3 Parts)

VII. VEDIC-BRAHMANIC SYSTEM

Vol. 8: The Bhagavadgita with the Sanatsujatiya and the Anugita
Vols. 29 & 30: The Grihya-Sutras: Rules of Vedic Domestic Ceremonies (2 Parts)
Vol. 42: Hymns of the Atharva Veda together with Extracts from the Ritual Books and the Commentaries
Vol. 7: The Institutes of Vishnu
Vol. 25: The Laws of Manu
Vol. 33: The Minor Law Books
Vols. 2 & 14: The Sacred Laws of the Aryas as Taught in the Schools of Apastamba, Gautama, Vasishtha and Baudhayana (2 Parts)
Vols. 12, 26, 41, 43 & 44: The Satapatha Brahmana According to the Text of the Madhyandina School (5 Parts)
Vols. 1 & 15: The Upanishads (2 Parts)
Vols. 34 & 38: The Vedanta Sutras (2 Parts)
Vol. 48: The Vedanta-Sutras (with the commentary by Ramanuja)
Vols. 32 & 46: Vedic Hymns (2 Parts)

VEDIC HYMNS

PART II
HYMNS TO AGNI (MANDALAS I-V)

Translated by
HERMANN OLDENBERG

MOTILAL BANARSIDASS PUBLISHERS
PRIVATE LIMITED • DELHI

8th Reprint: Delhi, 2013
First Published by the Oxford University Press, 1887

ISBN: 978-81-208-0147-9

MOTILAL BANARSIDASS
41 U.A. Bungalow Road, Jawahar Nagar, Delhi 110 007
8 Mahalaxmi Chamber, 22 Bhulabhai Desai Road, Mumbai 400 026
203 Royapettah High Road, Mylapore, Chennai 600 004
236, 9th Main III Block, Jayanagar, Bangaluru 560 011
Sanas Plaza, 1302 Baji Rao Road, Pune 411 002
8 Camac Street, Kolkata 700 017
Ashok Rajpath, Patna 800 004
Chowk, Varanasi 221 001

UNESCO COLLECTION OF REPRESENTATIVE WORKS— Indian Series
This book has been accepted in the Indian Translation Series of the UNESCO Collection of Representative Works, jointly sponsored by the United Nations Educational Scientific and Cultural Organization (UNESCO) and the Government of India

Printed in India

by RP Jain at NAB Printing Unit,
A-44, Naraina Industrial Area, Phase I, New Delhi–110028
and published by JP Jain for Motilal Banarsidass Publishers (P) Ltd,
41 U.A. Bungalow Road, Jawahar Nagar, Delhi-110007

RASHTRAPATI BHAVAN,
NEW DELHI-4
June 10, 1962

I am very glad to know that the Sacred Books of the East, published years ago by the Clarendon Press, Oxford, which have been out-of-print for a number of years, will now be available to all students of religion and philosophy. The enterprise of the publishers is commendable and I hope tne books will be widely read.

S. RADHAKRISHNAN

PREFATORY NOTE TO THE NEW EDITION

Since 1948 the United Nations Educational, Scientific and Cultural Organization (UNESCO), upon the recommendation of the General Assembly of the United Nations, has been concerned with facilitating the translation of the works most representative of the culture of certain of its Member States, and, in particular, those of Asia.

One of the major difficulties confronting this programme is the lack of translators having both the qualifications and the time to undertake translations of the many outstanding books meriting publication. To help overcome this difficulty in part, UNESCO's advisers in this field (a panel of experts convened every other year by the International Council for Philosophy and Humanistic Studies), have recommended that many worthwhile translations published during the 19th century, and now impossible to find except in a limited number of libraries, should be brought back into print in low-priced editions, for the use of students and of the general public. The experts also pointed out that in certain cases, even though there might be in existence more recent and more accurate translations endowed with a more modern apparatus of scholarship, a number of pioneer works of the greatest value and interest to students of Eastern religions also merited republication.

This point of view was warmly endorsed by the Indian National Academy of Letters (Sahitya Akademi), and the Indian National Commission for UNESCO.

It is in the spirit of these recommendations that this work from the famous series "Sacred Books of the East" is now once again being made available to the general public as part of the UNESCO Collection of Representative Works.

PUBLISHER'S NOTE

First, the man distinguished between eternal and perishable. Later he discovered within himself the germ of the Eternal. This discovery was an epoch in the history of the human mind and the *East was the first to discover it.*

To watch in the Sacred Books of the East the dawn of this religious consciousness of man, must always remain one of the most inspiring and hallowing sights in the whole history of the world. In order to have a solid foundation for a comparative study of the Religions of the East, we must have before all things, complete and thoroughly faithful translation of their Sacred Books in which some of the ancient sayings were preserved because they were so true and so striking that they could not be forgotten. They contained eternal truths, expressed for the first time in human language.

With profoundest reverence for Dr. S. Radhakrishnan, President of India, who inspired us for the task; our deep sense of gratitude for Dr. C. D. Deshmukh & Dr. D. S. Kothari, for encouraging assistance; esteemed appreciation of UNESCO for the warm endorsement of the cause; and finally with indebtedness to Dr. H. Rau, Director, Max Müller Bhawan, New Delhi, in procuring us the texts of the Series for reprint, we humbly conclude.

CONTENTS.

	PAGE
INTRODUCTION	xi
HYMNS, TRANSLATION AND NOTES:—	
Ma*nd*ala I, 1	1
12	6
13 Âprî Hymn	8
26	13
27	16
31	22
36	31
44	37
45	42
58	45
59	49
60	52
65	54
66	57
67	61
68	64
69	67
70	70
71	74
72	82
73	88
74	92
75	95
76	96
77	100
78	102
79	103
94	108

	PAGE
Ma*nd*ala I, 95	114
96	119
97	125
98	127
99	128
127	129
128	137
140	141
141	147
142 Âprî Hymn	153
143	157
144	160
145	164
146	167
147	170
148	173
149	176
150	178
188 Âprî Hymn	179
189	181
II, 1	186
2	193
3 Âprî Hymn	198
4	202
5	206
6	209
7	211
8	213
9	215
10	217
III, 1	219
2	228
3	232
4 Âprî Hymn	236
5	240
6	244
7	248
8	252
9	256

		PAGE
Mandala III,	10	259
	11	261
	12 To Indra-Agnî	263
	13	266
	14	268
	15	271
	16	273
	17	275
	18	277
	19	279
	20	281
	21	283
	22	285
	23	287
	24	289
	25	291
	26	292
	27	296
	28	300
	29	302
IV,	1	307
	2	316
	3	325
	4	331
	5	335
	6	340
	7	343
	8	346
	9	348
	10	350
	11	352
	12	354
	13	356
	14	358
	15	360
V,	1	363
	2	366
	3	371
	4	375

PAGE

Ma*nd*ala V, 5 Âprî Hymn 377
6 379
7 382
8 385
9 387
10 389
11 391
12 393
13 395
14 397
15 399
16 401
17 403
18 405
19 407
20 410
21 412
22 413
23 414
24 415
25 416
26 418
27 420
28 423

APPENDICES:—

I. Index of Words 427

II. List of the more important Passages quoted in the Notes 487

Transliteration of Oriental Alphabets adopted for the Translations of the Sacred Books of the East . . 497

INTRODUCTION.

IN preparing this volume, which contains the greater part of the Agni hymns of the Rig-veda, namely, those of the Ma*nd*alas I–V, the translator enjoyed the high advantage of Professor Max Müller's assistance, in the way stated in the Introduction to the first volume of Vedic Hymns, Sacred Books of the East, vol. xxxii, p. xxvii.

H. O.

KIEL:
November, 1895.

VEDIC HYMNS.

MA*ND*ALA I, HYMN 1.

ASH*T*AKA I, ADHYÂYA 1, VARGA 1–2.

1[1]. I magnify[2] Agni, the Purohita, the divine ministrant of the sacrifice, the Hot*ri* priest, the greatest bestower of treasures.

2. Agni, worthy to be magnified by the ancient *Ri*shis and by the present ones—may he conduct the gods hither.

3. May one obtain through Agni wealth and welfare day by day, which may bring glory and high bliss of valiant offspring.

4. Agni, whatever sacrifice and worship[1] thou encompassest on every side, that indeed goes to the gods.

5. May Agni the thoughtful Hot*ri*, he who is true and most splendidly renowned, may the god come hither with the gods.

6. Whatever good thou wilt do to thy worshipper, O Agni, that (work) verily is thine, O Aṅgiras

7. Thee, O Agni, we approach day by day, O (god) who shinest in the darkness[1]; with our prayer, bringing adoration to thee—

8. Who art the king of all worship, the guardian of *Ri*ta, the shining one, increasing in thy own house.

9. Thus, O Agni, be easy of access to us, as a father is to his son. Stay with us for our happiness.

NOTES.

The hymn is ascribed to Madhu*kkh*andas Vai*s*vâmitra, and may possibly belong to an author of the Vi*s*vâmitra family. See my Prolegomena, p. 261. Metre, Gâyatrî. The hymn has been translated and commented upon by M. M., Physical Religion, pp. 170–173.

Verse 1 = TS. IV, 3, 13, 3; MS. IV, 10, 5. Verse 3 = TS. III, 1, 11, 1; IV, 3, 13, 5; MS. IV, 10, 4 (IV, 14, 16). Verse 4 = TS. IV, 1, 11, 1; MS. IV, 10, 3. Verse 7 = SV. I, 14. Verses 7–9 = VS. III, 22–24; TS. I, 5, 6, 2; MS. I, 5, 3.

Verse 1.

Note 1. This verse being the first verse of the Rig-veda as we now possess it, seems already to have occupied the same position in the time of the author of the hymns X, 20–26. For, after a short benediction, the opening words of this collection of hymns are also agním î*l*e, 'I magnify Agni.' Comp. my Prolegomena, p. 231.

Note 2. The verb which I translate by 'magnify'—being well aware that it is impossible to do full justice to its meaning by such a translation—is î*d*. There seems to me no doubt that this verb is etymologically connected with the substantives ísh, 'food,' í*d*, í*d*â, írâ (not with the root ya*g* of which Brugmann, Indogermanische Forschungen I, 171, thinks). We need not ask here whether the connection between î*d* and ísh is effected by a 'Wurzeldeterminativ' (root-determinative) d—in this case we should have here î*d* for izhd, comp. nî*d*a for nizhda, pî*d* for pizhd, &c.; see Brugmann's Grundriss, vol. i, § 591—or whether î*d* is a reduplicated present of i*d* (of the type described by Brugmann, Grundriss, vol. ii, p. 854; comp. î́rte, &c.). The original meaning of î́*d*e at all events seems to be 'I give sap or nourishment.' Now in the Vedic poetry and ritual, the idea of sap or nourishment is especially connected with the different products coming from the cow, milk and butter. The footsteps of the goddess I*d*â drip with butter. The words 'agnim î*d*e' seem to me, consequently, originally to convey the idea of celebrating Agni by pouring sacrificial butter into the fire. There is a number of passages in the Rig-veda which, in my opinion, show clear traces of this original meaning of the verb. Thus we read X, 53, 2. yá*g*âmahai ya*gñ*íyân hánta devā́n ī́*l*âmahai ī́*d*yân ā́*g*yena, 'let us sacrifice (ya*g*) to the gods to whom sacrifice is due; let us magnify (î*d*) with butter those to whom magnifying is due.' V, 14, 3. tám hí *s*á*s*vanta*h* ī́*l*ate sru*k*ā́ devám gh*ri*ta*sk*útâ agním havyā́ya vó*l*h*ave, 'for all people magnify this god Agni with the butter-dripping sacrificial spoon that he may carry the sacrificial food.' V, 28, 1. devā́n ī́*l*ânâ havíshâ gh*ri*tā́*k*î, 'magnifying the gods with sacrificial food, (the spoon) filled with butter.' Comp. also I, 84, 18; VI, 70, 4; VIII, 74, 6; X, 118, 3. Then, by a gradual development, we find the verb î*d* or the noun î*l*enya connected with such instrumentals as girā́ or gîrbhí*h*, 'to magnify by songs,' or stómai*h* 'by praises,' námasâ 'by adoration,' and the like. The Rig-vedic texts, however, show us very clearly that even in such phrases the original meaning of î*d* was not quite forgotten. For the word is not used indifferently of any praise offered to any god whatever. No god of the Vedic Pantheon is praised so frequently and so highly by the poets of the Rig-veda as Indra. Yet, with very few exceptions, the word î*d* is avoided in connection with this god. The whole ninth Ma*nd*ala contains nothing but praises of Soma Pavamâna. Yet the word î*d* occurs, in the whole of this Ma*nd*ala, in two passages only (5, 3; 66, 1) of which one is contained in an Âprî verse transferring artificially to Soma such qualifications as belong originally to Agni. On the other hand, in the invocations addressed to Agni, this verb and its derivatives are most frequently used. We may conclude that the idea of celebration, as conveyed by these words, had a connotation which qualified them for the employment with regard to Agni, the god nourished by offerings of butter, much better than for being addressed to Indra, the drinker of the Soma juice, or to the god Soma himself.

Last comes, I believe, the meaning of *îd* as contained in a very small number of passages such as VII, 91, 2. índra-vâyû sustutí*h* vâm iyânấ mâr*d*îkám î*tt*e suvitám *k*a návyam, 'Indra and Vâyu! Our beautiful praise, approaching you, asks you for mercy and for new welfare.' Here the construction of *îd* is such as if in English the phrase, 'men magnify the gods for obtaining mercy,' could be expressed in the words 'men magnify the gods mercy.'

I conclude by quoting the more important recent literature referring to *îd*: Prof. Max Müller's note on V, 60, 1 (S. B. E. vol. xxxii, p. 354); Physical Religion, p. 170; Bezzenberger, Nachrichten von der Göttinger Gesellsch. d. Wissensch. 1878, p. 264; Bechtel, Bezzenberger's Beiträge, X, 286; Bartholomae, ibid. XII, 91; Arische Forschungen, II, 78; Indogermanische Forschungen, III, 28, note 1; Brugmann, Indogermanische Forschungen, I, 171; K. F. Johansson, Indogermanische Forschungen, II, 47. Comp. also Bartholomae, Arische Forschungen, I, 21; III, 52, and Joh. Schmidt, Kuhn's Zeitschrift, XXXII, 389.

Verse 4.

Note 1. 'Worship' is a very inadequate translation of adhvara, which is nearly a synonym of *yagña*, by the side of which it frequently stands. Possibly in the designation of the sacrifice as *yagña* the stress was laid on the element of prayer, praises, and adoration; in the designation as adhvara on the actual work which was chiefly done by the Adhvaryu.—Prof. Max Müller writes: 'I accept the native explanation a-dhvara, without a flaw, perfect, whole, holy. Adhvara is generally an opus operatum; hence adhvaryu, the operating priest.' Comp. Physical Religion, p. 171. Bury's derivation of adhvara from madhu (m̥̥dhu-ara, Bezzenberger's Beiträge, VII, 339) is much more ingenious than convincing.

Verse 7.

Note 1. I have translated dóshâvastar as a vocative which, as is rendered very probable by the accent, was also the opinion of the diaskeuasts of the Sa*m*hitâ text.

The author of the sacrificial formula which is given in Â*s*val. *S*raut. III, 12, 4 and *S*ânkh. G*ri*hy. V, 5, 4, evidently understood the word in the same way; there Agni is invoked as doshâvastar and as prâtarvastar, as shining in the darkness of evening and as shining in the morning. That this may indeed be the true meaning of the word is shown by Rig-veda III, 49, 4, where Indra is called kshapā́m vastā́, 'the illuminator of the nights' (kshapā́m is gen. plur., not as Bartholomae, Bezzenberger's Beiträge, XV, 208, takes it, loc. sing.). The very frequent passages, however, in which case-forms of doshā́ stand in opposition to words meaning 'dawn' or 'morning'—which words in most cases are derived from the root vas—strongly favour the opinion of Gaedicke (Der Accusativ im Veda, 177, note 3) and K. F. Johansson (Bezzenberger's Beiträge, XIV, 163), who give to dóshâvastar the meaning 'in the darkness and in the morning.' This translation very well suits all Rig-veda passages in which the word occurs. If this opinion is accepted, doshâvastar very probably ought to be written and accented as two independent words, doshā́ vástar. See M. M., Physical Religion, p. 173.

MA*ND*ALA I, HYMN 12.

ASH*T*AKA I, ADHYÂYA 1, VARGA 22–23.

1. We choose Agni as our messenger, the all-possessor, as the Hot*ri* of this sacrifice, the highly wise.

2. Agni and Agni again they constantly invoked with their invocations, the lord of the clans, the bearer of oblations, the beloved of many.

3. Agni, when born, conduct the gods hither for him who has strewn the Barhis (sacrificial grass)[1]; thou art our Hot*ri*, worthy of being magnified[2].

4. Awaken them, the willing ones, when thou goest as messenger, O Agni. Sit down with the gods on the Barhis.

5. O thou to whom Gh*ri*ta oblations are poured out, resplendent (god), burn against the mischievous, O Agni, against the sorcerers.

6. By Agni Agni is kindled (or, by fire fire is kindled), the sage, the master of the house, the young one, the bearer of oblations, whose mouth is the sacrificial spoon.

7. Praise Agni the sage, whose ordinances for the sacrifice are true, the god who drives away sickness.

8. Be the protector, O Agni, of a master of sacrificial food who worships thee, O god, as his messenger.

9. Be merciful, O purifier, unto the man who is rich in sacrificial food, and who invites Agni to the feast of the gods.

10. Thus, O Agni, resplendent purifier, conduct

the gods hither to us, to our sacrifice and to our food.

11. Thus praised by us with our new Gâyatra hymn, bring us wealth of valiant men and food.

12. Agni with thy bright splendour be pleased, through all our invocations of the gods, with this our praise.

NOTES.

This hymn is ascribed to Medhâtithi Kâ*n*va. It is the opening hymn of a collection which extends from I, 12 to 23 (not, as Ludwig, III, 102, believes, from I, 2 to 17; see my Prolegomena, p. 220). That the authorship of this collection belongs indeed to the Kanva family, whose poetical compositions are found partly in the first and partly in the eighth Ma*nd*ala, is shown by the text of 14, 2–5, and by other evidence; see Zeitschr. der Deutschen Morg. Gesellschaft, XXXVIII, 448.

The metre is Gâyatrî. It is possible, though I do not think it probable, that the hymn should be considered as consisting of T*rik*as. Verse 1 = SV. I, 3; TS. II, 5, 8, 5; V, 5, 6, 1; TB. III, 5, 2, 3; MS. IV, 10, 2. Verses 1–3 = SV. II, 140–142; AV. XX, 101, 1–3. Verse 2 = TS. IV, 3, 13, 8; MS. IV, 10, 1. Verse 3 = TB. III, 11, 6, 2. Verses 6, 8, 9 = SV. II, 194–196. Verse 6 = TS. I, 4, 46, 3; III, 5, 11, 5; V, 5, 6, 1; TB. II, 7, 12, 3; MS. IV, 10, 2 (3). Verse 7 = SV. I, 32. Verse 10 = VS. XVII, 9; TS. I, 3, 14, 8; 5, 5, 3; IV, 6, 1, 3; MS. I, 5, 1.

Verse 3.

Note 1. On v*r*iktábarhis, comp. RV. I, 116, 1; M. M., vol. xxxii, pp. 84 seq., 109; Geldner, P. G., Vedische Studien, I, 152.

Note 2. On î́*d*ya*h*, comp. the note on î*d*e I, 1, 1.

MA*N*D*A*LA I, HYMN 13.

ASH*T*AKA I, ADHYÂYA 1, VARGA 24–25.

Âprî Hymn.

1[1]. Being well lighted, O Agni, bring us hither the gods to the man rich in sacrificial food, O Hot*ri*, purifier, and perform the sacrifice.

2. Tanûnapât[1]! make our sacrifice rich in honey and convey it to-day to the gods, O sage, that they may feast.

3. I invoke here at this sacrifice Narâ*s*a*m*sa[1], the beloved one, the honey-tongued preparer of the sacrificial food.

4. O magnified[1] Agni! Conduct the gods hither in an easy-moving chariot. Thou art the Hot*ri* instituted by Manus[2].

5. Strew, O thoughtful men, in due order[1] the sacrificial grass, the back (or surface) of which is sprinkled with butter, on which the appearance of immortality[2] (is seen).

6. May the divine gates open, the increasers of *Ri*ta, which do not stick together, that to-day, that now the sacrifice may proceed.

7. I invoke here at this sacrifice Night and Dawn, the beautifully adorned goddesses, that they may sit down on this our sacrificial grass.

8. I invoke these two divine Hot*ri*s[1], the sages with beautiful tongues. May they perform this sacrifice for us.

9. I*l*â ('Nourishment'), Sarasvatî, and Mahî ('the great one')[1], the three comfort-giving goddesses, they who do not fail, shall sit down on the sacrificial grass.

10. I invoke hither the foremost, all-shaped Tvashtri to come hither; may he be ours alone.

11. O tree[1], let the sacrificial food go, O god, to the gods. May the giver's splendour be foremost.

12. Offer ye the sacrifice with the word Svâhâ to Indra in the sacrificer's house. Thereto I invoke the gods.

NOTES.

The hymn is ascribed, as the whole collection to which it belongs, to Medhâtithi Kâ*n*va (see the note on the preceding hymn). Its metre is Gâyatrî. Verses 1–4 = SV. II, 697–700. Verse 9 = RV. V, 5, 8. Verse 10 = TS. III, 1, 11, 1; TB. III, 5, 12, 1; MS. IV, 13, 10.

The hymn belongs to the class of Âprî hymns, which were classed by the ancient arrangers of the Sa*m*hitâ among the Agni hymns. The Âprî hymns, consisting of eleven or twelve verses, were destined for the Prayâ*g*a offerings of the animal sacrifice (comp. H. O., Zeitschrift der D. Morg. Gesellschaft, XLII, 243 seq.). They were addressed, verse by verse in regular order, partly to Agni, partly to different spirits or deified objects connected with the sacrifice, such as the sacrificial grass, the divine gates through which the gods had to pass on their way to the sacrifice, &c. The second verse was addressed by some of the *Ri*shi families to Tanûnapât, by some to Narâ*s*a*m*sa; in some of the hymns we find two verses instead of one (so that the total number of verses becomes twelve instead of eleven) addressed the one to Tanûnapât, the other to Narâ*s*a*m*sa. Bergaigne (Recherches sur l'histoire de la Liturgie Védique, p. 14) conjectures that some of the *Ri*shi families had only seven Prayâ*g*as. This opinion is based on the identical appearance of four verses (8–11) in the Âprî hymns of the Vi*s*vâmitras (III, 4) and of the Vasish*th*as (VII, 2), and on the diversity of metres used in two other Âprî hymns, IX, 5 and II, 3. To me this conjecture, though very ingenious, does not seem convincing.

With the text of the Âprî hymns should be compared the corresponding Praishas of the Maitrâvaru*n*a priest, i.e. the orders by which this priest directed the Hot*ri* to pronounce the Prayâ*g*a invocations. The text of these Praishas is given Taitt. Brâhm. III, 6, 2.

Comp. on the character and the historical and ritual position of the Âprî hymns, Max Müller, Hist. Anc. Sansc. Literature, p. 403 seq.; Roth, Nirukta, notes, p. 121 seq.; Weber, Indische Studien, X, 89 seq.; Ludwig V, 315 seq.; Hillebrandt, Das Altindische Neu- und Vollmondsopfer, 94 seq.; Schwab, Das Altindische Thieropfer, 90 seq.; Bergaigne, Recherches sur l'histoire de la Liturgie Védique, 13 seq.

Verse 1.

Note 1. Comp. Delbrück, Syntactische Forschungen, I, 97.

Verses 2, 3.

Note 1. Does Tanûnapât, lit. 'son of the body,' mean, as Roth and Grassmann believed, 'son of his own self' (comp. I, 12, 6. agnínâ agní*h* sám idhyate, 'by Agni Agni is kindled'), or is the meaning 'le propre fils' (Bergaigne, Rel. Védique II, 100)? Narâ*s*a*m*sa, which is nearly identical with the Avestic Nairyôsanha, means 'the song of men,' or 'praised by men' (Bergaigne, l. l. I, 305; M. M.'s note on VII, 46, 4). In III, 29, 11 it is said of Agni: 'He is called Tanûnapât as the foetus of the Asura; he becomes Narâ*s*a*m*sa when he is born.' Of course an expression like this is by no means sufficient to prove that the sacrificial gods Tanûnapât and Narâ*s*a*m*sa, as invoked in the Âprî hymns, are nothing but forms of Agni. Expressions which are constantly repeated in the Âprî verses show that the work of Tanûnapât, and likewise that of Narâ*s*a*m*sa, consisted in spreading gh*ri*ta or 'honey' over the sacrifice.

Verse 4.

Note 1. 'Magnified' is î*l*itá*h*; comp. the note on I, 1, 1. The third, or if both Tanûnapât and Narâ*s*a*m*sa are invoked, the fourth verse of the Âprî hymns is regularly addressed to Agni with this epithet î*l*ita.

Note 2. Manurhita, 'instituted by Manus,' not 'by men.' See Bergaigne, Religion Védique, I, 65 seq.

Verse 5.

Note 1. On ânushák, comp. Pischel, Vedische Studien, II, 125.

Note 2. The last Pâda is translated by Grassmann, 'wo der unsterbliche sich zeigt' (comp. Bergaigne, R.V. I, 194, note 1); by Ludwig, 'auf dem man das unsterbliche sieht.' To me it seems impossible to decide, so as to leave no doubt, whether am*ri*tasya is masculine or neuter. Comp. also Atharva-veda V, 4, 3; 28, 7; XIX, 39, 6-8, in which passages the phrase am*ri*tasya *k*ákshaṇam recurs.

Verse 8.

Note 1. The two divine Hot*ri*s are mentioned in the Rig-veda only in the eighth (or seventh) verse of the Âprîsûktas and besides in two passages, X, 65, 10; 66, 13, which do not throw any light on the nature of these sacrificial gods. They are called *g*âtavedasâ VII, 2, 7, purohitau X, 70, 7, bhisha*g*â Vâ*g*. Sa*m*h. XXVIII, 7. As regards the duality of these divine counterparts of the human Hot*ri* priest, possibly the 'two Hot*ri*s' should be understood as the Hot*ri* and the Maitrâvaru*n*a; the latter was the constant companion and assistant of the former in the Vedic animal sacrifice. Comp. Schwab, Altindisches Thieropfer, 96, 114, 117, &c.; H. O., Religion des Veda, 391.

Comp. on the two divine Hot*ri*s also Bergaigne, R.V. I, 233 seq.

Verse 9.

Note 1. On I*l*â, see H. O., Religion des Veda, pp. 72, 326.—With regard to Mahî Bergaigne (Rel. Védique, I, 322) has pronounced the opinion that 'Bhâratî et Mahî, qui, tantôt se remplacent, tantôt se juxtaposent tout en paraissant ne compter que pour une, se confondent aux yeux des *ri*shis.' But Pischel (Ved. Studien, II, 84 seq.) has shown that the eminent French scholar was wrong, and that really Mahî ('the great one') is independent of Bhâratî. Pischel's own opinion that Mahî is a name of the goddess Dhishaṇâ, does not seem to me to be established by sufficient reasons.—On the meaning of these three goddesses Prof. Max Müller writes: 'I should not fix on Nourishment as the true meaning of Iḷâ. Originally those three goddesses seem to be local: Iḷâ, the land or daughter of Manu, the Sarasvatî, and another river here called Mahî.'

Verse 11.

Note 1. To me it seems evident that the tree, or, to translate more literally, the lord of the forest (vanaspati) invoked in this Âprî verse can only be the sacrificial post (yûpa) to which the victim was tied before it was killed. The yûpa is called vanaspati in the Rig-veda (III, 8, 1. 3. 6. 11) as well as in the more modern Vedic texts (for inst., Taitt. Saṃh. I, 3, 6, 1).—In the Âprî hymn, IX, 5 (verse 10), the vanaspati is called sahasravalsa: with this should be compared III, 8, 11 (addressed to the yûpa): vánaspate satávalsaḥ ví roha sahásravalsâḥ ví vayám ruhema, 'O lord of the forest, rise with a hundred offshoots; may we rise with a thousand offshoots!'—In the Âprî hymn, X, 70 (verse 10), the rope (rasanâ) is mentioned by which the vanaspati should tie the victim; comp. with this expression the statements of the ritual texts as to the rasanâ with which the victim is tied to the yûpa; Schwab, Das Altindische Thieropfer, 81. Comp. also especially Taittirîya Brâhmaṇa III, 6, 11, 3.—In the Âprî hymns the vanaspati is frequently invoked to let loose the victim; in connection therewith mention is made of the sacrificial butcher (samitṛi), see II, 3, 10; III, 4, 10; X, 110, 10, and comp. Vâg. Saṃhitâ XXI, 21; XXVIII, 10. The meaning of these expressions becomes clear at once, if we explain the vanaspati as the sacrificial post. When they are going to kill the victim, they loosen it from the post; the post, therefore, can be said to let it loose. Then the butcher (samitṛi) leads the victim away. See the materials collected by Schwab, Thieropfer, p. 100 seq., and comp. also H. O., Religion des Veda, 257.

MANDALA I, HYMN 26.

ASHTAKA I, ADHYÂYA 2, VARGA 20–21.

1. Clothe thyself with thy clothing (of light), O sacrificial (god), lord of all vigour; and then perform this worship for us.

2. Sit down, most youthful god, as our desirable Hotri, through (our prayerful) thoughts[1], O Agni, with thy word[2] that goes to heaven.

3. The father verily by sacrificing procures (blessings) for the son[1], the companion for the companion, the elect friend for the friend.

4. May Varuna, Mitra, Aryaman, triumphant with riches (?)[1], sit down on our sacrificial grass as they did on Manu's.

5. O ancient Hotri, be pleased with this our friendship also, and hear these prayers.

6. For whenever we sacrifice constantly[1] to this or to that god, in thee alone the sacrificial food is offered.

7. May he be dear to us, the lord of the clan, the joy-giving, elect Hotri; may we be dear (to him), possessed of a good Agni (i. e. of good fire).

8. For the gods, when possessed of a good Agni, have given us excellent wealth, and we think ourselves possessed of a good Agni.

9. And may there be among us mutual praises of both the mortals, O immortal one, (and the immortals)[1].

10. With all Agnis (i. e. with all thy fires), O Agni, accept this sacrifice and this prayer, O young (son) of strength[1].

NOTES.

This hymn, as well as the whole collection to which it belongs, is ascribed to *S*una*h*s*e*pa Âg*î*garti (comp. 24, 12. 13). The metre is Gâyatrî. Bergaigne (Recherches sur l'histoire de la Sa*m*hitâ, II, 7) divides this hymn into T*rik*as, with one single verse added at the end. I cannot find sufficient evidence for this; the appearance in the Sâma-veda (II, 967–9) of a T*rik*a composed of the verses 10. 6. 7 of our hymn is rather against Bergaigne's opinion.

Verse 2.

Note 1. Mánmabhi*h* may possibly mean, 'with thy (wise) thoughts;' comp., for instance, III, 11, 8. pári ví*s*vâni súdhitâ agné*h* a*s*yâma mánmabhi*h*, 'may we obtain every bliss through Agni's (wise) thoughts,' or 'may we obtain all the blessings of Agni for our prayers.'

Note 2. Vá*k*as stands for vá*k*asâ. See the passages collected by Lanman, Noun-Inflection, 562, and comp. Roth, Ueber gewisse Kürzungen des Wortendes im Veda, 5; Joh. Schmidt, Die Pluralbildungen der indogermanischen Neutra, 304 seq. Ludwig also takes vá*k*as as instrumental.

Verse 3.

Note 1. Agni is the father, the mortal whose sacrifice he performs, the son.

Verse 4.

Note 1. Can ri*s*âdas be explained as a compound of ri (Tiefstufe of rai, as gu is the Tiefstufe of gau) and **s*ấdas, from the root *s*ad, 'to be triumphant'? Prof. Aufrecht (Bezzenberger's Beiträge, XIV, 33; see also Neisser, Bezz. Beitr. XIX, 143) connects ri- with the Greek ἐρι- (ἐρικυδής &c.); our hypothesis has the advantage of not leaving the limits of Sanskrit.—Comp. M. M.'s note on V, 60, 7; Ludwig, Ueber die neuesten Arbeiten auf dem Gebiete der Rig-veda-Forschung (1893), p. 7.

Verse 6.

Note 1. On *s*á*s*vatâ tánâ see Lanman, 480, 515, 518.

Verse 9.

Note 1. The comparison of verse 8 and the expression ám*ri*ta mártyânâm in the second Pâda of this verse seem to show that ubháyeshâm does not refer to two classes of mortals, the priests and their patrons, but to the mortals and the immortals. A genitive am*ri*tânâm, which would make this meaning quite clear, can easily be supplied. A Dvandva compound am*ri*tamartyā́nâm, which one could feel tempted to conjecture, would have, in my opinion, too modern a character.—Prof. Max Müller writes: 'I should prefer am*ri*ta martyânâm, not exactly as a compound, but as standing for am*ri*tânâm martyânâm. This seems to be Ludwig's opinion too.'

Verse 10.

Note 1. In the translation of sahasa*h* yaho I follow Geldner, Kuhn's Zeitschrift, XXVIII, 195; Ludwig's translation is similar.

MAN*D*ALA I, HYMN 27.

ASH*T*AKA I ADHYÂYA 2, VARGA 22-24.

A.

1. With reverence I shall worship thee who art long-tailed like a horse, Agni, the king of worship.

2. May he, our son of strength [1], proceeding on his broad way, the propitious, become bountiful to us.

3. Thus protect us always, thou who hast a full life, from the mortal who seeks to do us harm [1], whether near or afar.

4. And mayest thou, O Agni, announce to the gods this our newest efficient Gâyatra song.

5. Let us partake of all booty that is highest and that is middle (i. e. that dwells in the highest and in the middle world); help us to the wealth that is nearest.

6. O god with bright splendour, thou art the distributor. Thou instantly flowest for the liberal giver in the wave of the river, near at hand.

B.

7. The mortal, O Agni, whom thou protectest in battles, whom thou speedest in the races [1], he will command constant nourishment:

8. Whosoever he may be, no one will overtake him, O conqueror (Agni)! His strength [2] is glorious.

9. May he (the man), known among all tribes [3], win the race with his horses; may he with the help of his priests become a gainer.

C.

10. O *G*arâbodha[1]! Accomplish this (task) for every house[2]: a beautiful song of praise for worshipful Rudra[3].

11. May he, the great, the immeasurable, the smoke-bannered, rich in splendour, incite us to (pious) thoughts and to strength.

12. May he hear us, like the rich lord of a clan, the banner of the gods, on behalf of our hymns, Agni with bright light.

13. Reverence to the great ones, reverence to the lesser ones! Reverence to the young, reverence to the old[1]! Let us sacrifice to the gods, if we can. May I not, O gods, fall as a victim to the curse of my better[2].

NOTES.

The hymn is ascribed to *S*una*h*s*epa (see note on I, 26). The metre is Gâyatrî; the last verse is Trish*t*ubh.

The laws of arrangement of the Sa*m*hitâ show that this hymn, which has thirteen verses and follows after a hymn of ten verses belonging to the same deity, must be divided into a number of minor hymns. On the question of this division some further light is thrown by the metre. The first six verses and then again the verses 10–12 are composed in the trochaic form of the Gâyatrî metre; of the verses 7–9, on the other hand, not a single Pâda shows the characteristics of that metre. I believe, therefore, that the verses 1–6 form one hymn by themselves, or possibly two hymns of three verses each. Then follow two hymns: verses 7–9, 10–12. As to verse 13, which is composed in a different metre, it is difficult to determine its exact nature. It may be a later addition: though in that case we shall hardly be able to explain why it was placed at the end of the hymns addressed to Agni, to which god it contains no reference whatever. Or it may form part of the hymn 10–12: in that case we should have to consider this whole hymn, which would then violate the rules of arrangement, as an addition to the original collection.

We may add that the Sâma-veda gives the first twelve verses of this Sûkta so as to form four independent hymns: 1–3 = SV. II, 984–6; 4. 6. 5 = SV. II, 847–9; 7–9 = SV. II, 765–7; 10–12 = SV. II, 1013–15. Besides, verse 1 is found in SV. I, 17. Verse 4 = SV. I, 28; TÂr. IV, 11, 8. Verse 7 = VS. VI, 29; TS. I, 3, 13, 2; MS. I, 3, 1. Verse 10 = SV. I, 15. Comp. Bergaigne, Recherches sur l'histoire de la Sa*m*hitâ, II, pp. 7–8; H. O., Prolegomena, 225–226.

Verse 2.

Note 1. It requires a stronger belief in the infallibility of Vedic text tradition than I possess, not to change *s*ávasâ into *s*ávasa*h*. I do not think that I, 62, 9 (sánemi sakhyám svapasyámâna*h* sûnú*h* dâdhâra *s*ávasâ sudá*m*sâ*h*) furnishes a sufficient argument against this conjecture.

Verse 3.

Note 1. Grassmann reads aghaâyó*h* for the sake of the metre; Prof. Max Müller proposes ăghâyŏ*h*. I think that the missing syllable should be gained by disyllabic pronunciation of -ât in mártyât or rather mártiât. Comp. my Prolegomena 185 and the quotations given there in note 1.

Verses 7–9.

Note 1. It is not my intention to enter here into a new discussion on so frequently discussed a word as vâ*g*a. I have translated it in verses 7, 9 by 'race,' in verse 8 by 'strength.'

Note 2. The expression used in verses 7 and 8 should be compared especially with VII, 40, 3. sá*h* ít ugrá*h* astu maruta*h* sá*h* *s*ushmî́ yám mártyam p*ri*shada*s*vâ*h* ávâtha, utá îm agní*h* sárasvatî *g*unánti ná tásya râyá*h* paryetā́ asti.

Note 3. Visvakarshani, a frequent epithet of Agni, here refers to the mortal hero protected by Agni; comp. I, 64, 14 (vol. xxxii, p. 108); X, 93, 10 (visvákarshani srávah).

Verse 10.

Note 1. I think that Ludwig is right in taking Garâbodha for a proper name.

Note 2. Visé-vise may possibly depend on yagñíyâya, so that we should have to translate: 'Administer this task: a beautiful song of praise to Rudra who is worshipful for every house.'

Note 3. Rudra is here a designation of Agni, as the next verses show. Comp. Pischel-Geldner, I, 56.

Verse 13.

Note 1. The word âsiná, 'old,' occurring only here, is doubtful. In III, 1, 6; IV, 33, 3; X, 39, 4, sana or sanaya stands in contrast with yuvan. Shall we conjecture námah ắ sánebhyah?

Note 2. The last Pâda of this verse, mắ gyắyasah sámsam ắ vrikshi deváh ('May I not, O gods, neglect the praise of the greatest,' Muir, V, 12), offers some difficulty. It may be doubted whether ắ vrikshi belongs to â-vrig or to â-vrask.

Let us see what would be the meaning of the passage, if we were to decide for â-vrig. VIII, 101, 16 the cow speaks: devī́m devébhyah pári eyúshîm gắm ắ mâ avrikta mártyah dabhrákətâh, 'Me the goddess, the cow, who has come hither from the gods, the weak-minded mortal has appropriated.' Satapatha Brâhmana XIV, 9, 4, 3. ya evam vidvân adhopahâsam karaty â sa strînâm sukritam vriṅkte 'tha ya idam avidvân adhopahâsam karaty âsya striyah sukritam vriñgate, 'He who knowing this, &c., appropriates the good works of the women. But the women appropriate the good works of him who without knowing this,' &c. In Rig-veda X, 159, 5 also we probably have a form of â-vrig. There we find the triumphant utterance of a wife who has gained superiority over her fellow-wives: â avrîksham anyâsâm várkah, 'I have won for myself the splendour of the other wives.' We may conclude from these passages that our Pâda, if ấ vrîkshi is derived from â-vrig, would mean: 'May I not draw on myself the curse of my better.'

On the other hand we have a great number of passages—they have been collected by Ludwig, IV, 249 seq.—in which the verb â-vrask appears. Referring the reader for fuller information to Ludwig, I content myself here with selecting one or two of these passages. Taitt. Samh. II, 4, 11, 4. devatâbhyo vâ esha â vriskyate yo yakshya ity uktvâ na yagate. In translating this we should remember that vrask means 'to cut down;' â-vrask, therefore, must be 'to cut down so that the object reaches a certain destination.' I translate therefore: 'He who says, "I shall sacrifice," and does not sacrifice, is cut down for the deities,' —i. e. he is dedicated or forfeited to the deities and is thus destroyed (comp. a different explanation of â-vrask by Delbrück, Altindische Syntax, 143). In other passages not the dative but the locative is used for indicating the being to whom somebody is forfeited; see Atharva-veda XII, 4, 6. 12. 26; XV, 12, 6. 10.

A Rig-vedic passage containing â-vrask (with the dative) is X, 87, 18. ấ vriskyantâm áditaye durévâh, 'May the evil-doers be forfeited to Aditi.'

Several times we find the first person aor. med. in the same form as in our passage, â vrîkshi; see, for instance, the Nivid formula to the Visve devâh, Sâṅkhâyana Srautasûtra VIII, 21. In this Nivid, the text of which as given by Hillebrandt is not quite identical with that of Ludwig, we read according to Hillebrandt's edition: mâ vo devâ avisasâ mâ visasâyur â vrîkshi. This mâ . . . â vrîkshi looks quite similar to our passage. The same may be said of Taittirîya Samhitâ I, 6, 6, 1. yat te tapas tasmai te mâvrîkshi. Considering such passages it is difficult not to believe that it is the verb â vrask which we have before us in our verse. It must be admitted indeed that the accusative *s*a*m*sam does not agree with the construction of the later Vedic passages. Can the accusative stand in the ancient language of the Rig-veda in the same connection in which we have found the dative and the locative? So that â-vra*s*k (in the middle or passive) with the accusative would mean: to be cut down in the direction towards another being, i. e. being forfeited to that being? In that case the translation of our passage would be: 'May I not, O gods, fall as a victim to the praise (or rather, to the curse) of my better.' If this explanation of the accusative is thought too bold, we should propose to correct the text so as to get a dative or, which would suit the metre better, a locative: mấ *g*yấyasa*h* *s*á*m*sâya (or *s*á*m*se) ấ v*ri*kshi devâ*h*.

MA*ND*ALA I, HYMN 31.

ASH*T*AKA I, ADHYÂYA 2, VARGA 32-35.

1. Thou, O Agni, (who art) the first Aṅgiras *Ri*shi, hast become as god the kind friend of the gods. After thy law the sages, active in their wisdom[1], were born, the Maruts with brilliant spears.

2. Thou, O Agni, the first, highest Aṅgiras, a sage, administerest the law of the gods, mighty for the whole world, wise, the son of the two mothers[1], reposing everywhere for (the use of) the living[2].

3. Thou, O Agni, as the first, shalt become[1] manifest to Mâtari*s*van, through thy high wisdom, to Vivasvat. The two worlds trembled at (thy) election as Hot*ri*. Thou hast sustained the burthen; thou, O Vasu, hast sacrificed to the great (gods)[2].

4. Thou, O Agni, hast caused the sky to roar[1] for Manu, for the well-doing Purûravas, being thyself a greater well-doer. When thou art loosened by power (?)[2] from thy parents, they led thee hither before and afterwards again.

5. Thou, O Agni, the bull, the augmenter of prosperity, art to be praised by the sacrificer who raises the spoon, who knows all about the offering[1] and (the sacrifice performed with) the word Vasha*t*. Thou (god) of unique vigour art the first to invite[2] the clans.

6. Thou, O Agni, leadest forward the man who follows crooked ways[1], in thy company at the sacrifice[2], O god dwelling among all tribes, who in the strife of heroes, in the decisive moment for the

obtainment of the prize[3], even with few companions killest many foes in the battle[4].

7. Thou, O Agni, keepest that mortal[1] in the highest immortality, in glory day by day, (thou) who being thirsty thyself[2] givest happiness to both races (gods and men), and joy to the rich.

8. Thou, O Agni, praised by us, help the glorious singer to gain prizes. May we accomplish our work with the help of the young active (Agni). O Heaven and Earth! Bless us together with the gods.

9. Thou, O Agni, in the lap of thy parents, a god among gods, O blameless one, always watchful, be the body's creator and guardian to the singer. Thou, O beautiful one, pourest forth all wealth.

10. Thou, O Agni, art our guardian, thou art our father. Thou art the giver of strength; we are thy kinsmen. Hundredfold, thousandfold treasures come together in thee, who art rich in heroes, the guardian of the law, O undeceivable one.

11. Thee, O Agni, the gods have made for the living as the first living[1], the clan-lord of the Nahusha[2]. They have made (the goddess) I*l*â the teacher of men (manusha), when a son of my father is born[3].

12. Thou, O Agni, protect with thy guardians, O god, our liberal givers and ourselves, O venerable one! Thou art the protector of kith and kin[1] and of the cows, unremittingly watching over thy law.

13[1]. Thou, O Agni, art kindled four-eyed, as the closest guardian for the sacrificer who is without (even) a quiver[2] Thou acceptest in thy mind the hymn even of the poor[3] who has made offerings, that he may prosper without danger.

14. Thou, O Agni, gainest[1] for the widely-re-

nowned worshipper that property which is desirable and excellent. Thou art called the guardian and father even of the weak[2]; thou instructest the simple, thou, the greatest sage, the quarters of the world[3].

15. Thou, O Agni, protectest on every side like well-stitched armour the man who gives sacrificial fees. He who puts sweet food (before the priests), who makes them comfortable in his dwelling, who kills living (victims), he (will reside) high in heaven[1].

16. Forgive, O Agni, this our fault (?)[1], (look graciously at) this way which we have wandered from afar. Thou art the companion, the guardian, the father of those who offer Soma; thou art the quick one[2] who makes the mortals *Ri*shis[3].

17. As thou didst for Manus, O Agni, for Aṅgiras, O Aṅgiras, for Yayâti on thy (priestly) seat, as for the ancients, O brilliant one, come hither, conduct hither the host of the gods, seat them on the sacrificial grass, and sacrifice to the beloved (host).

18. Be magnified, O Agni, through this spell which we have made for thee with our skill or with our knowledge. And lead us forward to better things. Let us be united with thy favour, which bestows strength.

NOTES.

The *Ri*shi of the hymn is Hira*n*yastûpa Âṅgirasa. To him tradition ascribes the authorship of the collection I, 31–35, probably because in X, 149, 5 the poet invokes Savit*ri*, 'as Hira*n*yastûpa the Âṅgirasa has called thee, O Savit*ri*.' Vedic theologians of course tried to find out where this invocation of Hira*n*yastûpa to Savit*ri* was preserved, and the hymn, I, 35, seemed to agree best with the conditions of the case (comp. Zeitschrift der D. Morg. Ges. XLII, 230). By this and many similar cases it is made probable that at the time when the Anukrama*n*î was composed, all real knowledge as to authors to whom the collections of the first Ma*nd*ala belong, was lost.

The metre is *G*agatî; only the verses 8, 16, 18 are Trish*t*ubh. Verse 1 = VS. 34, 12. Verse 8 = MS. IV, 11, 1. Verse 12 = VS. 34, 13. With verse 16 comp. AV. III, 15, 4.

Verse 1.

Note 1. Vidmanā́pasa*h* seems to be nom. plur., not gen. sing. Comp. I, 111, 1. tákshan rátham . . . vidmanā́pasa*h*, 'they (the *Ri*bhus), active in their wisdom, have wrought the chariot.'

Verse 2.

Note 1. As to dvimâtā́ *s*ayú*h*, comp. III, 55, 6 (*s*ayú*h* parástât ádha nú dvimâtā́); Pischel, Vedische Studien, II, 50.—On Agni's two mothers and his double birth see Bergaigne, Religion Védique, II, 52.

Note 2. By 'living' I have translated âyú. See on this word, Bergaigne, Rel. Véd., I, 59 seq.

Verse 3.

Note 1. Probably Bergaigne (Rel. Véd. I, 55, note 2) is right in conjecturing bhava*h* for bhava. In this case we should have to translate: 'Thou as the first hast become manifest to Mâtari*s*van.'

Note 2. I believe that to mahá*h* we have to supply devā́n; see II, 37, 6; III, 7, 9; VI, 16, 2; 48, 4, &c. 'Can it not be an adverb? See vol. xxxii, p. 307; Lanman, p. 501,' M. M.

Verse 4.

Note 1. Comp. V, 58, 6. let Dyu (sky) roar down, the bull of the dawn. V, 59, 8. may Dyaus Aditi (the unbounded) roar for our feast.

Note 2. The translation of *s*vâtra is purely conjectural. It rests on the supposition that the word is related to *s*û*s*uve, *s*avas, &c. (thus Grassmann). Boehtlingk-Roth connect it with svad, which is phonetically impossible; they give the meaning 'schmackhaft,' and paraphrase our passage: das mit einer Lockspeise (z. B. mit einem Spahn) von den Reibhölzern abgenommene Feuer kann man hin und her tragen. Ludwig: mit Geprassel. I do not see how this translation would fit for a number of the passages in which the word occurs.

Verse 5.

Note 1. With the third Pâda compare VI, 1, 9. yá*h* ấhutim pári véda námobhi*h*.

Note 2. Avívâsasi cannot belong to the relative clause. The accent must be changed accordingly.

Verse 6.

Note 1. It is very curious to find here Agni as the protector of the v*ri*g*inavartani, the man who follows crooked ways. Ludwig tries to explain the passage by understanding the vidatha, in which Agni is here said to protect the sinner, as an asylum, but we have no reason to believe that the word could have this meaning. See the next note.

Note 2. On the derivation and meaning of vidátha various opinions have been pronounced in the last years, which have been collected by Prof. Max Müller in his note on V, 59, 2 (vol. xxxii p. 349 seq.; see also Bartholomae, Studien zur indogermanischen Sprachgeschichte, I, 41). Without trying to discuss here all different theories, I immediately proceed to state my own opinion, though I am far from claiming certainty for it. It will, however, I believe, solve the difficulties tolerably well. I propose to derive vidátha from vi-dhâ; the dh was changed into d by the same 'Hauchdissimilationsgesetz' (Brugmann, Grundriss der vergleichenden Grammatik, vol. i, p. 355 seq.), according to which Arian *bháudhati was changed into Sanskrit bódhati. No one will doubt that the operation of this 'Hauchdissimilationsgesetz' could be annihilated by opposite forces, but it must be admitted that the forms with 'Hauchdissimilation' could also remain intact. The verb vi-dhâ means 'to distribute, to arrange, to ordain;' thus the original meaning of vidátha must be, like the meaning of vidhấna, 'distribution, disposition, ordinance.' In V, 3, 6 we read vidátheshu áhnâm: this phrase receives its explanation by VII, 66, 11. ví yé dadhú*h* s*a*rádam mấsam ất áha*h*; ahorâtrấ*n*i vidádhat, X, 190, 2; mâsấm vidhấnam, X, 138, 6; *ri*tū́n . . . ví dadhau, I, 95, 3. We may call attention also to VI, 51, 2. véda yá*h* trī́*n*i vidáthâni eshâm devấnâm *g*ánma, 'he who knows their threefold division, the birth of the gods;' VI, 8, 1. prá nú vo*k*am vidáthâ *g*âtávedasa*h*, 'I will proclaim the ordinances of *G*âtavedas.' Within the sphere of the Vedic poets' thoughts, the most prominent example of something most artificially 'víhita' was the sacrifice (comp. ví yé dadhú*h* . . . ya*g*ñám, VII, 66, 11; *s*á*m*sâti ukthám yá*g*ate ví û dhâ*h*, IV, 6, 11; [the moon] bhâgám devébhya*h* ví dadhâti â-yán, X, 85, 19; and the following very significant passage: ya*g*ñásya tvâ vidáthâ p*rikkh*am átra káti hótâra*h* *ri*tu*s*á*h* ya*g*anti, Vâ*g*. Sa*m*h. XXIII, 57). Thus ya*g*ñá and vidátha, 'sacrifice' and 'ordinance,' became nearly synonymous (comp. III, 3, 3, &c.). It would be superfluous to quote the whole number of passages which show this, but I believe that an attentive reader will discern at least in some of them the traces of the original meaning of vidátha; see, for instance, II, 1, 4; III, 28, 4.—Finally vidátha seems to mean 'the act of disposing of any business' or the like; this meaning appears, I believe, in passages like the well-known phrase, b*ri*hát vadema vidáthe suvī́râ*h* (comp. suvī́râsa*h* vidátham ấ vadema): 'may we with valiant men mightily raise our voice at the determining (of ordinances, &c.).' Thus the words vidátha and sabhấ approach each other in their meaning; a person influential in council is called both vidathȳa and sabhéya (see Boehtlingk-Roth, s. v. vidathȳa).

Note 3. The exact meaning of paritakmya is not quite

free from doubt. Comp. Bartholomae, Bezzenberger's Beiträge, XV, 203, note 1.

Note 4. Prof. Max Müller translates this verse: 'Thou savest the man who has gone the wrong way in the thick of the battle, thou who art quick at the sacrifice; thou who in the strife of heroes, when the prize (or the booty) is surrounded (beset on all sides), killest,' &c.

Verse 7.

Note 1. The phrase begins as if a relative clause were to follow attached to the words 'that mortal.' But, instead of this, afterwards a relative clause follows referring to 'thou, O Agni.'

Note 2. Roth (Ueber gewisse Kürzungen des Wortendes, p. 4) and Bartholomae (Kuhn's Zeitschrift, XXIX, 559) think that a dative (like tâtṛishâṇáya) is required; Agni gives comfort to both thirsty races, gods and men. Roth takes tâtṛishâṇá[*h*] for an abbreviation of tâtṛishâṇáya; Bartholomae conjectures tâtṛisháya. It would be more easy to change the form into a dative with the ending -â (=-ai); comp. Kluge, Kuhn's Zeitschrift, XXV, 309; Pischel-Geldner, I, 61; Aufrecht, Festgruss an Böhtlingk, 1; J. Schmidt, Pluralbildungen, 234. But why not leave the nominative? Agni, being thirsty himself, quenches the thirst of other beings. Comp. J. Schmidt, Pluralbildungen, 309.

Verse 11.

Note 1. Âyúm âyáve. See verse 2, note 2.

Note 2. The names Nahus, Nahusha have much the same value as Manus, Manusha. But it seems that not all the Aryan tribes, but only a certain part of them, were considered as descendants of Nahus. Comp. Bergaigne, Rel. Védique, II, 324.

Note 3. The last words are very obscure. Mamaka occurs only in one other passage, belonging to the same collection of hymns, I, 34, 6: there the Asvins are invoked to bestow blessings on 'my son' (mámakâya sûnáve). 'When a son of my father is born' may mean 'When I am born,' or 'When a new issue is born within our tribe:' then—thus we may possibly supply—the goddess I*l*â, the teacher of mankind, will be the new-born child's teacher also. Another possible explanation would be to take Mamaka as a proper name. Or Prof. Max Müller may be right, who writes: 'Could not pitú*h* yát putrá*h* mámakasya *g*ấyate refer to Agni, who, in III, 29, 3, was called i*l*âyâ*h* putra*h*. Her father and husband (Manu) is also the father of mankind, therefore of the poet who says: Whenever the son of my father is born, they made I*l*â (his mother) the teacher of man.'

Verse 12.

Note 1. Trâtấ tokásya tánaye seems to be nothing else but trâtấ tokásya tánayasya, which would have had one syllable too much.

Verse 13.

Note 1. Comp. on this verse, Pischel, I, 216 seq.

Note 2. Agni is to protect the man who has no quiver, and cannot, therefore, protect himself. The four eyes of the divine guardian seem to signify that he can look in all directions, and perhaps also that he has the power of seeing invisible bad demons. The watchdogs of Yama also are four-eyed, X, 14, 10. 11; comp. H. O., Religion des Veda, 474, note 4. Comp. nishaṅgin, Rig-veda III, 30, 15; V, 57, 2; X, 103, 3.

Note 3. On kîrí, comp. Pischel loc. cit.

Note 4. Râtáhavya*h* means either a man who has made offerings, or a god to whom offerings are made. That it stands here in the first sense is shown with great probability by VIII, 103, 13, where the kîrí*h* râtáhavya*h* svadhvará*h* is described, the man who, though poor, makes offerings and is a good sacrificer. But if we are right in our translation of râtáhavya*h*, the verb vanóshi cannot belong to the relative clause; I propose to read vanoshi without accent. The way in which Pischel tries to explain the accent of vanóshi, by taking the words kîré*h k*it mántram mánasâ as a parenthesis, is too artificial.

Verse 14.

Note 1. I think that we should here, as in verse 13, read vanoshi without accent.

Note 2. This must be at least the approximate meaning of âdhra. 'For âdhrasya one expects radhrasya,' M. M.

Note 3. I think that the quarters of the world have nothing to do here, but that instead of prá dí*s*a*h* we should read (with Ludwig) pradí*s*a*h*. A similar mistake regarding the word pradi*s* occurs several times in the text of the Rig-veda. I propose to translate the corrected text: 'Thou instructest the simple, well knowing the (divine) commandments.' Comp. vayúnâni vidvắn, dûtyâni vidvắn, &c.

Verse 15.

Note 1. 'Der ist des himels ebenbild' (Ludwig). But this word upamắ is, as far as we can see, not very ancient. I take upamắ, with Boehtlingk-Roth, as an adverbial instrumental like dakshi*n*ắ, madhyắ, &c. Prof. Max Müller translates 'close or near to heaven.'

Verse 16.

Note 1. *S*ará*n*i designates in the Atharva-veda VI, 43, 3 a fault or defect, the exact nature of which cannot be determined. Boehtlingk-Roth propose Widerspänstigkeit, Hartnäckigkeit; Max Müller, Abweg, Fehltritt.

Note 2. On bh*ri*mi, comp. M. M.'s note on II, 34, 1.

Note 3. Comp. III, 43, 5. kuvít mâ *rí*shim papivắ*m*sam sutásya (supply kárase), 'Wilt thou make me a *R*ishi after I have drunk Soma?'

MANDALA I, HYMN 36.

ASHTAKA I, ADHYÂYA 3, VARGA 8–11.

1. We implore[1] with well-spoken words the vigorous[2] Agni who belongs to many people[3], to the clans that worship the gods[4], whom other people (also) magnify.

2. Men have placed Agni (on the altar) as the augmenter of strength. May we worship thee, rich in sacrificial food. Thus be thou here to-day gracious to us, a helper in our striving for gain, O good one!

3. We choose thee, the all-possessor, as our messenger and as our Hotri. The flames of thee, who art great, spread around; thy rays touch the heaven.

4. The gods, Varuna, Mitra, Aryaman, kindle thee, the ancient messenger. The mortal, O Agni, who worships thee, gains through thee every prize.

5. Thou art the cheerful Hotri and householder, O Agni, the messenger of the clans. In thee all the firm laws are comprised which the gods have made[1].

6. In thee, the blessed one, O Agni, youngest god, all sacrificial food is offered. Sacrifice then thou who art gracious to us to-day and afterwards[1], to the gods that we may be rich in valiant men.

7. Him, the king, verily the adorers approach reverentially. With oblations men kindle Agni, having overcome all failures.

8. Destroying the foe[1], they (victoriously) got through Heaven and Earth and the waters; they

have made wide room for their dwelling. May the manly (Agni)[2], after he has received the oblations, become brilliant at the side of Ka*n*va; may he neigh as a horse in battles.

9. Take thy seat; thou art great. Shine forth, thou who most excellently repairest to the gods. O Agni, holy god, emit thy red, beautiful smoke, O glorious one!

10. Thou whom the gods have placed here for Manu as the best performer of the sacrifice, O carrier of oblations, whom Ka*n*va and Medhyâtithi, whom V*ri*shan and Upastuta[1] (have worshipped,) the winner of prizes.

11. That Agni's nourishment has shone brightly whom Medhyâtithi and Ka*n*va have kindled on behalf of *Ri*ta[1]. Him do these hymns, him do we extol.

12. Fill (us with) wealth, thou self-dependent one, for thou, O Agni, hast companionship with the gods. Thou art lord over glorious booty. Have mercy upon us; thou art great.

13. Stand up straight for blessing us, like the god Savit*ri*, straight a winner of booty, when we with our worshippers and with ointments[1] call thee[2] in emulation (with other people).

14. Standing straight, protect us by thy splendour from evil; burn down every ghoul[1]. Let us stand straight that we may walk and live. Find out our worship[2] among the gods.

15. Save us, O Agni, from the sorcerer, save us from mischief, from the niggard. Save us from him

who does us harm or tries to kill us, O youngest god with bright splendour!

16. As with a club[1] smite the niggards in all directions, and him who deceives us, O god with fiery jaws. The mortal who makes (his weapons) very sharp by night, may that impostor not rule over us.

17. Agni has won abundance in heroes, Agni prosperity (for Kanva). Agni and the two Mitras (i.e. Mitra and Varuna) have blessed Medhyâtithi, Agni (has blessed) Upastuta in the acquirement (of wealth)[1].

18. Through Agni we call hither from afar Turvasa, Yadu, and Ugradeva. May Agni, our strength against the Dasyu, conduct Navavâstva, Brihadratha, and Turvîti[1].

19. Manu has established thee, O Agni, as a light for all people. Thou hast shone forth with Kanva, born from *Ri*ta, grown strong, thou whom the human races worship.

20. Agni's flames are impetuous and violent; they are terrible and not to be withstood. Always burn down the sorcerers, and the allies of the Yâtus, every ghoul[1].

NOTES.

The authorship of this hymn, and of the whole collection to which it belongs (I, 36–43), is ascribed to Kanva Ghaura. Numerous passages show indeed that it was the family of the Kanvas, or rather, to speak more accurately, a branch of that family, among which this group of hymns has been composed. But it is as great a mistake in this as in a number of similar cases to accept the founder of one of the great Brâhmanical families as an author of Vedic poems. Comp. Zeitschrift der Deutschen Morg. Gesellschaft, XLII, 215 seq.

The metre is alternately B*ri*hatî and Satob*ri*hatî, so that the hymn consists of strophes (Pragâtha) of two verses. Verse 1=SV. I, 59. Verse 9=VS. XI, 37; TS. IV, 1, 3, 3 (V, 1, 4, 5); TÂr. IV, 5, 2 (V, 4, 6); MS. II, 7, 3; IV, 9, 3. Verse 13=SV. I, 57; VS. XI, 42; TS. IV, 1, 4, 2 (V, 1, 5, 3); MS. II, 7, 4. Verses 13, 14=TB. III, 6, 1, 2; TÂr. IV, 20, 1; MS. IV, 13, 1. Verse 19=SV. I, 54.

Verse 1.

Note 1. Literally, we entreat for you. Comp. on this use of the pronoun va*h*, Delbrück, Altindische Syntax, 206. See also Neisser, Bezzenberger's Beiträge, XX, 64.

Note 2. The meaning of yahvá cannot be determined with full certainty.

Note 3. There is no sufficient reason to change with Ludwig (IV, 254) purû*n*ấm to Pûrû*n*ấm, and thus to convert the metrically correct Pâda into an irregular one.—Comp. Bollensen, Zeitschrift der Deutschen Morgenl. Gesellschaft, XXII, 593.

Note 4. On devayatî́nâm, comp. Lanman, p. 399.

Verse 5.

Note 1. 'On thee all the eternal works are united, i.e. depend, which the gods have wrought; such as sun, stars, lightning.' M. M.

Verse 6.

Note 1. With the third Pâda compare the third Pâda of verse 2. It is a galita.

Verse 8.

Note 1. The word 'the foe' (v*ri*tra) alludes to the name of the demon conquered by Indra; see H. O., Religion des Veda, 135, note 2.

Note 2. The metre would become more correct by reading v*ri*shabhá*h* instead of v*rí*shâ. Or V*rí*sha*n*i, 'with V*ri*shan'? Comp. verse 10.

Verse 10.

Note 1. Medhyâtithi or Medhâtithi is very frequently mentioned in connection with Ka*n*va.

V*ri*shan is taken as a proper name by Boehtlingk-Roth and by Grassmann (not by Ludwig) in VI, 16, 15. Possibly they are right, but in no case can V*ri*shan of the sixth book, named by the side of Dadhya*ñk* and Atharvan, be identified with any probability with the V*ri*shan mentioned in our passage, who evidently belongs to the ancestors of the Ka*n*vas.

Upastuta is mentioned again together with Ka*n*va and Medhyâtithi in verse 17 of our hymn, together with Ka*n*va in VIII, 5, 25. Comp. I, 112, 15; VIII, 103, 8; X, 115, 8. 9; Bergaigne, Rel. Véd., II, 448.

Verse 11.

Note 1. Comp. I, 139, 2. yát ha tyát mitrâvaru*n*âv *ri*tất ádhi âdadấthe án*ri*tam svéna manyúnâ; X, 73, 5. mándamâna*h* *ri*tất ádhi.

Verse 13.

Note 1. A*ñg*íbhi*h* can possibly mean 'who have salved themselves.' There is no reason to think of the anointing of the yûpa (sacrificial post), to which Sâya*n*a refers the word.

Note 2. On vi-hvâ, comp. Pischel-Geldner, I, 144. There must be a technical reason, unknown to me, for the connection in which this verb repeatedly occurs, as is the case in our passage, with the noun vâghat: comp. III, 8, 10 (see below); VIII, 5, 16. purutrấ *k*it hí vâm narâ vihváyante manîshí*n*a*h* vâghádbhi*h* a*s*vinâ ấ gatam.

Verse 14.

Note 1. The exact meaning of atrín is unknown.

Note 2. Geldner's conjectures on duvas seem rather bold

to me (Kuhn's Zeitschrift, XXVII, 233). Comp. vol. xxxii, pp. 203–206 (I, 165, 14).

Verse 16.

Note 1. On ghanéva, see Lanman, Noun-Inflection, 334.

Verse 17.

Note 1. On Medhyâtithi and Upastuta, see the note on verse 10. Aufrecht (Kuhn's Zeitschrift, XXVI, 612) believes that in mitrótá an abbreviation of the name Mitrâtithi (X, 33, 7) is contained; he translates: 'Agni has promoted Mitrâtithi, Medhyâtithi, and Upastuta in the acquirement of wealth.' This is very ingenious, but I do not think that the reason which Aufrecht gives is sufficient: it cannot be understood, he says, why Mitra (or Mitra and Varu*n*a) should be mentioned in a hymn exclusively addressed to Agni. But similar cases are quite frequent.—Prof. Max Müller writes: 'Could mitrâ stand for mitrâ*n*i? Agni has protected his friends and also Medhyâtithi.' Comp. also Lanman, p. 342.

Verse 18.

Note 1. On Turva*s*a and Yadu, comp. Muir, V, 286; Bergaigne, II, 354 seq.; Zeitschr. der D. Morg. Ges. XLII, 220. There is not the slightest reason for Ludwig's statement (IV, 254) that this hymn is a 'gebet um sig für den auf einem kriegszuge befindlichen Turvaçakönig.'

Ugradeva is not mentioned again. On Navavâstva and B*ri*hadratha, comp. X, 49, 6; VI, 20, 11; on Turvîti, the materials collected by Bergaigne, Rel. Véd., II, 358 seq.

Verse 20.

Note 1. See verse 14, note 1.

MANDALA I, HYMN 44.

ASHTAKA I, ADHYÂYA 3, VARGA 28–30.

1. Agni, at the rising of the dawn[1] bring splendid wealth, immortal *G*âtavedas, to the worshipper, (and bring hither) to-day the gods awakening with the dawn.

2. For thou art the accepted messenger, the bearer of sacrificial food, O Agni, the charioteer of worship. United with the two A*s*vins and with the Dawn bestow on us abundance of valiant heroes, and high glory.

3. We choose to-day as our messenger Agni, the Vasu, the beloved of many, whose banner is smoke, whose . . . [1] is light, at the dawning of the day, the beautifier of sacrifices[2].

4. I magnify at the dawning of the day Agni *G*âtavedas, the best, the youngest guest, the best receiver of offerings, welcome to pious people, that he may go to the gods[1].

5. I shall praise thee, O food on which everything lives, immortal one[1], Agni, the immortal protector, O holy god, the best sacrificer, O bearer of sacrificial food.

6. Be kind-spoken to him who praises thee, O youngest god, honey-tongued, the best receiver of offerings. Lengthening Praska*n*va's life, that he may reach old age, do homage[1] to the host of the gods.

7. The clans kindle thee, the all-possessing Hot*ri*:

therefore conduct hither speedily, much-invoked Agni, the provident gods—

8. Savit*ri*, the Dawn, the two A*s*vins, Bhaga, Agni[1], at the dawning (of the day), (at the end) of night[2]. The Ka*n*vas, having pressed Soma, inflame thee, the bearer of sacrificial food, O best performer of worship.

9. As thou, O Agni, art the lord of worship, the messenger of the clans, conduct hither to-day the gods awakening with the dawn, of sun-like aspect, that they may drink Soma.

10. Agni, rich in splendour! thou hast shone after the former dawns, visible to all. Thou art the guardian in the hamlets, the Purohita; thou belongest to men at the sacrifices[1].

11. O Agni, let us put thee down (on the altar) as Manus did, O god, to be the performer of the sacrifice, the Hot*ri*, the wise priest, the quick immortal messenger.

12. When thou, the Purohita of the gods, who art great like Mitra, goest on thy errand as messenger in their midst, then the flames of Agni shine like the roaring waves of the Sindhu[1].

13. Agni with thy attentive ears, hear me, together with the gods driven (on their chariots)[1] who accompany thee. May Mitra and Aryaman sit down on the sacrificial grass, they who come to the ceremony early in the morning.

14. May the Maruts, they who give rain, the fire-tongued increasers of *Ri*ta, hear my praise. May Varu*n*a, whose laws are firm, drink the Soma, united with the two A*s*vins and with the Dawn!

NOTES.

The hymn is ascribed to Praska*n*va Kâ*n*va, who is the reputed author of the whole group of the hymns, I, 44–50. It is certain that these hymns really belong to a branch of the great Ka*n*va family, for which the name Praska*n*va is characteristic. Comp. my Prolegomena, p. 260.

The metre is Bârhata Pragâtha. Verse 1 = SV. I, 40. Verses 1–2 = SV. II, 1130–1131. Verse 11 = TB. II, 7, 12, 6. Verse 13 = SV. I, 50; VS. 33, 15; TB. II, 7, 12, 5.

This Agni-hymn contains a number of allusions which show that it was destined for the morning service. The same may be said of the next hymn, I, 45, and of the whole collection of Praska*n*va hymns, which are addressed exclusively to the devâ*h* prâtaryâvâ*n*a*h*, viz. Agni in his special character as a matutinal deity, the two A*s*vins, the Dawn, the rising Sun. From the mention of the Soma tiroahnya 45, 10; 47, 1, and from other circumstances, Bergaigne has very ingeniously drawn the conclusion that in the Praska*n*va collection an ancient Â*s*vina*s*astra is preserved; see Recherches sur l'histoire de la Liturgie Védique, 45.

Verse 1.

Note 1. I believe that the text, I may perhaps not say requires, but very strongly invites, a slight correction. The tradition gives ágne vívasvat ushása*h* *k*itrám rấdha*h* amartya. To connect vívasvat with rấdha*h* and to make the genitive ushása*h* depend on rấdha*h* would give an expression which is not, strictly speaking, impossible but in every case very unusual. Nothing, on the other hand, is more frequent than combinations of the locative of a noun derived from vi-vas with the genitive ushása*h*, 'at the rising of the dawn' (ushása*h* vy̆ush*t*au, vy̆ush*t*ishu, vyúshi; comp. the phrase vásto usrấ*h* treated of by Kaegi, Festgruss an Böhtlingk, 48; vásto*h* usrấ*h*, Bartholomae, Bezzenberger's Beiträge, XV, 185). I think that such a phrase should be restored in our verse, and propose to read ágne vivásvan ushása*h*, &c. The word vivásvan occurs in VIII, 102, 22. agním îdhe vivásvabhi*h*. The expression used here would thus be similar to that of III, 15, 2. tvám na*h* asyā́*h* ushása*h* vyûsh*t*au . . . bodhi gopā́*h* ; comp. IV, 1, 5, &c.

Verse 3.

Note 1. The meaning of bhā́*h-rig*îka is quite uncertain. The accent would well agree with the explanation of the word as a possessive compound ; dhûmáketum bhā́*h-rig*îkam would then be exactly parallel : whose banner is smoke, whose *rig*îka is light. We have then gó-*rig*îka as an epithet of Soma, 'he whose *rig*îka the cows are,' i.e. 'whose *rig*îka is milk,' and âví*h-rig*îka as an epithet of Dadhikrâvan ('he whose *rig*îka is visible'). All this taken together is clearly insufficient for giving a result, and there is scarcely a better prospect for etymological guesses. Bergaigne's (Rel. Véd., I, 206) translation of *rig*îka by 'flèche' would do for bhā́*h-rig*îka, but it is not very tempting in the cases of gó-*rig*îka and âví*h-rig*îka. Roth (Zeitschrift der D. Morg. Ges. 48, 118) translates 'licht-glänzend.'

Note 2. Pischel's explanation of adhvara*s*rî (Vedische Studien, I, 53, 'Zum Opfer kommend') does not seem convincing to me.

Verse 4.

Note 1. Ludwig's translation 'dasz er die götter herbringe' is not exact. As to the real meaning of our passage, comp. VII, 9, 5. ágne yâhí dûtyam . . . devā́n á*kkh*a, 'Agni, go as a messenger . . . to the gods.'

Verse 5.

Note 1. Boehtlingk-Roth propose to read am*ri*tabho*g*ana. I think the traditional text is right. Agni is called vi*s*vasya bho*g*ana similarly, as it is said in I, 48, 10 (with regard to Ushas), ví*s*vasya hí prā́*n*anam *g*ī́vanam tvé. Am*ri*ta may be vocative s. neuter or masculine. Comp. Lanman, 339.

Verse 6.

Note 1. Benfey (Quantitätsverschiedenheiten, IV, 2, 27) and Ludwig take namasyấ for a first person.

Verse 8.

Note 1. If the accusative agním is right, as it probably is, Agni would be invoked to conduct Agni to the sacrifice. This is quite a possible idea. Comp. the formula of the 'devatânâm âvâhanam,' 'agnim agna âvaha, somam âvaha; agnim âvaha,' i. e. 'Agni, conduct hither Agni, conduct hither Soma, conduct hither Agni.' See Hillebrandt, Das Altindische Neu- und Vollmondsopfer, p. 84.

Note 2. Lanman, 482, takes kshápa*h* as an acc. plur. I think it is gen. sing., and the accent should be kshapá*h*. Comp. VIII, 19, 31; III, 49, 4, and the phrase aktó*h* vȳush*t*au.

Verse 10.

Note 1. Prof. Max Müller translates: 'Thou art the guardian in the hamlets, the chief-priest; thou art the human chief-priest at the sacrifices.'

Verse 12.

Note 1. With the third Pâda comp. IX, 50, 1, where it is said that the mighty strength of Soma shows itself 'síndho*h* ûrmé*h* iva svaná*h*,' i. e. 'like the roar of the waves of the Sindhu.'

Verse 13.

Note 1. I cannot follow the translation of Dr. Neisser, Bezzenberger's Beiträge, XVIII, 316.

MAṆḌALA I, HYMN 45.

ASHṬAKA I, ADHYÂYA 3, VARGA 31-32.

1. Sacrifice here, thou, O Agni, to the Vasus, the Rudras, and the Âdityas, to the (divine) host that receives good sacrifices[1], the Ghṛita-sprinkling offspring of Manu[2].

2. The wise gods, O Agni, are ready to listen to the worshippers: conduct them hither, the thirty-three, O lord of red horses, thou who lovest our praises.

3. As thou hast heard Priyamedha and Atri[1], O Gâtavedas, as thou hast heard Virûpa and Aṅgiras, thus hear the invocation of Praskaṇva, O lord of high laws.

4. The Mahikerus[1], the Priyamedhas have invoked for their protection the lord of worship, Agni with his bright splendour.

5. O thou to whom Ghṛita oblations are poured out, good (Agni), hear these praises with which the sons of Kaṇva invoke thee for their protection.

6. O Agni, whose glory is brightest, beloved of many, the people in the clans invoke thee, the radiant-haired, to convey the sacrificial food.

7. The priests have established thee, O Agni, in the striving for day[1], as their Hotṛi, the ministrant, the greatest acquirer of wealth, with attentive ears, the most widely extended[2].

8. The wise who have pressed Soma have made thee speed hither to the feast (which is offered to the gods), bringing great light[1] and sacrificial food, O Agni, on behalf of the mortal worshipper.

9. O strength-made, good (Agni), make the gods who come in the morning, the divine host, sit down here to-day on our sacrificial grass, O Vasu, to drink the Soma.

10. Sacrifice, O Agni, with joint invocations, and bring hither the divine host. This is the Soma, O rain-giving gods. Drink (the Soma) which has been kept over night[1].

NOTES.

The hymn is ascribed to Praska*n*va. It is evidently addressed to Agni in his matutinal character; comp. the note on I, 44. The metre is Anush*t*ubh. Verse 1 = SV. I, 96. Verse 6 = VS. XV, 31; TS. IV, 4, 4, 3; MS. II, 13, 7.

Verse 1.

Note 1. Comp. VIII, 5, 33. á*kkh*a svadhvarám *g*ánam.

Note 2. As to the gods being considered here as offspring of Manu, comp. especially X, 53, 6. mánu*h* bhava *g*anáya daívyam *g*ánam, 'become Manu, procreate the divine hosts.' See also Bergaigne, Rel. Védique, I, 69.

Verse 3.

Note 1. This passage is one of those which show that the Atris stood in especially friendly connection with the Ka*n*vas. Of the Priyamedhas the same may be said, or perhaps we may even go further and consider them as one branch of the Ka*n*vas. For a fuller discussion of these questions I refer to my paper, 'Ueber die Liedverfasser des Rig-veda,' Zeitschr. der D. Morg. Gesellschaft, XLII, 213 seq.

Verse 4.

Note 1. Máhikerava*h*, which I have translated as a proper name, may be an adjective belonging to Priyámedhâ*h*. Possibly it is derived from the root kar, 'to praise:' 'the

Priyamedhas with mighty hymns.' Comp. Bartholomae, Kuhn's Zeitschrift, XXVII, 341.

Verse 7.

Note 1. As gó-ish*t*i means 'the striving for cows,' thus dív-ish*t*i means 'the striving for day,' or possibly 'the striving for heaven.' Ludwig (III, 383) takes it for 'morgenopfer,' and it is true that most of the passages, in which the word occurs, are addressed to matutinal deities. Thus our passage belongs to a hymn addressed to the matutinal Agni; I, 48, 9 is addressed to Ushas; I, 139, 4; VII, 74, 1; VIII, 87, 3 to the A*s*vins; IV, 46, 1; 47, 1 to Vâyu who was invoked in the Praüga-*s*astra belonging to the Prâta*h*-savana, and who received the Soma offering before the other deities. There is, nevertheless, at least one passage which shows that Ludwig has gone too far: VIII, 76, 9. píba ít indra marútsakhâ sutám sómam dívish*t*ishu, 'Drink, O Indra, with the Maruts thy friends the Soma which has been pressed at the divish*t*is.' The Soma oblation offered to Indra Marutvat formed part of the second (midday) Savana.

Note 2. 'Sapráthastamam, the most renowned, répandu.' M. M.

Verse 8.

Note 1. Comp. IV, 5, 1. kathā́ dâ*s*ema agnáye b*ri*hát bhā́*h*, 'how may we offer great light to Agni?'—which seems to mean, 'how may we make Agni brilliant?' Thus in our passage the meaning seems to be: the priests kindle Agni and perform oblations.

Verse 10.

Note 1. The tirá*h*-ahnya Soma, which was kept from one day to the next day (not, as Ludwig translates, 'der von vorgestern'), was offered to the A*s*vins at the Atirâtra sacrifice. Comp. Rig-veda I, 47, 1; III, 58, 7; VIII, 35, 19; Kâtyâyana *S*rautasûtra XII, 6, 10; XXIV, 3, 42. There the commentary says, â*s*vina*s*astrakayâgasambandhina*h* *k*amasasthâ*h* somâ*h* pûrvadinanishpannatvât tirohnyâ ity u*k*yante.

MANDALA I, HYMN 58.

ASHTAKA I, ADHYÂYA 4, VARGA 23–24.

1. The strength-begotten immortal never grows tired[1], when he, the Hotri, has become the messenger of Vivasvat[2]. He passes through the air on the best paths. In the divine world he invites (the gods) with the sacrificial food.

2. Seizing his own food the undecaying, greedy (Agni) stands on the brushwood wishing to drink. When he has been sprinkled (with ghee), he shines like a racer with his back[1]. Thundering he has roared like the ridge of heaven.

3. As soon as[1] the Rudras, the Vasus have made him their Purohita, the immortal sitting down as Hotri, the conqueror of wealth, pressing forward like a chariot among the clans, among the Âyus[2], the god in due course discloses desirable boons.

4. Stirred by the wind he spreads among the brushwood lightly[1] (driven forward) by the sacrificial ladles, with his sickle[2], loudly roaring. When thou, O Agni, thirstily rushest on the wooden sticks like a bull[3], thy course, O never-aging god with fiery waves, becomes black[4].

5. He who has fiery jaws, stirred by the wind, blazes down on the forest[1] as a strong bull (rushes) on the herd. When he proceeds[2] with his stream of light to the imperishable atmosphere, then what is moveable and immoveable (and) the winged (birds) are afraid.

6. The Bhrigus have placed thee among men, who art beautiful like a treasure, who art easy to

invoke for people; thee the Hot*ri*, O Agni, the excellent guest, a delightful friend like Mitra to the divine race!

7. I worship with good cheer Agni the steward[1] of all treasures, whom the seven ladles[2] (of the priests), the worshippers choose as the Hot*ri*, the best sacrificer at the rites, and I pray for treasure[3].

8. Son of strength, great like Mitra, grant to-day flawless protection to us who magnify thee. Agni! guard from distress with strongholds of iron him who praises thee, O offspring of vigour!

9. Be a shelter to him who praises thee, O resplendent one; be protection, generous giver, to the generous. Agni! guard him who praises thee from distress. May he who gives wealth for our prayer, come quickly in the morning[1].

NOTES.

The hymn is ascribed to Nodhas Gautama, who is considered as the *Ri*shi of the whole collection, I, 58–64. This tradition is based on, and confirmed by, several passages of the text: I, 61, 14; 62, 13; 64, 1.

The metre is *G*agatî verses 1–5, Trish*t*ubh verses 6–9. None of the verses of this hymn occurs in the other Sa*m*hitâs.

Verse 1.

Note 1. I believe that Professor Aufrecht (Kuhn's Zeitschrift, XXV, 435) is right in reading nū́ *k*it saha*h*-*g*ā́*h* am*ri*ta*h* nú tandate. Comp. as to nū́ *k*it nú, I, 120, 2; VI, 37, 3; VII, 22, 8. Agni is frequently called átandra*h* dûtá*h* or similarly. Possibly we might read, instead of nú tandate, ní tandate, though parallel passages for the combination of this root with ní are not known.—Prof. Max

Müller's opinion is different. He writes: We say, der Funke schlägt oder fängt. Why should not the Hindu have said that Agni strikes out. That would be vi tundate, Agni schlägt aus im Augenblick. But even ni tundate may have been used in the sense of the spark striking down on the tinder—the atasâs, mentioned in verse 2—which he ignites. I should translate: 'The strength-begotten immortal strikes down or breaks forth (vi) quickly, whenever the Hot*ri* (Agni) becomes the messenger of the sacrificer (?).'

Note 2. I cannot follow Aufrecht in his translation 'zum boten des opfernden.' Comp. on Agni as the messenger of Vivasvat, Bergaigne, Rel. Védique, I, 87; H. O., Religion des Veda, 122, 275.

Verse 2.

Note 1. Literally, his back shines like a racer. On this kind of comparison, see Bergaigne, Mélanges Renier, 86; Pischel, Vedische Studien, I, 107.

Verse 3.

Note 1. Krâ*n*ấ: comp. von Bradke, Dyâus Asura, Ahura Mazdâ und die Asuras, p. 36; Pischel, Vedische Studien, I, 70.

Note 2. Bergaigne, Rel. Védique, I, 59 seq.

Verse 4.

Note 1. On v*ri*thâ, see Geldner, Vedische Studien, I, 116; Neisser, Bezzenberger's Beiträge, XIX, 148 seq.

Note 2. The meaning is: with his flames which are sharp like a sickle. S*rí**n*i is written here as a paroxytonon; in several other passages it is an oxytonon. Such differences are not quite rare, and there is no reason for taking on this account s*rí**n*yâ as an instr. plur. fem. of the adjective s*rí**n*ya, 'mit verkürzter Endung' (Geldner, loc. cit.). 'His sickle is the sharp edge of Agni.' M. M.—On *g*uhū́bhi*h*, comp. Pischel, Vedische Studien, II, 111.

Note 3. As to v*ri*shâyáse with the accusative, comp. Gaedicke, 74. RV. X, 44, 4. ûr*g*á*h* skambhám . . . v*ri*shâyase.

Note 4. With the last Pâda comp. IV, 7, 9. k*ri*sh*n*ám te éma rú*s*ata*h* purá*h* bhấ*h*.

Verse 5.

Note 1. That is, among the fuel.

Note 2. I think that we have here probably—(though, of course, this explanation can be avoided)—an anacoluthon. The poet began with the nominative (abhivrá*g*an), and then he changed the construction and went on as if he had begun with the ablative, taking sthâtú*h* *k*arátham (comp. Lanman, 422) as the subject instead of Agni.—Patatrí*n*a*h* seems to be nom. pl.; comp. I, 94, 11 (see below).

Verse 7.

Note 1. The translation of aratí is only approximative and conjectural.

Note 2. Comp. Pischel, Ved. Studien, II, 113.

Note 3. Comp. III, 54, 3. saparyấmi práyasâ yấmi rátnam.

Verse 9.

Note 1. The last Pâda is the standing conclusion of the Nodhas hymns.

MAN*D*ALA I, HYMN 59.

ASH*T*AKA I, ADHYÂYA 4, VARGA 25.

1. The other Agnis (the other fires) are verily thy branches, O Agni. In thee all the immortals enjoy themselves[1]. Vai*s*vânara! Thou art the centre[2] of human settlements; like a supporting column thou holdest men[3].

2. The head of heaven, the navel of the earth is Agni; he has become the steward[1] of both worlds. Thee, a god, the gods have engendered, O Vai*s*vânara, to be a light for the Ârya.

3. As in the sun the rays are firmly fixed, thus in Agni Vai*s*vânara all treasures have been laid down[1]. (The treasures) which dwell in the mountains, in the herbs, the waters, and among men—of all that thou art the king.

4. As the two great worlds to their son[1], like a Hot*ri*, like a skilful man, (we bring) praises—manifold (praises) to him who is united with the sun, to the truly strong one, new (praises) to Vai*s*vânara, the manliest god.

5. Thy greatness, O *G*âtavedas, Vai*s*vânara, has exceeded even the great heaven. Thou art the king of the human tribes; thou hast by fighting gained wide space for the gods.

6. Let me now proclaim the greatness of the bull whom the Pûrus worship as the destroyer of enemies[1]. Agni Vai*s*vânara, having slain the Dasyu, shook the (aerial) arena and cut down *S*ambara.

7. Agni Vaisvânara, extending by his greatness over all dominions, who is to be worshipped, the bright one, rich in loveliness, is awake (or, is praised) among the Bharadvâ*g*as, in the homestead of Puru*n*îtha *S*âtavaneya, with his hundredfold blessings.

NOTES.

The same *Ri*shi as in I, 58. Metre, Trish*t*ubh. None of the verses of this hymn occurs in the other Sa*m*hitâs.

Verse 1.

Note 1. Comp. VII, 11, 1. ná *ri*té tvát am*ri*tâ*h* mâdayante, 'the immortals do not enjoy themselves without thee.'

Note 2. Literally, 'the navel.' Comp. Muir, V, 214.

Note 3. Comp. IV, 5, 1 (see below). úpa stabhâyat upamít ná ródha*h*.

Verse 2.

Note 1. Comp. the remark on I, 58, 7 (note 1).

Verse 3.

Note 1. I cannot follow Prof. von Roth (Zeitschrift der D. Morgenl. Gesellschaft, XLVIII, 116), who explains dadhire as a third person sing. of dh*ri*.

Verse 4.

Note 1. The incompleteness both of the construction and of the metre shows that the text of the first Pâda is corrupt. I doubt whether it ever will be possible to restore the correct reading with full certainty, but I shall be glad if others succeed better than I did—and I may add, better than Prof. von Roth (Zeitschrift der D. Morg. Gesellschaft, XLVIII, 117 seq.) seems to me to have succeeded—in correcting and in interpreting the text. I think that after sûnáve ródasî clearly one syllable is wanted to complete the Pâda: possibly we should read therefore sûnáve ródasyo*h* (comp. verse 2, Pâda 2, aratí*h* ródasyo*h*, which words form the end of the Pâda). Agni, as is well known, is the son of the two worlds, the sûnú*h* ródasyo*h*. In the beginning of the Pâda b*ri*hatî́ must either refer to the two worlds: in this case we have to read b*ri*hatyó*h* (instead of b*ri*hatî́ iva); or b*ri*hatî́ may refer, as this adjective frequently does, to the gíra*h*, and we shall possibly have to read b*ri*hatî́*h* va*h* (as to va*h*, comp. Delbrück, Altindische Syntax, 206). But of course all these are mere guesses. In every case the verb on which the accusative gíra*h* depends ('we bring,' or something like that) must be supplied.

Verse 6.

Note 1. Or, as the killer of V*ri*tra. See H. O., Religion des Veda, 135, note 2.

MA*ND*ALA I, HYMN 60.

ASH*T*AKA I, ADHYÂYA 4, VARGA 26.

1. Mâtari*s*van brought (Agni) to Bh*ri*gu as a gift precious like wealth, of double birth[1], the carrier, the famous, the beacon of the sacrifice[2], the ready and immediately successful messenger.

2. Both follow his command, the U*s*i*g*s[1] offering sacrificial food, and the mortals. The Hot*ri* (Agni) has sat down before daybreak among the clans, the lord of the clans, whose leave should be asked, the performer of worship.

3. May our new, beautiful praise, born[1] from our heart, reach him the honey-tongued (Agni), whom the human priests in our settlement[2], the Âyus, offering enjoyment have engendered.

4. The U*s*i*g*[1], the purifier, the Vasu has been established among men, the best Hot*ri* among the clans, the domestic[2] master of the house in the house: Agni has become the treasure-lord of treasures.

5. Thus we, the Gotamas, praise thee, O Agni, the lord of treasures, with our (pious) thoughts, rubbing thee as (they rub down) a swift racer that wins the prize. May he who gives wealth for our prayer, come quickly in the morning[1].

NOTES.

*Ri*shi and metre are the same. No verse occurs in the other Sa*m*hitâs.

Verse 1.

Note 1. The celestial and the terrestrial birth of Agni. Comp. Bergaigne, Rel. Véd., II, 52.

Note 2. The text has vidáthasya. Comp. I, 31, 6, note 2.

Verse 2.

Note 1. On u*s*íg ('the willing one'), as denoting the mythical priests who have first established Agni and have sacrificed as the first, comp. Bergaigne, I, 57 seq. The ubháyâsa*h* seem to be these mythical ancestors and the actual sacrificers.

Verse 3.

Note 1. I propose to read *g*ấyamânâ. Comp. I, 171, 2. stóma*h* . . . h*ri*dấ tash*t*á*h* ; II, 35, 2. h*ri*dá*h* ấ sútash*t*am mántram ; VIII, 43, 2. ágne *g*ánâmi sush*t*utím ; V, 42, 13. gíram . . . *g*ấyamânâm, &c.—Comp. Lanman, 356.

Note 2. On the meaning of v*rig*ána, see Max Müller, vol. xxxii, pp. xx, 208, 304 ; Geldner, Vedische Studien, I, 139 seq., with my remarks, Göttinger Gelehrte Anzeigen, 1890, 410 seq.; Ludwig, Ueber Methode bei Interpretation des *Ri*g-veda, 27 seq. ; Colinet, Les Principes de l'Exégèse Védique d'après MM. Pischel et Geldner, 28 seq. ; von Bradke, Zeitschrift der Deutschen Morg. Gesellschaft, XLVIII, 500 ; Bechtel, Nachrichten der Göttinger Gesellschaft der Wiss., 1894, 392 seq.

Verse 4.

Note 1. See verse 2, note 1.

Note 2. Bartholomae's theory (Bezzenberger's Beiträge, XV, 194) that the stem dámûnas has been developed out of the phrase dámû na*h*, 'in our house,' does not carry conviction.

Verse 5.

Note 1. See I, 58, 9, note 1.

MA*N**D*ALA I, HYMN 65.

ASH*T*AKA I, ADHYÂYA 5, VARGA 9.

1[1]. Thee who hidest thyself in secret like a thief with an animal[2] (which he has stolen)—who hadst harnessed[3] adoration and carriedst adoration—

2. The wise unanimously followed by thy footmarks[1]. All (gods) deserving worship (reverentially) sat down near thee.

3. The gods followed the laws of *Ri*ta. There was an encompassing as the heaven (encompasses) the earth[1].

4. In the lap, in the womb of *Ri*ta, the waters nourish the fine child with praise, him who is well born.

5. Like good fortune, like a broad abode, like the fertile hill[1], like the refreshing stream,

6. Like a racer urged forward in the race, like the rapids of the Sindhu[1]—who can hold him back?

7. (He is) the kinsman of the rivers, as a brother of his sisters. He eats the forests as a king (eats, i. e. takes the wealth of) the rich[1].

8. When he has spread through the forests, driven by the wind, Agni shears the hair of the earth.

9. Sitting in the waters he hisses like a swan. (He is) most famous by his power of mind, he who belongs to the clans, awakening at dawn—

10. A performer of worship like Soma, the god born from *Ri*ta, like a young (?)[1] beast, far-extending, far-shining.

NOTES.

The authorship of the whole collection, I, 65–73, is ascribed to Parâ*s*ara *S*âktya. These hymns are addressed exclusively to Agni. The greater part of them (65–70) is composed in the Virâ*g* metre; comp. on this metre my Prolegomena, 95 seq. I have given there my reasons for considering that each verse consists of twenty, not of forty syllables.

This section ascribed to Parâ*s*ara has been treated of by Bollensen, Zeitschrift der D. Morg. Gesellschaft, XXII, 569 seq. No verse of these hymns composed in the metre Dvipadâ Virâ*g* (I, 65–70) occurs in the other Sa*m*hitâs.

Verse 1.

Note 1. Professor Max Müller proposes the following translation for verses 1 and 2: The wise (gods) together followed thee (Agni) when in hiding, by means of footsteps, as one follows a thief by the animal; they followed thee who accepts and carries adoration (to the gods). All the worshipful gods sat down (reverentially) near thee.

Note 2. There is no reason for reading with Bartholomae (Studien zur indogermanischen Sprachgeschichte, I, 48) pa*s*vấn (gen. plur.) ná tâyúm.

Note 3. Ludwig proposes yuvânám, which is quite unnecessary.—See also Gaedicke, 173.

Verse 2.

Note 1. We have here the well-known myth of the hidden Agni discovered by the gods. The 'wise ones,' (dhī́râ*h*) are no doubt the searching gods, the same who are called yá*g*atrâ*h* in the last Pâda, and who are expressly designated as devấ*h* in verse 3. Comp. Bergaigne, I, 110.

Verse 3.

Note 1. Regarding the construction, see Gaedicke, 192.—Professor Max Müller's opinion on this phrase differs from mine. He writes: 'I should prefer parîsh*t*i. But parish*t*i seems to mean a running about, reconnoitring, searching. "There was searching on earth as in heaven," lit. earth, like heaven, was reconnoitring-ground.'

Verse 5.

Note 1. Comp. VIII, 50, 2. girí*h* ná bhu*g*mấ. I believe that Boehtlingk-Roth, Bollensen, and Grassmann are right in correcting our passage accordingly; ra*n*vấ, p*ri*thvī́, *s*ambhú follow the gender of the corresponding substantives, and the same may be expected here. Comp. Lanman, 530. The meaning is that Agni yields nourishment to all beings as a mountain fertilises the country by the waters which come down from it; comp. VIII, 49, 2. giré*h* iva prá rásâ*h* asya pinvire dátrâ*n*i purubhó*g*asa*h*.

Verse 6.

Note 1. Regarding the construction, comp. Gaedicke, 252 seq.; Bergaigne, Mélanges Renier, 95. Joh. Schmidt (Die Pluralbildungen der indogerm. Neutra, 305) and Ludwig (V, 524) are wrong in taking kshóda*h* as a locative or as an instrumental respectively.

Verse 7.

Note 1. Comp. Pischel-Geldner, Vedische Studien, I, p. xvi.

Verse 10.

Note 1. Can *s*í*s*vâ be the nominative of a stem *s*í*s*van which stands by the side of *s*í*s*u as *ri*bhvan of *ri*bhú? Prof. Max Müller proposes: 'Large like a cow with young, like a pregnant cow.'

MAṆḌALA I, HYMN 66.

ASHṬAKA I, ADHYÂYA 5, VARGA 10.

1. Like unto excellent wealth, like unto the shine of the sun, like unto living breath, like unto one's own[1] son—

2. Like unto a quick takvan[1] he (Agni) holds the wood, like milk, like a milch cow[2], bright and shining.

3. He holds safety, pleasant like a homestead, like ripe barley, a conqueror of men,

4. Like a *Ri*shi uttering (sacred) shouts, praised among the clans; like a well-cared-for race-horse[1], Agni bestows vigour.

5. He to whose flame men do not grow accustomed[1], who is like one's own mind[2], like a wife on a couch, enough for all (happiness).

6. When the bright (Agni) has shone forth, he is like a white (horse [?])[1] among people, like a chariot with golden ornaments, impetuous in fights.

7. Like an army which is sent forward he shows his vehemence, like an archer's shaft with sharp point.

8. He who is born is one twin; he who will be born[1] is the other twin—the lover of maidens, the husband of wives[2].

9[1]. As cows go to their stalls, all that moves and we, for the sake of a dwelling, reach him who has been kindled.

10. Like the flood of the Sindhu[1] he has driven forward the downwards-flowing (waters)[2]. The cows lowed at the sight of the sun[3].

NOTES.

The same *Ri*shi and metre.

Verse 1.

Note 1. Comp. I, 166, 2; 185, 2; X, 39, 14. The second passage (nítyam ná sûnúm pitró*h* upásthe dyấvâ rákshatam p*ri*thivî na*h* ábhvât) would be sufficient to show that we cannot translate 'wie ein überlebender sohn' (Ludwig).

Verse 2.

Note 1. We do not know what animal the takvan is. Comp. I, 134, 5 with M. M.'s note.

Note 2. See Bergaigne, Mél. Renier, 101; Gaedicke, 253.

Verse 4.

Note 1. Comp. X, 101, 7. prî*n*îtá á*s*vân hitám *g*ayâtha.

Verse 5.

Note 1. Comp. VII, 4, 3. durókam agní*h* âyáve *s*u*s*o*k*a.

Note 2. Prof. Max Müller believes that kratu here means, 'like kart*ri*, a sacrificer, so that kratu*h* na nitya*h* sounds like sûnu*h* na nitya*h*, one's own sacrificing son. But all this is very obscure.'

Verse 6.

Note 1. The second Pâda is translated by Grassmann: 'wie Licht in Häusern;' by Ludwig: 'fast weiss, bei den menschenstämmen.' I think that there can be no doubt that the words *s*vetá*h* ná contain a comparison like all the other comparisons of which these hymns are full; this comparison is unduly effaced in Ludwig's translation. Nor is Grassmann right in translating *s*vetá*h* bei 'Licht;' the word is an adjective meaning 'white' and nothing else. We must supply here, as in many passages, a substantive, and I do not see any reason why this should not be that substantive with which *s*veta is most frequently combined in the Rig-veda, namely a*s*va; comp. I, 116, 6; 118, 9 [119, 10]; VII, 77, 3; X, 39, 10. In V, 1, 4 it is said of Agni: *s*vetá*h* vâ*g*î́ *g*âyate ágre áhnâm, 'the white racer is born in the beginning of the days.'

Verse 8.

Note 1. The traditional text is yamá*h* ha *g*âtá*h* yamá*h* *g*ánitvam. Ludwig translates 'bewältiger des gebornen, bewältiger auch des, was erst geboren wird.' It will scarcely be necessary to state the reasons which make against this translation. Yamá*h* . . . yamá*h* evidently means: 'the one twin . . . the other twin.' Now if we leave the text unchanged, we cannot but translate: 'the one twin is he who has been born, the other twin is that which will be born'—which sounds very strange. In I, 89, 10 we have áditi*h* *g*âtám áditi*h* *g*ánitvam; IV, 18, 4. antá*h* *g*âtéshu utá yé *g*ánitvâ*h*; X, 45, 10. út *g*âténa bhinádat út *g*ánitvai*h*. In all these cases *g*âtá and *g*ánitva stand parallel; there is no such difference as in our passage, according to the traditional text, between him (masc.) who is . . . and that (neuter) which will be . . . Thus I propose to read *g*ánitva*h*, of which conjecture Ludwig has thought also (see his note, IV, 259): that present Agni who has been born, and that future Agni who will be born, are twins.—Prof. Max Müller has discussed this passage in his Science of Language, II, 630 seqq. He interprets the twin who has been born as Agni representing the morning; the twin who will be born as the evening.

Note 2. The maidens very probably are the dawns (comp. Prof. Max Müller's discussion quoted in the last note). Are the wives the sacrificial ladles which approach Agni, or the offerings of ghee, or the prayers? See Bergaigne, Rel. Védique, II, 9 seqq.

Verse 9.

Note 1. This verse is very obscure, and I am quite aware of the merely tentative character of the translation which

I propose. I leave va*h* untranslated (comp. Delbrück, Altindische Syntax, 206), which must be done in most of the numerous verses beginning with the words tám va*h*. I then read *k*arathâ (comp. 68, 1 ; 70, 3. 7). Vasatyā́ seems to be either a dative similar to the newly-discovered datives in -â of a-stems, or we possibly should read vasatyaí (vasatyā́ in the Sa*m*hitâ-pâ*th*a).—Prof. Max Müller thinks of a correction *k*arâma*h* and would translate: 'To him (whom you know—va*h*) when lighted we go for our dwelling, as the cows reach their home.'

Verse 10.

Note 1. Comp. above, 65, 6.

Note 2. Or the downwards-streaming libations of Gh*ri*ta and the like? Comp. below, I, 72, 10 with note 4.

Note 3. Comp. below, 69, 10.

MANDALA I, HYMN 67.

ASHTAKA I, ADHYÂYA 5, VARGA 11.

1. Victorious[1] in the forests, a friend among men, he demands obedience like a king, the undecaying one[2].

2. Like good peace, like fortunate wisdom, may he (Agni) be a kind Hotri, a carrier of offerings.

3. Having taken in his hand all manly powers, he has made the gods fear, when sitting down in his hiding-place.

4. There the thoughtful men find him, when they have recited the spells which they had fashioned in their heart.

5. As the goat[1] (supports) the earth[2], thus he supports the earth[2]; he upholds the sky by his efficacious spells.

6. Protect the dear[1] footsteps of the cattle[2]. O Agni, thou who hast a full life, thou hast gone from covert to covert[3].

7. He who has seen him the hidden one, he who has got near to the stream of *Ri*ta[1]—

8. They who get him off, doing service to *Ri*ta, to him[1] he then indicates riches.

9. He who grows up with might within the plants, and within the children[1], and within the sprouting grass[2]—

10. The splendour [?] in the home of the waters[1], the full-lived. The sages made him as if building a seat.

NOTES.

The same *Ri*shi and metre.

Verse 1.

Note 1. '*G*âyu*h* : aus *g*yâyu*h*, wie der compar. *g*yâyân *g*yesh*th*a*h* zeigt,' Ludwig. But what shows that *g*yâyân is the comparative of *g*âyu*h* and that the utterly impossible change of *g*y into *g* is possible? Ludwig's translation 'überwindend' is right; comp. I, 119, 3.

Note 2. I propose to read a*g*uryá*h*. Prof. Max Müller conjectures—as Roth (Pet. Dict.) has done—that *s*rush*t*i may mean 'obedient, servant;' he translates: 'He desires a servant (or worshipper) who is not aged.'

Verse 5.

Note 1. On the mythical goat whose office it is to support the worlds, comp. I, 164, 6; VIII, 41, 10; X, 82, 6; Bergaigne, III, 21; H. O., Religion des Veda, 72.

Note 2. For 'earth' the text has two different words, kshấm and p*ri*thivī́m. Prof. Max Müller conjectures dyấm for kshấm: 'He, Agni, supports the earth, as the buck the sky.'

Verse 6.

Note 1. Literally, 'the dear footsteps;' but the meaning of priyá may be compared to that of the Homeric φίλος, his own.

Note 2. One could be tempted to refer the word pa*s*u to Agni, whose footsteps (padấni) the 'wise ones' follow (65, 2), and whom they find out in his hiding. Thus we could translate, 'Look at the dear footsteps of the beast.' But the comparison of 70, 6 makes it more probable that the imperative ní pâhi is addressed to Agni. I believe therefore that Grassmann is right in translating 'Die lieben Stätten der Heerden schütze.' Ludwig's translation is similar to this. Prof. Max Müller translates: 'Observe the footsteps of the animal (the stolen animal of the thief Agni).'

Note 3. With guhấ gúham comp. I, 53, 7. yudhấ yúdham, purấ púram.

Verse 7.

Note 1. Dhấrâm *ri*tásya: comp. V, 12, 2. *ri*tásya dhấrâ*h* ánu t*ri*ndhi pûrvî́*h*, 'open the many streams of *Ri*ta;' VII, 43, 4. *ri*tásya dhấrâ*h* sudúghâ*h* dúhânâ*h*, 'milking the streams of *Ri*ta flowing with plenty.' The stream of *Ri*ta seems to mean the stream of blessings (such as rain, ghee, &c.) which flows to mankind according to the eternal laws of *Ri*ta.

Verse 8.

Note 1. The poet passes over from the plural to the singular.

Verse 9.

Note 1. Bollensen's conjecture pra*g*ấsu (instead of pra*g*ấ*h* utá) seems very probable to me. Prof. von Roth (Ueber gewisse Kürzungen des Wortendes, p. 2) takes a different view.

Note 2. Comp. I, 95, 10 (see below); VII, 9, 3. apấm gárbha*h* prasvà*h* ấ vive*s*a, 'the son of the waters has entered upon the sprouting grass.'

Verse 10.

Note 1. 'Why not *k*iti*h* apâm dame, that is, the (burning) pile in the home of the waters.' M. M.

MAṆḌALA I, HYMN 68.

ASHṬAKA I, ADHYÂYA 5, VARGA 12.

1. Cooking[1] (the oblations?) the quick one has approached the sky. He has revealed the nights and what stands and moves[2]—

2. When he the god, alone of all these gods[1] encompassed (the others) by his greatness.

3. When thou, O god, hadst been born living from the dry (wood), then all (gods and men?) were pleased with thy wisdom.

4. They all obtained the name of divinity, of immortality[1], serving the *Ri*ta in due way.

5. The instigations of *Ri*ta, the thought of *Ri*ta[1]: they all performed the works of [?] the full-lived one[2].

6. Bestow wealth, thou who art the knowing one, on him who worships thee or who does service to thee[1].

7. He who sits down as the Hot*ri* among the offspring of Manu: he verily is the master of all these riches.

8. They longed together for the seed in their bodies[1], and the wise ones were concordant among each other in their minds.

9. They took pleasure in his will, as sons (take pleasure) in their father's (will), the quick ones who have listened to his command.

10. He who is rich in food has opened the gates of wealth[1]. The householder (Agni) has adorned the sky with stars.

NOTES.

The same *Ri*shi and metre.

Verse 1.

Note 1. Boehtlingk-Roth are wrong in deriving *s*rî*n*án (which should more correctly be written *s*ri*n*án, comp. my Prolegomena, 477) from the root *s*ri. They supply an object like *sok*i*h* and translate: 'Licht verbreitend hebt er sich zum Himmel.'

Note 2. Lanman, 422.

Verse 2.

Note 1. Bollensen conjectures devấnâm devá*h* (instead of devá*h* devấnâm) which seems to be right (comp. below, 69, 2), though this conjecture is not absolutely necessary (see my Prolegomena, 97).

Verse 4.

Note 1. Am*r*í*t*am belongs to nấma; comp. V, 57, 5. am*r*í*t*am nấma bhe*g*ire; X, 123, 4. vidát gandharvá*h* am*r*í-tâni nấma.

Verse 5.

Note 1. With *r*itásya dhîtí*h* comp. I, 71, 3; IV, 23, 8; IX, 76, 4; 97, 34; 111, 2.—Prof. Max Müller thinks that *r*ita should be taken as a name of Agni: 'for the righteous (Agni) are the prayers, for the righteous the devotion.'

Note 2. Is vi*s*vấyu*h* an adverb meaning 'eternally'? As vi*s*vấyu is an epithet of Agni frequently used in the Rig-veda and especially in the Parâ*s*ara hymns (see 67, 6. 10; 68, 5; 73, 4), one feels tempted to read vi*s*vấyo*h* (comp. IV, 42, 1. râsh*t*rám kshatríyasya vi*s*vấyo*h*).

Verse 6.

Note 1. Comp. III, 59, 2. yá*h* te âditya *s*íkshati vraténa.

Verse 8.

Note 1. Some light is thrown on this obscure verse by the hymn, I, 72, a hymn belonging, as our hymn does, to the Parâ*s*ara collection. It is shown by the second verse of that hymn (see below) that the searching ones, 'ámûrâ*h*,' are the gods who seek Agni. It seems probable, consequently, that the 'seed' is Agni (comp. I, 164, 35, where Soma is said to be v*rí*sh*n*a*h* á*s*vasya réta*h*, 'the seed of the manly horse'). Of the same searching gods in I, 72, 5 the expression sa*mg*ânânā́*h* is used; comp. sám *g*ânata in our passage.

Verse 10.

Note 1. Rā́ya*h* must be a genitive; comp. I, 72, 8. râyá*h* dúra*h* ví *ri*ta*g*ñā́*h* a*g*ânan. Probably the accent should be râyá*h*; comp., however, Lanman, 431.

MANDALA I, HYMN 69.

ASHTAKA I, ADHYÂYA 5, VARGA 13.

1. Bright, flaming, like the lover of the Dawn[1], he has, like the light of the sky, filled the two (worlds of Heaven and Earth) which are turned towards each other.

2. As soon as thou wert born thou hast excelled by thy power of mind; being the son of the gods thou hast become their father.

3. (Agni is) a worshipper (of the gods), never foolish, (always) discriminating; (he is) like the udder of the cows; (he is) the sweetness of food[1]—

4. Like a kind friend to men, not to be led astray[1], sitting in the midst, the lovely one, in the house;

5. Like a child when born, he is delightful in the house; like a race-horse which is well cared for[1], he has wandered across the clans[2].

6. When I call (to the sacrifice) the clans who dwell in the same nest with the heroes, may Agni then attain all divine powers[1].

7. When thou hast listened to these heroes, no one breaks those laws of thine.

8. That verily is thy wonderful deed that thou hast killed[1], with thy companions, (all foes), that, joined by the heroes, thou hast accomplished thy works[2].

9. Like the lover of the Dawn[1], resplendent and bright, of familiar form: may he (thus) pay attention to this (sacrificer).

10. Carrying (him) they opened by themselves the doors (of heaven). They all shouted at the aspect of the sun [1].

NOTES.

The same *Ri*shi and metre.

Verse 1.

Note 1. The lover of the Dawn is here the Sun. See Pischel, Vedische Studien, I, 31.

Verse 3.

Note 1. Agni is the sweetness of food (comp. V, 7, 6. svā́danam pitûnā́m); it is not probable that svā́dma and ū́dha*h* should depend on vi*g*ânán, as Ludwig believes.

Verse 4.

Note 1. I adopt Boehtlingk-Roth's conjecture ahûryá*h*. Âhū́rya*h* would mean, 'he who is to be led astray.'

Verse 5.

Note 1. See above, 66, 4.
Note 2. 'He has overcome the (hostile) clans.' M. M.

Verse 6.

Note 1. Perhaps devatvā́ is an instrumental, as Ludwig takes it. In this case we should have to translate: 'may Agni by his divine power attain everything.'—Prof. Max Müller translates this verse: 'When I with my men call the clans of the same nest (the gods), Agni will obtain all divine honours.'

Verse 8.

Note 1. The first hemistich of this verse has eleven syllables instead of ten and shows the regular Trish*t*ubh type. The same irregularity occurs in 70, 4. 10. As I have shown in my Prolegomena, p. 97, this metrical irregularity does not necessitate corrections of the text, and the comparison of X, 147, 1 (see next note), where it is said áhan yát vritrám . . . vivéh apáh, seems even to confirm the traditional reading. It cannot be denied, however, that the double yát and the use of áhan without an object raises some suspicion. In I, 34, 3; 186, 4 we have samâné áhan. Possibly we may read, tát tú te dámsah áhan samâné, 'this wonderful deed of thine has been accomplished on one and the same day (with that mentioned in verse 7).' I am fully aware of the uncertainty of such guesses. The removal of yát has already been proposed by Bollensen (Zeitschrift der Deutschen Morg. Gesellschaft, XXII, 592).

Note 2. Here we may correct the text with greater certainty than in the first hemistich, or to speak more accurately, we shall have to correct not the traditional text itself, but that ancient grammatical commentary on the text which has been preserved to us in the Padapâtha. The words vivérápâmsi of the Samhitâpâtha are written in the Padapâtha vivéh rápâmsi. Now we read IV, 19, 10. ápâmsi . . . nárya áviveshîh, 'thou hast performed manly works.' In X, 147, 1 we have áhan yát vritrám náryam vivéh apáh: here the adjective nárya clearly shows that apáh is a blunder for ápah, and we must translate, 'when thou hast killed Vritra and performed thy manly work.' This passage shows that in X, 76, 3 also vivéh apáh should be corrected (v. ápah). Thus we have three passages in which áviveshîh or vivéh has the object ápah, ápâmsi, and we may infer with full certainty that in our passage vivérápâmsi does not correspond to a Padapâtha reading vivéh rápâmsi but vivéh ápâmsi. The same may be said with regard to VI, 31, 3 (mushâyáh kakrám áviveh rápâmsi; Samh. ávive rápâmsi).

Verse 9.

Note 1. Comp. above, verse 1.

Verse 10.

Note 1. Comp. above, 66, 10.

MAN*D*ALA I, HYMN 70.

ASHT*A*KA I, ADHYÂYA 5, VARGA 14.

1. May we, the poor[1], succeed in many (pious) thoughts[2]. May Agni with his pure splendour attain everything—

2. He who understands the divine laws and the birth of the human race.

3. He who is the child of the waters, the child of the trees, the child of that which stands, and the child of that which moves.

4. Even in the rock (they have done homage [?]) to him, in his dwelling[1]. (He is) like a protector [?][2] of the clans, the immortal one, he who is of a good mind.

5. For he, Agni, (shows himself as) an earth-protecting (lord) of riches[1] to the man who satisfies him with well-spoken (prayers).

6. Protect, O knowing one, these beings, thou who knowest the birth of gods and men[1].

7. He whom many nights (and dawns), in their different forms[1], may increase, whom that which moves[2] and that which stands (increases), the god penetrated by *Ri*ta—

8. That Hot*ri* who has sat down in the sun[1], has been successfully worshipped[2] (by the human sacrificers), he who truly accomplishes all his works.

9. On the cows, on the trees thou hast conferred excellence. May all men bring us tribute in the sun[1].

10. In many places men have worshipped thee. They have brought (thee) to different places[1] as sons (divide) the property of an aged father[2].

11[1]. (He is) like a greedy man[2] who goes straight (to his aim), like a mighty archer, like a fearful avenger [?][3], impetuous in contests[4].

NOTES.

The same *Ri*shi and metre.

Verse 1.

Note 1. I adopt Bergaigne's opinion on the word arí (see Religion Védique, II, 218 seq.).

Note 2. The Padapâ*th*a has manîshấ instead of manîshấ*h*. See my Prolegomena, 385; Lanman, 363. Prof. Max Müller proposes to translate: 'May we by wisdom overcome many enemies!' He writes: 'Is not vanema almost a standing formula as applied to enemies? Let us conquer the enemies. The enemies are masculine in VII, 48, 3. ví*s*vân aryá*h* ... vanvan, feminine in VI, 16, 27. vanvánta*h* aryá*h* árâtî*h*. VIII, 39, 2. ví*s*vâ*h* aryá*h* árâtî*h*. X, 133, 3. ví*s*vâ*h* árâtaya*h* aryá*h*. IV, 50, 11. *g*a*g*astám aryá*h* vanúshâm árâtî*h* (repeated VII, 97, 9; cf. I, 29, 4).' For my translation I refer to II, 5, 7. stómam ... vanéma; II, 11, 12. dhíyam vanema; I, 122, 14. aryá*h* gíra*h*; X, 148, 3. aryá*h* vâ gíra*h* abhí ar*k*a vidvấn.

Verse 4.

Note 1. Or: even in the rock (they have done homage) to him, and in the (human) dwelling? I believe we must supply a verb on which the dative asmai depends. Ludwig proposes to read duro*n*ám: 'within the stone is his dwelling.' Comp. II, 1, 1; VI, 48, 5.

Note 2. I do not understand vi*s*ấm ná ví*s*va*h*. Ludwig translates 'er ist der menschen allgemeiner, unsterblicher fürsorger.' But ví*s*va does not mean 'allgemein,' and Ludwig omits ná, 'like.' One should expect a phrase like vi*s*ấm ná vi*s*páti*h*, which of course is metrically impossible. Is it too bold to correct ví*s*va*h* into vi*s*pấ*h*, a word hitherto not found in the texts, but formed exactly like stipấ, pa*s*upấ, tanûpấ and others?—Prof. Max Müller takes asmai as dependent on svâdhî́*h* and ví*s*va*h* as belonging at the same time to am*ri*ta*h* and to vi*s*ấm. He translates: 'To him also who dwells in the rock and in the house, every immortal like every one among men is well disposed.'

Verse 5.

Note 1. Comp. VII, 10, 5. sá hí kshápâvân ábhavat rayî*n*ấm.

Verse 6.

Note 1. Most probably we have here not the accusative mártân but the genitive mártâm, which was confounded by the arrangers of the traditional text with the accusative and treated according to the Sandhi rules which govern the ending -ân. See Lanman, Noun-Inflection, 353; Bartholomae, Studien zur indogermanischen Sprachgeschichte, I, 48.

Verse 7.

Note 1. Lanman (p. 422) takes kshapá*h* vírûpâ*h* as accusatives, and translates, 'Whom through many nights and mornings all beings worship.' I believe that they are nominatives, and that we should accentuate kshápa*h*. As vírûpa is a regular epithet of náktoshấsâ, I think that kshápa*h* is to be understood as an elliptic plural similar to the elliptic duals ushấsâ or áhanî (comp. Delbrück, Altindische Syntax, 102), and that it means, 'the nights (and mornings).'—Comp. VI, 38, 4. várdhân mấsâ*h* *s*aráda*h* dyấva*h* índram, 'May months, years, days increase Indra's greatness.'

Note 2. Of course *k*a rátham is a mistake for *k*arátham, as first pointed out by Benfey.

Verse 8.

Note 1. On the locative svar, see Lanman, 488; Joh. Schmidt in Kuhn's Zeitschrift, XXVII, 306; Bartholomae in Bezzenberger's Beiträge, XV, 42. Comp. X, 61, 14. svah ná yé trishadhasthé nishedúh.

Note 2. Comp. X, 53, 2. árâdhi hótâ nishádâ yágîyân.

Verse 9.

Note 1. Is it not more probable that tribute was brought to Agni (comp. V, 1, 10) than to the human worshippers? Possibly we should change svah nah (svar nah of the Samhitâpâtha) into svarnah, a vocative of the stem svarnri = svarnara. The translation would be, 'All men have brought tribute to thee, O sun-hero!'

Verse 10.

Note 1. Comp. V, 11, 4. agním nárah ví bharante grihégrihe.

Note 2. Regarding the metre, comp. above, 69, 8, note 1.

Verse 11.

Note 1. This verse may possibly be a later addition. See Bergaigne, Recherches sur l'Histoire de la Samhitâ, I, 61.

Note 2. On gridhnú, comp. Pischel, Ved. Studien, I, 231.

Note 3. Comp. I, 32, 14. áheh yâtâram.

Note 4. See above, 66, 6.

MAN*D*ALA I, HYMN 71.

ASH*T*AKA I, ADHYÂYA 5, VARGA 15–16.

1. The loving (women) have (amorously) excited [1] their lover, as wives of the same nest (house) their own husband. The sisters have delighted in the dark and in the red (goddess) [2], as the cows in the brightly shining dawn.

2. Our fathers, the Aṅgiras [1], have broken even the strong fortresses by their hymns, the rock by their shouting. They have opened to us the path of the great heaven; they have obtained day and sun and the shine of the dawn [2].

3. They founded the *Ri*ta; they set into motion the thought of it [1]. Thus then the widely-spread (prayers) [2] of the poor [3] which seek to obtain (wealth), which are free from thirst [4], the active, approach [5] the tribe of the gods [6], strengthening them by offering them delight.

4. When Mâtari*s*van had produced him by attrition, he, the reddish, the noble one, who was brought to many places [1], has come to every house. Then the Bh*ri*gu-like [2] has undertaken the messengership [3] (for the mortal) as for a mightier king, being attached to him.

5. When he had created sap to the great father Heaven, the knowing one stealthily approached the speckled (cows). The archer fiercely shot an arrow at him. The god turned his impetuous power against his daughter [1].

6. Augment, O Agni, twofold the strength of

the man who worships[1] thee in his house, or offers adoration to the loving one[2] day by day. May he whom thou incitest be united with riches[3].

7. Every nourishment goes towards Agni[1], as the seven young[2] rivers (flow) into the ocean. Our strength does not shine from kinsmen[3]. Do thou therefore who knowest this, procure among the gods kindness for us.

8[1]. When the sharp splendour[2] reached the lord of men to incite him[3], the bright sperm poured down from Heaven (or, from the god Dyaus)[4], Agni produced[5] and furthered the blameless, young, well-wishing host[6].

9. He who traverses the paths quickly[1] like thought, the Sun alone rules over wealth altogether. (There are) the two kings Mitra and Varu*n*a with graceful hands[2], who watch over the beloved ambrosia[3] in the cows.

10. Do not forget, O Agni, who art a sage possessed of knowledge[1], our paternal friendship. Old age impairs the appearance (of men) as a cloud (covers the sun or the sky). Before this curse (attains us), think thou (of us)[2].

NOTES.

The same *Ri*shi. Metre, Trish*t*ubh.

Though the hymns 71–73 are not composed in the Virâ*g* metre like the preceding hymns, it is shown by manifold evidence that they had the same origin. Verse 8 = VS. XXXIII, 11; TS. I, 3, 14, 6; MS. IV, 14, 15.

Verse 1.

Note 1. Comp. Geldner, Vedische Studien, II, 134.

Note 2. If the text is correct, the 'sisters' may either be the ten fingers which generate Agni by attrition (III, 29, 13; IV, 6, 8), or the streams of water among which Agni grows up, or streams of Gh*ri*ta or the like (comp. II, 5, 5; see below). Why these sisters are said to delight in the dark and in the bright goddess, the Night and the Dawn, remains doubtful.

But I think there are reasons which strongly recommend a correction of the text. In III, 55, 11 we read *s*yấvî *k*a . . . árushî *k*a svásârau, 'the two sisters, the dark one and the red one.' Is it not probable that in our passage also it is the sisters who are described as dark and red? The dark goddess and the red goddess of course are Night and Dawn, and Night and Dawn, as is well known, are sisters in Vedic poetry. And furthermore the 'sisters' are described in our verse as amorously exciting the god Agni: for it cannot well be doubted that the svásâra*h* of the third Pâda are identical with the u*s*atî́*h* of the first: similarly it is said in 70, 7—in a hymn belonging to the same collection with our Sûkta—that the Nights and Dawns augment Agni's greatness; in other passages Agni is represented as beloved by the Dawn, or as suckled by Night and Dawn (Bergaigne, Religion Védique, II, 14. 15). The 'sisters' then are stated in our verse to delight (a*g*ushran), probably in Agni: now we read in II, 2, 2. abhí tvâ náktî*h* ushása*h* vavâ*s*ire ágne vatsám ná svásareshu dhenáva*h*, 'The Nights and Dawns, Agni, have lowed at thee as the milch-cows in their stalls at their calves;' comp. Bergaigne, II, 15. Thus everything is clear, if we take the u*s*atî́*h* and the svásâra*h* for the bright and dark goddesses, i. e. for the Dawns and Nights. The correction of the text to which this interpretation leads, is svásâra*h* *s*yấvî*h* árushî*h* a*g*ushran, 'the dark and the red sisters have delighted (in Agni).' It is easy to understand that the corruption of the text was occasioned by the simile of the fourth Pâda. The words ushásam ná gấva*h* seemed to demand a parallel nominative and a parallel accusative in the third Pâda. The nominative was svásâra*h*, but there was no accusative. Thus probably arose the reading *s*yấvîm árushîm.

Verse 2.

Note 1. On the Aṅgiras as the fathers of the priestly tribes, see H. O., Religion des Veda, 278.

Note 2. The phrase ushásaḥ ketúḥ occurs several times in the Rig-veda. I think that ketúm usrā́ḥ means exactly the same; it has been shown by Kaegi, Festgruss an Boehtlingk, p. 49, and by Bartholomae, Bezzenberger's Beiträge, XV, 185, that a genitive sing. usrā́ḥ existed.

Verse 3.

Note 1. Ludwig refers asya to the sacrificer, Bollensen to Agni, and so does Sâyaṇa. I believe that asya should be explained as *ri*tásya; the phrase *ri*tásya dhîtí is frequently used, comp. IV, 23, 8; IX, 76, 4; 97, 34; 111, 2. See also Ludwig's note on III, 31, 1 (vol. v, p. 65).—Prof. Max Müller refers *ri*ta to Agni. 'One might translate it by righteous: They established the righteous (Agni), they moved his mind (made him attend?).'

Note 2. The substantive (of feminine gender) which is to be supplied to didhishvā́ḥ, át*ri*shyantîḥ, &c., seems to me to be gíraḥ or the like. Aryā́ḥ stands frequently together with gíraḥ.—Prof. Max Müller writes: 'Could not ari be a feminine like *k*arshaṇi and viś; see before, I, 70, 1. We should then translate, and then the people emulous, widely spread, never flagging [the stones also are called at*ri*shitâḥ at*ri*sh*n*agaḥ, X, 94, 11], and active go towards the gods.'

Note 3. See above, 70, 1, note 1.

Note 4. Are the prayers called 'free from thirst' because they are accompanied by libations of Gh*ri*ta, Soma, &c.?

Note 5. I believe that devā́n *g*ánma depends both on á*kkh*â and on vardháyantîḥ.

Note 6. Devā́n, or rather devā́m, is gen. plur.; see above, 70, 6, with note 1.

Verse 4.

Note 1. The place in which víbh*ri*taḥ stands would seem to show that it is an epithet of Mâtariśvan, and so it is understood by Ludwig and by Bergaigne (Rel. Véd. I, 54).

But it is Agni himself, not Mâtarisvan, who is very frequently mentioned as vibh*ri*ta or the like. As we read here, víbh*ri*ta*h* . . . g*ri*hé-g*ri*he, it is said in V, 11, 4. agním nára*h* ví bharante g*ri*hé-g*ri*he, 'the men carry Agni hither and thither, to every house;' comp. I, 70, 10; III, 55, 4; X, 1, 2; 45, 2; 80, 4. Thus I believe the poet means to say that Mâtari*s*van first kindled Agni, in one place of course, and that Agni then was brought to many places, to all human dwellings. I think that the text indeed can be understood in this way, if we suppose that the author, for the sake of the metre, allowed himself a hyperbaton or synchysis.

We must not omit to mention that the first Pâda of I, 148, 1 is nearly identical with our passage: máthît yát îm vish*táh* mâtarí*s*vâ. This Pâda is deficient by one syllable. If we were to read víbh*ri*ta*h*, as in our passage, this would lead indeed to the conclusion that there is no hyperbaton in our verse—for the verse, I, 148, 1, could not be explained in that way—but that víbh*ri*ta*h* refers to Mâtari*s*van. I think, however, that it is more than doubtful that the verse, I, 148, 1, really ought to be corrected in this way; whatever may have been the original form of that verse, it is quite possible, and even probable, that it differed from our passage just in that one word.

Note 2. The exact meaning of Bh*rí*gavâ*n*a is doubtful. It is, of course, derived from Bh*rí*gu as vásavâna, tákavâna, from vásu, táku. Agni is called Bh*rí*gavâ*n*a also in IV, 7, 4. Comp. Bergaigne, I, 54.

Note 3. With the words ấ dûtyam vivâya comp. IV, 9, 6. véshi ít u asya dûtyam.

Verse 5.

Note 1. This difficult verse evidently treats of the incest which the father Dyaus has committed with his daughter. Compare on this subject Bergaigne, Rel. Véd. II, 109 seq. Agni seems to be represented here as stimulating the desire of the father; the 'sap' (rása) probably is the sperm, comp. I, 105, 2.

In the second Pâda, Agni, having done, as it seems, some mischief, goes away to the 'speckled cows.' We cannot say who these speckled cows were; they evidently are identical with those mentioned in another passage treating of the same story, X, 61, 8.—Bergaigne paraphrases the second Pâda of our verse, wrongly in my opinion, 'Agni sort furtivement de cette fille, de cette vache, p*ri*s*an*î́.'

The archer who shoots at Agni (third Pâda) is not better known to us than the speckled cows. Bergaigne's opinion, 'que cet archer n'est autre que le père lui-même,' is not very convincing.

Verse 6.

Note 1. The traditional reading vibhấti ('he who shines for thee in his house') gives no satisfactory sense. I propose to read vidhấti. Cf. I, 120, 1. kathấ vidhâti ápra*k*etâ*h*.

Note 2. I have some doubts as to the correctness of u*s*atá*h* (Sa*m*hitâpâ*th*a, u*s*ató) ánu dyū́n. U*s*át, of course, is an epithet not of the days, but of Agni. But then we expect the dative. Correcting the text (u*s*até) is all the easier, because before a following vowel the dative and the genitive were, in the original pronunciation, identical (u*s*atá-ánu; see my Prolegomena, 447 sqq.); the spellings of the Sa*m*hitâpâ*th*a, u*s*ató ánu and u*s*até ánu, belong to the inventions of Vedic grammarians.

Note 3. Literally, May he whom thou incitest drive on the same chariot with riches. Comp. such expressions as rathī́*h* râyá*h* and the like.

Verse 7.

Note 1. Comp. IV, 44, 2. yuvó*h* vápu*h* abhí p*r*í́ksha*h* sa*k*ante; VII, 90, 5.

Note 2. Comp. I, 26, 10, note 1.

Note 3. Ludwig: nicht unter unsern freunden ward auszfündig gemacht die kraftspeise. Grassmann: nicht bei Verwandten ward uns Nahrung sichtbar. Wilson: Our food is not partaken of by our kinsmen. Griffith: Not by our brethren was our food discovered.—Ludwig and Grassmann translate as if the text had *g*âmíshu. What the instrumental means is shown, I believe, for instance, by IV, 14, 2. ví sū́rya*h* ra*s*míbhi*h* *k*ékitâna*h*, 'the sun shining with his rays.' Thus in our passage the poet seems to me to say, 'We have no strong kinsmen who might add lustre to our strength. Agni, procure thou strength to us.' Comp. X, 23, 7. vidmá hí te prámatim deva *g*âmivát, 'for we know, O god, thy providing care like that of a kinsman.' —Prof. Max Müller proposes the translation: 'Our wealth is not known by our kinsmen, i.e. we cannot support them as we ought.'

Verse 8.

Note 1. The poet returns here to the myth of which he had spoken in verse 5. Should the order of the verses be changed?—On our verse, compare Geldner, Ved. Studien, II, 34.

Note 2. Té*g*as seems to be here a synonym of rétas, as in the later language.

Note 3. Is the lord of men Agni? See the third Pâda.—Ishé I consider, with Geldner, as an infinitive.

Note 4. My translation rests on the supposition that dyaú*h* is to be corrected into dyó*h*; thus the ablative is obtained, of which the word abhī́ke is usually accompanied (comp. Lanman, 433; Collitz, Bezzenberger's Beiträge, X, 15). If we leave the reading dyaú*h*, this nominative will be the subject of the verb ā́na*t*. Then té*g*a*h* must be accusative dependent on ā́na*t*, and we can scarcely avoid making n*ri*pátim to depend on the infinitive ishé. This is the way which Geldner has followed in interpreting this passage. But I cannot consider this separation of n*ri*pátim from the verb ā́na*t* very probable.

Note 5. The exact meaning of *g*anayat seems to be here, 'he caused them to be born.' Comp. *S*atapatha Brâhma*n*a I, 7, 4, 4. yathâ tad devâ reta*h* prâ*g*anayan (comp. Aitareya Brâhma*n*a III, 34; see also Rig-veda X, 61, 7).

Note 6. This may be the host of the seven *Ri*shis. Comp. III, 31, 1–5; IV, 1, 12 seq. (?). Or the Maruts are alluded to (comp. below, 72, 4), though that seems to me less probable.

Verse 9.

Note 1. Literally, in one day. But sadyá*h* has already in the Rig-veda the secondary meaning 'immediately, quickly.'

Note 2. Comp. III, 56, 7. rấ*g*ânâ mitrấ-váru*n*â supâ*n*ī̂.

Note 3. See below, 72, 6.

Verse 10.

Note 1. Comp. VII, 18, 2: there the words abhí vidú*h* kaví*h* sán are identical with our text.

Note 2. Of the second hemistich Prof. Collitz has treated in Bezzenberger's Beiträge, X, 15, note. He paraphrases the meaning in the following way: 'Der Sinn des ganzen Verses ist: unsere Freundschaft mit dir, Agni, stammt aus alter Zeit. Nun sagt man zwar "im Alter ändert sich das Aussehn wie das der Wolke." Aber stehe du uns bei vor diesem Fluche.' I do not believe that this interpretation, though very ingenious, gives the real meaning of the Vedic poet.—Comp. I, 179, 1. minấti *s*ríyam *g*arimấ tanū̂nâm.

MA*ND*ALA I, HYMN 72.

ASH*T*AKA I, ADHYÂYA 5, VARGA 17–18.

1. He has brought down (i.e. surpassed) the wisdom of many a worshipper[1], he who holds in his hand all manly power. Agni has become the lord of treasures, he who brought together all (powers of) immortality.

2[1]. All the clever immortals when seeking did not find the calf though sojourning round about us. The attentive (gods), wearying themselves, following his footsteps[2], stood at the highest, beautiful[3] standing-place of Agni.

3. When the bright ones[1] had done service[2] to thee, the bright one, Agni, with Gh*ri*ta through three autumns, they assumed worshipful names; the well-born shaped their own bodies.

4. Acquiring (or, exploring?) for themselves the two great worlds, the worshipful ones brought forward their Rudra-like powers[1]. The mortal, when (beings) were in discord[2], perceived and found out Agni standing in the highest place.

5. Being like-minded they[1] reverentially approached him on their knees. Together with their wives they venerated the venerable one[2]. Abandoning their bodies they made them their own[3], the (one) friend waking when the (other) friend closed his eyes[4].

6. When the worshipful (gods) have discovered the thrice seven secret steps[1] (or, places) laid down in thee, they concordantly guard with them immor-

tality. Protect thou the cattle and that which remains steadfast[2] and that which moves.

7. Knowing, O Agni, the established orders[1] of (human) dwellings, distribute in due order gifts[2] that they may live. Knowing the ways which the gods go[3], thou hast become the unwearied messenger, the bearer of oblations.

8. They who knew the right way and were filled with good intentions, beheld from heaven the seven young[1] (rivers) and the doors of riches. Saramâ found the strong stable of the cows from which human clans receive their nourishment[2].

9. The Earth has spread herself far and wide with them who are great in their greatness, the mother Aditi, for the refreshment of the bird[1], with her sons who have assumed all powers of their own dominion[2], preparing (for themselves) the way to immortality.

10. When the immortals created the two eyes of heaven[1], they placed fair splendour in him (Agni)[2]. Then they rush down[3] like streams let loose. The red ones have recognised, O Agni, those which are directed downwards[4].

NOTES.

The same *Ri*shi and metre.—Verse 1 = TS. II, 2, 12, 1. Verse 3 = TB. II, 4, 5, 6. Verses 8–9 = TB. II, 5, 8, 10.

Verse 1.

Note 1. The meaning seems to me to be: by his wisdom he excels all human wisdom. Prof. Max Müller translates: 'Agni, who holds in his hand all that men desire, conquers (or, wins for himself) the praises of many a wise worshipper.' And the last Pâda: 'he who brought together all immortal blessings.'—On *s*a*s*vat, see VI, 61, 1; VII, 18, 18; VIII, 23, 28.

Verse 2.

Note 1. Here we have again the myth of the hidden Agni whom the gods seek. Agni is meant by the calf.

Note 2. Going on foot, Sâya*n*a.

Note 3. I follow Sâya*n*a, Bollensen, and Ludwig in taking *k*ā́ru as a locative.

Verse 3.

Note 1. 'Was not Sâya*n*a right in taking this verse as referring to the Maruts? Cf. VI, 48, 21. . . . su*g*âta also is an epithet of the Maruts, I, 88, 3; 166, 12.' M. M.

Note 2. As to the subjunctive, comp. Delbrück, Syntaktische Forschungen, I, p. 67. The Taittirîya Brâhma*n*a (II, 4, 5, 6) reads saparyán.

Verse 4.

Note 1. I follow the Padapâ*th*a which has rudríyâ. But possibly we may have the nom. plur. rudríyâ*h*: 'the worshipful Rudriyas (i.e. Maruts) rushed forward.'

Note 2. The translation of nemádhitâ is in jeopardy.

Verse 5.

Note 1. Probably the mortals, as Ludwig understands it. Comp. márta*h*, verse 4.

Note 2. The venerable one is Agni.

Note 3. Possibly the text is corrupt. In IV, 24, 3 we read ririkvā́*m*sa*h* tanvả*h* k*ri*n*vata trā́m, 'abandoning (i.e. risking) their bodies they took him (Indra) for their protector' (comp. I, 100, 7). Should svā́*h* have supplanted another word, for instance, trā́m? As the pronoun svá very frequently stands in apposition with tanū́, it may have found its way also into passages to which it did not belong.

Note 4. The meaning seems to be that whenever the attention of one of the friends relaxed, another friend watched instead of the first. See Zeitschrift der Deutschen Morgenl. Gesellschaft, XLIV, 328; Bartholomae, Studien zur indogerm. Sprachgeschichte, I, 95.

Verse 6.

Note 1. Sâya*n*a explains the trí*h* saptá padấ as the three times seven kinds of sacrifices, the seven Pâkaya*g*ñas, the seven Havirya*g*ñas, the seven Somaya*g*ñas. But this later system of the twenty-one forms of sacrifice can scarcely have existed at the time of the Rig-veda Sa*m*hitâ. Three times seven is a favourite number in Rig-vedic mysticism; comp. I, 191, 12. 14; IV, 1, 16; VII, 87, 4; VIII, 46, 26; 69, 7; 96, 2; IX, 70, 1; 86, 21; X, 64, 8; 90, 15. Possibly three times seven pieces of wood (samídha*h*) are alluded to, comp. X, 90, 15, but everybody who has studied Bergaigne's Arithmétique mythologique (Rel. Véd. II, 114 seq.; see especially p. 122) will admit that there are ever so many possible interpretations of a passage like this. Prof. Max Müller's translation is: 'The worshipful gods found in thee the twenty-one words which are hidden in thee. They guard with them the immortal (Agni).'—Instead of avidan (Padapâ*th*a) I think we must read ávidan.

Note 2. Ludwig certainly is wrong in translating 'hüte du den wandel von tier und pflanze.' The author of this group of hymns is very fond of the phrase sthâtú*h k*arátham and the like; see I, 68, 1; 70, 3. 7. The same phrase, in one or the other of its possible shapes, has evidently been used by him here also. The plural masculine sthât*r*ī́n is indeed very strange. Possibly J. Wackernagel is right in reading sthâtú*h* (Kuhn's Zeitschrift, XXV, 287; comp. Lanman, p. 422); the reading sthât*r*ī́*n* may be due to the neighbourhood of pa*s*ū́n. This sort of blunder is very frequent in the text of the Rig-veda. Prof. Max Müller suggests: the stabled cattle and what moves about (in the meadows).

Verse 7.

Note 1. On vayúna, comp. Pischel, Ved. Studien, I, 295. 300. 'The thoughts of human beings.' M. M.

Note 2. *S*urúdh : Pischel, Ved. Studien, I, 32. 50.

Note 3. 'Which lead to the gods?' M. M.

Verse 8.

Note 1. Comp. I, 26, 10, note 1.—'Beheld the seven young rivers coming down from heaven.' M. M.

Note 2. See Delbrück, Syntaktische Forschungen, I, 87.

Verse 9.

Note 1. The bird seems to be Agni.

Note 2. The Padapâ*th*a gives su-apatyấni. There is no doubt a word su-apatyá, 'blessed with good offspring.' This is frequently used together with such nouns as rayi, kshaya, ish ; it stands in several passages by the side of pra*g*âvat. See I, 117, 19; II, 2, 12; 4, 8; 9, 5; III, 3, 7; 16, 1; IV, 2, 11; X, 30, 12. But from this word should be distinguished sva-patyá, derived from svá-pati (X, 44, 1, &c.), 'a man's own dominion,' or 'own rulership;' comp. *g*âspatyá. This word is found here, and in some other passages, for instance, VII, 91, 3. ví*s*vâ ít nára*h* svapatyấni *k*akru*h*, 'the heroes have exercised all the powers of their own dominion;' VIII, 15, 10. satrấ ví*s*vâ svapatyấni dadhishe, 'thou hast assumed (Indra) all powers of thy own dominion altogether.'—Ludwig translates correctly, 'alle selbstherlichkeit.'

The Taittirîya Brâhma*n*a reads *k*akrú*h* for tasthú*h*. This reading evidently rests on Rig-veda IV, 34, 9; VII, 91, 3. There is no reason, however, for preferring this to the traditional reading of our Rik-text.

Verse 10.

Note 1. The sun and the moon? This very natural explanation will scarcely be modified on account of passages like the following (*S*atapatha Brâhma*n*a I, 6, 3, 38):

'These are the two eyes of the sacrifice, the (oblations of butter called) Âgyabhâgas.'

Note 2. Comp. below, 73, 4.

Note 3. It is not necessary to change the text; I believe, however, that the conjecture adhá*h* ksharanti (they stream downwards) would not be quite improbable. Comp. my Prolegomena, p. 369, note 1.—The subject seems to be the streams of sacrificial libations.

Note 4. Both expressions, 'the red ones' and 'those which are directed downwards,' are feminine. The red ones may be the dawns. But these cannot be called 'directed downwards.' I take, therefore, the one noun as a nominative, the other as an accusative. Cannot 'those which are directed downwards' be the libations of Gh*ri*ta and the like, which the dawns see?—Prof. Max Müller translates: 'People recognised the red netherward mares (of thee), O Agni.' He supplies *g*vâlâ*h* or takes arushî*h* as mares, cf. V, 56, 6.

MA*ND*ALA I, HYMN 73.

ASH*T*AKA I, ADHYÂYA 5, VARGA 19-20.

1. He who gives vigour like wealth acquired by the fathers[1], who is a good guide like the instruction of a sage, who is pleased (by worship) like a comfortably resting guest[2], (Agni) has crossed the (sacrificial) seat of the worshipper like a Hot*ri*.

2. He who being truthful like the god Savit*ri*[1] protects by his power of mind all settlements[2], praised by many like impetuous splendour[3], the truthful one has become dear like vital breath and worthy to be searched for[4].

3[1]. (Agni) who possessing every refreshment dwells on the earth like a god, like a king who has made himself (valiant) friends[2], like heroes who sit in front and under shelter, like a blameless wife beloved by her husband—

4. Thee, O Agni, who art constantly kindled in the house, men have worshipped in their firm dwellings. They have placed in him rich splendour[1]. Be thou possessed of all life, a supporter of riches[2].

5. May the liberal givers, O Agni, attain nourishment, may the rich[1] who bestow gifts (on us) attain to a full span of life. May we win in battles the booty of him who does not give[1], obtaining a (rich) share before the gods, that we may win glory[2].

6. The lowing milch-cows of *Ri*ta, assigned by Heaven, were exuberant with their full udders. The rivers imploring the favour (of the gods) from afar

have broken through the midst of the rock with their floods.

7. Imploring favour from thee, O Agni, the worshipful (gods) have won glory in the sky. They have made Night and Dawn of different shapes; they have joined the black and red colour (to Night and Dawn).

8. And may we, our liberal givers and ourselves, be the mortals whom thou furtherest to wealth, O Agni[1]. Like a shadow thou followest the whole world, having filled the two worlds (Heaven and Earth) and the air[2].

9. May we, O Agni, guarded by thee, conquer with our racers the racers, with our men the men, with our heroes the heroes (of our enemies). Being masters of the riches which their fathers[1] have conquered, may our rich (givers) reach a hundred winters.

10. May these hymns, O Agni, worshipper (of the gods), be grateful to thee, to thy mind and heart. May we be able to bridle thee, the well-harnessed wealth[1], acquiring the glory which the gods have assigned us.

NOTES.

The same *Ri*shi and metre.—Verse 5 = MS. IV, 14, 15. Verse 7 = TB. II, 7, 12, 5. Verse 10 = MS. IV, 14, 15.

Verse 1.

Note 1. Agni is compared to wealth acquired by the fathers, being himself pit*ri*vitta, found by the forefathers of the Brâhmanic tribes. Prof. Max Müller proposes to translate : 'wealth inherited from the fathers.'

Note 2. Comp. VII, 42, 4, and see also VI, 16, 42.

Verse 2.

Note 1. The first Pâda is identical with the fourth of IX, 97, 48. There the expressions are referred to Soma.

Note 2. On v*r*i*g*ána, comp. the quotations given above, I, 60, 3, note 2 ; cf. IX, 87, 2. v*r*i*g*ánam rákshamâ*n*a*h*.

Note 3. Comp. I, 64, 9. amáti*h* ná dar*s*atā́.

Note 4. Comp. II, 4, 1 (see below).

Verse 3.

Note 1. The first three Pâdas are nearly identical with III, 55, 21.

Note 2. As to the meaning of hitámitra, comp. X, 108, 3. mitrám ena dadhâma; see also X, 132, 5, and H. O., Religion des Veda, 186, note 1.

Verse 4.

Note 1. Comp. I, 72, 10 (see above).

Note 2. I cannot accept Pischel's translation of dharú*n*a*h* rayî*n*ā́m, 'der Reichtum fliessen lässt' (Vedische Studien, I, 40).—'Be thou, who art rich in all food, the protector of riches.' M. M.

Verse 5.

Note 1. On sûrí and arí, see Bergaigne, Rel. Véd. II, 218 seq. Aryá*h* may also be nom. pl. and mean '(we) the poor ones.'

Note 2. 'May we win in battles the booty of the enemy, setting aside a share for the gods to their glory.' M. M.

Verse 8.

Note 1. In the first Pâda one syllable is wanting. Perhaps the acc. plur. yā́n had here dissyllabic value.

Note 2. The last Pâda is identical with the second of X, 139, 2.

Verse 9.

Note 1. Comp. above, verse 1, note 1.

Verse 10.

Note 1. Comp. *s*akéma vâ*g*ína*h* yámam, II, 5, 1; ágne *s*akéma te vayám yámam devásya vâ*g*ína*h*, III, 27, 3. As sudhúr and sudhúra are epithets of horses, the poet of course could say, *s*akéma sudhúra*h* yámam te. But Agni is not only a horse; he is also wealth (II, 1, 12; IV, 2, 5, &c.). The combination of the two metaphors explains the curious expression sudhúra*h* râyá*h*.

MAṆḌALA I, HYMN 74.

ASHṬAKA I, ADHYÂYA 5, VARGA 21–22.

1. Going forward to the sacrifice let us repeat a prayer to Agni who hears us, may he be afar or with us—

2. He who foremost[1] in . . . .[2], when the human tribes met (in battle), has preserved his home to the worshipper.

3. And let the people say 'Agni is born, the slayer of foes (or, the slayer of Vritra), he who wins the prize in every battle.'

4. The man in whose home thou art a messenger, and to whose sacrificial food thou eagerly comest for feasting, to whose worship thou impartest wonderful power—

5. Such a man the people call a giver of good oblations, O Aṅgiras, a friend of the gods, O son of strength[1], and a possessor of a good Barhis (or sacrificial grass).

6. And thou shalt conduct them hither, the gods[1], that we may praise them, that they may eagerly come, O resplendent one, to the sacrificial offerings.

7. No noise[1] of the horses of the moving chariot[2] is heard any way, when thou goest on thy messengership, O Agni.

8. When guarded by thee the racer becomes fearless; the worshipper, O Agni, who is behind, gains the advantage[1] over him who is ahead.

9. And thou winnest, O Agni, brilliant, high bliss in strong heroes from the gods, O god, for the worshipper.

NOTES.

This hymn opens the section ascribed to Gotama Râhûga*n*a, and belonging indeed, as several passages show, to the family of the Gotamas (comp. Zeitschrift der D. Morg. Gesellschaft, XLII, 221). The metre is Gâyatrî.—Verse 1 =. VS. III, 11; TS. I, 5, 5, 1; MS. I, 5, 1 (I, 5, 5. 6). Verses 1-3 = SV. II, 729. 730. 732. Verse 3 = TS. III, 5, 11, 4; MS. IV, 10, 3.

Verse 2.

Note 1. Or pûrvyá*h*, 'the old Agni,' cf. IX, 96, 10? (M. M.)

Note 2. I have left untranslated the obscure word snî́hitîshu (Sâya*n*a, vadhakâri*n*îshu). It seems to be identical with snéhiti, which occurs VIII, 96, 13. ápa snéhitî*h* n*ri*mánâ*h* adhatta (the Sâma-veda has the reading snîh^c^). Here the verb ápa adhatta (comp. VI, 20, 5; X, 164, 3) and the comparison of the second hemistichs of the two following verses, 14 and 15, seem to show that the word means some kind of hostile powers, which would do very well for our passage.—In Taittirîya Âra*n*yaka IV, 23 the word snî́hiti occurs in an enumeration of the 'terrible substances' (ghorā́*h* tanúva*h*) of Agni.—Comp. Ludwig, Ueber die neuesten Arbeiten auf dem Gebiete der *Ri*gveda-Forschung, p. 93.

Verse 5.

Note 1. See above, I, 26, 10, note 1.

Verse 6.

Note 1. See Delbrück, Syntaktische Forschungen, I, 20, 111.

Verse 7.

Note 1. On upabdí, which literally means the noise produced by going, see Joh. Schmidt, Kuhn's Zeitschrift, XXV, 55; Hübschmann, Das indogermanische Vocal-system, 124.

Note 2. Yó*h* (comp. X, 176, 3?) seems to be a genitive of yú, 'the going one;' comp. sva-yú, *s*ubham-yú; Lanman, 401.

Verse 8.

Note 1. The last syllable of asthât has the value of two syllables.

MA*ND*ALA I, HYMN 75.

ASH*T*AKA I, ADHYÂYA 5, VARGA 23.

1. Accept gladly our most widely-sounding[1] speech, the most agreeable to the gods, thou who, in thy mouth, offerest the sacrificial food (to the gods).

2. And may we then pronounce to thee, O highest Aṅgiras, Agni, best worshipper, a prayer agreeable to thee and successful.

3. Who is thy kinsman among men, O Agni? Who performs worship to thee[1]? Who art thou, and where dost thou rest?

4. Thou, O Agni, art the kinsman, the dear friend ('Mitra') of men, a friend who is to be magnified by his friends.

5. Sacrifice for us to Mitra and Varu*n*a. Sacrifice to the gods, (a sacrifice conforming to) the great *Ri*ta[1]. Sacrifice, O Agni, to thy own house.

NOTES.

The same *Ri*shi and metre.—Verse 1 = TB. III, 6, 7, 1; MS. III, 10, 1 (IV, 13, 5). Verses 3–5 = SV. II, 885–887. Verse 5 = VS. XXXIII, 3; TB. II, 7, 12, 1.

Verse 1.

Note 1. Comp. VI, 68, 9. manma . . . saprátha*h*.

Verse 3.

Note 1. May we not take dâ*s*ú-adhvara as a compound with governed final member, like vidádvasu, sâdádyoni &c.?

Verse 5.

Note 1. Comp. Gaedicke, Der Accusativ im Veda, 159.

MA*ND*ALA I, HYMN 76.

ASH*T*AKA I, ADHYÂYA 5, VARGA 24.

1. What supplication is to thy mind's taste[1]? What (pious) thought may be, O Agni, most agreeable to thee? Or who has won for himself thy wisdom by sacrifices? Or with what thoughts may we worship thee[2]?

2. Come hither, Agni, sit down here as a Hot*ri*. Become our undeceivable leader[1]. May Heaven and Earth, the all-embracing, protect thee. Offer the sacrifice to the gods that they may be highly gracious to us.

3. Burn down all sorcerers, O Agni; become a protector of the sacrifices against imprecations. And conduct hither the lord of Soma (Indra) with his two bay horses. We have prepared hospitality for him, the good giver.

4. With words procuring offspring, carrying thee (to our sacrifice) with my mouth[1], I call[2] thee hither, and thou shalt sit down here with the gods. Perform the service of a Hot*ri* and of a Pot*ri*[3], O worshipful one. Be thou a giver and a father[4] of riches.

5. As thou didst perform sacrifice to the gods with the sacrificial food of the wise Manu[1], a sage together with sages, thus, O highly truthful Hot*ri*, perform thou the sacrifice to-day, O Agni, with thy joy-giving sacrificial ladle[2].

NOTES.

The same *R*ishi. Metre, Trish*t*ubh.

Verse 1.

Note 1. Sâya*n*a takes vára in the sense of 'holding back' (comp. I, 143, 5), and makes mánasa*h* depend on várâya. He says, 'he agne te tava manaso varâya nivâra*n*âyâsmâsv. avasthâpanâya kopetir bhuvat kîd*ris*am upagamana*m* bhavet.' The modern translators are evidently right in assigning to vára the meaning of 'wish' or the like (comp. VII, 59, 2. yá*h* va*h* várâya dấ*s*ati), but they differ as to whether mánasa*h* should be taken as belonging to várâya or to úpeti*h*. Ludwig translates, 'Welches nahen des geistes ist gegenstand der wal dir?' Grassmann, 'Welch Nahen ist nach deines Herzens Wunsche?' My opinion is that the tradition of the text is not quite free from suspicion. My doubts are based on VI, 21, 4. kás te yag*ñ*á*h* mánase *s*ám várâya, 'What sacrifice (O Indra) is agreeable to thy mind, to thy wish?' Here we have a question addressed to the god, beginning with kás te, quite similar to the question of our poet, which begins with kấ te. We have the word *s*ám, as in our passage *s*á*m*tamâ. We have várâya exactly as in our passage. We have, by the side of várâya, a case-form of mánas as in our passage. But we have the dative mánase instead of the genitive mánasa*h*. We may add that there are some other passages in which a dative of a similar meaning stands likewise by the side of várâya: thus, VIII, 82, 3. áram várâya manyáve bhúvat te indra *s*ám (comp. bhúvat agne *s*á*m*tamâ in our passage) h*r*idé, 'May it be, O Indra, according to thy wish and thy mood, may it be agreeable to thy heart;' VIII, 84, 4. várâya deva manyáve, 'to thy wish, O god, to thy mood.'

All this tends to raise the supposition that in our

passage also we should read mánase vârâya, which datives seem to depend on *sám*tamâ. We should then translate, 'What supplication, what (pious) thought may be, O Agni, most agreeable to thy mind and to thy wish?'

Note 2. This seems to be a Pâda of the defective type, with four syllables before the caesura and ending as if there were five syllables before the caesura; comp. my Prolegomena, 68 seq. It would be easy, however, to restore the normal metrical form, for instance, by reading túbhyam instead of te.

Verse 2.

Note 1. Pura*h*-etấ, literally, 'he who goes before somebody.'

Verse 4.

Note 1. It would be unnatural to give to the medium ấ huve the passive sense and not to translate it, as it must be translated in so many passages, 'I call (thee) hither.' But, if so, it is very difficult to avoid the conclusion that váhni*h* âsấ ('he who carries somebody with his mouth;' comp. I, 129, 5; VI, 11, 2; 16, 9; VII, 16, 9; X, 115, 3; see vol. xxxii, pp. 42 seq.) refers here not to Agni, the divine carrier, but to the human priest, who with his mouth, i.e. by his songs, carries Agni to his sacrifice. Váhni is used very frequently indeed of human worshippers, and generally the transferring of epithets of the divine priest Agni to human priests, and vice versa, is quite to the taste of Vedic poets.—Comp. on ấ huve and váhni*h* âsấ, Neisser, Bezzenberger's Beiträge, XVIII, 320 seq.; XX, 69, and below, I, 127, 8, note 1; S.B.E., vol. xxxii, p. 42. See also Delbrück, Altindische Syntax, 473, who very rightly observes: es liegt kein Grund vor, dem huvé den Character einer ersten Person zu versagen.

Note 2. On the accent of huvé, on which Ludwig bases very bold conclusions, see Delbrück, Altindische Syntax, 41; Weber, Indische Studien, XIII, 73.

Note 3. Comp. X, 3, 3.—On the priestly functions of the

Pot*ri*, see Weber, Indische Studien, X, 141, 366, 376 seq.; H. O., Religion des Veda, 391.

Note 4. On these vocatives, see Delbrück, Altindische Syntax, 106.

Verse 5.

Note 1. Manus is here a proper name; comp. Bergaigne, I, 65 seq. On his priestly character, comp. H. O., Religion des Veda, 275.

Note 2. On *g*uhvâ, comp. Pischel, Ved. Studien, II, 113. The ladle is meant for the flame of Agni.

MA*ND*ALA I, HYMN 77.

ASH*T*AKA I, ADHYÂYA 5, VARGA 25.

1. How shall we sacrifice to Agni? What words, agreeable to the god, shall be addressed to him, the luminous one, who, being immortal and righteous, the Hot*ri*, the best sacrificer, conveys the gods to the mortals[1]?

2. Bring hither by adoration the Hot*ri* who is most beneficial in sacrifices and righteous. When Agni repairs to the gods on behalf of the mortal[1], may he be attentive in his mind, and may he perform the sacrifice[2].

3. For he is wisdom[1], he is manly, he is straightforward; like Mitra he has become the charioteer of the mysterious[2]. Therefore the Aryan clans[3], longing for the gods, address him, the wonderful one, as the first at the sacrifices.

4. May that Agni, the manliest of men, triumphant with riches [?][1], come with help to our words, to our devotion, and (to the devotion) of those most powerful liberal givers who bent on the prize[2] have constantly stirred up our prayers[3].

5. Thus Agni, the righteous *G*âtavedas, has been praised by the priestly Gotamas[1]. May he augment their splendour and their strength. He the knowing one gains increase according to his desire.

NOTES.

The same *Ri*shi and metre.

Verse 1.

Note 1. The construction is yá*h* k*rin*óti devā́n mártyeshu. Comp., for instance, X, 40, 2. ká*h* vâm . . . k*rin*ute sadhásthe á. Ludwig translates: der unter den sterblichen der unsterbliche hotar . . . schafft die götter.—'Could it be ishk*rin*oti?' M. M.

Verse 2.

Note 1. The third Pâda of this verse has nine syllables instead of eleven. If we read, as several times must be done, mártyâya for mártâya, we get ten syllables, and the Pâda may belong to the defective type mentioned above, 76, 1, note 2.

Note 2. *K*a seems to me to stand here, as it several times does, in the first of the members of sentence connected by it. See Delbrück, Altindische Syntax, 475. Prof. Max Müller believes that it depends on yát: yát vé*h*, yát *k*a sá bódhâti, 'Bring hither the Hot*ri* . . . so that Agni may invite the gods . . . and that he (the mortal or Agni) may be attentive, &c.'

Verse 3.

Note 1. Grassmann gives to krátu here and in a number of other passages the meaning 'der Starke.' This is inadmissible; comp. Bergaigne, III, 304.

Note 2. Here we have again a Pâda of ten syllables (see verse 2, note 1), unless bhût has dissyllabic value. Prof. Max Müller translates this Pâda: 'like a friend he is the charioteer of enormous wealth.'

Note 3. Comp. I, 96, 3 (see below).

Verse 4.

Note 1. On ri*s*ắdas, comp. above, I, 26, 4, note 1.

Note 2. Comp. I, 92, 8. There Ushas receives the epithet vắ*g*aprasûtâ.

Note 3. Comp. VII, 87, 3. spá*s*a*h* Váru*n*asya . . . yé isháyanta mánma.

Verse 5.

Note 1. This is again a Pâda of ten syllables.

MA*ND*ALA I, HYMN 78.

ASH*T*AKA I, ADHYÂYA 5, VARGA 26.

1. O *G*âtavedas, who dwellest among all tribes, we the Gotamas (praise) thee with our song—we praise thee aloud with (songs full of) splendour.

2. Gotama[1] desirous of riches exalts thee, as thou art, with his song. We praise thee aloud with (songs full of) splendour.

3. We call thee, such as thou art, the highest winner of booty, as Aṅgiras did. We praise thee aloud with (songs full of) splendour.

4. (We praise) thee, the greatest destroyer of enemies (or, of V*ri*tra), who hurlest the Dasyus away—we praise thee, such as thou art, aloud with (songs full of) splendour.

5. We the Rahûga*n*as[1] have recited a honey-sweet speech to Agni. We praise thee aloud with (songs full of) splendour.

NOTES.

The same *Ri*shi. Metre, Gâyatrî.

Verse 2.

Note 1. This probably means, 'the descendant of Gotama.' See Zeitschrift der D. Morg. Gesellschaft, XLII, 202.

Verse 5.

Note 1. The Rahûga*n*as seem to be a branch of the Gotamas; see Â*s*valâyana *S*rautasûtra XII, 11, 1.

MAN*D*ALA I, HYMN 79.

ASH*T*AKA I, ADHYÂYA 5, VARGA 27–28.

I.

1. The golden-haired in the expanse[1] of the atmosphere, the roaring[2] snake, is hasting (through the air) like the wind; the brightly resplendent watcher of the dawn[3], he who is like the glorious, ever active and truthful (goddesses)[4].

2. By thy goings the beautifully-winged (birds) were disparaged[1]; the black bull[2] has roared, when here[3] (all this happened). He has come as if with the bounteous smiling (women)[4]. The mists fly, the clouds thunder.

3. When they have led him, who swells[1] with the milk of *R*ita, on the straightest paths of *R*ita, then Aryaman, Mitra, and Varu*n*a, he who walks round the earth[2], fill the leather-bag (the cloud) in the womb of the lower (atmosphere [?])[3].

II.

4. Agni, who art lord of booty, rich in cows, young son of strength[1], bestow on us, O *G*âtavedas, great glory.

5. Being lighted, a Vasu, a sage, Agni who is to be magnified by (pious) words, O (god) with many faces, shine to us so that riches may be ours.

6. Reigning[1] by night by thy own power, O Agni, and at the break of dawn, O god with sharp teeth, burn against the sorcerers.

III.

7. Bless us, O Agni, with thy blessings, when our Gâyatra song is brought forward (to thee), thou to whom reverence is due in all our prayers.

8. Bring us wealth, O Agni, which may be always conquering, excellent and invincible[1] in all battles.

9. Bestow on us, Agni, through thy kindness[1] wealth which may last all our life[2], and have mercy[3] on us that we may live.

IV.

10. O Gotama[1], bring forward purified words, bring songs to the sharp-flaming Agni, desirous of his favour.

11. May he who tries to harm us, whether nigh or afar, fall down. Do thou lead us alone to increase.

12. The thousand-eyed Agni, who dwells among all tribes, scares away the Rakshas. The praiseworthy Hot*ri* (Agni) is praised[1].

NOTES.

The same *Ri*shi. Metre, 1–3 Trish*t*ubh; 4–6 Ush*n*ih; 7–12 Gâyatrî.

What in the traditional text is one hymn, consists really of four independent hymns of three verses each. This is to be concluded from the well-known laws of arrangement of the Sa*m*hitâ, and is confirmed by the change of metre and by the reception of two of the four hymns into other Vedic Sa*m*hitâs: the second (verses 4–6) is found in the Sâma-veda II, 911–913; Vâ*g*. Sa*m*hitâ XV, 35–37; Taitt.

Sa*m*hitâ IV, 4, 4, 5; Maitr. Sa*m*hitâ II, 13, 8; the third (verses 7-9) in the Sâma-veda II, 874-876. Besides, verses 1-2 occur Taitt. Sa*m*h. III, 1, 11, 4-5; verse 2, Maitr. Sa*m*h. IV, 12, 5; verse 4, Sâma-veda I, 99; verses 8, 9, Maitr. Sa*m*h. IV, 12, 4; verse 9, Maitr. Sa*m*h. IV, 10, 6; Taitt. Br. II, 4, 5, 3.

Verse 1.

Note 1. As to visârá I think we should compare VII, 36, 1. ví sấnunâ p*ri*thivī́ sasre urvī́, 'The wide earth has expanded with her surface.' Prof. Max Müller observes with regard to this Pâda: when the sky sends forth the rain, the lightning appears.

Note 2. On dhúni, see vol. xxxii, p. 112 (I, 64, 5), and Geldner, Vedische Studien, I, 268. I do not take the word with Geldner for an epithet of Vâta, the wind, but of the snake, i. e. Agni, who very probably is to be understood here as in the whole T*rik*a, as the fire of the lightning.

Note 3. Perhaps we have here again a Pâda of ten syllables, of the type which occurs several times in the preceding hymns. Or possibly the text should be corrected: ushása*h* ná návedâ*h*, 'a knower (of sacrifices, comp. IV, 23, 4; V, 12, 3) like the dawns,' or ushásâm návedâ*h* (with dissyllabic -âm), 'a knower of the dawns.'—See Lanman, p. 565.

Note 4. The waters? Or the dawns?

Verse 2.

Note 1. On the nasalization of aminantañ in the Sa*m*hitâ text, see my Prolegomena, p. 471.

Note 2. I. e. Par*g*anya, the thundering cloud. Comp. V, 83, 1; VII, 101, 1; Bergaigne, Rel. Védique, III, 27 seq.

Note 3. Regarding yádi idám, comp. IV, 5, 11. There the verb belonging to yádi must be supplied; in the same way our passage must be interpreted also, unless we resort to changing the text and accentuating the verb nonâva, in which case the translation would be, 'when the black bull has bellowed here.'

Note 4. The women may be the showers of rain. Or they could be understood as the dawns, comp. ushásah návedâh, verse 1.

Verse 3.

Note 1. I propose to read píyânam.

Note 2. On párigmań, see Joh. Schmidt, Kuhn's Zeitschrift, XXV, 86; Bartholomae, Bezzenberger's Beiträge, XV, 27 seq.; Bergaigne, Rel. Véd. II, 505; and compare especially X, 93, 4. The word evidently is connected not with the verb gam, but with kshám, 'the earth,' of which we find the genitives gmáh and gmáh.

Note 3. It does not seem probable to me that úpara means here the lower pressing-stone, as Grassmann, Ludwig, and Pischel (Vedische Studien, I, 109) suggest (Grassmann: den Schlauch beim untern Pressstein. Ludwig: den schlauch . . . an des steines ort. Pischel: sie legen das Fell mitten auf den Stein). I propose to supply rágasah; comp. I, 62, 5. rágah úparam; IV, 1, 11. rágasah asyá yónau, and especially IV, 17, 14, where we find the 'womb of the atmosphere' (rágasah asyá yónau) mentioned, quite as in our passage, together with the leather-bag (tvák), i.e. the cloud.—Bergaigne (Rel. Véd. II, 505) translates and explains, 'arrose la peau dans le séjour de l'inférieur,' c'est-à-dire fait couler les eaux du ciel pour l'Agni terrestre.

Verse 4.

Note 1. See above, I, 26, 10, note 1.

Verse 6.

Note 1. Râgan seems to be the participle of râg; comp. VIII, 19, 31. kshapáh vástushu râgasi. Now it is very improbable that of this participle a vocative should occur; see Lanman, 509. I believe, therefore, that we should accentuate rấgan (comp. the remarks of Bartholomae, Bezzenberger's Beiträge, XV, 204).

Verse 8.

Note 1. Comp. IX, 63, 11. rayím . . . dushtáram.

Verse 9.

Note 1. As to su*k*etúnâ, comp. I, 159, 5.

Note 2. Comp. VI, 59, 9. rayím vi*s*vấyuposhasam.

Note 3. Mâr*d*îkám is a second object of dhehi, not an epithet of rayím. Comp. VIII, 7, 30.

Verse 10.

Note 1. Comp. above, 78, 2, note 1.

Verse 12.

Note 1. On the use of the middle of *gri* with passive meaning, comp. Delbrück, Altindische Syntax, 264.

MAN*D*ALA I, HYMN 94.

ASHT*A*KA I, ADHYÂYA 6, VARGA 30–32.

1. We have sent forward[1] with thoughtful mind this song of praise like a chariot to the worthy *G*âtavedas. For blissful is his care for us in his companionship. Agni! May we suffer no harm in thy friendship.

2. He prospers for whom thou performest the sacrifice; he dwells untouched[1]; he acquires abundance of heroes. He is strong; no distress overtakes him. Agni! May we suffer no harm in thy friendship.

3. May we be able to light thee. Prosper our prayers. The gods eat the sacrificial food that is offered in thee. Bring thou hither the Âdityas, for we long for them. Agni! May we suffer no harm in thy friendship.

4. Let us bring fuel and prepare sacrificial gifts for thee, awaking thy attention at each joint[1] (of the month). Help forward our prayers that we may live. Agni! May we suffer no harm in thy friendship.

5. (He is) the shepherd of the clans[1]; by his nightly light the creatures walk, the two-footed and four-footed. Thou art the bright, great splendour of dawn. Agni! May we suffer no harm in thy friendship.

6. Thou art the Adhvaryu and the ancient Hot*ri*, the Pra*s*âst*ri*[1], the Pot*ri*, the born Purohita[2]. Knowing the duties of every priest thou givest

success, O wise one. Agni! May we suffer no harm in thy friendship.

7. Thou who art beautiful, of like appearance on all sides, thou shinest forth even when afar like lightning. Thou seest, O god, even over the darkness of night. Agni! May we suffer no harm in thy friendship.

8. May the chariot of him who presses Soma, be to the front [1], O gods. May our curse overcome the malicious ones. Accept (O gods) this prayer and make it prosper. Agni! May we suffer no harm in thy friendship.

9. Strike away with thy weapons those who curse us, the malicious ones, all ghouls, be they near or afar. And make a good path to the sacrifice of him who praises thee. Agni! May we suffer no harm in thy friendship.

10. When thou hast yoked to thy chariot the two ruddy, red horses, whom the wind drives forward, and thy roaring is like that of a bull, then thou movest the trees with thy banner of smoke [1]. Agni! May we suffer no harm in thy friendship.

11. And when thy grass-consuming sparks are scattered, the winged (birds) [1] also fear the noise. Then all goes well with thee and thy chariots. Agni! May we suffer no harm in thy friendship.

12. He makes Mitra and Varu*n*a get refreshing drink. He mysteriously turns away the anger of the Maruts [1]. Be merciful towards us. May their mind be again (as it was before). Agni! May we suffer no harm in thy friendship.

13. Thou art god of the gods, a wonderful Mitra (i.e. friend, of the gods) [1]. Thou art the Vasu

of the Vasus, welcome at the sacrifice. May we be under thy most wide-reaching protection. Agni! May we suffer no harm in thy friendship.

14. That is thy glorious (nature) that when kindled in thy own house, and fed with Soma, thou art awake [1], the most merciful one. Thou bestowest treasures and wealth on the worshipper. Agni! May we suffer no harm in thy friendship.

15. May we be of those to whom thou, O possessor of beautiful wealth, O Aditi [1], art pleased to grant sinlessness in health and wealth [2], and whom thou wilt quicken with glorious strength and with abundance of progeny.

16. Do thou, O Agni, thou who knowest (how to grant) happiness, prolong our life here, O God! May Mitra and Varu*n*a grant us this, may Aditi, the Sindhu, the Earth, and the Sky [1]!

NOTES.

This hymn with the whole collection which it opens is ascribed to Kutsa Âṅgirasa. The metre is *G*agatî; the two last verses, as is frequently the case in *G*agatî-hymns (see H. O., Prolegomena, 144 seq.), are composed in Trish*t*ubh. The hymn has been translated by Prof. Max Müller, Physical Religion, p. 173.—Verse 1 = MS. II, 7, 3; SV. I, 66; AV. XX, 13, 3. Verses 1, 3, 4 = SV. II, 414. 416. 415.

Verse 1.

Note 1. Prof. Max Müller translates, 'Let us build up this hymn of praise.' To me it rather seems that the reading should be, as Boehtlingk-Roth have proposed, s. v. sam-hi, sám ahema. Comp. I, 61, 4. asmaí ít u stómam sám hinomi rátham ná tásh*t*â-iva, 'to him I send forward a song of praise as a carpenter (fits out) a chariot.' Compare besides, IX, 71, 5; I, 184, 4; II, 19, 7; VI, 45, 14, &c.

Verse 2.

Note 1. Comp. vol. xxxii, p. 65, I, 37, 1 note.

Verse 4.

Note 1. Párvan, 'joint,' seems to refer here, as it very frequently does in the later Vedic and post-Vedic texts, to the joints of the month, the sacrificial days of the full and change of the moon (the pârva*n*a-sacrifices). As to the temporal use of the instrumental, comp. *ri*tunâ and *ri*tubhi*h*; Delbrück, Altindische Syntax, p. 130.

Verse 5.

Note 1. Ludwig proposes the correction of vi*s*ā́m gopā́*h* into vi*s*ā́m gopá*h* (genitive). But I think it will be sufficient to write asyá accented. As to vi*s*ā́m gopā́*h*, comp. 96, 4.

Verse 6.

Note 1. The Pra*s*âst*ri* (or Upavakt*ri*), literally, 'the commander,' is the same priest who is more usually designated as the Maitrâvaru*n*a. All the priests mentioned here (with the exception of the Purohita, see next note) belong to the ancient system of the 'seven Hot*ri*s,' enumerated, for instance, II, 1, 2. Comp. H. O., Religion des Veda, 383 seq.

Note 2. The Purohita or house-priest does not, properly speaking, belong to the number of the priests officiating at a sacrifice (*ri*tvig*ah*), though of course the Purohita could act as a *ri*tvi*g*. Geldner (Vedische Studien, II, 144) seems to be wrong in concluding from our passage that 'already in the Rig-veda the Purohita, being the superintendent of the holy service, was a real *ri*tvi*g*, i. e. officiating priest.' Comp. H. O., loc. cit., 374 seq.; 379, note 2.

Verse 8.

Note 1. On pûrva*h*, comp. I, 34, 10; V, 31, 11.

Verse 10.

Note 1. The regular accentuation of a determinative compound ('banner of smoke') would be dhûmaketúnâ. But it is very natural that the traditional text gives the accent of the Bahuvrîhi ('he whose banner is smoke') which so frequently occurs.

Verse 11.

Note 1. As to patatrí*n*a*h*, comp. above, I, 58, 5.

Verse 12.

Note 1. Most probably the meaning is not that the Maruts are expected to turn away the anger of somebody else, but that the anger of the Maruts shall be turned away by Agni. Comp. I, 171, 1; VI, 66, 5; VII, 58, 5; Bergaigne, Religion Védique, II, 401. It seems, consequently, that we should read avayâtấ.—On ávayâtahe*l*â*h*, scil. Indra, see vol. xxxii, p. 292 (I, 171, 6), and also IV, 1, 4; VI, 66, 5.

The genitives Mitrásya Váru*n*asya may be understood as depending, together with Marútâm, on hé*l*a*h*. In this case the translation would be: 'He mysteriously turns away the anger of Mitra and Varu*n*a and of the Maruts in order that (men) may get refreshing drink.'

Verse 13.

Note 1. On the frequent identification of Agni with Mitra, see Bergaigne, Religion Védique, III, 134 seq.

Verse 14.

Note 1. On the root *g*ar used with regard to Agni, see the remarks of Dr. Neisser in Bezzenberger's Beiträge, XIII, 297 seq.

Verse 15.

Note 1. Agni is invoked here by the name of Aditi, with an evident allusion to the goddess Aditi, as granting freedom from bonds, which is the original meaning of Aditi. Comp. M. M., vol. xxxii, pp. 241, 260, 262; H. O., Religion des Veda, p. 204.

Note 2. Comp. III, 54, 19. On sarvátât (sarvátâti), see M. M.'s note, vol. xxxii, p. 260, note a, and compare Darmesteter, Haurvatât et Ameretât, p. 80. See also Lanman, p. 386.

Verse 16.

Note 1. The last hemistich is the regular conclusion of the Kutsa hymns.

MA*ND*ALA I, HYMN 95.

ASH*T*AKA I, ADHYÂYA 7, VARGA 1–2.

1. Two (sisters) of different shapes wander along, pursuing a good aim. The one and the other suckles the calf[1]. With the one (the calf) is golden, moving according to its wont[2]. With the other it is seen clear, full of fine splendour.

2. The ten unwearied[1] young women[2] have brought forth this widely-spread germ of Tvash*tri*[3]. Him, the sharp-faced (Agni) who is endowed with his own splendour, the shining one, they[4] carry around among men.

3. They celebrate his three births: one in the sea, one in heaven, one in the waters[1]. In the eastern region[2] he commanding determines the seasons of the dwellers on earth by his present power[3].

4. Who among you has understood this hidden (god)?[1] The calf has by itself given birth to its mothers[2]. The germ of many (mothers), the great seer, moving by his own strength, comes forward from the lap of the active ones[3].

5[1]. The fair (child Agni) grows up visibly in them in his own glory, standing erect in the lap of the down-streaming (waters). Both (Heaven and Earth) fled away in fear of (the son of) Tvash*tri*[2], when he was born, but turning back they caress the lion.

6. They caress him both, like two kind women; like lowing cows they have approached him in their own way. He has become the lord of all

powers [1], he whom they anoint with sacrificial gifts from the right side [2].

7. He raises his arms again and again like Savit*ri* [1]. He the terrible pressing on ranges both wings [2] (of his army). He raises up his bright vesture from himself alone [3]. He gives new garments to his mothers.

8. He assumes his fierce appearance which is above (i.e. the lightning ?), being united with the cows [1], the waters in his seat. The prayer purifies the bottom of the seer (?) [2]. This was the meeting among the gods [3].

9. The wide space encompasses thy base, the resplendent foundation [1] of the buffalo. Agni! Being kindled protect us with all thy undeceivable guardians who are endowed with their own splendour.

10. On the dry ground he produces a stream [1], a course, a flood. With his bright floods he reaches the earth. Whatever is old he receives into his belly. He moves about within the young sprouting grass [2].

11. Thus, O Agni, being strengthened by fuel, shine thou to us with wealth-giving shine, O purifier, for the sake of glory. May Mitra and Varu*n*a grant us this, may Aditi, Sindhu, the Earth, and the Sky!

NOTES.

The same *R*ishi. The metre is Trish*t*ubh.—Verse 1 = VS. XXXIII, 5; TB. II, 7, 12, 2. Verse 2 = TB. II, 8, 7, 4. Verse 5 = TB. II, 8, 7, 4; MS. IV, 14, 8.

Verse 1.

Note 1. The two females are evidently Night and Dawn

(comp. below, 96, 5). The calf is Agni whose bright appearance by night is contrasted here with his paler splendour by day (comp. below, 127, 5). The explanation of Professor Hillebrandt (Vedische Mythologie, I, 331) that 'das von ihnen wechselnd gesäugte Kalb der bald als Sonne bald als Mond erscheinende Lichtgott, d. h. Agni ist,' does not seem convincing to me.

Note 2. I cannot follow Hillebrandt (loc. cit. 335) in translating svadhā́vân 'an Labung reich.'

Verse 2.

Note 1. On feminine nominatives in -âsa*h* like átandrâsa*h*, see Lanman, Noun-Inflection, 362.

Note 2. The ten young women are the fingers which produce the fire by the attrition of woods.

Note 3. On Tvash*tri* as the father of Agni, see Hillebrandt, Vedische Mythologie, I, 522 seq.; Bergaigne, Rel. Véd., III, 47 seq.

Note 4. Hillebrandt (loc. cit.) takes the ten fingers as the subject of pári nayanti, which does not seem probable.

Verse 3.

Note 1. It is surprising that Agni's birth in the sea and his birth in the waters are distinguished. The poet's meaning is not quite clear. Prof. Max Müller thinks of the rising sun and the lightning in the clouds. Comp. H. O., Religion des Veda, 107.

Note 2. We ought to read pradí*s*am; comp. IV, 29, 3; IX, 111, 3.

Note 3. Comp. X, 85, 18, where it is said of the moon that she 'is born again, determining the seasons.' Thus it is possible that the poet understands here Agni as dwelling in the moon as light. Comp. on this identification Bergaigne, I, 159, and Hillebrandt, Ved. Mythologie, I, 330 seq. But this interpretation of our passage is by no means certain.

Verse 4.

Note 1. Possibly we should correct ká*h* idám va*h* ni*n*yám; comp. VII, 56, 4; 61, 5. The translation would be: 'Who among you has understood this secret?'—the secret that a calf should give birth to cows.

Note 2. In my opinion the mothers are the waters; the calf is Agni. The meaning must be, consequently, that, as Agni is born from the waters thus the waters are born from Agni. Agni—we may try to interpret the poet's meaning—sends his smoke to the sky. The smoke is charged to clouds; the clouds send forth water. Exactly the same meaning seems to be expressed in I, 164, 51. Comp. also Manu III, 76. agnau prâstâhuti*h* samyag âdityam upatish*th*ate, âdityâ*g* *g*âyate v*ri*sh*t*ir v*ri*sh*t*er anna*m* tata*h* pra*g*â*h*.—Prof. Max Müller observes: 'The mothers are day and night, or heaven and earth. The calf, the son, Agni, being born of the night gives birth to the day, and being born of the day (in the evening) gives birth to the night. Or it may be that Agni, light, makes Dyaus and P*ri*thivî to be visible.'—Prof. Hillebrandt's interpretation of our verse is quite different; see Vedische Mythologie, I, 335.

Note 3. I. e. the fire is born from the waters.

Verse 5.

Note 1. Comp. Hillebrandt, Ved. Myth., I, 371, 523.

Note 2. I. e. the son of Tvash*tri* (see above, verse 2) considered as identical with his father. Comp. Bergaigne, III, 47, and see also Aufrecht, Kuhn's Zeitschrift, I, 356.

Verse 6.

Note 1. On dáksha and its relation to krátu, comp. Geldner, Vedische Studien, I, 267.

Note 2. The poet seems to play upon words; 'power' is dáksha, 'from the right side' dakshi*n*atá*h* (i. e. approaching respectfully, dakshi*n*îk*ri*tya).

Verse 7.

Note 1. Comp. Bergaigne, Rel. Véd., III, 46.

Note 2. Observe the dual form sí*k*au ending in -au, not in -â. Comp. Lanman, Noun-Inflection, 576. Prof. Max

Müller translates here: 'He the terrible tries and stretches out the hems of his sleeves.' This may indeed be the meaning of si*k*.

Note 3. See Geldner, Vedische Studien, II, 189.

Verse 8.

Note 1. The cows of course are intended for the sacrificial food coming from the cow, such as milk and butter.

Note 2. The two nominatives, kaví*h* and dhî́*h*, can scarcely be right. The subject seems to be the prayer which cleanses, as it were, Agni, and thus augments his splendour (comp. IV, 15, 6; VIII, 103, 7). Possibly we should read kavé*h* budhnám. Comp., however, IX, 47, 4. svayám kaví*h* vidhartári víprâya rátnam i*kkh*ati yádi marm*rig*yáte dhíya*h*. In this difficult verse so much is clear that the seer (kaví*h*) is subject, and that he is stated to purify the prayers.

Note 3. The meaning seems to be that at the sacrificial fire all gods assemble.

Verse 9.

Note 1. On dhấman, comp. M. M., vol. xxxii, p. 383 seq. —Prof. Max Müller proposes the following translation: 'Thy wide effulgence goes round the firmament, the firm seat of the strong one (buffalo).'

Verse 10.

Note 1. Ludwig takes sróta*h* as a locative. But it is very improbable that we should have here a survival of the ancient locatives of stems in -s without a case-ending (Joh. Schmidt, Kuhn's Zeitschrift, XXVII, 306; Brugmann, Grundriss der vergl. Grammatik, vol. ii, p. 611). In Ludwig's opinion 'it follows from the corresponding gâtum ûrmim that srotas stands for srotasi as dhanvan for dhanvani.' But this is not convincing.

Note 2. On Agni as inhabiting the sprouting grass, comp. III, 5, 8; VII, 9, 3. 'I believe this refers to the blades of grass used as tinder to catch the sparks of fire.' M. M.

MANDALA I, HYMN 96.

ASHTAKA I, ADHYÂYA 7, VARGA 3-4.

1. Being born by strength[1] in the ancient way, lo! he (Agni) has assumed instantly all the qualities of a sage. The Waters and the Dhishanâ[2] have furthered the friend (Mitra[3]). The gods have held Agni as the giver of wealth.

2. By the ancient Nivid[1], by Âyu's[2] wisdom he has procreated these children of men. With his irradiating look[3] (he has procreated) the Sky and the Waters. The gods have held Agni as the giver of wealth.

3. The Âryan clans magnified[1] him as the first performer of sacrifices, as receiving offerings, as striving forward, the son of strength, the Bharata[2], the bestower of mighty rain (?)[3]. The gods have held Agni as the giver of wealth.

4. He, Mâtarisvan[1], the lord of bountiful prosperity, has found a path for (his ?) offspring, he who has found the sun, the shepherd of the clans, the begetter of the two worlds. The gods have held Agni as the giver of wealth.

5. Night and Dawn, who constantly destroy each other's appearance, suckle one young calf[1] unitedly[2]. The piece of gold[3] shines between Heaven and Earth. The gods have held Agni as the giver of wealth.

6. (He is) the base of wealth, the assembler of all goods[1], the beacon of sacrifice, the fulfiller of thought, the bird[2]. In order to guard their immor-

tality the gods have held him, Agni, as the giver of wealth.

7. Him who is now and who was formerly the abode of wealth, the earth[1] (i.e. the dwelling-place or support) of what is born and of what will be born, the shepherd and guardian of what is and of much that comes into being. The gods have held Agni as the giver of wealth.

8. May (Agni,) the giver of wealth, present us with quick wealth. May the giver of wealth (present us with wealth) united with strong men[1]. The giver of wealth (should grant us) food together with valiant heroes. The giver of wealth should grant us long life.

9 = 95, 11.

NOTES.

The same *Ri*shi and metre.—Verses 1, 2 = MS. IV, 10, 6. Verse 5 = VS. XII, 2; XVII, 70; TS. IV, 1, 10, 4; 6, 5, 2; 7, 12, 3; MS. II, 7, 8.

Verse 1.

Note 1. I.e. by the attrition of the woods, as sáhasa*h* putrá*h*.

Note 2. Two new discussions on dhishá*n*â have been given by Hillebrandt (Ved. Mythologie, I, 175 seq.; comp. the criticisms of Ludwig, Ueber die neuesten arbeiten auf dem gebiete der Ṛgveda-forschung, 85 seq.) and Pischel (Ved. Studien, II, 82 seq.). Hillebrandt arrives at the conclusion that dhishá*n*â is the Earth (in the dual, Heaven and Earth; in the plural, Heaven, Air, and Earth), and besides the Vedi, i. e. the excavated spot of ground which serves as a kind of altar for the sacrifice. Similar is

Pischel's opinion. He believes that the singular dhishá*n*â is everywhere to be interpreted as a proper name: the name of a goddess of wealth and prosperity. The dual dhishá*n*e means 'Heaven and Earth:' thus the original meaning of dhishá*n*â must have been, as Pischel concludes, either Heaven or Earth. He tries to show that it is Earth, and so does Prof. Hillebrandt. The goddess of wealth originally was a goddess of the earth conceived as the liberal giver of wealth. This goddess, Prof. Pischel thinks, was closely related to, or even identical with, the goddess Aditi, whom the same scholar also believes to be a personification of the Earth.

I must confess that even this close agreement of these two distinguished scholars has failed to convince me. It is quite true that the dual dhishá*n*e means Heaven and Earth, and it is possible that the singular may, at least in some passages, mean the Earth. But I cannot believe that this is the original meaning of the word. Originally, in my opinion, dhishá*n*â was an implement used at the sacrifice, more especially at the Soma sacrifice. The ádrî (Soma-stones) are said to rest in the lap of the dhishá*n*â (I, 109, 3). In a Ya*g*us Mantra referring to the sacrificial preparation of Soma (Vâ*g*asaneyi Sa*m*hitâ VI, 26) the dhishá*n*â, or more exactly the Dhishá*n*âs, as goddesses (dhishá*n*â*s* *k*a devî́*h*), are mentioned together with the sacrificial fire, the waters, and the grā́vâ*n*a*h*, the stones. In a similar connection we find a Ya*g*us formula pronounced when the Adhvaryu began to beat the Soma plants with the Upâ*ms*usavana stone (see Weber, Indische Studien, X, 370). There the Soma was addressed first, and then the two Dhisha*n*âs: 'Do not be afraid, do not be terrified, assume sap (O Soma!). O two Dhisha*n*âs! Being firm show firmness!' (Vâ*g*asaneyi Sa*m*hitâ VI, 35). Here the *S*atapatha Brâhma*n*a (III, 9, 4, 18) says, that some authorities refer the last words to the two boards (phalake) on which the pressing-stones rest (see Hillebrandt, Ved. Mythologie, I, 149 seq.). But the author of the Brâhma*n*a himself declares that Heaven and Earth are addressed; for as to the boards used for pressing the Soma, it would be of no consequence if they were broken.—Other passages in which the dhishá*n*â*h* are mentioned in connection with the preparation of the Soma, are Rig-veda IX, 59, 2; X, 17, 2. In the last passage 'the lap of the Dh.' is mentioned as in I, 109, 3 (see above). The dhishá*n*â was anointed, I, 102, 1. The dhishá*n*â is mentioned in connection with the waters which were fetched by the Adhvaryus and used at the sacrifice, X, 30, 6, and in connection with the sacrificial fire, III, 2, 1, and in our passage. I have therefore no doubt that according to the original meaning the Dhisha*n*â was, as stated above, a sacrificial implement used chiefly, though not exclusively, at the pressing of the Soma. I do not venture to determine the exact nature of this implement, but I think that from the passages collected above it will be evident that it was a sort of support on which the pressing-stones rested. A similar support may have been used for the vessel containing the sacrificial water, and for the sacrificial fire. This support was considered as yielding the Soma to Indra, as strengthening Indra, as inciting Indra and the gods to liberality towards men. Thus we have a goddess Dhisha*n*â who wears the aspect of a goddess of wealth. She is invoked as one of the Gnâs in I, 22, 10 with Hotrâ Bhâratî. Finally the Earth, the support of everything, was likened to this support of the pressing-stones and of the Soma; and Heaven and Earth were then considered as the two Dhisha*n*âs.

Note 3. Comp. above, 94, 13, note 1.

Verse 2.

Note 1. On the solemn formulas of invocation, called Nivids, see Haug's Aitareya Brâhma*n*a, p. 32 seq.; Weber, Indische Studien, IX, 355; H. O., Religion des Veda, 387, note 2. Of course, the Nivids which *S*âṅkhâyana (*S*rauta-sûtra VIII, 16–25) gives, cannot be those to which the poets of the Rig-veda several times allude.

Note 2. On Âyu as one of the mythical ancestors of

mankind, nearly related to Manu, see Bergaigne, Religion Védique, I, 59 seq.

Note 3. Ushas is called vivásvatî, III, 30, 13 (cf. Bergaigne, I, 86); we are justified, consequently, in translating vivásvatâ *k*ákshasâ, 'with the irradiating look.' But in giving this translation we should not forget that the poet no doubt at the same time intended to allude to the name of Vivasvat, the father of Yama.

Verse 3.

Note 1. The text has î*l*ata. Comp. above, I, 1, 1, note 2.

Note 2. Agni seems to be called Bharatá as belonging to the people of Bharatas. Comp. H. O., 'Buddha, sein Leben, seine Lehre, seine Gemeinde' (first edition), p. 414 seq. More usually Agni is designated as Bhárata.

Note 3. S*ri*prádânum. On dânu, the meaning of which I consider to be 'rain' or the like, comp. the discussion of Prof. Max Müller, vol. xxxii, 113 seq. The exact meaning of s*ri*prá, which should not be compared with the Greek λιπαρός, cannot be determined. The etymology is a very unsafe guide in such questions, and neither the connection with the root s*ri*p, 'to creep,' 'to crawl,' nor with the noun sarpís, 'butter,' seems to lead to a satisfactory result. The passages in which s*ri*prá or compounds of this adjective occur, point to a meaning like 'great,' 'mighty,' 'fine.' Thus s*ri*prábho*g*as seems to be something like purubhó*g*as or subhó*g*as; Indra's arms (karásna) are called both s*ri*prá (VIII, 32, 10) and p*ri*thú (VI, 19, 3); finally s*ri*prádânu, which is used here as an epithet of Agni, and VIII, 25, 5 of Mitra and Varu*n*a, does not seem to differ very much from sudânu.

Verse 4.

Note 1. Mâtari*s*van, the messenger of Vivasvat, who carried the fire from heaven to earth, was originally distinct from Agni, but is identified with him in several passages. See M. M., Physical Religion, p. 152; Bergaigne, Religion Védique, I, 52 seq.; H. O., Religion des Veda, 122.

Verse 5.

Note 1. Comp. above, 95, 1, and I, 113, 2. rúsadvatsâ. The calf, of course, is Agni.

Note 2. Literally, 'turned towards each other.'

Note 3. The gold is again Agni.

Verse 6.

Note 1. The first Pâda is identical with X, 139, 3.

Note 2. I prefer with Ludwig to take vé*h* as a nominative (comp. Lanman, Noun-Inflection, 375) instead of a genitive.

Verse 7.

Note 1. Compare the very obscure verse X, 31, 5. iyám sấ bhûyâ ushásâm iva kshấ*h*, 'may she be the earth, as it were, of the dawns.' 'She' may possibly be the earth, which would be designated here as a dwelling-place or support of the dawns.

Verse 8.

Note 1. Prof. Max Müller proposes another translation of sánara. He writes: 'One expects an opposition between turá and sánara. Sánara can hardly be the same as vîrávat in the next line. I should like to take sánara as a variety of sána and sanâtána. Give us fleeting, i.e. daily wealth, and give us old, i.e. lasting wealth!'

MAN*D*ALA I, HYMN 97.

ASHT*A*KA I, ADHYÂYA 7, VARGA 5.

1. Driving away evil[1] with thy light, Agni, shine upon us with wealth—driving away evil with thy light.

2. Longing for rich fields, for a free path, and for wealth, we sacrifice—driving away evil with thy light.

3[1]. When he stands forth as the most glorious one among them[2], and when our liberal lords excel—driving away evil with thy light—

4. When through thee, Agni, the liberal lords, and when through thee we may multiply with offspring—driving away evil with thy light—

5. When the rays of the mighty Agni go forth on all sides—driving away evil with thy light—

6. For thou indeed, (O god) whose face is turned everywhere, encompassest (the world) everywhere—driving away evil with thy light.

7. Do thou carry us, as with a boat, across hostile powers, (O god) whose face is turned everywhere—driving away evil with thy light.

8. Do thou carry us across (evil) to welfare, as across a stream with a boat[1]—driving away evil with thy light.

NOTES.

The same *Ri*shi. Metre, Gâyatrî. The hymn is addressed to Agni *Suk*i.—Verses 1–8 = AV. IV, 33, 1–8 : TÂ. VI, 11, 1–2. Verse 1 = TÂ. VI, 10, 1.

Verse 1.

Note 1. Lanman (Sanskrit Reader, p. 363) translates: 'Driving away with flames our sin.' But aghá is not exactly sin.

Verse 3.

Note 1. In this verse as well as in the verses 4 and 5—all commencing with the words prá yát—the principal clauses are wanting. As to the meaning, however, these clauses are supplied by the refrain; 'driving away evil' of course means 'may he drive away evil.'

Note 2. 'Among them' seems to mean 'among the liberal lords.'

Verse 8.

Note 1. Cf. Lanman, p. 434.

MA*ND*ALA I, HYMN 98.

ASH*T*AKA I, ADHYÂYA 7, VARGA 6.

1. May we dwell in the favour of (Agni) Vai*s*vânara. He indeed is a king, leading all beings to gloriousness [1]. As soon as born from here he looks over this whole world. Vai*s*vânara unites with the Sun [2].

2. Agni who has been looked and longed for [1] in Heaven, who has been looked for on Earth—he who has been looked for, has entered all herbs. May Agni Vai*s*vânara, who has strongly been looked for, protect us from harm by day and by night.

3. Vai*s*vânara! May this be true of thee: may wealth and liberal givers attend us! May Mitra and Varu*n*a grant us this, may Aditi, the Sindhu, the Earth, and the Sky!

NOTES.

The same *R*ishi. Metre, Trish*t*ubh.—Verse 1 = VS. XXVI, 7; TS. I, 5, 11, 3; MS. IV, 11, 1. Verse 2 = VS. XVIII, 73; TS. I, 5, 11, 1; IV, 4, 12, 5; 7, 15, 6; TB. III, 11, 6, 4; MS. II, 13, 11.

Verse 1.

Note 1. Comp. VI, 70, 1. bhúvanânâm abhi*s*ríyâ. Abhi*s*rî́ seems to mean, going or leading towards (abhí) gloriousness (*s*rî́). Prof. Pischel's opinion on the word is different; see Vedische Studien, I, 53 seq.

Note 2. As to yatate, comp. V, 4, 4. yátamâna*h* ra*s*míbhi*h* sū́ryasya; IX, 111, 3. sám ra*s*míbhi*h* yatate dar*s*atá*h* rátha*h*.

Verse 2.

Note 1. On the disappearance of Agni who is looked for everywhere, see M. M., Physical Religion, 264 seq.; Bergaigne, Rel. Védique, II, 75.

MA*ND*ALA I, HYMN 99.

ASH*T*AKA I, ADHYÂYA 8, VARGA 7.

1. Let us press Soma for *G*âtavedas[1]. May he burn down the property of the niggard[2]. May he, Agni, bring us across all troubles, across all difficulties, as across a stream with a boat.

NOTES.

The *Ri*shi is Ka*s*yapa Mârî*k*a. Metre, Trish*t*ubh.—Verse 1 = TÂ. X, 1.

Verse 1.

Note 1. This is one of the very rare passages in which Agni standing alone and not accompanied by Indra or the Maruts &c. is mentioned as drinking Soma. It seems as if this verse were not composed for the regular Soma sacrifice, but for a special occasion.

Note 2. Cf. Delbrück, Syntakt. Forschungen, I, 112.

MA*ND*ALA I, HYMN 127.

ASHT*A*KA II, ADHYÂYA 1, VARGA 12–13.

1. I deem Agni to be the munificent Hot*ri*, the Vasu, the Son of strength[1], *G*âtavedas, like a priest, *G*âtavedas[2]: the best performer of the sacrifice, the god who with his upright body that is turned towards the gods, and with his flame longs for the shine of the (boiling) ghee[3], of the butter that is offered in (the fire).

2. May we, the sacrificers, call thee hither, the best of sacrificers[1], the first of the Aṅgiras, O priest, with our prayers, with priestly prayers, O bright one[2]: thee who like the heaven encompassest the earth[3], the Hot*ri* of human tribes, the manly flame-haired, whom these folks—whom all folks should favour in order to speed him (to our sacrifice).

3. He indeed, shining mightily with his shining strength[1], becomes the conqueror of deceitful foes[2] —like an axe, the conqueror of deceitful foes[2]. He at whose onslaught[3] even what is strong melts away[4], steady things (waste away) like forests (which are burnt or bend down in the storm)[5]. Conquering he holds himself back; he does not proceed[6]. As with a conquering bow-man he proceeds[6].

4. Even what is firm gives way before him: thus it is known. With hottest kindling-sticks[1] one worships him[2] for winning his favour, one worships Agni for winning his favour. He who dives into many forests as if carving the wood with his flame, destroys even firm food[3] with his strength—he destroys even what is firm with his strength.

5. Let us place that power[1] of his in our neighbourhood[2]—(that power) which is more visible by night than by day[3]—(more visible) than by day to the unremitting[4] (worshipper). Therefore his life is a firm hold[5], like (a father's) safe refuge to a son: (the fires) that never grow old, tending to blessings enjoyed or not enjoyed (before)[6]—the fires that never grow old, tending (to such blessings).

6. He indeed makes a mighty noise like the host of the Maruts, . . .[1] on the rich fields, . . .[1] on the . . .[1]. He, the seizer, ate the offerings[2], he who has deservedly become the banner of the sacrifice. And when he joyously and joyfully (proceeds), all followed gladly on his path; men (have followed) his path as for a triumphal procession.

7. When forsooth the Kîstas[1] striving for heaven, when the Bh*ri*gus have addressed him paying reverence—the Bh*ri*gus producing him by attrition, with worship: Agni is the lord of goods, the bright one, who is their[2] supporter. May the wise one accept the wonted coverings[3]; may the wise one accept them.

8. We invoke thee, the lord of all people, the common master of the house of all, to enjoy (the sacrifice): (we call) thee who truly art carried by prayers as by a vehicle[1] to enjoy (the sacrifice): the guest of men in whose presence (they live) as before a father's (face), and all those immortals (attain) to strength, and the offerings among the gods (attain) to strength.

9. Thou, O Agni, art born, the mightiest by might[1], for the divine world, the strongest one, like wealth for the divine world. For thy delight is most strong, and thy power is most brilliant. And

they walk around thee[2], O (god) who never growest old, like obedient (servants), O (god) who never growest old.

10. Let your praise go forth to the great Agni, who is mighty in his might, who awakens at dawn, like a winner of cattle[1]—let it go forth to Agni. When (the worshipper) rich in offerings has loudly praised him[2] in all lands[3], he wakes[4] like a singer in front of the dawns[5], the flaming one (?), the Hot*ri* (in front) of the dawns[5].

11. Thus being seen by us, bring near to us, O Agni, graciously united with the gods, benignantly, great wealth benignantly. Make us behold great (bliss of valiant offspring[1]), O mightiest one, that we may obtain such enjoyment. Produce great bliss of valiant offspring, O bountiful Lord, (as fire is produced) by attrition, for those who praise thee, like a strong hero in thy might.

NOTES.

The *Ri*shi is Paru*kkh*epa Daivodâsi, the metre Atyash*t*i (verse 6 Atidh*ri*ti).—Verses 1–3 = SV. II, 1163–1165. Verse 1 = SV. I, 465; VS. XV, 47; TS. IV, 4, 4, 8; MS. II, 13, 8; AV. XX, 67, 3.

Verse 1.

Note 1. There is no doubt that the reading of the Rig-veda text vásum is correct; the Sâma-vedạ has váso*h*. Comp. H. O., Prolegomena, p. 280.

Note 2. 'Is it a play on the word? Like a priest knowing all things?' M. M.

Note 3. There is a metrical irregularity in this Pâda; it has six syllables instead of five before the caesura. The text, however, seems to be correct.

Verse 2.

Note 1. The first Pâda is Trish*t*ubh instead of *G*agatî. It would be easy to correct huvemahi, but that form is never found in the Rig-veda, though both huvema and havâmahe are frequent. Thus it is very probable that we have here a metrical irregularity of the type described by H. O., Prolegomena, p. 117.

Note 2. Comp. VIII, 60, 3. víprebhi*h* *s*ukra mánmabhi*h*.

Note 3. If the explanation of pári*g*man which we have adopted (see above, I, 79, 3, note 2) is correct, it will be impossible, of course, to accept Bergaigne's opinion (Rel. Véd., II, 505, note 1) that the accusative dyấm is governed by pári*g*mânam.

Verse 3.

Note 1. In the second Pâda one syllable is wanting. The text seems to be correct, and the irregularity apparently is the typical one described by H. O., Prolegomena, p. 68 seq.: the Pâda has the tetrasyllabic beginning (before the caesura), and it goes on as if the beginning had been pentasyllabic. Several Pâdas of the same irregular structure occur in our hymn, thus in verse 9: tvám (read tuám) agne || sáhasâ sáhantama*h*; verse 10: prá va*h* mahé || sáhasâ sáhasvate; usha*h*-búdhe || pa*s*u-sé ná agnáye.

Note 2. The comparison para*s*ú*h* ná, 'like an axe,' raises doubts as to the correctness of druham-tará*h*. Para*s*ú*h* seems to point to a compound containing the element drú, 'wood;' comp. below, 130, 4; VII, 104, 21. The second member of the compound would be han, which is frequently used with the meaning of cutting wood (II, 14, 2; X, 89, 7). Thus the reading would be dru-hántara*h* (comp. v*ri*tra-hántama*h*), 'a mighty wood-cutter.' As to this use of the comparative, see Delbrück, Altindische Syntax, p. 196.

Note 3. Comp. V, 7, 2. yásya sám*ri*tau.

Note 4. Prof. Max Müller (Science of Thought, p. 325) believes that the root *s*ru occurs here in the sense of shaking. To me it seems that this *s*rúvat is a misspelling for srúvat. The opinion of Pischel and Geldner (Vedische Studien, I, p. vi) is different.

Note 5. The meaning of the comparison which I have indicated by the words in parentheses, becomes clear from VIII, 40, 1. vánâ-iva vắte ít.

Note 6. The two last Pâdas are very obscure. In the last Pâda but one ná would seem to be comparative, not negative, because it has the same meaning in the last Pâda, and because its vowel does not coalesce with the following initial vowel (comp. Benfey's dissertation, 'Behandlung des auslautenden a in ná "wie" und ná "nicht."' But then instead of yamate a substantive meaning something like 'hero' would be required. And also instead of the instrumental dhanva-sáhâ one should expect to find a nominative; comp. Benfey, Vedica und Linguistica, p. 180, note 1.—Prof. Max Müller translates: 'Holding out (or resisting) he stands firm, he does not budge; holding his bow he does not budge.'

Verse 4.

Note 1. The words té*g*ish*th*âbhi*h* ará*n*ibhi*h* are repeated, probably by the same poet, below, 129, 5.

Note 2. It may be observed that several times in the Paru*kkh*epa hymns the parallelism between two subsequent Pâdas has corrupted the text, the reading of the one Pâda being wrongly introduced into the other. For instances I refer to I, 129, 11, where the last vaso has been added from the preceding Pâda, and to the last Pâda but one of I, 135, 4. Possibly our Pâda, which in its traditional form is metrically abnormal (comp., however, M. M.'s Hymns to the Maruts, 1st ed., p. cxii), has suffered damage in the same way. The comparison of I, 129, 5 would lead us to conjecture: té*g*ish*th*âbhi*h* ará*n*ibhi*h* ná ávase. 'One worships him in order that he may grant his favour as if (he were to help us) with hottest kindling-sticks. One worships Agni in order that he may grant his favour.'

Note 3. Comp. IV, 7, 10. sthirắ *k*it ánnâ dayate ví *g*ámbhai*h*. The food is the wood which Agni consumes.

Verse 5.

Note 1. See Prof. von Roth's translation of this verse, Zeitschrift der D. Morg. Gesellschaft, XLVIII, 117. On p*ri*ksham, comp. M. M., vol. xxxii, p. 302; Pischel, Vedische Studien, I, p. 96 seq. The translation of such a word can only be tentative.

Note 2. To úparâsu something like vikshú (IV, 37, 3) seems to be supplied.

Note 3. Comp. the Latin expression, 'argutius quam verius.' Pischel, Göttinger Gelehrte Anzeigen, 1884, p. 516 seq.; Delbrück, Altindische Syntax, p. 196.

Note 4. Ápráyus seems to be an anomalous formation, instead of ápráyu, unless we have to read áprâyuve. According to Pischel (Göttinger Gel. Anzeigen, 1890, p. 542), áprâyushe would mean 'dem der da lebt.' But I do not think that this áprâyus should be separated from áprâyu, which, as may be seen from I, 89, 1 compared with III, 5, 6 and X, 4, 7, is identical in meaning with, and evidently etymologically related to, áprayu*kkh*ant.

Note 5. Grábha*n*avat is the contrary of agrabha*n*á, I, 116, 5.

Note 6. Comp. III, 30, 7. ábhaktam *k*it bha*g*ate.

Verse 6.

Note 1. Ludwig: 'in den bebauten fluren zu verehren, auf den wüsten flächen zu verehren.' Prof. Max Müller observes with regard to ish*t*áni*h*: 'it stani*h*, or ish + stani*h* (ish-kartâ), much thundering.' For ấrtanâ he proposes the translation, 'ploughed field.' I have left both words untranslated.

Note 2. Ấdat is imperfect of ad; there is a play upon words (ấdat and â-dadí*h*).

Verse 7.

Note 1. Who the Kîstas (cf. Lanman, p. 346) are is not known. They seem, however, either to be identical with the Bh*ri*gus or to be another ancient and probably mythical family of priests like them. They are mentioned also in VI, 67, 10.

Note 2. 'Their' refers to 'goods.'

Note 3. The fuel and libations with which Agni is covered?

Verse 8.

Note 1. Vấhas and its compounds, such as stómavâhas. ukthávâhas, gírvâhas, have been treated of by Dr. Neisser in his ingenious article on váhni, Bezzenberger's Beiträge, XVIII, 301 seq. (comp. on váhni, vol. xxxii, p. 37 seq.). Dr. Neisser tries to show that by the side of váhni, derived from vah = Latin vehere, and meaning 'draught-horse' (and besides—though Dr. Neisser does not admit this, see p. 316—'a person that drives in a chariot'), there existed a second substantive váhni connected with the Greek εὔχεσθαι, and meaning both 'erhaben' and 'erhebend,' i. e. praising the gods (loc. cit., p. 314). With this second váhni he connects vấhas and its compounds. One of the principal arguments of Dr. Neisser is the fact quite correctly stated by him (p. 301), that 'the word váhni very frequently associates itself to the term hót*ri*, while it does not with the compounds havyaváh and havyavấhana.' This fact, indeed, points to the conclusion that 'those compounds belong to another sphere of ideas than váhni' (p. 302). But Dr. Neisser seems to me to go too far in concluding that váhni, standing as an epithet of Agni, is not derived from vah = vehere. Agni's action consists not only in carrying the sacrificial food to the gods, but also in carrying the gods to the sacrifice of men, and in coming to that sacrifice himself with his chariot and his horses. Nor do the words stómavâhas or ukthávâhas, if derived from vah = vehere, necessarily presuppose the admissibility of expressions such as 'uktham (stomam) vahati vipra*h* devân a*kkh*a' (p. 303), but those compounds may also rest on an idea conveyed by expressions such as 'uktham (stoma*h*) vahati devân upa ya*gñ*am,' which idea is quite Vedic. Thus stómavâhas in my opinion means, as an epithet of the god, 'carried by the stoma as by a vehicle' (comp. VII, 24, 5. eshá stóma*h* mahé ugrấya vấhe dhurí-iva átya*h* ná vâ*g*áyan adhâyi). or, as an epithet of the human worshippers, 'fitting out the stoma as a vehicle.' I believe that the words in question can thus be explained in conformity with the whole range of Vedic thought, and the artificial distinction of two different substantives váhni, &c., will be avoided. For special indications pointing in the same direction, which are furnished by the passages which contain the words here treated of, I refer to Bergaigne, Religion Védique, II, 286 seq., and to the article of Dr. Neisser himself, p. 321 seq.

Verse 9.

Note 1. On the metrical irregularity, see above, verse 3, note 1.

Note 2. Te seems to stand for the accusative, comp. Pischel, Zeitschrift der D. Morgenl. Gesellschaft, XXXV, 714 seq.; Delbrück, Altindische Syntax, 205. Or may the meaning be: 'and thy (worshippers) walk around thee . . . like obedient (servants)?'

Verse 10.

Note 1. On the metre, see above, verse 3, note 1. Prof. Max Müller translates, 'like a hunter for cattle.'

Note 2. The phrase ví*s*vâsu kshá̂su *g*óguve occurs also, V, 64, 2. The same hymn contains the word su-*k*etúnâ, which is found in the eleventh verse of our hymn.

Note 3. Literally, 'on all earths.' Comp. X, 2, 6. n*ri*vátî*h* ánu kshá̂*h*.

Note 4. *G*arate, 'he wakes,' at the same time can mean 'he sings,' and 'he is praised.' Comp. Neisser, Bezzenberger's Beiträge, XIII, 298.

Note 5. The translation 'dawn' is conjectural only. But it gives a good meaning in all the passages which contain the word *ri*shû*n*á̂m (besides our passage, V, 25, 1; VIII, 71, 15; X, 6, 1). Prof. Max Müller translates the last two Pâdas: 'he sings like Rebha at the head of all singers, like a clever Hot*ri* among the singers.'—Comp. Lanman, p. 424.

Verse 11.

Note 1. I supply suvî́ryam; see the last Pâda but one.

MANDALA I, HYMN 128.

ASHTAKA II, ADHYÂYA 1, VARGA 14-15.

1. He was born in Manu's firm law[1], the Hotri, the best sacrificer, according to the will of the Usigs[2], Agni, according to his own will. Always listening to him who wishes to be his friend, like a treasure to him who aspires to renown, the unbeguiled Hotri sat down in the abode of food (on the altar); enveloped[3] (he sat down) in the abode of food.

2. We render him attentive[1], the promoter of sacrifice, on the path of *Ri*ta, by adoration with offerings, in the divine world, by (adoration) with offerings[2]. In bringing us vigour he never becomes worn out with this body of his: he whom Mâtarisvan (has brought) to Manu from afar, the god whom he has brought from afar.

3. In his (own) way he moves in one moment round the terrestrial (space), the sudden devourer (emitting) his sperm, the bellowing bull emitting his sperm, the bellower[1], looking round with a hundred eyes, the god who quickly courses in the forests[2], taking his seat on the lower ridges, Agni, and on the highest ridges.

4. This highly wise Purohita, Agni watches sacrifice and service[1] house by house; by (the power of) his mind he is intent upon sacrifice. By (the power of) his mind helpful to him who desires food[2], he looks on all creatures, since he has been born, the guest adorned with ghee, (since) the helpful carrier (of the gods)[3] has been born.

5. When through his (Agni's) power the bounties grow in strength, with the roar of Agni[1] as with that of the Maruts[2]—like bounties offered to a vigorous man: then he by his greatness stirs up the gift of goods. May he protect us from misfortune and injury, from evil spell and injury.

6. The far-reaching[1] steward[2] has taken all goods[3] in his right hand, and strongly advancing does not let them loose; desirous of glory he does not let them loose. For every supplicant[4] thou hast carried the oblations to the gods[5]. For every righteous one he procures a treasure; Agni opens both folds of the door (for him).

7. He has been established as the most blissful one in the enclosures of men, Agni, at the sacrifices, like a noble lord of the clans, a beloved lord of the clans at the sacrifices: he rules over the oblations of men to which nourishing power has been imparted[1]. May he protect us from harm that comes from Varu*n*a, from harm[2] that comes from the great god.

8. They magnify Agni the Hot*ri*, the dispenser of goods. They have roused the beloved, the most shining steward[1] (of sacrifice); they have roused the carrier of oblations. The gods desirous of goods (have roused) him in whom all life dwells, who possesses all wealth, the Hot*ri*, the worshipful sage, the lovely one for the sake of bliss; with praises (they have roused), desirous of goods, the lovely one.

NOTES.

The same *Ri*shi and metre.—Verse 6 = TB. II, 5, 4, 4.

Verse 1.

Note 1. As to dhárîma*n*i, comp. IX, 86, 4, where it is said that the streams of Soma flow forward, 'dhárîma*n*i;' Bergaigne, III, 219. 'Domain, precinct, sanctuary?' M. M.

Note 2. The U*s*ig*a*s (comp. above, I, 60, 2, note 1) are closely related to the Bh*ri*gus; they are considered as the first sacrificers, the first worshippers of Agni. See Bergaigne, I, 57 seq.

Note 3. Enveloped in fuel and libations.

Verse 2.

Note 1. Comp. M. M.'s note, vol. xxxii, p. 437.

Note 2. Comp. Lanman, pp. 516, 518.

Verse 3.

Note 1. Prof. Max Müller translates the second and third Pâdas: 'again and again shouting, bellowing forth his sperm, yea, placing his sperm with bellowing.'

Note 2. Of course the fuel is alluded to.

Verse 4.

Note 1. Ya*gñ*ásya adhvarásya, 'sacrifice and service;' comp. above, I, 1, 4, note 1.

Note 2. The translation is doubtful. If the denominative ishûy is derived from íshu, the meaning must be 'to fly like an arrow,' or possibly 'to shoot arrows.' But I do not think that the poet can have meant to say that Agni acts as a vedhấ*h* and looks on all creatures 'for him who flies like an arrow,' or 'for him who shoots arrows.' We should rather have to write ishûyate without accent, so that the translation would be: 'By (the power of) his mind helpful (Agni) flies like an arrow; he looks on all creatures' (comp. VI, 3, 5, where it is said that Agni shoots arrows). But possibly ishûy, which is found only here, may be a synonym of ishudhy, see verse 6. It may be a denominative from ish, influenced by the type of verbs like *ri*g*û*y, kratûy, vasûy, &c. Then the accent can be retained, and the translation would be as given in the text ('to him who desires food').

Note 3. On váhni, comp. above, I, 127, 8, note 1.

Verse 5.

Note 1. The cerebral *n* in ave*n*a clearly points to the correction of the text agné*h* râve*n*a.

Note 2. The Maruts are called bho*g*ấ*h*, V, 53, 16 (stuhí bho*g*ấn, 'praise the liberal ones'). Here we have the corresponding abstract noun.

Verse 6.

Note 1. Víhâyas (comp. Bergaigne, Religion Védique, III, 287) seems to be formed like vímahas, ví*k*etas, vímanas. The meaning then will be 'of extended hâyas.' The substantive hâyas, which is not found in the texts separately, may be derived from *g*íhîte or from hinóti, and mean something like 'energy.' At all events it seems impossible to connect this adjective víhâyas with the substantive vihâyas, 'the aerial space,' belonging to the classical language.

Note 2. Comp. the remark above, I, 58, 7, note 2.

Note 3. I propose to read ví*s*vâ ví-hâyâ*h* aratí*h* vásû dadhe háste dákshi*n*e. Comp. IX, 18, 4. ấ yá*h* ví*s*vâni vấryâ vásûni hástayo*h* dadhé.

Note 4. Comp. Pischel, Vedische Studien, I, 191.

Note 5. Comp. VIII, 19, 1. devatrấ havyám óhire.

Verse 7.

Note 1. I*l*ấ k*ri*tá seems to be identical with íshk*ri*ta.

Note 2. Regarding the metre, comp. Lanman, p. 383.

Verse 8.

Note 1. Comp. I, 58, 7, note 1.

MANDALA I, HYMN 140.

ASHTAKA II, ADHYÂYA 2, VARGA 5–7.

1. For him who sits on the Vedi (i.e. on the sacrificial bed), whose foundations are pleasant, for the brilliant Agni bring forward[1] a receptacle[2], which is to him like a drink. Clothe[1] the bright one in prayer as in a garment, him whose chariot is light, whose colour is bright, the destroyer of darkness.

2. He who has a twofold birth[1], presses on towards the threefold food[2]; what he has eaten grows again after a year[3]. With the mouth and the tongue of the one he (shows himself as) the noble, manly one; with the other (mouth) the stubborn (Agni) wipes off the trees[4].

3. Both his mothers[1], dwelling together, immersed in darkness, and affrighted, proceed towards the young child who stretches forward his tongue, who sparkling moves about thirstily, whom men should attach to themselves, who agitates (the world), the increaser of his father[2].

4. Thy speedy (teams)[1] that strive to break loose for the benefit of the man who acts as men do, the swift ones, drawing black furrows—thy quick (horses), striving apart, the agile, swift runners, incited by the wind, are yoked.

5. When he stroking his wide course proceeds panting, thundering, roaring, then those sparkling (rays) of his fly about wildly, displaying wondrous darkness, a large sight[1].

6. When he bends down over the brown (plants)[1] like a busy (servant), he roars and approaches his

wives like a bull. Displaying his power he adorns his bodies with beauty; like a terrible beast, difficult to seize, he shakes his horns.

7. He clasps (the plants, &c.) that have been laid together and have been laid out[1]. Knowing them, while they know him, and being their own (friend or lover) he lies on them. They grow again and attain godhead. They produce together another shape of the parents[2].

8. The long-haired virgins[1] have embraced him. Having died they stand upright again for him (Agni) the living one (or, for him the Âyu). Delivering them of old age he proceeds roaring, procreating another vital spirit, an indestructible life.

9. Licking everywhere the upper garment of the mother[1], he spreads himself over the space with his mightily devouring warriors, giving strength to everything that has feet, licking and licking. The reddish white one[2] follows her ways[3].

10. Shine, O Agni, among our liberal lords, for thou art a mightily breathing bull, a friend of the house. Throwing down the (mothers) of the young child[1] thou hast shone, (a protector of thy friends) like a coat of mail in battles, hurrying around.

11. May this well-composed (prayer), O Agni, be more welcome to thee than a badly-composed one—more welcome than even a welcome prayer. With the bright light of thy body win thou treasures for us.

12. Grant us, Agni, for our chariot and for our house a ship which has its own rudders and which has feet[1], which may save our strong men and our liberal lords and our people, and which may be a shelter for us.

13. Approve, O Agni, our hymn alone. May Heaven and Earth and the Rivers, delightful by their own nature[1], going their way[2], (choose for us) bliss in cows and crops, long days; may the red (Dawns) choose food for us as a choice boon.

NOTES.

The *Ri*shi is Dîrghatamas Au*k*athya, the metre *G*agatî; the two last verses are Trish*t*ubh (comp. above the note on the metre of I, 94); the tenth verse, which is considered as either *G*agatî or Trish*t*ubh, begins with one *G*agatî Pâda which is followed by three Pâdas in Trish*t*ubh.—No verse occurs in the other Sa*m*hitâs.

Verse 1.

Note 1. Prá bharâ (Padap. prá bhara) and vâsayâ (Padap. vâsaya) may be 1st person.

Note 2. Possibly the 'womb' or 'receptacle' (yóni) here means gh*ri*ta or the like, for it is said of Agni that 'his womb is gh*ri*ta' (II, 3, 11), and he is called gh*ri*táyoni*h*. This receptacle 'is to him like a drink,' because he consumes the gh*ri*ta by which he is surrounded.

Verse 2.

Note 1. The terrestrial and the celestial birth. Comp. Bergaigne, I, 28 seq.

Note 2. Bergaigne (I, 29) translates: '. . . s'élance trois fois sur la nourriture,' which he explains as referring to 'the three sacrifices of the morning, the midday, and the evening.' But tri-v*ri*t clearly is an epithet of ánnam, not an adverb. The explanation of Sâya*n*a, who understands the threefold food as sacrificial butter, sacrificial cakes (puro*d*â*s*a), and Soma, may be correct.

Note 3. On the locative sa*m*vatsaré, comp. Delbrück, Altindische Syntax, p. 117.

Note 4. The last words evidently refer to Agni's tongue, i.e. his flames, wiping off as it were the firewood. But it is not clear what the tongue of the other one is. Sâya*n*a thinks of the sacrificial spoon conceived as the tongue of the officiating priest: which is very artificial, but perhaps not too artificial for a verse like this.

Verse 3.

Note 1. The 'two mothers' of Agni may be the two worlds (comp. Bergaigne, I, 238) or the two kindling-sticks. —Ubhấ (masc.) instead of ubhé is to be remarked.

Note 2. Agni increases the wealth of the worshipper who has lighted the fire and may thus be considered as Agni's father. Comp. *S*atapatha Brâhma*n*a XII, 5, 2, 15. Or the father may be Heaven; on Agni as imparting strength to Heaven, see I, 164, 51.

Verse 4.

Note 1. The verse begins with feminines; the *g*úva*h* (comp. I, 134, 1), literally the quick ones, seem to be something like the niyúta*h* of Agni. Then follow masculines; the horses of Agni are male (comp. Bergaigne, I, 143).

Verse 5.

Note 1. Comp. bhűri várpa*h* kárikrat, III, 58, 9.

Verse 6.

Note 1. The brown ones, according to Sâya*n*a, are the plants. They are called brown (babhru) also in X, 97, 1. 'Are they the dry leaves in which the spark is caught?' M. M.

Verse 7.

Note 1. Prof. Max Müller translates sa*m*stíra*h* vish*t*íra*h*, '(the flames) that are together and apart.'

Note 2. The parents seem to be Heaven and Earth, as Sâya*n*a explains.—Possibly pitró*h* depends on sá*k*â (comp.

pitróh sákâ, II, 17, 7; IV, 5, 10), 'being with their parents they produce a new shape.' Prof. Max Müller translates: 'They produce together a different shape of their parents.'

Verse 8.

Note 1. Should not the plants again be referred to? 'I think it refers to the gvâlâs, the flames that are hidden under the ashes and are lighted again.' M. M.

Verse 9.

Note 1. The mother is the Earth whose surface Agni licks.

Note 2. I believe the Dawn is alluded to whom the Vedic poets represent now as preceding Agni, now as following him. See Bergaigne, II, pp. 14, 15.

Note 3. For vartanî́r áha of the Samhitâpâtha the Padapâtha has vartaníh áha; comp. Rig-veda Prâtisâkhya, Sûtra 259. Vartanî́h of course is correct. Comp. X, 172, 1. gấvah sakanta vartanîm.

Verse 10.

Note 1. The mothers of the young child are very probably the mothers of Agni represented as a young child. They may be the Waters which Agni leaves resting on the surface of the earth while he himself rises to heaven. Or the mothers may be the woods or plants which he burns and thus throws them down as it were.

Verse 12.

Note 1. 'Which has feet in its own rudders,' M. M. That the ship has feet seems to mean only that it has the faculty of moving forward freely and quickly, and not that any real beings having feet are designated by this comparison. The ship that carries the worshippers across all dangers, is the protection and help which Agni grants, or the sacrifice which he helps to perform.

Verse 13.

Note 1. Comp. Geldner, Vedische Studien, I, 275.

Note 2. Yánta*h* seems to be corrupt; one or two syllables are wanting. Something like yâtáyanta*h* (IX, 39, 2) or vardháyanta*h*, or, as Prof. Max Müller proposes, vyánta*h* would do. He translates: 'May Heaven and Earth and the Rivers . . . accepting (vyánta*h*) sacrifices of milk and corn choose for us, and may the Dawns choose for us food as a boon for many days.'—Cf. Lanman, pp. 510, 539.

MANDALA I, HYMN 141.

ASHTAKA II, ADHYÂYA 2, VARGA 8-9.

1. Lo, that beautiful splendour of the god, when he was born of strength, has truly come to be a wondrous sight. Though he slinks away[1], the prayer goes straight to him[2]. They have led forward the flowing streams of *Ri*ta.

2. The powerful one[1], rich in food, the true (friend of men) has entered the wondrous (body)[2]. His second (form of existence) is in the seven kind mothers[3]. The ten young females[4] have brought the third (form) of this bull forth, him the guardian, in order to milk him.

3. When the rulers, the liberal lords brought him forth by their power out of the depth, out of the buffalo's shape[1], when from of old[2] at the purification of the sweet drink[3] Mâtaris*v*an produces the hidden one (i.e. Agni) by attrition—

4. When he is led forward from the highest father[1], he climbs up the . . .[2], the plants in his (or, in their ?) houses. When[3] both (Heaven and Earth or the two Ara*n*is ?) promote his birth, then the youngest one became bright by his heat[4].

5. Then he entered upon the mothers[1] in whom he the bright one grew up far and wide unimpaired[2]. When he has climbed up to the former (mothers) who from of old incite (him)[3], he runs down in the younger, later (or, nearer) ones.

6[1]. Then in the strivings for the day[2] they choose him Hot*ri*. As if to swell their good fortune they strive towards him [3], when praised by many he moves everywhere with wisdom and power to the gods and to the praise of mortals [4] for (bringing them) refreshing drink.

7. When he has scattered himself, the worshipful one, driven by the wind, like . . .[1], with the sound (which he produces) (?), he whom it is not possible to drive to a place (like cattle): on the flight of the burning one who speeds on his black way, whose birth is bright, who strays everywhere to the atmosphere . . .[2]

8. Like a chariot that goes forward, he goes to Heaven with his ruddy limbs, adorned with his locks of flames[1]. Then his black (clouds of smoke), O burning one (?), the liberal ones (?) (appear)[2]. The birds flee as before the fierceness of a hero[3].

9. Through thee indeed, O Agni, Varu*n*a whose laws are firm, Mitra and Aryaman, the givers of good rain, are glorious, when thou the mighty one hast been born, everywhere encompassing with wisdom (all beings), as the felly encompasses the spokes of a wheel.

10. Thou, O Agni, youngest (god), furtherest treasures and (the friendship of) the gods for him who performs worship, who presses Soma. May we thus establish thee the young one, O young (son) of strength, possessor of great treasures, like the winner in a race [1].

11. Make good fortune [1] swell for us like well-employed wealth belonging to the house, and like firm ability[2]—(fortune) which can hold both races [3] like reins: and being full of good-will in (the sphere of) *Ri*ta, (fill our) praise of the gods (with rich reward).

12. And may the brilliant, joyful Hot*ri* with quick horses, with a shining chariot hear us. May he, the wise Agni, lead us on the best leading (paths) to happy welfare and to bliss.

13. Agni has been praised with powerful[1] songs, he who has been brought forward furthermore for sovereignty. May both those our liberal lords and we ourselves spread out[2] (our power over all foes) as the sun (spreads out its light and by it destroys) the mist.

NOTES.

The same *R*ishi. The metre is *G*agatî; the two last verses again are Trish*t*ubh.—None of its verses occurs in the other Sa*m*hitâs.

Verse 1.

Note 1. The meaning seems to be that if Agni be unwilling to officiate at the sacrifice, the prayer nevertheless reaches its aim and induces him to do his duty as the divine Hot*ri*.

Note 2. The verb sâdh is very frequently connected with substantives such as dhíya*h* or the like. Comp. also matînấm *k*a sấdhanam, X, 26, 4.

Verse 2.

Note 1. It seems probable that p*ri*kshá*h* is the nominative of p*ri*kshá, and not the genitive of p*ri*ksh. Comp. VI, 8, 1, where it is said of Agni 'p*ri*kshásya v*ri*sh*n*a*h* arushásya.' On the meaning of p*ri*kshá, see above, I, 127, 5, note 1.

Note 2. The poet seems clearly to describe the second and third form of Agni's existence, his dwelling in the waters and his birth from the fire-sticks. But he is less explicit with regard to the first form. The epithet pitumā́n would seem to point to Agni as the sacrificial fire and the receiver of offerings. But it is rather strange that this form of the god should be distinguished from the Agni procreated by the ten females, i.e. produced by the ten fingers, by the attrition of the kindling-sticks.—Prof. Max Müller differs from me in referring the words dá*s*a-pramatim *g*anayanta yósha*n*a*h*, not to the third form of Agni, but to Agni in general. He translates: 'The powerful one, rich in food, rests always on that wondrous sight (Agni on the altar, gârhapatya Agni). The second rests in the seven kind mothers (vidyudrûpa; Agni in the clouds); the third is for milking the powerful one (Agni as the sun, âdityarûpa)—the ten maidens (the fingers) have brought forth the guardian.'

Note 3. Grassmann no doubt is right in proposing to read saptá *s*ivā́su. Of course the waters are alluded to.

Note 4. Read dá*s*a prámatim (Boehtlingk-Roth). On Agni as the son of the ten fingers, comp. Bergaigne, II, 7.

Verse 3.

Note 1. The buffalo Agni was hidden in the depth. Comp. X, 8, 1. apā́m upá-sthe mahishá*h* vavardha; I, 95, 9. budhnám vi-ró*k*amânam mahishásya dhā́ma.

Note 2. The preposition ánu seems to stand here with an ablative (pra-díva*h*).

Note 3. The literal meaning of mádhva*h* â-dhavé is indicated by passages such as I, 109, 4. ā́ dhâvatam má-dhunâ; IX, 11, 5. mádhâv ā́ dhâvata mádhu. Comp. also âdhavanîya. On the washing of the Soma which is technically designated by the verb â-dhâv, see H. O., Göttinger Gelehrte Anzeigen, 1890, p. 426 seq.; Hillebrandt, Vedische Mythologie, I, 216.—The purification of the sweet drink, at which Agni is produced, was probably achieved by the tempest.

Verse 4.

Note 1. The highest father is Heaven.

Note 2. The meaning of p*ri*kshúdha*h* is unknown.

Note 3. Yát is repeated twice, as yásya in X, 121, 2. yásya ví*s*ve upa-ā́sate pra-*s*ísham yásya devā́*h*.

Note 4. On gh*rin*ā́, comp. Lanman, Noun-Inflection, 335.

Verse 5.

Note 1. The mothers are the Waters.

Note 2. The reading, very probably, ought to be vivâv*ri*dhé.

Note 3. Boehtlingk-Roth believe that the reading ought to be sanâyúva*h* or sanâ-*g*úra*h*. Sanâ-*g*úra*h* (cf. sanâ-*g*úrâ pitárâ, IV, 36, 3) seems to me quite possible, although there is no positive necessity for abandoning the traditional reading.—The 'former' mothers may be the heavenly Waters; the mothers in whom Agni runs down are the rivers. Prof. Max Müller adds that the former mothers may possibly be 'the burnt pieces of wood. Agni runs up in them, then leaves them to burn new pieces.'

Verse 6.

Note 1. On the whole verse, compare Pischel, Vedische Studien, I, 217.

Note 2. Comp. above, I, 45, 7, note 1.

Note 3. The second Pâda is translated by Pischel: 'Wie in einen König drängen sie in ihn, wenn sie (Trank)opfer darbringen.' But verse 11 shows that bhágam depends on pap*rik*ânā́sa*h*.

Note 4. Comp. III, 16, 4. ā́ devéshu . . . ā́ *sám*se utá n*rin*ā́m.

Verse 7.

Note 1. The translation of hvârá*h* is quite uncertain. The same must be said of the rest of this Pâda.

Note 2. The sentence is incomplete.

Verse 8.

Note 1. On *s*íkvan (or *s*íkvas), comp. M. M.'s note, vol. xxxii, p. 318; Hübschmann, Vocalsystem, p. 186. The translation is only tentative.—Two syllables are wanting;

we may propose a reading like *s*ikvabhi*h* párishk*ri*ta*h* (comp. H. O., Prolegomena, 76, note 3).

Note 2. This passage is most obscure. The first words of the Pâda are the same as above, 140, 5. The 'black ones' probably are the dark clouds of smoke that surround Agni. But it is very strange that these clouds should be designated as sûráya*h*, 'liberal ones.' And the vocative (?) dakshi (Padapâ*th*a dhakshi), instead of which we should at least expect daksho or dakshin, is no less strange. The text seems thoroughly corrupt.

Note 3. See Lanman, p. 557.

Verse 10.

Note 1. Comp. Geldner, Vedische Studien, I, 121.

Verse 11.

Note 1. Comp. above, verse 6, Pâda 2.

Note 2. Comp. VIII, 24, 14. dáksham p*riñk*ántam.

Note 3. The human and the divine race. I do not believe that Dr. Neisser (Zur Vedischen Verballehre, 17) is right in interpreting yámati as an indicative.

Verse 13.

Note 1. The translation of *s*imîvadbhi*h* is only tentative. *S*imî (I, 151, 1) cannot be identical with *s*ámî.

Note 2. Ni*h* tatanyu*h* (nísh *t*atanyu*h*, Sa*m*hitâpâ*th*a) of course is derived from tan, not from stan. Comp. I, 105, 12. satyám tâtâna sűrya*h*; IV, 5, 13. sűra*h* vár*n*ena tatanan ushấsa*h*, &c.

MANDALA I, HYMN 142.

ASHTAKA II, ADHYÂYA 2, VARGA 10-11.

Âprî Hymn.

1. Being inflamed, Agni, bring hither to-day the gods to the man who holds forth the (sacrificial) ladle. Spin out the ancient thread (of sacrifice)[1] for the sacrificer who has prepared Soma.

2. Measure out, O Tanûnapât[1], the sacrifice rich in ghee, rich in honey, of a priest like me, of a sacrificer who has toiled hard.

3. The brilliant, purifying, wonderful Narâ*s*a*m*sa[1] mixes the sacrifice with honey three times a day, the god worthy of worship among the gods.

4. Agni, magnified[1] by us, bring hither the bright, beloved Indra. For this my prayer is addressed[2] to thee whose tongue is good.

5. (Priests) hold forth the (sacrificial) ladle, strewing the sacrificial grass at the decorous service of the sacrifice;—I[1] trim[2] (the sacrificial grass) which best receives the gods with its wide extent, a big shelter for Indra.

6[1]. May the divine doors open themselves, the increasers of *Ri*ta, the never sticking, large ones, the purifying, much-desired (doors), that the gods may come forth.

7. May Night and Dawn, of glorious appearance, the two neighbouring (goddesses), wearing beautiful ornaments[1], the young[2] mothers of *Ri*ta, sit down together on the sacrificial grass[3].

8. May the two divine Hot*ri*s, eager in praising (the gods), the sages with lovely tongues, perform

for us to-day this successful sacrifice which attains to Heaven.

9. The brilliant (goddess) placed among the gods, among the Maruts[1], Hotrâ Bhâratî[2], I*l*â, Sarasvatî, and Mahî[3]: may these worshipful (goddesses) sit down on the sacrificial grass.

10. May Tvash*tri*, inclined towards us, pour forth for us, in our navel[1], that wonderful seed with many treasures[2], plentiful by itself, for the sake of prosperity and wealth[3].

11. Letting go (the sacrificial food to the gods) sacrifice by thyself to the gods, O tree[1]. May[2] Agni make the offerings ready[3], the god among the gods, the wise one.

12. For Him who is accompanied by Pûshan and by the Maruts, by the Vi*s*ve devâ*h*, (by) Vâyu[1], who is moved by the Gâyatra song, for Indra pronounce the Svâhâ over the offering.

13. Come hither to the offerings over which the Svâhâ has been pronounced, in order to feast. Indra! Come hither! Hear our call! Thee they call at the worship.

NOTES.

The hymn is an Âprîsûkta. The same *Ri*shi. Metre, Anush*t*ubh. The whole hymn is closely related to I, 13.—Verse 10: cf. VS. XXVII, 20; TS. IV, 1, 8, 3; MS. II, 12, 6.

Verse 1.

Note 1. The third Pâda of this verse is identical with VIII, 13, 14.

Verse 2.

Note 1. Comp. I, 13, 2, note 1.

Verse 3.

Note 1. Comp. I, 13, 2, note 1.

Verse 4.

Note 1. 'Magnified' is î*l*itá*h*; comp. the note on I, 1, 1. The verse is addressed to the I*d*a*h*.

Note 2. The text has á*kkh*a . . . va*k*yáte. To me there seems to be no doubt that this is the passive of va*k*, not of va*ñk*. Comp. the name of the priest a*kkh*âvâka, and the phrase á*kkh*oktibhi*h* matînā́m, I, 61, 3; 184, 2. The same passive of va*k* is found III, 39, 1. matí*h* h*ri*dá*h* ā́ va*k*yá-mânâ (then follows á*kkh*a . . . *g*igâti); X, 47, 7 (stómâ*h*) . . . mánasâ va*k*yámânâ*h*.—It may be observed that in our passage as well as in III, 39, 1 and X, 47, 7, the forms va*k*yáte, va*k*yámânâ, va*k*yámânâ*h* are preceded by a vowel; and we may infer that the poet did not say u*k*yáte, &c., in order to avoid the hiatus.

Verse 5.

Note 1. The poet begins as if he intended to say, 'Priests . . . lay down the sacrificial grass.' But he continues, 'I lay down.' Dr. Neisser (Bezzenberger's Beiträge, XX, 60) tries to explain the difficulty in a way in which I cannot follow him.

Note 2. On the verb v*rig* technically connected with barhí*h*, see Geldner, Vedische Studien, I, 152 seq., and compare vol. xxxii, I, 38, 1, note 2; I, 64, 1, note 2.

Verse 6.

Note 1. With the whole verse compare I, 13, 6.

Verse 7.

Note 1. Pischel's opinion (Vedische Studien, II, 113 seq.) that pé*s*a*h* means 'Gestalt,' 'Form,' 'Farbe,' 'rûpa,' does not convince me.

Note 2. See Geldner, Kuhn's Zeitschrift, XXVIII, 195.

Note 3. Comp. VIII, 87, 4. ấ barhíh sîdatam sumát. Geldner (Vedische Studien, II, 190) translates: 'das schöne Opfergras.'

Verse 9.

Note 1. 'Should we read márteshu for marútsu?' M. M. This conjecture seems perhaps rather bold.

Note 2. Hotrâ Bhâratî, i.e. the personified Offering of the Bharatas, seems to be one goddess, more usually called simply Bhâratî. Comp. I, 22, 10; II, 1, 11; III, 62, 3; Bergaigne, Religion Védique, I, 322; H. O., Religion des Veda, 243, note 2. Pischel's opinion (Vedische Studien, II, 85) is different.

Note 3. See above, I, 13, 9, note 1.

Verse 10.

Note 1. On the navel as the symbol of the connection between father and son, see Bergaigne, I, 35, 36, and comp. the well-known name Nâbhânedishtha.

Note 2. For purú vấram very probably puruvấram should be read (Grassmann). See II, 40, 4. puruvấram . . . râyás pósham ví syatâm nấbhim asmé.

Note 3. With the last Pâda compare II, 40, 4, quoted in note 2, and II, 3, 9. pragấm Tváshtâ ví syatu nấbhim asmé; see also Taittirîya Samhitâ IV, 1, 8, 3. Tvashtri is generally considered as giving sons; see H. O., Religion des Veda, 234.

Verse 11.

Note 1. Comp. I, 13, 11, note 1.

Note 2. The second hemistich recurs I, 105, 14.

Note 3. See Neisser, Zur Vedischen Verballehre, 22.

Verse 12.

Note 1. The text has 'for Vâyu,' not 'for (the god) accompanied by Vâyu.' But there is no doubt that pûshanváte, &c., refers to Indra, and that Vâyu is named merely as a companion of Indra.

MAṆḌALA I, HYMN 143.

ASHṬAKA II, ADHYÂYA 2, VARGA 12.

1. I bring forward my most powerful, entirely new (pious) thought (i.e. hymn), the prayer of my words[1] to Agni, the son of strength; he is the child of the Waters[2], the beloved one, who together with the Vasus has sat down on the Earth as a Hot*ri* observing the appointed time (for sacrificing).

2. Being born in the highest heaven Agni became visible to Mâtari*s*van. By the power of his mind, by his greatness when kindled, his flame filled Heaven and Earth with light.

3[1]. His flames are fierce; never ageing are the flames of him who is beautiful to behold, whose face is beautiful, whose splendour is beautiful. The never sleeping, never ageing (rays) of Agni whose power is light, roll forward like streams across the nights (?)[2].

4. Him the all-wealthy, whom the Bh*ri*gus have set to work on the navel of the earth, with the whole power of the world[1]—stir up that Agni by thy prayers in his own house—(him) who alone rules over goods like Varu*n*a.

5. He who is not to be kept back like the roar of the Maruts, like an army[1] that is sent forward, like the thunderbolt of heaven—Agni eats with his sharp jaws, he chews, he throws down the forests as a warrior throws down his foes.

6. Would Agni eagerly come to our hymn? Would He the Vasu together with the Vasus fulfil our desire? Will He, the driver, stir our prayers

that they may be successful? (Thus thinking) I praise Him whose face is bright, with this my prayer.

7. He who has kindled him strives[1] towards Agni as towards Mitra (or, towards a friend)—(to Agni) whose face shines with ghee, the charioteer of *Ri*ta. May he who when kindled becomes a racer[2], shining at the sacrifices[3], lift up our bright-coloured prayer.

8[1]. Preserve us, O Agni, never failing with thy never-failing, kind and mighty guardians; protect our people all around with those undeceived, undismayed, never slumbering (guardians), O thou our wish[2]!

NOTES.

The same *Ri*shi. Metre, *G*agatî; the last verse Trish*t*ubh. The hymn has been translated by Kaegi, Siebenzig Lieder des Rigveda, p. 100.—Verse 7 = TB. I, 2, 1, 12.

Verse 1.

Note 1. Comp. VIII, 59, 6. vâ*k*á*h* mátim.

Note 2. Agni who is considered as born from the Waters, is identified several times with a god who, like Mâtari*s*van, in my opinion had an independent origin, with Apâm napât ('Child of the Waters'). Comp. Bergaigne, Rel. Védique, II, 17 seq.; H. O., Religion des Veda, 118 seq.

Verse 3.

Note 1. There is no sufficient reason for transposing verses 3 and 4 (Kaegi).

Note 2. Probably we should read áti aktū́n; comp. VI, 4, 5. áti eti aktū́n.—See Bergaigne, Mélanges Renier, p. 96.

Verse 4.

Note 1. Bhúvanasya seems to depend on ma*g*mánâ; comp. VII, 82, 5. bhúvanasya ma*g*mánâ.

Verse 5.

Note 1. Pischel (Vedische Studien, I, 231) seems to me to be right in denying that sénâ ever means 'Geschoss,' and in translating sénâ s*ri*sh*t*ấ 'exercitus effusus.' The opinion of Prof. von Bradke and Prof. Bloomfield is different; see Zeitschrift der Deutschen Morgenl. Gesellschaft, XLVI, 456; XLVIII, 549.

Verse 7.

Note 1. The text adds the dativus ethicus va*h*, 'for you' (comp. Delbrück, Altindische Syntax, 206), which can scarcely be translated.

Note 2. Geldner (Vedische Studien, I, 168) has shown that akrá very probably means 'horse.' Agni is very frequently compared to a horse.—Comp. Ludwig, Ueber die neuesten Arbeiten auf dem Gebiete der *Ri*gveda-Forschung, p. 54; Roth, Zeitschrift der D. Morg. Ges., XLVIII, 118.

Note 3. See above, I, 31, 6, note 2.

Verse 8.

Note 1. With Pâdas C D compare the verse VI, 8, 7. ádabdhebhi*h* táva gopấbhi*h* ish*t*e asmấkam pâhi trishadhastha sûrī́n.

Note 2. 'What is ish*t*e? Is it thou our wish, or thou our sacrifice?' M. M.

MA*ND*ALA I, HYMN 144.

ASH*T*AKA II, ADHYÂYA 2, VARGA 13.

1. The Hot*ri*[1] goes forward[2] (in order to fulfil) his duty by his wonderful power, directing upwards the brightly adorned prayer. He steps towards the (sacrificial) ladles which are turned to the right[3], and which first kiss his foundation[4].

2. They have greeted with shouts the streams of *Ri*ta[1] which were hidden at the birthplace of the god, at his seat. When He dwelt dispersed in the lap of the waters, he drank the draughts by (the power of) which he moves[2].

3. Two (beings) of the same age[1] try to draw that wonderful shape (Agni) towards themselves, progressing in turns towards a common aim[2]. Then he is to be proclaimed by us like a winner[3] (in a contest). The charioteer[4] (governs all things) as if pulling in the reins of a draught-horse.

4. He whom two (beings) of the same age[1] serve, two twins dwelling together in one common abode, the gray one has been born as a youth by night as by day[2], the ageless one who wanders through many generations of men.

5. The prayers, the ten fingers[1] stir him up. We, the mortals, call him, the god, for his protection. From the dry land he hastens to the declivities[2]. With those who approached him he has established new rules[3].

6. Thou indeed, O Agni, reignest by thy own nature over the heavenly and over the terrestrial

world as a shepherd (takes care of his cattle). These two variegated, great (goddesses) striving for gloriousness, the golden ones who move crookedly[1], have approached thy sacrificial grass.

7. Agni! Be gratified and accept graciously this prayer, O joy-giver, independent one, who art born in the *Ri*ta, good-willed one, whose face is turned towards us from all sides, conspicuous one, gay in thy aspect, like a dwelling-place rich in food[1].

NOTES.

The same *Ri*shi. Metre, *G*agatî.—No verse occurs in the other Sa*m*hitâs.

Verse 1.

Note 1. The Hot*ri* is Agni.

Note 2. Comp. III, 27, 7, where it is said of Agni: purástât eti mâyáyâ.—The poet says éti prá, and not prá eti, in order to avoid the hiatus.

Note 3. Comp. below, III, 6, 1. dakshi*n*â-vấ*t*.

Note 4. 'Which first, i.e. at the time when the sacrificial vessels are put down, kiss his dhâman (foundation), i.e. the place of Agni.' Sâya*n*a.

Verse 2.

Note 1. Comp. IX, 75, 3. abhí îm *ri*tásya dohánâ*h* anûshata, and VIII, 12, 32. nấbhâ ya*gñ*ásya dohánâ prá adhvaré. I take dohánâ*h* as acc. plur. of an abstract noun dohánâ formed like *g*ará*n*â, bhandánâ, &c. But possibly it might be the nom. plur. either of the same noun or of a nomen agentis dohána: 'the streams of *Ri*ta (the libations?) or the milkers of *Ri*ta, hidden at the birthplace of the god, have greeted him with shouts.' It would be difficult, however, to say why the milkers of *Ri*ta (i. e. the priests?) are called 'hidden at the birthplace of the god.' Prof. Max Müller thinks of a reading parîv*rí*ta*h*, 'surrounding Agni.' He refers the 'streams of *Ri*ta' (nom.) to the water, cf. I, 105, 12. *ri*tám arshanti síndhava*h*.

Note 2. Svadhā́*h* adhayat yā́bhi*h* ī́yate. In my opinion svadhā́ means 'the inherent power,' 'the power of moving according to one's own will,' and then the drink which confers this power on a being, especially on the dead ancestors.—Comp. M. M., vol. xxxii, p. 32 seq.; H. O., Religion des Veda, 531, note 2.

Verse 3.

Note 1. According to Sâya*n*a the two beings spoken of here and in the next verse are the Hot*ri* and the Adhvaryu.

Note 2. See I, 130, 5. ayu*ñg*ata samânám ártham ákshitam; III, 61, 3. samânám ártham *k*ara*n*îyámânâ.

Note 3. On bhága*h* ná hávya*h*, see Geldner, Vedische Studien, I, 121.

Note 4. The charioteer is Agni.

Verse 4.

Note 1. See verse 3, note 1.

Note 2. Comp. Gaedicke, Der Accusativ, p. 175. He translates: 'bei Tage noch bei Nacht ergrauend.'

Verse 5.

Note 1. Vrís (ἅπαξ λεγόμενον) is ranged in the Nigha*nt*us among the aṅgulinâmâni and explained by Sâya*n*a accordingly. The word seems indeed to mean 'finger.' Compare with our passage IX, 8, 4; 15, 8; 93, 1; 97, 57.

Note 2. Comp. I, 33, 4. dháno*h* ádhi vishu*n*ák té ví âyan, and especially X, 4, 3. dháno*h* ádhi pravátâ yâsi háryan. I cannot follow Pischel (Vedische Studien, II, 69 seq.) in explaining these passages. 'Over the heavenly expanse he hastens down towards us.' M. M.

Note 3. See Pischel, Vedische Studien, I, 300. Like Pischel I do not know who 'they who approached Agni' are. Possibly the worshippers or priests are alluded to. 'He received new praises with (or from) those who approached him.' M. M.

Verse 6.

Note 1. Sâya*n*a explains the two female beings here in question as Heaven and Earth. Does the 'crooked movement' refer to the daily revolution of the sky?

Verse 7.

Note 1. The last Pâda recurs X, 64, 11.

MAṆḌALA I, HYMN 145.

ASHṬAKA II, ADHYÂYA 2, VARGA 14.

1. Ask ye him. He has come. He knows. He the intelligent one moves forward; He moves along (his way) (?)[1]. In him all commands, all wishes dwell. He is the lord of strength, of mighty power.

2. They ask him. He himself[1] does not ask in turn what he, the wise one, has grasped by his own mind alone[2]. He does not forget the first word nor another word. Unconfused he adheres to his own power of mind.

3. To him go the sacrificial ladles, to him go the racers[1]. He alone may hear all my words. He who pronounces many praishas[2], the conqueror, the accomplisher of sacrifices whose blessings are flawless, the young child has assumed vigour.

4. When he has come together[1] (with his companions[2]), he goes to greet them[3]. As soon as born he steals upon (his prey) together with his companions. He strokes the . . .[4] to give him delight and joy, when the loving ones[5] approach him who stands on them[6].

5. He, the animal living in the water and walking in the forest[1], has been placed on the highest skin[2] (sky ?). He has proclaimed his rules to the mortals: for Agni, the knowing one, is intent upon *Ri*ta (Right) and is true.

NOTES.

The same *Ri*shi. Metre, *G*agatî; the last verse is Trish*t*ubh.—No verse occurs in the other Sa*m*hitâs.

Verse 1.

Note 1. The Samhitâ text has sấ nv̂ îyate, the Pada text, sáh nú îyate. Comp. Prâtisâkhya 314. I propose to read sấnu (= sá ánu) îyate.

Verse 2.

Note 1. See Geldner, Ved. Studien, II, p. 188.

Note 2. Possibly we should read svéna evá.

Verse 3.

Note 1. The text (árvatîh) implies that these race-horses are mares. Probably, as Sâyana explains, the prayers (stutayah) are alluded to. See on the prayers compared with horses, Bergaigne, II, 284 seq.

Note 2. Praishá is the technical designation of the sacrificial commands of one priest (or more especially, of the Maitrâvaruna) to another priest; comp. Schwab, Das Altindische Thieropfer, p. 90; H. O., Religion des Veda, 390.

Verse 4.

Note 1. Samấrata may be the third person of singular or of plural.

Note 2. I supply 'with his companions' in consideration of the second Pâda (yúgyebhih). It is difficult to say who Agni's companions are (the flames? the officiating priests?).

Note 3. Ludwig's conjecture, úpa stấyam karati, is very ingenious. 'He stealthily approaches them.'—On upasthayam, comp. also Bollensen, Zeitschrift der Deutschen Morgenl. Gesellschaft, XLVII, 586.

Note 4. The meaning of svântám, which occurs here and in the obscure passage X, 61, 21 (ádha gấvah úpamâtim kanấyâh ánu svântásya kásya kit párâ îyuh), is unknown. Possibly it is related to svâtrá, which means something like 'powerful' or 'prosperous.'

Note 5. The prayers? The oblations?

Note 6. Api-sthitám may have active or passive meaning, 'he who stands on somebody or something,' and 'he on whom somebody or something stands.'

Verse 5.

Note 1. The first Pâda (and probably also the fourth) belong to the metrical type described by H. O., Prolegomena, p. 68 seq.: the first part, before the caesura, consists of four syllables; and then the Pâda goes on as if it had the pentasyllabic opening.

Note 2. After Agni's abode in the Waters and in the wood has been mentioned in the first Pâda, the second Pâda possibly refers to his heavenly abode to which the adjective upamá ('highest') seems to point. Thus the 'highest skin' would be the sky. But Sâya*n*a, who refers it to the Vedi, may possibly be right. His explanation would very well agree with the second hemistich.

MA*ND*ALA I, HYMN 146.

ASH*T*AKA II, ADHYÂYA 2, VARGA 15.

1. I praise Agni who has three heads and seven rays (or reins)[1], who is without flaw, sitting in the lap of his parents[2] and of whatever moves or is firm, who has filled (with his light) all the lights of Heaven.

2. The big bull has grown up to them[1]; the ageless one who from here (from this world) distributes his blessings, the tall has stood up erect. He puts down his feet on the surface of the wide (Earth); his red ones[2] lick the udder (the cloud?).

3. Walking towards their common calf the two well-established[1] milch-cows[2] walk about in different directions. They measure interminable paths; they have invested themselves with all great desires.

4. Wise poets[1] follow his track[2] who in manifold ways protect the ageless one with their hearts. Wishing to acquire him they have searched the river[3]. He the Sun[4] became visible to them, to the men[5].

5. He is worthy to be looked for, round about in his race-courses, the noble who is to be magnified[1], the great one[2], in order that the small may live, as he, the all-visible liberal lord, has become a progenitor for those germs in many places.

NOTES.

The same *Ri*shi. The metre is Trish*t*ubh.—No verse occurs in the other Sa*m*hitâs.

Verse 1.

Note 1. Sâya*n*a refers the three heads of Agni to the three Savanas, or the three worlds, or the three sacrificial fires. The last explanation seems to be most probable. The seven reins (rays) are, according to Sâya*n*a, the seven metres or the seven flames of Agni. The last explanation is recommended by III, 6, 2 (see below). But it is possible also to think of the seven priests (sapta hotâra*h*).—Comp. II, 5, 2 (see below), and Taitt. Sa*m*hitâ I, 5, 3, 2 (to which passage Ludwig refers): saptá te agne samídha*h* saptá *g*ihvā́*h* saptá *rí*shaya*h* saptá dhā́ma priyā́*n*i, &c.

Note 2. The parents are Heaven and Earth.

Verse 2.

Note 1. The text has the dual feminine; no doubt Heaven and Earth are meant.

Note 2. The horses or flames of Agni.

Verse 3.

Note 1. On su-méka, comp. the article of Prof. Windisch in Festgruss an Böhtlingk, p. 114.

Note 2. The cows seem to be Night and Dawn; comp. above, I, 95, 1; 96, 5. Night and Dawn are called suméke, I, 113, 3.

Verse 4.

Note 1. The priests.

Note 2. I have translated padám nayanti in the way indicated by Atharva-veda XI, 2, 13. viddhásya padan*ī́h*-iva; comp. also Manu VIII, 44. Prof. Max Müller translates, 'Wise poets lead (Agni) to the ageless place, keeping many things in their heart—or, lead the ageless Agni to his place (the sacrifice).'

Note 3. They have tried to find Agni in his proper dwelling, in the water.

Note 4. The Sun is here identified with Agni.

Note 5. On the form n*rí*n standing for different cases, compare Lanman, Noun-Inflection, 430; Bergaigne, Religion Védique, I, 136, note 1; Pischel, Vedische Studien, I, 42, and Göttinger Gel. Anzeigen, 1890, p. 541 seq.; Hillebrandt, Zeitschrift der Deutschen Morgenl. Gesellschaft, XLVIII, 420. Here it seems most natural to take n*ri*ń, as Pischel has proposed, as standing for the dative plural. Bartholomae (Studien zur indogermanischen Sprachgeschichte, I, 118, comp. p. 48), referring to III, 14, 4, believes that n*ri*ń (or, more correctly, *n*ri*ḿ), both here and there is genitive plural, and that Agni is called 'the sun of men' because men are able to light this sun themselves. To me it seems very doubtful that this is a Vedic idea, and as to the verse III, 14, 4, I believe that n*ri*ń there is a regular accusative plural: Agni is called there, 'a sun that spreads out men over their dwellings.'

Verse 5.

Note 1. Î*l*ényya*h*. Comp. I, 1, 1, note 2.

Note 2. Agni may be called mahá*h*, 'the great one.' But it seems more natural to read mahé, the ancient pronunciation of which word before a word commencing with a vowel (mahá') coincided, or nearly coincided, with that of mahá*h*. The translation then would be: 'he who is to be magnified in order that the great and the small may live.'

MAN*D*ALA I, HYMN 147.

ASHT*A*KA II, ADHYÂYA 2, VARGA 16.

1. How, O Agni, have the resplendent ones worshipped thee, aspiring through the powers of the Âyu[1], when[2] the gods, obtaining kith and kin of both races[3] (human and divine ?), rejoiced in the song of *Ri*ta (or Right)[4] ?

2. Give heed to this my proffered hymn, O youngest one, which is most rich in liberal gifts[1], O self-dependent one! The one abuses thee, the other praises thee: I thy reverer revere thy body, O Agni[2]!

3. Thy guardians, O Agni, who saw and saved the blind son of Mamatâ from distress[1]—he the possessor of all wealth has saved them who have done good deeds[2]. The impostors, trying to deceive, have not deceived.

4. The niggard, O Agni, the harmful and malicious who injures us by falsehood: may the heavy spell recoil on him; may he injure his own body by his evil words[1].

5. And, O strong one, whatever mortal knowingly injures another mortal by falsehood: from such a one, O praised Agni, protect him who praises thee. Agni! Do not deliver us to distress.

NOTES.

The same *Ri*shi and metre.—Verse 2 = VS. XII, 42; TS. IV, 2, 3, 4; MS. II, 7, 10. Verse 3 = RV. IV, 4, 13; TS. I, 2, 14, 5; MS. IV, 11, 5.

Verse 1.

Note 1. The Âyu seems to be Agni himself. Or is it admissible to interpret âyó*h* as standing *metri causâ* for âyáva*h*? Then the hemistich would refer to the mythical sacerdotal tribe of the Âyus, the ancient worshippers of Agni. Comp., for instance, X, 7, 5; 46, 8. The translation would be, 'How, O Agni, have the resplendent Âyus worshipped thee, aspiring with their powers?'

Note 2. 'Because.' M. M.

Note 3. Comp. VIII, 103, 7. ubhé toké tánaye dasma vi*s*pate párshi rấdha*h* maghónâm.

Note 4. As to *ri*tásya sấman, comp. Vâ*g*. Sa*m*h. XXII, 2, and *ri*tásya *s*lóka*h*, Rig-veda IV, 23, 8. Our Pâda recurs IV, 7, 7 with the reading *ri*tásya dhấman.

Verse 2.

Note 1. With vá*k*asa*h* má*m*hish*th*asya compare má*m*hish*th*âbhi*h* matíbhi*h*, VIII, 23, 23.

Note 2. Cf. Aufrecht, Kuhn's Zeitschrift, III, 200.

Verse 3.

Note 1. Dîrghatamas the son of Mamatâ is the reputed author of this section of the first Ma*nd*ala which belongs indeed to a family of priests claiming descent from him. The story of the blindness of Dîrghatamas and of the distress into which he fell is told in the Mahâbhârata I, 4179 seq., ed. Calc.; comp. also Geldner, Vedische Studien, II, 145.

Note 2. Considering the construction of the whole verse from the grammatical point of view only, one will scarcely be tempted to translate otherwise than we have done. But it is rather strange that Agni is represented here as saving those very guardians by the aid of whom he has saved Mâmateya. The meaning which one should expect to find expressed, is rather that Agni, as he has saved Mâmateya by his guardians, has saved also, and will save, all pious worshippers. This meaning may be established if we consider the construction of the verse as similar, for instance, to that of I, 37, 12 (vol. xxxii, p. 64): máruta*h* yát ha va*h* bálam *g*ánân a*k*u*k*yavîtana, 'O Maruts, with such strength as yours, you have caused men to tremble.' Thus we may, I believe, translate here, 'Agni! With such guardians as thine who have seen and saved the blind son of Mamatâ from distress, he, the possessor of all wealth (i.e. Agni), has saved all those who have done good deeds.' Bergaigne (III, 191) understands the verse in the same way.

Verse 4.

Note 1. The Vedic idea of the evil deeds recoiling on the evil-doer himself has been treated of by Bergaigne, III, 190 seq.

MANDALA I, HYMN 148.

ASHTAKA II, ADHYÂYA 2, VARGA 17.

1. When Mâtarisvan . . .[1] had produced by attrition the Hotri, the . . .[2] who belongs to all gods, whom they have established among the human clans, shining like the sun, resplendent that (he might show his beautiful) shape—

2. They did not deceive him[1] who had granted a hymn (to the worshipper). Agni is my protection; therewith he is satisfied. They took pleasure in all his[2] works—(in the works) of the singer who brought praise.

3. Whom the worshipful (gods)[1] took and placed in his own seat (as priest) with their praises: him they[2] have carried forward, taking hold of him in their search, hastening like horses that draw a chariot.

4. The marvellous one destroys many things with his jaws. Then[1] the resplendent one shines in the forest. Then the wind blows after his flame day by day as after the arrow of an archer, after a weapon that has been shot.

5. Him whom no impostors, no harmful foes[1], no harm-doers may harm when he dwells in (his mother's) womb, him the blind ones bereft of sight did not damage by looking at him[2]. His own friends have protected him.

NOTES.

The same *Ri*shi and metre.—Verse 1 = MS. IV, 14, 15.

Verse 1.

Note 1. The first Pâda is identical with the first Pâda of I, 71, 4 (see our note there) with the exception of the word vish*táh*, instead of which that parallel passage has the reading ví-bh*ri*ta*h*. It seems impossible to explain vish*táh*, and the concurrence of the metrical irregularity in the same part of the Pâda—though metrical irregularities are not infrequent in this hymn—invites to a correction of the text. If ví-bh*ri*ta*h* in I, 71, 4 (see note there) refers to Mâtari*s*van, which I consider as doubtful, it would be easy to find for our passage an equivalent of that word little differing from the traditional vish*táh*, namely, ví-sthita*h*: 'when Mâtari*s*van, standing in different places, had produced him by attrition.' Of course whoever adopts a conjecture like this, can scarcely avoid understanding ví-bh*ri*ta*h* in I, 71, 4 as an epithet of Mâtari*s*van, not of Agni. Another way to correct our passage would be to put into the text a form derived from the root vish, 'to accomplish a work,' for instance, vish*t*yấ (to be read as trisyllabic): 'when Mâtari*s*van by his effort,' &c. Grassmann's ví-sita*h* is quite improbable.

Note 2. Vi*s*vá-apsum (Sa*m*hitâ text, vi*s*vấpsum), evidently an epithet of Agni the Hot*ri*, seems corrupt. Shall we read vi*s*vá-psum ('endowed with all food')—comp. VIII, 22, 12. hávam vi*s*vápsum vi*s*vávâryam—or vi*s*va-púsham (Sa*m*h., vi*s*vâpúsham, 'all-nourishing') or vi*s*vá-apasam ('doing all works')? Also vi*s*vá-psnyam may be thought of. It is impossible, of course, to arrive at any certain conclusion.

Verse 2.

Note 1. 'He' seems to be Agni. Sâya*n*a, however, explains: dadânam id agnaye kurvâ*n*am eva mâm. This would lead to a translation like this: '(The enemies) did not deceive (me, the worshipper) who had addressed a hymn (to Agni).'

Note 2. On 'his' Sâya*n*a remarks, 'ya*g*amânasya mama.' But the word may refer to Agni.

Verse 3.

Note 1. There is no reason for abandoning here the usual meaning of ya*g*ñíya. On the gods seeking after Agni, comp. Bergaigne, I, 110.

Note 2. It is very probable, to say the least, that 'they' are again the gods.

Verse 4.

Note 1. Is the first ất dissyllabic? More probably the Pâda is deficient by one syllable.

Verse 5.

Note 1. Two syllables are wanting before the caesura of the first Pâda.

Note 2. Was there a belief that a blind man by turning his blind eyes on somebody could do him harm? Possibly we might have to translate: 'Him (his foes) blind and bereft of sight did not damage though looking at him (i.e. though turning their blind eyes on him).'—Prof. Max Müller writes: 'Could it be: Even the blind saw, but did not injure him (andhấ*h* apa*s*yan ná dabhan); abhikhyấ, when he was seen, no longer in the womb?'

MA*ND*ALA I, HYMN 149.

ASH*T*AKA II, ADHYÂYA 2, VARGA 18.

1[1]. Towards great wealth this lord of the house[2] advances[3], the strong one in the abode of strong wealth. Let the stones honour him as he speeds forward.

2. He the manly (bull) as of men so of the two worlds, whose stream is drunk by living beings[1] in consequence of his renown—he who running forward has ripened in (his mother's) womb—

3. He who lighted up the . . .[1] stronghold, the racer, the sage, like a . . .[2] horse, shining like the sun, endowed with hundredfold life.

4. He who has a twofold birth (celestial and terrestrial), the flaming one has approached the threefold light, all spaces of the atmosphere, the Hot*ri*, the best sacrificer, in the abode of the Waters.

5. This is the Hot*ri* having a twofold birth[1] who has bestowed all the best gifts, out of desire of glory, on the quick mortal who worships him.

NOTES.

The same *Ri*shi. Metre, Virâ*g*.—Verses 3–5 = SV. II, 1124–1126.

Verse 1.

Note 1. My translation of this verse differs from that of Pischel, Ved. Studien, II, 100.

Note 2. On páti*h* dán, comp. Hübschmann, Vocalsystem, 142; Bartholomae, Arische Forschungen, I, 70; Joh. Schmidt, Kuhn's Zeitschrift, XXVII, 309; Pischel, Vedische Studien,

II, 93 seq.; Bartholomae, Indogermanische Forschungen, III, 100 seq.

Note 3. Comp. X, 93, 6. mahá*h* sá râyá*h* ấ îshate.

Verse 2.

Note 1. Comp. I, 80, 4, and similar passages, in which the waters are called *g*îvá-dhanyâ*h*, 'the prize (of contests) which living beings have gained.'

Verse 3.

Note 1. We do not know what nấrmi*n*î is. Possibly in this word two words, ná ármi*n*î, are contained, so that the particle ná would be repeated in each of the three Pâdas. The translation would then be: 'he who lighted up the ármi*n*î (?) like a stronghold.'

Note 2. I place no confidence in the attempts to find the meaning of a word like nabhanỹa*h* with the aid of etymology only. The same word occurs in I, 173, 1 as an epithet of the Sâman which the priest, who is compared to a bird, sings (gấyat sấma nabhanỹam yáthâ vé*h*). It occurs also in VII, 42, 1. prá krandanú*h* nabhanỹasya vetu. The connection in which these words stand, seems to show that the meaning is: 'the noise of the sacrificial fire shall arise;' very probably the fire is compared to a horse, and its noise to the neighing of that horse. Thus nabhanỹa would be in VII, 42, 1, quite as in our passage, an epithet of a horse. This epithet may refer either to the swift motion of the horse and of the Sâman ascending to the gods, or more probably to the gay voice of the horse, the loud noise of the Sâman.

Verse 5.

Note 1. Two syllables are wanting in the first Pâda.

MA*N*D*A*LA I, HYMN 150.

ASHT*A*KA II, ADHYÂYA 2, VARGA 19.

1. I thy indigent[1] worshipper say much to thee, O Agni, dwelling in thy protection as (in the protection) of a great impeller[2].

2. Away even from the libation of a rich man who is feeble, who is a niggard, who never comes forward and does not care for the gods.

3. The mortal (who worships thee ?), O priest, is brilliant, great, most powerful in heaven. May we, O Agni, addicted to thee, be always foremost.

NOTES.

The same *Ri*shi. Metre, Ush*n*ih.—Verse 1 = SV. I, 97.

Verse 1.

Note 1. On arí, see Bergaigne, Religion Védique, II, 218.

Note 2. Or, 'of the great impeller'—the Sun-god who impels or stimulates his horses ? Comp. VI, 6, 6 ?

MAN*D*ALA I, HYMN 188.

ASH*T*AKA II, ADHYÂYA 5, VARGA 8–9.

Âprî Hymn.

1. Being kindled thou reignest to-day, a god with the gods, O conqueror of thousandfold (wealth)! As messenger, as a sage, carry the oblations (to the gods).

2. O Tanûnapât! For him who walks in righteousness the sacrifice is anointed with honey. May he[1] grant thousandfold food.

3. Receiving libations, worthy of being magnified[1] bring hither to us the worshipful gods. Agni! Thou art a winner of thousandfold (bliss).

4. They have spread with might the eastward-turned sacrificial grass, blessing (our tribe) with a thousand men[1], (at the place) where you reign, O Âdityas!

5. The Prince, the Sovereign, the mighty ones, the eminent ones[1], the (Divine) Doors, which are many and more than many, have sent forth streams of ghee.

6. Adorned with gold, wearing beautiful ornaments you verily reign high[1] in your splendour. Sit down here, ye two Dawns[2].

7. May the two fine-voiced divine Hot*ri*s, the sages, perform as the first this sacrifice for us.

8. Bhâratî! I*l*â! Sarasvatî! All ye (goddesses) whom I invoke, promote us to splendour.

9. Tvash*t*ri indeed, the eminent (god) has shaped all forms, all cattle. Do thou by sacrifice produce their increase.

10. Yield up by thyself, O tree, (the sacrificial food) to the abode of the gods[1]. May Agni make the offerings relishable.

11. Agni going in front of the gods is anointed with this Gâyatra song; he shines when Svâhâ is pronounced (over the oblations).

NOTES.

The *Ri*shi is Agastya, the metre Gâyatrî. This Âprî hymn is closely related to hymn X, 110, the author of which no doubt knew and imitated our hymn.—No verses occur in the other Sa*m*hitâs.

Verse 2.

Note 1. I have taken dádhat as a third person, the subject being Tanûnapât. But it may be a participle referring to ya*gñ*á*h*: 'the sacrifice which procures thousandfold food is anointed with honey.'

Verse 3.

Note 1. The text has î́*d*ya*h*.

Verse 4.

Note 1. 'This is the Da*s*avîra sacrifice of the *S*âktyas. Ten valiant sons are born to those who perform it.' Pa*ñk*a-vi*ms*a Brâhma*n*a XXV, 7, 4.

Verse 5.

Note 1. These are evidently names of the divine doors.—As to the nominative dúra*h*, see Lanman, p. 486.

Verse 6.

Note 1. On adhi-vi-râ*g*, comp. IX, 75, 3. ádhi trip*ri*sh*th*á*h* ushása*h* ví râ*g*ati.

Note 2. I.e. Dawn and Evening.

Verse 10.

Note 1. Literally: 'to the abode, for the gods.' Comp. the corresponding verse (10) of the Âprî hymn X, 110. devā́nâm pā́tha*h*.

MAN*D*ALA I, HYMN 189.

ASH*T*AKA II, ADHYÂYA 5, VARGA 10–11.

1. Agni! Lead us to wealth on a good path, O god who knowest all rules. Drive away from us sin which leads us astray. We will offer to thee the fullest praise.

2. Agni! Thou who art young, help us safely across all difficulties. Be for us a broad, large, wide stronghold, for our kith and kin, with luck and weal[1].

3. Agni! Drive away from us all plagues. (Then) they shall plague[1] peoples who do not stand under Agni's protection (Give) us back again the earth, O god, together with all the immortals, O worshipful one, that it may go well with us.

4. Protect us, Agni, with thy unwearied guardians, thou who flamest in thy beloved seat. May no danger, O youngest of the gods, attain thy praiser, not now nor in future, O mighty one!

5. Do not deliver us, O Agni, to the harmful foe, to the greedy one, to the impostor, to misfortune. Do not surrender us, O mighty one, to one who has teeth, who bites, nor to one who has no teeth, nor to one who will hurt us.

6. May a (god) like thee, O Agni, who art born according to *Ri*ta, being praised spread out a shelter for the body (of the worshipper that protects) from every one who tries to harm or to revile him. For thou, O god, art a descrier[1] of everything that leads us astray.

7[1]. Thou, O Agni, distinguishing both (kinds of men, the pious and the impious, or the Aryans and the Dasyus[2]), eagerly approachest (Aryan) men at (the time of) the advancing (day)[3], O worshipful one. At (the time of) rest thou hast become governable to the man (or, to Manu; or, thou art to be praised by men[4]); thou art to be smoothed down like a horse[5] by the U*s*i*g*s.

8. We have pronounced our invocations, I the son of Mâna[1], before this mighty Agni. May we obtain (our wishes) through a thousand *Ri*shis. May we find a food-giving . . . rich in quickening rain[2].

NOTES.

The same *Ri*shi. Metre, Trish*t*ubh.—Verse 1=VS. V, 36; VII, 43; XL, 16; TS. I, 1, 14, 3; 4, 43, 1; TB. II, 8, 2, 3; TÂ. I, 8, 8; MS. I, 2, 13; IV, 10, 2; 14, 3. Verse 2= TS. I, 1, 14, 4; TB. II, 8, 2, 5; TÂ. X, 2, 1; MS. IV, 10, 1; 14, 3. Verse 3=TB. II, 8, 2, 4; MS. IV, 14, 3.

Verse 2.

Note 1. 'For health and wealth,' M. M.; see vol. xxxii, p. 193.

Verse 3.

Note 1. If the accent is correct (Sa*m*h. abhyámanta, Pad. abhí ámanta), the clause, though containing no subordinating word, must be understood as standing in logical dependence on the following, or—which in our case seems more probable—on the preceding clause. Examples of this kind have been collected by Delbrück, Altindische

Syntax, p. 43.—That k*ri*sh*t*î*h* should be nominative is very improbable; comp. Lanman, Noun-Inflection, 393. See also Leo Meyer, Kuhn's Zeitschrift, XVI, 9.

Verse 6.

Note 1. Prof. Max Müller (vol. xxxii, p. 229) translates, 'For thou, god, art the deliverer from all assaults;' he derives vishpá*t* 'from vi and spa*s*, to bind.'

Verse 7.

Note 1. This verse has been treated of by Geldner, Vedische Studien, II, 156, 158.

Note 2. Geldner (loc. cit., 156) proposes two explanations for ubháyân. It may refer either to the pious and the impious spoken of in the preceding verses, or to prapitvám and abhipitvám, which words Geldner believes to be masculine. I do not attach such weight to the Avestic frapithwô (Vend. III, 3) as to draw, with Geldner, a conclusion from this word on the gender of the Vedic prapitvá, and in every case I think that this explanation of ubháyân is very forced, while it is natural to refer ubháyân to the pious and impious, or as we may express it in conformity with Vedic ideas, to 'men' (comp. mánusha*h* Pâda 2, mánave Pâda 3), i.e. Aryans, and Dasyus (see VIII, 50, 8; 98, 6; IX, 92, 5). Then ubháyân ví vidvân would have exactly the same meaning as the words in I, 51, 8. ví *g*ânîhi ấryân yé *k*a dásyava*h*.

Note 3. On prapitvá we have the two ingenious discussions of Geldner, Vedische Studien, II, 155 seq., and of Bloomfield in the fifth series of his Contributions to the interpretation of the Veda, p. 24 seq. In my opinion Bloomfield has not succeeded in proving that the words ending in -pitvá (prapitvá, abhipitvá, sapitvá, &c.) contain the stem pitú, 'sap, drink, nourishment,' and that prapitvá means the morning-pressure of Soma, which is usually designated as prâta*h*savana, abhipitvá, the evening-pressure or the t*ri*tîya-savana. I do not think it necessary, however, to examine here the single points of his interesting and elaborate discussion, for it seems to me that Geldner has conclusively shown that the meaning of these words is different from what Bloomfield believes it to be: abhipitvá, as Geldner (p. 155) states, is 'Erholung,' 'Rast,' and 'die Zeit des Rastens,' 'Feierabend,' 'Abend;' prapitvá (p. 178), on the other hand, means 'Vorlauf,' 'das aufs Ziel Zugehen,' 'die vorgerückte Tageszeit.'

Note 4. *S*ắsya*h*, 'governable,' does not give an impossible meaning. But should we not have to correct *sá*m*s*ya*h* 'thou art to be praised by men?'

Note 5. On akrá*h*, comp. Vedische Studien, I, 168, and above, I, 143, 7.

Verse 8.

Note 1. Mâna is another name of Agastya. See Zeitschrift der Deutschen Morg. Gesellschaft, XLII, 221.

Note 2. On the last words of the hymn—the regularly repeated conclusion of the Agastya hymns—see M. M., vol. xxxii, p. xx, and also Bartholomae, Bezzenberger's Beiträge, XV, 212. I do not think it very probable that ishá is here the name of an autumn month, as found in the *S*atapatha Brâhma*n*a and others of the more modern Vedic texts; to me it would seem rather strange that such a prayer for the fertility of that month should have formed, among the Agastyas, the standing conclusion of their sacrificial hymns. But the names of the two months ishá and ûr*g*á seem to point to the existence of two adjectives meaning 'giving food' and 'giving sap.'—Then follows v*ri*gána, used as a masculine. Geldner (Vedische Studien, I, 151) indicates the following passages, in which he believes that this masculine v*ri*gána occurs: V, 44, 1; VI, 35, 5; VII, 32, 27; X, 27, 4; and the concluding Pâda of the Agastya hymns. Of these passages the two first seem to be open to doubt as to the correctness of the text. In V, 44, 1 the true reading may be pratî*k*înám v*rí*sha*n*am dohase; comp. verse 3, v*rí*shâ *sí*su*h*, and I, 173, 6, where possibly v*rí*sha*n*am should be read instead of v*ri*gánam (Göttinger

Gelehrte Anzeigen, 1890, 417). In VI, 35, 5 I propose to read *vrinagam* (Gött. Gel. Anzeigen, loc. cit., 416). In VII, 32, 27 and X, 27, 4 *vrigánâ* (Padap. *vrigánâh*; the letter d follows) and *vrigáneshu* seem to be masculine, though it is not absolutely impossible to see in these forms the nom. plur. and loc. plur. of the neuter *vrigána*. But I believe that any attempts to derive conclusions from these three passages on the meaning of the masculine *vrigána* are hopeless.

MAṆḌALA II, HYMN 1.

ASHṬAKA II, ADHYÂYA 5, VARGA 17–19.

1[1]. Thou, O Agni, the flaming one, (art born) from out the Heavens[2], thou (art born) from out the Waters and the stone (the flint); thou (art born) from out the forests and the herbs; thou art born bright, O Lord of men, (as belonging) to men[3].

2[1]. To thee, O Agni, belongs the Hot*ri*'s and the Pot*ri*'s office exercised at the appointed season; to thee belongs the office of the Nesh*tri*; thou art the Agnîdh[2] for the righteous. To thee belongs the office of the Pra*s*âst*ri*; thou actest as an Adhvaryu, and thou art the Brahman and the master of the house in our house[3].

3[1]. Thou, O Agni, art Indra, a bull among (all) beings. Thou art the wide-ruling Vish*n*u, worthy of adoration. Thou art the Brahman, a gainer of wealth, O Brahma*n*aspati[2]. Thou, O Vidhart*ri* (i. e. who keepest asunder all things), art united with Pura*m*dhi (or the Liberality of the gods)[3].

4. Thou, O Agni, art the king Varu*n*a whose laws are firm; thou becomest Mitra, the wondrous one, worthy of being magnified. Thou art Aryaman, the lord of beings, whom I may enjoy[1]. Thou, O god, art A*ms*a[2], desirous of distributing (goods) in the assembly[3].

5. Thou, O Agni, being Tvash*tri*, (grantest) to thy worshipper abundance in heroes. To thee, who art accompanied by the (divine) wives[1], who art great like Mitra, belongs relationship[2]. Thou,

the quick inciter[3], givest abundance in horses. Thou, rich in wealth, art the host of men[4].

6. Thou, O Agni, art Rudra, the Asura of the high Heaven[1]; thou, being the host of the Maruts, rulest over nourishment. Thou goest along with the flame-coloured Winds, bringing happiness to our home. Thou, being Pûshan, protectest thy worshippers by thy own might.

7. Thou, O Agni, art a giver of wealth to him who does service to thee[1]; thou art the god Savit*ri*, a bestower of treasures. Thou, being Bhaga, O lord of men, rulest over wealth. Thou art a protector in his house to him who has worshipped thee[2].

8. Towards thee, in the house, the lord of the clan, O Agni, the clans strive, towards thee, the bounteous king. Thou with the beautiful face possessest all things. Thou art equal to thousands, to hundreds, to ten (of others).

9. Thee, O Agni, men (make) their father by their sacrifices[1]; thee who shinest with thy body they (invite) to brotherhood by their (sacrificial) work. Thou becomest a son to him who has worshipped thee. As a kind friend thou protectest against attack.

10. Thou, O Agni, art *Ri*bhu, to be adored when near. Thou rulest over strength[1], over wealth rich in food. Thou shinest[2], thou burnest for the sake of giving (wealth). Thou art a hewer[3], an expander of sacrifice.

11. Thou, Agni, O god, art Aditi to the worshipper. Thou, being Hotrâ Bhâratî[1], growest strong by prayer. Thou art I*d*â, living a hundred winters, for (the increase of) ability. Thou, the killer of V*ri*tra, O Lord of wealth, art Sarasvatî[2].

12. Thou, O Agni, well kept, art the highest vital power. In thy lovely colour and in thy appearance (dwell all) beauties. Thou art great strength that carries us forward. Thou art abundant wealth, extending on all sides.

13. The Âdityas have made thee, O Agni, their mouth; the bright ones have made thee their tongue, O Sage. The Râti-sâ*k* gods (i.e. the 'bounteous' gods) accompany thee at the sacrifices. In thee the gods eat the offering which is offered to them.

14. In thee, O Agni, with (thy) mouth[1] all the guileless[2] immortal gods eat the offering which is offered to them. Through thee the mortals taste their drink. Thou hast been born, the bright one, as the child of the plants.

15[1]. Thou art united with them and equal to them in strength, O well-born Agni, nay, thou surpassest them, O god, when thy power[2] has expanded here in its greatness over Heaven and Earth, over both worlds.

16. The liberal lords who pour out, O Agni, over thy praisers gifts at the head of which there are cows[1], the ornament of which are horses: lead both ourselves and them to welfare. May we speak loud in the assembly[2], rich in valiant men.

NOTES.

The *Ri*shi is G*ri*tsamada, the metre *G*agatî.—Verse 1 = VS. XI, 27; TS. IV, 1, 2, 5; TÂ. X, 76, 1; MS. II, 7, 2. Verse 2 = RV. X, 91, 10. Verse 6 = TS. I, 3, 14, 1; TB. III, 11, 2, 1. Verse 13 = TB. II, 7, 12, 6.

Verse 1.

Note 1. Among the numerous texts which treat of the different origins of Agni (see Bergaigne, I, 20 seq.), especially the following two verses may be compared with this passage: VI, 48, 5. yám ấpa*h* ádraya*h* vánâ gárbham *ri*tásya píprati sáhasâ yá*h* mathitá*h* *g*ấyate n*rí*bhi*h* p*ri*thivyấ*h* ádhi sấnavi; X, 45, 1. divá*h* pári prathamám *g*a*gñ*e agní*h* asmát dvitī́yam pári *g*âtáveḍâ*h* t*ri*tī́yam apsú n*ri*máṇâ*h* á*g*asram índhâna enam *g*arate svâdhī́*h*.

Note 2. The text (dyúbhi*h* tvám â*s*u*s*ukshá*n*i*h*) seems to be corrupt. I believe that tvám, which is so frequently repeated through this verse and through the next verses, has been put here in the wrong place, and that we should read, dyúbhya*h* ấ *s*u*s*ukshá*n*i*h*.

Note 3. With the last words of this verse, comp. the conclusion of verse 14.

Verse 2.

Note 1. This whole verse is repeated, X, 91, 10.

Note 2. In my opinion there is no doubt that instead of the traditional reading, agnít, the correct form is agnī́t. The word is a compound of agní and idh and means 'the inflamer of the fire.' Cf. M. M., Hist. of A. S. L., 1859, pp. 450, 469.

Note 3. This is the most ancient list of the 'seven priests,' by the side of whom the g*ri*há-pati or 'master of the house' is mentioned as the eighth. Comp. the formula in which the Adhvaryu names the officiating priests, Kâtyâyana IX, 8, 8 seq., and see the remarks of Weber, Indische Studien, X, 141, 376, and my own exposition, Religion des Veda, 383 seq., 396. The 'Brahman' mentioned in our verse is the Brâhma*n*â*kkh*a*m*sin of the later ritual. Comp. Kâtyâyana IX, 8, 11; *S*atapatha Brâhma*n*a IV, 6, 6, 5.

Verse 3.

Note 1. On verses 3–6, see von Bradke, Dyâus Asura, p. 52 seq.

Note 2. B*ri*haspati or Brahma*n*aspati is the Brahman among the gods. But it is doubtful whether the title of Brahman in this connection should be understood in the later technical sense of the word, as the *Ri*tvi*g* who has to superintend the whole sacrifice. Comp. H. O., Religion des Veda, 396, note 1.

Note 3. Vidhart*ri* seems to be here another name of Bhaga; comp. VII, 41, 2. bhágam huvema . . . yá*h* vidhartā́). It is known that no god is so frequently mentioned in connection with Pura*m*dhi as Bhaga. The passages have been collected by Grassmann in his Dictionary, s. v. púra*m*-dhi.

Verse 4.

Note 1. Prof. von Bradke (Dyâus Asura, 53) believes that the text is corrupt; he thinks that the fourth Pâda may have occupied the place of a lost continuation of the relative clause, yásya sam-bhú*g*am. I cannot but share the feeling on which Prof. von Bradke's remark rests, though I do not believe that the solution of the difficulty which he proposes is very probable. Could not the correct reading be yâsi (instead of yásya) sam-bhú*g*am, 'thou goest to the enjoyment (of goods)?' Comp. VI, 71, 6, where the traditional text has vâmásya hí ksháyasya deva bhū́re*h*, and ksháyasya doubtless should be changed into ksháyasi.

Note 2. On A*m*sa, as one of the Âdityas, comp. Bergaigne, III, 39, 99.

Note 3. Vidáthe: comp. the note on I, 31, 6. It is tempting to conjecture vidhaté (comp. verse 5), but there is no necessity for such a conjecture. Comp., for instance, VI, 24, 2. vidáthe dâti vā́*g*am.

Verse 5.

Note 1. Gnâva*h* should be read without accent, as Grassmann, Prof. Weber, and M. Henry (Revue Critique, Jan. 12, 1891, p. 23) have seen. Cf. Lanman, 518, 519.

Note 2. The meaning probably is, 'Thou art related to the other gods and to men,' or 'Thou art related to us.' Comp. VIII, 27, 10; 73, 12.

Note 3. Agni seems to be identified here with Apâm napât, who frequently is called âsu-héman. Comp. Windisch, Festgruss an Roth, 143 seq.

Note 4. The men, of course, are the Maruts, as is shown by the well-known use of *s*árdha*h* (cf. vol. xxxii, p. 67 seq.).

Verse 6.

Note 1. Comp. von Bradke, Dyâus Asura, 53 seq.

Verse 7.

Note 1. As to ara*m*k*r*íte, cf. VIII, 67, 3.

Note 2. Or, thou art a protector to him who has worshipped thee in his house.—Among the various ways for explaining or removing the metrical deficiency of the last Pâda the correction dáme ấ (for dáme) is recommended by verse 8.

Verse 9.

Note 1. Ish*t*íbhi*h*, standing by the side of *s*ámyâ, seems to be derived from the root ya*g*. Thus î*g*é, î*g*âná stand by the side of *s*a*s*amé, *s*a*s*amâná.—Cf. ish*t*íbhi*h* matíbhi*h*, II, 18, 1.

Verse 10.

Note 1. The names of the three *Ri*bhus are *Ri*bhu, Vâ*g*a, Vibhvan. The word vấ*g*a used here evidently alludes to the second of these names.

Note 2. Bergaigne (Religion Véd., II, 406) no doubt is right in believing that the verb ví bhâsi ('thou shinest') alludes to the name Vibhvan. Comp. X, 91, 1. vibhú*h* vibhấvâ.

Note 3. Vi-*s*íkshu*h* again seems to convey an allusion to the *Ri*bhu myth. When dividing the cup of Tvash*tri* into four cups, the *Ri*bhus say, sákhe ví *s*iksha (IV, 35, 3). This ví *s*iksha and the corresponding adjective vi-*s*íkshu should be derived from the root *s*as, 'to cut to pieces.'

Verse 11.

Note 1. Here we have the three goddesses of the Âprî hymns, Bhâratî, I*d*â, and Sarasvatî. Of the goddess

Bhâratî the full name is given, Hotrâ Bhâratî, i.e. 'the Offering of the Bharatas.' Comp. Bergaigne, I, 322 seq.

Note 2. Comp. VI, 61, 7, where Sarasvatî is called v*ri*tra-ghnî.

Verse 14.

Note 1. Or 'through (thee who art their) mouth.'

Note 2. Comp. I, 19, 3. ví*s*ve devā́sa*h* adrúha*h*; vol. xxxii, pp. 53, 55.

Verse 15.

Note 1. On this verse, compare Pischel, Vedische Studien, I, 97.

Note 2. On p*ri*kshá*h*, see above, I, 127, 5, note 1.

Verse 16.

Note 1. On gó-agra, compare Pischel, Vedische Studien, I, 51.

Note 2. Vidáthe: comp. the note on I, 31, 6.

MA*N**D*ALA II, HYMN 2.

ASH*T*AKA II, ADHYÂYA 5, VARGA 20–21.

1. Increase *G*âtavedas by your sacrifice [1], worship Agni for ever with your offering and your prayer [2] —him who has been kindled, the receiver of good offerings, the solar hero, the heavenly Hot*ri*, the charioteer [3] in our settlements [4].

2. For thee Nights and Dawns have been lowing, O Agni, as milch-cows in the folds for their calf [1]. A steward [2], as it were, of Heaven, thou shinest on the human tribes, O bountiful one, on continuous nights [3].

3. The gods have set him to work, as a steward [1] of Heaven and Earth, endowed with wonderful power, at the bottom of the air: Agni who is well known like a chariot [2], brightly shining, deserving of praise like Mitra (or, like a friend) in (human) dwellings.

4. They have established him who grows in the air, in his house, the serpent [1] with beautiful splendour like gold [2], the winged (son?) of P*ri*sni [3] who lights up with his eyes both tribes (of gods and of men), like a guardian of the way (?) [4].

5. May he, the Hot*ri*, encompass the whole sacrifice. Men strive towards him with offerings and prayer. (Agni) with golden jaws [1], hurrying around in the growing (plants) [2], lighted up the two worlds like the Sky with the stars.

6. Thus mayst thou, being brightly kindled for our welfare or being exhausted (?) [1], shine upon us with thy wealth. Carry hither to us the two

worlds for the sake of happiness, Agni, O god, that they may eagerly partake[2] of the offering of the man (or, of Manus).

7. Give us, Agni, mighty, give us thousandfold (gifts). Open strength for us like a door[1] for the sake of glory. Make Heaven and Earth inclined towards us through (our) spell. Make the Dawns shine like the brilliant Sun.

8. Being kindled after dawns and nights may he shine with his red light like the sun, Agni, being a good sacrificer with the help of the offerings of man (or, of Manus)[1], the king of the clans, and the welcome guest of Âyu.

9. Thus, O Agni, ancient one, our human prayer has prospered among the immortals who dwell in the great heaven. May the cow[1] when milked, yield[2] freely to the singer in our settlements hundredfold (wealth) of all kinds.

10. May we, O Agni, (attain) bliss in valiant men by our racers, or may we shine over (all) people by our sacred spells. May our unconquerable lustre beam on high like the sun over the fivefold dwellings (of the five peoples).

11. Be thou, O mighty one, worthy of praise among us, (thou) from whom the well-born, liberal (lords) have sought nourishment[1], unto whom the strong ones, O Agni, go for sacrifice, who shinest in thy abode among (the worshipper's) own kith.

12. May we both, O *G*âtavedas, the praisers and the liberal (lords), be in thy protection, O Agni. Help us to good, resplendent, abundant wealth which is accompanied by offspring, by good progeny.

13 = II, 1, 16.

NOTES.

The same *Ri*shi and metre.—Verse 7 = TS. II, 2, 12, 6; MS. IV, 12, 2.

Verse 1.

Note 1. In this Pâda one syllable is wanting. It may be thought that the first word should be pronounced ia*gñ*éna. For supplying the missing syllable by conjecture there would, however, be many ways. Comp. also H. O., Hymnen des Rig-veda, I, p. 79.

Note 2. Tánâ girấ: comp. I. 38, 13 (vol. xxxii, p. 82).

Note 3. Dhû*h*-sádam. The exact meaning is, 'who occupies a decisive position.'

Note 4. V*rig*áneshu: comp. I, 60, 3, note 2.

Verse 2.

Note 1. Comp. VIII, 88, 1. abhí vatsám ná svásareshu dhenáva*h* índram gîrbhí*h* navâmahe.

Note 2. See I, 58, 7, note 1.

Note 3. See Lanman, p. 482; Gaedicke, p. 89. 'During continuous nights.' M. M.

Verse 3.

Note 1. See I, 58, 7, note 1.

Note 2. Cf. VIII, 84, 1. rátham ná védyam.

Verse 4.

Note 1. I follow the conjecture of Böhtlingk-Roth, who propose to read hvârám. Comp. Atharva-veda IV, 1, 2 (Â*s*valâyana *S*rautasûtra IV, 6, 3; *S*âṅkhâyana *S*rautasûtra V, 9, 7). surú*k*am hvârám. The meaning of the word is conjectural; comp. I, 141, 7, note 1. If we read hvâré, the translation could be 'brilliant like gold, in a hidden place.' (M. M.)

Note 2. Comp. Pischel, Vedische Studien, I, 52.

Note 3. Or, the winged (bird) of P*ris*ni? No other passages which make Agni the son (or the bird) of P*ris*ni are known to me.

Note 4. The accent of pâthás points to a genitive, dependent on pâyúm, of a word which is, however, different from pā́thas. Grassmann thinks that pâthás is a lengthening for pathás, but Lanman (Noun-Inflection, 470) is quite right in observing that this is hard to believe in the first syllable of a Pâda. Should we not correct the text and read pathá*h* (gen. sing. governed by pâyúm)? The reading pâthá*h* may be due to the influence of the neighbourhood of pâyúm.

Verse 5.

Note 1. See vol. xxxii, p. 301.

Note 2. Comp. X, 92, 1. *s*úshkâsu hári*n*îshu *g*árbhurat.

Verse 6.

Note 1. Ludwig translates sam-dadasvā́n: 'zum heile [dich selber] aufreibend;' Grassmann, 'oder seist erloschen du;' Gaedicke (p. 89), 'und wenn du verlöschest;' Griffith, 'a liberal giver;' Neisser (Bezzenberger's Beitr. XIX, 286), 'deine Kunst zusammennehmend.' Sâya*n*a says, 'sa*m*dadasvân samyak praya*kkh*an.' Prof. Max Müller suggests, 'being a liberal benefactor.'

Note 2. There was no reason for correcting devá-vîtaye as Ludwig once proposed. He has himself abandoned this conjecture.

Verse 7.

Note 1. As to this metaphor ('opening' strength or the like), comp. VIII, 5, 21. utá na*h* divyā́*h* ísha*h* ... ápa dvā́râ-iva varshatha*h*, and the passages collected by Dr. Hirzel, Gleichnisse und Metaphern im *R*ig-veda (Leipzig, 1890), 103.

Verse 8.

Note 1. The third Pâda is repeated in X, 11, 5.

Verse 9.

Note 1. The milch-cow of course is the prayer.

Note 2. Ishá*n*i seems to be an infinitive like parshá*n*i neshá*n*i tarîshá*n*i (Delbrück, Altindisches Verbum, 227; Neisser, Bezzenberger's Beiträge, XX, 43). I believe it to come from the root ish, 'to incite.' As to the syntactical peculiarities of these infinitives, comp. Delbrück, Altindische Syntax, 416.

Verse 11.

Note 1. Ishay is a denominative from ísh, as ûr*g*ay is derived from ū́r*g* (comp. Â*s*valâyana *S*rautasûtra V, 7, 3).

MA*ND*ALA II, HYMN 3.

ASH*T*AKA II, ADHYÂYA 5, VARGA 22–23.

Âprî Hymn.

1. Agni being kindled, set down on the earth, has stood up with his face towards all worlds. May the Hot*ri*, the purifier, the ancient, wise one, may god Agni sacrifice to the gods, he who is worthy (of being the sacrificer).

2. Narâ*s*a*m*sa, anointing the abodes (of the sacrifice), equal by his greatness to the three heavens, endowed with beautiful light, moistening the offering, his mind being intent on scattering gh*ri*ta—may he anoint the gods on the summit of sacrifice.

3. Being magnified[1] in our mind, Agni, sacrifice for us to-day to the gods before the human (sacrificer)[2], thou who art worthy (of being the sacrificer). Conduct hither the unshakable host of the Maruts. Sacrifice, O men, to Indra who sits on the Barhis.

4. O divine Barhis! On this (Barhis) which is large, rich in valiant men, which has been spread on this Vedi (or sacrificial altar) rich in gain, ready for wealth, which is anointed with gh*ri*ta, sit down, O Vasus, O Vi*s*ve devâs, O Âdityas[1] worthy of worship!

5. May the divine doors which are easily passable, open themselves wide when invoked with adoration. May they, the far-embracing, undecaying ones, open wide, purifying our glorious race[1] which is rich in valiant men.

6. May Dawn and Night, grown strong from of

old, joyful like two birds (?)[1], (do) their work well for us—they who weave, turned towards each other, the stretched-out warp, the ornamented form of the sacrifice[2], (the two goddesses) flowing with plenty, rich in milk.

7. May the two divine Hot*ri*s, the first ones, very knowing, very marvellous, perform the sacrifice rightly with their (sacrificial) verse. Sacrificing to the gods they anoint (them)[1], observing the right time, on the navel of the Earth, over the three ridges (of the three worlds).

8. May Sarasvatî, the accomplisher of our prayer, may the goddess I*l*â, all-victorious Bhâratî—may the three goddesses, according to their wont, sit down on this Barhis and protect it, the faultless shelter.

9. Through (the god's) hearing (our prayer) a manly son is born (to us), tawny-coloured, rich in gain, bringing vigour, loving the gods. May Tvash*tri* deliver for us a son, the navel (i.e. the tie that binds generations together), and may he then go to the abode of the gods.

10[1]. May the tree (i.e. the sacrificial post) stand by, letting loose (the offering which goes to the gods). May Agni make the offering ready in consequence of our prayers. May the prescient divine butcher carry the thrice-anointed offering to the gods.

11. He[1] is joined with gh*ri*ta[2]. His womb (on the altar) is gh*ri*ta. He rests on gh*ri*ta. His abode is gh*ri*ta. Carry hither (the gods) according to thy wont! Rejoice[3]! Carry, O bull, the offering, over which the Svâhâ has been spoken, (to the gods).

NOTES.

The same *Ri*shi. Metre, Trish*t*ubh ; verse 7 : *G*agatî.—Verse 9=TS. III, 1, 11, 2 ; TB. II, 8, 7, 4 ; MS. IV, 14, 8. Verse 11=VS. XVII, 88 ; TÂ. X, 10, 2.

Verse 3.

Note 1. The text has î*l*itá*h*. Comp. above, I, 1, 1, note 2.

Note 2. Comp. X, 53, 1. ní hí sátsat (scil. agní*h*) ántara*h* pű̂rva*h* asmát.

Verse 4.

Note 1. It is very probable that the poet intends to distinguish the Vasus, the Vi*s*ve devâs, and the Âdityas as three categories of gods. But then we should expect the accent ấdityâ*h*. Comp. VII, 51, 3. âdityấ*h* ví*s*ve marúta*h* *k*a ví*s*ve devấ*h* *k*a ví*s*ve; X, 125, 1. ahám rudrébhi*h* vásubhi*h* *k*arâmi ahám âdityaí*h* utá vi*s*vádevai*h*.

Verse 5.

Note 1. Comp. the G*ri*hya Mantra addressed to the Mekhalâ, of which it is said 'var*n*am pavitram punatî na*h* âgât,' *S*âṅkhâyana G*ri*hya II, 2, 1, &c.

Verse 6.

Note 1. The meaning of vayy̆a (comp. IX, 68, 8) is uncertain. Possibly it is derived from ví, 'the bird.' According to Sâya*n*a it would mean 'weavers' (vânaku*s*ale iva). Vayy̆eva may be vayy̆e iva (dual feminine), in spite of the artificial theory of the Prag*ri*hya vowels; see Lanman, p. 361 ; H. O., Hymnen des Rig-veda, I, 456. Or it may be vayy̆â iva, dual masculine or singular feminine (comp. VII, 2, 6).

Note 2. Comp. VII, 42, 1. adhvarásya pé*s*a*h*.

Verse 7.

Note 1. Comp. VIII, 39, 1. agní*h* devā́n anaktu na*h*.

Verse 10.

Note 1. With the first hemistich compare especially, III, 4, 10 (see below).

Verse 11.

Note 1. 'He' of course is Agni.

Note 2. Differing from M. M., vol. xxxii, p. 185, I take gh*ri*tam as an accusative.

Note 3. Comp. III, 6, 9 (see below).

MA*N**D*ALA II, HYMN 4.

ASHT*A*KA II, ADHYÂYA 5, VARGA 24-25.

1. I call for you Agni, shining with beautiful shine, praised with beautiful praise[1], the guest of the clans, the receiver of fine offerings, who is desirable like Mitra (or, like an ally), *G*âtavedas the god, among godly people.

2. The Bh*ri*gus worshipping him in the abode of the waters[1] have verily[2] established him among the clans of Âyu. Let him surpass all worlds, Agni, the steward of the gods[3], the possessor of quick horses.

3. The gods have established beloved Agni among the human clans as (people) going to settle (establish) Mitra[1]. May he illuminate the nights that are longing (for him), he who should be treated kindly by the liberal (worshipper) in his house.

4. His prosperity is delightful as good pasture (?)[1]; delightful is his appearance when the burning one is driven forward, he who quickly shaking his tongue among the plants waves[2] his tail mightily like a chariot-horse.

5. When they praised[1] to me the monstrous might of the eater of the forests[2], he produced his (shining) colour as (he has done) for the U*s*i*g*s[3]. With shining splendour he has shone joyously, he who having grown old has suddenly become young (again).

6. He who shines on the forests[1] as if he were thirsty, who resounded like water on its path, like (the rattle of the wheels) of a chariot[2]—he whose

path is black, the hot, the joyous one has shone, laughing [3] like the sky with its clouds.

7. He who has spread himself burning over the wide (earth), moves about like an animal, free, without a keeper. The flaming Agni, burning down the brushwood, with a black trail [1], has, as it were, tasted the earth.

8. Now in the remembrance of thy former blessings this prayer has been recited to thee at the third sacrifice [1]. Give to us, Agni, mighty strength with a succession of valiant men, with plenty of food; (give us) wealth with good progeny [2].

9. Give, O Agni, such vigour to thy praiser together with his liberal (lords), that the G*ri*tsamadas, rich in valiant men, victorious over hostile plots, attaining (their aim) in secret, may overcome through thee (their rivals) who get behind [1].

NOTES.

The *Ri*shi is Somâhuti Bhârgava, the metre Trish*t*ubh.—No verse occurs in the other Sa*m*hitâs.

Verse 1.

Note 1. To me there seems to be no doubt that the meaning of suv*ri*ktí is something like 'beautiful prayer,' 'beautiful song,' and then 'a god who is invoked with beautiful songs.' Thus suv*ri*ktáya*h* or other cases of the same word stand by the side of stómâ*h* . . . gíra*h*, VIII, 8, 22; of gíra*h*, I, 64, 1; VIII, 96, 10, comp. X, 64, 4; of bráhma, VII, 31, 11; 97, 9; of stómai*h*, VII, 96, 1; of dhîtíbhi*h*, VI, 61, 2; of á*kkh*oktibhi*h* matînấm, I, 61, 3, and so on. Comp. also VII, 83, 9. hávâmahe vâm v*ri*sha*n*â suv*ri*ktíbhi*h*; X, 41, 1. rátham . . . suv*ri*ktíbhi*h* vayám vŷush*t*â ushása*h* havâmahe; X, 80, 7. avo*k*âma suv*ri*ktím.

This being the meaning of the word, I cannot think it probable—and herein I differ from the opinion pronounced by Prof. Max Müller, vol. xxxii, p. 109—that it stands in connection with the verb v*ri*g in its well-known use referring to the Barhis. In my opinion (comp. also Geldner, Vedische Studien, I, 151) suv*ri*ktí may be connected with another use of v*ri*g, with the meaning of this verb 'to draw a god towards himself, averting him from other sacrificers' (materials regarding this use of v*ri*g have been collected by Geldner, loc. cit., 144). Or possibly the word may be derived, as Prof. von Roth believes, from *rik* (comp. suvita derived from i). It is true that the substantive *ri*kti does not occur by itself: but, as Prof. Max Müller remarks (loc. cit.), this would not be fatal to Prof. von Roth's etymology, because many other words in the Veda occur as uttarapadas only. If we accept this theory, we should of course have to separate suv*ri*ktí from námov*ri*kti and svâv*ri*kti.

Verse 2.

Note 1. Comp. X, 46, 2. imám vidhánta*h* apā́m sadhásthe.

Note 2. Literally, 'doubly.' 'In two places, in the abode of the waters and among the clans of man.' M. M. Compare, however, X, 46, 2 (see last note).

Note 3. Devā́nâm aratí*h*; comp. I, 58, 7, note 1.

Verse 3.

Note 1. The meaning seems to be that people going to settle anywhere, secure safety by ceremonies addressed to Mitra, i.e. possibly by concluding alliances which stand under the special protection of Mitra. Comp. IV, 33, 10; H. O., Religion des Veda, 186, note 1.—Mitra is kshetrasā́dhas, VIII, 31, 14.

Verse 4.

Note 1. Svásya-iva seems to be corrupt. Possibly we might read sûyávasâ-iva push*tíh*. In X, 11, 5 we read, sádâ asi ra*n*vá*h*, yávasâ-iva púshyate. IV, 16, 15. óka*h* ná ra*n*vā́ sud*ris*î-iva push*tíh*.—The translation of the traditional reading would be, 'His prosperity is delightful, like that of a person belonging to us.'

Note 2. Bháribhrat seems to be a participle: but then dodhavîti must be accented (dódhavîti).

Verse 5.

Note 1. On the verb pan, comp. Pischel, Vedische Studien, I, 199 seq.

Note 2. Vanád seems to be, as Grassmann has seen, a compound of ván, 'the forest' (comp. the genitive vanā́m, the locative vá*m*su), and of ád. Of Agni is said several times 'vánâni atti.'

Note 3. On the mythical ancestors designated as the U*s*i*g*as, see Bergaigne, I, 57 seq.

Verse 6.

Note 1. The forests, of course, are the fuel.

Note 2. To ráthyâ-iva probably *k*akrā́ (nom. plur.) is to be supplied.

Note 3. The 'laughing' of the sky is the lightning (Benfey, Vedica und Verwandtes, 138). The flames of Agni flash through the smoke as the lightning shines in the clouds.

Verse 7.

Note 1. See Geldner, Vedische Studien, II, 29 seq.; Roth, Zeitschrift der Deutschen Morgenländ. Gesellschaft, XLVIII, 107.

Verse 8.

Note 1. The text has t*ri*tī́ye' vidáthe (comp. I, 31, 6, note 2). Does this mean at the t*ri*tîya-savana? Three vidathas are spoken of also in VI, 51, 2; VII, 66, 10.

Note 2. On the metrical irregularity, comp. H. O., Die Hymnen des Rig-veda, I, 67.

Verse 9.

Note 1. 'May prevail, destroying through thee the neighbours lying in ambush.' M. M. To me gúhâ seems to be connected with vanvánta*h*.

MA*N**D*ALA II, HYMN 5.

ASH*T*AKA II, ADHYÂYA 5, VARGA 26.

1. The brilliant Hot*ri*[1] has been born[2], the father to protect the fathers[3], aspiring after noble wealth. May we be able to bridle the strong (horse)[4].

2. He the leader of the sacrifice towards whom the seven reins (or rays) are stretched, the Pot*ri* promotes, as (he has done) for Manu, the divine eighth (rein); all those (reins he promotes)[1].

3. Or when he has run along, and has recited the sacred words[1], and has pursued that (duty)[2], he has encompassed every kind of wisdom as the felly (encircles) the wheel.

4. For He has been born as the bright Pra*s*âst*ri*, with bright power of mind. (A man) who knows his firm laws, mounts up on them as on the branches (of a tree)[1].

5. The lively milch-cows were attached to his, the Nesh*tri*'s, (bright) colour[1]. Was it according to the wish of the three sisters who have gone there[2]?

6. When (coming) from the mother the sister has approached, bringing gh*ri*ta[1], the Adhvaryu rejoices at their[2] coming as corn (rejoices) at rain.

7. May He the *Ri*tvig (priest) himself make the *Ri*tvig (serve) for his own refreshment[1]. And may we readily gain the praise and the sacrifice[2]; we have offered it.

8. In order that He the knowing one (Agni) may readily serve all the worshipful (gods), this sacrifice, O Agni, which we have performed, rests in thee.

NOTES.

The same *Ri*shi. Metre, Anush*t*ubh.—Verse 3 = SV. I, 94; TS. III, 3, 3, 3; MS. II, 13, 5.

Verse 1.

Note 1. As the Hot*ri* is mentioned here, the following verses contain each the names of the other priests as given in II, 1, 2. Only the Agnîdh is left out; possibly the words svá*h* svấya dhấyase k*rin*utấm *ri*tvík *ri*tví*g*am (verse 7) contain an allusion to this priest, who may well be termed the *Ri*tvi*g* belonging to Agni and refreshing him.

Note 2. With the first Pâda of our verse, compare IX, 64, 10. índu*h* pavish*t*a *k*étana*h*.

Note 3. The meaning seems to be: Agni, who has protected the fathers, has been born again, and will do the same for the present sacrificer.

Note 4. The strong horse, of course, is Agni. Comp. III, 27, 3 (see below). On the construction (vâ*g*ína*h* yámam), see Delbrück, Altindische Syntax, p. 417.

Verse 2.

Note 1. On the seven rays or reins of Agni, see I, 146, 1, note 1. Besides the seven priests a mysterious eighth *Ri*tvi*g* priest is spoken of (X, 114, 9. kám *ri*tví*g*âm ash*t*amám *s*ū́ram âhu*h*); thus Agni has a mysterious eighth ra*s*mí (ray or rein) besides the seven. Comp. Bergaigne, Religion Védique, II, 144.

Verse 3.

Note 1. Vó*k*at bráhmâ*n*i: this seems to be an allusion to the Brahman priest (see verse 1, note 1).

Note 2. Vé*h* is third singular. See Joh. Schmidt, Kuhn's Zeitschrift, XXV, 91.

Verse 4.

Note 1. Comp. VIII, 13, 6. vayấ*h*-iva ánu rohate. Prof.

Max Müller (vol. xxxii, p. 207) translates, 'springs up like young sprouts.'

Verse 5.

Note 1. It is the Nesh*tri*'s office to lead the wife of the sacrificer to the place where the sacrifice is being performed. Thus Agni, the divine Nesh*tri*, is represented as accompanied by female beings, by the 'milch-cows,' meaning the oblations of gh*ri*ta, &c., or possibly the dawns.

Note 2. Are the 'three sisters' (comp. Bergaigne, I, 321; II, 107) identical with the milch-cows spoken of in the first hemistich? Ludwig (vol. iv, p. 166) very appropriately calls attention to the fact that three cows were milked at the sacrifice of the full and the new moon. Comp. Hillebrandt, Altindisches Neu- und Vollmondsopfer, p. 12 seq. Three dawns are mentioned in VIII, 41, 3.

Verse 6.

Note 1. The sister bringing gh*ri*ta seems to be the sacrificial spoon. Is the mother the milk-vessel or possibly the cow?

Note 2. Does 'their' refer to the mother and the sister (cf. Delbrück, Altindische Syntax, p. 102)? Or are 'the three sisters who have gone there' referred to?

Verse 7.

Note 1. The one *Ri*tvi*g* is Agni; the other possibly is the Agnîdh who refreshes the *Ri*tvi*g* Agni. See verse 1, note 1.

Note 2. After ất we should expect, instead of áram, another accusative, possibly *rík*am (see VII, 66, 11): 'may we master the praise, the sacrifice, and the verse.' Áram may have found its way into the text from verse 8.

MA*ND*ALA II, HYMN 6.

ASH*T*AKA II, ADHYÂYA 5, VARGA 27.

1. Accept, O Agni, this my piece of wood and this my sitting down (reverentially)[1], and hear these words of mine.

2. Let us worship thee, Agni, child of vigour, with this (piece of wood?)[1], O winner of horses[2], with this well-spoken (hymn), O well-born one.

3. May we thus as thy devoted servants pay devotion by our words to thee who acceptest words (of prayer), to thee who aspirest after wealth, O giver of wealth.

4. Thus be thou a liberal, bountiful lord, O lord of goods, O giver of goods. Drive hatred away from us.

5. Thus (give) us[1] rain from the sky; thus (give) us unattainable strength; thus (give) us thousandfold food.

6. To him who magnifies thee, who desires thy help, O youngest messenger, (invoked) by our word, best sacrificing Hot*ri*, come near.

7. For thou, Agni, O sage, who knowest both races (of gods and of men), passest (to and fro) between them, like a messenger belonging to thy own people[1], belonging to thy allies.

8. Thus gladden (the gods)[1] as the knowing one; sacrifice, O intelligent one, in due order, and sit down on this Barhis.

NOTES.

The same *Ri*shi. Metre, Gâyatrî.—Verse 4=VS. XII, 43; TS. IV, 2, 3, 4; MS. II, 7, 10.—The hymn has been translated by M. M., Selected Essays, II, p. 143.

Verse 1.

Note 1. It does not seem probable that upasád is to be translated here according to its meaning in the later ritual, as one of the preparatory ceremonies of the Soma sacrifice. See Weber, Indische Studien, X, 363; Hillebrandt, Vedische Mythologie, I, 300.

Verse 2.

Note 1. Ayā́ may be used adverbially: comp. III, 12, 2; VI, 17, 15; IX, 53, 2; 106, 14. But it is more probable that samídhâ or girā́ should be supplied from verse 1. Comp. II, 24, 1. ayā́ vidhema girā́; IV, 4, 15. ayā́ samídhâ vidhema.

Note 2. Comp. VIII, 61, 7. á*s*vam-ish*t*aye.

Verse 5.

Note 1. The conjecture sána*h*, proposed by Böhtlingk-Roth and Grassmann, is not necessary. The verb is to be supplied; comp. the passages collected by Pischel, Vedische Studien, I, 19.

Verse 7.

Note 1. *G*ányeva seems to be *g*ánya*h* iva, comp. II, 39, 1. dûtā́-iva hávyâ *g*ányâ purutrā́; IV, 55, 5. pā́t páti*h* *g*ányât á*m*hasa*h* na*h*.

Verse 8.

Note 1. Comp. VII, 17, 4. yákshat devā́n am*ri*tân piprá-yat *k*a; VIII, 39, 9. yákshat *k*a pipráyat *k*a na*h*.

MANDALA II, HYMN 7.

ASHTAKA II, ADHYÂYA 5, VARGA 28.

1. Bring us, O youngest god, Bhârata[1], Agni, the best, resplendent, much-desired wealth, O Vasu[2]!

2. May no malign power of a god or of a mortal overcome us. Help us across such hostile power.

3. And may we dive with thee across all hostile powers as across streams of water.

4. Bright, O purifier, worthy of adoration, Agni, thou shinest mightily; thou hast been worshipped by offerings of ghrita[1].

5. Thou, O Bhârata[1], Agni! hast been worshipped by us with offerings of heifers, of bulls, of eight-footed (cows)[2].

6. The old excellent Hotri who feeds on wood and drinks butter, he is the wonderful son of strength.

NOTES.

The same *Ri*shi and metre.—Verse 1=TS. I, 3, 14, 3; MS. IV, 11, 4. Verse 4=TS. I, 3, 14, 5. Verse 6=VS. XI, 70; TS. IV, 1, 9, 2; MS. II, 7, 7.

Verse 1.

Note 1. Agni Bhârata is Agni as the protector of the Bharata tribe or as invoked by that tribe.

Note 2. With the beginning of this verse, I, 44, 4 should be compared.

Verse 4.

Note 1. Comp. VIII, 19, 22. agni*h* gh*ri*tébhi*h* ấhuta*h*.

Verse 5.

Note 1. See verse 1, note 1.

Note 2. Roth (Petersb. Dictionary) supplies vâgbhi*h* or *ri*gbhi*h*; comp. VIII, 76, 12. vấ*k*am ash*t*ấpadîm. But there is no doubt that ash*t*ấpadî, standing by the side of va*s*ấ and ukshán, has the same meaning as in the later ritual, viz. a cow with calf.

MANDALA II, HYMN 8.

ASHTAKA II, ADHYÂYA 5, VARGA 29.

1. As one who runs a race[1] (praises) his chariots, praise thou the yoking of Agni (to the chariot of sacrifice), of the most glorious, bountiful (god)—

2. Who is the best leader for his worshipper, who undecaying makes the malign decay[1], the cheerful-faced who has been worshipped with offerings—

3. He who is praised in the houses on account of his beauty in the evening and at dawn, whose law is not set at nought,

4. The bright one who shines with his light as the Sun with his splendour, with his undecaying (flames)[1], he who is anointed (with ghrita).

5. The hymns have strengthened Agni the devourer[1] along (the extent of) his own royalty[2]. He has assumed every beauty.

6. May we unharmed stand under the protection of Agni, Indra, Soma, of the gods; may we overcome our foes.

NOTES.

The *Ri*shi is G*ri*tsamada; the metre is Gâyatrî, the last verse being Anush*t*ubh, as is frequently the case in Gâyatrî hymns (see H. O., Hymnen des Rig-veda, I, 146).—No verse occurs in the other Sa*m*hitâs.

Verse 1.

Note 1. Vâ*g*ayáti means 'he strives for vâ*g*a,' vâ*g*áyati 'he incites to quickness.' The accent is not always correct in the traditional text.

Verse 2.

Note 1. Comp. II, 16, 1. índram a*g*uryám *g*aráyantam.

Verse 4.

Note 1. As to a*g*árai*h*, 'the undecaying (flames),' comp. III, 18, 2; VI, 5, 4; 6, 2; VII, 3, 3; X, 87, 20.

Verse 5.

Note 1. That Agni should be identified here with the *Ri*shi Atri (see Bergaigne, II, 468) is very improbable. Possibly átri means simply 'the eater' (from ad), though the poet in calling him so may have intended to allude to the name of the *Ri*shi.

Note 2. Comp. I, 80, 1 seq. ár*k*an ánu svarā́*g*yam; 84, 10 seq. vásvî*h* ánu svarā́*g*yam.

MAN*D*ALA II, HYMN 9.

ASH*T*AKA II, ADHYÂYA 6, VARGA 1.

1. The Hot*ri* who is found on the Hot*ri*'s seat has sat down (there), the fierce, the resplendent, the dexterous one, the protector of (his own) infallible laws[1], the highest Vasu, he who brings thousandfold (gain), the pure-tongued Agni.

2. Be thou our messenger, be our protector far and wide; be thou, O bull, a leader towards greater wealth. O Agni! for the continuation of our children and of ourselves be thou an unremitting, brilliant protector.

3. May we worship thee at thy highest birth (-place), O Agni; may we worship thee with praises in thy lower abode. I honour the womb from which thou hast sprung. When thou hast been kindled, they have offered offerings in thee.

4. Agni, being the best sacrificer perform thou the sacrifice with the oblation. With thy readiness to hear (us) hail our gift, the wealth (which we offer). For thou art the treasure-lord of treasures; thou art the deviser of brilliant speech.

5. Thy wealth of both kinds[1] never fails, when thou art born (kindled) day by day, O wonderful one. Make thy singer, O Agni, rich in food; make him the lord of wealth with excellent offspring.

6. With this face of thine, as a bounteous (lord), a sacrificer to the gods, the best performer of sacrifices with happiness, as an undeceivable guardian and far-reaching protector, shine among us, O Agni, with light and wealth.

NOTES.

The same *Ri*shi. Metre, Trish*t*ubh.—According to an observation of Bergaigne's, hymns of six verses composed in Trish*t*ubh should precede hymns of the same extent composed in Gâyatrî. Though this law is not without exceptions (see H. O., Die Hymnen des Rigveda, I, 202 seq.), the suspicion is raised that the hymns 9 and 10 should each be divided into two T*rik*as.—Verse 1=VS. XI, 36; TS. III, 5, 11, 2; IV, 1, 3, 3; MS. II, 7, 3. Verse 2 =TS. III, 5, 11, 2; MS. IV, 10, 4. Verse 3=VS. XVII, 75; TS. IV, 6, 5, 4; MS. II, 10, 6. Verse 6=TS. IV, 3, 13, 2; MS. IV, 10, 5.

Verse 1.

Note 1. The long compound looks suspicious; possibly it should be read ádabdhavrata*h* prámati*h*.

Verse 5.

Note 1. Vásu and dhána frequently receive the epithet ubháya; see VI, 19, 10; VII, 82, 4; 83, 5; X, 84, 7. No doubt celestial and terrestrial goods are referred to, see II, 14, 11; V, 68, 3; VI, 59, 9; VII, 97, 10; IX, 19, 1; 100, 3.

MAN*D*ALA II, HYMN 10.

ASH*T*AKA II, ADHYÂYA 6, VARGA 2.

1. Agni is to be invoked as the first like a father, when he has been inflamed by Manus[1] in the abode of I*d*[2]. When he has invested himself with beauty, the wise immortal, he, the glorious strong (horse) is to be smoothed (by the worshippers as by grooms).

2. Agni with bright splendour, mayest thou hear my call with all my prayers, thou a wise immortal. The two tawny (horses) draw thy chariot or the two red (horses), or He the wide-ranging one has made the two ruddy (horses draw his chariot)[1].

3. They have generated the well-born (Agni) in her who lies on her back[1]. Agni became a germ in the manifoldly-adorned (wives)[2]. Even in the . . .[3] the wise one dwells by night uncovered in his powers[4].

4. I besprinkle with my offering, with Gh*ri*ta, Agni who abides turned towards all beings, who widely extends throughout, who is mighty in his vigour, who shows himself most capacious by the food (which he consumes), and robust[1].

5. I besprinkle Him who is turned towards (us) from all sides; may he gladly accept that with his benevolent mind. Agni, who is like a beautiful youth, who has the appearance of one eagerly striving, is not to be touched, when he hurries around with his body.

6. Mayst thou know the portion (belonging to thee), being strong through thy desire. With thee as our messenger may we speak like Manu. Gaining

wealth[1] I invoke with my (sacrificial) ladle, with my eloquence, the faultless Agni who mixes the honey-drink.

NOTES.

The same *Ri*shi and metre. On the position of this hymn in the collection and its division into T*rik*as, see the note on II, 9.—Verses 4-5=VS. XI, 23-24; TS. IV, 1, 2, 4. 5; MS. II, 7, 2.

Verse 1.

Note 1. Comp. VII, 2, 3. Mánunâ sámiddham.

Note 2. Í*d* is a synonym of í*d*â; i*l*á*h* padé means the same as í*l*âyâ*h* padé.

Verse 2.

Note 1. I cannot accept Prof. Lanman's scansion of this Pâda (Noun-Inflection, 342), utá arushā́ha *k*akre víbh*ri*tra*h*. In my opinion the only reading in conformity with the use of Vedic poets is utā́rushā́ áha, &c.

Verse 3.

Note 1. Comp. III, 29, 3 (see below). Of course the kindling-stick is alluded to.

Note 2. The wives are the plants.—Comp. Lanman, p. 548.

Note 3. The meaning of *s*íri*n*â (ἅπαξ λεγόμενον) is unknown. The Indian explanation ('night') of course is a guess, but this guess may be right.

Note 4. 'Uncovered by the night,' M. M. On máhobhi*h*, cf. vol. xxxii, p. 197.

Verse 4.

Note 1. See vol. xxxii, p. 212.

Verse 6.

Note 1. There is no reason for conjecturing dhanasā́m (Ludwig). Comp. X, 65, 10. indriyám sómam dhanasā́*h* u îmahe.

MAN*D*ALA III, HYMN 1.

ASH*T*AKA II, ADHYÂYA 8, VARGA 13–16.

1. Thou wilt have me, O Agni, as a strong (master) of Soma[1]: therefore thou hast made me the carrier (of the gods?) to perform worship at the sacrifice[2]. Sending my thoughts to the gods[3] I make the (press-) stone ready[4]; I toil, O Agni: find thou pleasure in thy own body[5].

2[1]. Eastward we have turned the sacrifice[2]; may the prayer increase. They honoured Agni with fuel and adoration. They have taught (him) the sacrificial ordinances of the sages of Heaven[3]. Though he (Agni) is clever and strong, they have sought a way for him.

3. He has conceived freshness[1], the wise one of pure[2] powers, he who is by his birth well allied with Heaven and Earth. The gods have found Agni the conspicuous one in the waters, in the work[3] of the sisters.

4. The seven young (wives)[1] made the blessed one grow who had been born white, ruddy in his growth. They ran up to him like mares[2] to a new-born foal. The gods wondered at Agni at his birth.

5. Spreading with his bright limbs to the aerial space, purifying his power[1] by wise purifications, clothing himself in light, the life of the waters[2], he creates mighty, perfect beauty.

6. He has gone to (the waters) who do not eat, the undeceived ones, the young (daughters) of Heaven who are not clothed and (yet) are not naked.

Here the former young (women) having the same origin, the seven sounds[1] have conceived one germ.

7. His compact masses assuming every shape are spread in the womb of ghee, in the streaming of honey. There the swelling milch-cows have stationed themselves. Great are the parents of the wonderfully mighty (Agni) who are turned towards each other[1].

8. Having been carried (in the waters) thou hast shone forth, O son of strength, assuming wonderful shapes brilliant and fierce. The streams of honey and ghee drip, where the male has grown by wisdom.

9. By (his) nature he has found his father's udder[1]; he has sent forth his streams and his showers[2]. Walking[3] hidden to his dear friends he has not been hidden to the young (daughters) of Heaven[4].

10. He bore (in his womb) the germ of the sire, of the father who begat him[1]. He, being one, sucked many (nurses) rich in milk[2]. Observe for this manly, bright one the two wives bound in kinship, belonging to men[3].

11. The great one has grown up in the wide unbounded space[1]. The Waters (have made) Agni (grow): for many glorious ones[2] (have come) together[3]. He lay in the womb of *Ri*ta, the domestic (god) Agni, in the work[4] of the uterine sisters.

12. Like a horse that carries (the prize), in the assembly of the great (waters)[1], visible to his son[2], he whose . . . is light[3]: he who as father begat the ruddy cows[4], he the son of the waters is the most manly, restless[5] Agni.

13. To him, the glorious son of the waters and of the plants, the blessed wood[1] has given birth, in his many shapes. Even the gods, for they agreed in

their mind, honoured him who had been born the most wonderful and strong.

14. Mighty rays of light like brilliant lightnings, milking (the sap of) immortality in the boundless stable, accompanied Agni whose . . . is light[1], who had grown up in his own house, as it were in secret.

15. I magnify thee, worshipping thee with offerings; I magnify (thee) desirous of thy friendship, of thy favour. Together with the gods give help to him who praises thee, and protect us with thy domestic faces.

16. As thy followers, O Agni, best leader, winning all precious (treasures), pressing onward with fertile glory, may we overcome the godless who seek to combat us.

17. Thou hast been here as the banner of the gods, Agni, joy-giving, knowing all wisdom. As the domestic (god) thou hast harboured the mortals. As the charioteer thou goest along straightway after the gods.

18. The immortal, the king, has sat down in the dwelling of the mortals, performing the sacrifices[1]. He the ghee-faced one has shone forth widely, Agni knowing all wisdom.

19[1]. Come to us with thy gracious friendship, speeding, great, with thy great blessings. Bestow on us plentiful victorious wealth; make our share glorious and adorned with fine speech.

20. These old births of thine, O Agni, and the recent ones I have told forth to thee the ancient one. These great libations (of Soma) have been prepared for the manly one; generation by generation *G*âtavedas has been placed (on the altar).

21. *G*âtavedas, placed (on the altar) generation

after generation, is kindled by the Visvâmitras, the indefatigable (or everlasting). May we dwell in the grace of him the worshipful, yea, in his blissful kindness.

22. Bring thou, O strong one, this sacrifice of ours to the gods, O wise one, as a liberal giver. Bestow on us, O Hot*ri*, abundant food; Agni, obtain by sacrificing mighty wealth for us.

23. Procure, O Agni, for ever, to him who implores thee, (the gift of) nourishment[1], the wonderful acquiring of the cow. May a son be ours, offspring that continues our race. Agni, may this favour of thine abide with us!

NOTES.

The *Ri*shi is Visvâmitra Gâthina, the metre Trish*t*ubh.—Verse 1 = MS. IV, 11, 2. Verse 19 = MS. IV, 14, 15. Verse 23=SV. I, 76; VS. XII, 51; TS. IV, 2, 4, 3; MS. II, 7, 11; IV, 11, 1; 12, 3.

Comp. on this hymn Geldner, Vedische Studien, I, 157 seq., and the article of Regnaud, Études Védiques, l'hymne III, 1 du Rig-Véda.

Verse 1.

Note 1. Vákshi, which is very frequent as 2nd person of vah, occurs also as belonging to vas (see VII, 98, 2. pîtím ít asya vakshi), and in this sense no doubt it is to be understood in our passage.—Ludwig and Geldner take tavásam vákshi agne as a parenthesis. G. translates: 'Du hast mich zu deinem Somaschenken—denn dich gelüstet nach dem starken, o Agni—bestellt, dass ich vor den Weisen opfern soll.' To me it seems more natural to understand the first Pâda as one continual clause; vákshi is accented on account of the logical dependence in which this clause stands, the clause being considered, even without a subordinating word, as a dependent one. See Delbrück, Altindische Syntax, p. 42; A. Mayr, Sitzungsberichte der phil. hist. Classe der Kais. Akademie der Wissenschaften, Vol. LXVIII (Vienna, 1871), 248, 259.—If we were to consider vákshi as a locative infinitive (see Bartholomae's theory on such infinitives, Indogermanische Forschungen, II, 271 seqq.), the translation would be: 'Thou hast made me, O Agni, a strong carrier of Soma at the carrying (of the oblations),' &c. I do not think, however, this interpretation of vákshi very probable, nor is it, as far as I can see, favoured by any passage which contains the word.—For sómasya tavásam, Prof. Max Müller suggests the translation 'strong of Soma,' i. e. full of Soma.

Note 2. The text has vidáthe.

Note 3. The traditional text has á*kkh*a dī́dyat, which means, 'shining towards or as far as the gods.' The verb dî with a*kkh*a occurs still in two other passages of this Ma*nd*ala, in 15, 5 and 55, 3. In the first of these passages the text seems to be correct: devā́n á*kkh*a dī́dyâna*h*, 'shining as far as the gods.' In the second passage I believe that we ought to read á*kkh*a dîdhye pûrvyā́*n*i, 'I think of the ancient things,' or more exactly, 'I send my thoughts to the ancient things.' In the same way it seems to me very probable that in our verse dī́dhyat would be the correct reading, for the participle refers to the priest who says of himself, 'I make the stone ready;' and this priest does not send his light (dī́dyat) but his thoughts (dī́dhyat) to the gods. Comp. I, 132, 5 = 139, 1. devā́n á*kkh*a ná dhîtáya*h*; III, 4, 3, and numerous passages which represent the mati, the gira*h*, &c., as going towards (á*kkh*a) the gods, such as III, 39, 1; 42, 3; VII, 10, 3; 36, 9; X, 43, 1; 47, 6.—Prof. von Roth (Zeitschrift der D. Morg. Ges., XLVIII, 108) speaks of the 'häufige Verwechslungen von Formen der beiden Wurzeln 2 dî scheinen und 1 dhî wahrnehmen, denken.' The reading dī́dyat in our verse, and didye III, 55, 3, may rest on the influence of III, 15, 5. devā́n á*kkh*â dī́dyâna*h*.

Note 4. On the accent of yu*ñg*é the same may be said as above (note 1) regarding the accent of vákshi.

Note 5. I. e. cause the fire to flare up.

Verse 2.

Note 1. The verses 2, 3, and 4 have been translated by Bergaigne, Religion Védique, I, 109.

Note 2. Many sacrificial rites are performed from west to east; comp. with regard to the Barhis, I, 188, 4; X, 110, 4; with regard to the sacrificial ladle, III, 6, 1; V, 28, 1; to the Havirdhânas, Vâ*g*as. Sa*m*hitâ V, 17. Thus the whole sacrifice is spoken of as proceeding in an eastward direction; see X, 66, 12. prấ*ñk*am na*h* ya*gñ*ám prá nayata; X, 87, 9. ya*gñ*ám prấ*ñk*am . . . prá naya.

Note 3. Comp. Mahâbhârata XIV, 280. tasmât svaya*m s*âdhi ya*gñ*e vidhânam. Vidátha indeed is here an equivalent of vidhâna.

Verse 3.

Note 1. The meaning seems to be that Agni won vigour (máya*h*) by dwelling in the waters (see Pâda 3); comp. the well-known words ấpa*h* hí sthá maya*h*-bhúva*h* (X, 9, 1), 'for you, O waters, give vigour.'

Note 2. More exactly, of purified faculties.

Note 3. The accent apási, instead of ápasi, looks very suspicious. It is easy, but perhaps too easy, to correct ápasi, as possibly in III, 6, 7. ápa*h* should be read for apá*h*. (In I, 31, 8; 151, 4 Grassmann is wrong in assuming a neutral stem apás- 'die Arbeit.') To me Ludwig's conjecture upási (in the lap of the sisters, i. e. of the waters) seems excellent. Upási occurs in V, 43, 7; X, 27, 13 in the meaning of upásthe. Thus upási svás*r*î*n*âm would be the same as apấm upásthe; comp. I, 144, 2; VI, 8, 4; IX, 86, 25; X, 45, 3; 46, 1. 2, &c.—Comp. below, verse 11, note 4.

Verse 4.

Note 1. Of course the seven wives are the rivers or waters.

Note 2. I cannot adopt Prof. Weber's conjecture asvâ*h* (Altiranische Sternnamen, 10). His translation is: 'Die Götter liefen zu dem wundersamen Agni bei seiner Geburt (neugierig) hinzu, wie die jungen Mädchen zu einem neugebornen Kinde.'

Verse 5.

Note 1. For krátum punânâ*h*, cf. III, 31, 16; VIII, 12, 11; 13, 1; 53, 6.

Note 2. I take pári as belonging to vásâna*h*; *sókih* and ấyu*h* are objects. Comp. X, 16, 5. ấyu*h* vásâna*h*; X, 53, 3. sá*h* ấyu*h* ấ agât surabhí*h* vásâna*h*.

Verse 6.

Note 1. The number of the seven sounds (comp. Sten Konow, Das Sâmavidhâna-brâhma*n*a, p. 33, note 3) seems to be connected with the seven *Ri*shis, see IX, 103, 3. vấ*nîh rí*shî*n*âm saptá (comp. IX, 62, 17). The seven sounds seem to be identified with the seven rivers also in III, 7, 1 (see below). Comp. Bergaigne, Religion Védique, II, 132; H. O., Religion des Veda, 117, note 1.

Verse 7.

Note 1. Heaven and Earth.

Verse 9.

Note 1. Comp. Bergaigne, Religion Védique, II, 99.

Note 2. See volume xxxii, 441 seq. (I, 2, 3, note 1).

Note 3. Here I believe we have an anacoluthon. The poet seems to have intended to say, 'Him who walked . . . the daughters of Heaven saw.'—Prof. Max Müller translates this hemistich: 'He found him (the father) moving along with dear friends, with the young maidens of Heaven—he was not hidden.'

Note 4. Agni was hidden to the gods but not to the waters.

Verse 10.

Note 1. The verse X, 3, 2, though very obscure, seems to contain a similar idea. Should the meaning be that

Agni bears in his womb the Dawn, the daughter of Heaven?

Note 2. The waters.

Note 3. This phrase, which I have translated as literally as possible, is very obscure. The two wives seem to be wives of Agni. Are they Night and Dawn (the two sabardúghe, III, 55, 12?), whose designation as 'belonging to men' seems not to be impossible? Or the two kindling-sticks (comp. V, 47, 5)? Or the two Darvis (V, 6, 9)?

Verse 11.

Note 1. Comp. V, 42, 17. uraú devâ*h* anibâdhé syâma.

Note 2. This is feminine.

Note 3. The phrase ya*s*ásá*h* sám hí pûrvî́*h* occurs also X, 46, 10. It may have been, as Geldner believes, a proverbial locution. But the verb which it is most natural to supply, seems to be gam (i, yâ), so that the meaning may have been: 'Many superior (wives) are wont to assemble,' i. e. where one such wife is, there will be many. This is applied here to the waters, in X, 46, 10 to such beings as ísha*h*, ûtáya*h* or the like. That ya*s*ás may be meant for the waters is shown by VII, 36, 6, where the ya*s*ása*h* vâva*s*ânấ*h*, mentioned by the side of Sarasvatî, evidently are the waters.—It should be observed that several expressions of this hymn have been made use of by the author of X, 46.

Note 4. Or rather 'in the lap' (upási). Comp. above, verse 3, note 3.

Verse 12.

Note 1. With regard to akrá*h* I adopt the translation proposed by Geldner (Ved. Studien, I, 168).—On the accent of mahî́nâm, see Lanman, p. 398.

Note 2. This seems to be the human worshipper. I cannot follow Prof. von Roth, Zeitschrift der D. Morg. Gesellschaft, XLVIII, 118, who explains sû*n*áve as a corrupt third person of the verb su.

Note 3. See above, I, 44, 3, note 1.

Note 4. The dawns.
Note 5. Comp. above, I, 36, 1, note 2.

Verse 13.

Note 1. Vánâ : the wood considered as a wife.

Verse 14.

Note 1. See verse 12, note 3.

Verse 18.

Note 1. The text has vidáthâni.

Verse 19.

Note 1. Comp. Kuhn, Kuhn's Zeitschrift, I, p. 445.

Verse 23.

Note 1. Í*l*âm, which more especially means the nourishing substance of the cow. Comp. H. O., Religion des Veda, 72, 326.—Prof. Max Müller translates : 'Procure to him who implores thee, O Agni, exuberant land for ever, rich in cows.'

MANDALA III, HYMN 2.

ASHTAKA II, ADHYÂYA 8, VARGA 17–19.

To Agni Vaisvânara.

1. For Vaisvânara, the increaser of *Ri*ta, for Agni we produce[1] a Dhishanâ[2] like purified ghee. And verily[3] by their prayer the invoking men (accomplish) him, the Hot*ri*, as the axe accomplishes a chariot.

2. By his birth he has given splendour to both worlds (Heaven and Earth). He became the praiseworthy son of his parents, Agni, the carrier of oblations, never ageing, with satisfied mind, undeceivable, the guest of men, rich in light.

3. Through the power of their mind, within the sphere of their superior strength the gods have procreated Agni by their thoughts. Desirous of winning the prize[1] I address Him who shines with his splendour, who is great in his light, as (one who desires to win the prize addresses his) race-horse.

4. Desirous of winning the choice, glorious, and praiseworthy prize (which is the gift) of the joy-giver, we choose the boon of the Bh*ri*gus[1], the U*sig*[2], who has the mind of a sage, Agni, who reigns with his heavenly light.

5. Men, having spread the sacrificial grass, holding the sacrificial ladle, have placed here in front (as Purohita), for the sake of (the divine) blessing, Agni renowned for strength, with great splendour, united with all the gods, the Rudra of sacrifices[1], who accomplishes the oblations of active (worshippers).

6. O (Agni) whose flame is purifying, around thy

dwelling, O Hotri, the men who at the sacrifices have spread the sacrificial grass, O Agni, seeking (how to do) honour (to thee), and (desiring) thy friendship, surround thee (reverentially);—bestow thou wealth on them!

7. He has filled the two worlds (Heaven and Earth) and the great Sun, when the active ones (i.e. the priests) held him fast who had been born. He the sage is led round for the performance of worship, like a racer for the winning of the prize[1], with satisfied mind.

8. Adore ye him, the giver of offerings, the best performer of worship; honour ye him the domestic *G*âtavedas. Agni, the charioteer of the mighty *Ri*ta, he who dwells among manifold tribes, has become the Purohita of the gods.

9. The immortal U*sig*s have purified three logs for the vigorous[1] Agni[2] who wanders round the earth[3]: of these they have placed one among the mortals for their enjoyment; two have passed into the sister world[4].

10. The food offered by men has sharpened him, the sage of the tribes, the lord of the tribes, as an axe. Busily he goes to the heights and to the depths. He has held fast the germ in these worlds.

11. He the generator, the strong one, stirs in the resplendent bellies like a roaring lion, Vai*s*vânara with his broad stream of light, the immortal, distributing goods and treasures to his worshipper.

12. Vai*s*vânara has mounted the firmament, the back of heaven, as of old, glorified by those who are rich in good thoughts. He, creating wealth for the creatures as of old, goes watchful round the common course.

13. The righteous, worshipful priest deserving of praise, the dweller in heaven[1] whom Mâtarisvan has established (on earth): him we approach whose way is bright and hair golden, the resplendent Agni, for the sake of ever new welfare.

14. Like the flaming one (the sun?) on his way, the quick one, of sun-like aspect, the banner of heaven, who dwells in light, who wakes at dawn—Agni the head of heaven, the unrepressed, him we approach with adoration, the strong one mightily.

15. The joy-giving, bright Hot*ri*, in whom is no falsehood, the domestic, praiseworthy dweller among all tribes, like a splendid chariot, wonderful to behold, established by Manus: him we constantly approach for the sake of wealth.

NOTES.

The same *Ri*shi. The metre is *G*agatî.—Verse 7 = VS. XXXIII, 75. Verse 9 = MS. I, 3, 35.

Verse 1.

Note 1. Literally, 'we generate.'

Note 2. On the meaning of this word, which I may be allowed to leave in its Sanskrit form, I refer to I, 96, 1, note 2.

Note 3. Literally, 'doubly.' Comp. below, III, 17, 5, note 1.

Verse 3.

Note 1. Vấ*g*a*m* sanishyán refers to the worshipper who desires to obtain vấ*g*a (quick strength, and the booty or prize obtained by it), and in the comparison, to the owner of a race-horse who desires to win the race.

Verse 4.

Note 1. Comp. I, 60, 1 (see above).

Note 2. Comp. Bergaigne, Religion Védique, I, 57 seq.

Verse 5.

Note 1. Comp. von Bradke, Dyâus Asura, p. 54.

Verse 7.

Note 1. Again, as in verse 3, vấgasâtaye means, with reference to the race, 'for the winning of the prize,' and with reference to sacrifice, 'for the obtainment of quick strength, of booty, &c.'

Verse 9.

Note 1. See above, I, 36, 1, note 2.

Note 2. Agni is stated here to have one terrestrial and two celestial forms: the fire belonging to men, and, it seems, sun and lightning. Comp. M. M., Physical Religion, 229; Bergaigne, Religion Védique, I, 22. With regard to the three forms of Agni, compare also H. O., Religion des Veda, 106 seq.

Note 3. On párigman, comp. above, I, 79, 3, note 2.

Note 4. Into the celestial world.

Verse 13.

Note 1. I read divikshayám (Bergaigne, Rel. Védique, I, 55, note). The blunder has been caused by X, 63, 5. dadhiré diví ksháyam.

MA*N*D*ALA III, HYMN 3.

ASH*T*AKA II, ADHYÂYA 8, VARGA 20-21.

TO AGNI VAI*S*VÂNARA.

1. They have worshipped Vai*s*vânara with his broad stream of light with prayers [1] and treasures in order that he may walk on firm ground. For immortal Agni honours the gods, and from of old he has not violated the laws.

2. The wonderful messenger goes between the two worlds (heaven and earth), the Hot*ri* who has sat down, the Purohita of Manus. He takes care of his wide dwelling day by day, Agni who, incited by the gods, gives wealth for our prayers.

3. The priests have exalted with their thoughts Agni, the banner of sacrifices, the achiever of sacrifice[1]. From him in whom they have put together their (sacrificial) works and their prayers, the sacrificer desires blessings.

4. The father of sacrifices, the miraculous lord of those who know prayers (?)[1], Agni, is the measure and rule[2] of the sacrificers; he has entered the two manifold-shaped worlds; the sage beloved by many people is glorified in his foundations.

5. The gods have established here in great beauty Agni the bright with his bright chariot, whose every law is golden[1], Vai*s*vânara who dwells in the waters, who finds the sun, the diver, the swift one covered with strength, the quick one.

6. Agni, spreading out with his thought the manifold-adorned sacrifice, together with the gods and

with the people of Manus, goes as a charioteer to and fro with (gods and men) who accomplish the sacrifice, the quick, domestic (god), the dispeller of curses.

7. Agni, be wakeful[1] in our life which may be blessed with offspring; swell with sap; shine upon us (plenty of) food. Stir up vigour and the great ones, O watchful (god). Thou art the U*s*ig (or willing one) of the gods, the good-minded (lord) of prayers.

8. The lord of the tribe, the vigorous[1] guest, the guider of prayers, the U*s*ig (or willing one) of those who invoke him, *G*âtavedas, the light of worship—him men constantly praise with adoration, with solicitations for their welfare.

9. The resplendent, joyous god, Agni on his chariot, has with his might encompassed the dwellings. May we honour in our house with beautiful prayers[1] his commands who is rich in manifold prosperity.

10. O Vai*s*vânara, I love thy statutes by which thou hast found the sun, O far-seeing one. When born thou hast filled the worlds, heaven and earth; Agni, thou encompassest all these (beings) by thyself.

11. For Vai*s*vânara's wonderful deeds he the sage alone has by his great skill mightily[1] let loose (his powers?). Agni has been born exalting both his parents, Heaven and Earth, rich in seed.

NOTES.

The same *Ri*shi and metre.—Verse 10 = MS. IV, 11, 1. Verse 11 = TS. I, 5, 11, 1.

Verse 1.

Note 1. A meaning like 'prayer' seems to recommend itself for most of the passages in which the substantive víp occurs, for instance, V, 68, 1. prá va*h* mitrấya gâyata váru*n*âya vipấ girấ; IX, 22, 3. eté pûtấ*h* vipa*sk*ítа*h* sómâsa*h* . . . vipấ ví ânasu*h* dhíya*h*; IX, 65, 12. ayấ *k*ittá*h* vipấ anáyâ hári*h* pavasva dhấrayâ; III, 10, 5 (see below), &c. As the verb vip means 'to be in trembling agitation,' the same word as a substantive may designate enthusiastic thoughts or prayers. Comp. vépate matî́, IX, 71, 3; X, 11, 6, and the nouns vípra, vipa*sk*ít, vipodhấ. We need not enter here upon the question, whether some concrete trembling or shaking objects also were designated as vípa*h*, and whether Bergaigne (Religion Védique, I, p. vii) is right in taking the víp áya*h*-agrâ, with which Trita killed the boar (X, 99, 6), as a 'prière à pointe de fer' (comp. Macdonell, Journ. R. Asiatic Society, 1893, p. 431; 1895, p. 185).—In our verse vípa*h* may be either nominative or accusative. I have translated it as an accusative; in the case of the nominative the translation would be: 'The prayers have worshipped Vai*s*vânara with treasures.'

Verse 3.

Note 1. The text has vidáthasya.

Verse 4.

Note 1. Ásura*h* vipa*h*-*k*ítâm. On the meaning of ásura, which implies the possession of secret, supernatural power, see H. O., Religion des Veda, 162 seq.—Comp. von Bradke, Dyâus Asura, pp. 64–65.

Note 2. 'Richtschnur und Weg der Opferer,' Pischel, Vedische Studien, I, 306.

Verse 5.

Note 1. Literally, 'whose rules are yellow.' The meaning is that Agni's whole sphere of activity bears the golden yellow colour. Sâyana gives the interesting remark 'haritvakam iti sâkhântaram,' but no doubt hárivratam is right.

Verse 7.

Note 1. Comp. Neisser, Bezzenberger's Beiträge, XIII, 297.

Verse 8.

Note 1. Comp. I, 36, 1, note 2.

Verse 9.

Note 1. Comp. II, 4, 1, note 1.

Verse 11.

Note 1. Prof. Max Müller proposes to translate, 'has sent forth his great song,' and observes, 'Might not brihat be like brihat sâma, a name of a hymn?'

MAN̩D̩ALA III, HYMN 4.

ASHT̩AKA II, ADHYÂYA 8, VARGA 22–23.

Âprî Hymn.

1. Log by log[1] be kind towards us. Flash by flash grant us thy, the Vasu's, favour[2]. Bring hither, O god, the gods that we may sacrifice. Sacrifice, O Agni, as a kind friend to thy friends.

2. Thou whom the gods, Varun̩a, Mitra, Agni, thrice every day bring hither by sacrifice day by day, Tanûnapât, make this our sacrifice honey-sweet, having its abode in ghee[1], (this sacrifice) which worships (the gods).

3. (Our adoring) thought rich in all boons goes forward for worshipping as the first the Hotr̩i of the sacred food (il̩), for saluting the strong bull with adoration and homage. May he, the best sacrificer, incited (by our prayers) sacrifice to the gods[1].

4. Upwards your[1] course has been directed at the worship; upwards (your) flames[2] are gone; ready (for receiving you) is the air[3]. Or the Hotr̩i has sat down at heaven's navel. We spread out the sacrificial grass which receives the gods.

5[1]. Choosing in their mind the sevenfold work of the Hotr̩is[2], enlivening everything (the gods) came hither in the right way. (The divine doors[3]) with men as their ornaments[4], born at the sacrifices[5], have come hither and thither to this sacrifice, many of them.

6. Hither (shall come) the two Dawns[1], the neighbourly (goddesses) of glorious appearance[2].

Of different forms, they both smile. (They shall come) that Mitra and Varu*n*a may be satisfied with us, and Indra accompanied by the Maruts with their powers [3].

7. I catch hold of the two divine Hot*ri*s first. The seven strong ones[1] rejoice according to their wont. Teaching the right, they proclaim the right, the guardians of law, contemplating the law.

8[1]. May Bhâratî, in concord with the Bhâratîs, I*l*â with the gods, Agni with men, Sarasvatî with all (beings) belonging to Sarasvatî (come) hither; may the three goddesses sit down on this sacrificial grass.

9. O divine Tvash*tri*, grant us and send forth this our seed which is to thrive: (the seed) from which a manly son is born able and skilful, who sets to work the press-stones, loving the gods.

10. O tree[1], send (the offering) forth to the gods. May Agni the slaughterer make the offering ready. May the same, the very true Hot*ri*, sacrifice according as he knows the generations of the gods.

11. Agni, being kindled, come hither, on one chariot with Indra, with the quick gods. May Aditi, the mother of noble sons, sit down on our sacrificial grass. With Svâhâ may the immortal gods rejoice.

NOTES.

The same *Ri*shi. Metre, Trish*t*ubh.—Verse 9 = TS. III, 1, 11, 1; MS. IV, 13, 10. Verse 10 = VS. XXVII, 21; TS. IV, 1, 8, 3; MS. II, 12, 6.

Verse 1.

Note 1. Agni is invoked as personified in each log of fuel which is put on the sacrificial fire.

Note 2. Comp. VII, 39, 1. sumatím vásva*h*.

Verse 2.

Note 1. Comp. II, 3, 11. gh*ri*tám asya yóni*h*.

Verse 3.

Note 1. Comp. X, 110, 3. sá*k* enân yakshi ishitá*h* yá*g*îyân (cf. also X, 110, 9).

Verse 4.

Note 1. The text has the dual vâm. But who are the two beings addressed? According to Sâya*n*a, Agni and the Barhis, which does not seem very probable. The structure of the phrase gives the impression—though this impression is by no means certain—that vâm, which belongs to gâtu, is to be supplied to *sok*î*m*shi also. If we are right in this supposition, are not the two beings in question the two first of the three sacred fires, the Âhavanîya and Gârhapatya? These two fires are frequently spoken of in the ritual texts as of a dyad, with the omission of the third fire.—Prof. Max Müller proposes to change vâm into vâ. According to him the meaning may be: Either the road has been made upward, i. e. the flames have gone upward to the sky, or Agni has sat down at heaven's navel.

Note 2. Comp. VII, 43, 2. ûrdhvấ *sok*î́*m*shi devayū́ni asthu*h*.

Note 3. Possibly the words ûrdhvấ *sok*î́*m*shi prásthitâ rá*g*â*m*si may form one clause, 'upwards (your) flames are gone towards the sky.' M. M.

Verse 5.

Note 1. On this verse, comp. Pischel, Vedische Studien, II, 115 seq.

Note 2. On the seven priests of the ancient Soma sacrifice, comp. H. O., Religion des Veda, 383 seq.

Note 3. That this subject is to be supplied, is shown by the regular composition of the Âprî hymns. It is confirmed by the word pûrvî́*h*, which is evidently an epithet of the divine doors; comp. I, 188, 5; VII, 2, 5.

Note 4. 'In human form.' M. M.

Note 5. The text has vidátheshu.

Verse 6.

Note 1. I. e. Night and Dawn.

Note 2. Comp. above, I, 142, 7.

Note 3. Comp. M. M., vol. xxxii, p. 196 seq.

Verse 7.

Note 1. Comp. above, I, 127, 5, note 1. Pischel (Vedische Studien, I, 96) may be right in taking the seven p*ri*kshā́sa*h* as the Aṅgiras, the saptá víprâ*h*.

Verse 8.

Note 1. The verses 8–11 are repeated in VII, 2, 8–11.

Verse 10.

Note 1. The tree is the sacrificial post (yûpa).

MA*ND*ALA III, HYMN 5.

ASH*T*AKA II, ADHYÂYA 8, VARGA 24–25.

1. Shining Agni has awoke over against the Dawns, the priest who traces the footsteps of the sages[1]. With his broad stream of light kindled by the pious, the carrier (of the gods) has opened the two doors of darkness.

2. Agni has grown strong by praises, by the speeches of the praisers, by hymns, the adorable one. Loving many aspects of *Ri*ta the messenger has shone up at the bursting forth of the Dawn.

3. Agni has been established among the tribes of men, the son of the waters, Mitra[1], acting in the right way. The delightful, worshipful one has reached the top; the priest has become one who should be invoked by prayers.

4. Agni becomes Mitra[1], when he has been kindled; he the Hot*ri* (Agni becomes) Mitra; he, *G*âtavedas, (becomes) Varu*n*a. The quick Adhvaryu, the domestic (god, Agni, becomes) Mitra, the Mitra (i.e. friend or ally) of the rivers and of the mountains.

5. He observes the deceiver's dear summit[1], the footstep of the bird[1]; the vigorous one[2] observes the course of the Sun. Agni observes at his (?) navel the seven-headed (song ?)[3]; tall (Agni) observes the enjoyment of the gods.

6. The *Ri*bhu[1] has created for himself a good name worthy of being magnified, he, the god who knows all laws. The skin of the herbs[2], the bird's footstep[3] rich in ghee: Agni watches (all) that, never failing.

7. Agni has approached the place[1] rich in ghee (the altar), with broad passages, (the place) longing (for him), longing (himself). He the resplendent, bright, tall purifier has made his two parents[2] new again and again.

8. As soon as born he has grown by the grass[1], when the sprouting (grass-)blades strengthen him with ghee. Like waters beautiful on their precipitous path, Agni, being in the lap of his parents, has escaped into wide space.

9. Receiving praise the vigorous one[1] has shone forth with his fuel, on heaven's summit, on the earth's navel. May Agni worthy of being magnified, (being) Mitra and Mâtarisvan, the messenger, carry hither the gods that they may receive our sacrifice.

10. The tall one has, by (receiving) fuel, upheld the firmament, Agni, becoming the highest of lights, when Mâtarisvan for the sake of the Bhrigus[1] kindled the carrier of oblations, (Agni) who dwelt in secret.

11 = III, 1, 23.

NOTES.

The same *Ri*shi and metre.—No verse occurs in the other Sa*m*hitâs.

Verse 1.

Note 1. On pada-vî́, comp. Pischel, Vedische Studien, I, 299.

Verse 3.

Note 1. Mitra has here and in verse 4 two meanings: it is the name of the god Mitra, with whom Agni is identified (Bergaigne, Religion Védique, III, 134 seq.), and it means also 'friend' or 'ally' (comp. H. O., Religion des Veda, 186, note 1). See von Bradke, Dyâus Asura, p. 13.

Verse 4.

Note 1. See verse 3, note 1.

Verse 5.

Note 1. All this is very enigmatical. In the parallel passage, IV, 5, 8, we have, instead of ripá*h* ágram, the reading rupá*h* ágram, which is confirmed by verse 7 of the same hymn (ágre rupá*h*) and by X, 13, 3 (pá*ñk*a padā́ni rupá*h* ánu aroham); in support of the reading ripá*h*, on the other side, the verse, X, 79, 3 (ripá*h* upásthe antá*h*), may be quoted. The meaning of rúp is unknown; ríp means 'deceit' and 'deceiver:' but what is the summit of the deceiver? Bergaigne (Religion Védique, II, 77 seq.) has tried to solve the riddle, but it is really hopeless.—The meaning of the following words, padá*m* vé*h*, is not quite so obscure; there is at least some probability that the bird is Agni himself (cf. below, III, 7, 7), or possibly the sun. The latter explanation is advocated by Prof. Max Müller, who writes: 'May it not be a description of sunrise? priyam ripa*h* agram I do not understand; but padam ve*h* is the place of the bird, as in I, 130, 3. ve*h* na garbham, the nest of the bird or of the sun. This nest is covered by a stone, is in fact the vra*g*a, which has to be opened to let out the light of day. It is also the yoni or the altar. Ripa*h* agram may possibly be the summit of the Pa*n*i or of V*ri*tra, X, 79, 3.'

Note 2. See above, I, 36, 1, note 2.

Note 3. Saptá-*s*îrshan ('seven-headed') occurs again in two other passages of the Rig-veda (VIII, 51, 4, and X, 67, 1); in both it is an epithet of words which signify 'hymn' or 'prayer' (arká, dhī́). Possibly a similar word should be supplied here. But why are the prayers called 'seven-headed?' Does this refer to unknown technicalities of the Vedic liturgy? Does it stand in connection with the seven tones of the scale, with the expression saptá dhîtáya*h*, with the number of the seven Hot*ri*s? 'Celui qui a sept têtes est sans doute un personnage équivalent à lui seul au groupe des sept prêtres,' says Bergaigne (II, 145), which is very ingenious, but should not be given as a doubtless fact. —Prof. Max Müller observes that saptasîrshan may be, like saptâsya, the vraga of Pani, opened by Agni, IV, 51, 4, and that Brihaspati is called saptâsya, IV, 50, 4, and saptagu, X, 47, 6.

Verse 6.

Note 1. Agni is here called *Ri*bhu in his quality as a skilful artisan. See Bergaigne, Religion Védique, II, 408.

Note 2. There seems to be no doubt that sasá (comp. sasyá) means 'herb' or possibly 'grain' in X, 79, 3; the text there has sasám ná pakvám; comp. I, 66, 2. yávah ná pakváh. The same meaning is quite admissible in I, 51, 3; V, 21, 4; VIII, 72, 3; though these passages are too uncertain for deciding anything. I cannot find any reason for believing that we have here and in IV, 5, 7; 7, 7 (see below), another word derived from the root sas, and meaning 'the sleeper.' At all events I neither pretend to know what mysteries are hidden under the 'skin of the herbs,' nor what stories may have happened to the 'peau du dormeur' (Bergaigne, II, 78 seq.).

Note 3. See verse 5, note 1.

Verse 7.

Note 1. Yónim, literally 'womb.'

Note 2. Probably Heaven and Earth.

Verse 8.

Note 1. Prof. Max Müller refers this to the grass of the barhis, or the tender blades in which the spark is caught and kept alive by ghee.

Verse 9.

Note 1. Comp. above, I, 36, 1, note 2.

Verse 10.

Note 1. I have adopted, though I do not believe it certain, Grassmann's opinion on the meaning of pári in this connection. Comp. H. O., Religion des Veda, 123, note 4.

MA*ND*ALA III, HYMN 6.

ASH*T*AKA II, ADHYÂYA 8, VARGA 26–27.

1. Bring forward, ye pious singers, stirred in your thoughts[1], (the ladle) which is turned towards the gods. Carrying (the sacrificial butter) from left to right[2] it turns eastward, rich in strength, bringing the offering to Agni, full of ghee.

2. When born thou hast filled the two worlds, nay thou hast even exceeded them, O friend of sacrifices[1]. May, O Agni, thy seven-tongued horses[2] move along, by the greatness of heaven and earth[3].

3. Heaven and Earth the worshipful[1] establish thee as Hot*ri* for the house, whenever the pious human tribes offering food magnify the bright light.

4. (Thou art) seated, the great one, in a firm place[1], between the two mighty Heavens[2], thou who art longed for—(between) the two united[3] never-ageing, inviolable wives, the two juice-yielding milch-cows[4] of the far-reigning one[5].

5. Thy, the great (god's) laws, O Agni, are great. Through the power of thy mind thou hast spread out the two worlds. Thou hast become a messenger at thy birth, thou, O bull, the leader of the tribes.

6. Or bind to the pole by means of thy (art of) harnessing the two long-maned, red (horses) of *Ri*ta, that swim in ghee[1], and carry hither, O god, all gods; perform splendid worship, O *G*âtavedas!

7[1]. Even from heaven thy shining lights have shone; thy splendour follows many resplendent dawns, when the gods, O Agni, praised the cheerful Hot*ri*'s work[2] who eagerly burns in the forests[3].

8. Whether it be the gods who rejoice in the wide air, or those who dwell in the heavenly light, or those who are helpful[1], ready to hear our call, and worshipful; or whether the horses of thy chariot, O Agni, have turned themselves hither—

9. Come hither with them, O Agni, on one chariot or on many chariots, for thy horses are powerful. Bring hither, after thy nature, the thirty and the three gods with their wives, and rejoice (in the Soma).

10. He is the Hot*ri* whose sacrifice even the two wide worlds salute over and over again for the sake of prosperity. Turned to the east[1], the two well-established[2] (goddesses, Heaven and Earth), the righteous, true ones stand as at the sacrifice[3] of (Agni) the right-born.

11 = III, 1, 23.

NOTES.

The same *R*ishi and metre.—Verse 1 = TB. II, 8, 2, 5; MS. IV, 14, 3. Verse 9 = AV. XX, 13, 4.

Verse 1.

Note 1. The translation of mananā́ is conjectural, and based only on the etymology. The passage ā́t ít rā́gânam manánâ*h* ag*ri*bh*n*ata, IX, 70, 3, does not help us much. 'Does not X, 47, 7. stómâ*h* h*ri*disp*rí*sa*h* mánasâ va*k*yá-mâna*h*, indicate the original reading, mánasâ va*k*yámânâm?' M. M.

Note 2. The srú*k*a*h* are called dakshi*n*âv*ŕi*ta*h*, I, 144, 1. By the word dakshi*n*âvā́*t* the poet probably intended to designate the ladle also as procuring a Dakshi*n*â (sacrificial fee) to the priest.

Verse 2.

Note 1. On práyagyu, see M. M., vol. xxxii, p. 335, and Pischel, Ved. Studien, I, 98.

Note 2. The flames of Agni.

Note 3. Comp. below, 7, 10. The meaning seems to be: by thy (Agni's) greatness which is equal to that of Heaven and Earth.

Verse 3.

Note 1. I refer yag*ñ*íyâsa*h*, though it is a plural, to Heaven and Earth. Comp. Delbrück, Altindische Syntax, 103.

Verse 4.

Note 1. The Padapâ*th*a has dhruvá*h*. I think it should be dhruvé, comp. II, 41, 5. dhruvé sádasi úttame . . . âsâte; IX, 40, 2. dhruvé sádasi sîdati.

Note 2. I.e. Heaven and Earth.

Note 3. Ấskra seems derived from â-sa*k* (Joh. Schmidt, Kuhn's Zeitschrift, XXV, 71).

Note 4. Or 'the two milch-cows which instantly give milk,' if sabar- is to be connected with the Greek ἄφαρ; comp. Bartholomae, Bezzenberger's Beiträge, XV, 17.

Note 5. Vish*n*u is not the only god who is called urugâyá, and there is no reason therefore why the epithet should not be referred here to Agni.

Verse 6.

Note 1. Comp. Lanman, Noun-Inflection, pp. 402, 413.—See below, IV, 2, 3.

Verse 7.

Note 1. See Geldner, Vedische Studien, I, 114 seq.

Note 2. Should the accent be ápa*h*? Comp. III, 1, 3, note 3.

Note 3. It is very probable that u*s*ádhak (comp. III, 34, 3; VII, 7, 2) is an epithet of Agni. We should expect the genitive; u*s*ádhak, which violates the construction, seems to stand metri causa. Or is usádhak an accusative singular neuter, so that the literal translation would be: 'When the gods praised the work, burning in the forests, of the Hotri'?

Verse 8.

Note 1. On ū́ma, comp. Pischel, Vedische Studien, I, 223.

Verse 10.

Note 1. Comp. above, II, 2, 7.

Note 2. See Windisch in the Festgruss an Boehtlingk, p. 114.

Note 3. There is one syllable above the number; the metre and meaning would be all right if we were to read adhvaré (for adhvaréva): '(the two goddesses) stand at the sacrifice,' &c. Prof. Max Müller explains: 'Adhvarā́-iva, like two sacrifices, like two sacrificial altars, barhis.'

MA*N*D*A*LA III, HYMN 7.

ASH*T*AKA III, ADHYÂYA 1, VARGA 1-2.

1. They who have risen out of the drink of the white-backed one, have entered the two parents, the seven sounds. The (all-)encompassing parents come together; they go forth to aspire after long life[1].

2. The milch-cows dwelling in heaven[1] are the mares of the manly one. He has bestridden the goddesses who carry the sweet (food)[2]. Thee who livest in peace in the abode of *Ri*ta, the one cow[3] circumambulates, making her way.

3. He has mounted the (mares)[1] that became well-manageable, the wise lord, the finder of riches. He with the dark blue back, with many faces, has made them depart from the drink of the brushwood[2].

4. Giving mighty vigour to the never-ageing son of Tvash*tri*[1], the streams[2] carry Him the firmly fixed one. Flashing in his abode with his limbs he has entered upon the two worlds as if they were one.

5. They know friendship towards the manly, the red one, and they delight in the command of ruddy (Agni), (the gods) shining from heaven, resplendent with bright shine, to whose host I*l*â belongs, the mighty praise.

6. And finding it out by following the noise they brought to the great one's great parents a song of praise, when the bull about nightfall (?) has grown strong according to the singer's own law[1].

7. With the five Adhvaryus the seven priests watch the beloved footstep which the bird has made[1]. Turned forwards the never-ageing bulls[2] rejoice: for they, being gods, have followed the laws of the gods.

8 = III, 4, 7.

9. The many (mares) are full of desire for the mighty stallion. For the manly, bright one, the reins easily direct (the horses)[1]. Divine Hot*ri*! Thou who art a great joy-giver and wise, bring hither the great gods and the two worlds[2].

10. The dawns, O wealth-giver, the mighty sacrificers[1], well spoken and bright have shone with wealth. And by the earth's greatness[2], O Agni, forgive us even committed sin[3], that we may be great.

11 = III, 1, 23.

NOTES.

The same *Ri*shi and metre.—No verse of this hymn occurs in the other Sa*m*hitâs.

Verse 1.

Note 1. On the meaning of this difficult verse conjectures only can be given. The white-backed one may be Agni. If this is right, 'they who have risen out of Agni's drink,' may be Agni's rays or flames (ye ra*s*maya*h* . . . prakarshe*n*odga*kkh*anti, Sâya*n*a); these flames enter upon the two mothers, i.e. Heaven and Earth, and upon the seven sounds, the sacrificial songs which are identified with the terrestrial and celestial seven rivers (comp. above, III, 1, 6). All this rests on the supposition that the traditional text is correct. Now Ludwig remarks with reference to the pronoun yé: 'Warscheinlicher ist, dass wir hier eine archaistische anwendung der form auf e für fem. vor uns haben,' and Griffith says that yé is 'apparently used for the feminine.' I do not believe in this possibility, but for yé (yá) the true reading may be yấ(*h*). In this case the seven vâ*n*îs would be subject: 'They who have risen out of the drink of the white-backed one, the seven sounds have entered the two parents.' The meaning of this may be: The sacrificial songs, rising as it were out of the offering made to Agni, and in the same way the streams of water which, in the shape of clouds of smoke rise out of the offering (comp. I, 164, 51), have gone to Heaven and Earth.

That the parents in the third Pâda are again Heaven and Earth is shown by X, 65, 8. parikshítâ pitárâ . . . dyấvâp*r*íthivî́. It may be observed that the author of X, 65 (see especially the verses 6–8) evidently imitated the expressions of the hymn, III, 7. 'The coming together of Heaven and Earth marks the beginning of the day and of the year.' M. M.

Verse 2.

Note 1. On divákshas, comp. Joh. Schmidt, Pluralbildungen der Neutra, 417 seq.

Note 2. The milch-cows, mares, or goddesses seem to be the celestial waters or Dawns.

Note 3. Comp. X, 65, 6, quoted at the end of this note. Is the cow (Vâ*k*, according to Sâya*n*a) the Dawn which daily returns in her due way? Or the butter offered to Agni? In our verse and in the parallel passage, X, 65, 6, the vartaní of the cow is mentioned; it may be observed that the vartaní of Ushas is referred to in X, 172, 1. 4. And Ushas is represented in I, 123, 9 as coming to the nishk*r*itá: comp. X, 65, 6. yấ gaú*h* vartaním pari-éti ni*h*-k*r*itám.

Verse 3.

Note 1. See verse 2.

Note 2. The meaning may possibly be the following. The Waters dwell in the plants as their sap (comp. H. O.,

Religion des Veda, 113). Agni, when burning or drinking as it were, the brushwood, destroys this dwelling of the Waters; he makes the Waters depart from the wood.

Verse 4.

Note 1. On Agni as the son of Tvash*tri*, see Hillebrandt, Vedische Mythologie, I, 522 seq.

Note 2. 'Could vaháta*h* be the suyámâ*h* of verse 3?' M. M.

Verse 6.

Note 1. Or, 'when the singer's bull . . . has grown strong according to his own law'? The bull, of course, is Agni.

Verse 7.

Note 1. See above, 5, 5. 6.

Note 2. The flames of Agni?

Verse 9.

Note 1. Ra*s*máya*h*, 'the reins,' at the same time means 'the rays' (of Agni). Suyâmắ*h* being an apposition to ra*s*máya*h*, one is tempted to derive it from the root yam, 'to direct,' but it may contain the word yắma, 'the way,' and mean 'having a good way.'—It is difficult to believe that ra*s*máya*h* suyâmắ*h* is a second subject of v*ri*shâyánte, in which case the translation would be: 'The many (mares) are desirous of the mighty stallion, the . . . reins (or rays) of the manly, bright one.'

Note 2. 'Bring hither to the two worlds the great gods.' M. M.

Verse 10.

Note 1. On p*ri*kshá-praya*g*a*h*, comp. M. M., vol. xxxii, p. 335; Pischel, Vedische Studien, I, 98.

Note 2. The meaning seems to be: By thy greatness which is equal to that of the earth.

Note 3. Comp. X, 63, 8. k*ri*tắt ák*ri*tât énasa*h*. See also I, 24, 9; VI, 51, 8.

MAN*D*ALA III, HYMN 8.

ASHT*A*KA III, ADHYÂYA 1, VARGA 3–4.

1. The worshippers of the gods anoint thee at the sacrifice, O lord of the forest[1], with heavenly honey[2]. When standing upright bestow wealth (on us) here, or when abiding in this mother's lap[3].

2. Situated in front of the kindled (fire), accepting our sacred spell which protects from old age and gives valiant offspring, driving away far from us lack of thoughts[1], rise up[2] for the sake of great prosperity.

3. Rise up, O lord of the forest, on the summit of the earth. Erected by skilful erection bestow splendour on (the worshipper) who fits out the sacrifice as a vehicle[1].

4. A well-clothed youth dressed has come hither. He becomes more excellent when born[1]. Wise sages full of pious thoughts, longing for the gods in their mind, bring him forth.

5. He who has been born is born[1] in the auspiciousness of days, growing up in the assembly and at the sacrifice[2]. Wise, active men purify him by pious thoughts; the priest approaching the gods raises his voice[3].

6. You whom the worshippers of the gods have fastened down (in the earth), or whom the axe has fashioned, O lord of the forest: may those divine posts[1] standing (here) take care to bestow on us treasures with offspring.

7. (The posts) which have been hewn on the earth and fastened down, and to which the sacrificial

ladles have been raised[1]: may they, giving bliss to our fields[2], eagerly seek precious goods for us among the gods.

8. May the Âdityas, the Rudras, the Vasus, the good leaders, Heaven and Earth, the Earth[1] and the Air—may the gods unanimously bless this sacrifice; may they raise up the banner of the sacrifice (the Yûpa).

9. Like swans ranging themselves in rows, arraying themselves in brightness the sacrificial posts have come to us. Led up by the sages they go forward as gods to the abode of the gods.

10. Like horns of horned animals the sacrificial posts with their head-pieces[1] are seen on the earth. Hearing (us) in the emulating call of the invoking (priests) may they protect us in the racings of battles.

11. O lord of the forest, rise with a hundred branches; may we rise with a thousand branches (offspring)—thou whom this sharpened axe has led forward to great prosperity.

NOTES.

The same *Ri*shi. The metre is Trish*t*ubh (verses 3 and 7 Anush*t*ubh).

This Sûkta is a collection of liturgical verses that refer to the erecting and anointing of the sacrificial post, and to the winding of a rope about it. See Aitareya Brâhma*n*a II, 2; Â*s*valâyana *S*rautasûtra III, 1, 8 seq.; *S*âṅkhâyana *S*rautasûtra V, 15, 2 seq.; Schwab, Das Altindische Thieropfer, 68 seq.; Bergaigne, Recherches sur l'Histoire de la Liturgie Védique, 16. On the ritual acts referring to the sacrificial post which seem to be connected with ancient tree-worship, comp. also H. O., Religion des Veda, 90 seq., 256.—Verses 1-5 = TB. III, 6, 1, 1. 3; MS. IV, 13, 1. Verse 3 = MS. I, 2, 11. Verse 4 = TÂ. I, 27, 2. Verse 10 = TB. II, 4, 7, 11. Verse 11 = TS. I, 3, 5, 1; VI, 3, 3, 3.

Verse 1.

Note 1. The tree of which the sacrificial post is made.

Note 2. The post is anointed with butter, see Schwab, l. c., 69. This butter is spoken of as honey also in the Yagus, which refers to this rite, 'May the god Savit*ri* anoint thee with honey,' Taittirîya Sa*m*hitâ I, 3, 6, 1.

Note 3. In the lap of the mother Earth.

Verse 2.

Note 1. Ámati has nothing to do with the verb am; it is the contrary of matí. See Rig-veda IV, 11, 6. ámatim . . . á*m*ha*h* . . . du*h*matím; X, 33, 2, and such passages of the younger Vedic Sa*m*hitâs as Vâ*g*. Sa*m*h. XVII, 54 (ápa ámatim du*h*matím bấdhamânâ*h*). The same is the opinion of Geldner (Ved. Studien, II, 184, note 4).

Note 2. The sacrificial post is addressed.

Verse 3.

Note 1. Comp. below, III, 24, 1.

Verse 4.

Note 1. The sacrificial post, round which a rope of grass (Schwab, Thieropfer, p. 49) is tied, is compared here with a well-dressed youth. This seems to contain an allusion to the Upanayana ceremony, at which the youth was invested with the sacred girdle, and which was considered as a second birth (comp. Pâda B: 'He becomes more excellent when born'). There is no doubt that this rite is as old and older than the Rig-veda; see H. O., Religion des Veda, 466 seq. It may be noted that several G*ri*hya-sûtras prescribe the use of our verse at the Upanayana (Âsvalâyana I, 20, 9, &c.).

Verse 5.

Note 1. Does this expression refer again to the second birth (see the preceding note)?

Note 2. The text has vidáthe.

Note 3. Comp. V, 76, 1. út víprâ*n*âm devayấ*h* vấ*k*a*h* asthu*h*. The conjecture devayấm easily suggests itself, but it is not necessary.

Verse 6.

Note 1. In the Rig-veda, sváru means the sacrificial post itself, not, as in the later ritual texts (Schwab, Thieropfer, pp. 11, 74), that splinter of the wood of the sacrificial post (yûpa*s*akala), with regard to which Kâtyâyana (VI, 3, 17) prescribes: 'Yûpa*s*akalam asyâm (scil. ra*s*anâyâm) avagûhati.' 'He hides the splinter of the wood of the sacrificial post in the rope (tied round the post).'—See Weber, Indische Studien, IX, 222.

Verse 7.

Note 1. Comp. below, IV, 6, 3.

Note 2. Comp. VIII, 71, 12. kshaítrâya sấdhase.

Verse 8.

Note 1. The Earth is mentioned twice, firstly together with the Heaven, in the compound Dyấvâ-Kshấmâ, and then separately as P*ri*thivî.

Verse 10.

Note 1. On the wooden head-piece of the sacrificial post (*k*ashấla), see Schwab, Das Thieropfer, p. 9.

MA*N*D*ALA III, HYMN 9.

ASHT*AKA III, ADHYÂYA 1, VARGA 5–6.

1. We, thy friends[1], have chosen thee for our protection, (we) the mortals (thee) the god, the offspring of the Waters, the blessed one with fine splendour[2], who gloriously advances, the unmenaced one.

2. When thou, finding pleasure in the wood, hast gone to thy mothers, the Waters, that return of thine, Agni, (to this world) should not be slighted, when dwelling afar thou hast come hither.

3. High above (all) pungent sharpness thou hast grown up[1], and verily thou art kind-hearted. Some go forward here and there; others sit around thee, in whose friendship thou abidest[2].

4. He who has passed beyond (all) failures, beyond all hindrances[1], the guileless, watchful ones[2] have found him as a lion (is found), when he had gone into the Waters;

5. He who had run as it were by his own might, Agni, who thus dwelt in concealment—Him Mâtari*s*van brought hither from afar, from the gods, when he had been produced by attrition (of the woods).

6. (And thus) the mortals have taken thee up, O carrier of sacrificial food towards the gods[1], because thou, O (god) belonging to Manus, protectest all sacrifices by the power of thy mind, O youngest one!

7[1]. This is something glorious; herein thy wonderful power shows itself even to the simple, that the cattle lie down round about thee when thou hast been kindled, O Agni, at the approach of darkness [2].

8. Make your offerings in (Agni), the best performer of worship, the sharp one who purifies with his flames[1]. Serve ye obediently the god, the quick messenger, the agile, the old, the adorable.

9 [1]. Three hundred and three thousand gods and thirty and nine did service to Agni. They sprinkled him with ghee and spread out for him the sacrificial grass: then they made him sit down as a Hot*ri*.

NOTES.

The same *Ri*shi. The metre is B*ri*hatî; the last verse is Trish*t*ubh.—Verse 1=SV. I, 62. Verse 2=SV. I, 53. Verse 9=VS. XXXIII, 7; TB. II, 7, 12, 2.

Verse 1.

Note 1. For this expression, compare I, 30, 7; VIII, 21, 2. 9.

Note 2. Comp. VIII, 19, 4. subhágam sud*í*ditim.

Verse 3.

Note 1. Comp. I, 81, 5. áti ví*s*vam vavakshitha; 102, 8. áti idám ví*s*vam bhúvanam vavakshitha.

Note 2. The different officiating priests seem to be alluded to.

Verse 4.

Note 1. Comp. I, 42, 7. áti na*h* sa*sk*áta*h* naya; VII, 97, 4. párshat na*h* áti sa*sk*áta*h*; Lanman, Noun-Inflection, 467.

Note 2. The gods who searched for Agni.

Verse 6.

Note 1. For devébhya*h* havyavâhana, comp. X, 118, 5; 119, 13; 150, 1.

Verse 7.

Note 1. Comp. Prof. von Schroeder's translation of this verse, Kuhn's Zeitschrift, XXIX, 205.

Note 2. Regarding apisarvaré, comp. VIII, 1, 29: Geldner, Vedische Studien, II, 178. I cannot adopt the conclusions of Prof. Bloomfield, Contributions to the Interpretation of the Veda, Fifth Series, p. 36. 'Wild animals run away from the fire at night, tame animals are attracted by it.' M. M.

Verse 8.

Note 1. For this Pâda, comp. VIII, 43, 31; 102, 11; X, 21, 1.

Verse 9.

Note 1. This verse is identical with X, 52, 6.

MAN*D*ALA III, HYMN 10.

ASHT*A*KA III, ADHYÂYA 1, VARGA 7–8.

1[1]. Thee, O Agni, the highest king of human tribes, the god, thoughtful mortals kindle at their worship.

2. Thee, O Agni, the *Ri*tvig, the Hot*ri*, they magnify at the sacrifices. Shine as the guardian of *Ri*ta in thy own house[1].

3. He indeed who may worship thee, the *G*âtavedas, with fuel, acquires abundance in valiant men, O Agni; he will prosper.

4. May He, the banner of the sacrifices, Agni, come hither with the gods, anointed by the seven Hot*ri*s[1] for the sake of the man who offers sacrificial food.

5. Bring ye forward an ancient, mighty speech to Agni, the Hot*ri*, who is like a worshipper bearing the lights of prayers[1].

6. May our prayers increase Agni, since he is born deserving of praises, the conspicuous one, for the sake of great strength and wealth.

7[1]. May Agni, as the best sacrificer at the worship (of men), perform the sacrifice to the gods for the man devoted to the gods. As a joyous Hot*ri* thou reignest (passing) beyond (all) failures.

8. Thus, O purifier, shine on us glorious abundance in heroes. Be the nearest (friend) to those who praise thee, for their welfare.

9. Thus the priests full of admiring praise, having awoke, kindle thee, the immortal carrier of sacrificial food, the increaser of strength.

NOTES.

The same *Ri*shi. The metre is Ush*n*ih.—Verse 5=SV. I, 98; TB. III, 2, 11, 1. Verse 7=SV. I, 100.

Verse 1.

Note 1. The first Pâda is identical with VIII, 44, 19.

Verse 2.

Note 1. Comp. above, I, 1, 8.

Verse 4.

Note 1. The most ancient list of officiating priests at the Soma sacrifice contained seven priests. See H. O., Religion des Veda, 383 seq. Hence Agni is called saptáhotâ, cf. III, 29, 14.

Verse 5.

Note 1. On víp, see the note on III, 3, 1. As to the 'lights' of the vipas, comp. vā́*k*a*h* *g*yóti*h*-agrâ*h*, VII, 101, 1, the expression *g*yoti*h*sh*t*oma—though this word is not known in the Rig-veda—and the materials collected by Bergaigne, Religion Védique, I, 285.

Verse 7.

Note 1. The second Pâda is identical with I, 15, 12.

MA*ND*ALA III, HYMN 11.

ASH*T*AKA III, ADHYÂYA 1, VARGA 9–10.

1. Agni is the Hot*ri*, the Purohita of our worship, he who dwells among many tribes, He knows the sacrifice in due order.

2. He, the immortal carrier of oblations, the U*sig*[1], the messenger, with satisfied mind, Agni sets himself in motion[2] (incited) by the thought (of praying men ?).

3. Agni takes heed[1] (of us) by the thought (the prayer ?), the banner of the sacrifice, the ancient one; for his purpose triumphs[2].

4. The gods have made Agni, the old-renowned son of strength, the *G*âtavedas, their carrier (towards the sacrifice)[1].

5. Agni the undeceivable one who goes before the human tribes, he is the quick chariot[1], ever new.

6. Overcoming all attacks, He, the uninjured mind (power) of the gods, Agni, is most mightily renowned.

7. Through the vehicle[1] (which carries the gods) towards the delights (of sacrifice), the worshipping mortal attains the dwelling-place[2] of (Agni) whose flames are purifying.

8. May we, the priests, by our prayers obtain all the blissful gifts of Agni *G*âtavedas.

9. Agni! May we win all the best things in (the trials of) strength. In thee the gods have established them[1].

NOTES.

The same *Ri*shi. The metre is Gâyatrî.—Verse 2=VS. XXII, 16; TS. IV, 1, 11, 4; MS. IV, 10, 1. Verses 5, 7, 6 =SV. II, 906–908. Verse 5=TB. II, 4, 8, 1.

Verse 2.

Note 1. Comp. Bergaigne, Religion Védique, I, 57 seq.

Note 2. On the intransitive use of *rin*váti, comp. Gaedicke, Der Accusativ im Veda, p. 53.

Verse 3.

Note 1. The meaning seems to be that Agni is intent on his purpose (ártham, Pâda 3); comp. I, 10, 2. tát índra*h* ártham *k*etati.

Note 2. Comp. Neisser, Bezzenberger's Beiträge, XX, 42.

Verse 4.

Note 1. See the note on I, 127, 8.

Verse 5.

Note 1. On Agni considered as a chariot, see Bergaigne, Religion Védique, I, 144.

Verse 7.

Note 1. Comp. I, 127, 8, note 1.

Note 2. Comp. above, III, 2, 6.

Verse 9.

Note 1. I.e. all the best things (Pâda 1); comp. VI, 5, 2. tvé vásûni . . . ắ îrire yag*ñ*íyâsa*h*.

MANDALA III, HYMN 12.

ASHTAKA III, ADHYÂYA 1, VARGA 11–12.

To Indra-Agnî.

1. Indra-Agnî, in consequence of our prayers come hither to the pressed (Soma), to the precious cloud[1]. Drink of it incited by our thoughts (i.e. by our prayers).

2. Indra-Agnî, the brilliant[1] sacrifice of him who praises you goes forward together (with the Soma libations, the praises, &c.). Thus drink this pressed (Soma)!

3. By this stirring sacrifice I choose Indra and Agni who show themselves as sages[1]; may they here satiate themselves with Soma.

4. I call the bounteous[1], the killers of foes[2], the united conquerors, unconquered, Indra-Agnî, the greatest winners of booty.

5. The praisers rich in hymns, knowing all the ways (of the sacrifice), laud you. Indra-Agnî, I choose the food (which you give).

6. Indra-Agnî, you have hurled down by one deed the ninety strongholds together of which the Dâsas were the lords.

7. Indra-Agnî, the thoughts (of the worshippers) go forward towards (you) from the work (of sacrifice) along the paths of *Ri*ta.

8. Indra and Agni, yours are powerful abodes and delights. You cross the waters: this is the deed which belongs to you[1].

9. Indra and Agni, you display the lights of heaven in your deeds of strength; that mighty deed of yours has been known far and wide.

NOTES.

The same *Ri*shi and metre. The hymn is addressed to the couple Indra and Agni.—Verses 1–3=SV. II, 19–21. Verse 1=VS. VII, 31; TS. I, 4, 15, 1; MS. I, 3, 17. Verses 4–6=SV. II, 1052–1054. Verses 5–8=SV. II, 925–928. Verse 5=MS. IV, 11, 1. Verse 6=TS. I, 1, 14, 1; MS. IV, 10, 5. Verses 9, 7, 8=SV. II, 1044–1045. Verse 9 =TS. IV, 2, 11, 1; 3, 13, 8; TB. III, 5, 7, 3; MS. IV, 10, 4; 11, 1.

Verse 1.

Note 1. 'Cloud,' of course, means that which comes from the cloud. In the Soma hymns of the ninth Ma*nd*ala, the word nábha*h* seems frequently to refer to the water with which the Soma is mixed (see IX, 69, 5; 71, 1. 3; 74, 4; 83, 5; 86, 14; 97, 21; Prof. Hillebrandt's opinion on these passages is different, see his Vedische Mythologie, I, 212). Perhaps we should go too far in believing that in our verse the poet invited the gods to come and drink that water, but possibly the mixture of water and of the juice of the Soma plant descending from heaven and nourished by the heavenly waters represented itself to the poet's mind as something coming from, and thus being identical with, the cloud.

Verse 2

Note 1. On *k*étana*h*, Prof. Max Müller remarks, 'perhaps which appeals to you . . . so that they take note of it.'

Verse 3.

Note 1. There may be doubts about kavi*kkh*ádâ. Prof. Max Müller remarks, 'is it, wishing for sages?' I think that my translation is recommended by X, 81, 1. prathama*kkh*át.

Verse 4.

Note 1. Comp. I, 169, 5. rấya*h* to*s*ấtamâ*h*; VIII, 38, 2. to*s*ấsâ rathayấvânâ . . . índrâgnî, and Brugmann in Kuhn's Zeitschrift, XXIV, 24.

Note 2. Or, the killers of V*ri*tra.

Verse 8.

Note 1. On aptúr and aptū́rya, comp. Pischel, Vedische Studien, I, 122 seq., and H. O., Göttingische Gelehrte Anzeigen, 1889, 4 seq.

MA*ND*ALA III, HYMN 13.

ASH*T*AKA III, ADHYÂYA 1, VARGA 13.

1. To this god Agni I sing[1] for you most powerfully. May he come to us with the gods; may he, the best sacrificer, sit down on the sacrificial grass.

2. The righteous one to whose skill the two worlds (Heaven and Earth) and (all) blessings cling —Him the men rich in offerings magnify, Him those who long for gain, that they may obtain his blessing.

3. He, the priest, is the guide of these (men)[1], and he indeed (is the guide) of sacrifices. Praise ye this Agni who is the giver, the winner of wealth.

4. May this Agni give us most blissful shelter for our (sacrificial) feast, whence he may shower wealth on us in heaven, the (human) dwellings[1], and in the waters.

5. The singers kindle Agni, the Hot*ri*, the lord of the tribes, the brilliant, the wonderful, with his excellent thoughts[1].

6. And mayst thou, the best invoker of the gods, help us in our spell, in our hymns. Shine bliss on us, Agni whom the Maruts strengthen[1], the greatest winner of thousandfold (wealth).

7. Now bestow on us thousandfold wealth with offspring and prosperity, splendid, most powerful, and undecaying abundance in heroes, O Agni!

NOTES.

The *Ri*shi is *Ri*shabha Vai*s*vâmitra. The metre is Anush*t*ubh.—Verses 6, 7=MS. IV, 11, 2.—Comp. concerning this hymn, Aitareya Brâhma*n*a II, 40.

Verse 1.

Note 1. Ar*k*a (ar*k*â) may be first or second person. Comp., for instance, VI, 16, 22. prá va*h* sakhâya*h* agnáye stómam . . . ár*k*a gấya *k*a vedháse; X, 50, 1. prá va*h* mahé . . . ár*k*a (Sa*m*hitâp. ár*k*â) vi*s*vấnarâya vi*s*vabhúve, and see Benfey, Die Quantitätsverschiedenheiten in den Sa*m*hitâ- und Pada-Texten der Veden, III, p. 8.—On the metre of the second Pâda, comp. my Prolegomena, p. 188.

Verse 3.

Note 1. Perhaps we should supply, on account of the preceding nominative, vípra*h* ('priest'): of these (priests).

Verse 4.

Note 1. Kshitíbhya*h* seems to me to be co-ordinated with diví and apsú ấ; comp. X, 89, 11. The locative kshitíshu would not have suited the metre as well as the dative. Prof. Max Müller proposes to translate: 'Whence he may shower wealth on our dwelling, whether he be in the sky or in the waters.'

Verse 5.

Note 1. Comp. X, 172, 2. ấ yâhi vásvyâ dhiyấ.

Verse 6.

Note 1. Comp. *S*âṅkhâyana *S*rautasûtra VIII, 16. indra*h* marutvân . . . marutstotra*h* marudga*n*a*h* marudv*ri*dha*h* marutsakhâ.

MAṆḌALA III, HYMN 14.

ASHṬAKA III, ADHYÂYA 1, VARGA 14.

1. The joy-giving Hot*ri* has taken his place at the sacrifices[1], He the true, the sacrificer, the highest sage, the worshipper. Agni whose chariot is lightning, the son of strength, whose hair is flame, has spread forth his light over the earth.

2. It[1] has been offered to thee—be pleased with the adoring speech[2]—to thee who is observant of it, O righteous, strong one. Bring hither thou who art wise, the wise (gods). Sit down on the sacrificial grass in the middle (of it) for bliss, O worshipful one!

3. To thee, Agni, Night and Dawn who further thy strength[1], shall hasten on the paths of the wind. When (the mortals) anoint the ancient one[2] with offerings, they[3] stand in the house as on a chariot-seat[4].

4. Mitra and Varu*n*a, O strong Agni, and all the Maruts shall sing to thee a pleasant song, when thou, O son of strength, standest with thy flames, a sun spreading out men[1] over the (terrestrial) dwellings.

5. We have given thee thy desire to-day, sitting down near thee adoringly with outstretched hands[1]: sacrifice thou to the gods as a priest with thy mind most skilled in sacrifice, with unerring thoughts, O Agni!

6. From thee indeed, O son of strength, proceed manifold divine blessings and gains[1]. Give us thousandfold true wealth according to thy guileless word, O Agni!

7. What we have done here for thee at this sacrifice, we mortals, O skilful and thoughtful god, take thou notice of all that, O (god) with the good chariot[1]; make all this (sacrificial food) here savoury, immortal Agni!

NOTES.

The same *Ri*shi. The metre is Trish*t*ubh.—Verse 5 = VS. XVIII, 75.

Verse 1.

Note 1. On vidátha, comp. I, 31, 6, note 2.

Verse 2.

Note 1. The subject to be supplied seems to be náma*h*-ukti*h*.

Note 2. The words náma*h*-uktim *g*ushasva form a parenthesis, as Ludwig has seen.

Verse 3.

Note 1. It is possible that here, as in several other passages, a confusion between the two verbs vâ*g*áyati and vâ*g*ayáti has taken place. If the reading were vâ*g*ayántî, we should have to translate, 'Night and Dawn who are striving together (as if running a race against each other?).'

Note 2. The ancient one is Agni.

Note 3. The two goddesses, Night and Dawn.

Note 4. The Padapâ*th*a has vandhúrâ-iva, which may be the dual of vandhúr (I, 34, 9). But more probably it should be vandhúre-iva (nom. dual, neuter or loc. sing.), comp. I, 64, 9. ấ vandhúreshu . . . tasthau; I, 139, 4. ádhi vâm sthấma vandhúre; III, 43, 1. vandhuresh*th*ấ*h*, and see III, 6, 10. adhvaréva. On contracted Prag*ri*hya vowels, see H. O., Die Hymnen des Rig-veda, I, p. 456.

Verse 4.

Note 1. On n*r*î*n* and the different theories proposed for this word, see above, I, 146, 4, note 5.

Verse 5.

Note 1. Comp. X, 79, 2. uttânáhastâ*h*.

Verse 6.

Note 1. For this hemistich, comp. VI, 13, 1; 34, 1.

Verse 7.

Note 1. The traditional text has tvám ví*s*vasya suráthasya bodhi, which can only mean, 'take thou notice of every one who has a good chariot'—which Bergaigne (Quelques observations sur les figures de rhétorique dans le Rig-veda, p. 15) explains: 'Le char en question est la prière qui amène le dieu au sacrifice.' I believe that the text is corrupt; instead of suráthasya I think we should read surathâsya (=suratha asya).

MANDALA III, HYMN 15.

ASHTAKA III, ADHYÂYA 1, VARGA 15.

1. Flaming with thy broad stream of light beat away fiends, sorcerers, plagues. May I dwell in the protection of the great, well-protecting (god), under the guidance of Agni who readily listens to our call.

2. Be thou our protector when this dawn shines forth, be thou (our protector) when the sun has risen. Cherish, O Agni, well-born in body, this praise of mine as (a man rejoices) in the birth (of a son), in his own offspring[1].

3. Beholding men, shine thou after many (dawns)[1], O bull, Agni, red in the dark (nights). O Vasu! Lead us and bring us across anguish. Help us, the U*sig*s[2], to wealth[3], thou youngest (of the gods)!

4. Shine, O Agni, thou the invincible bull, who hast conquered all strongholds and all delights, the leader of the first, the protecting[1], mighty sacrifice, O *G*âtavedas, best guide.

5. O singer, thou who art wise, brightly shining towards the gods[1], bring to us thy many perfect shelters, and gain like a victorious car[2]; Agni, (carry) thou (hither) towards us the two well-established[3] worlds (Heaven and Earth).

6. O bull, increase and rouse our gains. Agni! (Increase) for us the two worlds (Heaven and Earth) rich in milk, O god together with the gods, shining with beautiful shine! May a mortal's hatred never enclose us.

7 = III, 1, 23.

NOTES.

The *R*ishi is Utkîla Kâtya, the metre Trish*t*ubh.—Verse 1 = VS. XI, 49; TS. IV, 1, 5, 1; MS. II, 7, 5; III, 1, 6.

Verse 2

Note 1. Comp. VII, 1, 21. tánaye nítye; X, 39, 14. nítyam ná sûnúm tánayam dádhânâ*h*, and besides II, 26, 3. *g*ánena . . . visá̂ . . . *g*ánmanâ . . . putraí*h*; Hirzel, Gleichnisse und Metaphern im Rig-veda, 77.

Verse 3.

Note 1. For this expression, compare IV, 19, 8; IX, 71, 7; X, 31, 7, and especially III, 6, 7; VI, 39, 4.

Note 2. The poet compares himself and his friends with the mythical priestly tribe of the U*s*i*g*s (Bergaigne, Religion Védique, I, 57 seq.), using, as it seems, at the same time the word u*s*í*g*a*h* in its adjective sense 'the willing ones.'

Note 3. The Padapâ*th*a is right in giving râyé; comp. VIII, 26, 13. *s*ubhé *k*akrâte.

Verse 4.

Note 1. Is the text correct? I think that pâyó*h* should be corrected into pâyo or pâyú*h*: 'the leader and protector of the first mighty sacrifice.' The mistake may have been caused by the genitives which surround the word.

Verse 5.

Note 1. Geldner (Vedische Studien, I, 160) translates this hemistich: 'Die vielen sicheren Zufluchtsorte (= Opferplätze) bis zu den Göttern erleuchtend als Weiser, o Sänger.' I do not believe that *s*árma is the object of dī́dyâna*h*; and 'Zufluchtsorte = Opferplätze' is too much in the style of Sâya*n*a. I take á*kkh*idrâ *s*árma as depending on abhí vakshi; comp. I, 34, 6. tridhá̂tu *s*árma vahatam.

Note 2. For abhí vakshi vá̂*g*am, comp. III, 30, 11; VI, 21, 12.

Note 3. On suméka, comp. Windisch, Festgruss an Boehtlingk, 114.

MANDALA III, HYMN 16.

ASHTAKA III, ADHYÂYA 1, VARGA 16.

1. This Agni rules over abundance in valiant men, over great happiness. He rules over wealth consisting in offspring and cows; he rules over the killing of foes.

2. O Maruts[1], ye men, cling to this furtherer[2] who possesses joy-furthering boons—(the Maruts) who[3] in battles overcome ill-minded (foes), who have deceived the enemy[4] day by day.

3. As such, O bounteous Agni, prepare[1] us riches[2] and wealth in valiant men, which, O highly glorious one, may be most exalted, rich in offspring, free from plagues, and powerful.

4. The maker who victoriously (stands) over all beings, the maker who makes the praise arrive among the gods[1]: he stands firm among the gods, among the host of heroes, firm also in the praise of men.

5. Give us not up, Agni, to want of thought[1] nor to want of heroes nor to want of cows, O son of strength, nor to the scoffer. Drive away hostile powers[2].

6. Help us at this sacrifice, O blessed one, with mighty gain which is accompanied by offspring, O Agni! Let us be united with greater, gladdening, glorious wealth, O thou of mighty splendour!

NOTES.

The same *Ri*shi. The metre is Pragâtha, each Pragâtha distich being composed of one B*ri*hatî and one Satob*ri*hatî. The position of the Sûkta in the collection and the opening words of verse 3 show that the three Pragâthas are not independent. but form one hymn.—Verse 1 = SV. I, 60.

Verse 2.

Note 1. Comp. VII, 18, 25. imám nara*h* maruta*h* sa*s*-*k*ata ánu.

Note 2. The passages which Grassmann gives for the meaning of v*rí*dh, 'stärkend, erquickend,' I, 167, 4; X, 89, 10, are quite doubtful. Probably we should have to alter the accent and read v*ri*dhám.

Note 3. The relative clause seems to refer to the Maruts, not to the goods (rấya*h*).

Note 4. Comp. VI, 46, 10. yé . . . *s*átrum âdabhú*h*.

Verse 3.

Note 1. Literally, 'sharpen.'

Note 2. The genitive seems, as is also Prof. Ludwig's opinion, to be the partitive genitive, so that the literal meaning would be: 'Prepare us (a deal) of riches and of wealth,' &c. Comp. píba sutásya, 'drink of the pressed Soma,' &c.

Verse 4.

Note 1. On *k*ákri*h* devéshu ấ dúva*h*, comp. IV, 2, 9; VIII, 31, 9.

Verse 5.

Note 1. On ámati, comp. above, III, 8, 2, note.

Note 2. Comp. VI, 59, 8. ápa dvéshâ*m*si ấ k*ri*tam.

MANDALA III, HYMN 17.

ASHTAKA III, ADHYÂYA 1, VARGA 17.

1. He who is inflamed after the primitive ordinances, is anointed with ointments[1], the giver of all treasures, he whose hair is flame, whose stately robe is ghee, the purifier, skilled in sacrifice, Agni—that he may sacrifice to the gods.

2. As thou hast performed, O Agni, the Hotri's duty for the Earth, as thou hast done it for Heaven, O Gâtavedas, full of intelligence, in the same way sacrifice with this offering to the gods. Prosper this sacrifice to-day as thou hast done for Manus.

3. Thou hast three lives, O Gâtavedas, and three births from the Dawn[1], O Agni! Being wise, sacrifice with these to the favour of the gods, and bring luck and welfare to the sacrificer.

4. Praising Agni full of splendour, full of beauty, we adore thee, O Gâtavedas, deserving to be magnified. Thee the gods have made their messenger, their steward[1], and carrier of offerings, the navel of immortality.

5. O Agni, the Hotri who before thee was an excellent sacrificer, who verily[1] sat down and brought luck by himself[2]: sacrifice according to his rules, O intelligent one, and set down our sacrifice at the feast of the gods.

NOTES.

The *Ri*shi is Kata Vaisvâmitra, the metre Trish*t*ubh.—Verse 1 = TB. I, 2, 1, 10. Verse 3 = TB. III, 2, 11, 2;

MS. IV, 11, 1; 12, 5. Verse 4 = TB. III, 6, 9, 1; MS. IV, 13, 5.

Verse 1.

Note 1. Possibly the poet intended to allude also to the other meaning of aktúbhi*h*, which means both 'ointments' and 'nights.' The nights render Agni conspicuous and anoint (a*ñg*) him as it were with beauty. I do not believe that the existence of a Vedic word aktú, 'ointment,' should be denied; cf. Bechtel, Nachrichten d. Göttinger Ges. d. Wiss. 1894, p. 398.

Verse 3.

Note 1. See Bergaigne, Religion Védique, II, 14. Prof. Max Müller translates: Three lives are thine, the dawns are thy three birthplaces, or three dawns are thy birthplaces.

Verse 4.

Note 1. See above, I, 58, 7, note 1.

Verse 5.

Note 1. Literally, 'doubly.' Grassmann is right in observing that the Vedic poets show a certain predilection for the word dvitấ when speaking of Agni's being established and doing his work at the sacrifice. Prof. Max Müller thinks of Agni's two homes, earth and heaven.

Note 2. On the Hot*ri* more ancient than Agni, comp. Bergaigne, Religion Védique, I, 109. Probably this simply refers to the Agni or the fire used at former sacrifices.

MAN*D*ALA III, HYMN 18.

ASH*T*AKA III, ADHYÂYA 1, VARGA 18.

1. Be kind, O Agni, when we approach thee, as a friend a friend, as parents[1], a straight leader. For full of deceit are the tribes of men: burn thou against (all) malign powers so that they turn back.

2. Burn, O Agni, the nearer enemies, burn the curse of the distant evil-doer. Burn, O Vasu, seeing the unseen ones. May thy never-ageing, never-tiring flames[1] spread out.

3. Wishing for (thy blessings), O Agni, by fuel and ghee I offer this sacrificial food for (the attainment of) advancing power and of strength; worshipping thee with my spell as far as I have power (I offer) this divine prayer for the attainment of hundred(fold blessings).

4. (Shining) forth with thy flame, O son of strength, praised (by us), bestow mighty vigour on those who toil for thee, bright luck and welfare, O Agni, on the Vi*s*vâmitras! We have cleaned thy body many times.

5. Give us treasures, O best gainer of riches: such indeed art thou, Agni, when thou hast been kindled. In the blessed praiser's house thou hast placed, together with wealth, thy mighty(?) arms[1], thy marvellous shapes.

NOTES.

The same *Ri*shi and metre.—Verse 2 = TÂ. IV, 5, 5. Verse 3 = AV. III, 15, 3.

Verse 1.

Note 1. It is rather strange that Agni is compared with the two parents. Generally it is the two A*s*vins, or Heaven and Earth, or the pair of Indra and Varu*n*a, &c., who are compared with father and mother (see Hirzel, Gleichnisse und Metaphern im Rigveda, 71 seq.). No doubt in our verse the dual was chosen on account of the metre.—I do not think that Bollensen (Orient und Occident, II, 473) and Kirste (Bezzenberger's Beiträge, XVI, 297) are right in believing that a dative of pit*ri* is found here, and in translating: 'as a good (son) to his father.'

Verse 2.

Note 1. The meaning of ayā́sa*h* is doubtful; comp. Brugmann in Kuhn's Zeitschrift, XXIV, 24 seq.; M. M., vol. xxxii, p. 371 (VI, 66, 5); von Bradke, Festgruss an Roth, 124.

Verse 5.

Note 1. On s*ri*prá, see I, 96, 3, note 3. Karásna must mean something like 'arm,' though the exact meaning is doubtful. In VIII, 32, 10 the compound s*ri*prákarasna occurs. Prof. Max Müller writes: 'Thou hast brightly assumed a body with soft arms or with stretched-out arms, if we do not read s*ri*prakarasnâ.'

MANDALA III, HYMN 19.

ASHTAKA III, ADHYÂYA 1, VARGA 19.

1. I choose Agni as Hotri at this sacrificial meal, the clever sage all-knowing and not foolish. May he, the excellent sacrificer, sacrifice for us amid the host of the gods; may he obtain liberal boons (for us) for the sake of wealth and strength.

2. To thee, O Agni, I stretch forth the (ladle) rich in sacrificial food, splendid, full of gifts, full of ghee. From left to right, choosing the host of the gods [1], he has established the sacrifice with gifts and goods [2].

3. Whoever is favoured by thee, is blessed with the sharpest spirit. Favour him with good offspring, O god rich in favours [1]! Agni, may we, (dwelling) in the copiousness of manliest wealth, be rich in perfect praise of thee, the Vasu.

4. On thee indeed, O Agni, sacrificing men have put many faces of (thee) the god [1]. Bring hither then the host of the gods, O youngest one, when thou wilt sacrifice to-day to the divine host [2].

5. When the gods will anoint thee as the Hotri at the sacrificial meal making thee sit down for the sacrifice, be thou here, O Agni, our furtherer, and bestow glory on our bodies.

NOTES.

The *Ri*shi is Gâthin Kausika, the metre Trishtubh.—Verse 3 = TS. I, 3, 14, 6; MS. IV, 14, 15.

Verse 2.

Note 1. Comp. below, IV, 6, 3. This parallel passage shows that pradakshi*n*ít belongs to urâ*n*á*h*, not to a*s*ret. Agni is represented as choosing, i.e. inviting the host of the gods by moving around the sacrificial food from left to right. See concerning the Paryagnikara*n*a, which seems to be alluded to, Hillebrandt, Neu- und Vollmondsopfer, 42 seq.

Note 2. Or, 'with the (divine) givers and with the Vasus.'

Verse 3.

Note 1. Boehtlingk-Roth seem to be right in reading *s*iksho. Comp. VIII, 52, 8. yásmai tvám . . . *s*íksho *s*íkshasi dâ*s*úshe.

Verse 4.

Note 1. They have inflamed many fires, each of which is a face of the god Agni.

Note 2. Or, 'that thou mayest sacrifice,' &c. See Delbrück, Syntaktische Forschungen, I, 148.

MANDALA III, HYMN 20.

ASHTAKA III, ADHYÂYA 1, VARGA 20.

1. The carrier (of the gods)[1] calls by his hymns Agni, Ushas (dawn), the two Asvins, Dadhikrâ[2] at daybreak. May the gods rich in light, unanimously longing for our sacrifice, hear us.

2. Agni, threefold is thy strength; three are thy abodes; three are thy many tongues, O thou who art born in *Ri*ta! And three, O Agni, are thy bodies beloved by the gods. With these protect our prayers unremittingly.

3[1]. Agni! Many are the names, O *G*âtavedas, of thee the immortal one, O self-dependent god! And whatever the secret powers of the powerful[2] are, thou all-enlivener, in thee they have placed together (those) many (powers), O (god) after whose relations men ask[3].

4. Agni is the divine leader of the divine tribes like Bhaga, the guardian of the seasons[1], the righteous. May He, the killer of V*ri*tra[2], the ancient one, the possessor of all wealth, bring the singer across all troubles.

5. I invite hither[1] Dadhikrâ[2], Agni, and the goddess Ushas, B*ri*haspati and the god Savit*ri*, the Asvins, Mitra and Varu*n*a and Bhaga, the Vasus, Rudras, and Âdityas.

NOTES.

The same *Ri*shi and metre.—Verse 2 = TS. II, 4, 11, 2; III, 2, 11, 1; MS. II, 4, 4. Verse 3 = TS. III, 1, 11, 6.

Verse 1.

Note 1. The 'carrier' of the gods is the Hot*ri*. See above, I, 127, 8, note 1, and compare the article of Dr. Neisser quoted there. See also M. M., vol. xxxii, pp. 40–43 (I, 6, 5).

Note 2. On Dadhikrâ or Dadhikrâvan, the deified horse of Trasadasyu, see Pischel, Vedische Studien, I, 124; Ludwig, vol. iv, p. 79; H. O., Religion des Veda, 71. Prof. Max Müller writes, 'It seems to me some form of Agni generally in company with matutinal gods.'

Verse 3.

Note 1. The reader who compares this passage with 19, 4, will observe a general resemblance pointing to the conclusion that both verses belong to the same author.

Note 2. Mâyấ*h* mâyínâm : comp. concerning the idea of mâyấ, H. O., Religion des Veda, 163, 294.

Note 3. With p*ri*sh*t*abandhu, comp. bandhup*ríkh*, bandhveshá.

Verse 4.

Note 1. Perhaps *ri*tu-pấ*h* should be changed into *ri*ta-pấ*h*: 'the god who protects the *Ri*ta, the righteous.'

Note 2. Or 'the killer of foes.'

Verse 5.

Note 1. Possibly we have to read, on account of the metre, ihá hve.

Note 2. See above, verse 1, note 1.

MANDALA III, HYMN 21.

ASHTAKA III, ADHYÂYA 1, VARGA 21.

1. Take this our sacrifice to the immortals; accept graciously these offerings, O *G*âtavedas. O Agni, partake of the drops of fat and ghee, O Hot*ri*, having sat down as the first.

2. To thee, O purifier, the drops of fat mixed with ghee drip down. O (god) who followest thy own ordinances, give us the best boon for this feast to which the gods come eagerly.

3. To thee, the priest, O Agni, (belong) the drops dripping with ghee, O good one! Thou art kindled as the best *Ri*shi. Be a furtherer of our sacrifice!

4. For thee, O liberal one[1], full of power, the drops of fat and ghee drip down, O Agni! Praised by the sages thou hast come hither with mighty light. Accept graciously the offerings, O wise one!

5. For thee the richest fat[1] has been taken out from the midst. We give it to thee. On thy skin, O Vasu, the drops drip down. Accept them eagerly for each of the gods.

NOTES.

The same *Ri*shi. Verses 1 and 4 are Trish*t*ubh, verses 2 and 3 Anush*t*ubh, verse 5 Virâ*d*rûpâ Satob*ri*hatî.

The hymn belongs to the ritual of the animal sacrifice. It has to be recited, according to the prescription of the later Vedic texts, while the vapâ (omentum) of the sacrificial animal is roasted and the drops of fat drip down from it. See Schwab, Das Altindische Thieropfer, p. 114

seq., and the Sûtra texts quoted by him (for instance, Â*s*valâyana *S*rautasûtra III, 4, 1). Bergaigne (Recherches sur l'Histoire de la Liturgie Védique, 18) seems to be right in observing: 'Bien qu'il (l'hymne III, 21) soit récité tout d'une pièce dans le pa*s*ubandha, pendant la cuisson de la vapâ, pour les gouttes de graisse qui tombent dans le feu sa complexité métrique . . . le trahit et nous y fait voir une simple collection de vers liturgiques.' It may be observed, however, that the two last verses seem to form a distich of an irregular Pragâtha type; comp. H. O., Die Hymnen des Rigveda, vol. i, p. 118.—Verses 1–5 = TB. III, 6, 7, 1. 2; MS. IV, 13, 5.

Verse 4.

Note 1. On the word ádhrigu, cf. Bloomfield, American Or. Soc. Proceedings, March, 1894, p. cxxiii.

Verse 5.

Note 1. Vapâkhya*m* havi*h*, Sâya*n*a. This explanation is evidently correct. After the sacrificial animal has been killed, the omentum, which is very rich in fat, is first drawn out of its body and offered. See H. O., Die Religion des Veda, 360 seq.

MANDALA III, HYMN 22.

ASHTAKA III, ADHYÂYA 1, VARGA 22.

1. This is that Agni with whom the desiring Indra took the pressed Soma into his body. Having obtained thousandfold strength like a horse, a racer[1], thou art praised, O *G*âtavedas!

2[1]. Thy splendour, O Agni, which dwells in heaven and on earth, in the plants, O worshipful one, and in the waters, wherewith thou hast spread through the wide air—that light of thine is fierce, waving[2], man-beholding.

3. Agni, thou goest to the floods of heaven. Thou hast spoken to the gods who are liberal (?)[1]. (Thou goest) to the waters which (dwell) on high in the ether of the sun, and to those which approach below.

4. May the fires of the soil united with those on the hill-sides[1], without guile graciously accept our sacrifice and plentiful food free from all plague.

5 = III, 1, 23.

NOTES.

The same *R*ishi. The metre is Trish*t*ubh, except in verse 4 which is Anush*t*ubh.—A conjecture on the ritual use for which the hymn has been composed, see in the note on verse 4.—Verses 1–5 = VS. XII, 47–51; TS. IV, 2, 4, 2. 3; MS. II, 7, 11.—A sort of commentary on this hymn is found in the *S*atapatha Brâhma*n*a VII, 1, 1, 22 seq.

Verse 1.

Note 1. In the traditional text the words, 'a horse, a racer,' are accusatives. But it is the átya who attains (san) the vấga and who is called vâgín (comp. M. M., vol. xxxii, pp. 116, 442, and on sápti, ibid. p. 102): see I, 130, 6; III, 2, 7; 38, 1 (V, 30, 14; IX, 93, 1; 96, 15, &c.); VII, 24, 5; IX, 43, 5; 82, 2; 85, 5; 86, 3; 96, 20; X, 96, 10 (I, 52, 1, and III, 2, 3 do not contradict this). Pischel (Vedische Studien, I, 105) believes that átyam ná stands for átya*h* ná, which seems impossible to me. But I think that we should correct the text and read átya*h* ná sápti*h*. The preceding accusatives have caused the blunder.

Verse 2.

Note 1. Comp. Grassmann, Kuhn's Zeitschrift, XVI, 165.
Note 2. Comp. ketú*h* ar*n*avá*h* sū́ryasya, VII, 63, 2.

Verse 3.

Note 1. In the translation of dhísh*n*ya I have followed Pischel, Vedische Studien, II, 87, though this translation is quite uncertain. Should the meaning be: 'the gods who dwell on the dhish*n*ya altars'?

Verse 4.

Note 1. Agni purîshya, i.e. the fire dwelling in the soil (comp. Roth in Kuhn's Zeitschrift, XXVI, 64), is mentioned very frequently in the Mantras belonging to the Agni*k*ayana, i.e. to the construction of the brick altar. Agni is considered as residing in the soil used at that rite. Now in the Yagus texts the whole of our hymn occurs among the texts to be recited at the Agni*k*ayana (Taitt. Sa*m*h. IV, 2, 4, 2, &c.; comp. also Â*s*valâyana *S*rautasûtra IV, 8, 20). Perhaps we may conjecture, therefore, that the Agni*k*ayana rite in its simplest form was known already in the Rig-veda period, and that our hymn was destined for it.—The prâva*n*a fires (fires dwelling on the hill-sides) may be the fires dwelling in the rivers which run down the prava*n*as or descents.

MA*ND*ALA III, HYMN 23.

ASH*T*AKA III, ADHYÂYA 1, VARGA 23.

1. Produced by attrition, well preserved in his abode, the young sage, the leader of worship, Agni ever young in the forests[1] that grow old—*G*âtavedas, has here assumed immortality[2].

2. The two Bharatas[1], Deva*s*ravas and Devavâta, in the midst of wealth have produced by attrition Agni the skilful (god). Agni, look forth with mighty wealth, and then be[2] for us a guide of food day by day.

3[1]. The ten fingers have brought him to the birth, the ancient, beloved (Agni), well born in his mothers[2]. Praise, O Deva*s*ravas, the Agni of Devavâta who[3] should be the lord of people.

4. I have laid[1] thee[2] down in the best (place) of the earth[3], in the place of I*l*â[3], in the auspiciousness of days. O Agni, as the god who has belonged to Manus[4], shine with wealth on the D*ri*shadvatî, on the Âpayâ, on the Sarasvatî.

5 = III, 1, 23.

NOTES.

The *Ri*shis are Deva*s*ravas Bhârata and Devavâta Bhârata (see verse 2); the metre is Trish*t*ubh (verse 5 Satob*ri*hatî).—No verse occurs in the other Sa*m*hitâs.

Verse 1.

Note 1. The 'forests' are the fuel. 'Does the poet mean: Never consumed in the consumed wood or forests,

i. e. the fire burns and is kept alive while the wood is burnt up?' M. M.

Note 2. Or, 'he has received the drink of immortality'—which may refer to the ghee offered in the fire.

Verse 2.

Note 1. On the tribe of the Bharatas having their seats, as verse 4 seems to show, on the borders of the Sarasvatî and of the D*ri*shadvatî, see H. O., Buddha (first edition), 413 seq.

Note 2. This is an imperative in -tât, signifying, as Delbrück has shown (Syntaktische Forschungen, III, 2 seq.; Altindische Syntax, 363), an injunction to be carried out after something else has been done or has happened. Agni is first to look about (ví pa*s*ya), and shall then become (bhavatât) a guide of food, i. e. he shall lead plenty of food to the worshipper's house.—Prof. Max Müller translates ishấm netấ, 'a guide to food.'

Verse 3.

Note 1. Should this Satob*ri*hatî, standing alone among Trish*t*ubh verses, be considered as forming a distich together with verse 2? Comp. H. O., Die Hymnen des Rigveda, vol. i, p. 102, note 7.

Note 2. The woods.

Note 3. Agni, not Devavâta, is referred to.

Verse 4.

Note 1. Or, 'he has laid.' The form may be first or third person, present or perfect.

Note 2. Agni is addressed.

Note 3. The best place of the earth, the place of I*l*â (i. e. of the nourishment coming from the cow, of the ghee offered into Agni) is the sacrificial ground or more especially the spot on which the sacrificial fire is established.

Note 4. Or 'to men.' The Padapâ*th*a has mấnushe, but mấnusha*h* seems more probable.

MA*N**D*ALA III, HYMN 24.

ASH*T*AKA III, ADHYÂYA 1, VARGA 24.

1. Agni, be victorious in battles; thrust away the plotters. Difficult to overcome, overcoming malign powers, bestow splendour on (the worshipper) who fits out the sacrifice as a vehicle[1].

2. Agni, thou art kindled with nourishment[1], the immortal offerer of a feast (to the gods). Accept graciously our worship.

3. Agni, wakeful one, son of strength, into whom offerings are poured, sit down with thy splendour on this sacrificial grass of mine.

4. Agni, together with all Agnis, with the gods exalt our prayers and those who are respectful at the sacrifices.

5. Agni, give wealth to the worshipper, abundance in valiant men; further us[1] that we may be rich in sons.

NOTES.

The *R*ishi is Vi*s*vâmitra, the metre Gâyatrî, the first verse Anush*t*ubh. On this combination of a beginning Anush*t*ubh with Gâyatrîs following, comp. H. O., Die Hymnen des Rig-veda, vol. i, p. 148.—Verse 1 = VS. IX, 37. Verse 5 = TS. II, 2, 12, 6; MS. IV, 12, 2; 14, 6.

Verse 1.

Note 1. See above, III, 8, 3, and on *yagñávâhas*, I, 127, 8, note 1; Bergaigne, Religion Védique, II, 287, note 2.

Verse 2.

Note 1. *I/ấ*: especially designating the nourishment coming from the cow (personified as I*/*â), such as ghee.

Verse 5.

Note 1. Literally, 'sharpen us.'

MA*ND*ALA III, HYMN 25.

ASH*T*AKA III, ADHYÂYA 1, VARGA 25.

1. Agni, thou art for ever the wise son of Heaven and of the Earth, the all-wealthy one. In thy peculiar way[1] sacrifice here to the gods, O intelligent one!

2. Agni, the knowing, obtains (for his worshipper) heroic powers; he obtains (for him) strength, being busy for the sake of immortality. Bring then the gods hither, O (Agni), rich in food.

3. Agni, the wise, shines on Heaven and Earth, the two immortal goddesses who encompass all people—he who rules through his strength, and who is full of light through adoration.

4. Agni and Indra, come hither to the sacrifice in the house of the worshipper rich in pressed (Soma), never failing, ye two gods, at the drink of Soma.

5. Agni, thou art kindled in the house of the waters, (our) own (god), O son of strength, *G*âtavedas, who exaltest the abodes (in which thou dwellest) by thy blessing.

NOTES.

The same *Ri*shi. Metre, Virâ*g*.—Verse 4=MS. IV, 12, 6.

Verse 1.

Note 1. On *ri*dhak, see Pischel, Vedische Studien, II, 45.

MAṆḌALA III, HYMN 26.

ASHṬAKA III, ADHYÂYA 1, VARGA 26-27.

1. With our offerings revering in our mind Agni Vaiśvânara, the follower of truth, the finder of the sun—we, the Kuśikas[1], desirous of goods, call with our prayers the god who gives rain, the charioteer, the cheerful.

2. We call that beautiful Agni to help us, Vaiśvânara, Mâtariśvan the praiseworthy[1]; we the men (call) Bṛihaspati[2] for (the worship) of the divine host, the priest who hears us, the guest who swiftly glides along.

3. Vaiśvânara, neighing like a horse, is kindled by the women[1], by the Kuśikas, from age to age; may this Agni give us abundance in valiant men and in horses and treasures, he who wakes among the immortals.

4. May the Vâgas[1] come forward, the Agnis with their powers. United[2] they have harnessed the spotted deer for their triumphal procession[3]. The Maruts, mightily growing, the all-wealthy, make the mountains tremble, the unbeguiled ones.

5. The Maruts who possess the beauty of Agni[1], belong to all races of men. We implore their fierce, strong help. They are tumultuous, the sons of Rudra, clothed in rain, hot-spirited like lions[2], givers of rain.

6. We implore with our best praises every host, every troop (of the Maruts)[1], the splendour of Agni,

the power of the Maruts. With the spotted deer as horses [2], with gifts that cannot be taken away, they go to the sacrifice wise in the (sacrificial) ordinances [3].

7. Agni am I, by birth *G*âtavedas. Ghee is my eye; (the drink of) immortality is in my mouth. The threefold song [1] traversing the aerial space, the imperishable Gharma [2], the sacrificial food am I by name.

8. With three purifying strainers he (Agni) purified the song, with his heart the thought, discovering the light. The mightiest treasure he produced by the powers of his own nature, and then he looked over heaven and earth.

9. Carry him who is the inexhaustible spring with a hundred rills, who has knowledge of prayers (?), the father of (every speech) that should be uttered, the roaring one [1], gladly excited in the lap of his parents—carry him the truth-speaking across (all dangers), O ye two worlds!

NOTES.

Vi*s*vâmitra is the *Ri*shi of this Sûkta with the exception of the seventh verse of which the Âtman or Brahman is the *Ri*shi. The metre is *G*agatî verses 1–6, Trish*t*ubh verses 7–9.—Verse 5 = TB. II, 7, 12, 3. Verse 7 = VS. XVIII, 66; MS. IV, 12, 5.

The position of this Sûkta in the collection shows that it is to be divided into three independent hymns. This is confirmed by the metre, the first and second of these three hymns being in *G*agatî, the third in Trish*t*ubh, and also by the contents: the first hymn is addressed to Agni Vai*s*vânara, the second to Agni accompanied by the Maruts, the third contains mystical speculations about the nature and the deeds of Agni.

Verse 1.

Note 1. The Ku*s*ikas are identical with the Vi*s*vâmitras, or possibly the latter form one branch of the Ku*s*ikas; see H. O., Zeitschrift der Deutschen Morgenländischen Gesellschaft, XLII, 209.

Verse 2.

Note 1. On the relation of Mâtari*s*van to Agni, see above, I, 96, 4, note 1.

Note 2. B*ri*haspati, though in his origin distinct from Agni, is here identified with him, like Mâtari*s*van.

Verse 3.

Note 1. By the ten fingers. Comp. above, I, 71, 1.

Verse 4.

Note 1. I adopt the interpretation of Bergaigne (Religion Védique, II, 405, note 1) and Pischel (Vedische Studien, I, 46). Vấ*g*â*h* seems to be the proper name synonym with *Ri*bháva*h*; the Maruts may be called Vấ*g*â*h* as they are called several times *Ri*bhukshá*n*a*h*. But it is possible that we should have to translate simply, 'May the powers of strength,' &c.; comp. below, 27, 1.

Note 2. Possibly we have to supply, 'united with their spotted deer, with their beauty,' &c.; see II, 36, 2. ya*gñ*aí*h* sámmi*s*lâ*h* p*rí*shatîbhi*h* *ri*sh*tí*bhi*h*; VII, 56, 6. *s*riyấ sámmi*s*lâ*h*. Or the meaning may be, 'the Maruts united with Agni or with the Agnis;' comp. I, 166, 11. sámmi*s*lâ*h* índre.

Note 3. On *s*ubhé, see M. M., I, 87, 3, note 2 (vol. xxxii, p. 162).

Verse 5.

Note 1. Or, they receive their beauty through Agni.

Note 2. Of heshákratu the probable explanation has been given by Pischel, Vedische Studien, I, 48. See also von Bradke, Kuhn's Zeitschrift, XXVIII, 297.

Verse 6.

Note 1. Comp. V, 53, 11, vol. xxxii, p. 320.
Note 2. Comp. II, 34, 4, vol. xxxii, p. 302, note 5.
Note 3. The text has vidátheshu.

Verse 7.

Note 1. Comp. VIII, 51, 4. arkám saptásîrshâ*n*am . . . tridhā́tum uttamé padé. Is the song called tridhā́tu because it is sung by the three Udgât*ri*s (singers)? Or because it generally comprises three verses (see H. O., Zeitschrift der Deutschen Morgenländischen Gesellschaft, XXXVIII, 453)?

Note 2. The Gharma is the offering of hot milk brought to the A*s*vins. On the probable meaning of this offering, see H. O., Religion des Veda, 447 seq.

Verse 9.

Note 1. The translation of me*l*í (comp. IV, 7, 11; Atharva-veda XI, 7, 5; Taitt. Sa*m*h. V, 7, 8, 1) is quite conjectural.

MA*ND*ALA III, HYMN 27.

ASH*T*AKA III, ADHYÂYA 1, VARGA 28–30.

1. Forward (goes) your[1] strength tending heavenward, rich in offerings, with the (ladle) full of ghee. To the gods goes (the worshipper) desirous of their favour.

2. I magnify[1] with prayer Agni who has knowledge of prayers (?), the accomplisher of sacrifice, who hears us, and in whom (manifold wealth) has been laid down.

3. O Agni, may we be able to bridle thee the strong god[1]; may we overcome (all) hostile powers.

4. Agni, inflamed at the sacrifice, the purifier who should be magnified, whose hair is flame—him we approach (with prayers).

5. With his broad stream of light the immortal Agni, clothed in ghee, well served with oblations, is the carrier of offerings at the sacrifice.

6. Holding the (sacrificial) ladles, performing the sacrifice they have with right thought pressingly brought Agni hither[1] for help.

7. The Hot*ri*, the immortal god goes in front with his secret power[1], instigating the sacrifices[2].

8. The strong (horse, i.e. Agni) is set at the races. He is led forth at the sacrifices, the priest, the accomplisher of sacrifice.

9. He has been produced[1] by prayer, the excellent one. I have established[2] him, the germ of beings, for ever the father of Daksha[3].

10. I have laid thee down [1], the excellent one, with the nourishment [2] of Daksha, O thou who art produced by power, O Agni, thee the resplendent one, O U*s*ig [3].

11. The priests, eager to set to work the *Ri*ta [1], kindle with quick strength Agni the governor [2], him who crosses the waters [3].

12. I magnify [1] the child of vigour at this sacrifice, who shines under the heaven, the thoughtful Agni.

13. He who should be magnified and adored, who is visible through the darkness, Agni, the manly, is kindled [1].

14. Agni, the manly, is kindled, he who draws hither the gods like a horse. The (worshippers) rich in offerings magnify him.

15. We the manly ones will kindle thee the manly (god), O manly Agni who shinest mightily.

NOTES.

The same *Ri*shi. The metre is Gâyatrî.—The position of the hymn in the collection shows that it is to be divided into T*rik*as, and this is confirmed by the ritual use of several of these T*rik*as (see Bergaigne, Recherches sur l'Histoire de la Liturgie Védique, 19, note 1). Some of the T*rik*as at least, however, do not seem to form independent hymns; verse 10 very probably stands in connection with verse 9, and the same seems to be the case with verses 12 and 13. Ludwig (IV, 305) and Bergaigne (loc. cit.) consider the whole Sûkta as a collection of Sâmidhenîs or verses to be recited for each piece of wood thrown into the fire. Comp. Hillebrandt, Neu- und Vollmondsopfer, 77.—Verse 1

= TS. II, 5, 7, 2; TB. III, 5, 2, 1; MS. I, 6, 1; IV, 14, 3. Verses 2, 3 = TB. II, 4, 2, 4. 5; MS. IV, 11, 2. Verse 4 = TS. II, 5, 8, 6; TB. III, 5, 2, 3. Verses 5–6 = TB. III, 6, 1, 3; MS. IV, 10, 1 (verse 5 = MS. IV, 11, 2). Verses 7–9 = SV. II, 827–829. Verses 13–15 = SV. II, 888–890; TB. III, 5, 2, 2; AV. XX, 102, 1–3.

Verse 1.

Note 1. Of the priests and sacrificers?

Verse 2.

Note 1. The text has î*l*e.

Verse 3.

Note 1. Comp. above, II, 5, 1.

Verse 6.

Note 1. Comp. IV, 17, 18. vayám hí ấ te *k*akr*i*má sabấdha*h*.

Verse 7.

Note 1. Mâyáyâ: comp. H. O., Religion des Veda, 163, 294.

Note 2. Vidáthâni: comp. I, 31, 6, note 2.

Verse 9.

Note 1. This seems to mean, 'he has been set to work.'

Note 2. Ấ dadhe must be first person (comp. ní dadhe, verse 10) for the bhûtấnâm gárbha*h* is Agni.

Note 3. Or, the father of intelligence. Daksha is the personified intelligence. Comp. vol. xxxii, p. 245 seq.; Bergaigne, Religion Védique, III, 93 seq.

Verse 10.

Note 1. See above, III, 23, 4.

Note 2. The text has i*l*ấ, the same word as in 24, 2.—Prof. Max Müller observes, 'Could it be, ni tvâ dadhe i*l*â, I have placed thee on the altar with nutriment, son of the strength of Daksha?'

Note 3. Or, 'the willing one.'

Verse 11.

Note 1. 'Setting to work the Right (*Ri*ta)' means here 'performing the sacrifice.' The sacrifice is considered as a sphere especially pervaded by the power of *Ri*ta. Comp. H. O., Religion des Veda, 197.

Note 2. Yantúram (comp. VIII, 19, 2. agním î*l*ishva yantúram; Lanman, 486) must be the same as yantā́ram (comp. μάρτυρ? [M. M.] See de Saussure, Mémoire sur le Système Primitif des Voyelles, p. 207; but comp. also Kretschmer, Kuhn's Zeitschrift, XXXI, p. 447). To me it seems to be an accommodation to aptúram, facilitated probably by the influence of the genitive yantúr. See Lanman, Noun-Inflection in the Veda, p. 486; Wackernagel in Kuhn's Zeitschrift, XXV, 287.

Note 3. See Pischel, Vedische Studien, I, 122 seq.; H. O., Göttingische Gelehrte Anzeigen, 1889, p. 4 seq.

Verse 12.

Note 1. The text has î*l*e. In the same way î*l*ényaḥ verse 13, î*l*ate verse 14.

Verse 13.

Note 1. Observe sám idhyate here and verse 14, sám idhîmahi verse 15. The verses 13–15 form one T*rik*a.

MANDALA III, HYMN 28.

ASHTAKA III, ADHYÂYA 1, VARGA 31.

1. O Agni *G*âtavedas, accept graciously our offering, the sacrificial cake at the morning libation, O god who givest wealth for our prayers.

2. The sacrificial cake, O Agni, has been baked or made ready for thee: accept it graciously, O youngest (god).

3. Agni, accept eagerly the sacrificial cake which has been offered, which has stood overnight. Thou art the son of strength, established at the sacrifice.

4. At the midday libation, *G*âtavedas, accept here graciously the sacrificial cake, O sage. Agni, the wise ones do not diminish at the sacrificial distributions[1] the portion which belongs to thee, the vigorous one[2].

5. Agni, at the third libation take joyfully the sacrificial cake, O son of strength, which has been offered. And in thy admirable way place our wakeful sacrifice, blessed with treasures, before the immortal gods.

6. Agni, grown strong, O *G*âtavedas, accept graciously our offering, the sacrificial cake which has stood overnight.

NOTES.

The same *R*ishi. The metre is Gâyatrî in verses 1, 2, 6, Ush*n*ih in verse 3, Trish*t*ubh in verse 4, and *G*agatî in verse 5.—No verse occurs in the other Sa*m*hitâs.

This Sûkta and the following are, as their position at the end of the Anuvâka and the number of their verses show, later additions to the original collection. The 28th hymn contains verses destined for the offerings of sacrificial cakes to Agni at each of the three Savanas. Quite in the same way hymn 52, which also belongs to the later additions, refers to sacrificial cakes offered to Indra. The oblation of such cakes to Indra at each Savana is found also in the later Vedic ritual (comp. Kâtyâyana IX, 9, 2 seq.; Weber, Indische Studien, X, 369, 376), and several verses of III, 52 are indicated there as Puronuvâkyâ verses for those very offerings; see Â*s*valâyana *S*rautasûtra V, 4, 2. 3. After each cake-offering to Indra follows the Svish*t*ak*ri*t-oblation to Agni: and for these oblations Â*s*valâyana (loc. cit. Sûtra 6) prescribes verses 1, 4, and 5 of our hymn, according to the order of the three Savanas. From the text of the hymn it seems to be evident that verses 1–3 have been composed for the first, verse 4 for the second, and verses 5–6 for the third Savana. With this distribution the change of the metres evidently stands in connection. In accordance with the theories of the later Vedic theologians, we have here the Gâyatrî as the characteristic metre of the first, the Trish*t*ubh of the second, the *G*agatî of the third Savana.

Comp. also Â*s*valâyana VI, 5, 25, and the very ingenious but at the same time somewhat hazardous observations of Bergaigne, Recherches sur l'Histoire de la Liturgie Védique, 16 seq.

Verse 4.

Note 1. The text has vidátheshu.

Note 2. Comp. I, 36, 1, note 2.

MAṆḌALA III, HYMN 29.

ASHṬAKA III, ADHYÂYA 1, VARGA 32–34.

1[1]. This is the support on which the rubbing (for producing the fire) is performed[2]; the creative organ[3] has been prepared. Bring hither the house-wife[4]; let us produce Agni by rubbing in the old way.

2. In the two fire-sticks dwells *G*âtavedas, as the germ (lies) safe in pregnant women—Agni who should be magnified[1] day by day by wakeful men who bring offerings.

3. Place it[1] skilfully into her who lies extended[2]. Having conceived she has quickly given birth to the manly one. He whose summit is red—bright is his splendour—the son of I*l*â has been born in the (due) way[3].

4. In the place of I*l*â, on the navel of the earth we will lay thee down, *G*âtavedas, that thou, O Agni, mayst carry the offerings (to the gods).

5. Rub, ye men, the truthful sage, the wise, the immortal, the fair-faced. Bring forth, ye men, Agni, the banner of sacrifice, the first in the front, the gracious one.

6. When they produce him by rubbing with their arms, he shines forth flaming in the wood like a red race-horse. Like the bright one on the path of the A*s*vins[1] the unrestrained (Agni) spares the stones, burning the grass[2].

7. Agni, when born, shines forth resplendent, the racer, the priest, praised by the sages, the giver of rain, whom the gods placed in the sacrifices, to be

magnified, as the omniscient carrier of the sacrificial offerings.

8. Sit down, O Hot*ri*, in the space which is thine, as the knowing one. Place the sacrifice in the abode of good works (i.e. on the altar). Eagerly longing for the gods thou shalt worship the gods by offerings. Agni, bestow mighty vigour on the sacrificer.

9. Produce a mighty[1] smoke, ye friends. Without fail go forward towards strength. This Agni is the conqueror in battles, rich in valiant men, he by whom the gods have overpowered the Dasyus.

10. This is thy birth-place in due time whence born thou shonest forth; knowing it, O Agni, sit down on it, and make our prayers prosper.

11. He is called Tanûnapât as the Asura's germ. Narâ*s*a*m*sa he becomes when he is born, Mâtari*s*van when he has been shaped in the mother[1]. And he has become the rush of the wind in his swift course[2].

12. Rubbed forth by skilful rubbing, established by skilful establishing, as a sage, O Agni, perform excellent sacrifices. Sacrifice to the gods for him who is devoted to the gods[1].

13. The mortals have generated the immortal one, the . . .[1], advancing one with strong jaws. The ten unwedded sisters[2] united take care of the man (Agni) when he has been born.

14. He the god of the seven Hot*ri*s shone forth from of old, when he flamed up in his mother's lap, at her udder. Day by day the joyous one never closes his eyes, when he has been born from the Asura's (i.e. of the Heaven's ?) belly[1].

15. The onsets of (Agni) when he attacks his enemies, are like those of the Maruts. (He is) the

first-born (son) of the sacred spell. They know every (fire)[1]. The Ku*s*ikas have raised their brilliant spell; they have kindled Agni, every one in his house.

16. After we had chosen thee here to-day, O wise Hot*ri*, while this sacrifice was going on, thou hast firmly sacrificed and firmly laboured. Come to this Soma, expert and knowing!

NOTES.

The same *Ri*shi. The prevalent metre is Trish*t*ubh.—Verses 1, 4, 10, 12 are Anush*t*ubh; verses 6, 11, 14, 15, *G*agatî.

The Sûkta, which belongs to the later additions (see the note on hymn 28), consists of a number of verses and small groups of verses referring to the production of fire by the attrition of the two fire-sticks. The order in which the verses stand does not always agree with the natural order of the ritual acts.—Verse 2 = SV. I, 79. Verse 3 = VS. XXXIV, 14. Verse 4 = VS. XXXIV, 15; TS. III, 5, 11, 1; MS. I, 6, 2. 7; IV, 10, 4; 11, 1. Verse 8 = VS. XI, 35; TS. III, 5, 11, 2; IV, 1, 3, 3; MS. II, 7, 3; IV, 10, 4. Verse 10 = VS. III, 14; XII, 52; XV, 56; TS. I, 5, 5, 2; IV, 2, 4, 3; 7, 13, 5; TB. I, 2, 1, 16; II, 5, 8, 8; MS. I, 5, 1; 6, 1; AV. III, 20, 1. Verse 13 = TB. I, 2, 1, 19. Verse 16 = VS. VIII, 20; TS. I, 4, 44, 2; MS. I, 3, 38; AV. VII, 97, 1.

Verse 1.

Note 1. The verses 1–3 a, b have been translated by Muir, Original Sanskrit Texts, V, p. 209.

Note 2. On the adhimanthana*s*akala, the piece of wood on which the lower fire-stick is laid, see *S*atapatha Brâhma*n*a III, 4, 1, 20. so·dhimanthana*m* *s*akalam âdatte agner *g*anitram asîty atra hy agnir *g*âyate. Schwab, Das Altindische Thieropfer, p. 78 seq.

Note 3. Pra*g*ánana seems to be used in the concrete sense as the male organ. As such, the poet may have considered the so-called pramantha in the generation of Agni, which is described as having the shape of the male organ (Schwab, loc. cit., 78; see also Roth, Zeitschrift der Deutschen Morgenl. Gesellschaft, XLIII, 591). It does not seem very probable that the darbhapi*ñg*ûla of which Sâya*n*a thinks should be meant.

Note 4. Sâya*n*a explains this as meaning the Ara*n*i (fire-stick), i.e. the lower Ara*n*i, the receptacle of the upper fire-stick. In the Taittirîya Brâhma*n*a I, 2, 1, 13 the two Ara*n*is are addressed as mahî vi*s*patnî.

Verse 2.

Note 1. The text has î́*d*ya*h*.

Verse 3.

Note 1. The upper fire-stick or, more accurately, the pramantha.

Note 2. Comp. above, II, 10, 3. The lower Ara*n*i is alluded to, which is considered as a wife and more particularly as the nymph Urva*s*î (Kâtyâyana V, 1, 30, &c.).

Note 3. Prof. Pischel (Vedische Studien, I, 301) takes the genitive í*l*âyâ*h* as dependent on vayúne: 'wurde der Sohn geboren am Orte (Wege) der Opferspende.' To me it seems unnatural not to connect í*l*âyâ*h* with putrá*h*, which words are connected also by the Sandhi (the Sa*m*hitâ text has í*l*âyâs putró, not í*l*âyâ*h* putró).

Verse 6.

Note 1. For yā́man, cf. I, 37, 3; III, 2, 14; VI, 15, 5. Should not the bright one on the path of the A*s*vins be the sun? Sâya*n*a thinks of the chariot of the A*s*vins, which also may be right.

Note 2. Are the stones and the grass identical with the stones and grass-blades occurring in the later ritual of the agnyâdheya and agnimanthana (*S*atapatha Br. II, 1, 1, 8; III, 4, 1, 21; Kâtyâyana IV, 8, 16, &c.)?

Verse 9.

Note 1. Literally, a manly, strong, or bull-like smoke.

Verse 11.

Note 1. This is a play upon words (Mâtarí*s*vâ and ámimîta mâtári, 'he has been shaped in the mother').

Note 2. Von Bradke (Dyâus Asura, p. 51): des Windes Heerde (?) wird er, wenn er dahingleitet.

Verse 12.

Note 1. This Pâda is identical with I, 15, 12. It is a galita.

Verse 13.

Note 1. The meaning of asremán (comp. X, 8, 2. asremā́ vatsá*h* [i.e. Agni] *s*ímîvân arâvît) is unknown.

Note 2. The ten fingers.

Verse 14.

Note 1. Comp. von Bradke, loc. cit., 50.

Verse 15.

Note 1. Or prathama*g*ā́m bráhma*n*a*h* ví*s*ve ít vidu*h*: 'all (people) know him the first-born (son) of the sacred spell'? Comp. I, 34, 2. sómasya venā́m ánu ví*s*ve ít vidu*h*.—Prof. Max Müller writes: 'Prathama*g*â*h* is the wind, X, 168, 3. It might here refer to the Maruts, who are often said to sing prayers; they know all about Brahman (prayer).'

MAN*D*ALA IV, HYMN 1.

ASH*T*AKA III, ADHYÂYA 4, VARGA 12–15.

1. Thee, O Agni, the gods concordantly have ever set to work as their divine steward; with this intention[1] they have set thee to work. They have generated[2] thee, O worshipful one[2], the immortal among the mortals, the wise, god-loving god; they have generated every wise, god-loving (Agni)[3].

2. Do thou, [O Agni[1],] turn to brother Varu*n*a, towards the gods[2] with thy kindness[3], to (Varu*n*a) who accepts the sacrifice, to the eldest (god) who accepts the sacrifice, the righteous Âditya who supports the (human) tribes, the king who supports the (human) tribes.

3. O friend, turn to thy friend (Varu*n*a), as a wheel of a chariot[1] rapidly (follows) the swift (horse), for our sake, O wonderful one, rapidly. O Agni, find mercy (for us) with Varu*n*a, with the all-brilliant Maruts. Bless (us), O flaming one, that we may propagate ourselves, that we may press onward; bless us, O wonderful one!

4. Mayst thou, O Agni, who knowest Varu*n*a, deprecate for us the god's anger. Being the best sacrificer, the best carrier (of the gods), flaming, remove from us all hatred.

5. As such, O Agni, be for us the lowest[1] (god) with thy help, our nearest (friend) while this dawn shines forth. Being liberal (towards us), cause, by sacrificing, Varu*n*a to go away from us. Love mercy; readily hear our call.

6. His, the fortunate god's, appearance is excellent, and most brilliant among mortals. Like the bright, heated butter of the cow (the appearance) of the god is lovely, like the bountifulness of a milch-cow.

7. Three[1] are those highest, true, and lovely births of this god Agni. Being enveloped in the infinite[2] he has come hither, the bright, brilliant, shining Aryan.

8. He, the messenger, longs for all seats, the Hot*ri* with the golden chariot, with the lovely tongue, with the red horses, of marvellous appearance, brilliant, always lovely like an assembly abundant in food.

9. He, the kinsman of sacrifice, has enlightened men[1]. They lead him forward by a great rope[2]. He dwells in his (the mortal's) dwelling, accomplishing (his task). The god has obtained the companionship of the mortal.

10. May this Agni, the knowing one, lead us to the god-given treasure which belongs to him[1]. That (treasure) which all the immortals have created by their thought, which Dyaus, the father, the begetter (has created): that real (treasure) they have besprinkled[2].

11. He has been born in the dwellings as the first, at the bottom of the great (air)[1], in the womb of this air[2], footless, headless, hiding both his ends, drawing towards himself (his limbs?), in the nest of the bull[3].

12. The host[1] came forth wonderfully at first, in the womb of *Ri*ta, in the nest of the bull[2], lovely and young, of marvellous appearance, and brilliant[3]. Seven friends[4] were born for the bull.

13. Here our human fathers have sat down[1],

aspiring after *Ri*ta[2]. Invoking the dawns[3], they have driven out the milch-cows which dwelt in the rock-stable, in the prison.

14. Having rent the rock they cleaned themselves. Others around told forth that (deed) of theirs. Taking . . . as an instrument (?)[1], they sang triumphantly[2]. They found the light; they chanted their prayers.

15. Longing for the cows in their mind, those men, the U*s*i*g*s[1], have opened with godly words the fast-holding, closed rock, which enclosed and encompassed the cows, the firm stable full of cows.

16. They have devised the first name of the milch-cow; they have found the three times seven highest (names or essences) of the mother[1]. The hosts[2], understanding this, acclaimed. The red one[3] became visible through the brilliant (milk ?)[4] of the cow.

17. The confused[1] darkness disappeared; the sky appeared in splendour; the shine of the goddess Dawn rose up. The Sun ascended to the wide plains, beholding right and wrong deeds among the mortals.

18. Then, afterwards, being awoke they looked around; then they took that treasure given by Heaven, all the gods in all the houses. O Mitra, may true (fulfilment) belong to (our) prayer, O Varu*n*a!

19. I will address flaming Agni, the Hot*ri*, the supporter of everything[1], the best sacrificer. He has perforated, as it were, the pure udder of the cows, (and has made flow the milk) purified like the poured sap of the Soma shoots.

20. He, the Aditi (i. e. the freedom) of all the

worshipful gods, the guest[1] of all men, Agni, choosing (for us) the protection of all gods—may he, *G*âtavedas, be merciful.

NOTES.

The *Ri*shi is Vâmadeva, the metre Trish*t*ubh, except in verses 1–3, the metres of which are Ash*t*i, Ati*g*agatî, and Dh*ri*ti respectively.—Verses 4–5 = VS. XXI, 3–4; TS. II, 5, 12, 3; IV, 2, 11, 3; TB. III, 7, 11, 3; 12, 6; TÂ. II, 4, 4; IV, 20, 3; MS. IV, 10, 4; 14, 17. Verse 20 = VS. XXXIII, 16; TB. II, 7, 12, 5.—The hymn has been translated and commented upon by Bergaigne, Quarante Hymnes du Rig-véda, p. 11 seq.

This Sûkta seems to be composed of two independent hymns. Grassmann believed that the first three verses are the fragment of one hymn, and that verses 4–20 form a second hymn. His reason was that verses 1–3 are composed in metres similar to Atyash*t*i, while the rest are composed in Trish*t*ubh. I think that he was on the right way, but his opinion should be slightly modified. In verses 1–5 Agni is invoked to appease the anger of Varu*n*a; while, on the other hand, no allusion to Varu*n*a occurs in verses 6–20. I believe, therefore, that the first hymn should be considered as consisting of verses 1–5; it is composed in the metres of the Atyash*t*i class (1–3) with two concluding Trish*t*ubh verses (4, 5). The second hymn comprises the verses 6–20. The arrangers of the Sa*m*hitâ, however, considered these two hymns as one, as is shown by the position which they have assigned to it, before the second Sûkta, which has the same number of verses (20) as this first Sûkta. Comp. my Prolegomena, p. 141.

Verse 1.

Note 1. I.e. with the intention that he should act as the steward of the gods. As to íti krátvâ, comp. I, 138, 3. íti krátvâ bubhugriré. Delbrück, Altindische Syntax, p. 530, paraphrases íti krátvâ : mit Entschluss 'so sei es.'

Note 2. Sâyana, whom Ludwig follows, seems to be right in explaining yagata as a vocative ('yaganîya'), and ganata as 3rd plural ('aganayan'). Bergaigne takes both forms as 2nd plural imperative: 'honorez l'immortel chez les mortels; engendrez le Dieu qui honore les Dieux.'

Note 3. I cannot believe that Bergaigne is right in translating vísvam ấdevam, 'celui qui honore tous les Dieux.' His theory is that 'vísvam dépend . . . de ấ, qui logiquement gouverne le terme devá à l'accusatif,'

Verse 2.

Note 1. The metre shows, as Benfey (Vedica und Verwandtes, p. 19, note 1) has pointed out, that this vocative agne is a spurious addition.

Note 2. Should we not read devám? 'Turn to brother Varuna with thy kindness, towards the god who accepts the sacrifice.'

Note 3. Or 'for the sake of his kindness,' 'for winning his favour (for the mortals)'? Sumatî́ may be dative; see Lanman, p. 382; Brugmann, Grundriss der vergleichenden Grammatik, II, p. 602. Comp. I, 186, 10. ákkhâ sumnấya vavritîya devấn, 'may I turn to the gods for the sake of their favour.'

Verse 3.

Note 1. I believe that ráthyeva (Padapâtha ráthyâ-iva) stands for ráthyam-iva. Comp. Lanman, p. 331; Roth, Zeitschrift der Deutschen Morgenländischen Gesellschaft, XLVIII, p. 681 seq. Prof. Max Müller refers ráthyâ-iva to two horses; he translates: 'O friend, bring hither thy friend, as two swift chariot-horses bring rapidly a swift wheel.'

Verse 5.

Note 1. I.e. the nearest to men.

Verse 7.

Note 1. Literally 'thrice.' But I think that we should correct trî́ ('three'). The same blunder seems to occur in III, 56, 5. trî́ sadhásthâ sindhava*h* trí*h* (read trî́) kavînā́m, 'Three are your abodes, O rivers; three (are those) of the sages.' Comp. also III, 56, 8; I, 116, 4.

Note 2. This seems to mean, in the infinite sky.

Verse 9.

Note 1. Mánusha*h* seems to be acc. plur.; comp. VII, 86, 7. á*k*etayat a*k*íta*h*, 'he has enlightened the unenlightened ones.' Bergaigne takes mánusha*h* as a genitive depending on ya*gñ*ábandhu*h*, 'fils du sacrifice de Manus.'

Note 2. Bergaigne compares IX, 87, 1, where it is said that they lead Soma to the sacrificial grass like a horse by ropes (á*kkh*â barhí*h* ra*s*anā́bhi*h* nayanti). Sâya*n*a says, stutirûpayâ ra*gg*vâ, 'by a rope which has the shape of praises.'

Verse 10.

Note 1. Comp. below, verse 18.

Note 2. I. e. anointed, adorned. 'Poured down.' M. M.

Verse 11.

Note 1. Mahá*h* budhné seems to mean, mahá*h* rá*g*asa*h* budhné; comp. rá*g*asa*h* budhnám, I, 52, 6; budhné rá*g*asa*h*, II, 2, 3; mahá*h* rá*g*asa*h*, I, 6, 10; rá*g*asa*h* mahá*h*, I, 168, 6; mahî́ rá*g*asî, IX, 68, 3.

Note 2. With the second Pâda, compare IV, 17, 14. tva*k*á*h* budhné rá*g*asa*h* asyá yónau.

Note 3. The bull seems to be Agni himself. Comp. verse 12.

Verse 12.

Note 1. The word *s*árdha (or *s*árdha*h*? see note 3), which in most passages is applied to the host of the Maruts (see vol. xxxii, p. 67 seq.), seems here to refer to the company of the Aṅgiras or seven *Ri*shis, alluded to in the fourth

Pâda. The seven *Ri*shis, 'our fathers' (verse 13), have, with the aid of Agni, rent the mountain and delivered the cows or dawns (verses 13 seqq.; IV, 2, 15 seq.). Comp. H. O., Religion des Veda, p. 145 seq.

Note 2. The bull again seems to be Agni. Comp. verse 11, note 3.

Note 3. Do these epithets (comp. verse 8, Pâda 3) refer to the *s*árdha (host)? Or are they applied to Agni, so that we would have to translate: 'Lovely was the young one (Agni), of marvellous appearance, and brilliant'? In this way Bergaigne interprets the passage. If this translation is right, *s*árdha*h* may be considered as neuter, and the first Pâda could be translated: The first host came forth wonderfully.

Note 4. Evidently the seven *Ri*shis (see note 1). Bergaigne: Les sept prières? ou les sept rivières?

Verse 13.

Note 1. The seven *Ri*shis sat down for chanting and sacrificing, by which they have opened the mountain-prison of the cows.

Note 2. The mention of *Ri*ta in this connection is both Vedic and Avestic. Comp. Darmesteter, Ormazd et Ahriman, p. 146; H. O., Religion des Veda, p. 144, note 2.

Note 3. The cows in this myth seem to be a mythical representation of the dawns. Comp. M. M., Science of Language, II, p. 584; H. O., Religion des Veda, pp. 147, 149 seq.

Verse 14.

Note 1. Pa*s*váyantra (comp. *s*lókayantra, IX, 73, 6) is quite doubtful. Does there exist a stem pa*s*va, meaning possibly, 'the herd of cattle'? And can we translate, 'they who had their (battering- ?) machines directed on the cow-herds'? Or, 'holding the herds with their instruments (i.e. with the ropes used for drawing the cows out of the cavern)'?—Prof. Max Müller suggests the translation, 'the cattle-drivers,' and writes, 'Does it stand for pa*s*u-yantrâsa*h*? Yantra seems the same as yoktra, or something like it, cf. X, 94, 7, 8. Pa*s*uyantra would be they who hold the ropes of the cattle, who drive them away.' Bergaigne's translation, 'n'ayant rien (d'autre) pour conduire le bétail' (pa*s*u-ayantra), and that of Roth ('die der Sperre ledigen Thiere [pa*s*va*h* ayantrâsa*h*] erhoben ein Freudengeschrei,' Zeitschr. der D. Morg. Gesellschaft, XLVIII, 678), do not carry conviction, nor does a conjecture like pa*s*vấ yantắra*h* ('the leaders of the cattle together with the cattle itself shouted triumphantly'), seem to furnish a satisfying solution of the difficulty.

Note 2. See Geldner, Vedische Studien, I, 120.

Verse 15.

Note 1. On the U*s*i*g*s, compare Bergaigne's Religion Védique, I, 57 seq.

Verse 16.

Note 1. The mother seems again to be the cow, or more exactly the Dawn considered as the mother of the cows (mâtấ gávâm, IV, 52, 2. 3; VII, 77, 2), and as the mother of the *Ri*shis (IV, 2, 15). Comp. V, 45, 2. ấ ûrvất gávâm mâtấ *g*ânatī́ gât. The seven names of the cow are mentioned also in I, 164, 3, its three times seven names, in VII, 87, 4.

Note 2. Bergaigne (Quarante Hymnes, p. 14) and Pischel (Ved. Studien, II, 121 seq.) give to the word vrâ the meaning 'woman' (Bergaigne: 'femme,' particulièrement 'femme en rut,' 'femme amoureuse'). I prefer to follow the opinion of Bechtel, Nachrichten der Göttinger Gesellschaft der Wissenschaften, philolog.-historische Klasse, 1894, p. 393 seq. The hosts seem to be the assembly of the *Ri*shis.

Note 3. The dawn.

Note 4. Comp. IX, 81, 1 (H. O., Religion des Veda, p. 147, note 1). dadhnấ yát îm únnîtâ*h* ya*s*ásâ gávâm, 'When (the Somas) have been drawn, together with the brilliant curds of the cow.' The brilliant milk of the cow which the

*Ri*shis have obtained, seems to be considered as a magical means for procuring to men the aspect of the brilliant light of the dawn. Comp. H. O., Religion des Veda, p. 450.

Verse 17.

Note 1. On dúdhitam, comp. Geldner, Ved. Studien, II, 9, and see Rig-veda II, 17, 4; IV, 16, 4.

Verse 19.

Note 1. Comp. vol. xxxii, p. 330 (V, 54, 10, note 1).

Verse 20.

Note 1. 'Guest' is átithi*h*; the play on words (áditi*h* and átithi*h*) is untranslatable.

MA*ND*ALA IV, HYMN 2.

ASH*T*AKA III, ADHYÂYA 4, VARGA 16–19.

1. He who has been established as the steward among the mortals, the immortal, righteous one, and among the gods, being a god himself, the Hot*ri*, the best sacrificer shall mightily flame[1]; Agni shall rise up[1] with the offerings of Manus.

2. Here, O Agni, son of strength, thou goest for us to-day as a messenger, thou who art born, between the two races (of men and gods), having harnessed, O tall one, thy puissant, manly, brilliant (stallions)[1].

3. Harnessing the two mighty, red steeds that swim in ghee—(the steeds) of *Ri*ta, I think, that are most swift with their mind[1], the ruddy ones, thou goest (as a messenger) between you, the gods, and the tribes of men[2].

4. O Agni, with thy good horses, and thy good chariot, rich in bounties, bring hither from among them (the gods)[1] Aryaman, Varu*n*a, and Mitra, Indra and Vish*n*u, the Maruts and the A*s*vins, to him who offers good oblations.

5. This sacrifice, O Agni, is rich in cows[1], in sheep and horses, in manly friends; it is never to be despised; it is rich in nourishment, O wonderful lord[2], rich in offspring; it is long-lasting wealth, broad-based, with (brilliant) assemblies.

6[1]. Be a self-strong protector, O Agni, of the man who in the sweat of his brow brings fuel to thee[2], or heats his head desirous to worship thee. Deliver him from every harmful man.

7. The man who brings food to thee who art desirous of food, he who stirs up[1] the cheerful guest and rouses him, the godly man who kindles thee in his dwelling: to him may belong lasting and generous wealth.

8. The sacrificer who praises thee in the evening and in the morning and gratifies thee: that liberal man thou shouldst bring across all distress, like a well-impelled horse[1], (dwelling) in his house.

9. The man who worships thee, the immortal one, O Agni, and who honours thee, holding the sacrificial ladle—may he, the toiling (sacrificer), not be deprived of wealth; may no distress that comes from a harmful (foe), surround him.

10. That mortal whose well-ordered sacrifice thou, as the god, acceptest, O Agni, as a liberal giver, may his worship[1] be welcome, O youngest god, (the Hotri's work performed) for a worshipper whose helpers we may be.

11. May he, the knowing one, distinguish wisdom and folly of mortals[1], like straight and crooked backs (of horses)[2]. And for the sake of wealth and noble offspring, O god, grant us Diti and keep off Aditi[3].

12. The undeceived sages instructed the sage (Agni), setting him down in the dwellings of Âyu[1]. Hence mayst thou behold, O Agni, with thy eyes[2] these beings visible and secret (that move) on the Arya's ways[3].

13. Bring thou, O Agni, youngest (god), who art a good guide, a plentiful, brilliant treasure to the worshipper who presses Soma, who serves thee and toils, to help him, O brisk one, who fillest the dwellings of peoples.

14[1]. And whatsoever we have done, O Agni, out

of devotion for thee, with our feet[2], with our hands, with our bodies: (in those deeds of ours) the wise have held up the *Ri*ta, aspiring after it, like those who manage a chariot by means of the two pole-arms (?)[3].

15. And may we be born from the Dawn, the mother, as the seven priests[1], as the first worshippers among men[2]. May we be the Aṅgiras, the sons of Heaven. May we flaming break the rock which contains the prize of the contest[3].

16. And as our first, ancient fathers, O Agni, were aspiring after *Ri*ta[1]—they attained to pure devotion[2], chanting their litanies. Cleaving the earth they disclosed the red (cows).

17. The pious men, well performing the acts (of worship), resplendent, melting[1] the generations of the gods[2] like ore[3], kindling Agni, strengthening Indra, went along[4], besieging the stall of cows.

18. He looked (on the gods) as on herds of cattle[1] in a rich (pasture)[2], when the generations of the gods (were) near him, O mighty one[3]. After (the generations) of the mortals the Urva*s*îs[4] have pined, for the growing strong of the Arya[5], of the nearer Âyu[6].

19. We have done our work for thee; we have been good workers—the brilliant dawns have shone out *Ri*ta[1],—brightening[2] the perfect Agni who manifoldly shines with fine splendour, (brightening) the god's beautiful eye.

20. We have recited these hymns for thee, the sage, O Agni, worshipper (of the gods)[1]; accept them! Blaze up; make us wealthier. Bestow great wealth on us, O bountiful one!

NOTES.

The *Ri*shi is Vâmadeva, the metre Trish*t*ubh.—Verse 5=TS. I, 6, 6, 4; III, 1, 11, 1; MS. I, 4, 3. Verse 6=TÂ. VI, 2, 1. Verse 11=TS. V, 5, 4, 4. Verse 16=VS. XIX, 69; TS. II, 6, 12, 4. Verses 16–19=AV. XVIII, 3, 21–24.

Verse 1.

Note 1. On this use of these infinitives, comp. Delbrück, Altindische Syntax, p. 412.—Mánusha*h* seems to be genitive; comp. II, 2, 6. havyấ mánusha*h*; II, 2, 8. hótrâbhi*h* . . . mánusha*h*; I, 76, 5. mánusha*h* havírbhi*h*.

Verse 2.

Note 1. Comp. below, IV, 6, 9.

Verse 3.

Note 1. As to the horses of *Ri*ta, comp. above, III, 6, 6. In spite of the different accent there is no doubt that gh*ri*tasnúvâ, which occurs in that verse, is the same word as gh*ri*tásnû, in our verse, a compound of gh*ri*ta with a noun snu which seems to be different from sấnu, and connected with the root snâ (cf. gh*ri*tasnấ, IV, 6, 9; and see Bechtel, Hauptprobleme der Indogerm. Lautlehre, p. 211). V*ri*dhasnú, on the other hand, seems to be no compound, but an adjective formed like vadhasnu, nishatsnú. It is evident, however, that the poet here employed the two words v*ri*dhasnú and gh*ri*tásnu as parallel expressions.

Note 2. Read mártâm (for mártân; gen. plur.). Comp. below, verse 11; VI, 47, 16. vís*a*h manushŷân, where we ought to read manushŷâm. See Lanman, p. 353; Pischel, Vedische Studien, I, p. 44; Bartholomae, Studien zur Indogermanischen Sprachgeschichte, I, p. 48.

Verse 4.

Note 1. 'Could it be Mitrám eshám, the rapid Mitra?' M. M.

Verse 5.

Note 1. The meaning is, it is rich in reward consisting in cows, &c.

Note 2. The text has asura. Cf. H. O., Religion des Veda, p. 164.

Verse 6.

Note 1. With the first Pâda, comp. below, 12, 2.

Note 2. On svátavân, see Benfey, Vedica und Linguistica, p. 1 seqq; Lanman, p. 559; Joh. Schmidt, Kuhn's Zeitschrift, XXVI, p. 357 seq.; H. O., Prolegomena, p. 471.

Verse 7.

Note 1. Ni*s*íshat is not derived, as is the case for instance with ấ *s*ishâmahi, VIII, 24, 1, from (ni-)*s*âs (Grassmann, Ludwig), but from ni-*s*â (Böhtlingk-Roth); comp. VII, 3, 5. ni*s*í*s*ânâ*h* átithim. We must read, consequently, ni*s*í*s*at, formed like dádhat (3rd sg. subj. pres., or possibly nom. sing. part. pres.).

Verse 8.

Note 1. Böhtlingk-Roth conjecture harmyấvân 'im Hause, im Stall gehalten.' It is true that beasts may be kept in the harmya; comp. VII, 56, 16; X, 106, 5; Zimmer, Altindisches Leben, p. 149. But I do not think that 'being kept in the harmya' could be expressed by harmya-vat. Hemyấvat seems to be derived from the root hi, and to have the same meaning as â*s*uhéman; such a word very well fits into a phrase referring to a swift horse. Hemyấvat stands to hemán in the same relation as omyấvat to omán. All this was pointed out first by Ludwig (vol. iv, p. 22).

Verse 10.

Note 1. Literally the Hot*ri*'s work (performed for such a Ya*g*amâna).

Verse 11.

Note 1. I read mártâm (gen. plur.); comp. above, verse 3, note 2. It is possible, however, to leave the text unchanged; in this case the translation would be: 'May he, the knowing one, distinguish wisdom and folly, the (wise and foolish) mortals like straight and crooked backs (of horses).'

Note 2. Comp. vîtáp*ri*sh*th*a, 'straight-backed,' a frequent epithet of horses.

Note 3. For Prof. Max Müller's interpretation of this passage, comp. vol. xxxii, p. 256. See also Bergaigne, Rel. Védique, III, 97; Pischel, Vedische Studien, I, 297 seq. It is very strange that the poet should ask the god to keep off Aditi (comp. I, 152, 6. áditim urushyet) who must here be considered, consequently, as a malevolent deity. I think that this conception of Aditi is derived from the idea of this goddess as punishing sin; it is the same goddess who may free the sinner from the bonds of sin and who may fetter and destroy him. Keeping off Aditi seems to mean, consequently, removing from the mortal the danger of being bound by the fetters of sin; the idea is the same as above in IV, 1, 5, where Agni is invoked to make Varu*n*a, the son of Aditi, go away (comp. H. O., Religion des Veda, p. 336, note 1). In that case granting Diti would mean granting freedom from those same fetters. (On Diti, who very appropriately has been called a mere reflex of Aditi, see M. M., loc. cit.; Bergaigne, III, 97 seq.)

Verse 12.

Note 1. On Âyu, the mythical ancestor of the human race, see Bergaigne, Religion Védique, I, p. 59 seq.

Note 2. On pa*d*bhí*h*, comp. Pischel, Ved. Studien, I, 228 seq.; Bartholomae, Bezzenberger's Beiträge, XV, 3 seq.; Bloomfield, Contributions to the Interpretation of the Veda, Second Series, p. 32 seq. (American Journal of Philology, XI, 350 seq.). I believe that in our verse pa*d*bhí*h* should be derived from a noun pá*s*, and translated, 'with thy eyes,' while in verse 14 we ought to read padbhí*h*, and to translate, 'with the feet.'

Note 3. Pischel (Ved. Studien, I, 229, note 1) believes that aryá*h* is nom. sing., referring to Agni. But compare VI, 51, 2. *rig*ú márteshu v*rig*inấ *k*a pá*s*yan abhí *k*ash*t*e sû́ra*h* aryá*h* évân. This verse makes it very probable that aryá*h* is a genitive dependent on évai*h*, évân ('beholding right and wrong deeds among the mortals, the Sun looks upon the Arya's ways'). On the stem arí, 'the Arya,' see Pischel, Zeitschrift der Deutschen Morgenländischen Gesellschaft, XL, p. 125.

Verse 14.

Note 1. This verse has been commented upon by Pischel, Ved. Studien, I, 229 seq.

Note 2. On pa*d*bhí*h* or rather padbhí*h*, comp. verse 12, note 2.

Note 3. In translating bhurí*g* I have followed, though not without doubt, the theory of Pischel, Ved. Studien, I, 239 seq.—Pischel seems to be right in making *ri*tám depend both on yemu*h* (comp. IV, 23, 10) and on â*s*ushâ*n*ấ*h* (comp. above, IV, 1, 13, and below, verse 16).

Verse 15.

Note 1. The seven *Ri*shis or Aṅgiras, the sons of Heaven and the Dawn (cf. above 1, 16).

Note 2. n*rî́*n (or rather n*rî́*m) is genitive plural. See Lanman, p. 430; Pischel, Vedische Studien, I, p. 42.

Note 3. Here we have again the seven *Ri*shis breaking the mountain in which the cows were imprisoned.

Verse 16.

Note 1. The apodosis is wanting. As verse 15 shows, the meaning is: As our fathers have done their mighty deeds, aspiring after *Ri*ta, thus may we do the same.

Note 2. *S*ú*k*î́t (Padap. *s*ú*k*i ít) possibly stands for *s*ú*k*im ít; cf. Roth, Zeitschrift der Deutschen Morgenländischen Gesellschaft, XLVIII, p. 680. Or may we correct *s*ú*k*î ít...

dî́dhitî (instr. sing.), 'they went along in pure devotion'? Dî́dhiti seems to be what is called in III, 31, 1; IX, 102, 1. 8, *ri*tásya dî́dhiti*h*.

Verse 17.

Note 1. See Zimmer, Altindisches Leben, p. 252.

Note 2. Evidently the pious men, not the gods, form the subject. I propose to read, therefore, devā́m (gen. plur.) *g*ánimâ; cf. verse 18 devā́nâm yát *g*ánimâ. They kindle Agni; they strengthen Indra: in short, they treat the divine people as the smith treats the metal.

Note 3. I do not enter here upon the archaeological question as to the meaning of áya*h*. Comp. on this much-discussed question especially Max Müller, Biographies of Words, p. 252 seq.; Schrader, Sprachvergleichung und Urgeschichte (2nd ed.), p. 271 seq.; von Bradke, Methode der arischen Alterthumswissenschaft, p. 93 seq.

Note 4. Cf. X, 61, 13. parishádvâna*h* agman.

Verse 18.

Note 1. Pa*s*vá*h* is genitive sing.; it depends on yûthā́. Cf. V, 31, 1; VI, 19, 3.

Note 2. There is no reason for taking, as Lanman (p. 516) does, kshumáti as acc. plur. neut., which would be kshumā́nti. See Joh. Schmidt, Pluralbildungen der Indogermanischen Neutra, p. 237; Bartholomae, Kuhn's Zeitschrift, XXIX, p. 493. Bartholomae translates, 'bei einem wolhabenden.'

Note 3. Is this vocative ugra right? It would be easy to correct, with Ludwig, ugrā́ (' when the mighty generations of the gods were near him') or ugrá*h*, as suggested by Delbrück (Grassmann's Translation, vol. i, p. 573): 'the mighty one (Agni) looked on them,' &c.

Note 4. I believe that Geldner (Ved. Studien, I, 260, note 1) is right in contending that Urva*s*î, wherever it occurs, is the name of an Apsaras and nothing else. The name of Âyu, occurring in the fourth Pâda, confirms this; for Âyu, as is well known, is the son of Purûravas and of the nymph Urva*s*î. Geldner translates, 'Selbst mit den

Sterblichen hatten die Urvasîs Mitleid.' But I do not think that krip means 'having compassion.' In my opinion we should, with Ludwig, supply gánimâ to mártânâm, so that devấnâm gánimâ in the second Pâda corresponds with mártânâm (gánimâ) in the third. This gánimâ is an accusative which depends on akripran ('they pined after ...,' cf. IX, 85, 11. nấke suparnám upapaptivấmsam gírah venấnâm akripanta pûrvî́h; X, 74, 3. yé kripánanta rátnam). Thus the meaning seems to be: When the cows had been conquered, and when Agni looked over the generations of the gods that were near him, the Urvasîs, i. e. the Apsarases such as Urvasî, longed for the love of mortals such as Purûravas, and for the propagation of the human generations; they gave birth to children such as Âyu.

Note 5. Or 'of the indigent'? Or is aryáh nom. plur. fem. referring to the Urvasîs? Or nom. sing. masc. referring to Agni?

Note 6. On Âyu, see note 4. But I cannot tell why he is called the nearer Âyu. Is this nearer Âyu opposed, as a nearer or later (úpara) ancestor, to the pitárah párâsah pratnấsah, the Angiras, mentioned in verse 16? The same nearer Âyu (úpara which stands there in opposition to pû́rvâbhih) is mentioned also in I, 104, 4, connected, as it seems, with some Apsarases. I do not pretend to be able to interpret that very difficult verse, but I am convinced that it has been misinterpreted both by Roth (Siebenzig Lieder, p. vii) and by Bergaigne (I, 60).

Verse 19.

Note 1. I. e. the dawns have sent forth their shine, which is a visible manifestation of the eternal law of *Ri*ta.

Note 2. The construction is: we have been good workers, brightening &c. The words, 'the brilliant dawns have shone out *Ri*ta,' are a parenthesis.

Verse 20.

Note 1. The text is nearly identical with the first hemistich of I, 73, 10 (see above).

MA*ND*ALA IV, HYMN 3.

ASHT*A*KA III, ADHYÂYA 4, VARGA 20-22.

1. Draw Rudra hither for your protection[1], the king of sacrifice, the truly sacrificing Hot*ri* of the two worlds[2], the golden-coloured Agni, before the unseen thunderbolt (strikes you).

2. This is the home which we have prepared for thee as a well-dressed, loving wife (prepares the marriage-bed) for her husband[1]. Directed hitherward, dressed (in offerings and prayers ?)[2] sit down. These (sacrificial ladles or prayers ?) are turned towards thee, O most skilful one[3]!

3. To him who hears us, who is not proud, who beholds men, to the merciful, immortal god recite a prayer, O worshipper, a hymn—(to Agni) whom the presser (of Soma), the Madhu-presser, magnifies like the pressing-stone[1].

4. Thou who art well-intentioned, give heed to this our toiling[1], to this *Ri*ta[2], O observer of *Ri*ta! When will our hymns share in thy rejoicings? When will our friendship dwell in thy house?

5. How wilt thou, O Agni, before Varu*n*a, and how wilt thou, and which sin of ours wilt thou blame before Dyaus? How wilt thou speak to bountiful Mitra, to the Earth? What (wilt thou say) to Aryaman, to Bhaga?

6. What wilt thou say, O Agni, when thou hast grown strong on the Dhish*n*ya altars[1]? What to strong Vâta who goes forward in triumph[2]? To the Nâsatya[3] who goes round the earth[4], to . . .[5]? What, O Agni, to Rudra, the man-killer?

7. How (wilt thou speak) to great Pûshan who brings prosperity? What (wilt thou say) to martial Rudra, the giver of offerings[1]? What sin[2] wilt thou announce to wide-ruling Vish*n*u, what, O Agni, to the mighty weapon (of the gods)?

8. How wilt thou answer, when thou art asked, to the righteous[1] host of the Maruts? How to the mighty Sun, to the quick Aditi[2]? Accomplish thy work, O *G*âtavedas, thou who knowest the Heaven!

9. I magnify[1] the *Ri*ta of the cow[2] ruled by *Ri*ta and also by the raw one[3], the honey-sweet, ripe (milk), O Agni. Though being black this (cow) swells of bright drink, of . . .[4] milk.

10. With *Ri*ta indeed, with the milk of the back[1], the bull has been anointed, Agni the man. Without trembling he moved on bestowing his vigour. The speckled bull has poured out his bright udder[2].

11[1]. By the *Ri*ta the Aṅgiras have broken the rock and cleft it asunder; they have shouted together with the cows. Prosperously the men have surrounded[2] the Dawn. The Sun appeared when Agni (the fire) had been born[3].

12. By the *Ri*ta the immortal, uninjured[1] goddesses, the Waters, O Agni, with their honey-sweet waves have sped forward[2] for ever to flow (along their course), like a racer incited by shouting when (the race-horses) are let loose.

13. Go never on thy crooked way to the spirit (which avenges the guilt) of anybody[1], of a vassal who has trespassed, or of a friend. Require not (of us) a sinful brother's debt[2]. May we not have to suffer under the spirit which avenges a friend's or a (hostile) deceiver's guilt[3].

14. Protect us, O Agni, with all thy protection, thou who art protected, O martial one[1], and art gladdened (by us). Sparkle forth, and destroy even strong evil! Slay the Rakshas even though it has grown large.

15. Be gracious, O Agni, through these our hymns. Touch, O hero, this wealth moved by our prayers. And accept, O Aṅgiras, our sacred words. May the praise, beloved by the gods, resound to thee[1].

16. I, the priest, have rehearsed to thee the omniscient one, O Agni, worshipper (of the gods), all these songs, these inmost words, these recitations and words of wisdom, to thee the wise one, with prayers and hymns.

NOTES.

The same *R*ishi and metre.—Verse 1 = SV. I, 69; TS. I, 3, 14, 1; TB. II, 8, 6, 9; MS. IV, 11, 4. Verse 6 = MS. IV, 11, 4.

Verse 1.

Note 1. On the identification of Agni with Rudra, comp. Bergaigne, Rel. Védique, III, 36; von Bradke, Dyâus Asura, p. 54 (Rig-veda I, 27, 10; III, 2, 5; VIII, 72, 3).

Note 2. The second Pâda of this verse is identical with VI, 16, 46.

Verse 2.

Note 1. Cf. Hirzel, Gleichnisse und Metaphern im Rig-veda, p. 69.

Note 2. On párivîta*h* Sâya*n*a remarks, yash*t*avyadevais te*g*obhir vâ parivîta*h*. In the commentary on I, 128, 1, on the other hand, he says, *ri*tvigbhi*h* paridhibhir vâ parito vesh*t*ita*h*.

Note 3. I take su-apâka as a compound of su and a-pâka (comp. Vâg. Sa*m*h. XX, 44 = Taitt. Br. II, 6, 8, 4 = Maitr. Sa*m*h. III, 11, 1, where Tvash*t*ri is called apâká*h*). In Rig-veda VI, 11, 4 we read: ádidyutat sú ápâka*h* vibhấvâ; in VI, 12, 2. ấ yásmin tvé sú ápâke ya*g*atra, &c. Should we not correct in both passages suapâka*h*, suapâke?

Verse 3.

Note 1. The pressing-stone (grấvan) is frequently considered as speaking, as praising the gods. Cf. Hillebrandt, Vedische Mythologie, I, p. 152 sq.

Verse 4.

Note 1. The Padapâ*th*a has *s*ámyai. I think it should be *s*ámyâ*h*.

Note 2. I. e. to this sacrifice, which is considered as one of the chief manifestations of *Ri*ta. See H. O., Religion des Veda, p. 197.

Verse 6.

Note 1. At the Soma sacrifice fire burns on eight altars called Dhish*n*ya; see Weber, Indische Studien, X, pp. 366, 375.

Note 2. See vol. xxxii, p. 164.

Note 3. This is the only passage in the Rig-veda in which nâsatya occurs in the singular.

Note 4. On pári*g*man, cf. above, I, 79, 3 note.

Note 5. Kshé (cf. Lanman, pp. 440, 448, 534) is evidently corrupt. But neither Bollensen's conjecture, uksh*n*é, nor those of Ludwig (*k*akshe, yakshe), carry conviction.

Verse 7.

Note 1. It is very strange to find Rudra here designated as 'giver of offerings.' But it seems too bold to explain havi*h*-dé as a dative of havi*h*-ád ('eater of offerings').

Note 2. I read with Grassmann répa*h* ('sin') for réta*h* ('sperm').

Verse 8.

Note 1. The text has *ri*tấya, used as an adjective (see Bergaigne, Rel. Védique, III, 216).

Note 2. Aditi is masculine and seems to be an epithet ('unrestrained, free') of the Sun. Cf. vol. xxxii, p. 262; Bergaigne, III, 92. Probably at the same time the word is intended to allude to the goddess Aditi.

Verse 9.

Note 1. The text has î*l*e, on which Ludwig says, 'so viel wie nî*l*e.' Î*l*e of course cannot be the same as nî*l*e, but should we not conjecture nî*l*é? Cf. above, IV, 1, 11. v*ri*shabhásya nî*l*é, and IV, 1, 12. *ri*tásya yónâ v*ri*shabhásya nî*l*é. The translation would be, 'By *Ri*ta the *Ri*ta is restrained in the nest of the cow.'

Note 2. The '*Ri*ta of the cow,' if the reading is correct (see note 1), seems to be the milk.

Note 3. The 'raw one' is the cow as opposed to the ripe milk.

Note 4. The meaning of *g*ấmarya (*ἅπαξ λεγόμενον*) is unknown. Cf. Bergaigne, II, 398, note 1. Sâya*n*a reads *g*â amarye*n*a. 'I should prefer *g*â amartyena.' M. M.

Verse 10.

Note 1. Does this mean, with the milk that comes from the ridge of heaven? Cf. IV, 20, 4. sám ándhasâ mamada*h* p*ri*sh*th*ỹena.

Note 2. This Pâda seems to be an imitation of VI, 66, 1, where P*ri*sni ('the speckled one') is the mother of the Maruts: sak*ri*t *s*ukrám duduhe p*ri*sni*h* ũdha*h*. See vol. xxxii, p. 368.

Verse 11.

Note 1. Here we have again the same myth of the Angiras and the cows, to which so many allusions are found in the preceding hymns.

Note 2. The red cows of the myth are the dawns; the

Aṅgiras besiege the stronghold in which these cows are imprisoned.

Note 3. On the kindling of the fire as a charm by which the sun is made to rise, see H. O., Religion des Veda, p. 109 seq. The Aṅgiras kindle the fire for performing their sacrifice; thereby they make the sun rise.

Verse 12.

Note 1. The same epithet is applied to the waters also in X, 104, 8.

Note 2. The optative dadhanyu*h* is very strange. Probably we ought to read dadhanvu*h*.

Verse 13.

Note 1. The meaning seems to be that Agni is requested not to turn against the sacrificer a spirit which has to avenge the guilt committed by a third person. 'Why not read ya*g**ñ*am? Go not secretly to anybody's sacrifice, not of a hostile house, not of a friend. Do not require (of us) a sinful brother's debt. May we not feel the might of friend or foe.' M. M.

Note 2. Geldner (Ved. Studien II, 157) translates and interprets: 'tilge nicht, O Agni, die Schuld eines falschen Bruders,' nämlich die Schuld an die Manen, also dem Sinn nach 'mache ihn kinderlos.' This is quite unacceptable.

Note 3. The text is evidently corrupt. I propose to read: mấ sákhyu*h* yakshám mấ ripó*h* bhu*g*ema. Comp. V, 70, 4. mấ kásya adbhutakratû yakshám bhu*g*ema tanûbhi*h*.

Verse 14.

Note 1. I cannot adopt Bergaigne's opinion on sú*m*akha (Quarante Hymnes, p. 75).

Verse 15.

Note 1. Or, awake for thee.

MA*ND*ALA IV, HYMN 4.

ASH*T*AKA III, ADHYÂYA 4, VARGA 23–25.

1. Produce thy stream of flames like a broad onslaught. Go forth impetuous like a king with his elephant[1]; . . .[2] after thy greedy onslaught, thou art an archer; shoot the sorcerers with thy hottest (arrows).

2. Thy whirls fly quickly. Fiercely flaming touch (them). O Agni, (send forth) with the ladle[1] thy heat, thy winged (flames); send forth unfettered thy firebrands all around.

3. Being the quickest, send forth thy spies against (all evildoers). Be an undeceivable guardian of this clan. He who attacks us with evil spells, far or near, may no such (foe) defy thy track.

4. Rise up, O Agni! Spread out against (all foes)! Burn down the foes, O (god) with the sharp weapon! When kindled, O Agni, burn down like dry brushwood, the man who exercises malice against us.

5. Stand upright, strike (the foes) away from us! Make manifest thy divine (powers), O Agni! Unbend the strong (bows) of those who incite demons (against us)[1]. Crush all enemies, be they relations or strangers.

6. He knows thy favour, O youngest one, who makes a way for a sacred speech like this. Mayst thou beam forth to his doors all auspicious days and the wealth and the splendour of the niggard.

7. Let him, O Agni, be fortunate and blessed with good rain, who longs to gladden thee with

constant offerings and hymns through his life in his house. May such longing ever bring auspicious days to him.

8. I praise thy favour; it resounded here. May this song (which is like) a favourite wife, awaken for thee[1]. Let us brighten thee, being rich in horses and chariots. Mayst thou maintain our knightly power day by day.

9. May (the worshipper) here frequently of his own accord approach thee, O (god) who shinest in darkness[1], resplendent day by day. Let us worship thee sporting and joyous, surpassing the splendour of (other) people.

10. Whoever, rich in horses and rich in gold, approaches thee, O Agni, with his chariot full of wealth—thou art the protector and the friend of him who always delights in showing thee hospitality.

11. Through my kinship (with thee) I break down the great (foes) by my words[1]. That (kinship) has come down to me from my father Gotama. Be thou attentive to this our word, O youngest, highly wise Hot*ri*, as the friend of our house.

12. May those guardians of thine, infallible Agni, sitting down together protect us, the never sleeping, onward-pressing, kind, unwearied ones, who keep off the wolf, who never tire.

13[1]. Thy guardians, O Agni, who seeing have saved the blind son of Mamatâ from distress—He the possessor of all wealth has saved them who have done good deeds. The impostors, though trying to deceive, could not deceive.

14. In thy companionship we dwell, protected by thee. Under thy guidance let us acquire gain. Accomplish both praises[1], O (thou who art the)

truth! Do so by thy present power, O fearless one!

15. May we worship thee, O Agni, with this log of wood. Accept the hymn of praise which we recite. Burn down those who curse us, the sorcerers. Protect us, O (god) who art great like Mitra, from guile, from revilement, and from disgrace.

NOTES.

The hymn is addressed to Agni Rakshohan. The same *Ri*shi and metre.—Verses 1–15=TS. I, 2, 14, 1–6; MS. IV, 11, 5. Verses 1–5=VS. XIII, 9–13; MS. II, 7, 15.

Verse 1.

Note 1. On íbhena, cf. Pischel-Geldner, Vedische Studien, I, p. xv.

Note 2. The meaning of drû*n*âná*h*, which evidently should be pronounced dru*n*âná*h* (H. O., Prolegomena, p. 478), is uncertain. This verb is stated to occur still in one other passage, Maitr. Sa*m*h. II, 4, 2. tad ya eva*m* vidvânt surâm pibati na haina*m* drû*n*âti (dru*n*âti, two MSS.). But should we not read there hru*n*âti? [And possibly in our passage, as Prof. Max Müller observes, hrû*n*âná*h*?]

Verse 2.

Note 1. On *g*uhvâ, see Pischel, Vedische Studien, II, 113. Wherever butter is poured out with the ladle, the flames arise.

Verse 5.

Note 1. The third Pâda is identical with X, 116, 5 b.

Verse 8.

Note 1. Or 'resound to thee' (sám *g*areta). Cf. above, 3, 15. Shall we read, in consideration of this parallel passage, sám devávâtâ *g*aratâm iyám gī́*h* ('may this song beloved by the gods resound' or 'awaken')?

Verse 9.

Note 1. On dóshâvasta*h*, see above, I, 1, 7, note 1.

Verse 11.

Note 1. I have taken mahá*h* as acc. plural. If it is gen. singular, the translation will be: 'Through my kinship with the great (Agni) I break down (my foes) by my words.'

Verse 13.

Note 1. This verse is identical with I, 147, 3. See the notes there. The original place of this verse seems to be in the first Ma*nd*ala, because it mentions Mâmateya.

Verse 14.

Note 1. Probably the praise or song of the gods and of men. See vol. xxxii, p. 439.

MANDALA IV, HYMN 5.

ASHTAKA III, ADHYÂYA 5, VARGA 1-3.

1. How may we unanimously offer mighty light[1] to bountiful Agni Vaisvânara? With his mighty perfect growth he supports the high bank[2] like a pillar.

2. Do not reproach Him, the self-dependent one, who has given this bounty to me, the god to the mortal, the clever one to the simple, the wise immortal, the most manly, restless[1] Agni Vaisvânara.

3. Agni, the sharp-pointed, the mighty bull with thousandfold sperm, has proclaimed to me the great, doubly-powerful[1] Sâman, the prayer, having found, as it were, the hidden track of a cow[2].

4. May Agni, he who is rich in wealth, whose teeth are sharp, consume with his hottest flames those who violate the laws founded by Varuna, the beloved, firm (laws) of attentive Mitra.

5[1]. They who roam about like brotherless girls[2], of evil conduct like women who deceive their husbands, being wicked, sinful, and untrue—they have created for themselves this deep place[3].

6. On me, however small, but innocent, thou, O purifying Agni, hast fiercely placed this mighty, deep, vigorous prayer, like a heavy burden, this Prishtha[1], consisting of seven elements[2].

7. Let our prayer which purifies Him, through the power of mind (inherent in it), reach Him who is the common (property of all men) alike, the good (name?) of Prisni on the skin of the herbs, on the summit of the . . .[1].

8. What should be openly uttered by me of this speech? They secretly speak of that which is hidden[1]. When they have uncovered, as it were, the water of the cows[2], he guards the beloved summit of the . . .[3], the footstep of the bird[4].

9. He has found in secret that great face of the great ones which the bright cow accompanied[1], the ancient (face) shining in the abode of *Ri*ta, the quickly running, quickly moving.

10. And resplendent near his parents (Heaven and Earth), in their presence, he thought of the secret, good (name?) of P*ris*ni. The tongue of the manly, forward-bent flame (seized) that which was near at hand in the highest abode of the mother, the cow[1].

11. I speak, when being asked, *Ri*ta (i.e. truth), out of reverence (for Agni, or for the gods), out of hope[1] placed in thee, O *G*âtavedas, as I am here[2]. Thou rulest over all this wealth whatever (dwells) in heaven and earth.

12. Which of this wealth is ours, what treasure? Mayst thou who knowest it declare to us (that treasure), O *G*âtavedas! What is the highest (aim) of this our way, is hidden. We have not come scolding to an empty (?)[1] place.

13[1]. What is the limit, what the objects? What pleasant (wealth) may we obtain as swift (horses gain) the prize? When will the Dawns, the divine consorts of the immortal, expand over us with the sun's splendour?

14. And what do those insatiable ones here say, O Agni, with their sapless, feeble, weak speech that has to be listened to? Let them unarmed fall into nothingness.

15. The face of this kindled, manly Vasu has shone gloriously in the house. Clothed in brilliancy, with his shape beautiful to behold, the bountiful has shone like a house[1] with its wealth.

NOTES.

The hymn is addressed to Vaisvânara. The same *Ri*shi and metre.—No verse occurs in the other Sa*m*hitâs.

Verse 1.

Note 1. Cf. especially I, 45, 8 (above, p. 42). b*ri*hát bhā́*h* bíbhrata*h* havís*h*.

Note 2. Cf. vol. xxxii, p. 93 (I, 38, 11, note 2).

Verse 2.

Note 1. See above, I, 36, 1, note 2.

Verse 3.

Note 1. Dvibárhâ*h* is neuter. See Lanman, p. 560; Joh. Schmidt, Pluralbildungen der Indogermanischen Neutra, p. 132.

Note 2. Agni has discovered the Sâman which he proclaims to the mortal, like the track of a lost cow.

Verse 5.

Note 1. See H. O., Religion des Veda, p. 539.

Note 2. Abhrâtára*h* cannot be accusative plural fem., as Zimmer (Altindisches Leben, p. 419) seems to take it. The correct interpretation has been given by Pischel, Vedische Studien, I, p. 299.

Note 3. I.e. hell.

Verse 6.

Note 1. In the younger Vedic ritual certain Stotras are technically designated as p*ri*sh*th*a or 'backs' of the liturgies (see, for instance, Weber, Indische Studien, X, 385). Does the word stand here in the same sense? Or should we correct préshth*h*am?

Note 2. The seven tones of the scale?

Verse 7.

Note 1. This passage is obscure. The text runs thus: sasásya *k*árman ádhi *k*ā́ru p*r*í*s*ne*h* ágre rupá*h* árupitam (ā́rupitam Sa*m*hitâpâ*th*a) *g*ábâru. As to the first words, see III, 5, 6. To *k*ā́ru possibly a noun like nā́ma should be supplied (cf. below, verse 10). The last Pâda (cf. above, III, 5, 5, note 1) is simply untranslateable.

Verse 8.

Note 1. Of the milk alluded to in the third Pâda?—On ni*n*ík, cf. Lanman, p. 436; Joh. Schmidt, Pluralbildungen der Indogerm. Neutra, p. 397.

Note 2. The water of the cows is the milk, cf. X, 12, 3. Roth (Zeitschr. der D. Morgenl. Gesellschaft, XLVIII, 682): als sie den Schatz der Kühe entdeckt hatten (vâr iva=vâram iva).

Note 3. Rupá*h* ágram.

Note 4. Comp above, III, 5, 5 with note 1; III, 5, 6, note 2.

Verse 9.

Note 1. The sun, the face of the great gods (cf. I, 115, 1), accompanied by the dawn?

Verse 10.

Note 1. Is the meaning of all this that Agni, shining on the altar between heaven and earth, desires, and consumes with his flames, the oblation of butter which has its home in the udder of the cow?

Verse 11.

Note 1. On â*s*ásâ, see Lanman, p. 492 seq.; Bartholomae Indogermanische Forschungen, I, 182 seq.; Bechtel, Hauptprobleme der Indogerm. Lautlehre, p. 262. This noun is not to be derived from the root *s*âs, but from *sams*.

Note 2. Compare I, 79, 2 (with note 3).

Verse 12.

Note 1. Comp. X, 108, 7, where the Panis say to Saramâ: réku padám álakam ấ *g*agantha ('the place is empty (?); thou hast come in vain').

Verse 13.

Note 1. This verse has been treated of by Pischel, Ved. Studien, I, 306.

Verse 15.

Note 1. On this comparison, see Hirzel, Gleichnisse und Metaphern im Rigveda, p. 102 seq.

MA*N*D*A*LA IV, HYMN 6.

ASH*T*AKA III, ADHYÂYA 5, VARGA 4–5.

1. Stand upright for us, O Agni, Hot*ri* of the sacrifice, the best performer of sacrifices among the gods. For thou art the master of every thought; thou promotest the worshipper's prayer.

2. The unerring Hot*ri* has sat down among the people, joy-giving Agni, the wise one at the sacrifices[1]. Like Savit*ri* he has sent his light upward. Like a builder he has reared his smoke up to the sky.

3[1]. (The ladle) glowing, filled with gifts, with butter, is stretched forth. From left to right (does Agni move) choosing the divine people. Upright (stands) the (sacrificial) post like a new-born foal[2]; well-placed, well-established it anoints the victims[3].

4. After the sacrificial grass has been spread and the fire kindled, the delighted Adhvaryu has stationed himself upright. Agni, the Hot*ri*, chosen from of old, goes round thrice, like a shepherd.

5. As Hot*ri*, measuredly running, Agni, the joy-giving, sweet-tongued, the righteous, goes around by his own might. His flames run forward like race-horses; all beings are afraid when he has shone forth.

6. Beautiful, O fair-faced Agni, is thy aspect, who art terrible and manifold; pleasant (it is). As they have not hindered thy light by darkness, no bespatterers have left stains on thy body.

7. He whose mother (?)[1] has not been hindered from giving birth, nor his father and mother when-

ever they were incited (?)[2]: this Agni, the purifier, well-established like Mitra[3], has shone among the tribes of men,—

8. Agni, whom the twice-five sisters[1], dwelling together, have engendered among the human tribes, who awakes at dawn, who is bright like an elephant's (?)[2] tooth, whose mouth is beautiful, who is sharp like an axe.

9[1]. Agni, those golden horses of thine swimming in ghee, the red ones which go straight forward, the fleet ones, the brilliant, manly, wonderful horses, puissant stallions, have called hither the divine people.

10. Those victorious, never-tiring[1], fierce flames of thine, O Agni, which move about, hasten[2] to their goal like hawks; they roar mightily like the host of the Maruts.

11[1]. (This) hymn has been produced for thee, O Agni, when thou wert kindled. May (the priest) recite the litany; mayst thou distribute (treasures) to him who sacrifices. Men have set down Agni as the Hot*ri*, the U*s*ig*s*, adoring (Him), the praise of Âyu[2].

NOTES.

The same *R*ishi and metre.—Verse 6=TS. IV, 3, 13, 1.

Verse 2.

Note 1. The text has vidátheshu. Cf. above, I, 31, 6 note.

Verse 3.

Note 1. With the first hemistich compare above, III, 19, 2. See also VI, 63, 4.

Note 2. On akrá, see Geldner, Vedische Studien, I, 168.

Note 3. The meaning seems to be that the sacrificial post, which has been anointed itself, imparts ointment to the victim tied to it.

Verse 7.

Note 1. The meaning of sắtu is uncertain. Boehtlingk-Roth give 'receptaculum.' Joh. Schmidt (Kuhn's Zeitschrift, XXV, p. 29, cf. Hübschmann, Indogerm. Vocalsystem, p. 75) translates 'Mutterleib,' and connects the word with strî́. If 'womb' is right, it seems to be the womb from which Agni was born.

Note 2. Does this ish*t*áu belong to ish, 'to incite,' or to ish, 'to wish'? 'Whenever he (Agni) wishes.' M. M.

Note 3. On the well-established Mitra, comp. H. O., Religion des Veda, p. 186, note 1.

Verse 8.

Note 1. The ten sisters of course are the fingers.

Note 2. In translating atharyắa*h* ná dántam I have followed the opinion of Pischel (Vedische Studien, I, 99) on the meaning of atharî́, though his theory is very doubtful.

Verse 9.

Note 1. With this description of Agni's horses, comp. above, IV, 2, 2. 3.

Verse 10.

Note 1. On ayắsa*h*, cf. above, III, 18, 2, note 1.

Note 2. See Geldner, Kuhn's Zeitschrift, XXVII, 234.

Verse 11.

Note 1. The second hemistich of this verse is nearly identical with V, 3, 4.

Note 2. Cf. nárâ*s*a*m*sa, vol. xxxii, p. 439.

MANDALA IV, HYMN 7.

ASHTAKA III, ADHYÂYA 5, VARGA 6-7.

1. This (Agni) has been established here as the first by the establishers, the Hotri, the best sacrificer who should be magnified at the sacrifices, whom Apnavâna and the Bhrigus have made shine, brilliant in the woods, spreading to every house.

2. Agni! When will the splendour of thee, the god, appear in the right way? For verily the mortals have seized thee who shouldst be magnified in the houses.

3. Seeing the righteous, wise one, like the heaven with the stars, who produces joy at all sacrifices, from house to house—

4. The quick messenger of Vivasvat who rules over all human tribes: Him the Âyus have brought hither to every house, the light, him who belongs to the Bhrigus.

5. Him the knowing one they have set down in the right way as the Hotri, the gay one with his purifying flames, the best sacrificer with his seven (forms[1])—

6. Him who is enveloped in many mothers, in the wood[1], who does not rest thereon (?)[2], who is brilliant, though hidden in secret, easily to be found, and striving for all that is desired.

7. When the gods rejoiced in the . . . of the herbs[1], in that udder[2], in the foundation of Rita[3], the great Agni, to whom offerings are made with adoration, the righteous one, always approached eagerly for the sake of sacrifice.

8[1]. Thou, the knowing one, hast eagerly performed the messengership of the sacrifice, looking over both ends, over the two worlds. Thou goest as a messenger, chosen from of old, thou who knowest best the asçents to heaven.

9. Thy path is black. Light is before thee, the red one. Thy flame is speedy. This is one of the wonders: when the virgin conceives (thee as her) child[1], thou becomest a messenger, as soon as thou art born.

10. As soon as he is born, his strength shows itself, when the wind blows upon his flame. He turns his sharp tongue among the dry brushwood. Even solid food he tears to pieces with his teeth.

11. When he thirstily has grown strong by thirsty food[1], restless Agni appoints a thirsty messenger. Consuming (the wood) he follows the . . .[2] of the wind. He seems to drive forward a quick horse; the racer speeds along.

NOTES.

The same *Ri*shi. The metre is *G*agatî in verse 1, Anush*t*ubh in verses 2–6, Trish*t*ubh in verses 7–11.—Verse 1=VS. III, 15; XV, 26; XXXIII, 6; TS. I, 5, 5, 1; MS. I, 5, 1.

Verse 5.

Note 1. The seven flames or tongues of Agni? The seven Hot*r*is? The seven Ratnas?

Verse 6.

Note 1. Cf. IX, 107, 18. pári góbhi*h* úttara*h* sī́dan váneshu avyata.

Note 2. Possibly we might conjecture ấsritam, 'who rests thereon.'

Verse 7.

Note 1. On sasásya, cf. above, III, 5, 6, note 2. Víyutâ seems to be a locative standing parallel with the locative űdhan. We have here sasásya víyutâ . . . *ri*tásya dhấman, quite as in V, 21, 4 the two accusatives *ri*tásya yónim and sasásya yónim stand parallel. The meaning of víyutâ, however, seems to me quite uncertain. Is it an action-noun derived from vi-yu, 'to separate,' 'to keep off,' or from (vi-) vâ, 'to weave'? Professor Max Müller proposes: 'at the removal of the grass or tinder in which the spark is kept.

Note 2. sásmin űdhan; cf. below, 10, 8.

Note 3. Cf. above, I, 147, 1.

Verse 8.

Note 1. With this verse, compare below, hymn 8, verse 4.

Verse 9.

Note 1. The wood, the child of which is Agni.

Verse 11.

Note 1. I take ánnâ here as an instrumental.—Compare with our passage VII, 3, 4. t*ri*shú yát ánnâ samáv*ri*kta *g*ámbhai*h*; X, 79, 5. yá*h* asmai ánnam t*ri*shú âdádhâti; X, 91, 7. t*ri*shú yát ánnâ vévishat vitísh*th*ase; X, 113, 8. agní*h* ná *g*ámbhai*h* t*ri*shú ánnam ávayat.

Note 2. me*l*ím; cf. above, III, 26, 9.

MA*ND*ALA IV, HYMN 8.

ASH*T*AKA III, ADHYÂYA 5, VARGA 8.

1. I press on for you with my prayer to the all-possessing messenger, the immortal bearer of offerings, the best sacrificer.

2. He, the great one, knows indeed the place of wealth[1], the ascent to heaven; may he, (therefore,) conduct the gods hither.

3. He, the god, knows how to direct the gods for the righteous (worshipper), in his house. He gives (us) wealth dear (to us).

4. He is the Hot*ri*; he who knows the office of a messenger, goes to and fro (between men and gods), knowing the ascent to heaven.

5. May we be of those who have worshipped Agni with the gift of offerings, who cause him to thrive and kindle him.

6. The men who have brought worship to Agni, are renowned as successful by wealth and by powerful offspring.

7. May much-desired wealth come to us day by day; may gains arise among us.

8. He (Agni), the priest of the tribes, (the priest) of men, pierces (all hostile powers) by his might as with a tossing[1] (bow).

NOTES.

The same *Ri*shi. The metre is Gâyatrî.—Verse 1 = SV. I, 12; MS. II, 13, 5.

Verse 2.

Note 1. Comp. Pischel, Ved. Studien, II, 118.

Verse 8.

Note 1. Kshiprấ evidently is an instrumental. Cf. kshi prádhanvan, kshipréshu, kshipré*n*a dhánvanâ, II, 24, 8.

MA*ND*ALA IV, HYMN 9.

ASH*T*AKA III, ADHYÂYA 5, VARGA 9.

1. Agni, have mercy! Thou art great, who hast come to this pious man to sit down on the sacrificial grass.

2. He who cannot be deceived, the zealous, the immortal has among men become the messenger of all.

3. He, the joy-giving Hot*ri*, is led around the sacred seat at the heaven-aspiring sacrifices. And he sits down as the Pot*ri* also.

4. Agni sits down also as (the sacrificer's) wife[1] at the sacrifice, and as the master of the house in the house, and as the Brahman[2].

5. Thou zealously approachest as the Upavakt*ri*[1] of the people who perform the sacrificial service, and (thou approachest) the offerings of men.

6. And thou zealously performest the messengership for the man in whose sacrifice thou takest pleasure, in order to bear the mortal's offering (to the gods).

7. Find pleasure[1] in our rites, in our sacrifice, O Aṅgiras. Hear our call!

8. May thy unerring chariot, by which thou protectest the worshippers, encompass us from every side.

NOTES.

The same *R*ishi and metre.—Verse 1 = SV. I, 23. Verse 8 = VS. III, 36; MS. I, 5, 4. 5. 11.

Verse 4.

Note 1. 'Wir vermuten: utâgnâ agnir adhvare . . . die correctur dürfte evident sein.' Ludwig. The same conjecture has been proposed already in 1868 by Prof. Max Müller (Chips, 2nd ed., vol. iii, p. 157). In my opinion the traditional text is correct.

Note 2. The Brahman very probably is not the Brahman of the later ritual, but the Brâhma*n*â*kkh*a*m*sin. See H. O., Religion des Veda, p. 396.

Verse 5.

Note 1. The Upavakt*ri* is identical with the Pra*s*âst*ri* or Maitrâvaru*n*a of the later ritual. H. O., Religion des Veda, p. 390.

Verse 7.

Note 1. On *g*oshi, cf. Bartholomae, Studien zur Indog. Sprachgeschichte, I, 21.

MA*ND*ALA IV, HYMN 10.

ASH*T*AKA III, ADHYÂYA 5, VARGA 10.

1[1]. O Agni! May we to-day successfully perform, with thy heedfulness[2], this praise[3] which touches thy heart, which is like a horse, like auspicious power of the mind.

2. For verily thou, O Agni, hast become the charioteer of auspicious power of the mind, of real ability, and of the mighty *Ri*ta.

3. Through these our hymns direct thyself hitherwards to us like the sun with its light[1], O Agni, gracious with all thy faces.

4. May we to-day worship thee, O Agni, praising thee with these songs. Thy roarings thunder like (the thunder) of Heaven.

5. Thy sweetest aspect, O Agni, shines near us for glory's sake, now by day, now by night, like gold.

6. Like purified gh*ri*ta is thy stainless body; (it is) brilliant gold: that (body) of thine has shone[1], O self-dependent one, like gold.

7. For even a malice which one has committed, thou verily drivest away entirely, O righteous Agni, from the sacrificing mortal[1].

8. May our friendship, O Agni, our brotherhood with you, the gods, be blessed. This is our navel (i. e. relation) in our seat, in this udder[1].

NOTES.

The same *Ri*shi. The metre is stated to be Padapaṅkti (verses 4, 6, 7, Padapaṅkti or Ush*n*ih; verse 5, Mahâpadapaṅkti; verse 8, Ush*n*ih): see on this metre M. M., vol. xxxii, p. xcviii seq.; H. O., Prolegomena, p. 98; Kühnau, Die Trish*t*ubh-*G*agatî-Familie, p. 234 seq.—Verse 1=SV. I, 434; MS. I, 10, 3. Verses 1-3=SV. II, 1127-1129; VS. XV, 44-46. Verses 1-4=TS. IV, 4, 4, 7. Verse 1, 2, 4 = MS. II, 13, 8. Verse 3=MS. IV, 10, 2. Verse 6=TS. II, 2, 12, 7; MS. IV, 12, 4.

Verse 1.

Note 1. The Avasâna in this verse ought to stand before h*ri*disp*ris*am, not after this word, as the traditional text places it. *Ri*dhyâma, consequently, cannot be accented.

Note 2. Dr. Neisser's opinion on óha is different (Bezzenberger's Beiträge, XVIII, 312).

Note 3. I read stómam, which is frequently found as the object of the verb *ri*dh, and which in several passages receives the epithet h*ri*disp*ris*.

Verse 3.

Note 1. On the syntactical form of this comparison, see Bergaigne, Mélanges Renier, p. 95.

Verse 6.

Note 1. Or ro*k*ate, 'shines'?

Verse 7.

Note 1. The Avasâna ought to stand before mártât. Cf. above, verse 1, note 1.

Verse 8.

Note 1. Cf. above, IV, 7, 7. The meaning seems to be: in this sacrificial place, where the cows give milk.

MA*N*D*A*LA IV, HYMN 11.

ASH*T*AKA III, ADHYÂYA 5, VARGA 11.

1. Thy auspicious face, O mighty Agni, shines in the neighbourhood of the sun[1]. Brilliant to see, it is seen even by night. Soft to behold is the food in thy (beautiful) body[2].

2. O Agni, disclose (wise) thoughts for him who praises thee; (disclose) the opening, when thou, O strong-born, hast been praised with trembling. Grant unto us, O very great one, such a rich prayer as thou with all the gods wilt hold dear, O brilliant one.

3. From thee, O Agni, genius is born, from thee (wise) thoughts, from thee beneficent hymns. From thee comes wealth adorned with heroes[1] to the thus-minded mortal who worships thee.

4. From thee the racer is born that wins booty, whose energy expands round-about[1], the helpful, of true strength; from thee delightful wealth sent by the gods; from thee, O Agni, the swift and impetuous horse.

5. Thee, O Agni, the pious mortals seek to win by their prayers as the first, thee the god with agreeable speech, O immortal, who drivest away malice, the household god, the lord of the house, the wise one.

6. (Drive) far from us senselessness and anguish; (drive) far all ill-will from him whom thou attendest[1]. Be gracious at evening, Agni, son of strength, to him whom thou, the god, attendest with welfare.

NOTES.

The same *Ri*shi. Metre, Trish*t*ubh.—Verse 1 = TS. IV, 3, 13, 1.

Verse 1.

Note 1. Comp. above, IV, 10, 5. ro*k*ate upâké.

Note 2. Literally, 'in thy appearance' (rûpé). Thus the Soma is stated, IX, 16, 6, to purify itself rûpé avyáye, literally, 'in the appearance of the sheep,' i.e. in the filter made of sheep's hair.

Verse 3.

Note 1. See Lanman, p. 560; Pischel, Ved. Studien, II, 115.

Verse 4.

Note 1. On víhâyâ*h*, see V. Henry, Les livres VIII et IX de l'Atharva-véda (1894), p. 40 (AV. VIII, 2, 7).

Verse 6.

Note 1. Probably the correct Padapâ*th*a reading would be, as Prof. Bartholomae (Bezzenberger's Beiträge, XV, 190) has noticed, yám nipási (cf. Pâda d: yám . . . sá*k*ase). If yát is correct, the translation will be: '(drive) far all ill-will when thou protectest (us).'—Bartholomae proposes either to change asmát to asmât, or to interpret it as an equivalent of asmât. It is possible, though in my opinion not very probable, that the text should be changed. The ablative asmát very frequently depends on âré.

MA*ND*ALA IV, HYMN 12.

ASH*T*AKA III, ADHYÂYA 5, VARGA 12.

1. May the man who holds the sacrificial ladle and kindles thee, O Agni, who thrice prepares food for thee on this day, victoriously overcome (his foes) through his lustre, wise through the power of thy mind, O *G*âtavedas.

2 [1]. He who toiling brings fuel to thee, doing service to thy, the great (god's) face, O Agni, kindling thee at evening and at dawn—he prospers, obtains wealth, and destroys his enemies.

3. Agni is master of mighty royal power [1]; Agni (is master) of gain, of the highest wealth. He, the youngest, self-dependent (god) in the right way distributes treasures to the mortal worshipper.

4. Whatever sin, O youngest (god), we have committed against thee in thoughtlessness, men as we are [1], make thou us sinless before Aditi; release us from (every) guilt on all sides, O Agni!

5. Even from great guilt, O Agni, from the prison of gods and of mortals—let us, thy friends, never be harmed; grant luck and weal to kith and kin.

6 [1]. As you formerly have released, O Vasus, the buffalo cow bound by the foot, O worshipful gods, thus take away from us this distress. May, O Agni, our life be further prolonged.

NOTES.

The same *Ri*shi and metre.—Verse 4=TS. IV, 7, 15, 6; MS. III, 16, 5. Verse 5=MS. IV, 11, 1. Verse 6=TS. IV, 7, 15, 7; MS. III, 16, 5; IV, 11, 1.

Verse 2.

Note 1. With the beginning of this verse, comp. above, IV, 2, 6.

Verse 3.

Note 1. Comp. Roth, Zeitschr. der D. Morg. Ges., XLVIII, 114.

Verse 4.

Note 1. Grassmann is right in giving to purushatrấ the meaning 'unter den Menschen,' and in observing with reference to our passage: 'wo die Bedeutung "nach Menschenweise" (s. purushátâ) besser passt.' The same is the opinion of Böhtlingk-Roth. No doubt we should read purushátâ; cf. VII, 57, 4=X, 15, 6. yát va*h* ấga*h* purushátâ kárâma; IV, 54, 3. á*k*ittî yát *k*ak*ri*má . . . purushatvátâ.

Verse 6.

Note 1. This verse is identical with Rig-veda X, 126, 8.

MAṆḌALA IV, HYMN 13.

ASHṬAKA III, ADHYÂYA 5, VARGA 13.

1. Benevolent Agni has looked on the breaking of the shining dawns, on the bestowal of treasures. Come to the dwelling of the virtuous (mortal), ye Asvins. The god Sûrya rises with his light.

2. The god Savitṛi has sent his light upward[1], shaking his banner[2] like a warrior who fights for cows[3]. Varuṇa and Mitra follow the law, when they make the Sun rise on heaven.

3. Him whom (the gods) dwelling in firm peace, and never losing their object, have created for dispersing the darkness—Him, the Sun, the all-observer, the seven young fallow mares carry forward.

4. With (thy horses) most ready to run thou goest[1] forward, spreading out thy web (of light), removing (from the world) the black cloth (of darkness), O god. The rays of the Sun have shaken[2] the darkness, and have sunk it into the waters like a hide.

5. Unsupported, unattached, spread out downwards-turned—how is it that he[1] does not fall down? By what power of his does he move? Who has seen (that)? Erected as the pillar of Heaven he protects the firmament.

NOTES.

The same *Ri*shi and metre.—Verse 4=TB. II, 4, 5, 4.

This hymn and the next evidently form a couple. They have the same number of verses, and are composed in the same metre. They are both addressed to Agni in his matutinal character, or rather to the A*s*vins, who are invoked to partake of the matutinal oblation (13, 1; 14, 1. 4). The first verse of 13 is quite similar to that of 14; the same may be said of the second verses of the two hymns; the concluding verse of both is identical.

Verse 2.

Note 1. Cf. above, IV, 6, 2.

Note 2. Cf. Zend drafsha, 'banner.'

Note 3. Cf. IV, 40, 2. sátvâ bharishá*h* gavishá*h*.

Verse 4.

Note 1. The Sun is addressed.

Note 2. It is more natural to take dávidhvata*h* as nom. plur. than as gen. sing. (Ludwig).

Verse 5.

Note 1. The Sun.

MA*ND*ALA IV, HYMN 14.

ASH*T*AKA III, ADHYÂYA 5, VARGA 14.

1. Agni *G*âtavedas, the god, has looked on the dawns that shine with all their might[1]. Come hither, O Nâsatyas[2], wide-ruling (gods), on your chariot to this our sacrifice.

2. The god Savit*ri* has sent his shine upward, producing light for the whole world. The Sun, shining with his rays, has filled Heaven and Earth and the air.

3. The red one[1], carrying hither (bliss)[2], has come with her light, the great, brilliant one, shining with her rays. Ushas, the goddess, awakening (all beings) to welfare, goes along on her well-yoked chariot.

4. May those chariots and horses, most ready to drive, drive you[1] hither at the break of dawn. For these Somas are for you[1] that you may drink the honey-drink[2]. Rejoice, O manly ones, at this sacrifice.

5. = IV, 13, 5.

NOTES.

The same *Ri*shi and metre.—No verse of this hymn occurs in the other Sa*m*hitâs. On the parallelism in which IV, 14 stands to IV, 13, see the introductory note on IV, 13.

Verse 1.

Note 1. On máhobhi*h*, see vol. xxxii, p. 196 seq. (I, 165, 5, note 3). Here the word refers to the powerful light of the dawn, not of Agni, cf. VI, 64, 2. úsha*h* devi ró*k*amânâ máhobhi*h*.

Note 2. On the mention of the Nâsatyas (A*s*vins) in this connection, compare the introductory note on IV, 13.

Verse 3.

Note 1. The Dawn as before.

Note 2. That an object like 'bliss' is to be supplied, is shown by such passages as I, 48, 9. úsha*h* . . . âváhantî bhű̃ri asmábhyam saúbhagam; I, 92, 3. (the Dawns) ísham váhantî*h* suk*rí*te sudā́nave; I, 113, 15. (the Dawn) âváhantî póshyâ vā́ryâ*n*i.

Verse 4.

Note 1. The text has the dual of the pronoun. The A*s*vins are addressed.

Note 2. It is the peculiar character of the A*s*vins that they drink mádhu; see Hillebrandt, Vedische Mythologie, vol. i, p. 239 seq. H. O., Religion des Veda, p. 208, note 4; p. 367, note 2.

MANDALA IV, HYMN 15.

ASHTAKA III, ADHYÂYA 5, VARGA 15–16.

1. Agni, the Hotri, he who is a strong horse, is led around at our sacrifice, the god worshipful among the gods.

2. Agni goes thrice [1] around the sacrifice, like a charioteer, conveying the enjoyment [2] to the gods.

3. Agni, the lord of booty, the sage, has circumambulated the oblations, bestowing treasures on the worshipper.

4. This (is the Agni) who is kindled in the front for Devavâta's son, the Sriñgaya [1], the brilliant (god), the deceiver of foes.

5. May the strong mortal be the master of this (god), of an Agni like this, with sharp teeth and bountiful.

6 [1]. Him they clean day by day like a racer that wins (booty), like (Soma), the red young child of Heaven [2].

7. When Sahadeva's son, the prince, thought of me with two bay horses [1], I rose up like one who is called.

8. And immediately I accepted from Sahadeva's son, the prince, those adorable two bay horses which he offered me.

9. May this prince Somaka, Sahadeva's son, live long, for your sake, O divine Asvins!

10. Give long life, O divine Asvins, to this son of Sahadeva, the prince!

NOTES.

The same *Ri*shi. Metre, Gâyatrî.—Verses 1–3=TB. III, 6, 4, 1; MS. IV, 13, 4. Verse 3=SV. I, 30; VS. XI, 25; TS. IV, 1, 2, 5; MS. I, 1, 9.

The first three verses are characterised by the constant allusions to Agni's being carried around, and, in connection therewith, by the frequent repetition of the preposition pári. Probably these verses formed an independent Tri*k*a-hymn, the position of which would be according to the laws of arrangement of the Sa*m*hitâ; this Tri*k*a seems, consequently, to belong to the original collection of hymns. The verses 4–10, on the other hand, or at least the verses 7–10, would seem to be a later addition; the verses 4–6 can be considered as a Tri*k*a belonging to the original Sa*m*hitâ, though in this case it is difficult to explain why the verses 7–10, which do not contain any reference to Agni, have been inserted here at the end of the series of Agni hymns. Another argument against the separation of the verses 4–6 from the rest of the Sûkta is the mention of the prince *Sriñg*aya in verse 4: verses 7–10 refer to a prince Somaka Sâhadevya, and we know from the Aitareya Brâhma*n*a (VII, 34, cf. *S*atapatha Brâhma*n*a II, 4, 4, 4) that this prince also belonged to the *Sriñg*aya tribe.

Verse 2.

Note 1. Cf. above, IV, 6, 4.

Note 2. I.e. the offering which the gods enjoy.

Verse 4.

Note 1. This *Sriñg*aya Daivavâta is mentioned also in VI, 27, 7.

Verse 6.

Note 1. The first Pâda of this verse is identical with the first Pâda of VIII, 102, 12.

Note 2. The red young child of Heaven seems to be the Soma. The Soma frequently is called arushá ('red'), and is said to be cleansed by men; in IX, 33, 5; 38, 5, the expression div*áh* s*í*su*h* ('the young child of Heaven') is used with regard to him.

Verse 7.

Note 1. I. e. when he thought of presenting me with the two horses.

MA*ND*ALA V, HYMN 1.

ASH*T*AKA III, ADHYÂYA 8, VARGA 12–13.

1. Agni has been wakened by the fuel of men, in face of the Dawn who approaches like a milch-cow. His flames stream forward to the sky like quick (birds) that fly up to a branch.

2. The Hot*ri* has been wakened that there may be sacrifice for the gods. Gracious Agni has stood upright in the morning. When he has been kindled, his brilliant stream of flames has been seen. The great god has been released from darkness.

3. When he has wakened the string of the crowd (of worshippers)[1], the bright Agni anoints himself with bright cows[2]. Then the Dakshi*n*â is yoked, striving for gain[3]. He who stands upright has, by the sacrificial ladles, sucked her who lies extended[4].

4. Towards Agni the minds of the pious turn together as (all) eyes (turn) to the sun. When both Dawns of different colour[1] give birth to him, the white racer is born at the beginning of days.

5. For He, the noble one, has been born at the beginning of days, the red one has been laid down in the woods that have been laid down. Agni, the Hot*ri*, the best sacrificer, has sat down, bestowing his seven treasures on every house.

6. Agni, the Hot*ri*, the best sacrificer, sat down in the mother's lap, in the sweet-smelling place, the young sage growing up in many places, the righteous one, the supporter of tribes, and kindled in their midst.

7. They magnify with adorations that priest efficacious at sacrifices, Agni the Hot*ri*, who has spread himself over heaven and earth according to *Ri*ta; they groom (Agni), the own racer (of men), with Gh*ri*ta.

8. He who likes to be groomed, is groomed in his own (abode), the house-friend[1], praised by sages, our auspicious guest, the bull with a thousand horns who has the strength of such a one. O Agni! By this power thou surpassest all other (beings).

9. O Agni! Thou overtakest all other (beings) in one moment (for the sake of him) to whom Thou hast become visible as the fairest one, thou who shouldst be magnified, the wonderful, brilliant one, the beloved guest of human clans.

10. To thee, O youngest (god), the tribes bring tribute, O Agni, from near and far. Behold[1] the grace of the most glorious (god)! Mighty, O Agni, is thy great and glorious shelter.

11. Mount to-day, O shining Agni, the shining car, in the neighbourhood of the worshipful (gods). Knowing the paths, the wide air[1], bring hither the gods that they may eat the oblation.

12. We have pronounced an adoring speech to the holy sage, to the manly bull. Gavish*th*ira adoringly has sent his song of praise to Agni as the gold (i. e. the sun) far-reaching (is sent by the gods upward) to the sky.

NOTES.

The *Ri*shis are Budha Âtreya (cf. verse 1, ábodhi) and Gavish*th*ira Âtreya (cf. verse 12). The metre is Trish*t*ubh.—Verse 1 = SV. I, 73; AV. XIII, 2, 46; VS. XV, 24; TS.

IV, 4, 4, 1. Verses 1-2=MS. II, 13, 7. Verses 1-3=SV. II, 1096-1098. Verse 5=TS. IV, 1, 3, 4. Verse 6=MS. IV, 11, 1; TB. I, 3, 14, 1. Verse 9=TB. II, 4, 7, 10. Verse 10=MS. IV, 11, 4; TB. II, 4, 7, 9. Verse 12=MS. II, 13, 7; TB. IV, 4, 4, 2; VS. XV, 25.

Verse 3.

Note 1. The meaning seems to be: when Agni has set into motion the string (representing the prayers, &c.) by which the worshippers tie and instigate him and the other powers of the sacrifice. Cf. IV, 1, 9. prá tám (scil. agním) mahyấ rasanáyâ nayanti; IX, 87, 1. ásvam ná tvâ (scil. sómam) vâgínam margáyantah ákkha barhíh rasanấbhih nayanti. See also I, 163, 4. 5.

Note 2. I.e. with bright ghrita.

Note 3. The Dakshinâ or sacrificial gift offered by the Yagamâna to the ministrant priests, is represented here as a car which is yoked in the morning. Cf. Bergaigne, Rel. Védique, I, 128; III, 283.

Note 4. 'He who stands upright' is Agni; 'she who lies extended' seems to be the cow, i.e. the ghrita which Agni sucks by means of the sacrificial ladles.—See also Pischel, Vedische Studien, II, 113, from whose interpretation I differ.

Verse 4.

Note 1. I.e. Night and Dawn.

Verse 8.

Note 1. I cannot adopt the conjectures of Bartholomae (Bezzenberger's Beiträge, XV, 197) on své dámûnâh.

Verse 10.

Note 1. The human worshipper seems to be addressed; the 'most glorious one' is very probably Agni.

Verse 11.

Note 1. Vidvân, which may be construed with the genitive or with the accusative, stands here with both cases.

MA*ND*ALA V, HYMN 2.

ASH*T*AKA III, ADHYÂYA 8, VARGA 14–15.

1. The young mother carries in secret the boy confined[1]; she does not yield him to the father. People do not see before them his fading[2] face laid down with the Arâti[3].

2. Who is that boy, O young woman, whom thou, the Peshî[1], carriest? It is the queen who has borne him. Through many autumns the fruit of the womb has increased. I saw him born when his mother gave birth to him.

3. I saw him the gold-toothed, brilliant-coloured preparing his weapons far from his dwelling-place[1]. After I have offered to him the ambrosia cleared (from all impure mixture)[2]—what may the Indra-less, the hymnless do to me?

4. I saw him, the highly shining (Agni), walking far from his dwelling-place, like (a bull) together with the herd[1]. Those (women) have not held him, for he has been born. The young women become grey[2].

5. Who have separated my young bull from the cows that[1] had no cow-herd, not even a stranger? May those who have held him, let him loose. May he, the knowing one, lead the cattle towards us.

6. Him, the king of dwellings (?)[1], the dwelling-place of people, the Arâtis have laid down[2] among men. May the spells of Atri loose him. May the reproachers become reproachable (themselves).

7. Thou hast loosed the bound *S*una*h*s*e*pa from

the thousand sacrificial posts; for he toiled (worshipping thee). Thus, O Agni, loose from us the fetters, O knowing Hot*ri*, sitting down here.

8[1]. For thou hast gone away[2] from me, because thou wert angry; (this) the protector of the laws of the gods[3] has told me. (But) Indra, the knowing one, has looked after thee. Instructed by him, O Agni, I have come hither.

9. Agni shines with mighty light; he makes all things visible by his greatness. He conquers godless, wicked wiles. He sharpens his two horns in order to pierce the Rakshas.

10. And may the roarings of Agni mount up to the sky, with sharp weapons in order to kill the Rakshas. In his rapture his flames break down (everything); the godless hindrances do not hold him back.

11. This song of praise, O strong-born (Agni), I, the priest, have fashioned for thee, as a skilful workman (builds) a chariot[1]. If thou acceptest that (praise), O god Agni, may we conquer thereby waters together with the sun.

12. May the bull[1] with mighty neck, grown strong, with no foe to resist him, get together the niggard's wealth. Thus the immortal (gods) have spoken to this Agni: may he grant protection to the man who has spread the Barhis; may he grant protection to the man who brings offerings.

NOTES.

The *Ri*shi of verses 1, 3–8, 10–12 is Kumâra Âtreya, or V*ri*s*a* *G*âna; or both are the *Ri*shis of these verses. Of the verses 2 and 9 V*ri*s*a* alone is the *Ri*shi. The metre is

Trish*t*ubh (verse 12, *S*akvarî).—Verse 9=AV. VIII, 3, 24. Verses 9, 10=TS. I, 2, 14, 7. Verse 11=TB. II, 4, 7, 4.

A part of this hymn is very obscure. I do not think, as does Prof. Geldner (Festgruss an Roth, 192), that the story of the *S*â*t*yâyanakam (see Sâya*n*a's commentary, and compare Pa*ñk*avi*ms*a Brâhma*n*a XIII 3, 12), of the Purohita V*ris*a, who drives with the king on the royal chariot and kills a boy, throws any real light on the difficult points of the hymn. Nor does it seem to me that, as is the opinion of Prof. Hillebrandt (Zeitschrift der Deutschen Morgenländischen Gesellschaft, XXXIII, 248 seq.), the first six verses, which Hillebrandt considers as an independent hymn, contain a description of how the fire which they try to produce by the attrition of the Ara*n*is, does not appear. In my opinion the hymn—which is really one hymn as the tradition gives it—is a prayer of a person who suffers, who feels himself bound by the fetters of distress (verse 7) and persecuted by the power of Rakshas (verses 9, 10). Agni, formerly resplendent, has decayed and has forsaken him: may Agni be restored to his former might (verse 6), and may we ourselves be released from all distress (verse 7, &c.). Possibly the hymn is connected with the rite of Punarâdheya, where the sacrificial fire which has brought no luck to the sacrificer, is extinguished, and after an interval a new fire is established (H. O., Religion des Veda, p. 353). There may of course be other special points, beyond the reach of our conjectures, which, if known, would elucidate several of the obscure allusions so frequent in the first verses of the hymn.

Verse 1.

Note 1. The boy very probably is Agni.—With the words sámubdham gúhâ bibharti, cf. I, 158, 5. súsamubdham ava-ádhu*h*.

Note 2. Not without hesitation I translate minát as if it were the middle minânám. Possibly the word means: 'which violates (the ordinances),' i.e. which does not shine and bring luck to men as it usually does. Ná seems, as it usually does (cf. Delbrück, Altindische Syntax, p. 543), to belong to the whole clause, and not to minát.

Note 3. Böhtlingk-Roth and Grassmann conjecture aratnáu; Hillebrandt, arâtáu; Geldner (Festgruss an Roth, 192), árâtau. Geldner seems to be right (cf. verse 6), though it will scarcely be possible to determine what concrete being was here thought of. Geldner says, 'Gemeint ist die Pi*s*â*k*ikâ, welche die Gluth des Feuers entführt hat;' but, as has already been observed, I do not think that this traditional story on the meaning of our hymn is of any real value.

Verse 2.

Note 1. The meaning of Peshî is unknown. The word seems anyhow to describe the wrong mother as low or contemptible. Agni is degraded by sojourning with her, while his proper nature is glorious, for he is the queen's son.

Verse 3.

Note 1. Agni has forsaken his proper dwelling.

Note 2. On vip*ri*kvat, cf. Taitt. Sa*m*hitâ III, 1, 6, 2. yuná*g*mi tisrá*h* vip*ri*ka*h* sû́ryasya te; Vâ*g*. Sa*m*hitâ IX, 4. samp*ri*kau stha*h* sám mâ bhadré*n*a p*ri*ṅktam; vip*ri*kau stha*h* ví mâ pâpmánâ p*ri*ṅktam. Vi-p*rik* seems to mean, consequently, 'to free something from an admixture,' and am*ri*tam vip*ri*kvat seems to be ambrosia in which dwells the power of getting free from bad admixtures. Thus in the passage quoted from the Taitt. Sa*m*hitâ the Sun is referred to as thrice cleared from all impure elements. It is quite uncertain whether the expression used here refers or not to the myth of the churning of the ocean (Geldner, loc. cit.), and I do not think that we should translate am*ri*tam vip*ri*kvat, as Geldner does, 'das was sich als Nektar ausscheidet.'

Verse 4.

Note 1. I read with Böhtlingk-Roth sumádyûtham.

Note 2. The young women seem to be hostile beings of

the same kind as the young woman mentioned in verse 2. They try to seize Agni, but he has been born already; his fiery, unassailable nature has been formed. I do not pretend to know what it means that then those female foes become grey with age. 'I think they are the Dawns who hold Agni in the dark; but when he escapes and is actually born, they, the Dawns, become grey.' M. M.

Verse 5.

Note 1. The relative pronoun yéshâm seems to refer both to the bull (maryakám) and to the cows (góbhi*h*). The bull probably is Agni who has been separated from the cows, i.e. the oblations, prayers, &c. (?) 'Possibly the bull Agni, the rising sun, has been separated from the cows, the clouds or dawns.' M. M.

Verse 6.

Note 1. Vasấm rấ*g*ânam. I cannot follow the interpretation of Pischel, Vedische Studien, I, 210.

Note 2. Or ní dadu*h*, 'they have bound him'? Cf. áva s*ri*g*antu in the third Pâda, and níditam in verse 7.

Verse 8.

Note 1. The whole verse is nearly identical with X, 32, 6.

Note 2. I consider aíye*h* (cf. Bartholomae, Arische Forschungen, II, 72, 76; Studien zur Indogermanischen Sprachgeschichte, I, 21) as 2nd sing. pluperfect of the root i.

Note 3. Varu*n*a?

Verse 11.

Note 1. With the second Pâda compare I, 130, 6; V, 29, 15.

Verse 12.

Note 1. The bull of course is Agni.

MANDALA V, HYMN 3.

ASHTAKA III, ADHYÂYA 8, VARGA 16-17.

1. Thou, O Agni, art Varuna, when born; thou becomest Mitra when kindled. In thee, O son of strength, the Visvedevâs (dwell). Thou art Indra for the mortal worshipper.

2. Thou becomest Aryaman when thou bearest [1] the secret name of the maidens, O self-dependent one. They anoint (thee) with cows [2] like the well-established Mitra [3], when thou makest husband and wife one-minded.

3. For thy glory the Maruts have cleansed themselves [1], who are thy fair and brilliant offspring, O Rudra [2]! The footprint of Vishnu which is put down in the highest place: therewith thou protectest the secret name of the cows.

4. By thy beauty, O god, the gods are beautiful to behold [1]. Assuming many (powers or goods) they attached themselves to immortality. Men have set down Agni as the Hotri, the Usigs, honouring (him), the praise of Âyu [2].

5. There is no (other) Hotri before thee, a better sacrificer [1]; no one surpasses thee, O self-dependent one, by wisdom. And that house of which thou art the guest, he [2], O god, will overcome the mortals by his sacrifice.

6. May we overcome the mortals, O Agni, protected by thee, striving for wealth, awaking (thee) with offerings; may we (overcome mortals) in the contest, in the distribution [1] of days; may we (overcome them) by wealth, O son of strength!

7. If a man should turn upon us sin or guilt, bring ye the evil on him who pronounces evil spells (against us). Destroy, O knowing one, such a curse, O Agni, (of a man) who injures us by falsehood.

8. Thee, O god, the ancient (mortals) have made their messenger at the break of this (dawn), and have sacrificed with their oblations, when thou goest along, O Agni, in the abode of wealth, a god kindled by the mortals and by the Vasus.

9. Protect the father—drive away (evil) as the knowing one—(the father) who is considered[1] as thy son, O son of strength[2]. When, O sapient (Agni), wilt thou look upon us? When wilt thou, who knowest *Ri*ta, requite (human deeds)?

10. The father[1] adoring gives many names to thee, O Vasu, if thou shouldst take pleasure therein. Will not Agni, delighting in his divine power, grant us his favour, he who has grown strong?

11. Thou indeed, O Agni, youngest one, bringest thy praiser across all dangers. Thieves have been seen and deceitful men; dishonest people have come with unknown designs.

12. These our processions have been directed towards thee. Yes, to thee, the Vasu, this guilt has been confessed. Verily this Agni, grown strong, will never surrender us to the curse nor to him who does harm to us.

NOTES.

The *Ri*shi is Vasu*s*ruta Âtreya; the metre is Trish*t*ubh.—No verse of this hymn occurs in the other Sa*m*hitâs.

Verse 2.

Note 1. I think that we must read bíbharshi.

Note 2. I.e. with butter.

Note 3. On Mitra as the god of alliances, and the anointing of Mitra—possibly of an object that represents Mitra—see H. O., Religion des Veda, p. 186, note 1. Cf. also Pischel, Vedische Studien, I, 92 seq.

Verse 3.

Note 1. I.e. they have adorned themselves. Cf. VII, 39, 3. urā́v antárikshe mar*g*ayanta *s*ubhrā́*h*.

Note 2. Rudra of course is here a name of Agni.

Verse 4.

Note 1. Sud*rís*a*h*, which I have translated as nom. plur., may also be understood as gen. sing.: 'by thy beauty, who art beautiful to behold, O god, the gods, assuming, &c.'

Note 2. Cf. Narâ*s*a*m*sa.—This hemistich is nearly identical with IV, 6, 11.

Verse 5.

Note 1. Comp. above, III, 17, 5.

Note 2. The construction is rather free.

Verse 6.

Note 1. Vidátheshu áhnâm: cf. above, I, 31, 6, note 2 (p. 26 seq.).

Verse 9.

Note 1. See Neisser, Bezzenberger's Beiträge, XVIII, 310.

Note 2. Bergaigne (Religion Védique, II, 103) proposes to read yodhi without accent and to derive it, as Delbrück does, from yu (not from yudh); he translates the first hemistich: 'Protège-nous, écarte le père qui passe pour ton fils.' I think that he is right as to the verb yu, but that the accent of yódhi is correct; the words yódhi vidvā́n form a parenthesis. Agni is invoked to protect the father of the sacrificing tribe (comp. verse 10), or the father of

Agni himself, i.e. the sacrificer or the priest, who is himself considered, at the same time, as the son of Agni (see Bergaigne, I, 37 seq.; Geldner, Vedische Studien, I, 167).

Verse 10.

Note 1. 'The father' may either be the father spoken of in verse 9 (see verse 9, note 2). Or the word may refer to Agni: 'He who adores thee, gives many names to thee, if thou, the father, O Vasu, &c.'

MA*ND*ALA V, HYMN 4.

ASH*T*AKA III, ADHYÂYA 8, VARGA 18-19.

1. Thee, O Agni, the treasure-lord of treasures, I gladden at the sacrifices, O king! May we, striving for gain, conquer gain through thee; may we overcome the hostilities of mortals.

2. Agni, the bearer of oblations, our ever-young father, is mighty, brilliant, beautiful to behold among us. Shine (on us) food with a good household[1]. Turn all glory towards us[2].

3. Establish Agni as the Hot*ri*, the sage of the clans, the lord of human clans, the bright purifier, whose back is covered with ghee, the omniscient. May he obtain the best goods (for us) among the gods.

4. Enjoy thyself, O Agni, joined with I*d*â, uniting thyself with the rays of the sun. Enjoy our fuel, O *G*âtavedas, and bring the gods hither that they may eat our offerings.

5. Welcome, as our household-god and the guest in our dwelling, come to this our sacrifice as the knowing one. Dispelling, O Agni, all (hostile) attempts, bring to us the possessions of those who are at enmity with us.

6. Drive away the Dasyu with thy weapon, creating strength for thy own body. When thou bringest the gods across (to us), O son of strength, then, O manliest Agni, protect us in (our striving for) gain.

7. May we worship thee, O Agni, with hymns, with offerings, O purifier with glorious light. Stir for us wealth with all goods; bestow on us all riches!

8. Enjoy, O Agni, our sacrifice, our offering, O son of strength who dwellest in three abodes. May we be well-doers before the gods. Protect us with thy thrice-protecting shelter.

9. Bring us across all difficulties and dangers, O *G*âtavedas, as with a boat across a river. Agni, being praised with adoration as (thou hast been praised) by Atri, be a protector of our bodies.

10. When I, the mortal, call thee, the immortal, thinking of thee with humble mind[1], bestow glory on us, O *G*âtavedas; may I attain immortality, O Agni, with my offspring.

11. The well-doer to whom thou, O Agni *G*âtavedas, createst pleasant freedom, will happily attain wealth with horses and sons, with valiant men and cows.

NOTES.

The same *Ri*shi and metre.—Verse 1=TS. I, 4, 46, 2. Verse 2=TS. III, 4, 11, 1; MS. IV, 12, 6; 14, 15. Verse 5=AV. VII, 73, 9; TB. II, 4, 1, 1; MS. IV, 11, 1. Verse 9=TB. II, 4, 1, 5; TÂ. X, 2, 1; MS. IV, 10, 1. Verses 10, 11=TS. I, 4, 46, 1.

Verse 2.

Note 1. According to the traditional text, su-gârhapatyấ*h* must be an epithet of ísha*h*. But the conjecture of Böhtlingk-Roth, su-gârhapatyá*h*, has great probability: 'as the good protector of our household, shine food on us.' Cf. AV. XII, 2, 45=TB. I, 2, 1, 20.

Note 2. The second hemistich is nearly identical with III, 54, 22.

Verse 10.

Note 1. See Pischel, Vedische Studien, I, 221.

MAN*D*ALA V, HYMN 5.

ASHT*A*KA III, ADHYÂYA 8, VARGA 20–21.

Âprî Hymn.

1. Sacrifice sharp gh*ri*ta to the well-kindled light, to Agni *G*âtavedas.

2. May the unbeguiled Narâ*s*a*m*sa make this sacrifice ready; for he is a sage with honey in his hand.

3[1]. Agni, magnified by us, bring hither to our help the bright, beloved Indra, with easy-going chariots.

4. Soft like wool[1] spread thyself (O Barhis). The hymns have been sung to thee. Be to us for success, O beautiful (Barhis)!

5. O divine, easily passable doors, open yourselves for our protection. Fill the sacrifice (with bliss) further and further!

6. We approach (with prayers) Night and Morning, whose face is beautiful, the increasers of vital strength, the two young mothers of *Ri*ta.

7. On the wind's flight, magnified, ye two divine Hot*ri*s of man, come hither to this our sacrifice.

8[1]. I*l*â, Sarasvatî, and Mahî, the three comfort-giving goddesses, they who do not fail, shall sit down on the sacrificial grass.

9. Come hither as a friend, Tvash*tri*, and mighty in welfare, and also by thyself, protect us in every sacrifice.

10. Where thou knowest, O tree (i. e. sacrificial

post), the secret names of the gods, to that place make the offerings go.

11. Svâhâ to Agni and Varu*n*a! Svâhâ to Indra and the Maruts! Svâhâ to the gods for our offering!

NOTES.

The same *Ri*shi. Metre, Gâyatrî.—Verse 1=VS. III, 2. Verse 9=TS. III, 1, 11, 2. Verse 10=TB. III, 7, 2, 5.

Verse 3.

Note 1. The first hemistich is identical with I, 142, 4.

Verse 4.

Note 1. On ûr*n*a-mradâ*h*, see Lanman, Noun-Inflection, p. 560.

Verse 8.

Note 1. This verse is identical with I, 13, 9.

MAN*D*ALA V, HYMN 6.

ASH*T*AKA III, ADHYÂYA 8, VARGA 22–23.

1. I think of that Agni who is a Vasu, to whom the milch-cows go home, the swift horses (go) home, (our) own racers (go) home. Bring food to thy praisers!

2. He is Agni who is praised as the Vasu, he to whom the milch-cows come together, and the quickly running horses, and the well-born liberal patrons. Bring food to thy praisers!

3. For Agni, dwelling among all tribes, gives a racer to the clan. Agni (gives a racer) that is truly helpful for (winning) wealth[1]: he (the racer) being well cherished, will attain precious gain. Bring food to thy praisers!

4. May we kindle thee[1], Agni, O god, the brilliant, never ageing, in order that yon highly miraculous fuel of thine[2] may shine in the sky. Bring food to thy praisers!

5. To thee[1], O Agni, our oblation is offered with a *Rik*, O lord of bright splendour, highly brilliant, wonderful lord of the clan, carrier of oblations! Bring food to thy praisers!

6. Those Agnis make everything precious prosper in the Agnis; they drive forward (precious wealth); they incite it; they speed it hither in the due way[1]. Bring food to thy praisers!

7. Those flames of thine, O Agni, the racers, have boasted mightily—they who with the flight of their

hoofs have made tremble[1] the stables of the cows. Bring food to thy praisers!

8. Bring fresh food with fine dwellings, O Agni, to us, thy praisers! May we be of those who have praised (thee), who have thee as their messenger, house by house. Bring food to thy praisers!

9. Thou warmest in thy mouth, O highly brilliant one, the two (sacrificial) ladles full of butter. And mayst thou fill us (with gifts) at our hymns, O lord of strength! Bring food to thy praisers!

10. Thus[1] they have driven, they have led[2], Agni in the due way by prayers and sacrifices. May he bestow on us plenty of valiant men, and that plenty of swift horses (wished for)[3]. Bring food to thy praisers!

NOTES.

The same *Ri*shi. The metre is Paṅkti.—Verse 1=SV. I, 425. Verses 1-2=VS. XV, 41, 42; MS. II, 13, 7. Verses 1, 3, 2=SV. II, 1087-1089. Verse 3=TB. III, 11, 6, 4. Verse 4=SV. I, 419; AV. XVIII, 4, 88; MS. II, 13, 7. Verses 4, 5, 9=SV. II, 372-374; TS. IV, 4, 4, 6. Verse 9=VS. XV, 43; TS. II, 2, 12, 7.

Verse 3.

Note 1. At first sight the conjecture of Böhtlingk-Roth and Grassmann, rayím, is very tempting, cf. IX, 12, 9. rayím . . . su-âbhúvam; X, 122, 3. rayí*n*â . . . su-âbhúvâ. I believe, nevertheless, that on closer examination the traditional text will prove correct. Sá prîtá*h* evidently refers to the racer (vâ*g*ín) cf. I, 66, 4=69, 5. vâ*g*ī́ ná prîtá*h* (cf. also X, 101, 7. prî*n*îtá á*s*vân): then it follows that su-âbhúvam also refers to the racer, and râyé (cf. I, 100, 16; III, 53, 16) will be quite right.

Verse 4.

Note 1. Te stands for the accusative; see Pischel, Zeitschrift der Deutschen Morgenländ. Gesellschaft, XXXV, 715; Delbrück, Altindische Syntax, p. 205.

Note 2. This refers to the sun. By kindling the sacred fire men make the sun rise. See H. O., Religion des Veda, p. 110.

Verse 5.

Note 1. The pronoun 'to thee' stands twice, te in the first Pâda (where it is repeated from the first Pâda of verse 4, ắ te agne), and túbhyam (or rather túbhya) in the fourth Pâda, unless we construe te havi*h*.

Verse 6.

Note 1. See Pischel, Vedische Studien, II, 127.

Verse 7.

Note 1. See Gaedicke, Der Accusativ, p. 57.

Verse 10.

Note 1. On the nasalization of evắñ, cf. H. O., Prolegomena, p. 469 seq.

Note 2. Pischel (Vedische Studien, II, 127) explains a*g*u*h* as a*g*ush, the contrary of sa*g*ū́sh. Bartholomae (Studien zur Indogermanischen Sprachgeschichte, II, 159, note 2; cf. Indogermanische Forschungen, III, 108, note 1) conjectures á*g*ur (= á*g*man) yamu*h*: 'sie haben ihn jetzt auf seiner Bahn festgehalten.' I believe, as Sâya*n*a does, that this a*g*uryamu*h* contains two independent verbs, a*g*u*h* and yamu*h*, which are quite correct forms of the roots a*g* and yam (see Delbrück, Altindisches Verbum, p. 65). As to a*g*, cf. VI, 2, 8. a*g*yáse ágne vâ*g*ī́ ná; V, 30, 14. átya*h* ná vâ*g*ī́ raghú*h* a*g*yámâna*h*; as to yam II, 5, 1. *s*akéma vâ*g*ína*h* (i.e. agné*h*) yámam. But should not the accent be yamú*h*?

Note 3. The fourth Pâda is identical with VIII, 6, 24.

MA*ND*ALA V, HYMN 7.

ASH*T*AKA III, ADHYÂYA 8, VARGA 24–25.

1. O friends, (bring) together your united food and praise to Agni, the strongest (god) of (human) dwellings, the offspring of Vigour, the mighty one—

2. At whose onslaught[1], wherever it be, men rejoice in the seat of men, whom the worthy ones kindle, whom (human) creatures produce.

3. When we get together the food and the offerings of men, he has grasped, with the strength of his splendour, the rein of *Ri*ta.

4. He indeed produces light even by night to him who is afar, when he, the ever-young purifier, destroys the lords of the forest.

5. He at whose officiating (men) pour down the offering of their sweat on the paths—to Him who is noble by his own nature, the worlds have risen as to ridges (of hills)—

6. He whom the mortal has acquired, the much-desired (god), for the refreshment of every one, the sweetener of nourishment, the homestead for the Âyu—

7. He indeed, the beast, mows off deserts and habitable land like a mower, the golden-bearded with brilliant teeth, the *Ri*bhu of undecaying strength.

8. The bright one for whom (the gh*ri*ta) streams (quickly) like an axe[1], as at (the sacrifice of) Atri. Him the well-bearing mother has born, as soon as[2] she had enjoyed love[3].

9. He who satisfies thee for refreshment, O Agni

who drinkest butter: mayst thou bestow splendour, renown, and (wise) mind on such mortals [1].

10. Thus I have seized upon the spirit of Adhri*g* (?) as upon a head of cattle given by thee [1]. May then Atri, O Agni, overcome the Dasyus who do not give (to the Brahmans); may Isha overcome the men (who do not give).

NOTES.

The *Ri*shi is Isha Âtreya (cf. verse 10); the metre is Anush*t*ubh (verse 10, Pa*n*kti).—Verse 1 = VS. XV, 29; TS. II, 6, 11, 4; IV, 4, 4, 3; MS. IV, 11, 1. Verses 2, 3 = TS. II, 1, 11, 3; MS. IV, 12, 4.

Verse 2.

Note 1. Yásya sám-*ri*tau: see I, 127, 3.

Verse 8.

Note 1. With the expression svádhiti*h*-iva rî́yate (Lanman, Noun-Inflection, p. 375), compare V, 48, 4. rîtím para*s*ó*h*-iva. Of course we must ask: what is the thing that streams so brightly and quickly as an axe moves? The thing in question is stated to stream (rîyate) for Agni now as it did at Atri's sacrifice. The expression 'as at Atri's sacrifice' seems to show that something like prayers or libations is alluded to. The verb rîyate, on the other hand, seems to point either to rivers, or to streams of Soma or of Gh*ri*ta. Thus, considering that Gh*ri*ta is mentioned much more frequently in connection with Agni than Soma, we are led to the conclusion that the poet speaks here of streams of Gh*ri*ta. Should we not for *sú*k*ih* read *sú*k*i*, which would be here as in IV, 1, 6; VI, 10, 2; IX, 67, 12, an epithet of Gh*ri*ta? 'He for whom the bright (Gh*ri*ta) streams quickly like an axe.' The origin of the reading *súkih* may easily be accounted for; the word was thought to refer to Agni.—Another interpretation of this hemistich has been given by Benfey, Vedica und Linguistica, p. 177.

Note 2. Krâ*n*ấ: cf. I, 58, 3, note 1 (p. 47).

Note 3. 'Sobald sie den Liebesgenuss erlangt hatte.' Pischel, Ved. Studien, I, 71.

Verse 9.

Note 1. The first hemistich speaks of the worshipper in the singular, the second in the plural.

Verse 10.

Note 1. This hemistich is quite obscure. With manyúm ấ dade, cf., for instance, X, 48, 2. dásyubhya*h* pári n*ri*m*n*ám ấ dade. Adhrí*g*a*h* may be the genitive of a proper name, as I have translated it; but this is quite doubtful. Was the hymn intended for a charm in which the sacrificer seized a head of cattle which represented the spirit of an enemy, and thus deprived that enemy of his courage?

MAN*D*ALA V, HYMN 8.

ASHT*A*KA III, ADHYÂYA 8, VARGA 26.

1. Thee, O Agni, the men who love *Ri*ta have kindled, the ancient ones thee the ancient, for the sake of bliss, O (god) who art produced by strength; the highly-brilliant, worshipful, in whom all refreshment dwells, the household god, the lord of the house, the chosen.

2. Thee, O Agni, the clans have set down, the ancient guest, the flame-haired lord of the house, with mighty light, with many shapes, the winner of prizes, giving good shelter and good help, who is busy among the decayed (wood)[1].

3. Thee, O Agni, the human clans magnify, who knowest (the art of sacrificial) libations, who separatest (what was mixed)[1], the highest bestower of treasures, who, (though) dwelling in secret, O blessed one, (yet) art visible to all, mightily roaring, an excellent sacrificer, shining with ghee.

4. Thee, O Agni, the supporter, we always have praised with our songs and have sat down near thee with adoration. Thus being kindled, O Aṅgiras, be pleased with us, as a god through the mortal's brilliant (offering)[1], with thy glorious splendours.

5. Thou, O Agni, manifold-shaped, bestowest vigour on every house in thy ancient way, O much-praised one! Thou rulest with might over much food. This impetuousness of thine, when thou rushest forward impetuously, is not to be defied.

6. Thee, O Agni, when kindled, O youngest one, the gods have made their messenger and bearer of

oblations. Thee who extendest over wide spaces, who dwellest in ghee, into whom offerings are poured, they have made their eye, impetuous, stirring thoughts.

7. Thee, O Agni, on whom offerings of ghee are poured, (men) desirous of thy favour have kindled from of old with good fuel. Thus, grown strong, increased by the plants, thou spreadest thyself over the terrestrial spaces.

NOTES.

The same *Ri*shi. Metre, *G*agatî.—Verse 3 = TS. III, 3, 11, 2. Verses 6, 7 = TB. I, 2, 1, 12.

Verse 2.

Note 1. The Padapâ*th*a gives *g*arat-vísham. I prefer this explanation to *g*ara-dvísham ('who hates decay').

Verse 3.

Note 1. Agni is, in the later ritual, worshipped as 'separator' (víví*k*i), if the sacrificer's fires have become mixed with other fires. See Taittirîya Brâhma*n*a III, 7, 3, 5; *S*atapatha Brâhma*n*a XII, 4, 4, 2 (where this very verse is quoted), &c.

Verse 4.

Note 1. For ya*s*ásâ, Böhtlingk-Roth conjecture yá*s*asâ, which seems to me a conjectura nimis facilis. I think that the adjective ya*s*ásâ is right, and that a noun, meaning 'offering' or the like, should be supplied. Cf. above, IV, 1, 16, note 4.

MANDALA V, HYMN 9.

ASHTAKA IV, ADHYÂYA 1, VARGA 1.

1. Thee, O Agni, the god, mortals bringing offerings magnify. I deem thee the *G*âtavedas. Carry then the offerings (to the gods) in thy due way.

2. Agni is the Hot*ri* of the dwelling where they offer gifts and spread the sacrificial grass, he with whom sacrifices, with whom glorious gains assemble.

3. And he whom the kindling-stick has born, the young one, like a young (calf), the supporter of human clans, Agni the best sacrificer—

4. And thou showest thyself hard to seize like a son of ...[1], thou who art a burner of many woods, O Agni, like an animal (that consumes all grass) on a meadow[2].

5[1]. And he whose smoky[2] flames come together, when Trita in heaven blows upon him like a smelter, sharpens (him) as in smelting (him)[3]...

6. May I through thy protection, O Agni, and through the praises of Mitra—may we[1], like dispellers of malice, overcome the dangers of mortals.

7. Bring this wealth to us, O powerful Agni, to (these our) men. May he[1] give us dwelling; may he[1] give us prosperity; may he[1] help us in winning booty. And help us to grow strong in fights!

NOTES.

The *Ri*shi is Gaya Âtreya (cf. V, 10, 3); the metre is Anush*t*ubh (verses 4 and 7, Pańkti).—Verse 1 = TB. II, 4, 1, 4.

Verse 4.

Note 1. Putrá*h* ná hvâryá*n*âm. The meaning of hvâryá is conjectural. Cf. on hvârá, to which it very probably is related, I, 141, 7, note 1; II, 2, 4, note 1. Does hvâryá mean 'serpent,' or a kind of horse (VI, 2, 8. átya*h* ná hvâryá*h* *s*í*s*u*h*)?

Note 2. The last Pâda is identical with VI, 2, 9. Considering the occurrence of the word hvâryá here and in VI, 2, 8 (see note 1) we cannot believe that this is merely a casual coincidence.

Verse 5.

Note 1. On this verse, compare Neisser, Bezzenberger's Beiträge, XX, 40; Macdonell, Journal Roy. As. Soc., 1893, p. 446.

Note 2. Dhûmína*h* may be gen. sing.: 'he whose, the smoky (god's), flames.'

Note 3. Ludwig and Neisser (Bezz. Beitr., loc. cit.) regard dhmâtárî (Padap. dhmâtári) as a nom. sing. masculine. I think that Geldner (Vedische Studien, I, 146, note 1) and Bartholomae (Indogermanische Forschungen, I, 496, note 2) are right in explaining it as a locative infinitive. Compare also Johansson, Kuhn's Zeitschrift, XXX, 415; Joh. Schmidt, Pluralbildungen der Indogermanischen Neutra, p. 247. Macdonell translates, 'as in a smelting furnace.'

Verse 6.

Note 1. The poet, who has begun his sentence in the first person singular ('may I'), goes on in the plural.

Verse 7.

Note 1. 'He,' i. e. Agni, or 'it,' i. e. the wealth?

MAṆDALA V, HYMN 10.

ASHṬAKA IV, ADHYÂYA 1, VARGA 2.

1. Agni, bring us the mightiest splendour, O liberal one[1]! With wealth and plenty cleave a path for us to booty.

2. Thou, O wonderful Agni, (protect) us, through thy power of mind, through the bounteousness of thy strength. Upon thee mysterious power has entered. (Thou art) indeed[1] like worshipful Mitra.

3. Thou, O Agni, increase for our sake the dominion and the prosperity of those liberal givers, (of those) men who have accomplished liberalities (towards us) for our songs of praise.

4. They who adorn prayers for thee, O bright Agni, the givers of horses[1]: those men are powerful in their power, whose glory awakes by itself (shining) more mightily than even the sky[2].

5. Those shining flames of thine, Agni, go fiercely along, like lightnings (flashing) around the earth, like a thundering chariot bent on victory.

6. Now then, Agni, (come) for our protection, and for the reward of the urgent (worshipper)! May our liberal patrons pass across[1] all regions[2]!

7. Thou, O Agni, Aṅgiras, who hast been praised and who art being praised, bring us, O Hotṛi, wealth which overpowers (even) skilful men, to thy praisers, and thou shalt be praised by us. And help us to grow strong in fights[1].

NOTES.

The same *Ri*shi. Metre, Anush*t*ubh (verses 4, 7, Pañkti).—Verse 1 = SV. I, 81. The hymn seems to stand parallel with V, 9.

Verse 1.

Note 1. On adhrigo, compare above, III, 21, 4, note 1 (p. 284).

Verse 2.

Note 1. Krâ*n*ấ: see I, 58, 3, note 1 (p. 47); von Bradke, Dyâus Asura, p. 35; Pischel, Vedische Studien, I, 71.

Verse 4.

Note 1. *S*umbhánti á*s*va-râdhasa*h*; see X, 21, 2.

Note 2. On the ablative dependent on a positive, compare Speijer, Sanskrit Syntax, p. 78, and see also Delbrück, Grundriss der vergleichenden Grammatik (Brugmann), III, 1, 216; Pischel, Göttinger Gelehrte Anzeigen, 1884, 509.

Verse 6.

Note 1. On the use of this infinitive, see Delbrück, Altindische Syntax, p. 416.

Note 2. The last Pâda is identical with IV, 37, 7.

Verse 7.

Note 1. The last words are identical with those of V, 9, 16, 17.

MA*ND*ALA V, HYMN 11.

ASH*T*AKA IV, ADHYÂYA 1, VARGA 3.

1. The guardian of people, the watchful one, Agni, the highly dexterous, has been born, for the sake of new welfare. With ghrita on his face, with his mighty, heaven-touching (light) he, the bright one, brilliantly shines for the Bharatas.

2. Agni, the beacon of sacrifice, the first Purohita[1] men have kindled in the threefold abode[2]. (Driving) on the same chariot with Indra and with the gods, he, the highly wise Hot*ri*, has sat down on the Barhis for sacrificing.

3. Though not cleansed, thou art born bright from thy two mothers[1]. Thou hast arisen as the joy-giving sage belonging to Vivasvant[2]. They have strengthened thee by gh*ri*ta, O Agni, into whom oblations are poured. Smoke, reaching the sky, has become thy beacon.

4. May Agni straightway come to our sacrifice. Men carry Agni here and there, house by house. Agni has become the messenger, the carrier of oblations. Choosing Agni they choose a thoughtful (god).

5. For thee, O Agni, is this sweetest speech, for thee this prayer; may this one do thy heart good[1]! The prayers fill thee with power and strengthen thee, like great rivers the Sindhu.

6. Thee, O Agni, who wert hidden, dwelling here and there in every wood, the Aṅgiras have discovered[1]. Thus thou art born, produced by attrition, a mighty force. Thee, O Aṅgiras, they call the son of strength.

NOTES.

The *Ri*shi is Sutambhara Âtreya, the metre *G*agatî.—Verses 1, 6, 2=SV. II, 257–259; TS. IV, 4, 4, 2–3. Verses 1, 6, 5=MS. II, 13, 7. Verses 1, 6=VS. XV, 27–28. Verse 3=TB. II, 4, 3, 3.

Verse 2.

Note 1. This Pâda is identical with the first Pâda of X. 122, 4.

Note 2. The three sacrificial fires are alluded to.

Verse 3.

Note 1. The two kindling-sticks.

Note 2. Vivásvata*h* is genitive, not ablative, as Pischel, Vedische Studien, I, 241, believes. Agni opens his earthly career by doing service at the sacrifice of Vivasvant, i.e. originally, in my opinion, the first man. Comp. H. O., Religion des Veda, p. 122.

Verse 5.

Note 1. On the curious spelling manîshấ iyám in the Sa*m*hitâ text, instead of manî́sheyám, see the Rig-veda Prâti*s*âkhya 163; H. O., Prolegomena, p. 386.

Verse 6.

Note 1. The ancestors of the priestly tribes, being the first priests themselves, discover Agni.

MA*ND*ALA V, HYMN 12.

ASH*T*AKA IV, ADHYÂYA 1, VARGA 4.

1. To the mighty, sacrificial Agni, to the bull of *R*ita[1], the Asura, I bring this prayer and this song, which is turned towards him, to (him) the bull, as well-clarified gh*ri*ta (is poured) into his mouth at the sacrifice.

2. O knower of *R*ita, know the *R*ita! Bore for many streams of *R*ita. I (do) not (serve) a Yâtu[1] by violence nor by falsehood; I serve the *R*ita of the red bull[2].

3. How, O Agni, performing the *R*ita through *R*ita, mayst thou become a witness of our newest[1] hymn? The god, the protector of the seasons, knows of my seasons[2]. I (do) not (know another) lord but him who attains (for us) this wealth.

4. Who, O Agni, are thy fetterers to (fetter) the impostor[1]? What brilliant guardians were successful? Who, O Agni, drink the drink of falsehood? Who are the protectors of untrue speech?

5. These friends of thine, O Agni, turning themselves from (thee)[1], they who had been kind, have become unkind. They have harmed themselves by their own speeches, uttering wrong words to the righteous.

6. He who magnifies thy sacrifice, O Agni, by adoration, and serves[1] the *R*ita of the red bull: may a large, good dwelling come to him, to the offspring of the advancing Nahusha.

NOTES.

The same *Ri*shi; the metre is Trish*t*ubh.—No verse of this hymn occurs in the other Sa*m*hitâs.

Verse 1.

Note 1. The genitive *ri*tásya seems to depend on v*ri*sh*n*e, not on mánma. On the connection of Agni with the *Ri*ta, see Bergaigne, III, 229 seq.; H.O., Religion des Veda, 201.

Verse 2.

Note 1. A bad demon.

Note 2. Of Agni.

Verse 3.

Note 1. I think that návya*h* stands for návyasa*h*. Thus Ludwig translates: 'des neuen liedes.' It seems evident that it is not the nominative of návya, 'praiseworthy' (Böhtlingk-Roth, Grassmann).

Note 2. Probably we ought to read *ri*tapā́ *ri*tā́nâm. Cf. IV, 23, 4. devá*h* bhuvat nâvedâ*h* me *ri*tā́nâm, and see III, 20, 4, note 1 (above, p. 282). The translation will be: 'The god, the protector of *Ri*ta, knows of my (deeds of) *Ri*ta.'

Verse 4.

Note 1. Or ripáva*h*? 'Who, O Agni, are the impostors who fetter thee?'

Verse 5.

Note 1. On víshu*n*â*h*, compare V, 34, 6: ásunvata*h* víshu*n*a*h* sunvatá*h* v*ri*dhá*h*.

Verse 6.

Note 1. The second verse (*ri*tám sapâmi arushásya v*ri*sh*n*a*h*) shows with evidence that for sá pâti we ought to read sápâti (see Roth, Kuhn's Zeitschrift, XXVI, 49, and compare on the expression *ri*tam sap, Geldner, Vedische Studien, II, 135).

MA*ND*ALA V, HYMN 13.

ASH*T*AKA IV, ADHYÂYA 1, VARGA 5.

1. Praising we call[1] thee; praising let us kindle[1] thee, Agni, praising, for thy help.

2. Desirous of riches, we devise to-day an effective song of praise, of Agni the heaven-touching god[1].

3. May Agni take pleasure in our prayers, he who is the Hot*ri* among men. May he sacrifice[1] to the divine host.

4. Thou, O Agni, art widely extended, the gladly accepted, desirable Hot*ri*; through thee they spread out the sacrifice.

5. The priests make thee grow, O Agni, the greatest acquirer of wealth, the highly praised one. Bestow thou on us abundance of heroes.

6. Agni! Thou encompassest the gods as the felly (encompasses) the spokes (of a wheel). Thou strivest[1] for brilliant wealth.

NOTES.

The same *Ri*shi. The metre is Gâyatrî.—Verse 2=MS. IV, 10, 2 (cf. TS. V, 5, 6, 1). Verses 2–4=SV. II, 755–757. Verse 4=TB. II, 4, 1, 6; MS. IV, 10, 2. Verse 5=TS. I, 4, 46, 3; MS. IV, 11, 4. Verse 6=TS. II, 5, 9, 3. As the Sâma-veda forms a T*rik*a of the verses 2–4, not 1–3 or 4–6, we have here an instance of those liberties which the arrangers of the Sâma-veda not unfrequently took with regard to the Rig-veda text (see H. O., Zeitschrift der Deutschen Morgenländischen Gesellschaft, XXXVIII, 469 seq.); we have no reason, in such a case, to resort to such an expedient as changing the traditional order of verses in the Rig-veda text.

Verse 1.

Note 1. We have first the indicative, then the optative.

Verse 2.

Note 1. Divisp*ris*a*h* no doubt is genitive sing. referring to Agni, not nominative pl. referring to the worshippers.

Verse 3.

Note 1. Ludwig is right in observing here: 'eigentlich er spreche die yâ*g*yâs als einladung für die götter.'

Verse 6.

Note 1. On *riñg*ase, comp. Bartholomae, Indogermanische Forschungen, II, 281; Neisser, Bezzenberger's Beiträge, XX, 59. I take the form here as 2nd singular.

MANDALA V, HYMN 14.

ASHTAKA IV, ADHYÂYA 1, VARGA 6.

1. Awaken[1] Agni by thy song of praise, kindling (him) the immortal one. May he place our offerings among the gods.

2. Him, the immortal god, the mortals magnify at their sacrifices, the best sacrificer among the tribe of men.

3. Him indeed they all magnify, the god, with the (sacrificial) ladle that overflows with gh*ri*ta, Agni, in order that he may bear the oblation.

4. Agni when born has shone, killing the Dasyus, (killing) darkness by light. He has found the cows, the waters, the sun[1].

5. Worship Agni, the sage who should be magnified, whose back is covered with gh*ri*ta. May he come and hear my call[1].

6. They have made Agni grow by gh*ri*ta, him who dwells among all tribes, and by longing, eloquent praises.

NOTES.

The same *Ri*shi and metre.—Verse 1=TS. IV, 1, 11, 4; MS. IV, 10, 1; VS. XXII, 15. Verse 3=TS. IV, 3, 13, 8; MS. IV, 10, 1. Verse 4=MS. IV, 10, 2.

Verse 1.

Note 1. We have no reason and, unless we write bodhayâ, no right for taking bodhaya as an equivalent of bodhayâni (Ludwig).

Verse 4.

Note 1. Agni is considered here, as is done frequently, as the performer of deeds which properly belong to Indra (see H. O., Religion des Veda, 98 seq.). Indra is the conqueror of the cows and of the waters; as to the sun, it may be said of both gods with the same right that they have acquired it for mankind (Religion des Veda, 110 seq.; 150 seq.).

Verse 5.

Note 1. Although me can be accusative (Pischel, Zeitschrift der Deutschen Morgenländischen Gesellschaft, XXXV, 714 seq.), I have no doubt that it is here genitive, and depends on hávam. Cf. II, 24, 15. véshi me hávam; X, 61, 4. vîtám me ya*g*ñám.

MA*ND*ALA V, HYMN 15.

ASH*T*AKA IV, ADHYÂYA 1, VARGA 7.

1. I bring a prayer to the worshipper, the renowned sage, the glorious, ancient one. Agni is the highly gracious Asura, taking his seat in gh*ri*ta, the holder of wealth, supporting goods.

2. By *Ri*ta they have supported the supporting *Ri*ta, near the powerful (performer)[1] of sacrifice, in highest heaven, the men who sit[2] on the supporting support of the sky, and who with born (men) attained to the unborn.

3. Dispelling anguish[1] they spread out for the ancient one[2] his bodies[3], mighty vital power, difficult to overcome. May he, the new-born, traverse the spaces. They have stood round him as round an angry lion.

4. When thou carriest, spreading out, man after man like a mother, for their nourishment and for their sight, when thou growest old[1] assuming life after life, thou goest around by thyself in manifold shapes.

5. May gain protect now the boundaries of thy strength, the wide, firmly supporting milkstream[1] of wealth, O god! Putting down thy foot in secret like a thief[2], thou hast enlightened and freed Atri for the sake of wealth mightily[3].

NOTES.

The *Ri*shi is Dharu*n*a Âṅgirasa (cf. dharú*n*a*h* vásva*h* agní*h*, verse 1; *ri*tám dharú*n*am, divá*h* dhárman dharú*n*e, verse 2; dógham dharú*n*am, verse 5); the metre, Trish*t*ubh. —No verse of this hymn occurs in the other Sa*m*hitâs.

Verse 2.

Note 1. It may be asked whether *s*âká, beside its meaning 'the powerful (helper),' may also mean 'the power.' This would suit very well, V, 30, 10. sám tấ*h* (scil. gấ*h*) índra*h* as*rig*at asya *s*âkaí*h*; VI, 19, 4. tám va*h* índram *k*atínam asya *s*âkaí*h* ihá nûnám vâ*g*ayánta*h* huvema. The translation then would be: 'by the power of sacrifice.' Böhtlingk-Roth conjecture *s*ấke.

Note 2. I believe that sedúsha*h* stands for the nominative, cf. devấ*h* ábibhyusha*h*, I, 11, 5; S. B. E. XXXII, p. 28. This sedúsha*h* led on to a second accusative standing for the nominative, n*rî*n.—The men sitting on the support of the sky seem to be the forefathers who have established the universal laws, the Aṅgiras.

Verse 3.

Note 1. I consider a*m*hoyúva*h* as nom. plur. masc., but it may also be gen. sing. masc., or acc. plur. fem., as an epithet either of Agni or of his tanvã*h*.

Note 2. The ancient one (pûrvyá) seems to be Agni (cf. verse 1).

Note 3. Cf. VI, 46, 12. yátra *s*ũrâsa*h* tanvã*h* vitanvaté.

Verse 4.

Note 1. I think, like Ludwig, that *g*arase should be accented.

Verse 5.

Note 1. These are accusatives.—Cf. on this passage, Pischel, Vedische Studien, I, 39 seq.

Note 2. Cf. H. O., Prolegomena, p. 73.

Note 3. Cf. VI, 1, 2. mahá*h* râyé *k*itáyanta*h*.—See Geldner, Ved. Studien, I, 268.

MAN*D*ALA V, HYMN 16.

ASH*T*AKA IV, ADHYÂYA 1, VARGA 8.

1. Sing [1] (a song that gives) mighty vital power, to the light, to god Agni, whom the mortals have placed in front [2] like Mitra by their praises [3].

2. For he, Agni, the Hot*ri* of men, day by day, in the arms of Daksha, discloses the offering in the due way, as Bhaga [1] (discloses) a treasure.

3. (We abide [?]) in his praise, the liberal (god's), in his friendship, the mightily brilliant one's, in whom, the loudly roaring Aryan, all (beings) have put together their strength.

4. For verily, O Agni, (thou belongest [?]) to them [1] through thy bounteousness [2] in (bestowing) abundance of heroes. Him indeed, the vigorous one, his glory the two worlds could not encompass [3].

5. Now then, Agni, come hither and, being praised, bring treasure [1] to us who, we ourselves and our liberal givers, may acquire welfare together. And help us to grow strong in fights.

NOTES.

The *Ri*shi is Pûru Âtreya (cf. 17, 1); the metre Anush*t*ubh (verse 5, Pańkti). This hymn and V, 17 are parallel hymns; the concluding words of both are identical (see also V, 9, 7; 10, 7).—Verse 1 = SV. I, 88.

Verse 1.

Note 1. Ár*k*â may be first or second person.

Note 2. Dadhiré purá*h*: they have made him their Purohita.

Note 3. Comp. above, V, 9, 6.

Verse 2.

Note 1. On Bhaga, the divine Bestower or Dispenser of riches, cf. Herbert Baynes. The Biography of Bhaga (Actes du huitième Congrès intern. des Orientalistes, Sect. II, fasc. 1, pp. 83 seq.).

Verse 4.

Note 1. To them, i. e. the Maghavans. Compare below, 18, 3. 4.

Note 2. Ma*m*hánâ seems to be instrumental. Comp. 10. 2; 18, 2.

Note 3. Agni is himself yahvá; so ná cannot be the comparative particle, but it must be the negation. Similarly it is said in II, 16, 3 that Heaven and Earth cannot encompass the indriya of Indra; cf. also X, 27, 7.

Verse 5.

Note 1. Vấryam seems to depend on ấ bhara. With the whole phrase compare the first Pâda of V, 17, 5.

MANDALA V, HYMN 17.

ASHTAKA IV, ADHYÂYA 1, VARGA 9.

1. May the mortal truly by sacrifices, O god, (magnify) the stronger one for help; may the Pûru, when good service has been performed, magnify Agni (and thereby draw him) hither for his aid.

2. For thou art manifestly considered as his (i. e. Agni's) disposer, highly brilliant by thyself[1]: (magnify then Agni who is) a firmament of bright splendour, lovely beyond[2] thought[3].

3. (It is) yonder (sun?) who verily has been yoked by his (i. e. Agni's) light[1] through the impetuous speech[2]—(by the light of Agni) whose flames mightily shine as if (they were made to shine) by the sperm of heaven[3].

4. Through his, the wise one's, insight there is wealth on his, the wonderful (Agni's), chariot. And Agni is praised, he who is to be invoked among all peoples.

5. Now indeed our liberal lords have manifestly attained[1] treasure. Offspring of vigour! Protect us for the sake of victory! Help us to welfare! And assist us to grow strong in fights!

NOTES.

The same *Ri*shi and metre.—No verse occurs in the other Sa*m*hitâs.

Verse 2.

Note 1. I have translated the text in its traditional form, which I think is correct. On the vocative vidharman, comp. Delbrück, Altindische Syntax, p. 106. One could think, however, of reading vídharman as a locative, and sváya*s*astare, and of considering mányase as a first person, like ar*k*ase, &c.: 'For in his extension, brilliant by itself, I manifestly comprehend that firmament,' &c.

Note 2. Cf. VIII, 72, 3. antá*h* i*kkh*anti tám *g*áne rudrám pará*h* manîsháyâ. 'Ueber alle Vorstellung hinaus.' Ludwig.

Note 3. If we read sváya*s*astara*h*, vídharman, and explain mányase as second person, the following translation of this difficult verse may be attempted: 'Thou art manifestly, indeed, considered as very brilliant by thyself in its (the firmament's) extension: that firmament of bright splendour (I praise), lovely beyond thought.' It is not very probable, however, that ásya should refer to anything else but Agni.

Verse 3.

Note 1. Sâya*n*a, whom Ludwig follows, very probably is right in interpreting asáu as the sun.—On the Sandhi, compare Roth, Zeitschrift der Deutschen Morgenläṇd. Gesellschaft, XLVIII, 679.

Note 2. Through the sacred spell, by which the sun is made to rise through the kindling of the fire.—Cf. VIII, 17, 15. tu*g*ắ . . . *gri*bhắ.

Note 3. Does this mean that Agni's flames shine like lightning which receives its light from the waters of the cloud, the sperm of heaven? Cf. IX, 74, 1, where it is said of the Soma mixed with water: divá*h* rétasâ sa*k*ate.

Verse 5.

Note 1. I think that sa*k*anta should be accented, because it is connected with hí.

MA*N**D*ALA V, HYMN 18.

ASH*T*AKA IV, ADHYÂYA 1, VARGA 10.

1. May Agni, beloved of many, the guest of the house[1], be praised in the morning, the immortal who delights[2] in all offerings among the mortals.

2[1]. To Dvita who by the liberal power of his dexterousness carries away injury[2], this praiser of thine, O immortal, prepares Soma in the due way.

3. I call for your sake Him who flames through long life, with the speech that belongs to the liberal patrons[1] whose chariot moves uninjured, O giver of horses[2];

4. And in whom (dwells) brilliant thought, who guard the hymns of praise in their mouth, (whose) sacrificial grass is spread in the realm of the sun: they have invested themselves with glory.

5. On the liberal patrons who have given me fifty horses for my song of praise[1], bestow brilliant, mighty, high glory, O Agni; on those men (bestow glory) with (valiant) men, O immortal!

NOTES.

The *R*ishi is M*ri*ktavâhas Dvita Âtreya (see verse 2); the metre is the same.—Verse 1 = SV. I, 85. Verse 5 = TB. II, 7, 5, 2.

Verse 1.

Note 1. Vi*s*á*h* . . . átithi*h*: cf. above, V, 3, 5.

Note 2. On ran with the accusative, compare Gaedicke, p. 76.

Verse 2.

Note 1. Compare on this verse Macdonell, Journal Roy. As. Soc., 1893, p. 463 seq.

Note 2. Dvita, who seems to be identified with Agni, is, in the same way as Trita (see Bloomfield, Proceedings Amer. Or. Soc., March, 1894, p. cxix seqq.), supposed to take away human sin and all sorts of mischief and misfortune (cf. VIII, 47, 16. Tritấya *k*a Dvitấya *k*a úsha*h* dushvápnyam vaha). Thus he is invoked here as carrying away m*ri*̆ktá, i.e. injury.

Verse 3.

Note 1. The speech of the priest belongs to the sacrificer who has engaged him.

Note 2. This seems to be Agni, with an evident allusion to the human giver of horses (see verse 5).

Verse 5.

Note 1. Sadhástuti seems to be instrumental. Cf. Lanman, p. 381.

MANDALA V, HYMN 19.

ASHTAKA IV, ADHYÂYA 1, VARGA 11.

1. They are born for retirement[1]. Out of the cover he[2] has shone forth, being a cover himself. In the lap of the mother he looks about[3].

2. Causing him to discern (the pious and the impious ?), they have sacrificed. With unwinking eyes they protect his manly power. They have penetrated into the firm stronghold[1].

3. The people of *S*vaitreya[1], his clans, have thriven brilliantly. B*ri*haduktha with a golden ornament at his neck, is eager for the race as if by this honey-drink[2].

4. Like the dear milk of love[1]—(a thing) unrelated with two (things) related[2]—like the gharma vessel with booty in its belly—undeceived, the deceiver of all[3].

5. Sporting, O beam of light, appear to us, joined with the ash, with the wind. May those well sharpened . . . of his, standing on . . . , be sharp like . . .[1].

NOTES.

The *Ri*shi is Vavri Âtreya (cf. verse 1. prá vavré*h* vavrí*h* *k*iketa). The metre is Gâyatrî in verses 1, 2, Anush*t*ubh in verses 3, 4, Virâ*d*rûpâ in verse 5.—No verse occurs in the other Sa*m*hitâs.

This Sûkta seems to be anything rather than an ordinary Agni hymn. It may be a collection of verses belonging to an Âkhyâna, or of verses serving another purpose which we can scarcely hope to discover. In several parts of this

Sûkta I must content myself with translating the words without being able to elucidate the poet's meaning.

Verse 1.

Note 1. I translate the noun avasthấ in accordance with the Vedic meaning of the verb ava-sthâ. Possibly it means the secret parts, cf. avastha, AV. VII, 90, 3 (B.-R.). Ludwig translates: 'Ein zustand erzeugt einen andern,' and paraphrases, 'Nur zustände und formen, gestalten lernen wir kennen, das wesen des gottes bleibt uns verborgen.' This seems too modern. Prof. Max Müller proposes: 'The remnants (afterbirth) have been brought forth. Skin has shone forth from skin.'—On the question who are the beings 'born for retirement,' I do not venture any conjecture.

Note 2. Is Agni meant?

Note 3. Cf. X, 5, 1. (Agní*h*) asmát h*ri*dá*h* bhū́ri*g*anmâ ví *k*ash*t*e.

Verse 2.

Note 1. The meaning seems to be that the worshippers (possibly the first worshippers, the Aṅgiras), by discovering Agni and by worshipping him, have conquered the hostile strongholds.

Verse 3.

Note 1. *S*vaitreya is mentioned as a victorious hero also in I, 33, 14.

Note 2. Does this phrase allude to the rite of offering, at the Vâ*g*apeya sacrifice, to the horses that were going to run the sacred race, a naivâra *k*aru? In the Mantras connected with this rite the words occur: 'Drink of this honey-drink' (asyá mádhva*h* pibata). See Rig-veda VII, 38, 8; Taittirîya Sa*m*hitâ I, 7, 8, 2; Weber, Ueber den Vâ*g*apeya, p. 30.

Verse 4.

Note 1. The retas?

Note 2. Does this refer to an offering or the like, composed of two substances related among each other (such as milk and butter), and a third substance unrelated (such as rice)? Of course all this is absolutely uncertain.

Note 3. Is this Agni?

Verse 5.

Note 1. The meaning of dh*ri*shá*g*, vakshī́, vaksha*n*esthā́ is unknown.—On the first hemistich of this verse, compare Pischel Vedische Studien, II, 54.

MA*ND*ALA V, HYMN 20.

ASH*T*AKA IV, ADHYÂYA 1, VARGA 12.

1[1]. Whatever good, O Agni, best acquirer of gain, thou thinkest (fit), praise thou[2] that (good), which is celebrated in songs, among the gods as our share.

2. They, Agni, who do not set into motion for thee (prayers or offerings), when grown full of mighty strength[1], turn away to encounter the hatred and the tricks of him who follows another (i. e. a wrong) law[2].

3. We choose thee as our Hot*ri*, Agni, the giver of skill; offering delight (to thee) we call with our prayer (thee), the foremost at the sacrifices.

4. So that we, O strong one, (may be ready) for thy favour, for wealth and *Ri*ta, O highly wise one: thus may we day by day rejoice[1] with cows and rejoice with heroes.

NOTES.

The *Ri*shi is Prayasvanta Âtreya (cf. verse 3. práyasvanta*h* havâmahe), the metre Anush*t*ubh, verse 4 Pa*n*kti.—Verse 1 = VS. XIX, 64.

Verse 1.

Note 1. Professor Max Müller proposes to read vâ*g*asấtamam, as in IX, 98, 1. Pischel (Vedische Studien, I, 200) translates this verse: 'O Agni, das rühmenswerte Gut, das du für geeignet hältst, das preise du zugleich mit unsern Liedern (no gîrbhír yú*g*am) den Göttern an (diis vendita).' He explains: 'Agni soll den Göttern Gut bringen und sie veranlassen, es den Menschen für die Lieder zu schenken.' I cannot follow Pischel's theory about the identity of the roots pan and pa*n* (comp. about pa*n* the quotations collected by Bartholomae, Indogermanische Forschungen, III, 180); and the paraphrase 'diis vendita' seems inadmissible to me. I differ from Pischel, besides, in the interpretation of yú*g*am; cf. rayím . . . yú*g*am, IV, 37, 5; râyấ yu*g*ấ, VII, 43, 5; 95, 4.

Note 2. Neisser, Bezzenberger's Beiträge, XX, 55, explains panayâ as standing for panayâma, and compares V, 56, 2 (?).

Verse 2.

Note 1. On v*ri*dh with the genitive, compare Delbrück, Altindische Syntax, p. 158; Macdonell, Journal Roy. As. Soc., 1893, p. 433. Grassmann's conjecture v*rí*ddhâ(v) is a failure.

Note 2. With the second hemistich compare VS. XXXVIII, 20 (*S*atapatha Brâhma*n*a XIV, 3, 1, 9); TÂr. IV, 11, 4 (cf. V, 9, 7).

Verse 4.

Note 1. Syâma stands, as the accent shows, in an independent clause. Prof. Max Müller proposes to change the accent: 'So that we . . . may for thy favour, for wealth and *Ri*ta day by day rejoice with cows.'

MAN*D*ALA V, HYMN 21.

ASH*T*AKA IV, ADHYÂYA 1, VARGA 13.

1. Let us lay thee down, as Manus did. Let us kindle thee, as Manus did. O Agni Aṅgiras, sacrifice to the gods for the worshippers of the gods as (thou didst) for Manus.

2. For thou, O Agni, art kindled, highly pleased, among human people. To thee the (sacrificial) ladles proceed in due order, O well-born one who drinkest butter.

3. Thee all the gods unanimously have made their messenger. Serving thee, O sage, they magnify at the sacrifices (thee) the god.

4. Let the mortal magnify for your sake Agni, the god, with worship as is due to the gods. Being kindled, O brilliant one, shine! Sit down in the abode[1] of *R*ita; sit down in the abode[1] of herbs[2].

NOTES.

The *R*ishi is Sasa Âtreya (cf. verse 4); the metre is the same.—Verse 1 = TB. III, 11, 6, 3.

Verse 4.

Note 1. Literally 'in the womb.'

Note 2. On sasá, see III, 5, 6, note 2. Is the abode (or womb) of the herbs the Barhis? 'Is it satyasya?' M.M.

MAN*D*ALA V, HYMN 22.

ASHT*A*KA IV, ADHYÂYA 1, VARGA 14.

1. Lo, Visvasâman! Like Atri sing to him who purifies with his flames, to the Hot*ri* who should be magnified at the sacrifices, most delightful in the clan.

2[1]. Lay down Agni *G*âtavedas, the god, the priest. May the sacrifice which best encompasses the gods, proceed to-day in due order.

3. We, the mortals, approaching thee, the attentive-minded god, for thy help, have thought of thy desirable aid.

4. Agni, be intent on this—on this our word[1], O strong one. As such, O strong-jawed[2] lord of the house, the Atris strengthen thee by their praises; the Atris beautify thee by their prayers.

NOTES.

The *Ri*shi is Visvasâman (see verse 1); the metre is the same.—No verse of this hymn occurs in the other Sa*m*hitâs.

Verse 2.

Note 1. With this verse compare below, V, 26, 7. 8.

Verse 4.

Note 1. The verb *k*it stands here first with the genitive asyá, then with the accusative idám vá*k*a*h*.

Note 2. Compare vol. xxxii, p. 301 (II, 34, 3, note 3).

MA*ND*ALA V, HYMN 23.

ASH*T*AKA IV, ADHYÂYA 1, VARGA 15.

1. Agni, bring hither, through the power of thy splendour, powerful wealth which may manifestly prevail over all tribes in the (contests for) booty.

2. O powerful Agni! Bring hither that wealth powerful in battles. For thou art the true, wonderful giver of booty rich in cows.

3. For all men who have spread out the sacrificial grass, unanimously ask thee, the beloved Hot*ri* in the seats (of sacrifice), for many boons.

4. For he who dwells among all tribes, has invested himself with power against assault[1]. Agni! In these dwelling-places shine to us richly, O bright one, shine brilliantly, O purifier!

NOTES.

The *R*ishi is Dyumna Vi*s*va*k*arsha*n*i Âtreya (cf. verse 1); the metre is the same.—Verses 1-2 = TS. I, 3, 14, 6-7.

Verse 4.

Note 1. Is abhímâti (abhímâtî?) a dative? Should we read abhimâti-sahá*h* (cf. X, 83, 4) as a compound: 'he has been established as the conqueror of assaults.'

MANDALA V, HYMN 24.

ASHTAKA IV, ADHYÂYA 1, VARGA 16.

1. Agni, be thou our nearest (friend) and our kind, protecting guardian.

2. Agni is Vasu, renowned as Vasu (or, renowned by goods). Obtain, (and) bestow (on us), most brilliant wealth [1].

3. Listen to us then; hear our call; deliver us from every harmful man.

4. We entreat thee now, O brightest, shining (Agni), for thy grace, for our friends.

NOTES.

The *Ri*shis are the Gaupâyanas or Laupâyanas, Bandhu (verse 1), Subandhu (verse 2), *S*rutabandhu (verse 3), Viprabandhu (verse 4). The metre is Dvipadâ Virâ*g*.—Verses 1, 2, 4, 3 = VS. III, 25–26. Verses 1, 4, 2, 3 = MS. I, 5, 3. Verses 1, 2, 4 = SV. II, 457–459; VS. XV, 48; XXV, 47. Verses 1, 4, 2 = TS. I, 5, 6, 2–3; IV, 4, 4, 8. Verse 1 = SV. I, 448.

Verse 2.

Note 1. The accusative dyumáttamam rayím seems to depend both on á*kkh*â nakshi and on dâ*h*. I cannot find any reason for preferring the reading of SV. and TS. dyumáttama*h* (Ludwig).

MA*ND*ALA V, HYMN 25.

ASH*T*AKA IV, ADHYÂYA 1, VARGA 17–18.

1. Address thy song[1] for your sake to the god Agni, for his help. He is our Vasu. May the son of the dawns(?)[2] give us (wealth). May the righteous one help us across our enemies.

2. He is the true one, whom the men of old, whom the gods have kindled, the Hot*ri* with the delightful tongue, rich in splendour with glorious shine.

3. As such, with thy widest thought and with thy best favour, shine wealth on us, excellent Agni, for our beautiful praises[1].

4. Agni reigns among the gods, Agni among mortals, entering among them. Agni is the carrier of our offerings. Serve ye Agni with prayers!

5. Agni gives to the worshipper a son most mightily renowned, a knower of mighty spells, most excellent, unconquered, who brings renown to his lord[1].

6. Agni gives a good lord who is victorious in battles with his men; Agni (gives) a steed, swiftly running, victorious (in races), unconquered.

7. Sing mightily to Agni the (song) which may best bring him (to us), O (god) rich in splendour[1]! From thee (proceeds) wealth (mighty) like a buffalo-cow[2]; from thee proceed gains.

8. Thy brilliant flames resound mightily like the pressing-stone (of the Soma)[1]. And thy roaring arose like thunder by itself from heaven[2].

9. Thus we have paid homage, desirous of goods, to powerful Agni. May he, the highly wise one, help us, as with a ship, across all enemies.

NOTES.

The *R*ishis are the Vasûyava*h* Âtreyâ*h* (cf. verse 9); the metre is Anush*t*ubh. Verse 5=MS. IV, 11, 1. Verse 6 =MS. IV, 11, 1. Verse 7=SV. I, 86; VS. XXVI, 12; TS. I, 1, 14, 4. The Sûkta consists of hymns of three verses each.

Verse 1.

Note 1. On gâsi, comp. Neisser, Bezzenberger's Beiträge, XX, 70, note 1; Bartholomae, Indogermanische Forschungen, II, 278, 283.

Note 2. *R*ishû*n*ấm: comp. above, I, 127, 10, note 5.

Verse 3.

Note 1. On suv*ri*ktí, comp. above, II, 4, 1, note 1.

Verse 5.

Note 1. I.e. to his father? Or to his patrons?

Verse 7.

Note 1. This vocative very probably refers to Agni.

Note 2. Or 'like a king's consort'? It may be doubted whether the difference of accent (máhishî and mahishī́) holds good for the Rig-veda.—Comp. on máhishîva, Roth, Zeitschr. der Deutschen Morgenländ. Gesellschaft, XLVIII, 680.

Verse 8.

Note 1. B*ri*hat is not the name of the Sâman; cf. X, 64, 15 (100, 8). grấvâ yátra madhu-sút u*k*yáte b*ri*hát. Comp. Hillebrandt, Vedische Mythologie, I, p. 153.—The singular u*k*yate is explained by the connection with grấvâ.

Note 2. With the last Pâda comp. the conclusion of V, 52, 6 (vol. xxxii, p. 312).

MA*ND*ALA V, HYMN 26.

ASH*T*AKA IV, ADHYÂYA 1, VARGA 19-20.

1. Agni, purifier! With thy splendour, with thy delightful tongue, O god, bring hither the gods and perform the sacrifice.

2. Thee therefore we approach, who swimmest in gh*ri*ta[1], O (god) with brilliant light, thee of sun-like aspect. Bring hither the gods that they may feast.

3. Let us kindle thee, O sage, the brilliant offerer of feasts (to the gods), O Agni, the mighty (god) at the sacrifice.

4. Agni, come hither with all the gods to the gift of the offering. We choose thee as our Hot*ri*.

5. Bring to the sacrificer who presses (Soma), Agni, abundance of heroes. Sit down on the sacrificial grass together with the gods.

6. Being kindled, Agni, conqueror of thousandfold (wealth), thou makest the ordinances (of the world) thrive, the praiseworthy messenger of the gods.

7[1]. Lay down Agni *G*âtavedas, the carrier of offerings, the youngest, the god, the priest.

8. May the sacrifice which best encompasses the gods, proceed to-day in due order. Spread the sacrificial grass that (the gods) may sit down on it.

9. May the Maruts, the A*s*vins, Mitra and Varu*n*a sit down on this (sacrificial grass), the gods with all their folk.

NOTES.

The same *Ri*shis. Metre, Gâyatrî. Verses 1–3=SV. II, 871–873. Verse 1=TS. I, 3, 14, 8; 5, 5, 3; IV, 6, 1, 2; MS. I, 5, 1; II, 10, 1; IV, 10, 1; VS. XVII, 8. Verse 3 =TS. I, 1, 11, 2; VS. II, 4; comp. MS. I, 1, 12. Verse 7= MS. IV, 11, 1.

As V, 26, this Sûkta also consists of T*rik*a hymns.

Verse 2.

Note 1. Comp. above, IV, 2, 3, note 1.

Verse 7.

Note 1. With verses 7 and 8, compare above, V, 22, 2.

MA*ND*ALA V, HYMN 27.

ASH*T*AKA IV, ADHYÂYA 1, VARGA 21.

1. The good lord has presented me with two oxen together with a car, the most brilliant Asura among the liberal givers[1]. Tryaru*n*a, the son of Triv*ri*shan, O Agni Vai*s*vânara[2], has distinguished himself by (his gift of) ten thousand (cows?)[3].

2. To him who gives me one hundred[1] and twenty cows and two fallow steeds, harnessed and well-yoked, to Tryaru*n*a grant thy protection, Agni Vai*s*vânara, who art highly praised and grown strong.

3. Thus, O Agni, desiring thy favour[1], Trasadasyu[2] (sings) for the ninth time[3] to thee the youngest (god)—Tryaru*n*a who responds to my, the strong-born's, many hymns with (the gift of) a yoked (chariot)[4]—

4[1]. Who may thus announce me[2] to A*s*vamedha the liberal (prince): may he give to him who with his verse strives for gain; may he give to him who lives in the *Ri*ta for (acquiring) wisdom[3]—

5. A*s*vamedha whose gifts, a hundred speckled bulls, delight me like Soma juices with threefold admixture[1].

6. Indra-Agni! Bestow on A*s*vamedha, the giver of a hundred (bulls), abundance of heroes and mighty royal power, like the never-ageing Sun in heaven.

NOTES.

The *Ri*shis are Tryaru*n*a Traiv*ri*sh*n*a, Trasadasyu Paurukutsya, and A*s*vamedha Bhârata, or, according to others, Atri alone. The metre is Trish*t*ubh in verses 1–3, Anush*t*ubh in verses 4–6.

The position of this Sûkta shows that it is a later addition to the original collection.

Verse 1.

Note 1. With Delbrück, Grassmann, von Bradke (Dyaus Asura, p. 67) I read maghónâm instead of maghóna*h*. Cf. III, 3, 4. ásura*h* vipa*h*-*k*ítâm.

Note 2. On the invocation of Agni in Dânastutis, comp. H. O., Zeitschrift der Deutschen Morgenländischen Gesellschaft, XXXIX, 87.

Note 3. Geldner (Ved. Studien, I, 268) is right in observing: 'Hier ist unter sahasrâ*n*i eine bestimmte Geld- oder Wertsumme zu verstehen,' and in adding that it is not necessary that such a sum consisted in cows.

Verse 2.

Note 1. On *s*atắ, 'one hundred,' compare Delbrück, Altindische Syntax, p. 82.

Verse 3.

Note 1. Cf. X, 148, 3. sumatím *k*akânáh*h*.

Note 2. That is, very probably, a descendant of Trasadasyu.

Note 3. I do not adopt Sâya*n*a's explanation navama*m* = navatamâ*m*, though I do not know what the number 'nine' means here. Ludwig is absolutely right in observing 'dass man eben hier, wo es sich um specielle concrete, uns aber sonst her nicht bekannte verhältnisse und ereignisse handelt, eben sich bescheiden muss, nichts zu wissen.'—Prof. Max Müller believes that navish*th*âya makes navamam for navatamam excusable: 'to the newest god the newest song.'

Note 4. Sâya*n*a supplies to yuktena, not rathena, but manasâ.

Verse 4.

Note 1. I do not think that Ludwig is right in believing that with verse 4 a new, independent section begins.—Comp. on this verse, vol. xxxii, p. 304 (II, 34, 7, note 3).

Note 2. Me may be accusative, as it frequently is. Should it be a dative, we should have to translate: 'Who may tell A*s*vamedha for my sake.'

Note 3. Medhấm can scarcely depend on dádat; wisdom is not a gift which liberal princes may bestow on singers.

Verse 5.

Note 1. Of milk, curds, and barley. See Hillebrandt, Vedische Mythologie, I, p. 209.

MA*ND*ALA V, HYMN 28.

ASH*T*AKA IV, ADHYÂYA 1, VARGA 22.

1. Agni kindled has sent his light to the sky; turned towards the dawn he shines far and wide. (The sacrificial ladle) goes forward with adoration, rich in all treasures, magnifying the gods with sacrificial food.

2. Being kindled thou reignest over immortality; thou attendest for welfare the man who prepares the sacrificial food. He whom thou furtherest, acquires all wealth and puts in front hospitality (towards thee), O Agni[1].

3. Agni, show thy prowess for the sake of great bliss. May thy splendours be highest. Make our householdership easy to conduct[1]. Set thy foot on the greatness of those who show enmity to us.

4. I adore thy beauty, Agni, who hast been kindled, who art highly exalted. A bull, brilliant art thou. Thou art kindled at the sacrifices.

5. Being kindled, Agni into whom offerings are poured, sacrifice to the gods, best sacrificer, for thou art the carrier of oblations.

6. Sacrifice into (Agni); exalt Agni, while the sacrifice is going on. Choose him for your carrier of oblations.

NOTES.

The *Ri*shi is Vi*s*vavârâ Âtreyî (cf. verse 1); the metre is Trish*t*ubh in verses 1 and 3, *G*agatî in verse 2, Anush*t*ubh in verse 4, Gâyatrî in verses 5 and 6. Verse 3 = AV. VII, 73, 10; VS. XXXIII, 12; TS. II, 4, 1, 1; 5, 2, 4; MS. IV, 11, 1. Verse 5 = TS. II, 5, 8, 6. Verses 5–6 = TB. III, 5, 2, 3.

The Sûkta is a later addition to the original Sa*m*hitâ.

Verse 2.

Note 1. Should not dhatte be accented? 'He whom thou furtherest and (who) puts in front hospitality (towards thee), O Agni, acquires all wealth.'

Verse 3.

Note 1. Cf. X, 85, 23. sám *g*âspatyám suyámam astu devâ*h*. The additions to the single Ma*nd*alas seem, as a rule, to be of later origin than the hymns of the tenth Ma*nd*ala (see H. O., Prolegomena, p. 265); so it may be conjectured that the author of our verse imitated that passage of the great marriage hymn.

APPENDICES.

I. INDEX OF WORDS.

II. LIST OF THE MORE IMPORTANT PASSAGES QUOTED IN THE NOTES.

THE following is not (like the Index to vol. xxxii) a complete Index verborum to the hymns translated in this volume, but only an Index of all the words which can be of any importance. It contains all rare, difficult, and doubtful words, all words of any mythological importance, and especially all words about which something is said in the Notes.

Three figures refer to Ma*nd*ala, hymn, and verse, a small figure to a note. If a word occurs in a note only, the passage is put in parentheses.

M. W.

I. INDEX OF WORDS.

a, demonstr. pronoun: ayā́, II, 6, 2[1].

Á*ms*a, one of the Âdityas, II, 1, 4[2].

a*ms*ú, Soma shoot, IV, 1, 19.

a*m*ha*h*-yú, dispelling anguish, V, 15, 3[1].

a*m*hatí, distress, I, 94, 2.

á*m*has, evil, distress, anguish, I, 36, 14; 58, 8; 9; III, 15, 3; IV, 2, 8; 9; 3, 14; 11, 6; 12, 6.

aktú, night, I, 36, 16; 68, 1; 94, 5; II, 10, 3; III, 7, 6; IV, 10, 5; áti aktú*h* (conj. áti aktū́n), I, 143, 3[2].

aktú, ointment: aktú-bhi*h* a*g*yate, III, 17, 1[1].

akrá, a racer, I, 143, 7[2]; 189, 7[5]; III, 1, 12[1]; IV, 6, 3[2].

akshán, eye: *s*atám *k*ákshâ*n*a*h* akshá-bhi*h*, I, 128, 3.

akshí, eye: divá*h* akshī́ íti, I, 72, 10[1].

ákshita, imperishable, I, 58, 5.

ákshîyamâ*n*a, inexhaustible, III, 26, 9.

agótâ, want of cows, III, 16, 5.

ágopâ, without a keeper, II, 4, 7.

Agní, fire, and god of fire, I, 1, 1, &c.; III, 2, 9[2]; agním-agnim, I, 12, 2; agnínâ agní*h* sám idhyate, I, 12, 6; agne agníbhi*h*, I, 26, 10; agním (ā́ vaha ágne), I, 44, 8[1]; vayā́*h* ít agne agnáya*h* te anyé, I, 59, 1; índram agním, III, 12, 3; purîshyā́sa*h* agnáya*h*, III, 22, 4; ágne ví*s*vebhi*h* agní-bhi*h*, III, 24, 4; ágne índra*h* *k*a, III, 25, 4; agnáya*h* agníshu, V, 6, 6.

agni-*g*ihvá, fire-tongued: agni-*g*ihvâ*h*, I, 44, 14.

agnídh, the Agnîdh (priest): agnít (conj. agnī́t), II, 1, 2[2].

agni-*s*rī́, possessing the beauty of Agni, III, 26, 5[1].

ágra, summit: ripá*h* ágram, III, 5, 5[1]; ágre, at first, I, 31, 5; in front of, I, 127, 10.

agriyá, foremost: agriyám, I, 13, 10.

agrū́, virgin: agrúva*h*, I, 140, 8[1]; III, 29, 13[2].

aghá, evil, I, 97, 1[1]-8; 128, 5; V, 3, 7; harmful foe, I, 189, 5.

agha-yát, harmful, IV, 2, 6; 24, 3.

agha-yú, harmful, I, 27, 3[1]; 147, 4; IV, 2, 9.

aghá-*s*a*m*sa, attacking with evil spells, IV, 4, 3; V, 3, 7.

ághnyâ, cow, IV, 1, 6.

aṅgá: yát aṅgá, whatever, I, 1, 6.

Áṅgiras, N. of Agni, I, 1, 6; 31, 1; 17; 74, 5; IV, 2, 15; 3, 15; 9, 7; V, 8, 4; 10, 7; 11, 6; 21, 1; *g*yésh*th*am áṅgirasâm, I, 127, 2; áṅgira*h*-tama*h*, the highest Aṅgiras, I, 31, 2; 75, 2;—pl. the Aṅgiras (*Ri*shis), I, 71, 2[1]; IV, 3, 11[1]; V, 11, 6[1];—aṅgirasvát, I, 31, 17; 45, 3; 78, 3.

a*k*ítta, unseen, IV, 3, 1.

á*k*itti, folly, IV, 2, 11; thoughtlessness: á*k*itti-bhi*h*, IV, 12, 4.

a*kkh*âvâka, a certain priest, (I, 142, 4[2]).

á*kkh*idra, flawless, I, 58, 8; II, 3, 8; III, 15, 5.

á*kkh*idra-ûti, whose blessings are flawless, I, 145, 3.

á*k*yuta, unshakeable, II, 3, 3.

ag, to drive: út agate, he raises up, I, 95, 7; út âgan, they have driven out, IV, 1, 13; ắ agâti, may he lead, V, 2, 5; sám agâti, may he get together, V, 2, 12; agur yamuh, V, 6, 10[2].
agá, goat, I, 67, 5[1].
agára, undecaying, never ageing, I, 58, 2; 4; 127, 5; 9; 143, 3; 144, 4; 146, 2; II, 8, 4[1]; III, 2, 2; 6, 4; 8, 2; 18, 2; 23, 1; V, 4, 2.
ágasra, unwearied, I, 189, 4; III, 1, 21; 26, 7.
ágâta, unborn, V, 15, 2.
ágâmi, unrelated, IV, 4, 5; V, 19, 4.
agirá, agile, I, 140, 4; III, 9, 8.
aguryá, undecaying, I, 146, 4; II, 3, 5; 8, 2; III, 7, 4; 7; aguryám (conj. aguryáh), I, 67, 1[2].
ágñâta-keta, with unknown design, V, 3, 11.
ágma, course, III, 2, 12.
ágman, race, I, 65, 6.
ágra, plain: brihatáh ágrân, IV, 1, 17.
añg, to anoint, I, 95, 6, &c.;—samânagé, he has shaped, I, 188, 9; sám añgatah, II, 3, 7[1]; trídhâ sám-aktam, thrice-anointed, II, 3, 10; aktú-bhih agyate, III, 17, 1[1]; aṅkte, he anoints himself, V, 1, 3; anakti, IV, 6, 3[3].
añgí, ointment: añgí-bhih, I, 36, 13[1].
átandra, unwearied, I 72, 7; 95, 2[1]; IV, 4, 12.
atasá, brushwood, I, 58, 2; 4; II, 4, 7; III, 7, 3[2]; IV, 4, 4; 7, 10.
átithi, guest, I, 44, 4; 58, 6; 73, 1[2]; II, 2, 8; 4, 1; III, 2, 2; 3, 8; 26, 2; IV, 1, 20[1]; 2, 7; V, 1, 8; 9; 3, 5; 4, 5; 8, 2; 18, 1.
atûrta, unconquered, V, 25, 5.
atripá, insatiable, IV, 5, 14.
átka, vesture, I, 95, 7.
átya, racer: átyah ná prishthám rokate, I, 58, 2[1];—I, 65, 6; 149, 3; II, 4, 4; III, 2, 3; 7; 7, 9; átyam ná sáptim, III, 22, 1[1]; IV, 2, 3; V, 25, 6.
Átri, V, 2, 6; 7, 10;—pl. the Atris, V, 22, 4;—atri-vát, I, 45, 3[1]; V, 4, 9; 7, 8[1]; 22, 1.
átri, devourer, II, 8, 5[1].
atrín, ghoul, I, 36, 14[1]; 20; 94, 9.
átha, and, I, 26, 9.
atharí, elephant (?): atharyàh ná dántam, IV, 6, 8[2].
ad, to eat: ắdat, I, 127, 6[2].
adát, having no teeth, I, 189, 5.
ádabdha, undeceivable, I, 76, 2; 95, 9; 128, 1; 143, 8; II, 9, 6; III, 1, 6; IV, 4, 3; V, 19, 4.
ádabdhavrata-pramati, protector of infallible laws, II, 9, 1[1].
adás: asaú, yonder (sun), V, 17, 3[1].
ádâbhya, undeceivable, I, 31, 10; III, 11, 5; 26, 4; V, 5, 2.
Áditi, I, 94, 16; 95, 11; 98, 3; II, 1, 11; III, 4, 11; IV, 12, 4; mâtắ Áditih, I, 72, 9;—a name of Agni, I, 94, 15[1];—Freedom, IV, 1, 20[1];—áditim urushya, IV, 2, 11[3];—m., IV, 3, 8[2].
ádripita, undismayed, I, 143, 8; not proud, IV, 3, 3.
ádripta, never foolish, I, 69, 3.
ádeva, godless, III, 1, 16; V, 2, 9; 10.
ádeva-yu, not caring for the gods, I, 150, 2.
ádbhuta, mysterious, wonderful, I, 77, 3[2]; 94, 12; 13; 142, 3; 10; II, 7, 6; V, 10, 2; 23, 2;—secret, IV, 2, 12.
ádman, food, I, 58, 2.
ádri, rock, I, 70, 4[1]; 71, 2; 73, 6; 149, 1; IV, 1, 14; 15; 2, 15[3]; 3, 11;—press-stone, III, 1, 1.
adrúh, guileless, II, 1, 14[2]; III, 9, 4; 22, 4.
adroghá, guileless, III, 14, 6.
ádvayat, truthful, III, 29, 5.
ádvayâvin, in whom is no falsehood, III, 2, 15.
ádha, then: ádha ksharanti (for adháh ksharanti?), I, 72, 10[3].
ádhi, prep. with abl., on behalf of: ritắt ádhi, I, 36, 11[1].
ádhi-iti, remembrance, II, 4, 8.
adhi-mánthana, the support on which the rubbing (for producing the fire) is performed, III, 29, 1[2].
adhîvâsá, upper garment, I, 140, 9.
ádhrigu, liberal, III, 21, 4[1]; V, 10, 1.
Adhríg? V, 7, 10[1].
ádhvan, way, I, 31, 16; 71, 9; ádhvanah deva-yắnân, I, 72, 7[3].
adhvará, worship, rite, sacrifice, I, 1, 4[1]; 8; 12, 7, &c.: adhvarám yaga, I, 26, 1; pátih adhvarắnâm, I, 44, 9; ragantam adh-

varấ*n*âm, I, 45, 4; ya*gñ*ásya adhvarásya, I, 128, 4[1]; adhvarấ-iva (conj. adhvaré-iva), III, 6, 10[3]; adhvarásya pra-netấ, III, 23, 1.
adhvara-*s*rī́, beautifier of sacrifices, I, 44, 3[2].
adhvariy, to be as an Adhvaryu: adhvari-yasi, II, 1, 2.
adhvari-yát, performing the sacrificial service, IV, 9, 5.
adhvaryú, the Adhvaryu priest, I, 94, 6; II, 5, 6; III, 5, 4; IV, 6, 4; adhvaryú-bhi*h* pa*ñk*á-bhi*h*, III, 7, 7.
ánagna, not naked, III, 1, 6.
ánagni-trâ, not standing under Agni's protection, I, 189, 3.
ánadat, not eating, III, 1, 6.
anantá, infinite, IV, 1, 7[2].
anapa-v*r*i*g*yá, interminable, I, 146, 3.
anamîvá, free from plagues, III, 16, 3; 22, 4.
anarván, untouched, I, 94, 2; unattainable, II, 6, 5.
anavadyá, blameless, I, 31, 9; 71, 8; 73, 3.
anavabhrá-râdhas, with gifts that cannot be taken away, III, 26, 6.
ánasvat, together with a car, V, 27, 1.
ánâk*r*ita, whom it is not possible to drive to a place, I, 141, 7[1].
ánâga, sinless, IV, 12, 4.
anâgâ*h*-tvá, sinlessness, I, 94, 15.
ánâyata, unsupported, IV, 13, 5.
anâyudhá, unarmed, IV, 5, 14.
aniná, feeble, I, 150, 2.
anindrá, Indra-less, V, 2, 3.
áni-baddha, unattached, IV, 13, 5.
ani-bâdhá, unbounded, III, 1, 11[1].
ánibh*r*ish*t*a-tavishi, of undecaying strength, V, 7, 7.
ani-mâná, immeasurable, I, 27, 11.
ánimishat, never slumbering, I, 143, 8.
áni-misham, with unwinking eyes, V, 19, 2.
áni-mesham, unremittingly, I, 31, 12.
anirá, sapless, IV, 5, 14.
áni-v*r*ita, unrestrained, III, 29, 6.
anishaṅgá, without a quiver, I, 31, 13[2].
ánîka, face, II, 9, 6; III, 1, 15; 19, 4[1]; IV, 5, 9[1]; 15; 10, 3; 11, 1; 12, 2; V, 2, 1.
ánu prep. with ablat., I, 141, 3[2].
a[illegible]kthá, hymnless, V, 2, 3.
ánupa-kshita, undecaying, III, 13, 7.
anush*th*ú, by one's present power, I, 95, 3.
anush*th*uyấ, by one's present power, IV, 4, 14.
anu-satyá, follower of truth, III, 26, 1.
anu-svadhám, according to one's wont or nature, II, 3, 11; III, 6, 9.
ánûna, without flaw, I, 146, 1; II, 10, 6; III, 1, 5; IV, 2, 19; 5, 1.
án*r*i*g*u, sinful, IV, 3, 13.
an*r*itá, sinful, IV, 5, 5.
án*r*ita, falsehood, V, 12, 4.
anehás, unmenaced, III, 9, 1.
anta*h*-vidvấ*m*s, knowing, I, 72, 7.
ántama, nearest (friend), I, 27, 5; III, 10, 8; V, 24, 1.
ántara, closest, I, 31, 13; nearer, III, 18, 2;—in the midst, I, 44, 12.
antáriksha, air, I, 73, 8; III, 6, 8: 8, 8; 22, 2; IV, 14, 2; V, 1, 11.
ánti, nigh, I, 79, 11; 94, 9.
andhá, blind, I, 147, 3[1]; 148, 5[2].
ándhas, darkness, I, 94, 7.
ándhas, sap, IV, 1, 19.
ánna, food: sthirấ ánnâ, I, 127, 4[3]; IV, 7, 10; tri-v*r*ít ánnam, I, 140, 2[2]; ánnâ, instr., IV, 7, 11[1].
ánniyat, desirous of food, IV, 2, 7.
anyád-anyad, the one and the other, I, 95, 1.
anyá-vrata, following another law, V, 20, 2.
áp, pl., water, Waters, I, 36, 8; 95, 3[1]; 96, 1; 2; IV, 3, 12, &c.; gárbha*h* apấm, I, 70, 3; III, 1, 12; 13; 5, 3; apấm nápât, I, 143, 1[2]; III, 9, 1; apấm upá-sthe, I, 144, 2; apấm sadhá-sthe, I, 149, 4; II, 4, 2; ấyu*h* apấm, III, 1, 5; mât*r*i*h* apá*h*, III, 9, 2; ap-sú *s*ritám, III, 9, 4; apấm duro*n*é, III, 25, 5; ávindat apá*h*, V, 14, 4[1].
ápatya, offspring, I, 68, 7.
áparâ-*g*ita, unconquered, III, 12, 9; V, 25, 6.
ápari-v*r*ita, uncovered, II, 10, 3.
apa*s*yá, bereft of sight, I, 148, 5[2].
ápas, work, I, 68, 5; 69, 8[2]; 70, 8; II, 3, 6; III, 3, 3; 12, 7; IV, 2, 14; see apás.
apás, active, I, 31, 8; 71, 3; 95, 4; III, 2, 5; 7; 8, 5;—work:

apási (conj. upási), III, 1, 3[3]; 11[4]; apá*h* (conj. ápa*h*), III, 6, 7[2].
apasyú, ever active, I, 79, 1.
apấd, footless, IV, 1, 11.
apârá, boundless, III, 1, 14.
api-dhí, covering, I, 127, 7[3].
api-*s*arvará, approach of darkness, III, 9, 7[2].
api-sthitá, standing on, I, 145, 4[6].
ápûrvya, wonderful, III, 13, 5.
áp*rin*at, not giving, V, 7, 10.
ap-túr, crossing the waters, III, 27, 11[3].
ap-tṹrya, crossing the waters, III, 12, 8[1].
Ápnavâna, IV, 7, 1.
ápnasvat, rich: ápnasvatîshu urvárâsu, I, 127, 6.
ápya, living in the water, I, 145, 5.
ápra-âyu(s), unremitting, I, 127, 5[4].
áprati-skuta, unrepressed, III, 2, 14.
ápra-d*ri*pita, unconfused, I, 145, 2.
apra-m*ri*shyá, not to be despised, IV, 2, 5.
ápra-yu*kkh*at, never failing, unremitting, I, 143, 8; II, 9, 2; III, 5, 6; 20, 2.
ápra-vîtâ, virgin, IV, 7, 9[1].
apsu-sád, dwelling in the waters, III, 3, 5.
abhi-khyấ, looking at, I, 148, 5[2].
abhi-*gñ*ú, on one's knees, I, 72, 5.
abhí-dyu, striving for heaven, I, 127, 7; III, 27, 1.
abhi-pitvá, the time of rest, I, 189, 7[2,3].
abhí-mâti, plotter, III, 24, 1; assault, V, 23, 4[1].
abhimâti-sáh, victorious over hostile plots, II, 4, 9.
abhi-yú*g*, attack, III, 11, 6; V, 4, 5.
abhí-*s*asti, curse, I, 71, 10; V, 3, 7; 12.
abhi*s*asti-*k*ấtana, dispeller of curses, III, 3, 6.
abhi*s*asti-pấvan, protector against imprecations, I, 76, 3.
abhi-*s*rî́, leading to, or striving for, gloriousness, I, 98, 1[1]; 144, 6.
abhísh*t*i, victory, V, 17, 5.
abhish*t*i-k*r*ít, helpful, IV, 11, 4.
abhi-hrút, injury, I, 128, 5; anything leading astray, I, 189, 6[1].
abhî́ke with ablat., I, 71, 8[4].
abhrá, cloud, I, 79, 2.
abhrât*rí*, brotherless: abhrâtára*h*, IV, 5, 5[2].
ábhva, wondrous, I, 140, 5; monstrous might, II, 4, 5.
am, to plague: abhí ámanta, I, 189, 3[1].
áma, vehemence, I, 66, 7; fear: áme dhât, I, 67, 3.
amáti, impetuous splendour, I, 73, 2[3].
ámati, lack of thoughts, senselessness, III, 8, 2[1]; 16, 5; IV, 11, 6.
ámartya, immortal, I, 44, 1; 11; 58, 3; III, 2, 11; 10, 9; 11, 2; 24, 2; 27, 5; 7; IV, 1, 1; 8, 1; 9, 2; V, 4, 10.
ámardhat, never failing, III, 25, 4.
áma-vat, violent, impetuous, I, 36, 20; IV, 4, 1.
amítra, enemy, III, 18, 2; IV, 4, 4; 12, 2.
amitra-dámbhana, deceiver of foes, IV, 15, 4.
amitra-yúdh, attacking the enemies, III, 29, 15.
áminat, innocent, IV, 5, 6.
amîva-*k*ấtana, driving away sickness: amîva-*k*ấtanam, I, 12, 7.
ámîvâ, plague, I, 189, 3; III, 15, 1.
ámûra, not foolish, unerring, wise, I, 68, 8[1]; 72, 2: 141, 12; III, 19, 1; 25, 3; IV, 4, 12; 6, 2; 11, 5.
ám*ri*kta, uninjured, inviolable, III, 6, 4; 11, 6; IV, 3, 12[1].
am*rí*ta, immortal (Agni), I, 26, 9[1]; 44, 5[1]; 58, 1; 70, 4[2], &c.;—pl. the immortal gods, I, 59, 1, &c.;—immortality, I, 13, 5[2]; 68, 4[1]; 72, 1[1]; 6; III, 1, 14; 23, 1[2]; 25, 2; V, 3, 4; 28, 2; am*rí*tasya nấbhim, III, 17, 4;—ambrosia, I, 71, 9[3]; III, 26, 7; V, 2, 3[2].
am*ri*ta-tvá, immortality, I, 31, 7; 72, 9; 96, 6; V, 4, 10.
ám*ri*tyu, immortal, III, 2, 9.
áyas, ore, IV, 2, 17[3].
ayấ, thus, III, 12, 2.
ayấs, never-tiring (flame), III, 18, 2[1]; IV, 6, 10.
ará, spoke of a wheel, I, 141, 9; V, 13, 6.
arakshás, benevolent, II, 10, 5.
ára*n*a, stranger, V, 2, 5.
ará*n*i, kindling-stick, I, 127, 4[1]; III, 29, 2; V, 9, 3.

aratí, steward (?), I, 58, 7^{1}; 59, 2; 128, 6; 8; II, 2, 2; 3; 4, 2; III, 17, 4; IV, 1, 1; 2, 1; V, 2, 1^{3}.

áram, enough, I, 66, 5; dấ*s*at áram, he satisfies, I, 70, 5; readily, II, 5, 7^{2}; 8; purú vâ áram (conj. puruvấram), I, 142, 10^{2}.

aram-k*ri*t, doing service, II, 1, 7^{1}.

ấrariva*m*s, niggardly, I, 147, 4; 150, 2; III, 18, 2.

árâti, malign power, II, 7, 2; III, 18, 1; 24, 1; IV, 4, 4; árâtau (conj. for arataú), V, 2, 1^{3}; pl., V, 2, 6.

arâti-yát, niggard, I, 99, 1^{2}.

arâti-ván, malicious, I, 147, 4.

árâvan, niggard: árâv*n*a*h*, I, 36, 15; 16.

arí, poor: aryá*h*, I, 70, $1^{1,2}$; 71, 3^{2}; 150, 1^{1};—he who does not give, niggard, I, 73, $5^{1,2}$; II, 8, 2; IV, 4, 6; V, 2, 12.

arí, the Arya: aryá*h*, IV, 2, 12^{3}; 18^{5}.

árish*t*a, uninjured, V, 18, 3.

árishyat, unharmed: árishyanta*h*, II, 8, 6.

aru*n*á, red, I, 73, 7; II, 1, 6.

aru*n*î, the red (cow, or Dawn), I, 140, 13; IV, 1, 16^{3}; 2, 16; 14, 3^{1}.

árupita? IV, 5, 7^{1}.

arushá, red, ruddy, I, 36, 9; 141, 8; II, 2, 8; III, 1, 4; 7, 5; 15, 3; 29, 6; IV, 15, 6^{2}; V, 1, 5; arushấ, the two ruddy horses, I, 94, 10; II, 10, 2^{1}; IV, 2, 3; arushấsa*h*, I, 146, 2^{2}; IV, 6, 9; arushásya v*r*íshna*h*, V, 12, 2^{2}; 6;—árushîm (conj. árushî*h*?), I, 71, 1^{2}; árushî*h*, I, 72, 10^{4}.

arushá-stûpa, whose summit is red, III, 29, 3.

árûkshita, soft, IV, 11, 1.

arepás, stainless, IV, 10, 6.

arká, song, I, 141, 13; III, 26, 7^{1}; 8; IV, 3, 15; 10, 3; V, 5, 4.

ar*k*, to sing, praise: ar*k*an, III, 14, 4; ár*k*âmi, IV, 4, 8; ân*r*i*k*ú*h*, V, 6, 8; ár*k*anta*h*, V, 13, 1; ár*k*a, V, 16, 1^{1}; 22, 1; 25, 7;—abhí kârám ar*k*an, they sang triumphantly, IV, 1, 14^{2};—prá ar*k*anti, III, 12, 5; prá ar*k*a, I sing, III, 13, 1^{1}.

ar*k*í, flame, I, 36, 3; 20, &c.

ar*k*ís, flame, IV, 7, 9; V, 17, 3.

ár*n*a, flood: divá*h* ár*n*am, III, 22, 3.

ar*n*avá, waving, III, 22, 2^{2}.

ár*n*as, wave, IV, 3, 12.

ártha, aim, I, 144, 3^{2}; III, 11, 3^{2}; IV, 6, 10.

árbha, small, I, 146, 5.

arbhaká, little: arbhakébhya*h*, I, 27, 13.

ármi*n*î in nấrmi*n*î? (I, 149, 3^{1}).

aryá, Aryan, IV, 1, 7; (2, 12^{3}; 18^{5};) V, 16, 3.

Aryamán, I, 26, 4; 36, 4; 44, 13; 79, 3; 141, 9; II, 1, 4; IV, 2, 4; 3, 5; V, 3, 2.

arvấñ*k*: arvấñ*k*am yákshva, sacrifice and bring hither, I, 45, 10.

árvat, horse, I, 27, 9; 73, 9; 145, 3^{1}; II, 2, 10; IV, 15, 6; V, 6, 1; 2.

árvan, horse, I, 149, 3; IV, 7, 11; 11, 4.

arhá*n*â, deservedly, I, 127, 6.

árhat, worthy, I, 94, 1; II, 3, 1; 3; V, 7, 2.

av, to protect, bless, help: ávâ*h*, I, 27, 7; avisha*h*, III, 13, 6, &c.

áva: agné*h* ávena for agné ráve*n*a, I, 128, 5^{1}.

avadyá, disgrace, IV, 4, 15.

aváni, course, I, 140, 5;—river, V, 11, 5.

avamá, lowest (god), IV, 1, 5.

ávara, later (or, nearer), I, 141, 5;—lower, II, 9, 3.

ávasâna, not clothed, III, 1, 6.

avástât, below, III, 22, 3.

ava-sthấ, retirement, V, 19, 1^{1}.

avasyú, desiring help, II, 6, 6.

avit*rí*, helper, I, 36, 2; 44, 10; III, 19, 5.

ávi-mat, rich in sheep, IV, 2, 5^{1}.

avishyát, wishing to drink, I, 58, 2.

avishyú, greedy, I, 189, 5.

avîratâ, want of heroes, III, 16, 5.

av*r*iká, without danger, I, 31, 13;—keeping off the wolf, IV, 4, 12.

a*s*, to eat: prá a*s*âna, III, 21, 1.

a*s*atrú, without a foe, V, 2, 12.

a*s*áni, thunderbolt, I, 143, 5.

a*s*ás, cursing, IV, 4, 15.

á*s*iva, unkind, V, 12, 5.

a*s*îrshán, headless, IV, 1, 11.

á*s*man, stone (flint), II, 1, 1; III, 29, 6.

á*s*ma-vra*g*a, dwelling in the rock-stable, IV, 1, 13.
á*s*ramish*th*a, never tiring, IV, 4, 12.
á*s*rita, not resting on (?), IV, 7, 6[2].
a*s*va-dấvan, giver of horses, V, 18, 3[2].
á*s*va-pe*s*as, the ornament of which are horses, II, 1, 16.
á*s*vam-ish*t*i, winner of horses, II, 6, 2[2].
Á*s*va-medha, N. p., V, 27, 4–6.
á*s*va-râdhas, giver of horses, V, 10, 4[1].
á*s*vâ, mare, III, 1, 4; 7, 2[2].
a*s*vín, rich in horses, IV, 2, 5[1]; V, 4, 11.
A*s*vínau, du., the two A*s*vins, I, 44, 2; 8; 14; III, 20, 1; 5; 29, 6[1]; IV, 2, 4; 13, 1; 15, 9; 10; V, 26, 9.
á*s*vya, of the horses, I, 74, 7.
áshâ*l*h*a, invincible, III, 15, 4.
ash*t*amá, eighth (rein or priest of Agni), II, 5, 2[1].
ash*t*ấ-padî, eight-footed (i. e. cow with calf), II, 7, 5[2].
as, to be: prá astu, may it be foremost, I, 13, 9;—satá*h* *k*a bhávata*h* *k*a, I, 96, 7; tvám tấn sám *k*a práti *k*a asi, thou art united with them and equal to them, II, 1, 15.
as, to throw: ava-ásya, I, 140, 10.
ásat, nothingness, IV, 5, 14;—untrue, V, 12, 4.
asanấ, weapon, I, 148, 4.
asamaná, striving apart, I, 140, 4.
ásam-dita, unfettered, IV, 4, 2.
ásam-m*ri*sh*t*a, not cleansed, V, 11, 3.
asa*s**k*át, not sticking together, I, 13, 6; 142, 6.
ásasat, never sleeping, I, 143, 3.
ásita, black, IV, 13, 4.
ásu, vital spirit, I, 140, 8.
ásura, the Asura, miraculous lord, II, 1, 6; III, 3, 4[1]; 29, 14[1]; IV, 2, 5[2]; V, 12, 1; 15, 1; 27, 1.
asuryà, mysterious power, V, 10, 2.
ásta, stall, I, 66, 9;—home: ástam yánti, V, 6, 1.
ásta-tâti, homestead, V, 7, 6.
ást*ri*, archer, I, 66, 7; 70, 11; 71, 5[1]; 148, 4; IV, 4, 1.
ást*ri*ta, indestructible, I, 140, 8.
áspandamâna, without trembling, IV, 3, 10.
asmád, pers. pronoun: asmấkam astu, may he be ours, I, 13, 10; prá va*h* îmahe, we entreat for you, I, 36, 1[1]; va*h* untranslated, I, 66, 9[1]; sá*h* na*h*, thus (give) us, II, 6, 5[1]; âré asmát, IV, 11, 6[1].
asma-drúh, he who deceives us: asma-dhrúk, I, 36, 16.
asmadryàk, turned towards us, V, 4, 2.
asma-yú, inclined towards us, I, 142, 10.
asrídh, not failing, I, 13, 9; V, 5, 8.
ásredhat, unerring, III, 14, 5.
asremán? III, 29, 13[1].
ásvapna*g*, never sleeping: ásvapna*g*a*h*, IV, 4, 12.
áhan, day, I, 71, 2; dîrghấ áhâ, I, 140, 13; áhna*h*, by day, IV, 10, 5; ágre áhnâm, V, 1, 4; 5.
áhi, snake, I, 79, 1.
ahûryá, not to be led astray: ahûryá*h* (conj. for âhû́rya*h*), I, 69, 4[1].
áhraya, fearless, I, 74, 8; glorious, III, 2, 4.
áhrayâ*n*a, fearless, IV, 4, 14.

âké, near, II, 1, 10.
ấ-kshita, habitable, V, 7, 7.
ấgas, sin, IV, 3, 5; 12, 4; V, 3, 7; 12.
â-*g*ấni, birth: tisrá*h* â-*g*ấnî*h*, III, 17, 3[1].
ất, then, I, 148, 4[1].
â-táni, an expander: ya*g*ñám â-táni*h*, II, 1, 10.
âtithyá, hospitality, I, 76, 3; IV, 4, 10; V, 28, 2.
âtmán, vital breath: âtmấ-iva *s*éva*h*, I, 73, 2.
â-dadí, seizer: ấdat â-dadí*h*, I, 127, 6[2].
Âdityá, IV, 1, 2; pl., the Âdityas, I, 45, 1; 94, 3; 188, 4; II, 1, 13; 3, 4[1]; III, 8, 8; 20, 5.
ấ-deva, godly, II, 4, 1; devám ấ-devam, IV, 1, 1[3].
â-dhavá, purification, I, 141, 3[3].
â-dh*ri*sh, attack, II, 1, 9.
âdhrá, weak: âdhrásya, I, 31, 14[2].
ânushák, in due order, I, 13, 5[1]; 58, 3; 72, 7; II, 6, 8; III, 11, 1; IV, 4, 10; 7, 2; 5; 12, 3; V, 6, 6[1]; 10; 9, 1; 16, 2; 18, 2; 21, 2; 22, 2; 26, 8.
âp: pári âpa, he has won, I, 76, 1.
Âpayấ, N. of a river, III, 23, 4.
âpí, companion, I, 26, 3; 31, 16; IV, 3, 13.

â-p*ri*kk*h*ya, whose leave should be asked, I, 60, 2.
ā̃pya, companionship, I, 36, 12; III, 2, 6.
âmá, raw, IV, 3, 9³.
ā̃-ya*g*ish*th*a, best performer of sacrifices, II, 9, 6.
ā̃yasa, of iron, I, 58, 8.
âyú, the living, I, 31, 2²; 11; 66, 1; 140, 8; 147, 1¹;—lively: âyúva*h* dhenáva*h*, II, 5, 5;—Âyú, N. p., I, 96, 2²; II, 2, 8; 4, 2; IV, 2, 12¹; 18⁴,⁶; V, 7, 6; *s*ám*s*am âyó*h*, IV, 6, 11²; V, 3, 4²; pl., the Âyus, I, 58, 3²; 60, 3; IV, 7, 4;—n., life, III, 3, 7.
ā̃yudha, weapon, V, 2, 3.
ā̃yus, life: ví*s*vam ā̃yu*h*, I, 73, 5; ā̃yu*h* apā̃m, III, 1, 5²; dîrghám ā̃yu*h* pra-yákshe, III, 7, 1; trî́*n*i ā̃yû*m*shi, III, 17, 3¹, &c.
â-ródhana, ascent, IV, 7, 8; 8, 2; 4.
ā̃rtanâ? I, 127, 6¹.
ā̃rtvi*g*ya, duty of a priest, I, 94, 6.
ā̃rya, the Aryan, I, 59, 2; ví*s*a*h* ā̃rî*h*, I, 77, 3³; 96, 3.
âví*h*-*rig*îka, (I, 44, 3¹).
âví*h*-tya, visible, I, 95, 5.
âví*s*, manifest: âví*h* bhava, I, 31, 3¹; âví*h* babhū̃tha, V, 1, 9; âví*h* k*rin*ute, V, 2, 9.
â-*s*ás, hope: â-*s*ásâ, IV, 5, 11¹.
ā̃*s*â, region, V, 10, 6.
â*s*iná, old (?), I, 27, 13¹.
â*s*ú, swift racer, I, 60, 5; IV, 7, 11.
â*s*u-á*s*vya, plenty of swift horses, V, 6, 10.
â*s*u-yā̃, quickly, IV, 4, 2.
â-*s*u*s*ukshá*n*i, flaming, II, 1, 1.
â*s*ushâ*n*á, aspiring after, IV, 1, 13.
â*s*u-héman, quick inciter, II, 1, 5³.
âs: úpa âsate, they approach reverentially, I, 36, 7; III, 2, 6;—sam-ā̃sate, they lie down round about, III, 9, 7.
ā̃s, mouth: âsā̃, I, 76, 4¹; 140, 2; II, 1, 14¹; in the presence of, IV, 5, 10; manifestly, V, 17, 2; 5; 23, 1.
âsán, mouth, I, 75, 1; III, 26, 7; V, 6, 9; 18, 4.
âsā̃, face: yásya âsayā̃, in whose presence, I, 127, 8.
âsā̃t, adv., near, I, 27, 3.
â-sutí, drink, II, 1, 14.
âsurá, of the Asura: gárbha*h* âsurá*h*, III, 29, 11.
ā̃skra, united, III, 6, 4³.
âsyà, mouth, II, 1, 13; V, 12, 1.
ā̃-huta, see hu.
â-hū̃rya, to be led astray: â-hū̃rya*h* (conj. ahûryá*h*), I, 69, 4¹.

i: ayate, he proceeds, I, 127, 3⁶; yánta*h*, corrupt for vyánta*h*? I, 140, 13²; saním yaté, striving for gain, V, 27, 4;—ádhi ihi, think thou (of us), I, 71, 10²;—sá*h* nú îyate (Sa*m*hitâ: sâ nvî̀yate), conj. sā̃nu (= sá ánu) îyate, I, 145, 1¹;—ánta*h* ī̃yase, thou passest between, II, 6, 7;—ápa aíye*h*, V, 2, 8;—úpa ā̃ imasī̃, we approach, I, 1, 7;—pari-etā̃, will overtake, I, 27, 8;—pra-yatí ya*gñ*é, adhvaré, while the sacrifice is going on, III, 29, 16; V, 28, 6; pra-yaí devébhya*h*, that the gods may come forth, I, 142, 6; éti prá, I, 144, 1²;—ná práti-itaye, not to be withstood, I, 36, 20;—sám yanti, come together, I, 31, 10; see sam-yát.
í*d*, nourishing power, sacred food: i*l*ā̃ k*r*itā̃ni, I, 128, 7; i*l*á*h* padé, I, 128, 1; II, 10, 1²; hótâram i*l*á*h*, III, 4, 3.
Í*l*â, 'Nourishment,' N. of a goddess, I, 13, 9¹; 31, 11³; 142, 9; 188, 8; II, 1, 11¹; 3, 8; III, 1, 23¹; 4, 8; 7, 5; 27, 10²; V, 4, 4; 5, 8; í*l*âyâ*h* padé, III, 23, 4³; 29, 4; i*l*ā̃, instr., III, 24, 2; í*l*âyâ*h* putrá*h*, III, 29, 3³.
í*l*â-vat, rich in nourishment, IV, 2, 5.
itá*h*-ûti, who from here distributes his blessings, I, 146, 2.
íti, thus: íti krátvâ, with this intention, IV, 1, 1¹.
itthā̃, truly, I, 36, 7; 141, 1; V, 17, 1; itthā̃ dhiyā̃, with right thought, III, 27, 6.
itthā̃-dhî, thus minded, IV, 11, 3.
idám, this: asmai (after the plural yé), I, 67, 8¹; asmai (verb to be supplied), I, 70, 4¹; yádi idám, when here (all this happened), I, 79, 2³; yádi idám, as I am here, IV, 5, 11²;

there, II, 5, 5; eshâm (conj. eshám), IV, 2, 4[1].
idấ *k*it-idấ *k*it, now-now, IV, 10, 5.
idhmá, fuel, I, 94, 4; III, 18, 3.
in: inóshi, thou drivest away, IV, 10, 7;—prá ainot, he has driven forward, I, 66, 10.
iná, strong, I, 149, 1.
índu, Soma, V, 18, 2.
Índra, I, 13, 12; 142, 4; 5; 12; 13; II, 1, 3; 3, 3; 8, 6; III, 4, 6; 11; 22, 1; 25, 4; IV, 2, 17; V, 2, 8; 3, 1; 5, 3; 11; 11, 2; índram agním, III, 12, 3.
Índrâgnî, du., III, 12, 1; 2; 4-9; V, 27, 6.
Índrâvísh*n*û, du., Indra and Vish*n*u, IV, 2, 4.
inv, to stir up, to further: ínvati, I, 128, 5; ínvata*h*, I, 141, 4; invasi, I, 94, 10; 141, 10; V, 28, 2; ínvanta*h*, III, 4, 5; invire, V, 6, 6.
íbha, elephant, IV, 4, 1[1].
íbhya, rich, I, 65, 7.
iva: svéna-iva, read svéna evá? I, 145, 2[2].
ish, to long, seek: i*kkh*ánta, I, 68, 8; i*kkh*ánta*h*, I, 72, 2; îshu*h*, III, 1, 2.
ish, to incite: ishé, infin., I, 71, 8[3]; isháyanta mánma, they have stirred up our prayers, I, 77, 4[3]; ishá*n*i, II, 2, 9[2]; ishitá, III, 3, 2; 4, 3; 12, 1.
ísh, food, I, 12, 11; 27, 7; 36, 11, &c.; V, 6, 1-10; ishấm netấ, III, 23, 2[2].
ishá, food-giving, I, 189, 8[2].
Ishá, N. p., V, 7, 10.
isha*n*y: isha*n*yanti, they speed it hither, V, 6, 6[1].
ishay, to seek nourishment: isháyanta, II, 2, 11[1].
ishirá, vigorous, quick, I, 128, 5; III, 2, 13; 5, 4.
ishudhyát, supplicant: ishudhyatê, I, 128, 6[4].
ishuy, to fly like an arrow, to shoot arrows (?): ishûyate, I, 128, 4[2].
ishu-yát, desiring food (?), I, 128, 4[2].
ish*t*áni? I, 127, 6[1].
ish*t*í, wish, search, I, 143, 8[2]; 145, 1; 148, 3; IV, 4, 7.
ish*t*í, sacrifice, II, 1, 9[1].
ish*t*í, incitement (?), IV, 6, 7[2].

î: prá îmahe va*h*, we entreat for you, I, 36, 1[1];—ấ îmahe, we implore, III, 26, 5.
î*d*, to magnify: î*l*e, I, 1, 1[2]; 44, 4; III, 1, 15; 27, 2; 12; IV, 3, 3; 9[1]; ấ*l*ate, I, 36, 1; 128, 8; III, 6, 3; 10, 2; 13, 2; 27, 14; V, 1, 7; 8, 3; 9, 1; 14, 2; 3; 21, 3; î*l*ata, I, 96, 3[1]; î*tt*e, V, 12, 6; ấ*l*ita, V, 17, 1; 21, 4; ấ*l*âna, II, 6, 6; 28, 1; î*l*itá, I, 13, 4[1]; 142, 4[1]; II, 3, 3; V, 5, 3; 7.
î*l*énya, to be magnified, I, 79, 5; 146, 5; III, 27, 13; V, 1, 9; 14, 5.
ấ*d*ya, worthy of being magnified: ấ*d*ya*h*, I, 1, 2; 12, 3[2]; 75, 4; 188, 3; II, 1, 4; III, 2, 2; 5, 6; 9; 9, 8; 17, 4; 27, 4; 29, 2; 7; IV, 7, 1; 2; V, 22, 1.
îr: îratâm, may they arise, IV, 8, 7; îrayádhyai, he shall rise up, IV, 2, 1[1];—â-îriré, they have raised, set to work, I, 143, 4; III, 11, 9; 29, 15;—ní erire, they have roused, I, 128, 8; II, 2, 3; IV, 1, 1.
ấvat, like this, IV, 4, 6; 15, 5.
î*s*, to rule: î*s*ata, I, 36, 16; II, 7, 2; vásva*h* î*s*e, I, 71, 9; yấvat ấ*s*e, as far as I have power, III, 18, 3.
î*s*âná, master, lord, I, 73, 9; 79, 4; 141, 3.
îsh: îshate, they flee, I, 141, 8;—ấ îshate, he advances, I, 149, 1[2].

ukthá, hymn, litany, I, 27, 12; 71, 2; 140, 13; II, 8, 5; III, 5, 2; 13, 6; 20, 1; IV, 3, 4; 16; 6, 11; 11, 3; V, 4, 7; 6, 9; 18, 4.
ukthávâhas, (I, 127, 8[1]).
uktha-*s*ás, chanting litanies, IV, 2, 16.
ukthín, rich in hymns, III, 12, 5.
ukthyà, praiseworthy, I, 79, 12; III, 2, 13; 15; 10, 6; 26, 2; V, 26, 6.
uksh, to sprinkle: aúkshan, III, 9, 9; satyám ukshan, IV, 1, 10.
uksh, to grow. See vaksh.
ukshán, bull, I, 146, 2; II, 7, 5; III, 7, 6; 7[2]; V, 27, 5.
ugrá, strong, mighty, I, 127, 11; III, 26, 5; IV, 2, 18[3].
Ugrá-deva: ugrá-devam, I, 36, 18[1].

u*k*átha, hymn, I, 73, 10; 143, 6; IV, 2, 20; V, 12, 3.
uttânâ: uttânấ, lying extended on her back, II, 10, 3[1]; III, 29, 3[2]; V, 1, 3[4];—nyàñ uttânấ*h*, spread out downwards-turned, IV, 13, 5.
uttânấ-hasta, with outstretched hand, III, 14, 5[1].
ut-vát: ut-váta*h* ni-váta*h*, to the heights and to the depths, III, 2, 10.
útsa, spring, III, 26, 9.
udanyấ, of water, II, 7, 3.
údyata-sru*k*, the sacrificer who raises the spoon, I, 31, 5.
und, to moisten: havyám undán, II, 3, 2.
upa-ấbh*ri*t, the bringing: ûrgấm upa-ấbh*ri*ti, I, 128, 2.
úpa-iti, approaching, supplication, I, 76, 1[1]; III, 18, 1.
upa-kshet*rí*, follower, III, 1, 16.
upabdí, noise produced by going, I, 74, 7[1].
upa-mấ, high up, I, 31, 15[1].
upamấ, likeness, (I, 31, 15[1]).
upa-mấda, enjoyment, III, 5, 5.
upa-mít, supporting, I, 59, 1[3]; pillar, IV, 5, 1.
úpara, lower, I, 79, 3[3]; 128, 3; úparâsu, in our neighbourhood, I, 127, 5[2]; úparasya, nearer, IV, 2, 18[6]; úparân, getting behind, II, 4, 9[1].
upa-vaktrí, the U. priest, IV, 9, 5[1].
upás, lap: upási (conj. for apási), (III, 1, 3[3]; 11[4]).
upa-sád, sitting down (reverentially), II, 6, 1[1].
Upa-stutá, I, 36, 10[1]; 17[1].
úpa-stuti, praise, I, 148, 2.
upá-stha, lap, I, 95, 4; 5; pitró*h* upá-sthe, I, 31, 9; 146, 1; III, 5, 8; 26, 9; apấm upá-sthe, I, 144, 2; mâtú*h* upá-sthe, III, 8, 1; 29, 14; V, 1, 6; 19, 1.
upa-sthấyam *k*arati, he goes to greet them, I, 145, 4[3].
úpâka, neighbouring, I, 142, 7; III, 4, 6.
upâké, near at hand, I, 27, 6; IV, 10, 5; 11, 1.
úpeti, see úpa-iti.
ubh: ubdhám, closed, IV, 1, 15;—sám-ubdham, confined, V, 2, 1[1].
ubhá, both: ubhấ for ubhé, I, 140, 3[1]; ubhé íti toké íti tánaye, I, 147, 1[3].
ubháya, both, I, 26, 9[1]; 31, 7; ubháyân, both (kinds of men, the pious and the impious), I, 189, 7[2]; of both kinds (wealth), II, 9, 5[1].
urú, wide: urú ksháyâya *k*akrire, I, 36, 8; urvî́, the wide (Earth), I, 146, 2; II, 4, 7; urú, wide space, III, 1, 11[1].
uru-gâyá, wide-ruling, II, 1, 3; III, 6, 4[5]; IV, 3, 7; 14, 1.
uru-*g*ráyas, extending over wide spaces, V, 8, 6.
uru-vyáñ*k*, far-reaching, V, 1, 12.
uru-*s*á*m*sa, widely-renowned: uru-sá*m*sâya, I, 31, 14.
urushy, to guard, deliver: urushya, I, 58, 8; 9; IV, 2, 6; to keep off: áditim urushya, IV, 2, 11[3]; urushyát, he has escaped into wide space, III, 5, 8.
urvárâ, field, I, 127, 6.
Urvá*s*î: urvá*s*î*h*, IV, 2, 18[4].
urviyấ, far and wide, I, 141, 5; II, 3, 5; III, 1, 18; V, 28, 1.
ulkấ, firebrand, IV, 4, 2.
u*s*, see va*s*.
u*s*ádhak, eagerly burning, III, 6, 7[3].
U*s*íg, (Agni) the U*s*ig (or willing one), III, 3, 7; 8; 11, 2[1]; 27, 10[3];—pl., the U*s*igs, mythical priests, I, 60, 2[1]; 4; 128, 1[2]; 189, 7; II, 4, 5[3]; III, 2, 4[2]; 9; 15, 3[2]; IV, 1, 15[1]; V, 3, 4.
ush, to burn down: ush*n*án, II, 4, 7;—ní oshatât, burn down, IV, 4, 4.
ush, to shine. See vas.
usha*h*-búdh, awakening with the dawn, I, 44, 1; 9; 65, 9; 127, 10; III, 2, 14; IV, 6, 8.
ushár, dawn: usrấ*h*, gen. sing., I, 71, 2[2].
ushás, dawn, I, 71, 1; 94, 5; ushása*h* návedâ*h*, I, 79, 1[3]; vásto*h* ushása*h*, I, 79, 6; doshấ ushási, II, 8, 3; IV, 2, 8; práti doshấm ushásam, IV, 12, 2; ushása*h* vi-roké, III, 5, 2; ushása*h* ví-ush*t*au, III, 15, 2; IV, 1, 5; 14, 4;—Dawn, the goddess, I, 44, 1[1]; 2; 8; 14; III, 17, 3[1]; 20, 1; IV, 2, 15; 3, 11[2]; V, 1,

1; 28, 1; ushá*h* *g*ârá*h*, lover of the Dawn, I, 69, 1[1]; 9; devî́ ushấ*h*, III, 20, 5; IV, 1, 17; 14, 3; doshấm ushásam, Night and Morning, V, 5, 6;—du., nákta *k*a ushásâ, I, 73, 7; ushásau, the two Dawns, Night and Dawn, I, 188, 6[2]; III, 4, 6[1]; 14, 3; V, 1, 4;—ushása*h*, the Dawns, I, 44, 10; II, 2, 2; 7; 8; III, 5, 1; IV, 1, 13[3]; 2, 19; 5, 13; 14, 1; ushá*h* vibhâtî́*h*, III, 6, 7; ushása*h* ûshu*h*, III, 7, 10; ushásâm ágram, IV, 13, 1.
ushásânáktâ, Dawn and Night, II, 3, 6.
usrá, bright, I, 69, 9.
usrấ, milch-cow, IV, 1, 13; see also ushar.
usríyâ, ruddy cow, III, 1, 12[4]; IV, 5, 8[2]; 9.

ûtí, blessing, protection, I, 36, 13, &c.
ū́dhan, udder, I, 69, 3[1]; 146, 2; III, 29, 14; IV, 1, 19; 3, 10; pitú*h* ū́dha*h*, III, 1, 9[1]; sásmin ū́dhan, IV, 7, 7[2]; 10, 8[1].
ū́ma, helpful, III, 6, 8[1].
ûr*g*: máhi ûr*g*áyantî́*h*, giving mighty vigour, III, 7, 4.
ū́r*g*, vigour: ûr*g*âm pate, I, 26, 1; ū́r*g*a*h* napât, I, 58, 8; II, 6, 2; III, 27, 12; V, 7, 1; 17, 5; ûr*g*á*h* putrám, I, 96, 3; ûr*g*ấ pinvasva, III, 3, 7.
ū́r*n*a-mradas, soft like wool, V, 5, 4[1].
ûr*n*u: ví ûr*n*ot, he has revealed, I, 68, 1; ví aur*n*ot, he has opened, I, 68, 10.
ûrdhvá, straight, standing erect, I, 36, 13; 14; 95, 5, &c.
ûrmí, wave, I, 27, 6; 44, 12; 95, 10.
ū́rmyâ, night, II, 4, 3.
ûrvá, stable, stall, prison, I, 72, 8; III, 1, 14; IV, 2, 17; 12, 5.
ûh: ûhé, he is considered, V, 3, 9[1].

ri, to go, &c.: *rin*vati, he procures, I, 128, 6; he hastens, I, 144, 5; arta tmánâ divá*h*, arose, V, 25, 8[2];—abhí âru*h*, they ran up to, III, 1, 4;—ut-ấritha, thou hast sprung, II, 9, 3; út iyarti vấ*k*am, he raises his voice, III, 8, 5[3]; út arta, it rose up, IV, 1, 17; út aram, IV, 15, 7;—prá ârú*h*, they have risen, III, 7, 1; prá iyarmi, I stretch forth, III, 19, 2; prá ârta, it came forth, IV, 1, 12;—ví *rin*vati, he discloses, I, 58, 3; ví *rin*van, they opened, I, 69, 10; ví *rin*vati, he opens, I, 128, 6; V, 16, 2;—sam-ấrata, he has come together, I, 145, 4[1]; sám *rin*vati, it accomplishes, III, 2, 1; he sets himself in motion, III, 11, 2[2]; sám-*ri*ta*h*, erected, IV, 13, 5.
*rí*kvan, singer, III, 13, 5.
*ri*gmíya, praiseworthy, III, 2, 4.
rik, see ar*k*.
rík, hymn, (sacrificial) verse, I, 36, 11; II, 3, 7; V, 6, 5; 27, 4.
rig, *riñg*, to press on, strive forward: *riñg*asâná, I, 58, 3; 96, 3; *riñg*án, I, 95, 7; *riñg*ate, I, 141, 6; 143, 7; II, 1, 8; 2, 5; *riñg*ase, I press on, IV, 8, 1;—abhí *rig*yate, I, 140, 2;—ấ *riñg*ase, V, 13, 6[1];—ní *riñg*ate, he throws down, I, 143, 5; ní *riñg*e, I catch hold, III, 4, 7.
*rig*îka, (I, 44, 3[1]).
*rig*ú, rightly, II, 3, 7; right deeds, IV, 1, 17.
*rig*u-áñ*k*, going straight forward, IV, 6, 9.
*rig*u-mushká, puissant, IV, 2, 2; 6, 9.
*rig*u-yát, righteous, V, 12, 5.
*rin*á, debt, IV, 3, 13[2].
*ri*tá, the *Ri*ta, Right, I, 1, 8; 75, 5[1]; 79, 3; 141, 1; 11; III, 4, 7; 6, 6; IV, 1, 13[2]; 2, 3[1]; 14[3]; 16; 19[1]; 3, 4[2]; 9–12; 5, 11; V, 1, 7; 12, 1[1]; 6[1]; 15, 2; 20, 4; *ri*tất ádhi, on behalf of *Ri*ta, I, 36, 11[1]; *ri*tásya vratấ, I, 65, 3; *ri*tásya yóni, I, 65, 4; III, 1, 11; IV, 1, 12; V, 21, 4; dhấrâm *ri*tásya, I, 67, 7[1]; V, 12, 2; *ri*tấ sápanta*h*, I, 67, 8; 68, 4; *ri*tásya présha*h* *ri*tásya dhîtí*h*, I, 68, 5[1]; dádhan *ri*tám, I, 71, 3[1]; *ri*tásya dhenáva*h*, I, 73, 6; *ri*tásya pathấ, I, 128, 2; yahvî́ íti *ri*tásya, mâtárâ, I, 142, 7; V, 5, 6; *ri*tásya dhû*h*-sádam, I, 143, 7; *ri*tásya dohánâ*h*, streams of *Ri*ta, I, 144, 2[1]; rathî́*h* *ri*tásya, III, 2, 8; IV, 10, 2; *ri*tásya sấman, I, 147,

1[4]; *ri*tám yaté, I, 188, 2; pûrvî*h* *ri*tásya sam-d*rís*a*h*, III, 5, 2; *ri*tásya sádasi, III, 7, 2; gopâ*h* *ri*tásya, III, 10, 2; *ri*tásya pathyâ*h* ánu, III, 12, 7; *ri*tásya yóge vanúsha*h*, eager to set to work the *Ri*ta, III, 27, 11[1]; *ri*téna *ri*tám ní-yatam, IV, 3, 9[1,2]; *ri*tásya padé, IV, 5, 9; *ri*tásya dhâman, IV, 7, 7[3]; *ri*tásya ra*s*mím, V, 7, 3; *ri*téna, in the right way, III, 4, 5; 5, 3;—adj., righteous, IV, 3, 8[1].

*ri*ta-*k*ít, intent upon *Ri*ta (Right), I, 145, 5; IV, 3, 4; V, 3, 9.

*ri*tá-*g*âta, born in or from the *Ri*ta: *ri*tá-*g*âta*h*, I, 36, 19; 144, 7; 189, 6; III, 6, 10; 20, 2.

*ri*ta-*g*ñá, knowing the right way, I, 72, 8.

*ri*ta-pâ, protecting the *Ri*ta, (III, 20, 4[1]; V, 12, 3[2]).

*ri*tá-pra*g*âta, born from *Ri*ta, I, 65, 10.

*ri*tá-pravîta, penetrated by *Ri*ta, I, 70, 7.

*ri*tay, to perform the *Ri*ta: *ri*táyan *ri*téna, V, 12, 3.

*ri*ta-yát, righteous, II, 1, 2; IV, 8, 3; V, 27, 4.

*ri*ta-yú, loving *Ri*ta, V, 8, 1.

*ri*tá-van, righteous, I, 77, 1; 2; 5; III, 2, 13; 6, 10; 13, 2; 14, 2; 20, 4; IV, 1, 2; 2, 1; 6, 5; 7, 3; 7; 10, 7; V, 1, 6; 25, 1.

*ri*ta-v*rí*dh, increaser of *Ri*ta, I, 13, 6; 44, 14; 142, 6; III, 2, 1.

*ri*tú, season, I, 95, 3[3]; V, 12, 3[2].

*ri*tu-thâ, observing the right time, II, 3, 7.

*ri*tu-pâ, guardian of the seasons, III, 20, 4[1]; V, 12, 3[2].

*ri*tvíg, ministrant, priest, I, 1, 1; 44, 11; 45, 7; 60, 3; II, 5, 7[1]; III, 10, 2; V, 22, 2; 26, 7.

*ri*tvíya, at the appointed season, I, 143, 1; II, 1, 2; III, 29, 10.

*ri*dh, to accomplish: *ri*dhyâma, I, 31, 8; IV, 10, 1[1].

*rí*dhak, in one's peculiar way, III, 25, 1[1].

*Ri*bhú, II, 1, 10[1]; III, 5, 6[1]; V, 7, 7.

*rí*shi, a *Ri*shi, I, 1, 2; 31, 1; 66, 4; III, 21, 3; sahásram *rí*shibhi*h*, I, 189, 8.

*ri*shi-k*rí*t, making (one) a *Ri*shi, I, 31, 16[3].

*ri*shú, pl., dawns (?), I, 127, 10[5]; V, 25, 1[2].

*ri*shvá, tall, I, 146, 2; III, 5, 5; 7; 10; IV, 2, 2.

éka: éka*h*-eka*h*, every one, III, 29, 15.

éka-âyu, of unique vigour, I, 31, 5.

éna, variegated: énî íti, I, 144, 6[1].

énas, sin, I, 189, 1; III, 7, 10[3]; IV, 12, 4; 5; V, 3, 7.

éman, course, path, I, 58, 4[4]; IV, 7, 9.

éva, way: évai*h*, in due way, I, 68, 4; 95, 6; évena, in his way, I, 128, 3; aryá*h* évai*h*, IV, 2, 12[3]; —the going, I, 79, 2.

evá, thus, I, 76, 5; 77, 5; 95, 11; III, 17, 2; evâm̐, Sa*m*h., V, 6, 10[1].

eshá, rapid, (IV, 2, 4[1]).

óka, homestead, I, 66, 3.

o*g*âyámâna, displaying his power, I, 140, 6.

ó*g*ish*th*a, richest: ó*g*ish*th*am méda*h*, III, 21, 5[1].

óshadhî, herb, I, 59, 3; 98, 2; II, 1, 1; 4, 4; III, 1, 13; 5, 8[1]; 22, 2; V, 8, 7.

óha, heedfulness, IV, 10, 1[2].

Ká*n*va, I, 36, 8; 10[1]; 11; 17; 19; ká*n*vâsa*h*, I, 44, 8; Ká*n*vasya sûnáva*h*, I, 45, 5.

katidhâ *k*it, everywhere, I, 31, 2.

kadâ *k*aná, never, I, 150, 2.

kan: tásya *k*âkan, therewith he is satisfied, I, 148, 2; *k*akâná*h*, loving, III, 5, 2; kânisha*h*, take joyfully, III, 28, 5; *k*akâná*h*, delighting, desiring, V, 3, 10; 27, 3[1];—â *k*ake, he desires, III, 3, 3; â *k*ake, I love, III, 3, 10.

kanyâ, maiden, I, 66, 8[1]; kanînâm, V, 3, 2.

káya: káyasya *k*it, of whomsoever, I, 27, 8; káyâ, how, V, 12, 3.

kar, to praise, (I, 45, 4[1]).

karásna, arm: s*ri*prâ karásnâ, III, 18, 5[1].

karma*n*yà, able, III, 4, 9.

kárman, work, deed, I, 31, 8; III, 12, 6.

kalyâ*n*a, beautiful, I, 31, 9.

kaví, sage, I, 12, 6; 7; 13, 2; 8, &c.; I, 95, 8[2]; dhîrâsa*h* kavá-ya*h*, I, 146, 4[1].

kaví-kratu, having the mind of a sage, thoughtful, I, 1, 5; III, 2, 4; 14, 7; 27, 12; V, 11, 4.
kavi-khád, showing himself as a sage, III, 12, 3[1].
kaví-tama, the highest sage, III, 14, 1.
kavi-prasastá, praised by sages, V, 1, 8.
kavi-sastá, praised by the sages, III, 21, 4; 29, 7.
kavyátâ, wisdom, I, 96, 2.
kâ: kấyamânah, finding pleasure, III, 9, 2. See kan.
kấmya, of love: dugdhám ná kấmyam, V, 19, 4[1].
kârá, race: bhágam ná kâré, I, 141, 10[1];—triumph: abhí kârám arkan, IV, 1, 14[2].
kârú, singer, I, 31, 8; 9; 148, 2; II, 2, 9; III, 6, 1.
kấvya, quality of a sage, wisdom, I, 72, 1[1]; 96, 1; II, 5, 3; III, 1, 8; 17; 18; IV, 3, 16; 11, 3; V, 3, 5.
kấshthâ, pl., the (aerial) arena, I, 59, 6; race-course, I, 146, 5.
kíyat, however small, IV, 5, 6.
kîrí, poor, humble, I, 31, 13[3]; V, 4, 10[1].
Kîstá: Kîstấsah, the Kîstas, I, 127, 7[1].
kúpaya, agitating, I, 140, 3.
kumârá, prince, IV, 15, 7–10; boy, V, 2, 1[1]; 2.
kúlisa, axe, III, 2, 1.
Kusiká, pl., the Kusikas, III, 26, 1[1]; 3; 29, 15.
kûkit-arthín, striving for all that is desired, IV, 7, 6.
kri, to make, &c.: yagñám krinotana, I, 13, 12; krinuhi, I, 31, 8; kridhí nah râyé, help us to wealth, III, 15, 3[3]; krinóti devấn mártyeshu, he conveys the gods to the mortals, I, 77, 1[1]; kárikratah, displaying, I, 140, 5[1]; kritáh (read párishkritah?), adorned, I, 141, 8[1]; dhiyấ kakre, III, 27, 9[1]; krántah, IV, 2, 14; ákarma te, we have done our work for thee, IV, 2, 19;—áram karat, he may readily serve, II, 5, 8; urú kakrire, they have made wide room for, I, 36, 8; satrấ kakrânấh, I, 72, 1;—ấ krinóshi, thou givest, I, 31, 7; ấ krinudhvam, bring hither, I, 77, 2;—ápa ấ kridhi, drive away, III, 16, 5[2];—ní kah, he has brought down (i. e. surpassed), I, 72, 1[1];—párikrita, made ready, III, 28, 2;—sám akrinvan tégase, they have sharpened, III, 2, 10; see krânấ.
kridhú, weak, IV, 5, 14.
krip: akripran, they have pined, IV, 2, 18[4].
kríp, body, I, 127, 1; 128, 2.
krishtí, human race, I, 36, 19; 59, 5; 74, 2; 189, 3;—tribe, clan, V, 1, 6; 19, 3:—dwelling, II, 2, 10.
krishná, black, I, 58, 4[4]; 73, 7; 141, 8[2]; krishnáh vrishabháh, I, 79, 2[2]; darkness, I, 140, 5; krishnấsu, in the dark nights, III, 15, 3.
krishná-adhvan, whose path is black, II, 4, 6.
krishná-gamhas, speeding on his black way, I, 141, 7.
krishna-prúta, immersed in darkness, I, 140, 3.
krishná-vyathi, with a black trail, II, 4, 7[1].
krishná-sîta, drawing black furrows, I, 140, 4.
klip: kakripánta dhîbhíh, they chanted their prayers, IV, 1, 14.
kéta, desire, I, 146, 3.
ketú, light, shine, splendour, I, 36, 14; IV, 7, 4; 14, 2; V, 7, 4; ketúm usrấh, I, 71, 2[2];—ketú, beacon, banner, I, 27, 12; III, 1, 17; 2, 14; V, 11, 3; vidáthasya, I, 60, 1; yagñásya, I, 96, 6; 127, 6; III, 11, 3; 29, 5; V, 1, 2; yagñấnâm, III, 3, 3; adhvarásya, III, 8, 8; adhvarấnâm, III, 10, 4.
kévala, alone, I, 13, 10.
kesín, long-haired, I, 140, 8; long-maned, III, 6, 6.
krátu, power of mind, wisdom, I, 65, 9; 67, 2; 68, 3; 69, 2; 73, 2; 77, 3[1]; 128, 4; 141, 6; 9; 143, 2; 145, 2; II, 5, 4; III, 2, 3; 6, 5; 9, 6; 11, 6; IV, 5, 7; 10, 1; 2; 12, 1; V, 10, 2; 17, 4;—mind, I, 66, 5[2]; will, I, 68, 9; íti kratvâ, with this intention, IV, 1, 1[1];—power, I, 127, 9; 128, 5; III, 1, 5[1].

krand, to neigh, bellow, roar: krándat, I, 36, 8; a*k*ikradat, I, 58, 2; kánikradat, bellowing, I, 128, 3[1]; krándan, III, 26, 3.
kram: pári akramît, he has circumambulated, IV, 15, 3.
krâ*n*ấ, as soon as, I, 58, 3[1]; V, 7, 8[2]; indeed, V, 10, 2[1].
krî*d*, to sport: krî*l*anta*h*, IV, 4, 9; krî*l*an, V, 19, 5.
kshatrá, royal power, IV, 4, 8; V, 27, 6.
kshatríya, royal power, IV, 12, 3[1].
ksháp, night: ksháp*ah* (conj. kshapá*h*), I, 44, 8[2]; kshapá*h* (conj. ksháp*ah*), nights and dawns, I, 70, 7[1]: kshapá*h*, by night, I, 79, 6; ksháp*ah* sam-yáta*h*, II, 2, 2[3].
kshapấ-vat, earth-protecting, I, 70, 5[1].
kshám, earth, (I, 79, 3[2]); III, 8, 7.
ksháya, dwelling, I, 36, 8; 74, 4; 144, 7; III, 2, 6; 3, 2; 11, 7[2]; V, 9, 2; 12, 6; 23, 4; diví ksháyam (conj. divikshayám), III, 2, 13[1].
kshar, to flow: ksharasi, I, 27, 6; ksharanti, I, 72, 10.
kshấ, earth, I, 67, 5[2]; 95, 10; 96, 7[1]; 189, 3; ví*s*vâsu kshấsu, I, 127, 10[2,3].
kshấman, earth, IV, 2, 16.
kshi, to dwell: ksheti, I, 94, 2; ksheshyánta*h*, going to settle, II, 4, 3[1]; ksháya*h*, III, 8, 1; kshepayat, may he give us dwelling, V, 9, 7;—p*ri*thivî́m upa-kshéti, he dwells on the earth, I, 73, 3;—prati-kshiyántam, who abides turned towards, II, 10, 4;—to rule: ksháyan, III, 25, 3; kshayasi, IV, 5, 11.
kshití, dwelling, human settlement, I, 59, 1; 65, 5; 72, 7; 73, 4; II, 2, 3; III, 3, 9; 13, 4[1]; 14, 4; IV, 5, 15[1]; V, 7, 1;—tribe, III, 18, 1; V, 1, 10; kshitî́nấm, daívînâm, III, 20, 4.
kshíp, finger: dá*s*a kshípa*h*, III, 23, 3.
kshiprấ, a tossing (bow?), IV, 8, 8[1].
kshî, to fail: kshîyate, II, 9, 5.
kshu-mát, rich in food, II, 1, 10; 4, 8; 9, 5; IV, 2, 18[2].
kshé? IV, 3, 6[5].
kshétra, dwelling-place, V, 2, 3[1]; 4.
kshetra-sấdhas, giving bliss to our fields, III, 8, 7[2].
kshéma, safety, peace, I, 66, 3; 67, 2.
kshema-yát, living in peace, III, 7, 2.
kshóda, stream, I, 65, 5; 6[1]; 10.

khá, opening, IV, 11, 2.
khyâ: práti akhyat, he has looked on, IV, 13, 1; 14, 1;—ví akhyan, they looked around, IV, 1, 18.

ga*n*á, troop: ga*n*ám-ga*n*am, III, 26, 6; crowd, V, 1, 3.
gá*n*ya, belonging to the host, III, 7, 5.
gabhîrá, deep, IV, 5, 5[3]; 6.
gam, to go: *g*agamyât, I, 58, 9; pari-sádanta*h* agman, IV, 2, 17[4];—á*kkh*a gamema, we may obtain, IV, 5, 13;—sám-gatâni, comprised, I, 31, 5[1]; sam-*g*agmânấsu k*ri*sh*t*íshu, when the human tribes met (in battle), I, 74, 2; mánasâ sám *g*agmú*h*, they agreed in their mind, III, 1, 13.
gáya, home, I, 74, 2; dominion, V, 10, 3.
gárbha, womb, I, 65, 4; 148, 5;—fruit of the womb, germ, I, 95, 2; 4; 146, 5; II, 10, 3; III, 1, 6; 10[1]; 2, 10; 29, 2; 11; V, 2, 2; bhûtấnâm gárbham, III, 27, 9;—child, son: gárbha*h* apấm, vánânâm, &c., I, 70, 3; III, 1, 12; 13; 5, 3; gárbha*h* vîrúdhâm, II, 1, 14; dádhate gárbham, IV, 7, 9[1].
garbhí*n*î, pregnant, III, 29, 2.
garh, to blame: garhase, IV, 3, 5.
gavishá, see go-ishá.
gávish*t*i, see gó-ish*t*i.
Gávish*th*ira, V, 1, 12.
gávya, of the cows, I, 72, 8; IV, 2, 17;—bliss in cows, I, 140, 13.
gavyát, longing for the cows, IV, 1, 15.
gâ, to go: pra-*g*í*g*ata*h*, coming forward, I, 150, 2.
gâ, to sing: á*kkh*a agním gâsi, V, 25, 1[1].
gâtú, path, course, I, 71, 2; 72, 9; 95, 10; 96, 4; III, 1, 2; 4, 4.
gâyatrá, Gâyatra song, I, 12, 11; 27, 4; 79, 7; 188, 11.
gâyatrá-vepas, moved by the Gâyatra song, I, 142, 12.
gâh, to dive: áti gâhemahi, II, 7, 3.
gír, praise, prayer, I, 26, 5; 59, 4[1]; II, 2, 1[2], &c.

girí, hill, I, 65, 5.
gírva*n*as, loving praises, I, 45, 2; II, 6, 3.
gu: *g*óguve, he has loudly praised, I, 127, 10[2].
gur: *g*ugurvá*n*î íti, eager in praising, I, 142, 8;—abhí *g*uguryâ*h*, approve, I, 140, 13.
gurú, heavy: mántra*h* gurú*h*, I, 147, 4.
guh, to hide: guhámâna*h*, IV, 1, 11.
gúh, covert: guhā́ gúham, I, 67, 6[3].
gúhâ, in secret, I, 65, 1; 67, 3; II, 4, 9[1]; III, 1, 9; 14; V, 2, 1; 15, 5; gúhâ bhávantam, sántam, the hidden one, I, 67, 7; 141, 3; III, 5, 10; V, 8, 3; gúhâ hitám, hidden, IV, 5, 8[1]; 7, 6; V, 11, 6.
gúhya, secret, I, 72, 6; IV, 5, 10; V, 3, 2; 3; 5, 10.
g*ri*, to praise, I, 44, 6, &c.; g*rin*îte, he is praised, I, 79, 12[1];—desh*n*ám abhí g*rin*îhi, hail our gift, II, 9, 4; abhí g*rin*îtá*h*, they salute, III, 6, 10; gíra*h* abhí g*rin*ā́ti, he responds to my hymns, V, 27, 3.
g*ri*: *g*âg*ri*-vā́*m*sa*h*, having awoke, III, 10, 9; á*g*îgar íti, he has awakened, V, 1, 3[1]. See *gri*.
g*ri*tsa, clever, III, 1, 2; 19, 1; IV, 5, 2.
G*ri*tsa-madá: g*ri*tsa-madā́sa*h*, II, 4, 9.
g*ri*dhnú, greedy, I, 70, 11[2].
g*ri*há-pati, master of the house, I, 12, 6; 36, 5; 60, 4; II, 1, 2[3]; IV, 9, 4; 11, 5; V, 8, 1; 2.
gó, cow, I, 31, 12, &c.; 95, 8[1]; V, 1, 3[2]; 3, 2[2]; ástam ná gā́va*h*, I, 66, 9; ū́dha*h* ná gónâm, I, 69, 3; puru-dá*m*sam saním gó*h*, III, 1, 23; ékâ gaú*h*, III, 7, 2[3]; gúhyam nā́ma gónâm, V, 3, 3; ávindat gā́*h*, V, 14, 4[1]; ánasvantâ gā́vâ, two oxen with a car, V, 27, 1.
gó-agra, at the head of which are cows, II, 1, 16[1].
go-ishá, fighting for cows, IV, 13, 2[3].
gó-ish*t*i, 'striving for cows,' battle, I, 36, 8; (45, 7[1]).
gó-*ri*gîka, (I, 44, 3[1]).
Gótama, I, 79, 10; IV, 4, 11; pl., the Gotamas, I, 60, 5; 77, 5; 78, 1; 2[1].
gopā́, shepherd, guardian, protector, I, 96, 7; II, 9, 2; 6; III, 15, 2; V, 2, 5; 11, 1; 12, 4; gopā́m *ri*tásya, I, 1, 8; III, 10, 2; vi*s*ā́m gopā́*h*, I, 94, 5[1]; 96, 4.
gó-mat, rich in, or consisting in, cows, I, 79, 4; III, 16, 1; IV, 2, 5[1]; V, 4, 11; 24, 2; vra*g*ám gó-mantam, full of cows, IV, 1, 15.
gaurī́, buffalo cow: gauryàm, IV, 12, 6.
gnā́, wife, IV, 9, 4[1].
gnā́vat, accompanied by the divine wives: gnā́va*h* (conj. gnâva*h*), II, 1, 5[1].
grábha*n*a-vat, a firm hold, I, 127, 5[5].
grā́ma, hamlet, I, 44, 10.
grā́van, pressing-stone (of the Soma), IV, 3, 3[1]; V, 25, 8[1].

ghaná, club, I, 36, 16[1].
gharmá, offering of hot milk to the A*s*vins, III, 26, 7[2]; the gharma vessel, V, 19, 4.
ghush: ghóshi, it resounded, IV, 4, 8.
gh*ri*, to besprinkle: *g*ígharmi, II, 10, 4; 5.
gh*rin*á, heat: gh*rin*ā́, I, 141, 4[4].
gh*ri*tá, the Gh*ri*ta, or ghee, I, 72, 3; 127, 1, &c.; II, 3, 11[2]; 5, 6[1]; gh*ri*tā́ni aksharan, I, 188, 5; gh*ri*tám ná pûtám, III, 2, 1; gh*ri*tébhi*h* ā́-huta*h*, worshipped by offerings of gh*ri*ta, II, 7, 4[1]; *s*ú*k*i gh*ri*tám ná taptám, IV, 1, 6.
gh*rí*ta-âhavana, to whom gh*ri*ta oblations are poured out, I, 12, 5; 45, 5.
gh*ri*tá-nir*n*ig, whose stately robe is ghee, III, 17, 1; 27, 5.
gh*ri*tá-p*ri*sh*th*a, whose back is covered with ghee, I, 13, 5; V, 4, 3; 14, 5.
gh*ri*tá-pratîka, whose face shines with ghee, I, 143, 7; III, 1, 18; V, 11, 1.
gh*ri*tá-prasatta, taking his seat in ghee, V, 15, 1.
gh*ri*ta-prúsh, gh*ri*ta-sprinkling, I, 45, 1; II, 3, 2.
gh*ri*tá-yoni, having his abode in ghee, (I, 140, 1[2]); III, 4, 2[1]; V, 8, 6.
gh*ri*tá-vat, rich in ghee, I, 142, 2; III, 5, 6; 7; 21, 2.

ghr*i*ta-*s*k*ú*t, dripping with ghee, III, 21, 3; V, 14, 3.
ghr*i*ta-*s*rî, adorned with ghee, I, 128, 4; V, 8, 3.
ghr*i*ta-snâ, swimming in ghee, IV, 6, 9.
ghr*i*ta-snú, swimming in ghee, III, 6, 6[1]; IV, 2, 3[1]; V, 26, 2.
ghr*i*tâ*k*î, (the ladle) full of ghee, III, 6, 1; 19, 2; 27, 1; IV, 6, 3; V, 28, 1.
ghr*í*shvi, brisk, IV, 2, 13.
ghorá, terrible, IV, 6, 6.
ghósha, noise, III, 7, 6.

*k*a, and: *k*a rátham for *k*arátham, I, 70, 7[2]; (in the first member), I, 77, 2[2].
*k*ákri, maker, III, 16, 4.
*k*aksh, to look: *s*atám *k*ákshâ*n*a*h* akshábhi*h*, I, 128, 3;—ánu *k*a*k*áksha, V, 2, 8;—abhí *k*akshase, V, 3, 9;—ví *k*ash*t*e, I, 98, 1; V, 19, 1[3];—na*h* kr*i*dhi sam*k*ákshe, make us behold, I, 127, 11.
*k*áksha*n*a, appearance, I, 13, 5.
*k*ákshas, look, sight, I, 96, 2[3]; V, 15, 4.
*k*at, to hid: *k*átantam, I, 65, 1;—prá *k*âtáyasva, drive away, V, 4, 6.
*k*atu*h*-akshá, four-eyed: *k*atu*h*-akshá*h*, I, 31, 13[2].
*k*átu*h*-pad, four-footed, I, 94, 5.
*k*ána*h*-hita, with satisfied mind, III, 2, 2; 7; 11, 2.
*k*ánas: *k*ána*h* dhâ*h*, accept, I, 26, 10.
*k*andrá, gold, II, 2, 4[2].
*k*andrá-ratha, with a shining chariot, I, 141, 12; III, 3, 5.
*k*ar, to move, walk: *k*aráthâya *g*î-váse, that we may walk and live, I, 36, 14; *k*arâthâ (conj. *k*aráthâ), I, 66, 9[1]; *k*árata*h* dhruvásya, of whatever moves or is firm, I, 146, 1; gúhâ *k*árantam, III, 1, 9[3];—ní*h* *k*arati, he comes forward, I, 95, 4;—te pári *k*aranti, they walk around thee, I, 127, 9[2];—ví *k*aranti, spread around, I, 36, 3;—abhí ví *k*aranta, they have come hither and thither, III, 4, 5.
*k*arátha, all that moves, (I, 66, 9[1]); sthâtú*h* *k*arátham, I, 58, 5[2]; 68, 1; 70, 7[2]; sthâtâm *k*aráthâm, I, 70, 3; sthâtr*î*n *k*arátham *k*a, I, 72, 6[2].
*k*arish*n*ú, speedy, IV, 7, 9.
*k*árman, skin: sasásya *k*árma, III, 5, 6[2]; 7[1];—*k*árma-iva, like a hide, IV, 13, 4.
*k*arsha*n*í, human tribe, I, 127, 2; III, 6, 5; 10, 1; IV, 7, 4; 8, 8; V, 23, 1.
*k*arsha*n*i-dhr*i*t, supporting the human tribes, IV, 1, 2.
*k*arsha*n*i-prâ, filling the dwellings of people, IV, 2, 13.
*k*ashâla-vat, with head-pieces, III, 8, 10[1].
*k*âyú, respectful, III, 24, 4.
*k*âru, beautiful, I, 58, 6, &c.; *k*âru, loc., I, 72, 2[3].
*k*âru-pratîka, cheerful-faced, II, 8, 2.
*k*i: ni-*k*âyya, revering, III, 26, 1;—ví *k*inavat, may he distinguish, IV, 2, 11.
*k*ikitvít-manas, attentive-minded, V, 22, 3.
*k*it, to shine, light up: *k*itáyantam, II, 2, 4; *k*itayat, II, 2, 5; *k*itayema, II, 2, 10; *k*itré*n*a *k*ikite bhâsâ, II, 4, 5; *k*iketa, II, 4, 6; *k*ékitâna*h*, resplendent, III, 29, 7; *k*iketa, he has distinguished himself, V, 27, 1;—prá *k*iketa, he has shone forth, V, 19, 1;—ví *k*ikite, it shines, I, 71, 7[3].
*k*it, to see, watch, be intent on: *k*ikéta, I, 67, 7; *k*íketat asmai, may he pay attention to this (sacrificer), I, 69, 9; *k*itáyanta*h*, awaking attention, I, 94, 4; *k*etati, I, 128, 4; III, 11, 3[1]; *k*étate, III, 14, 2; *k*ikitâná*h* a*k*íttân, seeing the unseen ones, III, 18, 2; *k*étata*h*, attentive, IV, 5, 4; *k*ikiddhí, V, 22, 4[1]; *k*etayat, he has enlightened, IV, 1, 9[1]; *k*itáyan, enlightening, V, 15, 5[3]; *k*ikitvân, knowing, I, 68, 6, &c.;—â *k*iketa, he has understood, I, 95, 4;—*k*eti prá, it has been known, III, 12, 9;—ví *k*itáyanta*h*, causing to discern, V, 19, 2;—sam-*k*ikitvân, looking over, IV, 7, 8.
*k*iti, pile, (I, 67, 10[1]).
*k*ittá, mind, V, 7, 9.

*k*itti, splendour (?), I, 67, 10[1].
*k*ítti, thought, III, 2, 3; 3, 3; wisdom, IV, 2, 11.
*k*itrá, bright, excellent, I, 66, 1; 6, &c.
*k*itrá-bhânu, with bright splendour, I, 27, 6; II, 10, 2; V, 26, 2.
*k*itrá-yâma, whose way is bright, III, 2, 13.
*k*itrá-*s*o*k*is, of bright splendour, V, 17, 2.
*k*itrá*s*rava*h*-tama, whose glory is brightest, I, 1, 5; 45, 6.
*k*ud, to quicken, promote: *k*odáyâsi, I, 94, 15; *k*odayata, I, 188, 8.
*kri*t: ví *kri*tánti, they get off, I, 67, 8.
*k*étana, brilliant, II, 5, 1[2]; III, 12, 2;—n., splendour, light, I, 13, 11; III, 3, 8; IV, 7, 2.
*k*étish*th*a, most famous, I, 65, 9; most shining, I, 128, 8; most brilliant, V, 27, 1.
*k*odá, driver, I, 143, 6.
*k*odayát-mati, stirring thoughts, V, 8, 6.
*k*yu: ấ tvâ a*k*u*k*yavu*h*, they have made thee speed hither, I, 45, 8.

*kh*ad, to show oneself: *kh*adayati, III, 9, 7.
*kh*âyấ, shadow, I, 73, 8.

*gath*ára, belly, I, 95, 10; III, 2, 11; 22, 1; 29, 14[1].
*g*an, to be born: *g*a*gñ*ânấ*h*, I, 12, 3; *g*âtá*h* and *g*áni-tva*h*, I, 66, 8[1]; *g*anayat, he caused to be born, I, 71, 8[5]; *g*âtásya *k*a *g*ấyamânasya *k*a kshấm, the earth (i.e. the support) of what is born and what will be born, I, 96, 7[1]; *g*ấyemahi, we may multiply with offspring, I, 97, 4; *g*anâmasi, III, 2, 1[1]; *g*âtá*h* *g*âyate, III, 8, 5[1]; *g*anata, they have generated, IV, 1, 1; *g*âtấn ubháyân, the two races (of men and gods), IV, 2, 2; *g*ánitos, from giving birth, IV, 6, 7;—ấ *g*ấyamânam (conj. *g*ấyamânâ), I, 60, 3[1];—pra*g*a*gñ*i-vấn, generator, III, 2, 11.
*g*ána, man, people, I, 36, 2, &c.; daívyam *g*ánam, the divine host, I, 31, 17; 44, 6; 45, 1[1,2]; 9; 10; V, 13, 3; *g*ánâya *s*á*s*vate, I, 36, 19.
*g*ánas, tribe: *g*ánasî íti ubhé íti, both tribes (of gods and of men), II, 2, 4.
*g*áni, wife, I, 66, 8; *g*ánaya*h* sánî*l*â*h*, I, 71, 1;—woman, III, 26, 3[1]; IV, 5, 5.
*g*anit*r*í, begetter, I, 76, 4[4]; *g*anitấ, ródasyo*h*, I, 96, 4; pitú*h* *k*a gárbham *g*anitú*h* *k*a, III, 1, 10[1]; dyaú*h* pitấ *g*anitấ, IV, 1, 10.
*g*áni-tva, who will be born: *g*ánitvam (conj. *g*áni-tva*h*), I, 66, 8[1].
*g*ániman, birth, III, 1, 4; 20; trí*h* *g*ánimâni, IV, 1, 7;—devấnâm *g*ánimâni, III, 4, 10; IV, 2, 17; 18;—offspring, V, 3, 3.
*g*anús, birth: *g*anúshâ, by birth, by nature, I, 94, 6; III, 1, 3; 9; 2, 2; *g*anúsham, I, 141, 4.
*g*antú, people, human creature, I, 45, 6, &c.; mấnusha*h* *g*antúbhi*h*, III, 3, 6.
*g*ánman, birth: mấnushasya *g*ánasya *g*ánma, I, 70, 2; devấnâm *g*ánma, I, 70, 6; *g*ánma-iva nítyam tánayam, III, 15, 2[1];—birthplace: paramé *g*ánman, II, 9, 3;—race: ubháyâya *g*ánmane, I, 31, 7; divyấya *g*ánmane, I, 58, 6; devấn (i.e. devấm) *g*ánma, I, 67, 3[5,6]; *g*ánmanî íti ubhé íti, I, 141, 11[3]; *g*ánma ubháyâ, II, 6, 7; *g*ánman-*g*anman, generation by generation, III, 1, 20; 21.
*g*ánya, belonging to one's own people: *g*ányâ-iva (conj. *g*ánya*h*-iva), II, 6, 7[1].
*g*ábâru? IV, 5, 7[1].
*g*ámbha, jaw, I, 143, 5; 148, 4; IV, 7, 10.
*g*ar, see *gri*.
*g*ará*n*a, sound (?), I, 141, 7[1].
*g*arat-vísha, busy among the decayed (wood), V, 8, 2[1].
*G*arâ-bodha, N. pr.: *G*árâ-bodha, I, 27, 10[1].
*g*arit*r*í, praiser, I, 189, 4; II, 9, 5; III, 7, 6[1]; 12, 2; 5; 15, 5; V, 3, 11.
*g*arimán, old age, I, 71, 10.
*g*ávish*th*a, most swift, IV, 2, 3.
*g*ấ, people: na*h* *g*ấ*h*, I, 143, 8.
*g*â*h*-patyá, householdership, V, 28, 3[1].

gâgrivi, watchful: gâgrivih, I, 31, 9; III, 2, 12; 3, 7; 24, 3; 26, 3; 28, 5; 29, 2; V, 11, 1.
Gâtá-vedas, I, 44, 1; 5; 45, 3, &c.; 127, 1[2].
gâna, birth: trîni gânâ, I, 95, 3.
gâmarya?, IV, 3, 9[4].
gâmí, kinsman, I, 31, 10; 65, 7; 71, 7[3]; 75, 3; 4; IV, 4, 5; V, 19, 4; gâmînâm svásrînâm, uterine sisters, III, 1, 11; lokám gâmím, the sister world, III, 2, 9[4].
gâyâ, wife, I, 66, 5; IV, 3, 2[1].
gâyú, victorious, I, 67, 1[1].
gârá, lover, I, 66, 8; 69, 1[1]; 9.
gi, to conquer, to gain: gayati, I, 36, 4;—sam-gigîvân, III, 15, 4.
ginv, to stir: ginvate, III, 2, 11; ginva, III, 3, 7; 15, 6;—úpa prá ginvan, they have excited, I, 71, 1[1].
gívri, aged, I, 70, 10.
gihmá, down-streaming, I, 95, 5.
gihvâ, tongue, I, 140, 2; II, 1, 13; 4, 4; III, 20, 2; IV, 5, 10; 7, 10; V, 26, 1.
gîrá, quick, I, 44, 11; III, 3, 6.
gîrá-asva, with quick horses, I, 141, 12; II, 4, 2.
gîrá-dânu, rich in quickening rain, I, 189, 8.
gîv, to live: gîváse, I, 36, 14; 72, 7; 79, 9; gîvâtave, I, 94, 4.
gîvá, living, I, 68, 3;—life, I, 140, 8.
gîvá-dhanya, the prize (of contests) which living beings have gained, (I, 149, 2[1]).
gîvápita-sarga, whose stream is drunk by living beings, I, 149, 2[1].
gîva-yâgá, a sacrifice of living (victims), I, 31, 15.
gur, see gri.
gush, to be pleased, accept gladly: gushasva, I, 12, 12; 75, 1; 144, 7; gushanta, I, 68, 3; 9; a-gushran, I, 71, 1, &c.; gushanta pánthâm, they followed gladly his path, I, 127, 6; tanvàm gushasva, III, 1, 1[5]; goshi, find pleasure, IV, 9, 7[1];—práti goshayete iti, they caress, I, 95, 5; 6.
gúshta, welcome, I, 44, 2; 4;—grateful, I, 73, 10.
guhú-âsya, whose mouth is the sacrificial spoon, I, 12, 6.
guhurâná, leading astray, I, 189, 1.
guhû, sacrificial ladle, I, 58, 4[2]; 76, 5[2]; 145, 3; II, 10, 6; IV, 4, 2[1]; V, 1, 3; saptá guhvàh, I, 58, 7[2].
gû, to speed, incite: gunâh, I, 27, 7; gunâsi, I, 71, 6; gûgu-vat, impetuous, IV, 11, 4.
gû, speedy: gúvah, I, 140, 4[1].
gûtí, speeding, I, 127, 2;—solicitation, III, 3, 8;—yagñásya gûtyâ, stirring, III, 12, 3.
gûrni, flaming (?), I, 127, 10.
gûrv, to consume: ni-gûrvan, IV, 7, 11.
gri, to grow old: gûryati, I, 128, 2; gugurvân, II, 4, 5; gûryat-su, III, 23, 1; garáyan, making decay, II, 8, 2[1]; garase, V, 15, 4[1].
gri, to praise: garate, he is praised (?), I, 59, 7;—sám te gareta, may it resound to thee, IV, 3, 15[1].
gri, to be awake: garate, I, 59, 7; 127, 10[4]; gárase, I, 94, 14[1]; gárasva, III, 3, 7[1];—sám garatâm, may it awaken, IV, 4, 8[1].
gétri, conqueror, I, 66, 3; V, 25, 6.
génya, noble, I, 71, 4; 128, 7; 140, 2; 146, 5; II, 5, 1; V, 1, 5.
gósha, desire: gósham â, I, 77, 5.
gohûtra, to be invoked, II, 10, 1.
gñâ, to know: â gânîta, accept, I, 94, 8;—pra-gânán, prescient, II, 3, 10; ánu pra-gânán, III, 26, 8;—vi-gânán, discriminating, I, 69, 3[1];—sám gânata, they were concordant, I, 68, 8[1]; sam-gânânâh, being like-minded, I, 72, 5.
gyâyas, better, I, 27, 13.
gyéshtha, the first, I, 127, 2; eldest, IV, 1, 2.
gyotíh-ratha, whose chariot is light, I, 140, 1.
gyótis, light, I, 36, 19; 59, 2; III, 26, 8; diváh gyótih, I, 69, 1; vipâm gyótîmshi, III, 10, 5[1]; vidánta gyótih, IV, 1, 14; svàh ná gyótih, IV, 10, 3[1].
gráyas, space, I, 95, 9; 140, 9; V, 8, 7.

tákvan, N. of an animal, I, 66, 2[1].
taksh, to fashion: hridâ tashtân mántrân, I, 67, 4; tatáksha, III, 8, 6; ataksham, V, 2, 11.

ta*/*ít, lightning, I, 94, 7.
tát-o*g*as, having the strength of such a one, V, 1, 8.
tan, to spin out, stretch out: tántum tanushva, I, 142, 1; tántum tatám, II, 3, 6; tanvânâ*h* ya*g*-*ñ*ám, III, 3, 6;—áva tanuhi, unbend, IV, 4, 5;—â-tatántha, thou hast spread, III, 22, 2;—áti ní*h* tatanyu*h*, may they spread out, I, 141, 13[2];—ví tanvate, V, 13, 4; 15, 3[3].
tán, continuation: *s*á*s*vatâ tánâ, constantly, I, 26, 6[1]; tánâ, for ever, I, 77, 4; II, 2, 1[2]; III, 25, 1; 27, 9;—tokásya na*h* táne tanū́nâm, II, 9, 2.
tánaya, offspring, I, 96, 4; III, 15, 2[1];—tokásya tánaye, of kith and kin, I, 31, 12[1]; toké íti tánaye, I, 147, 1[3]; tokā́ya tánayâya, I, 189, 2; IV, 12, 5.
tanayitnú, thunderbolt, IV, 3, 1.
tánâ, see tán.
tanū́, body: tanvà*h*, I, 31, 12; 72, 3; 5[3]; i*kkh*ánta réta*h* mithá*h* tanū́shu, I, 68, 8[1]; táne tanū́nâm, II, 9, 2; tanvàm *g*ushasva, III, 1, 1[5]; tanvā̀ su-*g*âta, III, 15, 2; tanū́-bhi*h*, IV, 2, 14; tanvà*h* tanvate ví, V, 15, 3[3].
tanû-k*rí*t, the body's creator: tanû-k*rí*t, I, 31, 9.
Tánû-napât, 'son of the body,' I, 13, 2[1]; 142, 2; 188, 2; III, 4, 2; 29, 11.
tanû-rú*k*, shining with his body, II, 1, 9.
tántu, thread (of sacrifice), I, 142, 1;—tántum tatám, warp, II, 3, 6;—web (of light), IV, 13, 4.
tand, to grow tired: tandate (by conjecture), I, 58, 1[1].
tanyatú, thunder, V, 25, 8.
tap, to burn, heat: tápo íti, tápa, III, 18, 2; tatápate, IV, 2, 6.
tápish*th*a, hottest, IV, 4, 1; 5, 4.
tápu, hot, II, 4, 6.
tápu*h*-*g*ambha, with fiery jaws, I, 36, 16; 58, 5.
tápus, heat: tápû*m*shi, IV, 4, 2.
tama*h*-hán, destroyer of darkness, I, 140, 1.
támas, darkness: dvā́râ támasa*h*, III, 5, 1; tirá*h* támâ*m*si dar-*s*atá*h*, III, 27, 13.
tará*n*i, strongly advancing, triumphant, I, 128, 6; III, 11, 3[2]; 29, 13; IV, 4, 12.
táras, advancing power, III, 18, 3.
tárut*ri*, a winner, I, 27, 9.
tárus: dákshasya tárusha*h*, of superior strength, III, 2, 3.
tavás, strong, III, 1, 1[1]; 2; 13.
tavishá, powerful, III, 12, 8.
távishî, strength, I, 128, 5; III, 3, 5; 26, 4.
távya*m*s, most powerful, I, 143, 1; V, 17, 1.
tâyú, thief, I, 65, 1; V, 15, 5[2].
tâvaká, thy, I, 94, 11.
tigitá, sharp, I, 143, 5.
tigmá, sharp, IV, 6, 8; 7, 10; V, 19, 5.
tigmá-anîka, sharp-faced, I, 95, 2.
tigmá-âyudha, with sharp weapons, V, 2, 10.
tigmá-*g*ambha, with sharp teeth, I, 79, 6; IV, 5, 4; 15, 5.
tigmá-bh*ri*sh*t*i, sharp-pointed, IV, 5, 3.
tigmá-*s*o*k*is, sharp-flaming, I, 79, 10.
tigmá-heti, with the sharp weapon, IV, 4, 4.
ti*g*, to sharpen: té*g*amâna*h*, sharpened, III, 8, 11.
titvishâ*n*á, rushing forward impetuously, V, 8, 5.
tir, see t*ri*.
tirá*h*-ahnya, kept over night, I, 45, 10[1]; III, 28, 3; 6.
tirá*h*-hita, dwelling in concealment, III, 9, 5.
tira*s*kā́, throughout, II, 10, 4.
tirás, through, III, 27, 13.
tu: tûtâva, he is strong, I, 94, 2.
tu*g*, to stir, press onward: tutu*g*yā́t, I, 143, 6; tú*ñg*amânâ*h*, III, 1, 16; tu*g*é, IV, 1, 3.
tú*g*, impetuous: tu*g*ā́ girā́, V, 17, 3[2].
túturi, conqueror, I, 145, 3.
tud, to strike: ní tundate (conj. nú tandate), I, 58, 1[1].
turá, quick, I, 68, 9; 96, 8; III, 4, 11; IV, 3, 8.
turī́pa, seed, I, 142, 10; III, 4, 9.
Turvá*s*a, I, 36, 18[1].
Turvī́ti, I, 36, 18[1].
tuvi-grá, mightily devouring, I, 140, 9.
tuvi-grī́va, with mighty neck, V, 2, 12.
tuvi-*g*âtá, strong-born, IV, 11, 2; V, 2, 11; 27, 3.

túvi-dyumna, highly glorious, III, 16, 3; 6.
tuví-brahman, knower of mighty spells, V, 25, 5.
tuvísravah-tama, most mightily renowned, III, 11, 6; V, 25, 5.
túvishmat, mighty, IV, 5, 3.
tuvi-sván, loudly roaring, V, 26, 3.
tuvi-svanás, roaring mightily, IV, 6, 10; V, 8, 3.
tuvi-sváni, loudly roaring, I, 58, 4; 127, 6.
tűrni, swift, III, 3, 5; 11, 5.
tűrni-tama, quickest, IV, 4, 3.
tri, to get through, to overcome: ataran, I, 36, 8; táran, III, 24, 1; turyấma, V, 9, 6; tarîshấni, may they pass across, V, 10, 6[1]; tuturyât, may he traverse, V, 15, 3;—titirvấmsah áti srídhah, I, 36, 7; áti tarema, III, 27, 3;—with prá, to prolong, promote: pra-tirán, I, 44, 6; prá tira, I, 94, 16; III, 17, 2; prá tirasi, IV, 6, 1; prá tấri pra-tarám, IV, 12, 6;—ví târit, he has crossed, I, 69, 5[2]; 73, 1; vitáritratâ, progressing, I, 144, 3.
trína, grass, III, 29, 6.
trid, to perforate: atrinat, IV, 1, 19;—ánu trindhi, V, 12, 2.
trip, to satiate oneself: sómasya trimpatâm, III, 12, 3.
trish, to be thirsty: tatrishânáh, I, 31, 7[2]; átrishyantîh, free from thirst, I, 71, 3[2],[4]; tatrishânáh, II, 4, 6.
trishú, thirsty, greedy, I, 58, 2; 4; IV, 4, 1; 7, 11.
trishu-kyút, moving about thirstily, I, 140, 3.
trishtá, pungent sharpness, III, 9, 3.
tégas, sharp splendour, I, 71, 8[2]; sharpness: sám akrinvan tégase, III, 2, 10.
tégishtha, hottest, I, 127, 4[1].
tégîyas, sharpest, III, 19, 3.
toká, children: toká tánaya, kith and kin, I, 31, 12[1]; 147, 1[3]; 189, 2; IV, 12, 5; nítye toké, II, 2, 11; tokásya táne tanűnâm, II, 9, 2; tokấya tugé, IV, 1, 3.
toká-vat, with offspring, III, 13, 7.
todá, an or the impeller, I, 150, 1[2].
tosá, bounteous, III, 12, 4[1].
tmánâ, by oneself, by one's own power, I, 69, 10; 79, 6, &c.
tmányâ, thyself, I, 188, 10.
tráyah-trimsat, thirty-three (gods), I, 45, 2.
Trasádasyu, V, 27, 3[2].
trâ: trâsate, may he protect, I, 128, 5; 7.
trấ, protector, (I, 72, 5[3]).
trâtrí, protector, I, 31, 12; V, 24, 1.
trí, three, I, 13, 9, &c.; trî́ rokanấni, the threefold light, I, 149, 4; tisrí-bhyah ấ váram, II, 5, 5[2]; tisráh devîh, II, 3, 8; III, 4, 8; V, 5, 8; trî́ni sata trî́ sahásrâni trimsát ka devấh náva ka, III, 9, 9; trî́ni ấyûmshi, tisrấh â-gấnîh, III, 17, 3[1]; trî, tisrấh, III, 20, 2.
trimsát, thirty: trimsátam trî́n ka devấn, III, 6, 9.
Trí-aruna, V, 27, 1-3.
trí-âsir, with threefold admixture (Soma), V, 27, 5[1].
Tritá, V, 9, 5.
tri-dhấtu, threefold: arkáh tri-dhấtuh, III, 26, 7[1].
tri-mûrdhán, having three heads, I, 146, 1[1].
tri-várûtha, thrice-protecting, V, 4, 8.
tri-vishti, thrice, IV, 6, 4; 15, 2[1].
tri-vrít, threefold: tri-vrít ánnam I, 140, 2[2].
trís, thrice: tríh saptá, I, 72, 6[1]; tríh áhan, III, 4, 2; tríh (read trî́?), IV, 1, 7[1].
tri-sadhasthá, dwelling in three abodes, V, 4, 8;—threefold abode, V, 11, 2[2].
Traivrishná, the son of Trivrishan, V, 27, 1.
tvák, skin, III, 21, 5;—leather-bag (cloud), I, 79, 3[3];—tvakí upamásyâm, I, 145, 5[2].
tvád, pers. pron.: tvé íti, in thee, I, 26, 6; 36, 5[1]; 6; te, acc., I, 127, 9[2]; V, 6, 4[1]; te túbhyam, V, 6, 5[1].
tvadrík, directed towards thee, V, 3, 12.
Tváshtri, N. of a god, I, 13, 10; 95, 2[3]; 5[2]; 142, 10; 188, 9; II, 1, 5; 3, 9; III, 4, 9; V, 5, 9.
tvấ-ûta, guarded by thee, I, 73, 9; 74, 8; III, 19, 3; IV, 4, 14; V, 3, 6.

tvấ-dâta, given by thee, V, 7, 10.
tvấ-dûta, with thee as messenger, II, 10, 6; V, 6, 8.
tvâ-yấ, desire of worshipping thee, IV, 2, 6; 14.
tvấ-vat, like thee: tvấ-vân, I, 189, 6.
Tvâsh*tr*á, son of Tvash*tri*, III, 7, 4[1].
tvish, see titvishâ*n*á.
tvíshi, impetuous power, I, 71, 5; V, 8, 5.
tveshá, impetuous, fierce, I, 36, 20; 66, 6; 70, 11; 95, 8; 143, 3; II, 9, 1; III, 22, 2; 26, 5; IV, 6, 10; V, 8, 6.
tveshátha, fierceness, I, 141, 8.
tveshá-pratîka, with sharp point, I, 66, 7.
tsar: tatsâra, he steals upon (his prey), I, 145, 4;—áva tsarat, he stealthily approached, I, 71, 5.

da*ms*, to bite: dá*s*ate, I, 189, 5.
da*m*sánâ, wonderful deed, III, 3, 11; wonderful power, III, 9, 7.
dá*m*sas, wonderful deed, I, 69, 8.
dáksha, mind, I, 68, 8;—power, ability, skill, I, 76, 1; 95, 6[1]; 141, 11[2]; III, 2, 3; 13, 2; IV, 10, 2; V, 10, 2; 18, 2; 20, 3; dáksham (conj. yakshám), IV, 3, 13[3]; Dáksha personified, III, 27, 9[3]; 10; V, 16, 2;—skilful, I, 59, 4; III, 14, 7.
dáksha-pati, lord of power, I, 95, 6.
dákshas, ability, II, 1, 11.
dakshấyya, to be treated kindly, II, 4, 3.
dakshi*n*atás, from the right side, I, 95, 6[2].
dákshi*n*â, the sacrificial gift, V, 1, 3[3].
dakshi*n*â-âv*rí*t, turned to the right, I, 144, 1[3].
dakshi*n*â-vấh, carrying from left to right, III, 6, 1[2].
dágdh*ri*, burner, V, 9, 4.
datvát, having teeth, I, 189, 5.
Dadhí-krấ, III, 20, 1[2]; 5.
dán, house: páti*h* dán, lord of the house, I, 149, 1[2].
dánta, tooth: atharyà*h* ná dántam, IV, 6, 8[2].
dabh, to deceive: dípsanta*h* ná debhu*h*, I, 147, 3; dadabhanta, I, 148, 2; dabhan, I, 148, 5;—*s*átrum â-dabhú*h*, III, 16, 2.
dábha, deceiver, V, 19, 4[3].
dabhrá, few, I, 31, 6.
dám, house: dám-su, I, 141, 4.
dáma, house, I, 1, 8, &c.; II, 1, 7[2]; 8; *k*ítti*h* apấm dáme, I, 67, 10[1]; dáme-dame, house by house, I, 128, 4; IV, 7, 3; V, 1, 5; 6, 8.
dámûnas, domestic, friend of the house, I, 60, 4[2]; 68, 9; 140, 10; 141, 11; III, 1, 11; 17; 2, 15; 3, 6; 5, 4; IV, 4, 11; 11, 5; V, 1, 8[1]; 4, 5; 8, 1.
dám-pati, master of the house, I, 127, 8; V, 22, 4;—dám-patî, husband and wife, V, 3, 2.
dámya, domestic, III, 1, 15; 2, 8.
day, to bestow: dayasva, I, 68, 6;—ví dáyamâna*h*, distributing, III, 2, 11; ví dayate, he tears to pieces, IV, 7, 10.
dárvî, sacrificial ladle, V, 6, 9.
dar*s*atá, conspicuous, beautiful, I, 36, 9; 141, 1; 144, 7; III, 1, 3; 10, 6; 27, 13.
dá*s*a-pramati: dá*s*a-pramatim, read: dá*s*a prámatim, I, 141, 2[4].
da*s*asy: sám da*s*asya, forgive, III, 7, 10.
das: sam-dadasvấn, being exhausted (?), II, 2, 6[1].
dasmá, wonderful, I, 77, 3; 148, 4; II, 1, 4; 9, 5; III, 1, 7; 3, 2; IV, 1, 3; 6, 9; V, 6, 5; 17, 4.
dasmát, possessed of wonderful power, I, 74, 4.
Dásyu, I, 36, 18; 59, 6; V, 4, 6; pl., the Dasyus, I, 78, 4; III, 29, 9; V, 7, 10; 14, 4.
dah, to burn: daha, I, 12, 5, &c.; dhákshat, burning, II, 4, 7;—ánu dhakshi, II, 1, 10;—prá dhakshi, I, 76, 3;—práti dahatât, burn against, III, 18, 1;—sám daha, I, 36, 14; 20.
dâ, to give: ánu du*h*, they give way, I, 127, 4;—ná párâ dât, he will not surrender, V, 3, 12.
dâ, to bind: ní-dadu*h*, (V, 2, 6[2]); ní-ditam, V, 2, 7.
dâ (do), to cut, to shear: dâti, I, 65, 8; V, 7, 7.
dât*rí*, giver, I, 13, 11.
dất*ri*, mower, V, 7, 7.
dấna, gift, V, 27, 5.
dâván: dâváne, for the sake of giving, II, 1, 10.

dâs, to offer, worship: dadấsa, I, 36, 4, &c.; yáh túbhyam dấsât, I, 68, 6; dâsat, IV, 2, 9; dấsat yáh asmai áram, who satisfies him, I, 70, 5; námah dấsât, I, 71, 6; agnáye dâshti ávase, I, 127, 4[2].
dấs, worship, I, 127, 7.
dâsú-adhvara, performing worship, I, 75, 3[1].
dâsvấms, worshipper, liberal giver, I, 1, 6; 27, 6, &c.
dâs: abhi-dấsati, he tries to harm, I, 79, 11.
dâsá-patnî, (strongholds) of which the Dâsas are the lords, III, 12, 6.
dấsvat, munificent, I, 127, 1; II, 4, 3; IV, 2, 7; V, 9, 2.
Díti, IV, 2, 11[3].
didrikshénya, worthy to be looked for, I, 146, 5.
didrikshéya, visible, III, 1, 12.
didyú, arrow, I, 71, 5.
didyút, shaft, I, 66, 7.
didhishấyya, worthy to be searched for, desirable, I, 73, 2[4]; II, 4, 1.
didhishú, seeking to obtain, I, 71, 3[2].
dív, see dyú.
divah-rúk, shining from heaven, III, 7, 5.
divákshas, dwelling in heaven, III, 7, 2[1].
dívâ-tarât, more than by day, I, 127, 5[3].
divi-kshayá, dweller in heaven: divi-kshayám (conj. for diví kshá-yam), III, 2, 13[1].
divítmat, going to heaven, I, 26, 2.
dívishti, the striving for day, I, 45, 7[1]; 141, 6: — heaven-aspiring sacrifice, IV, 9, 3.
divi-spris, attaining to Heaven, I, 142, 8; V, 11, 1; 13, 2[1].
divyá, heavenly, I, 143, 5; 144, 6; III, 2, 4: — divine: divyấya gánmane, I, 58, 6.
dís, quarter of the world: dísah, I, 31, 14[3]; prá dísam (for pra-dísam), I, 95, 3[2].
dî, dîdî, to shine, I, 36, 11, &c.; rayím asmấsu dîdihi, shine upon us with thy wealth, II, 2, 6; dìdayet, may he illuminate, II, 4, 3; dî́dyat (conj. dî́dhyat), III, 1, 1[3]; devấn ákkha dî́dy-ânah, brightly shining towards the gods, III, 15, 5[1]; dî́dyatam brihát, III, 27, 15.
dîdi-vấms, resplendent, I, 12, 5; 10, &c.
dî́divi, shining, I, 1, 8.
dîdhiti, (adoring) thought, devotion, III, 4, 3; IV, 2, 16[2]; V, 18, 4.
dîrghá, long-lasting: dîrgháh rayíh, IV, 2, 5.
dîrghá-âyus, long living, IV, 15, 9; 10.
dìrghấyu-sokis, flaming through long life, V, 18, 3.
duh-itá, trouble, misfortune, danger, I, 99, 1; 128, 5; III, 20, 4; V, 3, 11; 4, 9; 9, 6.
duh-uktá, evil word, I, 147, 4.
duh-éva, of evil conduct, IV, 5, 5; V, 2, 9.
duh-gá, trouble, I, 99, 1; 189, 2.
duh-gáha, difficulty, V, 4, 9.
duh-gríbhi, difficult to seize, I, 140, 6.
duh-gribhîy: duh-gribhîyase, thou showest thyself hard to seize, V, 9, 4.
duh-dábha, undeceivable, III, 2, 2; IV, 9, 2; 8.
dúh-dhita, badly-composed (prayer), I, 140, 11.
duh-dhî́, malicious, I, 94, 8; 9; III, 16, 2.
duh-matí, hatred, ill-will, III, 15, 6; IV, 11, 6.
duh-sámsa, one who curses, I, 94, 9.
dugdhá, milk, V, 19, 4[1].
dukkhúnâ, misfortune, I, 189, 5.
dúdhita, confused, IV, 1, 17[1].
dúr, gate, door, I, 68, 10; II, 2, 7[1]; IV, 4, 6; dúrah, the doors (of heaven), I, 69, 10; 188, 5[1]; râyáh dúrah, I, 72, 8.
duritá, see duh-itá.
duróka-sokis, he to whose flame men do not get accustomed, I, 66, 5[1].
duroná, house, I, 69, 4; 5; 70, 4[1], &c.
durgá, see duh-gá.
dúryâ, pl., dwelling, IV, 1, 9; 18; 2, 12.
dúvas, worship, I, 36, 14[2]; III, 2, 6; 16, 4; IV, 2, 9; 8, 6.
duvasaná, hastening, IV, 6, 10[2].
duvasy, to exalt: duvasyati, I, 78, 2; III, 3, 1; duvasyan, III, 1, 2; 13; duvasyáta, III, 2, 8; V, 28, 6.

dush, to violate: dûdushat, III, 3, 1.
dustára, invincible, I, 79, 8[1]; II, 2, 10; III, 24, 1; V, 15, 3.
duh, to milk: doháse, I, 141, 2; am*ri*tam dúhânâ*h*, III, 1, 14.
duhit*ri*, daughter, I, 71, 5[1].
dûtá, messenger (Agni), I, 12, 1; 8; 36, 3-5; 44, 2; 3; 9; 11; 58, 1; 60, 1; 72, 7; 74, 4; 188, 1; II, 6, 6; 7; 9, 2; III, 3, 2; 5, 2; 9; 6, 5; 9, 8; 11, 2; 17, 4; IV, 1, 8; 2, 2; 7, 4; 9; 11; 8, 1; 9, 2; V, 3, 8; 8, 6; 11, 4; 21, 3; 26, 6.
dûtyà, the work of a messenger: dûtyàm (yấsi), I, 12, 4; 44, 12; 74, 7; messengership, I, 71, 4[3]; IV, 7, 8; 8, 4; 9, 6.
dûré-bhâ, far-shining, I, 65, 10.
d*ri*, to rend: dad*ri*-vấ*m*sa*h*, IV, 1, 14.
d*rilh*á, strong, I, 71, 2; 72, 8.
d*ris*îka, beautiful, I, 27, 10;—sight, I, 66, 10; 69, 10.
d*ris*ya, visible, IV, 2, 12.
d*ri*shát-vatî, N. of a river, III, 23, 4.
devá, god, I, 1, 2, &c.; devá*h* devébhi*h*, devanâm, &c., I, 1, 5; 13, 11; 31, 1; 9; 68, 2[1]; 94, 13; 142, 11; II, 3, 1; IV, 15, 1; devám-devam, this or that god, I, 26, 6; bhúva*h* devấnâm pitấ putrá*h* sán, I, 69, 2; devấnâm *g*ánma, I, 70, 6; devấn (i. e. devấm) *g*ánma, I, 71, 3[5,6]; IV, 1, 2[2]; 2, 17[2]; pấtha*h* devébhya*h*, I, 188, 10[1]; devấnâm *g*ánimâni, III, 4, 10; devấnâm gúhyâ nấmâni, V, 5, 10; devấsa*h* sárvayâ vi*s*ấ, V, 26, 9;—vísve devấ*h*, II, 3, 4[1]; V, 3, 1; 26, 4;—divine, I, 1, 1; III, 20, 4; dvấra*h* devî́*h*, I, 13, 6; II, 3, 5; V, 5, 5; déva barhi*h*, II, 3, 4; dhíyam devî́m, III, 18, 3; devî́*h* pátnî*h*, IV, 5, 13.
deva-avî́, eagerly longing for the gods, III, 29, 8.
devá-kâma, loving the gods, II, 3, 9; III, 4, 9.
devá-*g*ush*t*a, agreeable to the god, I, 77, 1.
devá-*g*ûta, sent by the gods, IV, 11, 4.
devá-tâti, the divine world, host of the gods, I, 127, 9; 141, 10; III, 19, 2; 4; 26, 2; IV, 6, 3; 9; devá-tâtâ, among the gods, I, 58, 1; 95, 8[3]; 128, 2; III, 19, 1; IV, 6, 1.
deva-trấ, to the gods, I, 128, 6[5]; III, 1, 22;—among the gods, III, 8, 7; V, 20, 1.
deva-tvá, divinity, I, 68, 4; 69, 6[1].
devadryấ*ñk*, turned towards the gods: devadrî́*k*îm, III, 6, 1[2].
devápsara*h*-tama, most agreeable to the gods, I, 75, 1.
devá-bhakta, god-given, IV, 1, 10.
deva-yagyấ, worship as is due to the gods, V, 21, 4.
deva-yát, worshipping, or longing for, the gods, pious, I, 36, 1[4]; 77, 3; III, 5, 1; 6, 1; 3; 8, 1; 4; 6; 10, 7; 29, 12; IV, 2, 17; 11, 5; V, 1, 4; 21, 1.
deva-yấ, approaching the gods, III, 8, 5[3].
deva-yấna, (the ways) which the gods go: ádhvana*h* deva-yấnân, I, 72, 7[3].
deva-yú, godly, IV, 2, 7; 9, 1.
devá-vâta, beloved by the gods, III, 20, 2; IV, 3, 15;—Devavâta, N. p., III, 23, 2.
deva-vấhana, drawing hither the gods, III, 27, 14.
deva-vî́tama, most excellently repairing to the gods, I, 36, 9.
devá-vîti, feast of the gods, I, 12, 9; III, 17, 5; 21, 2.
devávya*k*a*h*-tama, which best receives the gods with its wide extent, I, 142, 5; IV, 26, 8; V, 22, 2.
devá-vya*k*as, receiving the gods, III, 4, 4.
deva-*s*ás, for each of the gods, III, 21, 5.
Devá-*s*ravas, N. p., III, 23, 2; 3.
deva-hū́tama, best invoker of the gods, III, 13, 6.
deváhûti, invocation of the gods, I, 12, 12.
devấ*ñk*, turned towards the gods, I, 127, 1.
devî́, goddess, I, 13, 9; III, 7, 2[2]; 25, 3; IV, 14, 3; tisrá*h* devî́*h*, II, 3, 8; III, 4, 8; V, 5, 8.
devyà, godhead, I, 140, 7.
desh*n*á, gift, II, 9, 4.
Daiva-vâtá, (Agni) of Devavâta, III, 23, 3;—son of Devavâta, IV, 15, 4[1].
daívya, divine, I, 27, 12; II, 5, 2;

III, 20, 4; daívyâ hótârâ, I, 13, 8[1]; 142, 8; 188, 7; II, 3, 7; III, 4, 7; V, 5, 7; daívyam gánam, host of the gods, I, 31, 17; 44, 6; 45, 1[1,2]; 9; 10; V, 13, 3; daívyâni vratấ, I, 70, 2; daívyah samitấ, II, 3, 10; mádhunâ daívyena, III, 8, 1[2]; vákasâ daívyena, IV, 1, 15; daívyâni, divine powers, IV, 4, 5.
do, see dâ.
dógha, milkstream, V, 15, 5[1].
doshấ, evening: doshấ ushási, II, 8, 3; IV, 2, 8; práti doshấm ushásam, IV, 12, 2; V, 5, 6; doshấ, at evening, IV, 11, 6.
dóshâ-vastar, shining in the darkness, I, 1, 7[1]; IV, 4, 9[1].
dohána, stream (?), I, 144, 2[1].
dyấvâkshấmâ, du., Heaven and Earth, I, 96, 5; 140, 13; III, 8, 8[1].
dyấvâprithivî́, du., Heaven and Earth, I, 31, 8; II, 1, 15; 2, 3; 7; III, 3, 11; 25, 3; 26, 8; IV, 14, 2.
dyú, sky, heaven, Heaven, I, 31, 4[1], &c.; 67, 5[2]; upa-mấ divấh, I, 31, 15[1]; diváh ná sấnu, I, 58, 2; mûrdhấ diváh, I, 59, 2; III, 2, 14; diváh brihatáh, I, 59, 5; 71, 2; dyaúh ná bhū́ma, I, 65, 3[1]; diváh gyótih, I, 69, 1; mahé pitré divé, I, 71, 5[1]; IV, 1, 10; dyaúh (conj. dyóh), I, 71, 8[4]; diváh akshī́ íti, I, 72, 10[1]; párigmânam-iva dyấm, I, 127, 2[3]; dyấvâ prithivī́ íti, Heaven and Earth, I, 143, 2; vísvâ diváh rokanấ, I, 146, 1; III, 6, 8; 12, 9; dyú-bhih tvám (conj. dyú-bhyah), II, 1, 1[2]; ásurah maháh diváh, II, 1, 6; diváh-iva aratíh, II, 2, 2; dyaúh ná strí-bhih, II, 2, 5; IV, 7, 3; tisráh dívah, II, 3, 2; diváh kavînấm, III, 1, 2; diváh prithivyấh, III, 1, 3; 6, 2[3]; 3; 25, 1; IV, 5, 11; diváh yahvī́h, III, 1, 6; 9[4]; diváh prishthám, III, 2, 12; diví ksháyam (conj. divikshayám) III, 2, 13[1]; ketúm diváh, III, 2, 14; diváh nâbhâ, III, 4, 4; várshman diváh, III, 5, 9; dyấvâ, III, 6, 4[2]; diváh árnam, III, 22, 3; diváh putrấh, IV, 2, 15; diváh kikitvấn, IV, 3, 8; diváh â-ródhanâni, IV, 7, 8; 8, 2; 4; diváh skambhấh, IV, 13, 5; diváh sísum, IV, 15, 6[2]; diváh kit brihát, more mightily than even the sky, V, 10, 4[2]; diváh dhárman, V, 15, 2[2]; diváh ná rétasâ, V, 17, 3[3].
dyú, day: divé-dive, day by day, I, 1, 3; 7, &c.; diváh pū́rvah, before daybreak, I, 60, 2; ánu dyū́n, day by day, I, 71, 6; 148, 4; III, 23, 2; IV, 4, 8; 9; dívâ náktam, I, 98, 2; 144, 4[2]; tríh ấ diváh, I, 142, 3; dyúbhih, day by day, III, 3, 2; V, 16, 2.
dyukshá, heavenly, II, 2, 1.
dyut, to shine: ví abhí dyaut, mayest thou beam forth, IV, 4, 6;—ví didyutah, make shine, II, 2, 7; ví adyaut, thou hast shone forth, III, 1, 8; 18; ví didyutânáh, flashing, III, 7, 4;—sám adyaut, III, 5, 2.
dyú-bhakta, assigned by Heaven, I, 73, 6; IV, 1, 18.
dyu-mát, brilliant, I, 74, 9; II, 7, 1; 9, 6; III, 10, 8; 13, 7; V, 23, 4.
dyumát-tama, most brilliant, V, 24, 2[1].
dyumná, splendour, I, 73, 4, &c.; dyumnaíh, with (songs full of) splendour, I, 78, 1–5; dyumnásya sávasâ, V, 7, 3.
dyumná-vat, brilliant, III, 29, 15.
dyumnín, brilliant, I, 36, 8.
dyumnín-tama, most brilliant, I, 127, 9.
drapsá, spark, I, 94, 11;—banner, IV, 13, 2[2].
dravát, see dru.
dravinah-dás, giver of wealth, II, 6, 3.
dravinah-dấ, giver of wealth, I, 96, 1–8; II, 1, 7.
drávinas, wealth, I, 96, 8;—wealth-giver, III, 7, 10.
dravinasyú, aspiring after wealth, II, 6, 3; V, 13, 2.
dru, to run: dravát, speedily, I, 44, 7; drávatâm, III, 14, 3; drûnânáh? IV, 4, 1[2].
drú-anna, feeding on wood, II, 7, 6.
drúh, guile, IV, 4, 15.
dru-hántara, a mighty woodcutter, (I, 127, 3[2]).
druham-tará, conqueror of deceitful foes, I, 127, 3[2].

dvayá, falsehood, I, 147, 4; 5; V, 3, 7; 12, 2.
dvā̃r, door: dvā̃ra*h* devī̃*h*, the divine doors, I, 13, 6; 142, 6; II, 3, 5; V, 5, 5; dvā̃râ, the two folds of the door, I, 128, 6; dvā̃râ támasa*h*, III, 5, 1.
dví*h* pá*ñk*a, twice five, IV, 6, 8[1].
dvi-*g*ánman, of double birth (Agni), I, 60, 1[1]; 140, 2[1]; 149, 4; 5.
Dvitá, V, 18, 2[2].
dvitā̃, forsooth, verily, I, 127, 7; II, 4, 2[2]; III, 2, 1[3]; 17, 5[1].
dvi-pád, two-footed, I, 94, 5.
dvi-bárhas, twofold, I, 71, 6;—doubly-powerful, IV, 5, 3[1].
dvi-mât*rí*, having two mothers, I, 31, 2[1].
dvísh, hostile power, I, 97, 7; II, 7, 2; 3; III, 15, 1.
dvesha*h*-yút, driving away malice, IV, 11, 5; V, 9, 6.
dvéshas, hatred, malice, II, 6, 4; IV, 1, 4; 10, 7; V, 20, 2;—hostile power, III, 16, 5[2]; 27, 3.

dhakshi (Sa*m*hitâ: dakshi), voc. (?), O burning one (?), I, 141, 8[2].
dhákshu, burning, II, 4, 4.
dhakshús, burning, I, 141, 7.
dhan: dhanáyan, they set into motion, I, 71, 3;—dadhanyu*h* (read dadhanvu*h*?), IV, 3, 12[2].
dhána, prize, I, 31, 6; 8; 36, 4.
dhanam-*g*ayá, winning the prize, I, 74, 3.
dhana-sā̃, gaining wealth, II, 10, 6[1].
dhana-sp*rí*t, winner of prizes, I, 36, 10; V, 8, 2.
dhanín, rich, I, 150, 2;—containing the prize of the contest, IV, 2, 15[3].
dhánus, dry land: dháno*h* ádhi, I, 144, 5[2].
dhánya, precious, III, 1, 16.
dhanv, to run along: dadhanvé, II, 5, 3; dadhanvu*h*, (IV, 3, 12[2]).
dhánvan, dry ground, I, 95, 10;—desert, V, 7, 7.
dhanva-sáh, a conquering bowman, I, 127, 3[6].
dham, to melt: dhámanta*h*, IV, 2, 17[1];—úpa dhámati dhmâtári, V, 9, 5[3].
dháriman, firm law, I, 128, 1[1].
dharú*n*a, supporter: dharú*n*a*h* rayî*n*ā̃m, I, 73, 4[2]; supporting, V, 15, 1; 2; 5[1];—firm ground, III, 3, 1.
dhar*n*así, firm, I, 141, 11;—supporter, V, 8, 4.
dhar*n*í, supporter, I, 127, 7.
dhart*rí*, supporter, V, 1, 6; 9, 3.
dhárman, law, ordinance, III, 3, 1; V, 26, 6; prathamā̃ ánu dhárma, III, 17, 1; ánu dhárma, III, 17, 5;—support, V, 15, 2.
dhâ, to put, place, give: dadhiré, I, 26, 8, &c.; *k*ána*h* dhâ*h*, accept, I, 26, 10; dadhire, have been laid down, I, 59, 3[1]; dádhâna*h*, obtaining, I, 73, 5[2]; mā̃ki*h* na*h* du*h*-itā̃ya dhâyî*h*, do not deliver us to distress, I, 147, 5; dádhat, 3rd pers. or part., I, 188, 2[1]; dadhire purá*h*, they have placed in front (as Purohita), III, 2, 5; dhishva, III, 6, 6; didhishantu, may they bestow, III, 8, 6; dhā̃mahe, may we acquire, V, 16, 5;—ā̃ dadhe, I have established, III, 27, 9[2];—ní dadhe, he has established, I, 36, 19; ní dadhe, I have laid down, III, 23, 4[1]; 27, 10[1]; ní dadhu*h* (conj. ní dadu*h*?), V, 2, 6[2]; ní dhatte purá*h*, V, 28, 2[1];—vi-dhā̃ti, he worships (conj. for vi-bhā̃ti), I, 71, 6[1]; ví dhâ*h*, distribute, I, 72, 7; IV, 6, 11; ví dadhau, he determines, I, 95, 3.
dhâ, to suckle: dhâpáyete íti, I, 96, 5; adhayat, I, 144, 2; III, 1, 10; V, 1, 3[4];—úpa dhâpayete íti, I, 95, 1.
dhât*rí*, establisher, IV, 7, 1.
dhā̃na: pári dhā̃nam aktó*h*, about nightfall (?), III, 7, 6.
dhā̃man, foundation, I, 95, 9[1]; 144, 1[4]; III, 3, 4; IV, 7, 7;—abode, II, 3, 2; 11;—statute, law, III, 2, 10; 7, 6; IV, 5, 4;—form: saptá dhā̃ma-bhi*h*, IV, 7, 5[1].
dhā̃yas, prospering, I, 31, 13;—refreshment, refreshing drink, I, 72, 9; 94, 12; 141, 6; II, 5, 7; V, 7, 6; 9; 15, 4.
dhā̃râ, stream: dhā̃râm *ri*tásya, I, 67, 7[1]; V, 12, 2; dhā̃râ*h* udanyā̃*h*-iva, II, 7, 3; dhā̃râ*h*, III, 1, 8; 9.

dhâv : ní dhâvate, he runs down, I, 141, 5.
dhâsí, drink, I, 140, 1[2]; III, 7, 1[1]; 3[2]; IV, 3, 9; V, 12, 4.
dhitá-van, in whom (wealth) has been laid down, III, 27, 2.
dhiyam-dhấ, thoughtful, I, 67, 4; 72, 2.
dhiyấ-vasu, giving wealth for prayer, I, 58, 9; 60, 5; III, 3, 2; 28, 1.
Dhishá*n*â, N. of a goddess, I, 96, 1[2]; III, 2, 1[2].
dhísh*n*ya, liberal (?), III, 22, 3[1].
dhísh*n*yâ, the Dhish*n*ya altar, IV, 3, 6[1].
dhî, to think : devấn á*kkh*a dî́dhyat (conj. for dî́dyat), III, 1, 1[3];—ánu vratám dî́dhyânâ*h*, contemplating the law, III, 4, 7.
dhî́, (pious) thought, prayer, I, 1, 7; 27, 11, &c.; 95, 8[2]; III, 11, 2; 3; 12, 1; yantấram dhînấm, III, 3, 8; dhiyấ *k*akre, III, 27, 9[1]; *k*akr*i*pánta dhîbhí*h*, IV, 1, 14.
dhîtí, thought, I, 68, 5[1]; 71, 3[1]; III, 12, 7; 13, 5; V, 25, 3; devotion, I, 77, 4; pious thought, i. e. hymn, or prayer, I, 143, 1; 144, 5; IV, 5, 7.
dhî́ra, wise, I, 65, 2[1], &c.
dhúni, roaring, I, 79, 1[2].
dhur, to harm : ádhûrshata, V, 12, 5.
dhúr, pole, III, 6, 6.
dhû, to shake : ádhûnot, I, 59, 6; davidhâva, I, 140, 6; dodhavîti, he waves, II, 4, 4[2]; adhûnutam, you have hurled down, III, 12, 6; dávidhvat, shaking, IV, 13, 2; dávidhvata*h*, having shaken, IV, 13, 4[2];—ava-dhûnushé, thou hurlest away, I, 78, 4.
dhû*h*-sád, charioteer, I, 143, 7; II, 2, 1[3].
dhûmá, smoke, I, 36, 9; III, 29, 9; IV, 6, 2; V, 11, 3.
dhûmá-ketu, whose banner is smoke, I, 27, 11; 44, 3.
dhû́ma-ketu, banner of smoke, I, 94, 10[1].
dhûmín, smoky, V, 9, 5[2].
dhûrtí, mischief, I, 36, 15; 128, 7.
dh*ri*, to hold : dâdhấra, I, 65, 3, &c.;—ni-dhâráyanta*h*, setting down, IV, 2, 12.
dh*ri*tá-vrata, whose laws are firm, I, 44, 14; 141, 9; II, 1, 4.
dh*ri*sh : ấ dadharshît, may he defy, IV, 4, 3; ná â-dh*rí*she, not to be defied, V, 8, 5.
dh*ri*shá*g*? V, 19, 5[1].
dh*ri*shatấ, fiercely, I, 71, 5; IV, 4, 2; 5, 6.
dh*ri*sh*n*u-yấ, fiercely, V, 10, 5.
dhénâ, stream, I, 141, 1; shower, III, 1, 9[2].
dhenú, milch cow, I, 66, 2; 73, 6; II, 2, 2; 9[1]; 5, 5[1]; III, 1, 7; 6, 4; IV, 1, 6; 16; dhenû́ íti, I, 146, 3[2]; divákshasa*h* dhenáva*h*, III, 7, 2[2].
dhmâ, see dham.
dhmât*rí*, smelter, V, 9, 5.
dhra*g* : úpa dhrá*g*antam, speeding forward, I, 149, 1.
dhrá*g*îmat, hasting, I. 79, 1.
dhruvá, firm, I, 36, 5[1], &c.; *k*árata*h* dhruvásya, I, 146, 1; dhruvé (for Pada : dhruvá*h*), III, 6, 4[1].
dhruvá-kshema, dwelling in firm peace, IV, 13, 3.
dhva*m*s : dhvasáyantam, sparkling, I, 140, 3; dhvasáyanta*h*, I, 140, 5.
dhvasmán, bespatterer, IV, 6, 6.
dhv*ri*, see dhur.

ná, 'like,' and ná, 'not,' I, 127, 3[6].
nákis, not, I, 27, 8; 69, 7.
nákta, Night : náktâ *k*a ushásâ, I, 73, 7; náktam, by night, I, 98, 2; 127, 5; 144, 4[2]; V, 7, 4.
nakta-yấ, by night, IV, 11, 1.
nákti, Night : náktî*h* ushása*h*, II, 2, 2.
Náktoshásâ, du., Night and Dawn, I, 13, 7; 96, 5; 142, 7.
naksh, to reach : nákshante, I, 66, 9;—abhí nakshati, I, 95, 10.
nad : nấnadat, roaring, I, 140, 5; III, 2, 11.
nápât, offspring : ū́r*g*a*h* napât, I, 58, 8; II, 6, 2; III, 27, 12; V, 17, 5;—apấm nápât, the child of the Waters, I, 143, 1[2]; III, 9, 1.
náptri, offspring : ûr*g*á*h* náptre, V, 7, 1.
nabhanyà? I, 149, 3[2].
nábhas, cloud, I, 71, 10; II, 4, 6; III, 12, 1[1].
nam : â-námam, to direct, IV, 8, 3.
náma*h*-ukti, praise, I, 189, 1; III, 14, 2[2].
námas, adoration, reverence, I, 1, 7,

&c.; námasâ, adoringly, III, 14, 5.
namasy, to worship, adore: namasyánti, I, 36, 19; namasyá, I, 44, 6[1]; namasyan, I, 72, 5; namasyáta, III, 2, 8; namasyâmah, III, 17, 4; namasyántah, adoring, IV, 6, 11.
namasyà, to be adored, venerable, I, 72, 5[2]; II, 1, 3; 10; III, 5, 2; 27, 13.
namasvín, adorer, I, 36, 7.
Nárâsámsa, 'song of men' or 'praised by men,' I, 13, 3[1]; 142, 3; II, 3, 1; III, 29, 11; V, 5, 2.
nárya, manly power, I, 72, 1[1].
náva, new, young, I, 31, 8, &c.;—návyams, návyasî, I, 27, 4; 60, 3; 141, 5; 143, 1; III, 2, 13; návîyasâ, I, 12, 11;—návyah, gen., V, 12, 3[1];—návishtha, youngest, V, 27, 3.
nava-gâ, new-born, IV, 6, 3.
náva-gâta, new-born, V, 15, 3.
navatí, ninety: navatím púrah, III, 12, 6.
navamám, for the ninth time, V, 27, 3[3].
Náva-vâstva, I, 36, 18[1].
návedas, watcher: ushásah návedâh, I, 79, 1[3];—witness, V, 12, 3.
návya, young, I, 141, 10; 189, 2.
nas, to attain: nasate, V, 4, 11;—â ânat, I, 71, 8.
nas: nésat, it disappeared, IV, 1, 17.
Náhusha, N. of a clan, I, 31, 11[2]; V, 12, 6.
Nahus, (I, 31, 11[2]).
nâka, sky, firmament: pipésa nâkam stríbhih, I, 68, 10;—III, 2, 12; 5, 10; IV, 13, 5; V, 1, 1; 17, 2.
nânâ-rathám, on many chariots, III, 6, 9.
nândî, delight: nândyè, I, 145, 4.
Nâbhânedishtha, (I, 142, 10[1]).
nâbhi, navel, centre, I, 59, 1[2]; 142, 10[1]; III, 5, 5; IV, 10, 8; nâbhih prithivyâh, I, 59, 2; 143, 4; II, 3, 7; III, 5, 9; 29, 4; pra-gâm nâbhim, II, 3, 9; divâh nâbhâ, III, 4, 4; amrítasya nâbhim, III, 17, 4.
nâman, name: deva-tvám nâma, amrítam nâma, I, 68, 4[1]; nâmâni dadhire yagñíyâni, I, 72, 3; prathamám nâma dhenóh, IV, 1, 16; gúhyam nâma, V, 3, 2; 3; 5, 10; bhûri nâma dadhâti, V, 3, 10.
nârî, wife, I, 73, 3.
nârminî? I, 149, 3[1].
nâvâ, boat: nâváyâ, I, 97, 8[1].
Nâsatya, IV, 3, 6[3];—du., the Asvins, IV, 14, 1[2].
nims, to kiss: nímsate, I, 144, 1[4].
ní-kâma, desirous of, III, 1, 15.
niksh: vi-níkshe, to pierce, V, 2, 9.
ni-kirá, watchful, III, 9, 4.
niník, secretly, IV, 5, 8[1].
ninyá, hidden, I, 95, 4[1]; inmost, IV, 3, 16.
nítya, one's own, I, 66, 1[1]; 5; 71, 1; 140, 7; 148, 3; 5; II, 2, 11;—true (friend of men), I, 141, 2[2];—nítyam, constantly, I, 73, 4.
nítya-aritra, with its own rudders, I, 140, 12[1].
nid: nidânâh, scolding, IV, 5, 12.
níd, scoffer, III, 16, 5;—revilement, IV, 4, 15.
ninitsú, who tries to revile, I, 189, 6.
ninditrí, reproacher, V, 2, 6.
níndya, reproachable, V, 2, 6.
ni-mísh, closing of the eyes, I, 72, 5[4].
ni-vákana, invocation, I, 189, 8;—recitation, IV, 3, 16.
ni-vát, depth: ut-vátah ni-vátah, III, 2, 10.
ni-vártana, return, III, 9, 2.
ni-víd, the Nivid formula, I, 96, 2[1].
nishká-grîva, with a golden ornament at his neck, V, 19, 3.
ní-hita, laid down, I, 72, 6.
nî, to lead: padám nayanti, they follow his track, I, 146, 4[2];—pári nayanti, they carry around, I, 95, 2[4]; pári nîyate, he is led around, IV, 15, 1.
nîlá, nest, IV, 1, 11; 12.
nîthá, song, IV, 3, 16.
nîtha-víd, knowing all the ways, III, 12, 5.
nîla-prishtha, with the dark blue back, III, 7, 3.
nu, to low, roar: návanta, I, 66, 10; nonâva, I, 79, 2;—to shout (hymns of praise): návanta, I, 69, 10;—abhí prá nonumah, I, 78, 1–5; abhí anûshata, they have greeted with shouts, I, 144, 2; IV, 1, 16; abhí anûshata,

(the hymns) have been sung, V, 5, 4;—sám navanta, IV, 3, 11.
nú, now: nú *k*it nú, I, 58, 1[1]; nú *k*a purấ *k*a, I, 96, 7.
nû́tana, present, recent, I, 1, 2; III, 1, 20.
nûnám, now: adyá nûnám *k*a, I, 13, 6; nûnám aparám, now and in future, I, 189, 4.
n*ri*, man: n*rî́*n (for various cases), I, 146, 4[5]; III, 14, 4[1]; IV, 2, 15[2]; V, 15, 2[2]; nara*h* marutah, III, 16, 2[1]; *sám*se n*rin*ấm, III, 16, 4.
n*ri*-*k*ákshas, beholding men, III, 15, 3; 22, 2; IV, 3, 3.
n*rí*-tama, manliest, I, 59, 4; 77, 4; III, 1, 12; 19, 3; IV, 5, 2; V, 4, 6.
n*ri*-páti, lord of men, I, 71, 8[3]; II, 1, 1; 7.
n*ri*-pé*s*as, (the divine doors) with men as their ornaments, III, 4, 5[3,4].
n*ri*mn*á*, manly power, I, 67, 3; V, 19, 2.
n*ri*-vát, with men, V, 18, 5.
n*ri*vát-sakhi, rich in manly friends, IV, 2, 5[1].
n*ri*-sádana, seat of men, V, 7, 2.
n*ri*-hán, man-killer, IV, 3, 6.
net*rí*, leader, III, 15, 4; 20, 4; ishấm netấ, III, 23, 2[2].
nédish*th*a, near, nearest, I, 127, 11; IV, 1, 5.
nemá-dhiti, discord, I, 72, 4[2].
nemí, felly, I, 141, 9; II, 5, 3; V, 13, 6.
nésha-tama, best leading, I, 141, 12.
nésh*tri*, the N. priest, II, 5, 5[1].
nesh*t*rá, office of the Nesh*tri* (priest), II, 1, 2.
naú, boat: nâvấ-iva, I, 97, 7; 99, 1; V, 25, 9; síndhum ná nâvấ, V, 4, 9; nấvam nítya-aritrâm pat-vátîm, I, 140, 12[1].
nyá*ñk*, directed downwards: nî́*k*î*h*, I, 66, 10[2]; 72, 10[4].

pakvá, ripe, I, 66, 3; IV, 3, 9.
pa*k*atá, baked, III, 28, 2.
pá*ñk*an, five: ádhi pá*ñk*a k*ri*sh*t*íshu, over the fivefold dwellings (of the five peoples), II, 2, 10.
pa*ñk*â*s*át, fifty, V, 18, 5.
pat: patyate, he rules, I, 128, 7; patyase, thou possessest, II, 1, 8.
pat, to fly: pátanti míha*h*, I, 79, 2.
patangá, winged (flames), IV, 4, 2.
patatrín, winged, I, 58, 5[2]; 94, 11.
patará, winged: p*ri*snyâ*h* patarám, II, 2, 4.
páti, lord, I, 26, 1, &c.; páti*h* dán, I, 149, 1[2];—husband, I, 66, 8; 71, 1; IV, 3, 2[1].
páti-gush*t*â (nấrî), (a wife) beloved by her husband, I, 73, 3.
pati-ríp, deceiving her husband, IV, 5, 5.
pátnî, consort: devî́*h* pátnî*h*, IV, 5, 13.
pátnî-vat, together with the wife, I, 72, 5; III, 6, 9.
pátman, flight, I, 141, 7; V, 5, 7.
pat-vát, having feet, I, 140, 9; pat-vátîm nấvam, I, 140, 12[1].
pátvan, flight, V, 6, 7.
pathyấ, path, III, 14, 3.
pad, to fall: padîsh*t*á, I, 79, 11;—áva padyate, IV, 13, 5.
pád, foot: padá*h* ní dadhâti, I, 146, 2; pad-bhí*h* (conj. for pa*t*-bhí*h*), IV, 2, 14[2].
padá, footstep, footmark, track, I, 65, 2; 67, 6[2]; IV, 5, 3; padám nayanti, they follow his track, I, 146, 4[2]; padám vé*h*, III, 5, 5[1]; 6; IV, 5, 8[4]; padám Vísh*noh* upa-mám, V, 3, 3;—standing-place, abode: padé paramé, I, 72, 2; 4; trí*h* saptá gúhyâni padấ, steps or places, I, 72, 6[1]; i*l*á*h* padé, I, 128, 1; *ri*tásya padé, IV, 5, 9; mâtú*h* padé paramé, IV, 5, 10.
pada-vî́, following the footsteps, I. 72, 2[2]; III, 5, 1[1].
pan, to praise: pánanta, II, 4, 5[1]; panáyanta, III, 6, 7; panaya, V, 20, 1[1,2].
pánish*th*a, most wonderful, III, 1, 13.
pánîya*ms*, highly miraculous, V, 6, 4.
panú, praise, I, 65, 4.
páyas, milk, I, 66, 2; 79, 3; IV, 3, 9; 10.
páyasvat, rich in milk, II, 3, 6.
par, see p*ri*.
pára, distant, III, 18, 2.
para*h*-pấ, a protector far and wide, II, 9, 2; 6.
para*s*ú, axe, I, 127, 3; IV, 6, 8.

parás, beyond: paráh manîsháyâ, V, 17, 2[2].
parástât, on high, III, 22, 3.
parâ-vátah, from afar, I, 36, 18; 73, 6; III, 9, 5.
pári, prep., from, I, 31, 4;—for the sake of, III, 5, 10[1].
pari-kshít, encompassing, III, 7, 1.
pári-gman, walking round the earth, I, 79, 3[2]; 127, 2[3]; III, 2, 9[3]; IV, 3, 6[4]; V, 10, 5.
pári-takmya, the decisive moment, I, 31, 6[3,4].
pari-bắdh, hindrance, V, 2, 10.
pari-bhű, encompassing, I, 1, 4; 97, 6; 141, 9; III, 3, 10.
pári-vîta, enveloped, I, 128, 1[3]; III, 8, 4[1]; IV, 1, 7.
párishti, encompassing, I, 65, 3[1].
párînas, abundance, III, 24, 5; V, 10, 1.
parîshti, searching, (I, 65, 3[1]).
parushá, speckled, V, 27, 5.
párvan, joint (of the month): párvanâ-parvanâ, I, 94, 4[1].
palitá, grey, I, 144, 4; fem. páliknî, V, 2, 4[2].
pavítra, purification, III, 1, 5;—purifying strainer, III, 26, 8.
pas, to see: áti pasyasi, I, 94, 7;—pári apasyanta, they have searched, I, 146, 4;—ví pasya, look forth, III, 23, 2[2].
pás, eye: pat-bhíh, IV, 2, 12[2]; pat-bhíh (conj. pad-bhíh), IV, 2, 14[2].
pasú, animal, beast: pasvắ ná tâyúm, I, 65, 1[1,2]; pasúh ná sísvâ, I, 65, 10; (Agni), II, 4, 7; V, 7, 7; cattle, I, 67, 6[2]; 72, 6; III, 9, 7; IV, 2, 18[1]; V, 2, 5; victim, IV, 6, 3.
pasu-pắ, shepherd, I, 144, 6; IV, 6, 4.
pasu-sắ, winner of cattle, I, 127, 10[1].
pasvá-yantra, taking . . . as an instrument (?), IV, 1, 14.
pastyầ, dwelling, IV, 1, 11.
pâ: sáh pâti (conj. sápâti), V, 12, 6[1].
pắka, simple, I, 31, 14; III, 9, 7; IV, 5, 2.
pắgas, stream of light, I, 58, 5; III, 14, 1; 15, 1; 29, 3; IV, 4, 1; V, 1, 2.
pắthas, abode, I, 188, 10[1]; II, 3, 9; III, 8, 9; pâtháh (conj. patháh?), II, 2, 4[4].
pâyú, guardian, I, 31, 12; 13; 95, 9; 143, 8; 147, 3; 189, 4; II, 1, 7; 2, 4; III, 15, 4[1]; IV, 2, 6; 4, 3; 12; V, 12, 4.
pắrthiva, dweller on earth, I, 95, 3;—the terrestrial (space), I, 128, 3; 144, 6; gráyâmsi pắrthivâ, V, 8, 7.
pâvaká, purifier, I, 12, 9; 10; 13, 1; 60, 4; 95, 11; 142, 3; 6; II, 3, 1; 7, 4; III, 5, 7; 10, 8; 17, 1; 21, 2; 27, 4; IV, 5, 6; 6, 7; V, 4, 3; 7; 7, 4; 26, 1.
pắvaka-soki, whose flame is purifying, III, 2, 6.
pâvaká-sokis, purifying with his flames, III, 9, 8[1]; 11, 7; IV, 7, 5; V, 22, 1.
pắsa, fetter, V, 2, 7.
pitú, food, I, 69, 3; V, 7, 6.
pitu-mát, rich in food, I, 141, 2[2]; 144, 7; IV, 1, 8.
pitrí, father: mahé pitré divé, I, 71, 5; pitúh paramắt (Heaven), I, 141, 4[1]; pitúh ka ganitúh ka, III, 1, 10[1]; pitắ yagñắnâm, III, 3, 4;—V, 3, 9[2]; 10[1];—du., parents, I, 140, 7[2]; III, 7, 1[1]; 18, 1[1]; pitróh upá-sthe, I, 146, 1[2]; III, 26, 9; mâtárâ pitárâ, IV, 6, 7;—pitárah Áṅgirasah, I, 71, 2[1]; pitắ pitrí-bhyah ûtáye, II, 5, 1[3]; pitárah manushyầh, IV, 1, 13[1]; pitárah párâsah pratnắsah, IV, 2, 16.
pitri-vittá, acquired by the fathers, I, 73, 1[1]; 9.
pítrya, paternal: sakhyắ pítryâni, I, 71, 10.
pinv, to swell: pínvamânâh, III, 1, 7; pinvasva, III, 3, 7.
pis, to adorn: pipésa, I, 68, 10.
pisáṅga-rûpa, tawny-coloured, II, 3, 9.
pîy, to abuse: pîyati, I, 147, 2.
putrín, with sons, V, 4, 11.
púnar: púnah astu sáh asmai, may it (the spell) recoil on him, I, 147, 4; púnah, give us back, I, 189, 3.
púr, stronghold: pûh-bhíh ắyasîbhih, I, 58, 8;—I, 149, 3; 189, 2; III, 12, 6; 15, 4; V, 19, 2.
purah-etrí, leader, I, 76, 2[1]; III, 11, 5.
purah-gắ, going in front, I, 188, 11.
purah-sád, sitting in front, I, 73, 3.
puráh-hita, the Purohita, I, 1, 1;

44, 10[1]; 12; 58, 3; 94, 6[1],[2]; 128, 4; III, 2, 8; 3, 2; 11, 1; V, 11, 2.
Púram-dhi, Liberality of the gods, II, 1, 3[3].
purás, in front: dadhiré purá*h*, III, 2, 5; V, 16, 1[2].
purã́, before (with gen.), I, 71, 10; —formerly, I, 96, 7.
purîshyà, of the soil: purîshyẫsa*h* agnáya*h*, III, 22, 4[1].
purú, many, I, 36, 1[3], &c.; III, 4, 5[3]; purú vâ áram (conj. puru-vã́ram), I, 142, 10[2]; ánu pûrvī́*h*, III, 15, 3[1];—mightily, I, 127, 3.
puru-anîka, with many faces, I, 79, 5.
puru-kshú, rich in food, I, 68, 10; III, 25, 2.
puru-*k*andrá, rich in splendour, I, 27, 11; II, 2, 12; III, 25, 3; V, 8, 1.
puru-trã́, in many places, I, 70, 10; 146, 5.
puru-dá*m*sa, wonderful, III, 1, 23.
puru-drúh, full of deceit, III, 18, 1.
purudhá-pratîka, with many faces, III, 7, 3.
purudhã́, manifoldly, IV, 2, 19.
puruni*h*-sthá, growing up in many places, V 1, 6.
Puru-nîthá, N. pr., I, 59, 7.
puru-pé*s*a, manifoldly-adorned, II, 10, 3[2].
puru-pé*s*as, manifold-adorned, III, 3, 6.
puru-pra*s*astá, praised by many, I, 73, 2.
puru-priyá, beloved of many, I, 12, 2; 44, 3; 45, 6; III, 3, 4; V, 18, 1.
puru-praishá, he who pronounces many Praishas, I, 145, 3[2].
puru-rṹpa, of all kinds, manifold-shaped, II, 2, 9; V, 8, 2; 5.
puru-vásu, rich in wealth, II, 1, 5.
puru-vã́ra, with many treasures, bountiful: puru-vã́ram (conj. for purú vâ áram), I, 142, 10[2]; —II, 2, 2; IV, 2, 20; 5, 15.
puruvã́ra-push*t*i, lord of bountiful prosperity, I, 96, 4.
purusha-trã́: conj. purusha-tã́, men as we are, IV, 12, 4[1].
puru-stutá, praised by many, I, 141, 6; V, 8, 5.
puru-sp*r*íh, much desired, I, 142, 6; II, 7, 1; IV, 8, 7; V, 7, 6.
puru-hûtá, much-invoked, I, 44, 7.
Purûrávas, I, 31, 4.
puro*l*ã́*s*, sacrificial cake, III, 28, 1-6.
puróhita, see purá*h*-hita.
push, to make prosper: pushyasi, I, 94, 6; V, 26, 6; pushyata, I, 94, 8; pushyati, III, 10, 3; púshyanta*h*, causing to thrive, IV, 8, 5.
push*t*í, prosperity, I, 65, 5; 77, 5; II, 4, 4; V, 10, 3.
push*t*i-mát with prosperity, III, 13, 7.
push*t*im-bhará, bringing prosperity, IV, 3, 7.
push*t*i-várdhana, augmenter of prosperity, I, 31, 5.
pû, to purify: punânã́*h*, II, 3, 5; krátum punâná*h*, III, 1, 5[1]; punánti, III, 8, 5; ápupot, III, 26, 8;—abhí punatī́, IV, 5, 7.
pûtá, purified, I, 79, 10.
pûtá-daksha, of pure powers, III, 1, 3[2].
Pûrú, the Pûrus, I, 59, 6; V, 17, 1.
pṹrva, former, ancient, I, 1, 2, &c.; pûrva-vát, as for the ancients, I, 31, 17;—divá*h* pṹrva*h*, before daybreak, I, 60, 2; to the front, I, 94, 8[1]; mã́nushât pṹrva*h*, II, 3, 3[2]; tvát hótâ pṹrva*h*, III, 17, 5;—eastern: pṹrvâm ánu pra-dí*s*am, I, 95, 3.
pûrvá-thâ, in the old way, III, 29, 1.
pûrvyá, ancient, I, 26, 5; 94, 6; III, 14, 3[2]; 23, 3; V, 15, 3[2];—foremost, I, 74, 2[1].
Pûshán, II, 1, 6; IV, 3, 7.
pûsha*n*-vát, accompanied by Pûshan, I, 142, 12.
p*ri* or par, to bring across: piparshi, thou leadest forward, I, 31, 6[4]; párshi, II, 7, 2; párshat, III, 20, 4; pip*ri*tam, III, 26, 9; parshati dvishá*h*, may he help us across our enemies, V, 25, 1; 9;—áti pâraya, I, 97, 7; áti parsha, I, 97, 8; áti parshat, I, 99, 1.
p*ri*, to fill: pûrdhi, I, 36, 12; paprã́, I, 69, 1;—âpapri-vã́n, I, 73, 8; 146, 1; ã́ ap*ri*nat, III, 2, 7; ã́ ap*ri*na*h*, III, 3, 10; ã́ aprâ*h*, IV, 14, 2;—prá-pra p*ri*nîtana,

fill (with bliss) further and further, V, 5, 5.
pr*i*ksh, nourishment, I, 71, 7[1]; 73, 5; II, 1, 6.
pr*i*kshá, power, I, 127, 5[1]; II, 1, 15[2]; —powerful, I, 141, 2[1]; saptá pr*i*kshâsa*h*, III, 4, 7[1].
pr*i*kshá-prayag, mighty sacrificer, III, 7, 10[1].
pr*i*kshúdh: pr*i*kshúdha*h*? I, 141, 4[2].
pr*i*k: pri*ñk*anti, they fill, I, 79, 3; pri*ñk*áte, they grow, I, 128, 5; papr*ik*ânâsa*h*, swelling, I, 141, 6[3]; papr*ik*âsi, make swell, I, 141, 11[2];—támase vi-pr*i*k*e*, for dispersing the darkness, IV, 13, 3; vi-pr*i*kvat, cleared from admixture, V, 2, 3[2];—sam-pri*ñk*ânâ*h*, being united, I, 95, 8.
pr*i*t, battle, I, 27, 7; 79, 8; V, 9, 7; 10, 7; 16, 5; 17, 5.
pr*i*tanâ, battle, III, 16, 2; 24, 1.
pr*i*tanâ*g*ya, racing of battle, III, 8, 10.
pr*i*tanâ-yú, seeking to combat, III, 1, 16.
pr*i*tanâ-sáh, powerful in battles, III, 29, 9; V, 23, 2.
pr*i*tanyát, foe, II, 8, 6.
pr*i*tsutí, hostility, V, 4, 1.
pr*i*thivî, earth, Earth: nâbhi*h* pr*i*thivyâ*h*, I, 59, 2; III, 29, 4; agní*h* dâti róma pr*i*thivyâ*h*, I, 65, 8; kshâm and pr*i*thivîm, I, 67, 5; dyâvâ pr*i*thivî íti, Heaven and Earth, I, 143, 2; divá*h* pr*i*thivyâ*h*, III, 1, 3; mahinâ pr*i*thivyâ*h*, III, 7, 10[2]; várshman pr*i*thivyâ*h*, III, 8, 3; váre â pr*i*thivyâ*h*, III, 23, 4[3]; divá*h* sûnú*h* pr*i*thivyâ*h*, III, 25, 1;—Earth, I, 72, 9; 94, 16; 95, 11; 98, 3; III, 8, 8[1]; 17, 2; IV, 3, 5.
pr*i*thú, broad, I, 65, 5; II, 1, 12.
pr*i*thu-pâ*g*as, with broad stream of light, III, 2, 11; 3, 1; 5, 1; 27, 5.
pr*i*thú-pragâ*n*a, with broad passages, III, 5, 7.
pr*i*thú-pragâman, proceeding on his broad way, I, 27, 2.
pr*i*thu-budhná, broad-based, IV, 2, 5.
pr*i*sanî, the speckled (cow), I, 71, 5[1].
prí*s*ni, speckled, IV, 3, 10[2];—Pr*i*sni, the mother of the Maruts, II, 2, 4[3]; IV, 5, 7[1]; 10.
pr*i*shat-a*s*va, with the spotted deer as horses, III, 26, 6[2].
pr*i*shatî, the spotted deer, III, 26, 4[2].
pr*i*sh*t*a-bandhu, after whose relations men ask, III, 20, 3[3].
pr*i*sh*th*á, back, I, 58, 2[1]; IV, 2, 11[2]; ridge, V, 7, 5;—a certain Stotra? IV, 5, 6[1].
pr*i*sh*th*yà, of the back: páyasâ pr*i*sh*th*yèna, IV, 3, 10[1].
pé*s*as, the ornamented form: ya*gñ*ásya pé*s*a*h*, II, 3, 6[2].
Péshî, V, 2, 2[1].
pótr*i*, the Potr*i* priest, I, 94, 6; II, 5, 2; IV, 9, 3.
potrá, service of a Potr*i*, I, 76, 4[3]; II, 1, 2.
pósha, welfare, I, 1, 3; V, 5, 9.
poshayitnú, which is to thrive, III, 4, 9.
pyai, to swell: pîpáyanta, they were exuberant, I, 73, 6; pîpayat, may he augment, I, 77, 5; píyâna*h* (conj. píyânam), I, 79, 3[1]; pîpâya, it has prospered, II, 2, 9; pîpyânâ*h*, rich in milk, III, 1, 10[2];—prá pîpaya, increase, III, 15, 6.
pra-avitr*i*, protector, I, 12, 8; furtherer, III, 21, 3.
pra-avís, zealous, IV, 9, 2.
pra-ketá, splendour, I, 94, 5.
prá-*k*etas, provident, wise, I, 44, 7; 11; II, 10, 3; III, 25, 1; 29, 5.
pra*kh*, to look for: pr*i*sh*t*á*h*, I, 98, 2[1].
pra-*g*ánana, the creative organ, III, 29, 1[3].
pra-*g*â, children: pra-*g*â*h* utá (conj. pra-*g*âsu), I, 67, 9[1]; pra-*g*âm ví syatu, may he deliver a son, II, 3, 9.
pra*g*â-vat, procuring offspring, I, 76, 4; pra*g*â-vat râdhas, abundance of progeny, I, 94, 15; accompanied by offspring, II, 2, 12; III, 8, 6; 16, 6; rich in offspring, III, 16, 3; IV, 2, 5.
pra-tára*n*a, carrying forward, II, 1, 12.
prá-tavas, strong, IV, 3, 6.
práti, equal to, II, 1, 8; 15; 3, 2.
pratîtya, to be listened to, IV, 5, 14.
pratná, old: pratnám, I, 36, 4; II, 7, 6; III, 9, 8.
pratná-thâ, in the ancient way, I, 96, 1; III, 2, 12; V, 8, 5.

pratyáñk, turning back, I, 95, 5; II, 3, 1; III, 18, 1.
prath, to spread out: prathâyan nrîn, III, 14, 4; paprathânáh, V, 15, 4;—ví prathantâm, may they open wide, II, 3, 5; ví prathasva, spread thyself, V, 5, 4.
prathamá: prathamâ ánu dhárma, after the primitive ordinances, III, 17, 1.
prathama-gâ, first-born (son), III, 29, 15[1].
pra-dakshinít, from left to right, III, 19, 2[1]; IV, 6, 3.
pra-díva, ancient, II, 3, 1.
pra-dívas, from of old, I, 141, 3[2]; IV, 6, 4; 7, 8; V, 8, 7.
pradís, commandment: pradísah, (I, 31, 14[3]).
pra-dís, region: pra-dísam (conj. for prá dísam), I, 95, 3[2].
prá-nîti, guidance, III, 15, 1; IV, 4, 14.
pra-netrí, leader, II, 9, 2; III, 23, 1.
pra-pitvá, the time of the advancing day, I, 189, 7[2,3].
prá-bharman, the bringing forward, I, 79, 7.
pra-bhû, eminent: pra-bhvîh (dúrah), I, 188, 5[1]; 9.
prá-bhûti, copiousness, III, 19, 3.
prá mati, guardian, I, 31, 9; 10; 14; 16; 141, 2[4];—kindness, I, 71, 7; care, I, 94, 1.
prá-mahas, highly exalted, V, 28, 4.
prá-yagyu, friend of sacrifices, III, 6, 2[1].
prá-yata, forward-bent, IV, 5, 10.
práyata-dakshina, giving sacrificial fees, I, 31, 15.
pra-yantrí, giver, I, 76, 4[4].
práyas, joy, delight, feast, I, 31, 7; 45, 8; 58, 7[3]; 71, 3; III, 11, 7; 12, 8; IV, 5, 6; 15, 2[2].
práyasvat, offering enjoyment, I, 60, 3; III, 6, 3; V, 20, 3.
pra-yâ, onset, III, 29, 15.
pravaná, hill-side, III, 22, 4.
pra-vát, declivity, I, 144, 5[2];—precipitous: pra-vátâ, III, 5, 8.
pra-vâkya, to be openly uttered, IV, 5, 8.
pra-víd, finding out, III, 7, 6.
pra-sámsya, deserving of praise, II, 2, 3; 11.
pra-sastá, praised, glorious, precious, I, 36, 9; 60, 1; 66, 4.
prá-sasti, praise, I, 26, 9; 70, 9; 74, 6; 148, 3; V, 9, 6; 16, 1.
pra-sâstrí, the Prasâstri priest, I, 94, 6[1]; II, 5, 4.
pra-sâstrá, office of the Prasâstri priest, II, 1, 2.
pra-sísh, command, I, 145, 1.
pra-sáh, power, V, 23, 1.
prá-siti, onslaught, IV, 4, 1.
pra-sû, sprouting grass, I, 67, 9[2]; 95, 10[2]; III, 5, 8.
Práskanva, I, 44, 6; 45, 3.
prá-svanita, roaring, I, 44, 12[1].
pra-hoshá, libation, I, 150, 2.
prâkâ-gihva, stretching forward his tongue, I, 140, 3.
prâkîna, eastward-turned (barhís), I, 188, 4.
prâñk, inclined towards, II, 2, 7;—eastward: prâñkam yagñám kakrima, III, 1, 2[2]; prâkî íti, III, 6, 10[1];—turned forwards, III, 7, 7.
prâná, breath: âyuh prânáh, I, 66, 1.
prâtah-yâvan, coming early in the morning, I, 44, 13; 45, 9.
prâtah-sâvá, morning libation, III, 28, 1.
priyá, beloved, I, 13, 3, &c.; dear = φίλος, I, 67, 6[1]; saptá priyâsah, seven friends, IV, 1, 12; priyám tvâ krinávate, he gratifies thee, IV, 2, 8.
priyá-dhâma, whose foundations are pleasant, I, 140, 1.
Priyá-medha: priyamedha-vát, I, 45, 3[1]; priyá-medhâh, I, 45, 4[1].
prî, to please: prînânáh, I, 73, 1; píprîshati, he longs to gladden, IV, 4, 7;—â piprayah, gladden (the gods), II, 6, 8[1].
prîtá, well-cared for, I, 66, 4[1]; 69, 5.
prush, to sprinkle, shower: prushitá, I, 58, 2; prushnávat, III, 13, 4.
pretrí, friend, I, 148, 5.
présha, instigation, I, 68, 5[1].
praishá, sacrificial command of a priest, (I, 145, 3[2]).

phalgvà, feeble, IV, 5, 14.

bát, lo! I, 96, 1; 141, 1.
bándhana, fetterer, V, 12, 4.
bandhútâ, kinship, IV, 4, 11.
babhrí, carrying (the prize), III, 1, 12.

babhrū́, brown (plants), I, 140, 6[1].
bárhish*th*am, most powerfully, III, 13, 1.
barhíshmat, he who has spread the Barhis, V, 2, 12.
barhís, the sacrificial grass, I, 12, 4; 13, 5; 7; 9, &c.; prâ*k*ī́nam barhí*h*, I, 188, 4; déva barhi*h*, II, 3, 4; mádhye ā́ barhí*h*, III, 14, 2.
barhi-sád, sitting on the Barhis, II, 3, 3.
balí, tribute, I, 70, 9; V, 1, 10.
bahú, many: bahvī́*h* *k*a bhū́yasî*h* *k*a yā́*h* dúra*h*, I, 188, 5.
bahulá, large, I, 189, 2.
bâdh, to drive away: bā́dhamâna*h*, III, 8, 2; bā́dhasva, beat away, III, 15, 1.
bâhú, arm, III, 29, 6.
budh, to take notice: bodhi, III, 14, 7; V, 24, 3; sá*h* *k*a bódhâti, may he be attentive, I, 77, 2[2];—to think: bódhat, IV, 15, 7[1];—ábodhi, he has been awakened, V, 1, 1; 2; búdhyamânâ*h*, awaking, V, 3, 6; bodhaya, awaken, V, 14, 1[1];—ví bodhaya, awaken, I, 12, 4.
budhná, bottom, base, I, 95, 8[2]; 9; 96, 6; II, 2, 3; mahá*h* budhné rágasa*h*, IV, 1, 11[1];—depth, I, 141, 3[1].
b*r*ihát, great: b*r*ihát bhā́*h*, I, 45, 8[1]; b*r*ihatī́ ivéti b*r*i°, I, 59, 4[1]; ā́ b*r*ihát vadema, loud, II, 1, 16; mightily, III, 3, 11[1]; V, 25, 8[1].
B*r*ihát-uktha, V, 19, 3.
b*r*ihat-úksh, mightily growing, III, 26, 4.
b*r*ihát-ketu, with mighty light, V, 8, 2.
b*r*ihát-diva, dwelling in the great heaven, II, 2, 9.
b*r*ihát-bhânu, with bright light, I, 27, 12; 36, 15.
B*r*ihát-ratha, I, 36, 18[1].
B*r*íhaspáti, III, 20, 5; 26, 2[2].
bradhná, ruddy, III, 7, 5.
brahmán, the Brahman (priest), II, 1, 2[3]; 3[2]; IV, 9, 4[2].
bráhman, (sacred) spell, I, 31, 18; II, 2, 7; 10; III, 8, 2; 13, 6; 18, 3; V, 2, 6; prathama-*g*ā́*h* bráhma*n*a*h* III, 29, 15[1];—sacred word, II, 5, 3[1]; IV, 3, 15; 4, 6;—prayer, hymn: vo*k*éma bráhma, I, 75, 2; brahma*n*a*h* pate, Brahma*n*aspati, II, 1, 3; ákâri bráhma, IV, 6, 11.
brû: upa-bruvé, I invoke, I, 188, 8.

bhága, good fortune, I, 141, 6[3]; 11[1];—love, V, 7, 8[3];—a winner (in a contest), I, 141, 10[1]; 144, 3[3];—Bhaga, the god, I, 44, 8; II, 1, 7; III, 20, 4; 5; IV, 3, 5; V, 16, 2[1].
bha*g*, to obtain: bhá*g*anta ... nā́ma, I, 68, 4; bhaktám ábhaktam áva*h*, blessings enjoyed or not enjoyed (before), I, 127, 5[6];—ā́ na*h* bha*g*a, let us partake, I, 27, 5.
bhadrá, good, I, 1, 6; fortunate, I, 67, 2; blissful, I, 94, 1; glorious, I, 94, 14, &c.
bhadra-*s*o*k*i, with glorious light, V, 4, 7.
bhand: bhándamâne íti, of glorious appearance, I, 142, 7; III, 4, 6[2]; bhándamâna*h*, glorified, III, 2, 12; bhandate, he is glorified, III, 3, 4.
bhándish*th*a, most glorious, I, 97, 3; V, 1, 10[1].
Bharatá, Agni the B., I, 96, 3[2]; pl., the Bharatas, V, 11, 1.
Bharát-vâ*g*a, the Bharadvâ*g*âs, I, 59, 7.
bhárgas, splendour, I, 141, 1.
bharv, to chew: bhárvati, I, 143, 5.
bhas: prá babhasat, may he consume, IV, 5, 4.
bhásman, ash, V, 19, 5.
bhâ, to shine: ánu bhâsi, III, 6, 7;—vi-bhā́ti, he shines (conj. vidhā́ti), I, 71, 6[1]; ví bhâsi, thou shinest, II, 1, 10[1, 2]; ví bhâhi, I, 95, 11.
bhā́*h*-*r*i*g*îka, whose *r*i*g*îka (?) is light, I, 44, 3[1]; III, 1, 12; 14.
bhâgá, share, portion, I, 73, 5[2]; II, 10, 6; III, 1, 19.
bhâga-dhéya, portion, III, 28, 4.
bhâ*g*ayú, desirous of distributing (goods), II, 1, 4.
bhā́-tvakshas, whose power is light, I, 143, 3.
bhânú, ray, I, 36, 3; 97, 5; III, 1, 14; flame, I, 143, 3; V, 1, 1; light, splendour, II, 2, 8, &c.

bhânu-mát, shining, V, 1, 11.
bhā́ma, splendour, III, 26, 6;—flame, V, 2, 10.
bhâmín, luminous, I, 77, 1.
bhârá, burthen, I, 31, 3.
Bhā́rata, (Agni) of the Bharata tribe, II, 7, 1[1]; 5;—Bhā́ratâ, the two Bharatas, III, 23, 2[1].
Bhā́ratî: Hótrâ Bhā́ratî, I, 142, 9[2]; II, 1, 11[1];—I, 188, 8; II, 3, 8; bhā́ratî bhā́ratîbhi*h*, III, 4, 8.
bhā́s, light: br*i*hát bhā́*h*, I, 45, 8[1]; IV, 5, 1[1];—II, 4, 5; IV, 7, 9.
bhiksh, to implore, I, 73, 6; 7.
bhid: áva bhet, he cut down, I, 59, 6.
bhug: bhó*g*ate, receives nourishment, I, 72, 8[2]; bhu*g*é, to enjoy, I, 127, 8; 11; bhú*g*am, for the enjoyment, III, 2, 9;—yásya sam-bhú*g*am, whom I may enjoy, II, 1, 4[1].
bhugmán, fertile: bhú*g*ma (conj. bhugmā́), I, 65, 5[1].
bhur: *g*árbhurat, hurrying around, II, 2, 5; *g*árbhurâ*n*a*h*, II, 10, 5; bhuránta, they have made tremble, V, 6, 7[1];—pari-*g*árbhurâ*n*a*h*, hurrying around, I, 140, 10.
bhura*n*yú, quick, I, 68, 1.
bhurí*g*, pole-arm (?), IV, 2, 14[3].
bhúvana, world, I, 31, 2; 73, 8; II, 3, 1; III, 2, 10; 3, 10; IV, 14, 2; bhúvanasya magmánâ, I, 143, 4[1];—being, I, 98, 1; III, 16, 4.
bhû: satá*h* *k*a bhávata*h* *k*a, of what is and what comes into being, I, 96, 7;—bhavatât, be, III, 23, 2[2];—pári bhúvat, he encompassed, I, 68, 2; pári babhûtha, thou hast excelled, I, 69, 2.
bhū́man, earth, I, 65, 3[1]; II, 4, 7;—being: etā́ bhū́ma, I, 70, 6;—world: ví*s*vâni bhū́ma, II, 4, 2;—V, 7, 5.
bhū́ya*m*s, many, I, 31, 6.
bhū́ri, rich, I, 73, 4;—bhū́ri kr*í*tva*h*, many times, III, 18, 4.
bhûri-po*sh*ín, rich in manifold prosperity, III, 3, 9.
bhū́ri-retas, rich in seed, III, 3, 11.
bhū́ri-varpas, manifold-shaped, III, 3, 4.
bhū́r*n*i, quick, I, 66, 2; III, 3, 5.
bhûsh, to be busy: bhū́shan, I, 140, 6; III, 25, 2;—úpa bhûshema, may we honour, III, 3, 9;—pári bhûshasi vratám, thou administerest the law, I, 31, 2; pári bhûshanti, they celebrate, I, 95, 3; pári bhûshati, he takes care of, III, 3, 2; pári bhûshatha*h*, you display, III, 12, 9.
bh*ri*, to bring: náma*h* bháranta*h*, I, 1, 7; bhā́r íti bhā́*h*, I, 128, 2; bibharshi (conj. víbharshi), V, 3, 2[1];—út-bh*ri*ta, taken out, III, 21, 5;—prá *g*abhrire, I, 72, 4; prá bhara (Sa*m*hitâ: bharâ), 2nd or 1st person, I, 140, 1[1]; prá-bh*ri*ta, proffered, I, 147, 2;—ví bharanta, they have brought to different places, I, 70, 10[1]; ví-bh*ri*ta*h*, brought to many places, I, 71, 4[1]; dispersed, I, 144, 2; ví bháribhrat, quickly shaking, II, 4, 4[2].
Bh*rí*gavâ*n*a, Bh*ri*gu-like, I, 71, 4[2];—belonging to the Bh*ri*gus, IV, 7, 4.
Bh*rí*gu, I, 60, 1;—bh*ri*gava*h*, the Bh*ri*gus, I, 58, 5; 127, 7; 143, 4; II, 4, 2; III, 2, 4[1]; 5, 10; IV, 7, 1.
bh*rí*mi, quick, I, 31, 16[2].
bhó*g*ana, food: ví*s*vasya bho*g*ana, O food on which everything lives, I, 44, 5[1];—possession, V, 4, 5.
bho*g*yà, bounty, I, 128, 5.
bhramá, whirl, IV, 4, 2.
bhrâ*g*, to shine: bhrâ*g*ante, I, 44, 12; ábhrâ*t*, I, 66, 6; IV, 6, 5.
bhrā́*g*at-*r*ish*t*i, with brilliant spears, I, 31, 1.
bhrā́t*ri*, brother, I, 65, 7; bhrā́taram váru*n*am, IV, 1, 2; bhrā́tu*h* *ri*nám, IV, 3, 13[2].
bhrâtrá, brotherhood, II, 1, 9; IV, 10, 8.

ma*m*hánâ, bountifulness, IV, 1, 6; V, 10, 2; ma*m*hánâ, instr., V, 16, 4[2]; 18, 2.
má*m*hish*th*a, most rich in liberal gifts, I, 147, 2[1].
makshú, quickly, I, 58, 9, &c.
maghá, wealth, III, 13, 3;—liberal boon, III, 19, 1;—liberality, V, 10, 3.
maghá-vat, generous, I, 58, 9; 140, 10.

maghá-van, liberal giver, I, 31, 12; 58, 9; 73, 5; 8; 77, 4; 98, 3; 127, 11; 140, 12; 141, 13; 146, 5; II, 6, 4; V, 16, 3; 18, 3; 5; maghóna*h* (conj. maghónâm), V, 27, 1[1].
ma*g*mán, greatness, power, I, 128, 5; 141, 6; 143, 2; 4[1]; II, 1, 15.
matí, (pious) thought, I, 60, 5; III, 26, 8;—prayer, I, 141, 1; 142, 4; III, 5, 3; IV, 3, 16; vâ*k*á*h* matím, I, 143, 1[1].
math or manth, to produce by attrition: máthît, I, 71, 4; 148, 1; mathnánta*h*, I, 127, 7; máthî*h*, I, 127, 11; mathâyáti, I, 141, 3; mathitá, III, 9, 5; ámanthish*t*âm, III, 23, 2; manthâma, III, 29, 1; mánthata, III, 29, 5; mánthanti, III, 29, 6; mathyámâna*h*, V, 11, 6;—ní*h*-mathita*h*, produced by attrition, III, 23, 1; 29, 12.
mad or mand, to be pleased, rejoice: mándasva (with gen.), I, 26, 5; mâdayante, I, 59, 1[1]; mâdáyasva, II, 3, 11[3]; III, 6, 9; madanti, III, 4, 7; 7, 7; mâdayantâm, III, 4, 11; mádantam, III, 26, 9; mâdayethâm, IV, 14, 4;—abhí prá mande, I gladden, V, 4, 1.
mád, pronoun: me, acc., V, 27, 4[2].
máda, delight, I, 127, 9; V, 2, 10.
mádhu, sweet drink: mádhva*h* âdhavé, I, 141, 3[3];—honey, I, 142, 3; 188, 2; III, 1, 7; 8; mádhunâ daívyena, III, 8, 1[2];—honey-drink, V, 19, 3[2].
mádhu-*g*ihva, honey-tongued, I, 13, 3; 44, 6; 60, 3.
madhu-péya, honey-drink, IV, 14, 4[2].
madhu-p*ri*k, mixing the honey-drink, II, 10, 6.
mádhu-mat, rich in honey, I, 13, 2; 142, 2; honey-sweet, I, 78, 5; III, 4, 2; IV, 3, 9; 12;—sweet (food), III, 7, 2.
mádhumat-tama, sweetest, V, 11, 5.
mádhu-va*k*as, sweet-tongued, IV, 6, 5.
madhu-sút, Madhu-presser, IV, 3, 3.
mádhu-hastya, with honey in his hand, V, 5, 2.
madhyatá*h*, out from the midst, III, 21, 5.
madhyamá, middle: madhyaméshu, I, 27, 5.
man: manvata, they have devised, IV, 1, 16; mányase, thou art considered, V, 17, 2[1,3].
mananá, thought, III, 6, 1[1].
mánas, thought: mána*h* ná sadyá*h*, I, 71, 9; mind: mánasa*h* várâya, I, 76, 1[1]; gh*ri*ta-prúshâ mánasâ, his mind being intent on scattering gh*ri*ta, II, 3, 2; mánasâ sám *g*agmú*h*, they agreed in their mind, III, 1, 13.
manîshấ, (pious) thought: manîshấ (Pada text for manîshấ*h*?), I, 70, 1[2]; 76, 1; III, 8, 5; prayer, IV, 5, 3; 6, 1; V, 11, 5[1];—thoughtful mind, I, 94, 1;—wise thoughts, IV, 11, 2; 3;—pará*h* manîsháyâ, beyond thought, V, 17, 2[2].
manîshín, thoughtful man, I, 13, 5; III, 10, 1.
mánu, man, I, 96, 2; 140, 4; V, 2, 12;—mánave, to the man, or to Manu, I, 189, 7[4];—Manu, N.p., I, 31, 4; 36, 10; 19; 68, 7; 128, 2.
mánu*h*-hita, instituted by Manus, I, 13, 4[2]; III, 2, 15.
Mánu-*g*âta, offspring of Manu, I, 45, 1[2].
Manu-vát, like Manu, II, 10, 6.
mánusha, man, I, 31, 11[2].
manushyà, man, I, 59, 4;—belonging to men, III, 1, 10.
Manushvát, as for Manu, I, 31, 17; II, 5, 2; III, 17, 2; as Manus did, I, 44, 11; V, 21, 1.
mánus, man, (I, 31, 11[2]); I, 36, 7; III, 26, 2; IV, 1, 9[1]; 6, 11; V, 3, 4; 5, 7; mánusha*h*, (Aryan) men, I, 189, 7[2];—mánusha*h*, of the man, or, of Manus, II, 2, 6; 8;—Manus, N. p., I, 26, 4; 76, 5[1]; 128, 1; II, 10, 1; IV, 2, 1[1]; mánusha*h* purá*h*-hita*h*, III, 3, 2;—Mánusha*h* *g*antú-bhi*h*, III, 3, 6; manót*ri*, deviser, II, 9, 4.
mántra, hymn, I, 31, 13; spell, I, 67, 4; 5; 147, 4; prayer, I, 74, 1.
mand, see mad.
mandrá, joy-giving, cheerful, I, 26, 7, &c.; lovely, delightful, V, 17, 2; 26, 1.

mandrá-*g*ihva, with lovely tongues, I, 142, 8; — with agreeable speech, IV, 11, 5;—with the delightful tongue, V, 25, 2.
mandrá-tama, most delightful, V, 22, 1.
mandrá-tara, a great joy-giver, III, 7, 9.
mánman, thought, I, 26, 2[1]; III, 14, 5; IV, 6, 1;—prayer, I, 77, 4; 127, 2; 140, 1; 11; 148, 2; II, 4, 8; III, 11, 8; IV, 3, 3; 15; 5, 6; 11, 2; V, 12, 1.
manma-sã́dhana, fulfiller of thought, I, 96, 6.
manyú, spirit, V, 7, 10[1].
mámaka, mine, I, 31, 11[3].
maya*h*-bhṹ, comfort-giving, I, 13, 9; III, 16, 6; IV, 11, 4; V, 5, 8.
máyas, happiness, I, 31, 7; freshness, III, 1, 3[1].
Marút: marúta*h*, the Maruts, I, 31, 1; 44, 14; 94, 12; 128, 5; 142, 9[1]; III, 26, 4-6; 29, 15; IV, 1, 3; 2, 4; V, 3, 3; 5, 11; 26, 9; marútâm-iva svaná*h*, I, 143, 5; marútâm *s*árdha*h*, II, 3, 3; IV, 3, 8; ví*s*ve marúta*h*, III, 14, 4; nara*h* maruta*h*, III, 16, 2[1].
marútvat, accompanied by the Maruts, I, 142, 12; III, 4, 6.
marút-v*ri*dh, whom the Maruts strengthen, III, 13, 6[1].
márta, mortal, man: mártân (for mártâm, gen. plur?), I, 70, 6[1]; IV, 2, 3[2]; 11[1]; mártâya (for mártyâya?), I, 77, 2[1]; mártam *s*á*m*sam, praise of mortals, I, 141, 6[4].
mártya, the mortal, I, 26, 9[1]; mártyeshu devã́n k*rin*óti, I, 77, 1[1]; devásya mártyasya *k*a, II, 7, 2.
márya, manly, I, 77, 3.
maryaká, young bull, V, 2, 5[1].
márya-*s*rî, like a beautiful youth, II, 10, 5.
maryã́dâ, limit, IV, 5, 13.
mah: mamahantâm, may they grant, I, 94, 16; 95, 11; mamahe me, he has presented me, V, 27, 1;—to exalt: mahayanta, III, 3, 3; maháyan, III, 3, 11; mahaya, III, 24, 4: maháyamâna*h*, III, 25, 5;—sám mahema (conj. sám ahema), I, 94, 1[1].
máh, great: mahá*h* (acc. pl.), I, 31, 3[2], &c.; IV, 4, 11[1]; mahî́nâm, of the great (waters), III, 1, 12[1].
máh, greatness: mahé, III, 7, 10.
mahá, great: mahá*h*, I, 146, 5[2].
mahán, greatness: mahnã́ mahátbhi*h*, I, 72, 9.
máhas, power: máha*h*-bhi*h*, II, 10, 3[4]; III, 4, 6[3]; with all their might, IV, 14, 1[1];—mightily: mahá*h* râyé *k*itáyan, V, 15, 5[3].
máhi, great, I, 79, 4.
Máhi-keru: máhi-kerava*h*, I, 45, 4[1].
mahi-tvá, greatness, might, I, 59, 5; 6; mahi-tvã́, I, 67, 9; 68, 2; growth, III, 1, 4.
mahiná, greatness, III, 6, 2; 7, 10[2].
mahimán, greatness, I, 59, 7.
mahi-ratna, possessor of great treasures, I, 141, 10.
mahi-vrata, lord of high laws, I, 45, 3.
mahishá, buffalo, I, 95, 9[1]; 141, 3[1].
máhishî, queen, V, 2, 2[1]; buffalo-cow, V, 25, 7[2].
Mahî́, 'the Great One,' N. of a goddess, I, 13, 9[1]; 142, 9; V, 5, 8.
mâ, to create, produce: amimîta, he produced, II, 4, 5; mimîte, III, 1, 5; ámimîta (mâtári), he has been shaped, III, 29, 11[1]; mímânam, preparing, V, 2, 3;—úpa mâsi, measure out, I, 142, 2;—ví rá*g*a*h* mame, he passes through the air, I, 58, 1; vimã́na*h*, traversing, III, 26, 7;—sam-mã́ya, building, I, 67, 10.
mấkis, not, I, 147, 5.
Mâtarí*s*van, I, 31, 3; 60, 1; 71, 4[1]; 96, 4[1]; 128, 2; 141, 3; 143, 2; 148, 1; III, 2, 13; 5, 9; 10; 9, 5; 26, 2[1]; 29, 11[1].
mât*rí*, mother: mâtã́ Áditi*h*, I, 72, 9; mother (Earth), I, 140, 9[1]; mâtú*h*, II, 5, 6[1]; mâtú*h* upásthe, III, 8, 1[3]; 29, 14; V, 1, 6; ámimîta mâtári, III, 29, 11[1]; trí*h* saptá mâtú*h* paramã́*n*i, IV, 1, 16[1]; mâtú*h* ushása*h*, IV, 2, 15; mâtú*h* gó*h*, IV, 5, 10[1]; mâtã́ yuvatí*h*, V, 2, 1; 2; mâtã́-iva, V, 15, 4;—du., ubhã́ mâtárâ, I, 140, 3[1]; mâtárâ samî́*k*î́, the parents turned towards each other (Heaven and Earth), III, 1, 7[1]; parents, III, 2, 2; 5, 7[2]; 7, 1[1]; V, 11, 3[1]; mâtárâ pitárâ,

IV, 6, 7; yahvî íti *ri*tásya mâtárâ, V, 5, 6;—pl., mothers, I, 95, 7; 141, 5[1]; vatsá*h* mâtr*î*h *g*anayata, I, 95, 4[2]; saptá *s*ivẫsu mât*ri*shu, I, 141, 2[2]; mât*rî*h apá*h*, III, 9, 2; sú-*g*âtam mât*ri*shu, III, 23, 3; *s*á*s*vatîshu mât*ri*shu, IV, 7, 6.

mẫdhyandina, midday: mẫdhyandine sávane, III, 28, 4.

Mẫna, N. p.: mẫnasya sûnú*h*, I, 189, 8[1].

mânavasyát, acting as men do, I, 140, 4.

mẫnusha, man, I, 58, 5, &c.;—belonging to men, I, 44, 10[1]; 128, 7; human, I, 59, 5; 60, 3; mẫnushasya *g*ánasya *g*ánma, I, 70, 2; mẫnushî ví*s*, I, 72, 8; dhî̃*h* mẫnushâ, II, 2, 9; human (sacrificer): mẫnushât pû̃rva*h*, II, 3, 3[2];—belonging to Manus, III, 9, 6; mẫnushe (conj. mẫnusha*h*), III, 23, 4[4].

Mâmateyá, son of Mamatâ, I, 147, 3[1].

mâyẫ, wonderful power, I, 144, 1;—secret power, III, 20, 3[2]; 27, 7[1];—wile, V, 2, 9.

mâyín, powerful, III, 20, 3.

Mẫruta, of the Maruts: *s*árdha*h* mẫrutam, I, 127, 6; II, 1, 6; IV, 6, 10.

mâr*g*âlyà, liking to be groomed, V, 1, 8.

mâr*d*iká, mercy, I, 79, 9[3].

mẫ-vat, like me, I, 142, 2.

mẫhina, mighty, III, 6, 4; 7, 5.

mi, to erect: mîyámâna*h*, III, 8, 3;—ni-mimyú*h*, they have fastened down, III, 8, 6; ní-mita, III, 8, 7.

miksh, to mix: mimikshati, I, 142, 3; ghr*i*tám mimikshe, he is joined with ghr*i*ta, II, 3, 11[2].

mitá-dru, measuredly running, IV, 6, 5.

mitrá, friend, I, (36, 17[1]); 67, 1; 75, 4;—friend or Mitra, the god, I, 96, 1[3]; II, 2, 3; 4, 1; III, 5, 3;—Mitra, the god, I, 26, 4; 36, 4; 44, 13; 58, 6; 77, 3[2]; 79, 3; 94, 12[1]; 13[1]; 16; 95, 11; 98, 3; 141, 9; 143, 7; II, 1, 4; III, 4, 2; 6; 5, 9; 14, 4; IV, 1, 18; 2, 4; 3, 5; 5, 4; 6, 7[3]; 13, 2; V, 3, 1; 2[3]; 9, 6; 10, 2; 16, 1; 26, 9; mitrẫ, the two Mitras i.e. Mitra and Varu*n*a, I, 36, 17[1]; ksheshyánta*h* ná mitrám, II, 4, 3[1]; mitrá*h* agní*h* bhavati, III, 5, 4.

mitra-mahas, great like Mitra, I, 44, 12; 58, 8; II, 1, 5; IV, 4, 15.

Mitrẫvárunau, du., Mitra and Varu*n*a, I, 71, 9[2]; 75, 5; III, 20, 5.

mítrya, belonging to one's allies, II, 6, 7.

mithẫs, mutually, I, 26, 9;—together, I, 68, 8.

mithuná, twin, I, 144, 4.

miyédha, sacrificial meal, III, 19, 1; 5.

miyedhya, sacrificial, I, 26, 1;—holy: I, 36, 9; 44, 5.

mish: ní mishati, he closes his eyes, III, 29, 14.

míh, mist, I, 79, 2; 141, 13.

mî, to break (a law): minanti, I, 69, 7; yásya vratám ná mî̃yate, II, 8, 3;—to impair: minâti, I, 71, 10;—minát, fading, V, 2, 1[2];—ẫ aminanta (Sa*m*hitâ text: °ntañ), they were disparaged, I, 79, 2[1];—âmémyâne ity â-mémyâne, constantly destroying, I, 96, 5;—prá minanti, they diminish, III, 28, 4; pra-minatá*h*, trespassing, IV, 3, 13; prá minẫti, he destroys, V, 7, 4.

mî*dh*vá*m*s, bountiful, I, 27, 2; II, 8, 1; III, 16, 3; IV, 3, 5; 5, 1; 15, 5.

mu*k*, to loosen: mú*k*yase, I, 31, 4.

múd, joy, I, 145, 4.

mumukshú, striving to break loose, I, 140, 4.

muhu*h*-gír, the sudden devourer, I, 128, 3.

mûrdhán, head: mûrdhẫ divá*h*, I, 59, 2; III, 2, 14; mûrdhẫnam tatápate, IV, 2, 6;—summit: mûrdhán ya*g*ñásya, II, 3, 2.

mr*i*, to die: mamrúshî*h*, I, 140, 8.

mr*i*: prá mr*i*nîhi, crush, IV, 4, 5.

mr*i*ktá-vâhas, carrying away injury, V, 18, 2[2].

mr*i*gá, animal, I, 145, 5.

mr*ik*, to injure: mar*k*áyati, mr*i*kshîsh*t*a, I, 147, 4; 5; V, 3, 7.

mr*ig*, to rub: mar*g*áyanta*h*, I, 60, 5; marmr*ig*énya, to be smoothed down, I, 189, 7; II, 10, 1;—to clean, brighten: marmr*ig*má, III, 18, 4; marmr*ig*ata, IV, 1,

14; mármrigatah, IV, 2, 19; margayema, IV, 4, 8; marmrigyánte, IV, 15, 6; margayanta, they have cleansed themselves, V, 3, 3[1];—to groom: mriganti, V, 1, 7; mrigyate, V, 1, 8;—pári marmrigyate, purifies, I, 95, 8[2].

mrid, to be merciful: mrilaya, I, 12, 9; mrila, I, 36, 12; 94, 12; IV, 9, 1.

mrilayát-tama, most merciful, I, 94, 14.

mrilîká, mercy, IV, 1, 3; 5.

mris: abhí mrisate, he strokes, I, 145, 4; ná abhi-mríse, not to be touched, II, 10, 5.

mrish, to forgive: mîmrishah, I, 31, 16; to forget: mấ prá marshishthâh, I, 71, 10; ná tát pramríshe, it should not be slighted, III, 9, 2.

melí, roaring (?), III, 26, 9[1]; IV, 7, 11[2].

métri, builder, IV, 6, 2.

médas, fat, III, 21, 1; 2; 4; 5[1].

médha, sacrifice, I, 77, 3.

medhấ, wisdom, V, 27, 4.

médhira, wise, I, 31, 2; 127, 7; 142, 11; III, 1, 3; 21, 4.

médhya, holy, V, 1, 12.

Médhya-atithi, I, 36, 10[1]; 11; 17[1].

ménâ, woman, I, 95, 6.

yaksh with prá, to aspire after: pra-yákshan vásu, II, 5, 1; prayákshe, III, 7, 1.

yakshá, a spirit, IV, 3, 13[1],[3] (bis).

yag, to sacrifice: yákshi, I, 13, 1; 31, 17; 36, 6; yáshtave, I, 13, 6; yagñám yakshatâm, I, 13, 8; arvấñkam yákshva, I, 45, 10; yágadhyai, III, 4, 3; áyagah hotrám, III, 17, 2; yát yágâsi, III, 19, 4[2]; dhruvám ayâh, III, 29, 16; yagáthâya, see yagátha;—áva yakshva, cause, by sacrificing, to go away, IV, 1, 5;—ấ yágati, procures (blessings) by sacrificing, I, 26, 3; â-yágase, I, 94, 2; ấ yaga, produce by sacrifice, I, 188, 9; ấ yagasva, obtain by sacrificing, III, 1, 22; â-yágante, they bring hither by sacrifice, III, 4, 2; ấ yakshat, V, 13, 3[1].

yagatá, to be worshipped, worshipful, I, 59, 7; 128, 8; II, 5, 8; III, 5, 3; IV, 1, 1[2]; 15, 8; V, 1, 11; 8, 1.

yágatra, deserving worship, worshipful, I, 65, 2[1], &c.

yagátha, the sacrificing, sacrifice: yagáthâya, III, 4, 1; 5, 9; 17, 1; 19, 5; V, 1, 2; 11, 2.

yágamâna, sacrificer, I, 127, 2; V, 26, 5.

yágishtha, best sacrificer, I, 36, 10; 44, 5; 58, 7; 77, 1; 127, 1; 128, 1; 149, 4; II, 6, 6; III, 10, 7; 13, 1; 14, 5; IV, 1, 4; 19; 2, 1; 7, 1; 5; 8, 1; V, 14, 2.

yágîyams, the best, or excellent, sacrificer, II, 9, 4; III, 4, 3; 17, 5; 19, 1; IV, 6, 1; V, 1, 5; 6; 3, 5.

yagñá, sacrifice, I, 1, 1; 4[1], &c.; II, 2, 1[1]; yagñấnâm adhvarasríyam, I, 44, 3[2]; mûrdhán yagñásya, II, 3, 2; yagñásya netári, II, 5, 2; rudrám yagñấnâm, III, 2, 5[1]; ketúm yagñấnâm, III, 3, 3; 11, 3; 29, 5; pitấ yagñấnâm, III, 3, 4; yagñám-yagñam, III, 6, 10; yagñásya netấ prathamásya, III, 15, 4.

yagñá-bandhu, kinsman of sacrifice, IV, 1, 9[1].

yagñá-vat, performing the sacrifice, III, 27, 6.

yagñá-vanas, accepting the sacrifice, IV, 1, 2.

yagñá-vâhas, fitting out the sacrifice as a vehicle, III, 8, 3[1]; 24, 1[1].

yagña-sấdh, performer or promoter of sacrifices, I, 96, 3; 128, 2.

yagña-sấdhana, accomplisher of sacrifices, I, 145, 3.

yagñíya, worshipful, I, 27, 10[2]; 72, 3; 4; 6; 73, 7; 148, 3[1]; II, 3, 4; III, 1, 21; 2, 13; 6, 3; IV, 1, 20; V, 10, 2;—sacrificial, V, 12, 1.

yágyu, sacrificer, I, 31, 13; III, 19, 4.

yágvan, sacrificer, I, 13, 12; III, 14, 1.

yat: yatate, he ranges (the wings of his army), I, 95, 7[2]; he unites with, I, 98, 1[2]; yátânâh, ranging themselves, III, 8, 9;—yátate, he stands firm, III, 16, 4;—

yâtayâse, thou wilt requite, V, 3, 9.
yáta*h*, since, I, 128, 4.
yatá-sru*k*, holding forth the sacrificial ladle(s), I, 142, 1; 5; III, 2, 5; 27, 6; IV, 2, 9; 12, 1;—to which the sacrificial ladles have been raised, III, 8, 7[1].
yád, adv. when (repeated twice), I, 141, 4[3].
yádi, when: yádi idám, when here (all this happened), I, 79, 2[3];—as I am, IV, 5, 11[2].
Yádu, I, 36, 18[1].
yantúr, governor, III, 27, 11[2].
yant*rí*, guider: yantắram dhînẩm, III, 3, 8;—guide, III, 13, 3.
yam, to command: yántâ, I, 27, 7;—to hold: yayantha, I, 59, 1; yámati, it can hold, I, 141, 11[3]; yemânám, fast-holding, IV, 1, 15; yemu*h*, they have held up, IV, 2, 14;—to bridle: *s*akéma yámam, I, 73, 10[1]; II, 5, 1[4]; III, 27, 3; yamate, he holds himself back, I, 127, 3;—áyâmi te, it has been offered to thee, III, 14, 2[1];—to lead: a*g*ur yamu*h*, V, 6, 10[2];—â-yemiré, they have turned themselves hither, III, 6, 8;—út ya*m*yamîti, he raises again and again, I, 95, 7; út ya*m*sate, may he lift up, I, 143, 7;—ní-yata, ruled, IV, 3, 9;—with prá, to bestow: prá ya*m*si, III, 1, 22; prá yandhi, bestow, IV, 2, 20; prá-yatâ, IV, 15, 8;—ví ya*m*sat, may he spread out, I, 189, 6;—sám aya*m*sta, he pulls in (the reins), I, 144, 3.
yamá, twin: yamá*h* ha *g*âtá*h* yamá*h* *g*áni-tvam, I, 66, 8[1].
Yayâti: yayâti-vát, I, 31, 17.
yáva, barley, I, 66, 3; corn, II, 5, 6.
yávasa, meadow, V, 9, 4.
yavasa-ád, grass-consuming, I, 94, 11.
yávish*th*a, the youngest (god, Agni), I, 26, 2; 44, 4; 141, 4; 10; 147, 2; 189, 4; II, 6, 6; 7, 1; III, 15, 3; 19, 4; IV, 2, 10; 13; 4, 6; 11; 12, 3; 4; V, 1, 10; 3, 11.
yávish*th*ya, youngest (Agni), I, 36, 6; 15; 44, 6; III, 9, 6; 28, 2; V, 8, 6; 26, 7.
yávya, bliss in crops, I, 140, 13.
ya*s*á*h*-tama, most glorious, II, 8, 1.
ya*s*ás, bringing glory, glorious, I, 1, 3; 31, 8; 60, 1; II, 3, 5; III, 1, 19; V, 15, 1; ya*s*ása*h* (fem.), III, 1, 11[2,3]; ya*s*ásâ gó*h*, through the brilliant (milk?) of the cow, IV, 1, 16[4]; mártasya ya*s*ásâ, through the mortal's brilliant (offering), V, 8, 4[1].
yá*s*asvat, glorious, I, 79, 1[4]; III, 16, 6.
yahú, young son: sahasa*h* yaho íti, I, 26, 10[1]; 74, 5[1]; 79, 4.
yahvá, vigorous, I, 36, 1[2]; III, 2, 9[1]; 3, 8; 5, 5; 9; 28, 4; IV, 5, 6; V, 16, 4[3]; restless, III, 1, 12[5]; IV, 5, 2; 7, 11;—young, V, 1, 1;—yahvî́*h*, new, I, 59, 4;—saptá yahvî́*h*, I, 71, 7[2]; 72, 8[1]; III, 1, 4[1]; IV, 13, 3;—divá*h* yahvî́*h*, young (daughters), III, 1, 6; 9[4];—yahvî́ íti mâtárâ, I, 142, 7[2]; V, 5, 6.
yâ, to go: yẩmi rátnam, I pray for treasure, I, 58, 7[3]; yẩsat, may he drive on, I, 71, 6[3];—á*kkh*a yâhi, come hither, I, 31, 17; devẩn á*kkh*a yẩtave, I, 44, 4[1];—ava-yâtẩm (conj. ava-yâtẩ), I, 94, 12[1]; áva yâsisîsh*th*â*h*, mayest thou deprecate, IV, 1, 4.
Yâtú, a bad demon, V, 12, 2[1].
yâtu-*g*ú, inciting demons, IV, 4, 5.
yâtu-mẩvat, ally of the Yâtus: yâtu-mẩvata*h*, I, 36, 20.
yẩt*ri*, avenger (?), I, 70, 11[3].
yẩma, procession, V, 3, 12.
yẩman, way, III, 2, 14; 29, 6[1].
yu: yúyûshata*h*, they try to draw towards themselves, I, 144, 3;—yuyodhí, drive away, I, 189, 1; 3; II, 6, 4; yódhi, V, 3, 9[2];—ẩ yuvámâna*h*, seizing, I, 58, 2; â-yóyuvâna*h*, drawing towards himself, IV, 1, 11;—ví yoshat, may he be deprived of, IV, 2, 9.
yú, going: yó*h*, I, 74, 7[2].
yuktá, see yu*g*.
yuktá-grâvan, who sets to work the press-stones, III, 4, 9.
yugá, generation, tribe: mẩnushâ yugẩ, I, 144, 4; II, 2, 2;—age: yugé-yuge, III, 26, 3.
yu*g*, to harness, yoke: yu*g*ânám, I, 65, 1[1,3]; áyukthâ*h*, I, 94, 10; ayukshata, III, 26, 4; dákshi*n*â

yugyate, V, 1, 3[3]; yuktá, V, 27, 2; 3[4];—to join: nrí-bhih yuktáh, I, 69, 8;—yuñgé, I make ready, III, 1, 1[4].
yúg, share: yúgam, V, 20, 1[1].
yúgya, companion: yúgyebhih, I, 145, 4[2].
yúdh, the fighting, I, 59, 5; battle, I, 140, 10; V, 25, 6.
yuvatí, young woman: dása yuvatáyah, I, 95, 2[2];—III, 1, 6; V, 2, 1; 2; 4[2].
yúvan, young, I, 12, 1; 27, 13; 71, 8; 141, 10; 144, 4; III, 23, 1; IV, 1, 12; V, 1, 6; yúvâ suvấsâh, III, 8, 4[1];—see yávishtha, yávishthya.
yushmád, pron.: vah, dativus ethicus, I, 143, 7[1]; vâm, III, 4, 4[1].
yûthá, herd, I, 58, 5; IV, 2, 18; V, 2, 4[1].
yū́pa, sacrificial post, (I, 13, 11[1]); V, 2, 7.
yóga, the yoking, II, 8, 1;—setting to work, III, 27, 11.
yogyấ, the harnessing, III, 6, 6.
yóni, womb, I, 149, 2; II, 3, 11; 9, 3; ritásya yónau, I, 65, 4; III, 1, 11; IV, 1, 12; V, 21, 4[1]; úparasya yónau, I, 79, 3[3]; ghritásya yónau, III, 1, 7; rágasah yónau, IV, 1, 11;—couch, I, 66, 5;—receptacle, I, 140, 1[2];—birthplace, I, 144, 2; III, 29, 10;—abode: samâné yónâ, I, 144, 4; su-kritásya yónau, III, 29, 8;—place, III, 5, 7[1]; home, IV, 3, 2.
yóshan, young female: dása yóshanah, I, 141, 2[4]; abhrâtárah ná yóshanah, IV, 5, 5[2].
yós: sám yóh, with luck and weal, I, 189, 2; III, 17, 3; 18, 4; IV, 12, 5.

ramh, to hasten: rarahâṇấh, I, 148, 3.
rámhyâ, rapidly, IV, 1, 3.
rákshas, pl., rákshâmsi, the Rakshas (devils), I, 79, 12; IV, 3, 14; V, 2, 9; 10.
rakshás, sorcerer, I, 36, 15; 76, 3; 79, 6; III, 15, 1; IV, 4, 1; 4, 15.
rakshasvín, sorcerer, I, 12, 5; 36, 20.
raghú, swift, IV, 5, 13.
raghu-drú, quickly running, I, 140, 4; V, 6, 2.
raghu-yát, quickly moving, IV, 5, 9.
raghu-syád, swift runner, I, 140, 4; III, 26, 2; IV, 5, 9; V, 25, 6.
rágas, air, atmosphere, aerial space, I, 58, 1; 5; 79, 1; 141, 7; 149, 4; II, 2, 3; 4; III, 1, 5; 4, 4[3]; 26, 7; rágasah yónau, IV, 1, 11[2].
rágishtha, straightest, I, 79, 3.
ran, to rejoice, delight: ranáyanta, I, 147, 1; rananti, III, 7, 5; ranáyanta, IV, 7, 7; havyấ rányati, V, 18, 1[2].
rána, battle: ráne-rane, I, 74, 3.
ranv, to be joyful: ranvité íti, II, 3, 6.
ranvá, pleasant, lovely, I, 65, 5; 66, 3–5; 128, 8; II, 4, 4; IV, 1, 8;—gay, joyous, cheerful, I, 144, 7; II, 4, 6; III, 26, 1; IV, 7, 5; V, 7, 2.
rátna, treasure: yấmi rátnam, I, 58, 7[3]; vásu rátnâ, III, 2, 11; kridhí rátnam, III, 18, 5.
ratna-dhấ, bestower of treasures, II, 1, 7.
ratna-dhấtama, highest bestower of treasures, I, 1, 1; V, 8, 3.
ratna-dhéya, bestowal of treasures, IV, 13, 1.
rátna-vat, blessed with treasures, III, 28, 5.
rátha, chariot: rátham-iva védyam, II, 2, 3[2]; ráthah ná sásnih, like a victorious car, III, 15, 5.
rathirá, charioteer, III, 1, 17; 26, 1.
rathī́, drawing a chariot: ásvâsah rathyàh, I, 148, 3; III, 6, 8;—charioteer, I, 77, 3; III, 3, 6; IV, 15, 2; rathī́h adhvarấnâm, I, 44, 2; rathī́h ritásya, III, 2, 8; IV, 10, 2.
ráthya, of a chariot: átyah ráthyah, II, 4, 4; ráthyâ-iva (supply kakrấ?), II, 4, 6[2]; kakrám ráthyâ-iva (rather ráthyam-iva?), IV, 1, 3[1].
rad, to cleave: rátsi, V, 10, 1.
radhrá: radhrásya for âdhrásya, (I, 31, 14[2]).
rápas: rápâmsi, Pada text instead of ápâmsi, I, 69, 8[2].
rabh: sám rebhire, they have embraced, I, 140, 8;—abhí sám rabhante, they take care of, III, 29, 13.

rábhas, vigour, I. 145, 3.
rabhasá, robust, II, 10, 4^1; fierce, III, 1, 8.
rám-su, joyously, II, 4, 5.
rám-su*g*ihva, with lovely tongue, IV, 1, 8.
rayí, riches, treasures: kshapấ-vân rayî*n*ấm, I, 70, 5^1.
rayi-páti, treasure-lord: rayi-páti*h* rayî*n*ấm, I, 60, 4; 72, 1; II, 9, 4.
rayi-víd, gainer of wealth, II, 1, 3; III, 7, 3.
rayisháh, conqueror of wealth, I, 58, 3.
ráva, shouting, roaring, I, 71, 2; 94, 10; agné ráve*n*a (Pada: agné*h* ávena), I, 128, 5^1.
ra*s*anấ, rope, (I, 13, 11^1); IV, 1, 9^2; V, 1, 3^1.
ra*s*mí, ray, I, 59, 3; IV, 13, 4; 14, 2; 3; V, 19, 5;—saptá ra*s*máya*h*, seven rays or reins, II, 5, 2;—rein, I, 141, 11; III, 7, 9^1; *ri*tásya ra*s*mím, V, 7, 3.
rása, sap, I, 71, 5^1.
Ráhûga*n*a, plur., the Rahûga*n*as, I, 78, 5^1.
râ, to give: râsate, I, 96, 8; rarishe, II, 1, 5; rarimá, II, 5, 7; rárâ*n*â*h*, a liberal giver, III, 1, 22; IV, 1, 5; 2, 10.
râ*g*, to be king or lord: rấ*g*antam adhvarấ*n*âm, I, 1, 8; 45, 4; râ*g*asi, I, 36, 12; 188, 1; râ*g*an (conj. rấ*g*an), I, 79, 6^1;—virấ*g*atha, I, 188, 4;—ádhi virấ*g*ata*h*, you reign high, I, 188, 6^1.
rấ*g*an, king, I, 59, 3; 5, &c.; rấ*g*ânâ mitrấváru*n*â, I, 71, 9^2; rấ*g*â Váru*n*a*h*, II, 1, 4; IV, 1, 2; rấ*g*â vi*s*ấm, II, 2, 8; vasấm rấ*g*ânam, V, 2, 6^1.
râtá-havya, who has made offerings: râtá-havya*h*, I, 31, 13^4;—to whom offerings are made, IV, 7, 7.
râtí, gift, I, 60, 1; II, 1, 16; III, 2, 4; 19, 2^2.
râtínî, full of gifts, III, 19, 2; IV, 6, 3.
Râti-sấ*k*, pl., the Râtisâ*k* or 'bounteous' gods, II, 1, 13.
rấtrî, night, I, 94, 7.
râdh, to worship: árâdhi, I, 70, 8^2;—mấ na*h* rîradha*h*, give us not up, III, 16, 5.
rấdhas, abundance, wealth, I, 94, 15; II, 9, 4.
rấdhya, beneficent, IV, 11, 3.
rấmyâ, night, II, 2, 8.
râyá*h*-kâma, desirous of riches, I, 78, 2.
ri, to let loose: ári*n*ât, III, 3, 11^1;—svádhiti*h*-iva rî́yate, it streams, V, 7, 8^1;—ní ri*n*âti, he destroys, I, 127, 4; 148, 4.
ri*k*: ririkvấ*m*sa*h*, abandoning, I, 72, 5^3;—with prá, to exceed: prá riri*k*e, I, 59, 5; prá ri*k*yase, II, 1, 15; prá rikthâ*h*, III, 6, 2.
ríp, deceiver: priyám ripá*h* ágram, III, 5, 5^1.
ripú, impostor, I, 36, 16; 147, 3; 148, 5; 189, 5; IV, 3, 13^3; V, 3, 11; ripáve (conj. ripáva*h*?), V, 12, 4^1.
ririkshú, who tries to harm, I, 189, 6.
ri*s*ấdas, triumphant with riches (?), I, 26, 4^1; 77, 4^1.
rish, to do harm: ríshata*h*, I, 12, 5; 36, 15; mấ rishâma, may we suffer no harm, I, 94, 1–14; IV, 12, 5; resháyanti, I, 148, 5; ríshate, I, 189, 5; V, 3, 12.
rísh, harm, I, 98, 2.
risha*n*yú, harmful foe, I, 148, 5.
rih, to lick: rérihat sádâ, licking and licking, I, 140, 9; rihánti ū́dha*h*, I, 146, 2;—pári rihán, licking everywhere, I, 140, 9.
rî, see ri.
ru: róruvat, roaring, I, 140, 6.
rukmá, gold, I, 96, 5^3; IV, 10, 5; 6; V, 1, 12.
rukmín, with golden ornaments, I, 66, 6.
ru*k*, to shine: ro*k*ate, I, 58, 2, &c.; rurukvấn, I, 149, 3; su-rú*k*â ru*k*âná*h*, III, 15, 6; ro*k*ata, IV, 10, 6^1;—áti ro*k*ase, thou shinest forth, I, 94, 7;—prá aro*k*ayat, it filled with light, I, 143, 2;—viró*k*amânam, I, 95, 2; 9; ví ro*k*ase, II, 7, 4; ví-ruru*k*ú*h*, they have made shine, IV, 7, 1.
ru*g*, to break: ru*g*an, I, 71, 2; ádrim ru*g*ema, IV, 2, 15^3;—ví ru*g*a, destroy, IV, 3, 14.
Rudrá, a name of Agni, I, 27, 10^3; IV, 3, 1^1; rudrám ya*g*ñấnâm,

III, 2, 5[1];—Rudra, the father of the Maruts, II, 1, 6; IV, 3, 6; 7; V, 3, 3[2];—pl., the Rudras, I, 45, 1; 58, 3; III, 8, 8; 20, 5.
Rudríya, Rudra-like: rudríyâ, I, 72, 4[1];—pl., the sons of Rudra, III, 26, 5.
rudh: ví ródhat, he grows up, I, 67, 9.
rúp: rupá*h*? IV, 5, 7[1]; 8.
rú*s*at, bright, brilliant, III, 29, 3; IV, 3, 9; 5, 15; 11, 1; V, 1, 2;—red, IV, 7, 9.
rú*s*at-ûrmi, with fiery waves, I, 58, 4[4].
ruh: vayấ*h*-iva ánu rohate, he mounts up as on the branches (of a tree), II, 5, 4[1].
rûpá, appearance, I, 71, 10; 95, 8; IV, 11, 1[2].
réku, empty (?), IV, 5, 12[1].
rék*n*as, property, I, 31, 14.
re*g*, to tremble: áre*g*etâm, I, 31, 3; re*g*ante, they roll forward, I, 143, 3.
rétas, seed, sperm, I, 68, 8[1]; 71, 8; 128, 3; réta*h* (read répa*h*), IV, 3, 7[2]; divá*h* ná rétasâ, V, 17, 3[3].
répas, sin: répa*h* (conj. for réta*h*), IV, 3, 7[2]; stain, IV, 6, 6.
rebhá, singer, I, 127, 10[5].
revát, rich: revấn, I, 27, 12;—revát, with riches, I, 79, 5; 95, 11; II, 2, 6; 9, 6; III, 7, 10; 18, 4; 5; 23, 2; 4; V, 23, 4.
resha*n*á, harm-doer, I, 148, 5.
raí, wealth: rấya*h*, gen., I, 68, 10[1]; yấsat râyấ sa-rátham, I, 71, 6[3]; râyá*h* dúra*h*, I, 72, 8; râyá*h* su-dhúra*h*, I, 73, 10[1]; râyá*h* *s*i*s*îhi, III, 16, 3[2].
roká, shining light, III, 6, 7.
ro*k*aná, light: ví*s*vâ divá*h* ro*k*anấ, I, 146, 1; III, 12, 9; divá*h* ro*k*ané, III, 6, 8; trî́ ro*k*anấni, I, 149, 4; ut-tamá*h* ro*k*anấnâm, III, 5, 10; ro*k*ané sū́ryasya, III, 22, 3.
ro*k*ana-sthấ, dwelling in light, III, 2, 14.
ro*k*ís, splendour, V, 26, 1.
ródasî, du., the two worlds, Heaven and Earth, I, 31, 3, &c.; I, 59, 2; 4[1]; III, 7, 9[2]; V, 16, 4[3].
ródhas, bank, IV, 5, 1[2].
róman, hair, I, 65, 8.
róhita, red (horses), I, 94, 10; II, 10, 2; III, 6, 6; IV, 2, 3; 6, 9.
rohit-a*s*va, lord of red horses, I, 45, 2; IV, 1, 8.

loká, world: lokám *g*âmím, III, 2, 9[4];—své u loké, space, III, 29, 8;—surabhaú u loké, in the sweet-smelling place, V, 1, 6; lokám syonám, pleasant freedom, V, 4, 11.

váktva, (speech) to be uttered, III, 26, 9.
vákvan? I, 141, 7[1].
vákvara, moving crookedly: vákvarî íti, I, 144, 6[1].
vaksh, to grow: ukshitá, I, 36, 19; II, 3, 6; V, 8, 7; ukshámâ*n*am rá*g*asi, II, 2, 4; vavakshe, III, 5, 8; vaváksha, IV, 7, 11;—áti vavakshitha, III, 9, 3[1];—abhí vavakshe, he has grown up, I, 146, 2.
vaksha*n*e-sthấ? V, 19, 5[1].
vakshátha, growth, IV, 5, 1.
vakshî́? V, 19, 5[1].
va*k*, to pronounce (a prayer): vo*k*éma, I, 74, 1; 75, 2; va*k*yáte, I, 142, 4[2];—ánu vó*k*at bráhmâ*n*i, II, 5, 3[1];—with prá, to announce: prá vo*k*a*h*, I, 27, 4; pra-vó*k*ati, V, 27, 4; prá vavâ*k*a, he indicates, I, 67, 8.
vá*k*as, word: vá*k*a*h*, instr., I, 26, 2[2]; adroghé*n*a vá*k*asâ satyám, according to thy guileless word, III, 14, 6;—prayer, I, 26, 10, &c.
va*k*asyấ, eloquence, II, 10, 6.
va*k*asyú, eloquent, V, 14, 6.
va*ñk*, to stir: va*k*yámâna, III, 6, 1; va*k*yántâm, may they move along, III, 6, 2.
vat: ápi vâtayâmasi, we render attentive, I, 128, 2[1].
vatsá, calf, I, 72, 2[1]; 95, 1[1]; 4[2]; 146, 3; II, 2, 2.
vadhá, weapon, I, 94, 9; V, 4, 6.
van, to accept: vanóshi, I, 31, 13[4]; vanishî́sh*t*a, I, 127, 7; vaner íti vane*h*, II, 6, 1; vanvâná*h*, III, 8, 2;—to gain, win: vanóshi, I, 31, 14[1]; vavne, I, 36, 17; vanéma, I, 70, 1[2]; II, 5, 7; vanvánta*h*, attaining (their aim), II, 4, 9; vanate, may he obtain, III, 19, 1; V, 4, 3;—to conquer, overcome: vanuyâma, I, 73, 9;

vanavat, V, 3, 5; vanuyâma, V, 3, 6;—vanúsha*h*, addicted to, eager, I, 150, 3; III, 27, 11; vavána*h*, thou wilt hold dear, IV, 11, 2;—to grant: vanate, V, 3, 10;—ấ vanase, win thou, I, 140, 11;—sám vánâmahe, we get together, V, 7, 3.
vána, forest = fuel, wood, I, 58, 5[1]; II, 4, 6[1]; III, 1, 13[1]; 9, 2; 23, 1[1]; váne ấ vîtám, IV, 7, 6[1];—tree: gárbha*h* vánânâm, I, 70, 3; 9;—forest: vánâ-iva yát sthirám, I, 127, 3[5];—I, 128, 3[2], &c.
vanád, eater of the forests, II, 4, 5[2].
vanargú, walking in the forest, I, 145, 5[1].
vánaspáti, lord of the forest, tree (i.e. sacrificial post), I, 13, 11[1]; 142, 11[1]; 188, 10; II, 3, 10; III, 4, 10[1]; 8, 1[1]; 3; 6; 11; V, 5, 10;—vánaspátîn prá minấti, V, 7, 4.
vánitri, winner, III, 13, 3.
vanín, wooden stick, I, 58, 4;—tree, I, 94, 10; 140, 2.
vand, to worship, salute: vandádhyai, I, 27, 1; III, 4, 3.
vandấru, reverer, I, 147, 2; V, 1, 12.
vándya, venerable, I, 31, 12; 79, 7; II, 7, 4.
vandhúra, chariot-seat: vandhúre-iva (conj. for vandhúrâ-iva), III, 14, 3[4].
vap: ấ ûpishe, thou pourest forth, I, 31, 9.
vapú*h*-tara, very marvellous, II, 3, 7.
vápusha: vápushâya darsatám, wonderful to behold, III, 2, 15.
vapushy, to wonder: vapushyan, III, 1, 4.
vapushyà, of marvellous appearance, IV, 1, 8; 12; V, 1, 9.
vápus, a wondrous sight, wonder, I, 141, 1; IV, 7, 9; wondrous body, wonderful shape, I, 141, 2[2]; 144, 3; 148, 1; III, 1, 8; 18, 5.
vaya*h*-k*ri*t, giver of strength: vaya*h*-k*rí*t, I, 31, 10.
vaya*h*-dhấ, giving vigour, I, 73, 1; II, 3, 9; IV, 3, 10.
vaya*h*-v*rí*dh, increaser of vital strength, V, 5, 6.
váyas, vigour, strength, vital power, I, 66, 4, &c.; váya*h*-vaya*h*, life after life, V, 15, 4.
vayấ, branch, I, 59, 1; II, 5, 4[1]; V, 1, 1.
vayí, weaver (?): vayyầ-iva, (II, 3, 6[1]).
vayúna, established order, rule: vidvấn vayúnâni, I, 72, 7[1]; 189, 1; III, 5, 6; vayúnâ návâ adhita, I, 144, 5[3]; 145, 5; vayúnam vâghátâm, III, 3, 4[2]; vayúne, in the due way, III, 29, 3[3];—kấ vayúnâ, what are the objects, IV, 5, 13.
vára, wish: mánasa*h* várâya, to thy mind's taste, I, 76, 1[1]; a choice boon, I, 140, 13; tis*rí*-bhya*h* ấ váram, according to the wish of the three (sisters), II, 5, 5; desire, II, 10, 6.
vára, the holding back: ná várâya, he is not to be kept back, I, 143, 5.
várivas, wide space, I, 59, 5.
Váru*n*a, I, 26, 4; 36, 4; 44, 14; 79, 3; 94, 12[1]; 16; 95, 11; 98, 3; 128, 7; 141, 9; 143, 4; II, 1, 4; III, 4, 2; 6; 5, 4; 14, 4; IV, 1, 2–5; 18; 2, 4; 3, 5; 13, 2; V, 3, 1; 5, 11; 26, 9.
várûtha, shelter, I, 58, 9; 148, 2; 189, 6.
varûthyà, protecting, V, 24, 1.
váre*n*ya, elect, desirable, excellent, I, 26, 2; 3; 7, &c.
vár*k*as, splendour, III, 8, 3; 22, 2; 24, 1.
vár*n*a, colour, I, 73, 7; II, 1, 12; 4, 5;—(bright) colour, splendour, II, 5, 5; IV, 5, 13;—appearance, I, 96, 5;—race, II, 3, 5[1].
vartaní, way: vartanî̀*h* (Pada: vartaní*h*), I, 140, 9[3];—III, 7, 2.
várdhana, increaser: várdhanam pitú*h*, I, 140, 3[2].
várpas, sight, shape, I, 140, 5[1]; 7; 141, 3.
várman, armour, I, 31, 15; 140, 10.
varshá-nirnig, clothed in rain, III, 26, 5.
várshish*th*a, most powerful, III, 13, 7; 16, 3; 26, 8; V, 7, 1.
várshman, summit: várshman divá*h*, III, 5, 9; várshman p*ri*thivyấ*h*, III, 8, 3.
vavấtâ, a favourite wife, IV, 4, 8.
vavrá, prison, IV, 1, 13.

vavrí, cover, V, 19, 1.
vaś, to be willing, long for, love: uśatá*h*, I, 12, 4; uśatî́*h* uśántam, I, 71, 1; uśatấ*h* (read uśaté?), I, 71, 6[2]; uśmási, I, 94, 3; uśatî́*h*, I, 145, 4[5]; II, 4, 3; vákshi, III, 1, 1[1]; uśántam uśânấ*h*, III, 5, 7; vâvaśânấ*h*, III, 20, 1; vâvaśâna, III, 22, 1; uśatî́, loving, IV, 3, 2;—ánu vash*t*i, I, 127, 1;—abhí vash*t*i, IV, 1, 8.
vaśấ, heifer, II, 7, 5.
vaśín, lord, III, 23, 3.
váshaṭ-k*ri*ti, the word Vasha*t*, I, 31, 5.
vas, to shine: u*kkh*ántîm, I, 71, 1; ûshu*h*, III, 7, 10; *ri*tám avasran, IV, 2, 19[1].
vas, to clothe: vásishva, I, 26, 1; vâsaya (Sa*m*hitâ: vâsayâ), clothe, or I clothe, I, 140, 1[1]; śríyam vásâna*h*, II, 10, 1; śukrấ vásânâ*h*, arraying themselves in brightness, III, 8, 9; rúśat vásâna*h*, clothed in brilliancy, IV, 5, 15;—pári vásâna*h*, III, 1, 5[2].
vas, to dwell: avâsayat, he has made depart, III, 7, 3;—práti avâsaya*h*, thou hast harboured, III, 1, 17;—sam-vásânâ*h*, dwelling together, IV, 6, 8.
vás, dwelling (?): vasấm rấ*g*ânam, V, 2, 6[1].
vasatí, dwelling, I, 31, 15; 66, 9[1].
vásana, garment, I, 95, 7.
vasavyà, wealth, II, 9, 5[1].
vásish*th*a, the highest Vasu, II, 9, 1.
vásu, excellent: vásvîbhi*h* dhîtí-bhi*h*, III, 13, 5[1];—wealth, treasure, goods, I, 27, 5, &c.; víśva*h* vásu*h* (conj. víśvâ vásû), I, 128, 6[3]; vásva*h* rấ*g*ati, I, 143, 4; vásu rátnâ, III, 2, 11; goods, or Vasus, III, 19, 2[2];—see vásyas.
Vásu, ep. of Agni, I, 31, 3; 44, 3; 45, 9; 60, 4; 79, 5; 127, 1[1]; II, 7, 1; III, 4, 1[2]; 15, 3; 18, 2; 19, 3; 21, 5; IV, 5, 15; V, 3, 10; 12; 6, 1; 2; 24, 2; 25, 1; vásu*h* vásûnâm asi, I, 94, 13; vásu*h* vásu-bhi*h*, I, 143, 6;—pl., the Vasus, a class of gods, I, 45, 1; 58, 3; 143, 1; II, 3, 4[1]; III, 8, 8; 19, 2[2]; 20, 5; IV, 12, 6; V, 3, 8.
vásu-dâvan, giver of goods, II, 6, 4.
vásu-dhiti, dispenser of goods, I, 128, 8.
vásu-dhiti, place of wealth, IV, 8, 2[1].
vásu-pati, lord of wealth, II, 1, 11; 6, 4; V, 4, 1.
vasu-yấ, desire for wealth, I, 97, 2.
vasu-yú, desirous of goods, I, 128, 8; III, 26, 1; V, 3, 6; 25, 9.
vasuvít-tama, the greatest acquirer of wealth, I, 45, 7.
vásu-śravas, renowned as Vasu (or, as goods), V, 24, 2.
vástu, daybreak: vásto*h* ushása*h*, I, 79, 6.
vast*rí*, illuminator: kshapấm vastấ, (I, 1, 7[1]).
vástra, clothing, I, 26, 1.
vásman, cloth, IV, 13, 4.
vásyas, better things, I, 31, 18;—bliss, I, 141, 12; welfare, II, 1, 16;—greater wealth, II, 9, 2;—wealthier, IV, 2, 20.
vah, to carry: vákshi, (III, 1, 1[1]); havyấya vó*ḷh*ave, I, 45, 6; III, 29, 4;—abhí vakshi vấ*g*am, III, 15, 5[2];—ấ vakshati, may he conduct, I, 1, 2; ấ vakshat, may he carry hither, III, 5, 9; ấ vakshi, bring, III, 14, 2; â-váhantî, carrying (bliss), IV, 14, 3[2].
vahát, stream, III, 7, 4[2].
váhish*th*a, (horses) most ready to drive, IV, 13, 4; 14, 4.
váhni, driven (on a chariot): váhni-bhi*h* devaí*h*, I, 44, 13[1];—carrier (of the gods), I, 60, 1; 128, 4[3]; III, 1, 1; 5, 1; 11, 4[1]; 20, 1[1];—carrying: váhni*h* âsấ, I, 76, 4[1];—horse: váhnaya*h*, III, 6, 2[2];—váhni and vấhas, (I, 127, 8[1]).
váhni-tama, best carrier (of the gods), IV, 1, 4.
vâ, to blow: vấta*h* ánu vâti, I, 148, 4;—áva vâti, he blazes down, I, 58, 5.
vâ: vivâsasi, thou winnest, I, 74, 9;—â-vívâsati, (who) invites, I, 12, 9; 58, 1; â-vívâsasi, thou invitest, I, 31, 5[2];—ấ vivâsanti, they seek to win, IV, 11, 5.
vâ, to weave: sa*m*váyantî íti sam-váyantî, II, 3, 6.
vâghát, worshipper, I, 31, 14; 36, 13[2]; 58, 7; IV, 2, 13; invoking,

III, 2, 1; 3, 8; 8, 10; sacrificer, III, 3, 4.
vâ̆k, word, I, 79, 10.
vâ̆ga, strength, I, 27, 8[1,2]; 11; 77, 5; II, 1, 10[1]; 12; 2, 7; 4, 8; 6, 5; III, 10, 6; 11, 9; 19, 1; 22, 1; 25, 2; 3; 27, 1; 11; 29, 9; vâ̆gasya pátiḥ, I, 145, 1;—deed of strength, III, 12, 9;—booty, I, 27, 5, &c.;—prize, gain, III, 2, 3[1]; 4, &c.; abhí vakshi vâ̆gam, III, 15, 5[2];—race (striving for gain, contest for booty), I, 27, 7[1]; 9[1]; 36, 2; III, 27, 7; V, 23, 1.
Vâ̆ga, pl., the Vâgas, III, 26, 4[1].
vâ̆ga-gaṭhara, with booty in its belly, V, 19, 4.
vâ̆ga-pati, lord of booty, IV, 15, 3.
vâ̆ga-prasûta, bent on the prize, I, 77, 4[2].
vâgam-bhará, winning the prize, I, 60, 5; winning booty, IV, 11, 4.
vâgay, to run a race: vâgayán-iva, II, 8, 1[1];—to further strength: vâgáyantî íti, III, 14, 3[1];—to drive forward: vâgayate, IV, 7, 11;—to strive for gain: vâgayántî, V, 1, 3; vâga-yántaḥ, V, 4, 1.
vâga-yú, bent on victory, V, 10, 5;—eager for the race, V, 19, 3.
vâ̆ga-vat, bestowing strength, I, 31, 18.
vâ̆ga-sravas, renowned for strength, III, 2, 5.
vâga-sâ̆tama, highest winner of booty, I, 78, 3; III, 12, 4; V, 13, 5; 20, 1[1].
vâ̆ga-sâti, winning of the prize, III, 2, 7[1].
vâgín, strong, II, 2, 11; III, 6, 1;—the strong horse, racer, I, 66, 4[1], &c.; II, 5, 1[4]; III, 27, 3[1]; ásvaḥ ná vâgî́, III, 29, 6.
vâ̆gina, strength, III, 20, 2.
vâ̆ṇî, sound: saptá vâ̆ṇîḥ, III, 1, 6[1]; 7, 1[1].
vâ̆ta, wind, I, 79, 1; 148, 4; IV, 7, 10; 11; vâ̆taiḥ aruṇaíḥ, II, 1, 6; vâ̆tasya pathyâ̆bhiḥ, III, 14, 3; vâ̆tasya sárgaḥ, III, 29, 11[2]; vâ̆tasya pátman, V, 5, 7; Vâta, the god, IV, 3, 6.
vâ̆ta-kodita, stirred by the wind, I, 58, 4; 141, 7.
vâ̆ta-gûta, stirred or driven by the wind, I, 58, 4; 65, 8; 94, 10; 140, 4.
vâmá, happy, I, 141, 12;—pleasant (wealth), IV, 5, 13.
Vâyú, the god, I, 142, 12[1];—vâyú, wind, V, 19, 5.
vâ̆r, water, II, 4, 6; usríyâṇâm vâ̆ḥ-iva, IV, 5, 8.
vâ̆ra, treasure, I, 128, 6; V, 16, 2.
vâ̆ra, tail, II, 4, 4.
vâraṇá, stubborn, I, 140, 2.
vâ̆ra-vat, long-tailed, I, 27, 1.
vâ̆rya, excellent wealth, treasure, I, 26, 8; III, 8, 7; V, 16, 5[1]; 17, 5; desirable boon, I, 58, 3; III, 21, 2; V, 23, 3; best gifts, I, 149, 5; III, 11, 9.
vâs, to roar, low: avâsayaḥ, I, 31, 4[1]; vâvasânâ̆ḥ, I, 73, 6; vavâsire, II, 2, 2.
vâsrá, lowing, I, 95, 6.
vâ̆has, vehicle, (I, 127, 8[1]); III, 11, 7[1].
vâ̆hishṭha, which may best bring, V, 25, 7.
vi, to weave. See vâ.
ví, bird: vér íti véḥ, I, 72, 9[1]; 96, 6[2]; III, 5, 5[1]; 6; III, 7, 7[1]; IV, 5, 8[4]; váyaḥ, I, 141, 8; vayyâ̆-iva? II, 3, 6[1].
ví, away from, I, 150, 2.
ví-adhvan, straying everywhere, I, 141, 7.
vi-úsh, the break of dawn, V, 3, 8.
ví-ushṭi, dawning: ví-ushṭishu, I, 44, 3; 4; 8; III, 20, 1; ushásaḥ ví-ushṭau, at the break of dawn, III, 15, 2; IV, 1, 5; 14, 4.
ví-oman, heaven: paramé ví-omani, I, 143, 2; V, 15, 2.
vi-gâhá, diver, III, 3, 5.
vi-kakshaṇa, far-seeing, III, 3, 10.
ví-karshaṇi, dwelling among all tribes, I, 31, 6[4]; 78, 1; 79, 12; III, 2, 8; 11, 1.
ví-ketas, wise, I, 45, 2; II, 10, 1; 2; IV, 5, 2; 7, 3.
vig: vevigé íti, they are affrighted, I, 140, 3.
vigâ̆-van, continuing our race: sûnúḥ tánayaḥ vigâ̆-vâ, III, 1, 23.
vid, to find: vévidânâḥ, acquiring (or, exploring?), I, 72, 4; avidan (conj. ávidan), I, 72, 6[1].
vid, to know: yáthâ vidé, as it is

known, I, 127, 4; vidvā́n, knowing (with gen. and acc.), V, 1, 11[1];—pári véda, I, 31, 5[1]; —ví vidvā́n, distinguishing, I, 189, 7.

víd, knowledge: vidā́, I, 31, 18.

vidátha, sacrifice, I, 31, 6[2]; 60, 1[2]; 143, 7; III, 1, 1[2]; 18; 3, 3; 4, 5; 8, 5; 14, 1[1]; 27, 7[2]; IV, 6, 2; tr*i*tī́ye vidáthe, II, 4, 8[1]; —vidáthâ, sacrificial ordinances, III, 1, 2[3]; 26, 6[2];—sacrificial distribution, III, 28, 4; vidátheshu áhnâm, V, 3, 6[1];—assembly, II, 1, 4[3]; 16[2].

vidathyā̀, influential in council, (I, 31, 6[2]).

vidú*h*-tara*h*, the greatest sage, I, 31, 14; II, 3, 7.

vidús, possessed of knowledge, I, 71, 10[1].

vidmanā́-apas, active in wisdom, I, 31, 1[1].

vi-dyút, lightning, III, 1, 14; V, 10, 5.

vidyút-ratha, whose chariot is lightning, III, 14, 1.

vidh, to worship: vidhema, I, 36, 2; vidhatá*h*, I, 73, 1, &c.

vidh, vyadh, to pierce, to shoot: vídhya, IV, 4, 1.

Vidhartr*i*, he who keeps asunder all things, II, 1, 3[3].

ví-dharman, sphere, III, 2, 3;—disposer, V, 17, 2[1,3].

vip, to tremble: prá vepayanti, they make tremble, III, 26, 4.

víp, prayer, III, 3, 1[1]; 7; vipā́m gyótī*m*shi, III, 10, 5.

vipa*h*-*k*ít, knowing prayers, III, 3, 4[1]; 26, 9; 27, 2.

vipanyā́: vipanyā́yâ, in thy admirable way, III, 28, 5; vipanyā́, wonderfully, IV, 1, 12.

vipanyú, full of admiring praise, III, 10, 9.

vípra, priest, I, 27, 9, &c.; saptá víprâ*h*, III, 7, 7; IV, 2, 15[1].

vi-bhaktr*i*, distributor: vi-bhaktā́, I, 27, 6.

vi-bhâtí, resplendent, III, 6, 7.

vibhā́-van, resplendent, I, 58, 9; 59, 7; 66, 2; 69, 9; 148, 1; 4; III, 3, 9; IV, 1, 8; 12; V, 1, 9; 4, 2.

vibhâ-vasu, rich in splendour, I, 44, 10; III, 2, 2; V, 25, 2; 7[1].

vi-bhú, mighty, I, 31, 2; 141, 9; III, 6, 9; V, 4, 2; 5, 9; vibhvī́*h* (dúra*h*), I, 188, 5[1];—far-extending, I, 65, 10;—spreading, IV, 7, 1.

ví-bhr*i*tra, widely-spread, I, 71, 3[2]; 95, 2; wide-ranging, II, 10, 2.

ví-bhrâsh*t*i, shine, I, 127, 1.

vibhva-sáh, overpowering skilful men, V, 10, 7.

vi-mā́na, measure, III, 3, 4[2].

ví-yutâ? IV, 7, 7[1].

vi-rā́*g*, Prince, I, 188, 5.

virúkmat, shining, I, 127, 3.

ví-rûpa, of different shapes or forms, I, 70, 7[1]; 73, 7; 95, 1; III, 1, 13; 4, 6;—of different colour, V, 1, 4[1].

Vírûpa: virûpa-vát, I, 45, 3.

vi-roká, the bursting forth: ushása*h* vi-roké, III, 5, 2.

vivásvat, irradiating: vívasvat (conj. vivásvan), I, 44, 1[1]; vivásvatâ *k*ákshasâ, I, 96, 2[3].

Vivásvat, N. pr., I, 31, 3; 58, 1[1,2]; IV, 7, 4; V, 11, 3[2].

vivásvan, the shining forth: vívasvat (conj. vivásvan) ushása*h*, at the rising of the dawn, I, 44, 1[1].

vívi*k*i, separating, V, 8, 3[1].

ví*s*, house, clan, tribe: vi*s*é-vi*s*e, I, 27, 10[2], &c.; vi*s*ā́m ná ví*s*va*h*, I, 70, 4[2]; mā́nushî ví*t*, I, 72, 8; rā́*g*â vi*s*ā́m, II, 2, 8; vi*s*ā́m kavím vi*s*pátim, III, 2, 10; pura*h*-etā́ vi*s*ā́m mā́nushî*n*âm, III, 11, 5; ví*s*a*h* mártân, IV, 2, 3[2]; vi*s*á*h* átithi*h*, V, 18, 1; devā́sa*h* sárvayâ vi*s*ā́, the gods with all their folk, V, 26, 9.

vi-*s*íkshu, a hewer, II, 1, 10[3].

vi*s*páti, lord of the clans, I, 12, 2; 26, 7; 27, 12; 31, 11; 60, 2; 128, 7; II, 1, 8; III, 2, 10; 3, 8; 13, 5; V, 4, 3; 6, 5.

vi*s*pátnî, housewife, III, 29, 1[4].

vi*s*pā́, lord of clans, (I, 70, 4[2]).

ví*s*va, every one: vi*s*ā́m ná ví*s*va*h*, I, 70, 4[2]; ví*s*vam idám, this whole world, I, 98, 1; ví*s*ve devā́*h*, II, 3, 4[1]; V, 3, 1; 26, 4; ví*s*vam ít vidu*h*, III, 29, 15[1].

vi*s*vá-apsu? I, 148, 1[2].

vi*s*vá-âyu, having a full life, or, in whom all life dwells, I, 27, 3; 67, 6; 10; 73, 4; 128, 8; vi*s*vá-

âyu*h* (conj. vi*s*vá-âyo*h*), I, 68, 5[2].
vi*s*vá-âyus, adv., eternally (?), (I, 68, 5[2]).
vi*s*vá-k*r*ish*t*i, extending over all dominions, I, 59, 7; belonging to all races of men, III, 26, 5.
vi*s*vá-*k*árshan*i*, dwelling among all tribes, I, 27, 9[3]; III, 2, 15; V, 6, 3; 14, 6; 23, 4.
vi*s*vá-*g*anya, encompassing all people, III, 25, 3.
vi*s*vata*h*-mukha, whose face is turned everywhere, I, 97, 6; 7.
vi*s*vá-tûrti, all-victorious, II, 3, 8.
vi*s*vá-thâ, everywhere, I, 141, 9.
vi*s*vá-dar*s*ata, visible to all, I, 44, 10; 146, 5; V, 8, 3.
vi*s*vá-deva, accompanied by the Vi*s*ve devâ*h*, I, 142, 12.
vi*s*vá-devya, belonging to all gods, I, 148, 1; united with all the gods, III, 2, 5.
vi*s*vádhâ, everywhere, I, 141, 6; always, V, 8, 4.
vi*s*vá-dhâyas, possessing every refreshment, I, 73, 3; V, 8, 1.
vi*s*vá-bharas, supporter of everything, IV, 1, 19[1].
vi*s*vá-bhânu, all-brilliant, IV, 1, 3.
vi*s*vam-invá, all-embracing, I, 76, 2; —all-enlivener, III, 20, 3.
vi*s*vá-rûpa, all-shaped, I, 13, 10; assuming every shape, III, 1, 7.
vi*s*vá-vâra, rich in all boons, III, 4, 3; giver of all treasures, III, 17, 1; with all goods, V, 4, 7; rich in all treasures, V, 28, 1.
vi*s*va-víd, all-knowing, III, 19, 1;—omniscient, III, 29, 7; V, 4, 3.
vi*s*vá-vedas, all-possessor, possessor of all wealth, I, 12, 1; 36, 3; 44, 7; 128, 8; 143, 4; 147, 3; III, 20, 4; 25, 1; 26, 4; IV, 8, 1.
vi*s*vá-*s*rush*t*i, always listening, I, 128, 1.
Vi*s*va-sâman, V, 22, 1.
Vi*s*vấmitra, pl., the Vi*s*vâmitras, III, 1, 21; 18, 4.
vi*s*vấyu-poshas, lasting all our life, I, 79, 9[2].
vi*s*vấhâ, day by day, III, 16, 2.
vish, to accomplish: vivi*dd*h*i*, I, 27, 10; vévishat, busy, III, 2, 10.
víshu*n*a, manifold, IV, 6, 6;—turning oneself from one, V, 12, 5[1].
víshu-rûpa, in manifold shapes, V, 15, 4.
vish*t*á? I, 148, 1[1].
Vísh*n*u, II, 1, 3; IV, 3, 7; V, 3, 3.
vishpá*s*, descrier: vishpá*t*, I, 189, 6[1].
víshvak, in all directions, I, 36, 16; IV, 4, 2.
vi-sârá, expanse, I, 79, 1[1].
vi-stír, laid out: vi-stíra*h*, I, 140, 7[1].
vi-havá, the emulating call, III, 8, 10.
ví-hâyas, far-reaching, I, 128, 6[1]; whose energy expands roundabout, IV, 11, 4[1].
vî, to accomplish, pursue, perform eagerly: vivé*h* rápâ*m*si (rather vivér ápâ*m*si), I, 69, 8[2]; véshi (hotrám), I, 76, 4; vé*h*, II, 5, 3[2]; IV, 7, 8;—to come or approach eagerly, to move: véshi, I, 74, 4; 189, 7; IV, 9, 5; 6; vé*h*, he repairs, I, 77, 2; IV, 7, 7; vetu, I, 77, 4; véti, I, 141, 6; vîtáye, that they may eagerly come or partake, I, 74, 6; II, 2, 6[2]; see also vîtí;—vîhí, accept eagerly, III, 28, 3;—vyánta*h*, tending to I, 127, 5; vyantu, may they eagerly seek, III, 8, 7; vîhí m*ril*î*k*ám, love mercy, IV, 1, 5; mấ ve*h*, require not, IV, 3, 13;—ấ dûtyàm vivâya, he has undertaken the messengership, I, 71, 4[3];—úpa vetu, may he come, V, 11, 4;—prá-vîta, having conceived, III, 29, 3;—práti vihi, accept eagerly, III, 21, 5.
vî, to envelop. See vyâ.
vî́, eager: vî́*h*, I, 143, 6.
vî*l*ú, strong, safe, I, 127, 3; 5; IV, 3, 14;—fortress, I, 71, 2.
vî*l*ú-*g*ambha, with strong jaws, III, 29, 13.
vîtá, straight, IV, 2, 11.
vîtí, (sacrificial) feast: vîtáye, I, 13, 2; 74, 4; 142, 13; III, 13, 4; V, 26, 2.
vîtí-hotra, offerer of a feast (to the gods), III, 24, 2; V, 26, 3.
vîrá, hero, a manly son, I, 73, 3, &c.
vîrá-pe*s*as, adorned with heroes, IV, 11, 3[1].
vîrá-vat, with valiant heroes, I, 12, 11; 96, 8; III, 24, 5; V, 4, 11.

vîrávat-tama, high bliss of valiant offspring, I, 1, 3.
vîrúdh, plant, I, 67, 9; 141, 4; gárbha*h* vîrúdhâm, II, 1, 14.
vîryà, mighty deed, III, 12, 9;—heroic power, III, 25, 2.
v*ri*, to choose: v*rin*îmahe, I, 12, 1, &c.; v*rin*îté, he demands, I, 67, 1;—urâ*n*á*h*, choosing, III, 19, 2; IV, 6, 3; chosen, IV, 6, 4; 7, 8.
v*ri*, to hold back, hinder: varâte, I, 65, 6; váranta, IV, 6, 6; ávâri, IV, 6, 7;—ápa v*ri*dhi, open, II, 2, 7; ápa âvar íty âva*h*, he has opened, III, 5, 1; ápa vrán, they have uncovered, IV, 5, 8; ápa vran, they disclosed, IV, 2, 16;—kấmam â-várat, would he fulfil our desire, I, 143, 6;—pári-v*ri*ta, hidden, I, 144, 2;—see ûr*n*u.
v*ri*ktá-barhis, having spread the sacrificial grass, I, 12, 3[1]; III, 2, 5; 6; V, 23, 3;—where they spread sacrificial grass, V, 9, 2.
v*rig*ána, settlement, I, 60, 3[2]; 73, 2[2]; II, 2, 1[4]; 9;—enclosure, I, 128, 7;—masc.? I, 189, 8[2].
v*rig*iná, wrong, dishonest, IV, 1, 17; V, 3, 11; 12, 5.
v*rig*iná-vartani, following crooked ways, I, 31, 6[1,4].
v*riñg*, to trim: v*riñg*é, I, 142, 5[2];—to turn: v*rin*ákti, IV, 7, 10;—ấ v*ri*kshi, may I draw on myself, (I, 27, 13[2]);—pári v*rin*akti, he spares, III, 29, 6.
v*ri*trá, foe, I, 36, 8[1].
v*ri*tra-hátha, the killing of foes, III, 16, 1.
v*ri*tra-hán, slayer of foes or of V*ri*tra, I, 59, 6[1]; 74, 3; II, 1, 11; III, 12, 4[2]; 20, 4[2].
v*ri*trahán-tama, the greatest destroyer of enemies (or of V*ri*tra), I, 78, 4.
v*rí*thâ, lightly, I, 58, 4[1];—wildly, I, 140, 5.
v*ri*ddhá *s*o*k*is, mightily brilliant, V, 16, 3.
v*ri*dh, to increase, grow, &c.: várdhamânam, increasing, I, 1, 8, &c.; vav*ri*dhasva, be magnified, I, 31, 18; v*ri*dhé, for welfare, prosperity, III, 3, 8; 6, 10; IV, 2, 18; v*ri*ddhá, grown full of, V, 20, 2[1];—várdhanti, they nourish, I, 65, 4;—vardhayâmasi, we extol, I, 36, 11; vardhaya gíra*h*, make prosper, III, 29, 10;—ví vav*ri*dhe (conj. vivav*ri*dhé), I, 141, 5[2].
v*rí*dh, furtherer, III, 16, 2[2].
v*ri*dhá, helper, furtherer, (III, 16, 2[2]); IV, 2, 10.
v*ri*dhasâná, growing: v*ri*dhasânấsu, in the growing (plants), II, 2, 5[2].
v*ri*dha-snú, mighty, IV, 2, 3[1].
v*rí*shan, manly, bull, I, 36, 8[2]; 10[1], &c.; III, 29, 9[1]; *ri*tásya v*rí*sh*n*e, V, 12, 1[1]; arushásya v*rí*sh*n*a*h*, V, 12, 2[2].
V*rí*shan, N. pr., I, 36, 10[1].
v*ri*shabhá, bull (Agni), I, 31, 5, &c.; I, 141, 2[2]; IV, 1, 11[3]; 12[2]; V, 2, 12[1]; k*ri*sh*n*á*h* v*ri*shabhá*h*, I, 79, 2[2].
v*ri*shay: v*ri*sha-yáse, thou rushest on (acc.) like a bull, I, 58, 4[3];—v*ri*sha-yánte, they are full of (sexual) desire, III, 7, 9.
v*ri*sh*t*í, rain, II, 5, 6; 6, 5.
védas, property, I, 70, 10; 99, 1; V, 2, 12.
védi, sacrificial altar: védî íti asyấm, II, 3, 4.
vedi-sád, sitting on the sacrificial bed, I, 140, 1.
védya, well known: rátham-iva védyam, II, 2, 3[2];—renowned, V, 15, 1.
vedha*h*-tama, best worshipper, I, 75, 2.
vedhás, worshipper, I, 60, 2; 65, 10; 69, 3; 72, 1[1]; 73, 10; III, 10, 5; 14, 1; IV, 2, 15; 20; 3, 3; 16; 6, 1;—helpful, I, 128, 4 (bis).
vépas, trembling, IV, 11, 2.
ve*s*á, vassal, IV, 3, 13.
vésha*n*a, officiating, V, 7, 5.
Vai*s*vânará, I, 59, 1–7; 98, 1–3; III, 2, 1; 11; 12; 3, 1; 5; 10; 11; 26, 1–3; IV, 5, 1; 2; V, 27, 1[2]; 2.
vó*l*h*ri*, draught-horse, I, 144, 3.
vyá*k*asvat, far-embracing, II, 3, 5.
vyá*k*sh*th*a, most capacious, II, 10, 4.
vyáthis, track, IV, 4, 3.
vyadh, see vidh.
vyâ (vî), to envelop: ava-vyáyan, re-

moving, IV, 13, 4;—ā̆ vîtám, enveloped, IV, 7, 6[1];—párivîta, dressed (in offerings and prayers?), IV, 3, 2[2].
vyòman, see ví-oman.
vra*g*, to go: vavrā̆*g*a, III, 1, 6;—abhi-vrá*g*an, proceeding, I, 58, 5[2]; abhivrá*g*at-bhi*h*, approaching, I, 144, 5[3].
vra*g*á, stable, IV, 1, 15; V, 6, 7.
vratá, law, I, 31, 1; 2; 12; 65, 3; 69, 7; II, 8, 3; III, 3, 9; 4, 7; 6, 5; 7, 7; IV, 13, 2; vratā̆ dhruvā̆, I, 36, 5[1]; II, 5, 4; daívyâni vratā̆, I, 70, 2;—ánu vratám, according to his will, I, 128, 1;—duty, I, 144, 1.
vrata-pā̆, guardian of the law, I, 31, 10; III, 4, 7; V, 2, 8[3].
vra*sk*: mā̆*g*yā̆yasa*h* *s*á*m*sam ā̆ v*r*ikshi, may I not fall as a victim to the curse of my better, I, 27, 13[2]; v*r*ik*n*ā̆sa*h*, hewn, III, 8, 7.
vrā̆, host, IV, 1, 16[2].
vrā̆ta, host: vrâtam-vrâtam, III, 26, 6.
vrâdh: vrâdhanta, they have boasted, V, 6, 7.
vrā̆dhan-tama, most powerful, I, 150, 3.
vrí*s*, finger: dá*s*a vrí*s*a*h*, I, 144, 5[1].

*s*a*m*s, to recite: á*s*a*m*san, I, 67, 4; mánma *s*a*m*si, II, 4, 8;—to teach: *ri*tám *s*á*m*santa*h*, III, 4, 7.
*s*á*m*sa, curse, I, 27, 13[2]; 94, 8; III, 18, 2; *s*á*m*sât aghā̆t, from evil spell, I, 128, 5;—praise, I, 141, 6[4]; 11; *s*á*m*se n*ri*nā̆m, III, 16, 4; ubhā̆ *s*á*m*sâ, IV, 4, 14[1]; *s*á*m*sam âyó*h*, IV, 6, 11[2]; V, 3, 4[2].
*s*ak, to be able: *s*aknávâma, I, 27, 13; *s*akéma yámam, I, 73, 10[1]; II, 5, 1[4]; III, 27, 3; *s*akema sam-ídham, I, 94, 3;—to help to: *s*agdhi (with gen.), II, 2, 12; III, 16, 6; *s*agdhí svastáye, V, 17, 5.
*s*ákti, skill: *s*áktî, I, 31, 18.
*s*agmá, mighty, I, 143, 8.
*s*a*k*î-vat, full of power, III, 21, 4.
*s*atá, hundred: *s*atā̆ *k*a vi*m**s*atím *k*a, V, 27, 2[1].
*s*atá-âtman, endowed with hundredfold life, I, 149, 3.
*s*atadā̆van, giver of a hundred (bulls), V, 27, 6.
*s*atá-dhâra, with a hundred rills, III, 26, 9.
*s*atá-val*s*a, with a hundred branches, III, 8, 11.
*s*ata-séya, attainment of hundredfold blessings, III, 18, 3.
*s*atá-hima, living a hundred winters, II, 1, 11.
*s*atá-himâ, pl., a hundred winters, I, 73, 9.
*s*atín, hundredfold, I, 31, 10; II, 2, 9; *s*atínîbhi*h*, with his hundredfold blessings, I, 59, 7.
*s*átru, enemy: *s*átrum â-dabhú*h*, III, 16, 2[4].
*s*atru-yát, being at enmity, V, 4, 5; 28, 3.
*s*ad, to be glorious: *s*â*s*adré, I, 141, 9.
*s*aphá, hoof, V, 6, 7.
*s*am, to toil (esp. in performing worship): *s*a*s*amâná, who has toiled hard, I, 141, 10; 142, 2; III, 18, 4; IV, 2, 9; 13; a*s*amish*th*â*h*, III, 29, 16; á*s*amish*t*a, he toiled, V, 2, 7.
*s*ám, bliss, luck: *s*ám yó*h*, with luck and weal, I, 189, 2; III, 17, 3; 18, 4; IV, 12, 5; *s*ám na*h* *s*o*k*a, III, 13, 6; *s*ám k*ri*dhi, IV, -, 3; *s*ám ásti, he satisfies, V, 7, 9; *s*ám h*ri*dé, V, 11, 5.
*s*amây, to toil: *s*am-âyé, III, 1, 1.
*s*ámi, toiling, (sacrificial) work: *s*ámyâ, II, 1, 9[1]; *s*ámyai (read *s*ámyâ*h*?), IV, 3, 4[1].
*s*amit*rí*, the sacrificial butcher, or slaughterer, (I, 13, 12[1]); II, 3, 10; III, 4, 10.
*s*am-gayá, bringing happiness to our home, II, 1, 6.
*s*ám-tama, most agreeable, beneficial, blissful, I, 76, 1[1]; 77, 2; 128, 7; III, 13, 4.
*S*ámbara, I, 59, 6.
*s*am-bhú, refreshing, I, 65, 5; bringing luck, III, 17, 5
*s*ayú, reposing, I, 31, 2.
*s*ará*n*i, fault (?), I, 31, 16[1].
*s*arád, autumn: tisrá*h* *s*aráda*h*, I, 72, 3.
*s*áru, weapon, IV, 3, 7.
*s*árdha, host, I, 71, 8[6]; IV, 1, 12[1,3]; *s*árdhâya marútâm, IV, 3, 8.
*s*árdhas, host: *s*árdha*h* mā̆rutam, I,

127, 6; II, 1, 6; IV, 6, 10; marútâm *s*árdha*h*, II, 3, 3; narã́m *s*árdha*h*, II, 1, 5[4]; *s*árdha*h* divyám, III, 19, 4;—*s*árdha*h*, m. or n.? IV, 1, 12[1,3].
*s*árman, shelter, protection, I, 58, 8, &c.; *s*árma*n*i syâm, III, 15, 1; á*kkh*idrâ *s*árma, III, 15, 5[1].
*s*arma-sád, sitting under shelter, I, 73, 3.
*s*áryâ, arrow, I, 148, 4.
*s*ávas, strength, might, power: *s*ávasâ (conj. *s*ávasa*h*), I, 27, 2[1], &c.; *s*ávasa*h* *s*ushmí*n*a*h* páti*h*, I, 145, 1; *s*avasa*h* pate, V, 6, 9.
*s*ávish*th*a, most powerful, I, 77, 4; mightiest, I, 127, 11.
*s*á*s*vat: *s*á*s*vatâ tánâ, constantly, I, 26, 6[1]; *s*á*s*vatî*h*, constant, I, 27, 7; *g*ánâya *s*á*s*vate, all people, I, 36, 19; *s*á*s*vata*h*, many, I, 72, 1[1].
*s*a*s*vat-tamám, for ever, III, 1, 23.
*s*astí, hymn, praise, IV, 3, 3; 15.
*s*â, to sharpen, further: *s*i*s*íhi, III, 16, 3[1]; 24, 5[1]; *s*i*s*îte, V, 2, 9; 9, 5;—áti *s*i*s*îte, I, 36, 16;—ni-*s*íshat, he stirs up, IV, 2, 7[1].
*s*âká, powerful, V, 15, 2[1].
*S*âta-vaneyá, N. pr., I, 59, 7.
*s*âs, to teach, instruct: *s*a*s*âsu*h*, III, 1, 2; IV, 2, 12;—ánu-*s*ish*t*a, instructed, V, 2, 8;—prá *s*ã́ssi, thou instructest, I, 31, 14; pra-*s*ã́sat, commanding, I, 95, 3.
*s*ã́s, command, I, 68, 9.
*s*ã́sana, command, III, 7, 5.
*s*ã́sanî, teacher, I, 31, 11.
*s*ã́sus, command, instruction, I, 60, 2; 73, 1.
*s*ã́sya, governable, I, 189, 7[4].
*s*íkvan, plur., locks of flames, I, 141, 8[1].
*s*iksh, to help one to, to favour with a thing (gen.): *s*íksha, I, 27, 5; III, 19, 3; yá*h* te *s*íkshât, who does service to thee, I, 68, 6[1].
*s*ikshú, rich in favours: *s*ikshó*h* (conj. *s*iksho), III, 19, 3[1].
*s*iti-p*ri*sh*th*á, white-backed, III, 7, 1[1].
*s*ímî-vat, powerful (?), I, 141, 13[1].
*s*iri*n*â? II, 10, 3[3].
*s*ivá, kind, bounteous, gracious, blessed: I, 31, 1; 79, 2; 143, 8; III, 1, 9; 19; IV, 10, 8; 11, 6; V, 24, 1.
*s*í*s*u, the young one: pa*s*ú*h* ná *s*í*s*vâ, like a pregnant cow, (I, 65, 10[1]); young calf, I, 96, 5[1]; the young child (Agni), I, 140, 3; 145, 3; V, 9, 3; a foal, III, 1, 4; divá*h* *s*í*s*um, (Soma) the child of heaven, IV, 15, 6[2].
*s*í*s*u-matî, the mother of the young child, I, 140, 10[1].
*s*í*s*van (?), young: pa*s*ú*h* ná *s*í*s*vâ, I, 65, 10[1].
*s*îrá, sharp, III, 9, 8.
*s*ukrá, bright, I, 12, 12, &c.;—brightness: *s*ukrã́ vásânâ*h*, III, 8, 9.
*s*ukrá-var*n*a, whose colour is bright, I, 140, 1; 143, 7.
*s*ukrá-*s*o*k*is, brightly shining, II, 2, 3.
*s*u*k*, to shine forth, flame up: *s*ó*k*asva, I, 36, 9; *s*u*s*ukvã́n, flaming, I, 69, 1; *s*u*k*áyanta*h*, the resplendent ones, I, 147, 1; *s*u*s*u*k*ânã́, I, 149, 4; *s*ám na*h* *s*o*k*a, III, 13, 6; á*s*o*k*at, III, 29, 14; *s*u*k*ádhyai, IV, 2, 1[1];—to kindle: *s*u*k*ánta*h* agním, IV, 2, 17;—ápa na*h* *s*ó*s*u*k*at aghám, driving away evil with thy light, I, 97, 1–8;—*s*u*s*ugdhí ã́ rayím, shine upon us with wealth, I, 97, 1;—ví *s*ó*s*u*k*âna*h*, flaming, III, 15, 1.
*s*ú*k*, flash: *s*u*k*ã́-*s*u*k*â, flash by flash, III, 4, 1.
*s*ú*k*i, brilliant, bright, I, 31, 17, &c.; V, 7, 8[1]; *s*ú*k*im *s*ú*k*aya*h*, I, 72, 3[1]; *s*ú*k*i ít (for *s*ú*k*im ít?), IV, 2, 16[2].
*s*ú*k*i-*g*anman, whose birth is bright, I, 141, 7.
*s*ú*k*i-*g*ihva, pure-tongued, II, 9, 1.
*s*ú*k*i-dant, with brilliant teeth, V, 7, 7.
*s*ú*k*i-pe*s*as, brightly adorned, I, 144, 1.
*s*ú*k*i-pratîka, whose face is bright, I, 143, 6.
*s*ú*k*i-bhrâ*g*as, brightly resplendent, I, 79, 1.
*s*ú*k*i-var*n*a, brilliant-coloured, V, 2, 3.
*S*úna*h*-*s*épa, V, 2, 7.
*s*unám, prosperously, IV, 3, 11.
*s*ubh, to adorn, beautify: *s*umbhánti, V, 10, 4[1]; 22, 4.
*s*úbh, a triumphal procession, I, 127, 6; III, 26, 4[3].
*s*ubham-yã́, going in triumph, IV, 3, 6[2].
*s*ubhrá, beautiful, III, 26, 2.
*s*urúdh, gift, I, 72, 7[2].
*s*ush, see *s*vas.

*s*úshka, dry (wood), I, 68, 3.
*s*úshma, roaring, IV, 10, 4;—power, V, 10, 4; 16, 3.
*s*ushmín, mighty, powerful, I, 145, 1; III, 16, 3; V, 10, 4.
*s*ushmín-tama, strongest, I, 127, 9.
*s*ū́ra, mighty, I, 70, 11;—hero, IV, 3, 15.
*s*ū́ra-sâti, strife of heroes: *s*ū́ra-sâtâ, I, 31, 6.
*s*ûshá, song of praise, III, 7, 6.
*sri*ṅga, horn, III, 8, 10; V, 2, 9.
*sri*ṅgín, horned animal, III, 8, 10.
*sri*dh: *s*ardha, show thy prowess, V, 28, 3.
*s*éva, a kind friend, I, 58, 6; 69, 4; 73, 2;—friendship, III, 7, 5.
*s*é-v*ri*dha, joy-furthering, III, 16, 2.
*s*ésha, offspring, V, 12, 6.
*s*óka, flame, IV, 6, 5.
*s*o*k*í*h*-ke*s*a, whose hair is flame, I, 45, 6; 127, 2; III, 14, 1; 17, 1; 27, 4; V, 8, 2.
*s*o*k*ish*th*a, brightest, V, 24, 4.
*s*o*k*íshmat, flaming, II, 4, 7.
*s*o*k*ís, splendour, flame, I, 12, 12, &c.
*sk*ut, to drip down: *sk*otanti, III, 1, 8; 21, 2; 4; 5.
*s*yā́va, dark: *s*yā́vîm (conj. *s*yā́vî*h*?), I, 71, 1²; *s*yâvā́, the two tawny horses, II, 10, 2.
*s*yetá, reddish, I, 71, 4.
*s*yená, hawk, IV, 6, 10.
*s*yénî, the reddish white one, I, 140, 9².
*s*rath, to let loose: *sis*rathat, I, 128, 6;—ví *sis*ratha*h*, release from, IV, 12, 4.
*s*ram: *sas*ramâ*n*á*h*, toiling, IV, 12, 2.
*s*ramayú, wearying oneself, I, 72, 2.
*s*ravayát-pati, who brings renown to his lord, V, 25, 5¹.
*s*rávas, glory, renown, I, 31, 7, &c.; *s*rávase, I, 73, 5².
*s*ravasyà, glorious, II, 10, 1.
*s*ravasyát, aspiring to renown, I, 128, 1.
*s*ravasyā́, desire of glory, I, 128, 6; 149, 5.
*s*ravasyú, glorious, V, 9, 2.
*s*ravā́yya, glorious, celebrated, I, 27, 8; 31, 5; V, 20, 1.
*s*râ, see *s*rî.
*s*ri, to rest, abide: asi *s*ritá*h*, I, 75, 3; III, 9, 3; *sis*riyâ*n*á, dwelling here and there, V, 11, 6;—a*s*ret, he has spread forth, established, III, 14, 1; 19, 2;—to send: ûrdhvám a*s*ret, he has sent upwards, IV, 6, 2; 13, 2; 14, 2; a*s*ret, he has sent, V, 1, 12; 28, 1;—ū́t *s*rayasva, rise up, III, 8, 2;—with ví, to open (intr.): ví *s*rayantâm, I, 13, 6; 142, 6; II, 3, 5; ví *s*rayadhvam, V, 5, 5.
*s*rî, to cook: *s*rî*n*án, I, 68, 1¹; *sis*rîtá, he has ripened, I, 149, 2; *s*rî*n*îshe, thou warmest, V, 6, 9.
*s*rī́, splendour, beauty, glory, I, 72, 10², &c.; *s*ríyam vásâna*h*, II, 10, 1; *s*riyé, gloriously, IV, 5, 15.
*s*ru, to hear: *s*rudhi, I, 26, 5, &c.; *s*rúvat (conj. srúvat), it melts away, I, 127, 3⁴; *s*róshamâ*n*â*h*, hearing, III, 8, 10;—ví *srin*vire, they are renowned, IV, 8, 6.
*s*rúti, glory, II, 2, 7.
*s*rut-kar*n*a, with attentive ears, I, 44, 13; 45, 7.
*s*rútya, glorious, I, 36, 12.
*s*rush*t*í, obedience, I, 67, 1²; III, 9, 8;—hearing, readiness to hear, I, 69, 7; II, 3, 9; 9, 4.
*s*rush*t*î-ván, ready to listen, hearing, I, 45, 2; III, 27, 2;—obedient, I, 127, 9.
*s*re*n*i-*s*ás, in rows, III, 8, 9.
*s*vas, to hiss: *s*vásiti ap-sú, I, 65, 9;—abhi-*s*vasán, panting, I, 140, 5;—â*s*ushâ*n*ā́*h*, aspiring after, I, 147, 1; IV, 2, 14; 16.
*s*vásîvat, mightily breathing, I, 140, 10.
*s*vâtrá, power (?), I, 31, 4².
*s*vântá? I, 145, 4⁴.
*s*vetá, white (horse?), I, 66, 6¹;—*s*vetám *g*a*g*ñânám, who had been born white (Agni), III, 1, 4.
*S*vaitreyá, V, 19, 3¹.

sa*m*yát-vîra, with a succession of valiant men, II, 4, 8.
sa*m*vatsará, year: sa*m*vatsaré, after a year, I, 140, 2³.
sákman, company: sákman (loc.), I, 31, 6⁴.
sa-kshíta, dwelling together, I, 140, 3.
sákhi, friend, I, 31, 1; 75, 4; III, 9, 1¹; sákhâ sákhye, I, 26, 3; III, 18, 1; sákhâ sákhyu*h* nimíshi rákshamâ*n*â*h*, I, 72, 5⁴; gúhâ sákhi-bhi*h*, III, 1, 9³.

sakhi-yát, wishing to be a friend, I, 128, 1.
sakhyá, friendship, I, 26, 5; 71, 10; 94, 1-14; III, 9, 3; IV, 10, 8.
sagh, to sustain: ásaghno*h*, I, 31, 3.
sa*k* (sa*s*k), to be united with, accompany: sá*k*asva na*h*, stay with us, I, 1, 9; sa*k*ase, II, 1, 3; sa*s*kire, II, 1, 13;—to attend, worship: sa*k*ante, I, 59, 6; sá*k*anta, I, 73, 4; sa*k*antâm, I, 98, 3;—to follow: sa*k*ante, I, 60, 2; sisakshi, I, 73, 8;—to hold, cling, adhere: sisakti, I, 66, 2; sa*k*ate (krátvâ), I, 145, 2; sá*k*ante, III, 13, 2; sa*s*kata, III, 16, 2;—sa*k*anta, they have attained, V, 17, 5[1];—ánu sa*k*ate vartanî́*h*, she follows her ways, I, 140, 9[3];—ápa sa*s*kire, they turn away to encounter, V, 20, 2;—abhí sa*k*ante, go towards, I, 71, 7[1];—ấ sắ*k*yam, whom men should attach to themselves, I, 140, 3.
sá-*k*anas, graciously united, I, 127, 11.
sá*k*â, together with: sá*k*â sán, being attached, I, 71, 4;—III, 12, 2; IV. 5, 10.
sa-*g*âtyà, relationship, II, 1, 5[2].
sa-*g*ítvan: sa-*g*ítvânâ, united conquerors, III, 12, 4.
sa-*g*úsh, united with: sa-*g*ū́*h*, I, 44, 2; 14.
sa-*g*ósha, unanimous, concordant, I, 65, 2; 72, 6.
sa-*g*óshas, in concord with, unanimous, III, 4, 8; 8, 8; 20, 1; 22, 4; IV, 5, 1; V, 4, 4; 21, 3; 23, 3.
sá*mg*ñâta-rûpa, of familiar form, I, 69, 9.
sáttri, sitting down, III, 17, 5.
sát-pati, lord of beings, II, 1, 4;—a good lord, V, 25, 6; 27, 1.
satyá, true, truthful, I, 1, 5; 73, 2; 79, 1; 98, 3; k*ri*nván satyắ, I, 70, 8; satyấm, true (fulfilment), IV, 1, 18;—satyám, verily, I, 1, 6;—efficacious, I, 67, 5;—real, IV, 1, 10.
satyá-girvâhas, truly carried by prayers as by a vehicle, I, 127, 8[1].
satyá-tara, highly truthful, I, 76, 5; III, 4, 10.
satyá-tâti, truth, IV, 4, 14.
satyá-dharman, whose ordinances are true, I, 12, 7.
satyá-manman, truthful, I, 73, 2.
satya-yâ*g*, truly sacrificing, IV, 3, 1.
satya-vâ*k*, truth-speaking, III, 26, 9.
satyá-*s*ushma, truly strong, I, 59, 4; IV, 11, 4.
satrắ, altogether, I, 71, 9;—together: satrắ *k*akrâ*n*á*h*, I, 72, 1.
satrâ-sáha, always conquering, I, 79, 7.
sátvan, warrior, I, 140, 9; IV, 13, 2[3].
sad, to sit: úpa sîdan, they reverentially approached, I, 72, 5;—pari-sádanta*h*, besieging, IV, 2, 17[4].
sádana, (priestly) seat, I, 31, 17;—seat, abode, I, 95, 8; 96, 7.
sa-d*rí*s, of like appearance, I, 94, 7.
sádman, seat, I, 67, 10; the (sacrificial) seat, I, 73, 1; IV, 1, 8; 9, 3; V, 23, 3.
sadyá*h*-artha, immediately successful, I, 60, 1.
sadyás, instantly, I, 27, 6, &c.; quickly, I, 71, 9[1].
sadhani-tvá, companionship, IV, 1, 9.
sa-dhanî́, companion: sa-dhanyà*h*, IV, 4, 14.
sadha-mắd, rejoicing, V, 20, 4.
sadha-mắdya, sharing in rejoicings, IV, 3, 4.
sadhá-stuti, song of praise, V, 18, 5[1].
sadhá-stha, abode, II, 9, 3; III, 6, 4; 7, 4; 12, 8; 23, 1; 25, 5; apắm sadhá-sthe, I, 149, 4; II, 4, 2; trî́ sadhá-sthâ, III, 20, 2.
sadhryà*ñk*, together, IV, 4, 12.
san, to win: sanéma, I, 73, 5; 189, 8; sanishyán, sanishyánta*h*, desirous of winning, III, 2, 3[1]; 4; 13, 2; sanishâmahe, III, 11, 9; sasa-vắn, having obtained, III, 22, 1; sasa-vắ*m*sa*h*, successful, IV, 8, 6; sanishanta, they were successful, V, 12, 4;—see also sâ.
sána, old, I, (27, 13[1]); 95, 10; III, 1, 6; 20.
sanakắt, from of old, III, 29, 14.
sanátâ, from of old, II, 3, 6; III, 3, 1.
sanáya, ancient, III, 20, 4.
sánara, united with strong men, I, 96, 8[1].
sána-*s*ruta, old-renowned, III, 11, 4.

sanâ-*g*ú, inciting from old, I, 141, 5[3].
saní, efficient, I, 27, 4;—saní, gain: sanáye, I, 31, 8; sanim gó*h*, the acquiring of the cow, III, 1, 23; saním yaté, V, 27, 4.
sánit*ri*, a gainer, winner: sánitâ, I, 27, 9; 36, 13; sanitú*h*, V, 12, 3.
sá-nî*l*a, dwelling in the same nest, I, 69, 6; 71, 1.
sanutár, far, V, 2, 4.
sánemi, entirely, IV, 10, 7.
santya (voc.), good, I, 36, 2; 45, 5; 9; III, 21, 3.
sap, to serve, worship: *ri*tấ sápanta*h*, I, 67, 8; 68, 4; sapema, IV, 4, 9; sapâmi, V, 12, 2; sápâti (Pada: sa*h* pâti), V, 12, 6[1];—to attach oneself: sapanta, V, 3, 4.
sapátnî, the two wives, III, 1, 10[3]; 6, 4.
sapary, to worship, do service: saparyáti, I, 12, 8; saparyấmi práyasâ, I, 58, 7[3]; saparyấn, I, 72, 3[2]; saparyáta*h*, I, 144, 4; saparyéma saparyáva*h*, II, 6, 3; saparyata, III, 9, 8; V, 14, 5; 25, 4; asaparyan, III, 9, 9; saparyánta*h*, V, 21, 3;—ấ saparyán, IV, 12, 2;—ví saparyan, I, 70, 10.
saparyú, devoted servant, II, 6, 3.
saptá-*g*ihva, seven-tongued, III, 6, 2[2].
saptá-dhâtu, consisting of seven elements, IV, 5, 6[2].
saptán, seven: saptá *g*uhvà*h*, I, 58, 7; yahvî*h*, I, 71, 7; 72, 8[1]; III, 1, 4[1]; ra*s*máya*h*, II, 5, 2[1]; vấ*n*î*h*, III, 1, 6[1]; 7, 1[1]; hotrấ*n*i, III, 4, 5[2]; p*ri*kshấsa*h*, III, 4, 7[1]; víprâ*h*, III, 7, 7; IV, 2, 15[1]; hót*ri*-bhi*h*, III, 10, 4[1]; priyấsa*h*, IV, 1, 12; dhấma-bhi*h*, IV, 7, 5[1]; rátnâ, V, 1, 5;—trí*h* saptá, I, 72, 6[1]; IV, 1, 16[1].
saptá-ra*s*mi, having seven rays (or reins), I, 146, 1[1].
saptá-*s*iva: saptá-*s*ivâsu, read: saptá *s*ivấsu, I, 141, 2[3].
saptá-*s*îrshan, seven-headed, III, 5, 5[3].
saptá-hot*ri*, the god of the seven Hot*ri*s, III, (10, 4[1]); 29, 14.
sápti, racer: átyam ná sáptim, III, 22, 1[1].
saprátha*h*-tama, most widely extended, I, 45, 7[2]; most widely-sounding, I, 75, 1[1]; most wide-reaching, I, 94, 13.
sa-práthas, widely extended: *s*árma sa-prátha*h*, a big shelter, I, 142, 5;—V, 13, 4.
saba*h*-dúgha, juice-yielding, III, 6, 4[4].
sábandhu, bound in kinship, III, 1, 10.
sa-bấdh, pressing: sa-bấdha*h* ấ *k*akru*h*, III, 27, 6[1].
sa-bấdhas, urgent, V, 10, 6.
sabhấ-vat, with (brilliant) assemblies, IV, 2, 5.
sám, together: ya*s*ása*h* sám hí pûrvî*h*, many glorious ones have come together, III, 1, 11[3].
sama, every, V, 24, 3.
samád, contest: tveshá*h* samát-su, I, 66, 6; 70, 11.
sá-manas, one-minded, V, 3, 2.
samanấ, alike, IV, 5, 7.
sám-antam, in the neighbourhood of, V, 1, 11.
sa-manyú, concordant, IV, 1, 1.
samáyâ, through the midst, I, 73, 6.
sa-maryá, assembly, III, 8, 5;—contest, V, 3, 6.
samâná, companion, I, 69, 8[1];—common, I, 127, 8, &c.; samânám ártham, I, 144, 3[2].
sám-iti, meeting, I, 95, 8.
sam-ithá, battle, I, 73, 5;—assembly, III, 1, 12.
sam-ídh, log of wood, fuel, I, 95, 11; II, 6, 1; III, 1, 2; 10, 3; IV, 4, 15; V, 1, 1; 4, 4; 6, 4[2]; tisrá*h* sam-ídha*h*, III, 2, 9; samít-samit, log by log, III, 4, 1[1].
samudrá, ocean, I, 71, 7; 95, 3[1].
sám-*ri*ti, battle, I, 31, 6;—onslaught, I, 127, 3[3]; V, 7, 2[1].
sám-okas, dwelling together, I, 144, 4.
sam-gámana, assembler, I, 96, 6.
sám-tarutra, victorious, III, 1, 19.
sam-d*rís*, the shine (of the sun), I, 66, 1;—appearance, aspect, II, 1, 12; III, 5, 2; IV, 1, 6; 6, 6.
sám-d*r*ish*t*i, aspect, I, 144, 7; II, 4, 4; IV, 10, 5.
sam-bhú*g*a, enjoyment, (II, 1, 4[1]).
sám-mi*s*la, united, III, 26, 4[2].
samyá*ñk*, turned towards each other: sam*î*kî íti sam-î*k*í, I, 69, 1; 96, 5[2]; II, 3, 6; III, 1, 7[1];—united:

sam-îkîh, III, 29, 13; sam-yâñkam, V, 7, 1.
sam-yát: ksházpah sam-yátah, on continuous nights, II, 2, 2[3].
sam-rấg, the Sovereign, I, 188, 5; III, 10, 1.
sam-rấgat, king: sam-rấgantam, I, 27, 1.
sam-vát, space, V, 15, 3.
sam-sád, companionship, I, 94, 1;—assembly, IV, 1, 8.
sam-stír, laid together: sam-stírah vi-stírah, I, 140, 7[1].
sam-sthá, abode, V, 3, 8.
sam-hát, a compact mass, III, 1, 7.
sayấvan, accompanying, I, 44, 13.
sá-yoni, having the same origin, III, 1, 6.
sarany, to speed: saranyán, III, 1, 19.
sa-rátham, on one chariot with, I, 71, 6[3]; III, 4, 11; 6, 9; V, 11, 2.
Sarámâ, I, 72, 8.
Sárasvatî, N. of a goddess, I, 13, 9[1]; 142, 9; 188, 8; II, 1, 11[1],[2]; 3, 8; III, 4, 8; V, 5, 8;—N. of a river, III, 23, 4.
sárîman, swift course, III, 29, 11[2].
sárga, rush: vấtasya sárgah, III, 29, 11[2];—the letting loose, IV, 3, 12.
sárga-pratakta, urged forward, I, 65, 6.
sarpíh-âsuti, drinking butter, II, 7, 6; V, 7, 9; 21, 2.
sarpís, butter, I, 127, 1; V, 6, 9.
sarvá-tâti, health and wealth, I, 94, 15.
sávana, libation, III, 1, 20; tritîye sávane, III, 28, 5; mấdhyandine sávane, III, 28, 4.
sá-vayas, of the same age, I, 144, 3[1]; 4.
Savitri, I, 36, 13; 44, 8; 73, 2; 95, 7[1]; II, 1, 7; III, 20, 5; IV, 6, 2; 13, 2; 14, 2.
sask, see sak.
saskát, hindrance, III, 9, 4[1].
sasá, herbs, III, 5, 6[2]; IV, 5, 7[1]; 7, 7[1]; V, 21, 4[2].
sasahí, victorious, III, 16, 4.
sásni, victorious, III, 15, 5.
sa-srút, flowing, I, 141, 1.
sah, to overcome, be victorious: sahvấn, III, 11, 6; sáhasva, III, 24, 1; ásahanta, III, 29, 9; sasấha, V, 25, 6;—abhí sasáhat, it may prevail, V, 23, 1;—nih-sáhamânah, conquering, I, 127, 3;—pra-sákshat, victorious, IV, 12, 1.
sahah-krita, produced by strength, I, 45, 9; III, 27, 10; V, 8, 1.
sahah-gâ, strength-begotten, I, 58, 1.
sahah-vridh, augmenter of strength, I, 36, 2; III, 10, 9.
sáhan-tama, mightiest, I, 127, 9.
sahantya, conqueror, I, 27, 8.
sáhamâna, victorious, IV, 6, 10.
sáhas, strength: sahasah yaho íti, I, 26, 10[1]; 74, 5[1]; 79, 4; sûno íti sahasah, I, 58, 8; 127, 1; 143, 1; III, 1, 8; 11, 4; 24, 3; 25, 5; 28, 3; 5; IV, 2, 2; 11, 6; V, 3, 9; 4, 8; sáhasâ gấyamânah, I, 96, 1[1]; sáhasah yátah gáni, I, 141, 1; sahasah yuvan, O young (son) of strength, I, 141, 10; sáhasah putráh, II, 7, 6; III, 14, 1; 4; 6; 16, 5; 18, 4; V, 3, 1; 6; 4, 6; 11, 6;—sáhah, (Agni our) strength, I, 36, 18;—sáhasâ, strongly, I, 98, 2;—might, power, I, 127, 9; 10; V, 1, 8; devásya sáhasâ, V, 3, 10; abhí-mâti sáhah dadhé, V, 23, 4[1];—violence, V, 12, 2.
sahasâná, mighty, strong, I, 189, 8; II, 10, 6; V, 25, 9.
sáhasâ-vat, mighty, strong, I, 189, 5; III, 1, 22; V, 20, 4.
sahasin, strong, IV, 11, 1.
sahasya, strong, I, 147, 5; II, 2, 11; V, 22, 4.
sahásra, thousand: sahásrâni satấ dása, II, 1, 8; sahásrât yúpât, V, 2, 7; dasá-bhih sahásraih, V, 27, 1[3].
sahasra-akshá, thousand-eyed, I, 79, 12.
sahasra-git, conqueror of thousandfold wealth, I, 188, 1; V, 26, 6.
sahasram-bhará, bringing thousandfold gain, II, 9, 1.
sahásra-retas, with thousandfold sperm, IV, 5, 3.
sahásra-vat, thousandfold, III, 13, 7.
sahásra-valsa, with a thousand branches, III, 8, 11.
sahásra-vîra, blessing with a thousand men, I, 188, 4[1].
sahásra-sringa, with a thousand horns, V, 1, 8.

sahasra-sā́, a winner of thousandfold bliss, I, 188, 3.

sahasra-sā́tama, the greatest winner of thousandfold wealth, III, 13, 6.

sahasrín, thousandfold, I, 31, 10; 188, 2; II, 2, 7.

sáhasvat, mighty, strong, I, 97, 5; 127, 10; 189, 4; III, 14, 2; 4; V, 7, 1; 9, 7; 23, 2.

sáhîyas, mightier, I, 71, 4.

sáhûti, joint invocation, I, 45, 10.

sahvát, strong, I, 58, 5.

sâ: sísâsanta*h*, wishing to acquire, I, 146, 4.

sâ: ánava-syanta*h* ártham, never losing their object, IV, 13, 3;—ví syatu, may he pour forth, I, 142, 10; pra-*g*ā́m ví syatu, may he deliver a son, II, 3, 9; ví syasva, send forth, III, 4, 9; ví sâhi, disclose, IV, 11, 2.

sâtí, acquirement (of wealth), success, I, 36, 17; 143, 6; V, 5, 4; 9, 7.

sā́tu, womb, mother (?), IV, 6, 7[1].

sâdh, to prosper (intr.): sâdhati, I, 94, 2;—sā́dhate matí*h*, the prayer goes straight to him, I, 141, 1[2]; sā́dhan, straightway, III, 1, 17;—to prosper (tr.), further: sâdháya, I, 94, 3; pra-tarám sâdhaya, I, 94, 4; sâdhan, I, 96, 1;—to accomplish, perform: sâdháyantî dhíyam, II, 3, 8; sā́dhan, III, 1, 18; 5, 3.

sā́dhat-ish*t*i, accomplishing the oblations, III, 2, 5; 3, 6.

sā́dhana, performer: ya*g*ñásya (vidáthasya) sā́dhanam, I, 44, 11; III, 3, 3; 27, 2; 8;—giver, V, 20, 3.

sā́dhish*th*a, best, I, 58, 1.

sâdhú, good, I, 67, 2;—going straight (to his aim), I, 70, 11; straightforward, I, 77, 3; III, 18, 1;—real, IV, 10, 2; efficacious, V, 1, 7.

sâdhu-yā́, straightway, V, 11, 4.

sânasí, successful, winning (booty), I, 75, 2; IV, 15, 6.

sā́nu, ridge, I, 128, 3; divá*h* ná sā́nu, I, 58, 2; ádhi sā́nushu trishú, II, 3, 7;—surface, I, 146, 2;—top, III, 5, 3.

sā́man, song: *ri*tásya sā́man, I, 147, 1[4];—the Sâman, IV, 5, 3.

sā́m-râ*g*ya, sovereignty, I, 141, 13.

sā́rathi, charioteer (Agni), I, 144, 3[4].

sârasvatá, beings belonging to Sarasvatî, III, 4, 8.

Sâha-devyá, Sahadeva's son, IV, 15, 7–10.

si*m*há, lion, I, 95, 5; III, 9, 4; 11; 26, 5; V, 15, 3.

sí*k*, wing (of an army): sí*k*au, I, 95, 7[2].

si(*ñ*)*k*: ní-siktam, poured down, I, 71, 8;—pári-sikta, poured, IV, 1, 19.

sitá, bound: padí sitā́m, IV, 12, 6.

sidh, to scare away: sedhati, I, 79, 12.

sidhrá, successful, I, 142, 8; effective, V, 13, 2.

síndhu, river, stream, I, 27, 6; 72, 10; 73, 6; 97, 8; 99, 1; 143, 3; 146, 4[3]; III, 5, 4; V, 4, 9; *g*âmí*h* síndhûnâm, I, 65, 7; pl., the Rivers, I, 140, 13;—the river Sindhu, I, 44, 12[1]; 94, 16; 95, 11; 98, 3; V, 11, 5; síndhu*h* ná kshóda*h*, I, 65, 6[1]; 10.

simá, self, I, 95, 7[3]; 145, 2[1].

sîv, see syû.

su, to bear. See sû.

su, to press Soma: sunvata*h*, I, 94, 8; sunavā́ma, I, 99, 1; sunvaté, I, 141, 10; V, 26, 5; sómam sutám, III, 22, 1.

su-agní, possessed of a good Agni (fire): su-agnáya*h*, I, 26, 7; 8 (bis).

su-áñ*k*, fleet, IV, 6, 9.

su-adhvará, best performer of worship, I, 44, 8; 127, 1; II, 2, 8; III, 2, 8; 9, 8; V, 9, 3; 28, 5;—receiving good sacrifices, I, 45, 1[1];—ya*g*ñé su-adhvaré, at the decorous service of the sacrifice, I, 142, 5;—splendid worship, III, 6, 6; 29, 12; V, 17, 1.

su-anîka, with beautiful face, II, 1, 8; IV, 6, 6.

su-apatyá, with good offspring, I, 72, 9[2]; II, 2, 12; 4, 8; 9, 5;—blessed with offspring, III, 3, 7; consisting in offspring, III, 16, 1;—good offspring, III, 19, 3.

su-ápas, good worker, IV, 2, 19; V, 2, 11.

su-apasyā́, great skill, III, 3, 11.

su-apâka, most skilful, IV, 3, 2[3].
su-ar*k*ís, endowed with beautiful light, II, 3, 2.
su-ártha, pursuing a good aim, I, 95, 1;—well-employed, I, 141, 11.
su-ávas, giving good help, V, 8, 2.
su-á*s*va, with good horses, IV, 2, 4;—rich in horses, IV, 4, 8; 10.
su-á*s*vya, abundance in horses, II, 1, 5; III, 26, 3.
su-âdhî́, of a good mind, kind, well-wishing, I, 67, 2; 70, 4[2]; 71, 8;—with good intentions, I, 72, 8; IV, 3, 4;—full of pious thoughts, III, 8, 4;—longing, V, 14, 6.
su-âbhū́, truly helpful: râyé su-âbhúvam, V, 6, 3[1].
su-ẫsa, whose mouth is beautiful, IV, 6, 8.
sú-âhuta, best receiver of offerings, I, 44, 4; 6; III, 27, 5.
su-uktá, well-spoken (prayer), I, 36, 1; 70, 5; II, 6, 2.
su-upâyaná, easy of access, I, 1, 9.
su-kárman, well performing the acts (of worship), IV, 2, 17.
su-kîrtí, beautiful praise, I, 60, 3;—glory, V, 10, 4.
su-k*r*ít, well-doing: su-k*r*íte suk*r*ít-tara*h*, I, 31, 4; righteous, I, 128, 6; who has done good deeds, I, 147, 3[2]; virtuous, well-doer, IV, 13, 1; V, 4, 8; 11.
su-k*r*itá, good works, III, 29, 8.
su-ketú, bright, III, 7, 10.
su-krátu, highly wise, I, 12, 1; 128, 4; III, 1, 22; IV, 4, 11; V, 11, 2; 20, 4; 25, 9;—full of good-will, I, 141, 11; 144, 7; III, 3, 7.
sukratu-yẫ, high wisdom, I, 31, 3.
su-kshití, with fine dwellings, V, 6, 8.
su-kshetriyẫ, desire for rich fields, I, 97, 2.
su-khá, easy-going, V, 5, 3.
sukhá-tama, easy-moving: sukhá-tame (ráthe), I, 13, 4.
su-gá, a good path, I, 94, 9;—going well, I, 94, 11.
sugâtu-yẫ, desire for a free path, I, 97, 2.
su-gârhapatyá, with a good household, V, 4, 2[1].
su-*k*andrá, resplendent, I, 74, 6; IV, 2, 19; V, 6, 5; 9.
su-*k*etúnâ, through thy kindness, I, 79, 9[1]; benignantly, I, 127, 11.
sú-*g*âta, well born, I, 65, 4; 72, 3[1]; II, 1, 15; 2, 11; 6, 2; III, 15, 2; 23, 3; V, 6, 2; 21, 2.
su-*g*ihvá, with beautiful tongue(s), I, 13, 8; 142, 4.
su-*g*ûr*n*í, glowing, IV, 6, 3.
su-*g*yótis, rich in light, III, 20, 1.
sutá, the pressed (Soma), III, 12, 1; 2.
sutá-vat, rich in pressed (Soma), III, 25, 4.
sutá-soma, having pressed Soma, I, 44, 8; 45, 8; 142, 1; IV, 2, 13.
su-túka, quick, I, 149, 5.
su-dá*m*sas, endowed with wonderful power, II, 2, 3.
su-dáksha, highly dexterous, II, 9, 1; III, 4, 9; 23, 2; V, 11, 1.
sudár*s*a-tara, more visible, I, 127, 5[3].
su-dẫnu, giving good rain, I, 44, 14; 45, 10; 141, 9; III, 26, 1; 5; 29, 7;—blessed with good rain, IV, 4, 7.
su-dẫvan, good giver, I, 76, 3.
su-dína, auspicious day, IV, 4, 6; 7.
sudina-tvá, auspiciousness of days, III, 8, 5; sudina-tvé áhnâm, III, 23, 4.
su-dî̃diti, with fine splendour, III, 9, 1[2].
su-dîtí, resplendent, III, 2, 13; 17, 4; 27, 10; V, 25, 2;—glorious splendour, V, 8, 4.
sudúgha, flowing with plenty, II, 3, 6; su-dúghâ*h* usrẫ*h*, IV, 1, 13.
su-d*r*í*s*, full of beauty, III, 17, 4; V, 3, 4[1].
su-d*r*í*s*îka, beautiful to behold, V, 4, 2.
sud*r*í*s*îka-rûpa, with his shape beautiful to behold, IV, 5, 15.
su-devá, a friend of the gods, I, 74, 5.
su-dógha, rich in milk, III, 15, 6.
su-dyút, brilliant, I, 140, 1; 143, 3.
su-dyumná, splendid, III, 19, 2.
su-dyótman, brilliant, I, 141, 12; II, 4, 1.
su-dravi*n*as, possessor of beautiful wealth, I, 94, 15.
sú-dhita, well-composed (prayer), I, 140, 11;—blissful gift, III, 11, 8;—well-preserved, III, 23, 1; lying safe, III, 29, 2;—well-ordered, IV, 2, 10;—well-placed,

IV, 6, 3; well-established, IV, 6, 7[3]; V, 3, 2.
su-dhī́, wise, IV, 2, 14.
su-dhúr, well-harnessed: râyá*h* su-dhúra*h*, I, 73, 10[1]; hárî íti su-dhúrâ, well-yoked, V, 27, 2.
suni*h*-máth, skilful rubbing, III, 29, 12.
su-nidhā́, skilful establishing, III, 29, 12.
su-nîthá, the best leader, II, 8, 2; III, 8, 8.
su-pátha, good path, I, 189, 1.
su-par*n*á, beautifully-winged, I, 79, 2.
su-pâ*n*í, with graceful hands, I, 71, 9[2].
su-putrá, with noble sons, III, 4, 11.
sú-pûta, well-clarified, V, 12, 1.
su-pé*s*as, wearing beautiful ornaments, I, 13, 7; 142, 7[1]; 188, 6.
supra-ayaná, easily passable, II, 3, 5; V, 5, 5.
supra-avyà, ready, I, 60, 1.
su-prátîka, whose face is beautiful, I, 94, 7; 143, 3; III, 29, 5; V, 5, 6.
su-prátûrti, gloriously advancing, III, 9, 1.
su-pránîti, a good guide, I, 73, 1; III, 1, 16; 15, 4; IV, 2, 13.
su-prayás, receiver of good offerings, II, 2, 1; 4, 1.
su-bándhu, well-allied, III, 1, 3.
su-barhís, possessor of good sacrificial grass, I, 74, 5.
su-bhága, blessed, I, 36, 6; III, 1, 4; 13; 9, 1[2]; 16, 6; 18, 5; IV, 1, 6; 4, 7; V, 8, 3.
su-bhára, rich in gain, II, 3, 4; 9.
sú-bh*ri*ta, well kept, II, 1, 12.
sú-makha, martial, IV, 3, 7; 14[1].
su-mát, together, I, 142, 7[3];—see sumát-yûtha.
su-matí, favour, I, 31, 18, &c.; III, 4, 1[2]; V, 27, 3[1]; kindness: su-matī́, IV, 1, 2[3].
sumát-yûtha, together with the herd: sumát-yûtham (conj. for su-mát yûthám), V, 2, 4[1].
sumát-ratha, on his chariot, III, 3, 9.
su-mánas, gracious, kind-hearted, I, 36, 2, &c.;—joyous, IV, 4, 9.
su-mánman, rich in good thoughts, III, 2, 12.
su-mahas, very great, IV, 11, 2.
sú-miti, skilful erection, III, 8, 3.
su-m*ri*l*î*ká, merciful, IV, 1, 20; 3, 3.
su-méka, well-established, I, 146, 3[1]; III, 6, 10[2]; 15, 5[3]; IV, 6, 3.
su-medhás, wise, II, 3, 1; III, 15, 5.
sumná, blessing, III, 2, 5; 3, 3;—favour, grace, V, 3, 10; 24, 4;—pleasant, III, 14, 4.
sumna-yú, desirous of favour, I, 79, 10; III, 27, 1; V, 8, 7.
su-yá*g*, excellent sacrificer, V, 8, 3.
su-ya*gñ*á, skilled in sacrifice, III, 17, 1.
su-yáma, well-manageable, III, 7, 3; (4[2]); V, 28, 3[1].
su-yávasa, good pasture: suyávasâ-iva, conj. for svásya-iva, II, 4, 4[1].
su-yâmá, easily directing, III, 7, 9[1].
su-yú*g*, well-yoked, IV, 14, 3.
su-rá*n*a, joyous, III, 3, 9; 29, 14.
su-rátha, with good chariot: su-ráthasya (conj. su-ratha asya), III, 14, 7[1];—IV, 2, 4;—rich in chariots, IV, 4, 8.
surabhí, sweet-smelling, V, 1, 6.
su-rā́dhas, rich in wealth, IV, 2, 4; 5, 4.
su-rukmá, adorned with gold, I, 188, 6.
su-rú*k*, with beautiful splendour, II, 2, 4; III, 2, 5; 7, 5; 15, 6; IV, 2, 17.
su-rétas, fertile, III, 1, 16.
su-vár*k*as, full of fine splendour, I, 95, 1.
su-vā́*k*, adorned with fine speech, III, 1, 19;—well-spoken, III, 7, 10.
su-vā́*k*as, fine-voiced, I, 188, 7.
su-vā́sas, well-clothed, III, 8, 4; IV, 3, 2.
suvitá, welfare, I, 141, 12; 189, 3; II, 2, 6; III, 2, 13; IV, 14, 3; V, 11, 1.
su-vidátra, bounteous, II, 1, 8; 9, 6.
su-vī́ra, rich in heroes, in valiant men, I, 31, 10; II, 1, 16; 3, 4; 5; 4, 9; III, 29, 9;—giving valiant offspring, III, 8, 2.
su-vī́rya, abundance in heroes, bliss of valiant offspring, I, 36, 6; 17, &c.; I, 127, 11[1];—host of heroes, III, 16, 4.
su-v*ri*ktí, praised with beautiful praise, II, 4, 1[1];—beautiful prayer, or praise, III, 3, 9; V, 25, 3[1].
su-véda, easily to be found, IV, 7, 6.

su-*s*ám*s*a, kind-spoken, I, 44, 6.
su-*s*árman, well-protecting, III, 15, 1; V, 8, 2.
su-*s*astí, best praise, III, 26, 6.
su-*s*ipra, strong-jawed, V, 22, 4[2].
sú-*s*i*s*vi, fine child, I, 65, 4.
su-*s*éva, propitious, I, 27, 2; kind, gracious, II, 1, 9; III, 29, 5; IV, 4, 12; V, 15, 1.
su-*s*óka, with pure splendour, I, 70, 1.
su-*s*rî́, in great beauty, III, 3, 5.
sú-sa*m*s*i*ta, well-sharpened, V, 19, 5.
su-sanit*ri*, best gainer, III, 18, 5.
su-sa*m*dr*ís*, beautiful to behold, I, 143, 3.
sú-samiddha, well-kindled, I, 13, 1; V, 5, 1.
su-samídh, good fuel, V, 8, 7.
su-sû́, well-bearing, V, 7, 8.
sú-sûta, well-born, II, 10, 3.
sú-stuta, highly praised, V, 27, 2.
su-stutí, rich in perfect praise, III, 19, 3.
su-háva, easy to invoke, readily hearing (our) call, I, 58, 6; III, 6, 8; 15, 1; IV, 1, 5.
su-havís, offering good oblations, IV, 2, 4.
su-havyá, giver of good oblations, I, 74, 5.
su-hira*n*yá, rich in gold, IV, 4, 10.
sû, to give birth: súvâte íti, they give birth, V, 1, 4;—ásûta, V, 2, 2; 7, 8.
sû́, a progenitor, I, 146, 5.
sûktá, see su-uktá.
sûd, to further: sûdáyat, I, 71, 8; súsûda*h*, I, 73, 8;—to shape: ásûdayanta, I, 72, 3;—to make ready: susûdati, I, 142, 11[3]; V, 5, 2;—sûdayâti, III, 4, 10;—sûdaya, accomplish, IV, 4, 14;—sûdayâti prá, may he make ready, II, 3, 10.
sûnú, son, I, 1, 9, &c.; I, 59, 4[1]; III, 1, 12[2]; sûno íti sahasa*h*, I, 58, 8; 127, 1; III, 1, 8; 11, 4; nítya*h* sûnú*h*, I, 66, 1[1].
sûnu-mát, rich in sons, III, 24, 5.
sûn*ri*tâ-vat, rich in loveliness, I, 59, 7.
sû́ra, Sun, I, 71, 9; 141, 13; 149, 3; III, 15, 2.
sûrí, the rich man, liberal lord or patron, I, 31, 7, &c.; I, 73, 5[1]; 141, 8[2].
sû́rya, the sun, or Sun, I, 59, 3; 98, 1; 146, 4[4]; III, 14, 4; IV, 1, 17; 13, 1–4; 14, 2; V, 1, 4; 4, 4; *k*ára*n*am sû́ryasya, III, 5, 5; ro*k*ané sû́ryasya, III, 22, 3; diví sû́ryam-iva a*g*áram, V, 27, 6.
s*ri*, to run: sasrâ*n*á*h*, I, 149, 2; sas*ri*vấ*m*sam-iva, III, 9, 5;—prá sarsrâte íti, they go forth, III, 7, 1; prá sisrate, they stream forward, V, 1, 1; pra-sársrâ*n*asya, advancing, V, 12, 6;—ví sasru*h*, they have broken through with their floods, I, 73, 6.
s*rig*, to let loose: sénâ-iva s*ri*sh*t*ấ, like an army that is sent forward, I, 66, 7; 143, 5[1]; s*rig*át didyúm asmai, he shot an arrow at him, I, 71, 5; s*ri*sh*t*ấ*h*, I, 72, 10;—áva s*rig*a, let go, I, 13, 11; ava-s*rig*án, letting go (the sacrificial food to the gods), I, 142, 11; II, 3, 10; mấ áva s*rig*a*h*, do not deliver, I, 189, 5;—úpa s*rig*a, yield up, I, 188, 10; upa-s*rig*ánti, they pour out, II, 1, 16;—ví s*rig*á, emit, I, 36, 9;—sá*m* na*h* s*rig*a, let us be united, I, 31, 18; III, 16, 6.
S*ríñg*aya, son of Devavâta, IV, 15, 4[1].
s*rí*n*i*, sickle: s*r*i*n*yâ, I, 58, 4[2].
s*ri*prá, mighty (?), III, 18, 5[1].
s*ri*prá-dânu, bestower of mighty rain (?), I, 96, 3[3].
sénâ, army, I, 66, 7; sénâ-iva s*ri*sh*t*ấ, I, 143, 5[1].
sót*ri*, presser (of Soma), IV, 3, 3.
sóma, Soma (juice), I, 44, 14; 45, 10; 99, 1[1]; III, 12, 3; 22, 1; 29, 16; sómasya tavásam, III, 1, 1[1]; sómâ*h*, IV, 14, 4; V, 27, 5[1];—Soma, the god, I, 65, 10; II, 8, 6.
sóma-âhuta, fed with Soma, I, 94, 14.
Sómaka, Sahadeva's son, IV, 15, 9.
sóma-pati, lord of Soma (Indra), I, 76, 3.
sóma-pîti, drinking of Soma: sóma-pîtaye, I, 44, 9.
soma-péya, drink of Soma, I, 45, 9; III, 25, 4.
somyá, one who offers Soma, I, 31, 16.
saúbhaga, prosperity, delight, happiness, I, 36, 17; III, 8, 2; 3; 11; 15, 4; 16, 1; V, 28, 3.

saubhaga-tvá, happiness, I, 94, 16.
saumanasá, graciousness, I, 76, 2; kindness, III, 1, 21.
skambhá, pillar, IV, 13, 5.
stan, to thunder: stanáyan, I, 58, 2; 140, 5; stanáyanti abhrấ, I, 79, 2; prá stanayanti, IV, 10, 4.
stabhu-yámâna, firmly fixed, III, 7, 4.
sta(m)bh, to uphold: tastámbha, I, 67, 5;—út astambhît, he has upheld, III, 5, 10;—úpa stabhâyat, he supports, IV, 5, 1; stabhâyat úpa dyấm, he has reared... up to the sky, IV, 6, 2.
stấyam, stealthily: úpa stấyam *k*arati, conj., (I, 145, 4[3]).
stu, to praise: stávâna*h*, praised, I, 12, 11; 31, 8, &c.
stubh: pra-stubhâná*h*, incited by shouting, IV, 3, 12.
stúbhvan, uttering (sacred) shouts, I, 66, 4.
st*ri*, to strew: st*rin*îta, I, 13, 5; st*rin*ânấsa*h* barhí*h*, I, 142, 5.
st*rí*, star: pipé*s*a nấkam st*rí*bhi*h*, I, 68, 10; dyaú*h* ná st*rí*-bhi*h*, II, 2, 5; IV, 7, 3.
stená, thief, V, 3, 11.
stoká, drop, III, 21, 1–5.
stot*rí*, praiser, I, 58, 8; II, 1, 16; III, 5, 2.
stóma, praise, song of praise, I, 12, 12, &c.; stómai*h* (conj. stómam), IV, 10, 1[3].
stómavâhas, (I, 127, 8[1]).
sthâ, to stand: ûrdhvá*h* tísh*th*a, I, 36, 13;—abhí tish*th*a, set thy foot on, V, 28, 3;—ấ tasthú*h*, they have assumed, I, 72, 9[2];—úpa sthât, he has approached, I, 68, 1; see upa-sthấyam;—prá-sthitâ, ready, III, 4, 4[3];—abhí prá asthât, he gains advantage, I, 74, 8[1];—with ví, to spread: ví tish*th*ate, I, 58, 4; ví tasthe, I, 72, 9; ví ásthât, I, 65, 8; 141, 7; ví ásthiran, they are scattered, I, 94, 11; ví tish*th*ase, V, 8, 7.
sthâtú, what stands: sthâtú*h* *k*arátham, what is movable and immovable, I, 58, 5[2]; 68, 1[2]; 70, 7[2]; (72, 6[2]).
sthât*rí*, that which stands: sthâtấm *k*aráthâm, I, 70, 3; what remains steadfast: sthât*rî́n*, I, 72, 6[2].
sthirá, solid: sthirấ *k*it ánnâ, IV, 7, 10.
sthû́*n*â, a column: sthû́*n*â-iva upamít, I, 59, 1[3].
snî́hitî? I, 74, 2[2].
snéhiti, (I, 74, 2[2]).
spá*s*, spy, IV, 4, 3;—observer: spá*s*am ví*s*vasya *g*ágata*h*, IV, 13, 3.
spârhá, desirable, lovely, I, 31, 14; II, 1, 12; IV, 1, 6; 7; 12.
sp*ri*: aspar íty aspa*h*, thou hast freed, V, 15, 5;—áva sp*ri*dhi, protect, V, 3, 9.
sp*ris*, to touch: sp*ris*anti, I, 36, 3.
sp*ri*hayát-var*n*a, having the appearance of one eagerly striving, II, 10, 5.
sphâtí, increase, I, 188, 9.
sphur, to sparkle: práti sphura, IV, 3, 14.
smát-ûdhnî, with full udders, I, 73, 6.
smi, to smile, laugh: smáyamânâbhi*h*, I, 79, 2[4]; smáyamâna*h* (dyaú*h*), II, 4, 6[3]; smayete íti, III, 4, 6.
syû: syûtám, well-stitched, I, 31, 15.
syona-k*rí*t, making comfortable, I, 31, 15.
syona-*s*î́, comfortably resting, I, 73, 1[2].
sravát, river: sravâta*h* saptá yahvî́*h*, I, 71, 7.
sravátha, streaming, III, 1, 7.
sridh: ásredhanta*h*, without fail, III, 29, 9.
srídh, failure, I, 36, 7; III, 9, 4; 10, 7.
sru, to flow: srúvat (conj. for *s*rúvat), it melts away, I, 127, 3[4].
srú*k*, sacrificial ladle, I, 144, 1; V, 14, 3; 21, 2.
srótas, stream, I, 95, 10[1].
svá: tanvà*h* k*rin*vata svấ*h*, I, 72, 5[3]; svásya-iva, conj. suyávasâ-iva, II, 4, 4[1].
sva*h*-d*ris*, of sun-like aspect, I, 44, 9; III, 2, 14; V, 26, 2.
svà*h*-nara, the solar hero, II, 2, 1;—realm of the Sun, V, 18, 4.
svà*h*-vat, together with the sun, I, 59, 4; V, 2, 11.
sva*h*-víd, finding the sun, I, 96, 4; III, 3, 5; 10; 26, 1.

svá-gûrta, delightful by their own nature, I, 140, 13.
svá-*g*enya, noble by his own nature, V, 7, 5.
svá-tavat, self-strong, IV, 2, 6.
svad, to taste: svadante, II, 1, 14; asvadayat, II, 4, 7;—to make relishable, savoury: sisvadat, I, 188, 10; svada, III, 14, 7.
svá-dharman, following his own ordinances, III, 21, 2.
svadhấ, inherent power: svadhấbhi*h*, by one's self, by the power of his own nature, I, 95, 4; III, 26, 8; svadhấyâ, according to their wont, II, 3, 8; III, 4, 7; by himself, III, 17, 5; by his own power, IV, 13, 5;—svadhấ*h* adhayat, he drank the draughts, I, 144, 2[2].
svadhấ-vat, self-dependent, I, 36, 12; 144, 7; 147, 2; III, 20, 3; IV, 5, 2; 10, 6; 12, 3; V, 3, 2; 5; moving according to one's wont, I, 95, 1[2]; moving by his own strength, I, 95, 4.
svá-dhiti, axe, III, 2, 10; 8, 6; 11; V, 7, 8[1].
svan, to resound: svânît, II, 4, 6.
svaná, noise, I, 94, 11.
sva-patyá, a man's own dominion: sva-patyấni (conj. for su-apatyấni), I, 72, 9[2].
sváya*s*a*h*-tara, highly brilliant by oneself, V, 17, 2[1],[3].
svá-ya*s*as, endowed with his own splendour, I, 95, 2; 5; 9.
sva-yú, free, II, 4, 7.
svár, sun, or Sun: sûra*h* ná sam-d*ri*k, I, 66, 1; svà*h* d*ris*îke, I, 66, 10[3]; 69, 10; svà*h* (loc.), I, 70, 8[1]; 9[1]; svà*h* vividu*h*, I, 71, 2; svà*h* ná, I, 148, 1; II, 2, 7; 8; 10; 8, 4; svà*h* mahát, III, 2, 7; sûré, IV, 3, 8; âví*h* svà*h* abhavat, IV, 3, 11[3]; sûra*h* vár*n*ena, IV, 5, 13; svà*h* ná *g*yóti*h*, IV, 10, 3[1]; ávindat gấ*h* apá*h* svá*h*, V, 14, 4[1].
sva-rấ*g*, king, I, 36, 7.
sva-rấ*g*ya, royalty, II, 8, 5[2].
sváru, sacrificial post, III, 8, 6[1]; 9; 10; IV, 6, 3.
svar*n*ri, sun-hero: svar*n*a*h* (?), (I, 70, 9[1]).
svártha, see su-ártha.
svásara, fold, II, 2, 2.
svás*ri*, sister, I, 65, 7; II, 5, 6[1]; svásâra*h*, I, 71, 1[2]; tisrá*h*, II, 5, 5[1]; dá*s*a, III, 29, 13[2]; dví*h* pá*ñk*a, IV, 6, 8[1]; apási svás*rîn*âm, III, 1, 3[3]; 11.
svastí, happiness, welfare, I, 1, 9, &c.; svastí-bhi*h*, safely, I, 189, 2;—with welfare, happily, II, 9, 6; IV, 11, 6; V, 4, 11.
svấdana, sweetener, V, 7, 6.
svâdu-kshádman, having sweet food, I, 31, 15.
svấdman, sweetness, I, 69, 3[1].
svâná, roaring, V, 2, 10; 25, 8;—thundering, V, 10, 5.
svânín, tumultuous, III, 26, 5.
svấhâ, the word Svâhâ, I, 13, 12; III, 4, 11; V, 5, 11; svấhâ havyám kartana, pronounce the Svâhâ over the offering, I, 142, 12.
svấhâ-k*ri*ta, (offerings) over which the Svâhâ has been pronounced, I, 142, 13; II, 3, 11.
svấhâ-k*ri*ti, pronouncing Svâhâ, I, 188, 11.
svid, to sweat: sisvidâná*h*, IV, 2, 6.
svéda, sweat, V, 7, 5.

ha*m*sá, swan, I, 65, 9; III, 8, 9.
han, to kill, slay: há*m*si, I, 31, 6; *g*ígh*â*msata*h*, I, 36, 15; áhan (without an object), I, 69, 8[1];—ví *g*ahi, smite, I, 36, 16.
har: háryamâ*n*a, longed for, III, 6, 4;—práti harya, accept graciously, I, 144, 7; práti háryâ*h*, thou acceptest, V, 2, 11.
hári, golden, I, 95, 1;—bay horse, fallow steed: hári-bhyâm, I, 76, 3; IV, 15, 7[1]; hárî íti, IV, 15, 8; V, 27, 2.
hári-ke*s*a, whose hair is golden, III, 2, 13.
harít, pl., the golden horses, IV, 6, 9[1]; harítа*h* saptá yahví*h*, the seven young fallow mares, IV, 13, 3.
hári-vrata, whose every law is golden, III, 3, 5[1].
haryatá, delightful, III, 5, 3.
háva, invocation, I, 45, 3.
havi*h*-ádya, eating the oblation, V, 1, 11; 4, 4.
havi*h*-k*ri*t, preparer of the sacrificial food, I, 13, 3.

havi*h*-dắ, giver of offerings, IV, 3, 7[1].
havi*h*-pati, master of sacrificial food, I, 12, 8.
havi*h*-vắh, bearer of oblations, I, 72, 7.
havís, sacrificial food, I, 12, 10, &c.
havíshmat, rich in sacrificial food, offering sacrificial food, I, 12, 9, &c.; I, 128, 2[2].
hávîman, invocation, I, 12, 2.
hávya, to be proclaimed: bhága*h* ná hávya*h*, I, 144, 3[3];—to be invoked, III, 5, 3; V, 17, 4.
havyá, sacrificial food: havyắya vó*l*have, I, 45, 6;—I, 74, 4, &c.
havyá-dâti, giver of offerings, III, 2, 8;—gift of offerings, IV, 8, 5; V, 26, 4.
havya-vắh, bearer of oblations, carrier of offerings, I, 12, 2; 6; 44, 8; 67, 2; 128, 8; III, 2, 2; 5, 10; 10, 9; 11, 2; 17, 4; 27, 5; 29, 7; IV, 8, 1; V, 4, 2; 6, 5; 28, 5.
havya-vắhana, carrier of oblations, I, 36, 10; 44, 2; 5; V, 8, 6; 11, 4; 25, 4; 28, 6; devébhya*h* havya-vâhana, III, 9, 6[1].
haskart*r*í, producing joy, IV, 7, 3.
hâ, to give (up to): *g*ahâti, I, 95, 7.
hâ: ut-*g*íhânâ*h*, flying up, V, 1, 1.
hi, to incite, stir up: hinvatu, I, 27, 11; hinuhi, I, 143, 4; hinvanti, I, 144, 5; hiyâná, driven forward, II, 4, 4; hinvé, he speeds along, IV, 7, 11; hinvire, they drive forward, V, 6, 6;—sám ahema (conj. for sám mahema), we have sent forward, I, 94, 1[1].
hitá-mitra, who has made himself (valiant) friends, I, 73, 3[2].
híra*n*ya, gold, IV, 10, 6.
híra*n*ya-ke*s*a, golden-haired, I, 79, 1.
híra*n*ya-danta, gold-toothed, V, 2, 3.
hira*n*yáya, golden: hira*n*yáyî íti, I, 144, 6.
híra*n*ya-ratha, with the golden chariot, IV, 1, 8.
híra*n*ya-rûpa, golden-coloured, IV, 3, 1.
hiri-*s*iprá, with golden jaws, II, 2, 5[1].
híri-*s*ma*s*ru, golden-bearded, V, 7, 7.
hu, to offer, sacrifice: hûyate, I, 26, 6, &c.; *g*uhure, II, 9, 3;—ắ-huta*h*, worshipped by offerings, into whom offerings are poured, I, 36, 8, &c.; II, 7, 4[1]; 5; III, 24, 3, &c.; â-*g*úhvâna*h*, receiving libations, I, 188, 3; ắ *g*uhota, with Acc., make offerings in, III, 9, 8.
hurás, on a crooked way, IV, 3, 13.
h*ri*, to take: vi-háran, spreading out, IV, 13, 4.
h*ri*, to be angry: h*rin*îyámâna*h*, V, 2, 8.
h*r*íd, heart, mind, I, 60, 3, &c.
h*r*idi-sp*r*í*s*, touching the heart, IV, 10, 1[3].
h*ri*sh: hárshat, joyous, I, 127, 6;—ut-harsháyanti, they delight, V, 27, 5.
h*r*íshîvat, joyful, I, 127, 6.
hé*l*as, anger, I, 94, 12[1]; IV, 1, 4.
hemyắ-vat, well-impelled, IV, 2, 8[1].
heshá-kratu, hot-spirited, III, 26, 5[2].
hót*ri*, the Hot*ri* priest, I, 1, 1; 5, &c.; I, 94, 6; II, 9, 1; III, 17, 5; hótârâ daívyâ, I, 13, 8[1]; 142, 8; 188, 7; II, 3, 7; III, 4, 7; V, 5, 7;—saptá hót*ri*-bhi*h*, III, 10, 4.
hot*ri*-vū́rya, election as Hot*ri*, I, 31, 3.
hot*ri*-sádana, the Hot*ri*'s seat, II, 9, 1.
hotrá, service of a Hot*ri*, the Hot*ri*'s office, I, 76, 4; II, 1, 2; III, 17, 2; saptá hotrắ*n*i, III, 4, 5[2].
hotra-vắh, carrier of offerings, V, 26, 7.
hótrâ, oblation, I, 36, 7; II, 2, 8;—Hótrâ Bhâratî, I, 142, 9[2]; II, 1, 11[1];—the Hot*ri*'s work, worship, IV, 2, 10[1].
hotrâ-víd, knowing the art of sacrificial libations, V, 8, 3.
hru, see hv*ri*.
hváras, tricks, V, 20, 2.
hvârá, serpent (?), I, 141, 7[1]; hvâré (conj. hvârám), II, 2, 4[1].
hvâryá? V, 9, 4[1].
hv*ri*: úpa hvárate, he slinks away, I, 141, 1[1];—hrû*n*âná*h*? (IV, 4, 1[2]).
hve, to call, invoke. huvema, I, 127, 2[1]; ihá huve (read ihá hve?), III, 20, 5[1];—váhni*h* âsâ ắ huvé, I, 76, 4, [1,2];—vi-hváyâmahe, we call (thee) in emulation (with other people), I, 36, 13[2].

II. LIST OF THE MORE IMPORTANT PASSAGES QUOTED IN THE NOTES.

RIG-VEDA.

	PAGE
I, 1, 8	260
6, 10	312
10, 2	262
11, 5	400
15, 12	260, 306
19, 3	192
22, 10	122, 156
24, 9	251
26, 10	86
27, 10	327
29, 4	71
30, 7	257
31, 8	224
32, 14	73
33, 4	162
33, 14	408
34, 2	306
34, 3	69
34, 6	28, 272
34, 9	269
34, 10	112
37, 3	305
37, 12	172
38, 13	195
42, 7	257
44, 4	211
47, 1	44
48, 9	359
48, 10	40
51, 3	243
51, 8	183
52, 1	286
52, 6	312
53, 7	63
60, 1	231
61, 3	155, 203
I, 61, 4	110
62, 5	106
62, 9	18
64, 1	203
64, 5	105
64, 9	90, 269
64, 14	19
66, 2	243
66, 4	380
69, 2	65
69, 5	380
70, 7	76
70, 10	78
71, 1	294
71, 3	65
71, 4	174
72	66
72, 5	66
72, 8	66
76, 5	319
80, 4	177
81, 5	257
84, 18	3
88, 3	84
89, 1	134
89, 10	59
92, 3	359
92, 8	101
95, 1	168
95, 3	27
95, 9	150
95, 10	63
96, 3	101
96, 5	168
100, 7	84
100, 16	380

	PAGE
I, 102, 1	122
102, 8	257
104, 4	324
105, 2	78
105, 12	152, 162
105, 14	156
109, 3	121, 122
109, 4	150
111, 1	25
112, 15	35
113, 2	124
113, 3	168
113, 15	359
115, 1	338
116, 1	7
116, 4	312
116, 5	134
116, 6	59
118, 9	59
119, 3	62
119, 10	59
120, 1	79
120, 2	46
122, 14	71
123, 9	250
127, 5	192
128, 1	327
129, 5	98, 133
129, 11	133
130, 3	242
130, 4	132
130, 5	162
130, 6	286, 370
132, 5	223
134, 1	144
134, 5	58
135, 4	133
138, 3	310
139, 1	223
139, 2	35
139, 4	269
142, 7	239
143, 5	97
143, 7	184
144, 1	245
146, 1	207
147, 3	334
148, 1	78
151, 1	152
151, 4	224
152, 6	321
158, 5	368
159, 5	107
163, 4; 5	365
164, 3	314

	PAGE
I, 164, 6	62
164, 35	66
164, 51	117, 144, 250
166, 2	58
166, 11	294
166, 12	84
167, 4	274
168, 6	312
169, 5	265
171, 1	112
171, 2	53
171, 6	112
173, 1	177
173, 6	184
179, 1	81
184, 2	155
184, 4	111
185, 2	58
186, 4	69
186, 10	311
188, 4	224
188, 5	239
II, 1, 1	71
1, 2	111
1, 4	27
1, 11	156
1, 12	91
2, 2	76
2, 3	312
2, 6	319
2, 8	319
3, 9	156
3, 11	143, 238
4, 1	90
5, 1	91, 381
5, 2	168
5, 5	76
5, 7	71
11, 12	71
14, 2	132
14, 11	216
16, 1	214
16, 3	402
17, 4	315
17, 7	145
18, 1	191
19, 7	111
24, 1	210
24, 8	347
24, 15	398
26, 3	272
34, 4	295
35, 2	53
36, 2	294
37, 6	25

	PAGE
II, 39, 1	210
40, 4	156
41, 5	246
III, 1, 6	19
2, 1	122
2, 3	286
2, 5	327
2, 7	286
2, 14	305
3, 4	421
4, 3	223
4, 10	201
5, 6	134
5, 8	118
6, 1	161, 224
6, 2	168
6, 6	319
6, 7	224, 272
6, 9	201
6, 10	269
7, 1	225
7, 9	25
8, 1; 3; 6; 11	12
8, 10	35
8, 11	12
10, 5	234
11, 8	14
12, 2	210
14, 4	169
15, 2	40
15, 5	223
16, 4	151
18, 2	214
24, 1	254
27, 1	294
27, 3	91, 207
27, 7	161
28, 4	27
29, 3	29, 218
29, 11	10
29, 13	76
29, 14	260
30, 7	134
30, 11	272
30, 13	123
30, 15	29
31, 1	323
31, 1-5	80
31, 16	225
34, 3	246
38, 1	286
39, 1	155
43, 1	269
43, 5	30
49, 4	5, 41

	PAGE
III, 53, 16	380
54, 3	48
54, 19	113
54, 22	376
55, 3	223
55, 4	78
55, 6	25
55, 11	76
55, 12	226
55, 21	90
56, 5	312
56, 7	81
56, 8	312
58, 7	44
58, 9	144
59, 2	65
61, 3	162
62, 3	156
IV, 1, 4	112
1, 5	40
1, 6	383
1, 9	365
1, 11	106, 329
1, 12	329
1, 12 seq.	80
2, 3	246
2, 5	91
2, 9	274
2, 15	314
4, 15	210
5, 1	44, 50
5, 7	242, 243
5, 8	242
5, 10	145
5, 11	105
5, 13	152
6, 3	255, 280
6, 8	76
6, 9	319
6, 11	27, 373
7, 4	78
7, 7	171, 243
7, 9	48
7, 10	133
7, 11	295
9, 6	78
11, 6	254
14, 2	80
15, 6	118
16, 4	315
16, 15	204
17, 14	106, 312
17, 18	298
18, 4	59
19, 8	272

	PAGE
IV, 19, 10	69
20, 4	329
23, 4	105, 394
23, 8	65, 77, 171
23, 10	322
24, 3	84
29, 3	116
33, 3	19
33, 10	204
34, 9	86
35, 3	191
36, 3	151
37, 3	134
37, 5	411
37, 7	390
40, 2	357
42, 1	65
44, 2	79
50, 4	243
50, 11	71
51, 4	243
52, 2; 3	314
54, 3	355
55, 5	210
V, 1, 4	59
1, 10	73
3, 4	342
3, 6	27
4, 4	127
6, 9	226
7, 2	132
7, 6	68
11, 4	73, 78
12, 2	63
12, 3	105
14, 3	3
21, 4	243, 345
25, 1	136
28, 1	3, 224
29, 15	370
30, 10	400
30, 14	381
31, 1	323
31, 11	112
34, 6	394
42, 13	53
42, 17	226
43, 7	224
44, 1	184
45, 2	314
47, 5	226
48, 4	383
53, 11	295
53, 16	140
56, 2	411
V, 56, 6	87
57, 2	29
57, 5	65
58, 6	25
59, 8	25
64, 2	136
68, 1	234
68, 3	216
70, 4	330
76, 1	255
83, 1	105
VI, 1, 2	400
1, 9	26
2, 8	381, 388
2, 9	388
3, 5	139
4, 5	158
5, 2	262
5, 4	214
6, 2	214
6, 6	178
8, 1	27, 149
8, 7	159
10, 2	383
11, 2	98
11, 4	328
12, 2	328
13, 1	270
15, 5	305
16, 2	25
16, 9	98
16, 15	35
16, 22	267
16, 27	71
16, 42	90
16, 46	327
17, 15	210
19, 3	123, 323
19, 4	400
19, 10	216
20, 5	93
20, 11	36
21, 4	97
21, 12	272
24, 2	190
27, 7	361
31, 3	69
34, 1	270
35, 5	184, 185
37, 3	46
38, 4	72
39, 4	272
45, 14	111
46, 10	274
46, 12	400

	PAGE
VI, 47, 16	319
48, 4	25
48, 5	71, 189
48, 21	84
51, 2	27, 205, 322
51, 8	251
59, 8	274
59, 9	107, 216
61, 1	84
61, 2	203
61, 7	192
63, 4	341
64, 2	359
66, 1	329
66, 5	112
67, 10	134
68, 9	95
70, 1	127
70, 4	3
71, 6	190
VII, 1, 21	272
2, 3	218
2, 5	239
2, 6	200
2, 7	11
2, 8-11	239
3, 3	214
3, 4	345
3, 5	320
4, 3	58
7, 2	246
9, 3	63, 118
9, 5	40
10, 5	72
11, 1	50
16, 9	98
17, 4	210
18, 2	81
18, 18	84
18, 25	274
22, 8	46
24, 5	135, 286
31, 11	203
32, 27	184, 185
36, 1	105
36, 6	226
38, 8	408
39, 1	238
39, 3	373
40, 3	18
42, 1	177, 200
42, 4	90
43, 2	238
43, 4	63
43, 5	411

	PAGE
VII, 48, 3	71
51, 3	200
56, 4	116
56, 6	294
56, 16	320
57, 4	355
58, 5	112
59, 2	97
61, 5	116
63, 2	286
66, 10	205
66, 11	27, 208
77, 2	314
77, 3	59
82, 4	216
82, 5	159
83, 5	216
83, 9	203
86, 7	312
87, 3	101
87, 4	314
90, 5	79
91, 2	4
91, 3	86
95, 4	411
96, 1	203
97, 4	257
97, 9	71, 203
97, 10	216
98, 2	222
101, 1	105, 260
104, 21	132
VIII, 1, 29	258
5, 16	35
5, 21	196
5, 25	35
5, 33	43
6, 24	381
7, 30	107
8, 22	203
12, 11	225
12, 32	161
13, 1	225
13, 6	207
13, 14	154
15, 10	86
17, 15	404
19, 1	140
19, 2	299
19, 4	257
19, 22	212
19, 31	41, 106
21, 2; 9	257
22, 12	174
23, 23	171

	PAGE
VIII, 23, 28	84
24, 1	320
24, 14	152
25, 5	123
26, 13	272
27, 10	190
31, 9	274
31, 14	204
32, 10	123, 278
35, 19	44
38, 2	265
39, 1	201
39, 2	71
39, 9	210
40, 1	133
41, 3	208
41, 10	62
43, 2	53
43, 31	258
44, 19	260
47, 16	406
49, 2	56
50, 2	56
50, 8	183
51, 4	242, 295
52, 8	280
53, 6	225
59, 6	158
60, 3	132
61, 7	210
67, 3	191
71, 12	255
71, 15	136
72, 3	243, 327, 404
73, 12	190
74, 6	3
76, 9	44
76, 12	212
82, 3	97
84, 1	195
84, 4	97
87, 4	156
88, 1	195
96, 10	203
96, 13	93
98, 6	183
101, 16	19
102, 11	258
102, 12	361
102, 22	40
103, 7	118, 171
103, 8	35
103, 13	29
IX, 5, 3	3
5, 10	12

	PAGE
IX, 8, 4	162
11, 5	150
12, 9	380
15, 8	162
16, 6	353
18, 4	140
19, 1	216
22, 3	234
33, 5	362
38, 5	362
39, 2	146
40, 2	246
43, 5	286
47, 4	118
50, 1	41
53, 2	210
59, 2	122
62, 17	225
63, 11	106
64, 10	207
65, 12	234
66, 1	3
67, 12	383
68, 3	312
68, 8	200
69, 5	264
70, 3	245
71, 1; 3	264
71, 3	234
71, 5	111
71, 7	272
73, 6	313
74, 1	404
74, 4	264
75, 3	161, 180
76, 4	65, 77
81, 1	314
82, 2	286
83, 5	264
85, 5	286
85, 11	324
86, 3	286
86, 4	139
86, 14	264
87, 1	312, 365
87, 2	90
92, 5	183
93, 1	162
96, 10	93
96, 20	286
97, 21	264
97, 34	65, 77
97, 48	90
97, 57	162
98, 1	410

	PAGE
IX, 100, 3	216
102, 1; 8	323
103, 3	225
106, 14	210
107, 18	344
111, 2	65, 77
111, 3	116, 127
X, 1, 2	78
2, 6	136
3, 2	225 seq.
3, 3	98
4, 3	162
4, 7	134
5, 1	408
6, 1	136
7, 5	171
8, 1	150
8, 2	306
9, 1	224
11, 5	196, 204
11, 6	234
12, 3	338
13, 3	242
14, 10; 11	29
15, 6	355
16, 5	225
17, 2	122
21, 1	258
22, 2	390
23, 7	80
26, 4	149
27, 4	184, 185
27, 7	402
27, 13	224
30, 6	122
31, 5	124
31, 7	272
32, 6	370
33, 2	254
33, 7	36
39, 4	19
39, 10	59
39, 14	58, 272
40, 2	100
41, 1	203
44, 1	86
44, 4	48
45, 1	189
45, 2	78
45, 10	59
46, 2	204
46, 8	171
46, 10	226
47, 6	243
47, 7	155, 245
X, 48, 2	384
49, 6	36
50, 1	267
52, 6	258
53, 1	200
53, 2	3, 73
53, 3	225
53, 6	43
61, 4	398
61, 7	80
61, 8	79
61, 13	323
61, 14	73
61, 21	165
63, 5	231
63, 8	251
64, 4	203
64, 11	163
64, 15	417
65	250
65, 6	250
65, 8	250
65, 10	11, 218
66, 12	224
66, 13	11
67, 1	242
70, 7	11
70, 10	12
73, 5	35
74, 3	324
76, 3	69
79, 2	270
79, 3	242, 243
79, 5	345
80, 4	78
80, 7	203
81, 1	264
82, 6	62
83, 4	414
84, 7	216
85, 18	116
85, 19	27
85, 23	424
87, 9	224
87, 18	20
87, 20	214
89, 7	132
89, 10	274
89, 11	267
90, 15	85
91, 1	191
91, 7	345
91, 10	189
92, 1	196
93, 4	106

	PAGE		PAGE
X, 93, 6	177	X, 118, 5	257
93, 10	19	119, 13	257
94, 7; 8	314	121, 2	151
94, 11	77	122, 3	380
96, 10	286	122, 4	392
97, 1	144	123, 4	65
99, 6	234	125, 1	200
100, 8	417	126, 8	355
101, 7	58, 380	132, 5	90
103, 3	29	133, 3	71
104, 8	330	138, 6	27
106, 5	320	139, 2	90
108, 3	90	139, 3	124
108, 7	339	147, 1	69
110	180	148, 3	71, 421
110, 3	238	150, 1	257
110, 4	224	159, 5	19 seq.
110, 9	238	164, 3	93
110, 10	180	168, 3	306
113, 8	345	172, 1	145
114, 9	207	172, 1; 4	250
115, 3	98	172, 2	267
115, 8; 9	35	176, 3	94
118, 3	3	190, 2	27

ATHARVA-VEDA.

IV, 1, 2	195	XI, 2, 13	168
V, 4, 3	11	7, 5	295
28, 7	11	XII, 2, 45	376
VI, 43, 3	30	4, 6; 12; 26	20
VII, 90, 3	408	XV, 12, 6; 10	20
VIII, 2, 7	353	XIX, 39, 6–8	11

VÂ*G*ASANEYI-SA*M*HITÂ.

V, 17	224	XX, 44	328
VI, 26	121	XXII, 2	171
35	121	XXIII, 57	27
IX, 4	369	XXVIII, 7	11
XVII, 54	254	XXXVIII, 20	411

MAITRÂYA*N*ÎYA-SA*M*HITÂ.

II, 4, 2 333

TAITTIRÎYA-SA*M*HITÂ.

I, 3, 6, 1	12, 254	III, 1, 6, 2	369
5, 3, 2	168	IV, 1, 8, 3	156
6, 6, 1	20	2, 4, 2	286
7, 8, 2	408	V, 7, 8, 1	295
II, 4, 11, 4	20		

AITAREYA-BRÂHMA*N*A.

	PAGE
II, 2	253
40	267
III, 34	80
VII, 34	361

*S*ATAPATHA-BRÂHMA*N*A.

I, 6, 3, 38	86
7, 4, 4	80
II, 1, 1, 8	306
4, 4, 4	361
III, 4, 1, 20	304 seq.
4, 1, 21	306
9, 4, 18	121
IV, 6, 6, 5	189
VII, 1, 1, 22 seq.	285
XII, 4, 4, 2	386
5, 2, 15	144
XIV, 3, 1, 9	411
9, 4, 3	19

TAITTIRÎYA-BRÂHMA*N*A.

I, 2, 1, 13	305
2, 1, 20	376
III, 7, 3, 5	386

PA*Ñ**K*AVI*M**S*A-BRÂHMA*N*A.

XIII, 3, 12	368
XXV, 7, 4	180

TAITTIRÎYA-ÂRA*N*YAKA.

IV, 11, 4	411
23	93
V, 9, 7	411

Â*S*VALÂYANA-*S*RAUTASÛTRA.

III 1, 8 seq.	253
4, 1	284
12, 4	5
IV, 8, 20	286
V, 7, 3	197
XII, 11, 1	102

*S*ÂṄKHÂYANA-*S*RAUTASÛTRA.

V, 15, 2 seq.	253
VIII, 16	267
VIII, 21	20

KÂTYÂYANA-*S*RAUTASÛTRA.

IV, 8, 16	306
VI, 3, 17	255
IX, 8, 8 seq.	189
IX, 8, 11	189
XII, 6, 10	44
XXIV, 3, 42	44

*S*ÂṄKHÂYANA-G*R*IHYASÛTRA.

II, 2, 1	200
V, 5, 4	5

MANU.

VIII, 44	168

MAHÂBHÂRATA.

XIV, 280	224

TRANSLITERATION OF ORIENTAL ALPHABETS ADOPTED FOR THE TRANSLATIONS OF THE SACRED BOOKS OF THE EAST.

CONSONANTS.	MISSIONARY ALPHABET.			Sanskrit.	Zend.	Pehlevi.	Persian.	Arabic.	Hebrew.	Chinese.
	I Class.	II Class.	III Class.							
Gutturales.										
1 Tenuis	k	...	....	क	𐬐	[illegible]	ک	ک	כּ	k
2 " aspirata	kh	...	....	ख	𐬑	[illegible]	...	...	כ	kh
3 Media	g	...	....	ग	𐬔	[illegible]	گ	...	גּ	...
4 " aspirata	gh	...	....	घ	𐬖	[illegible]	...	...	ג	...
5 Gutturo-labialis	q	...	....	...	....	...	ق	ق	ק	...
6 Nasalis	ṅ (ng)	...	....	ङ	{ 𐬣 (ng) / 𐬢 (N) }	...	...	...	...	...
7 Spiritus asper	h	...	....	ह	𐬵 (𐬓 *hv*)	[illegible]	ه	ه	ה	h, hs
8 " lenis	'	...	....	...	....	...	ا	ا	א	...
9 " asper faucalis	‘h	...	....	...	....	...	ح	ح	ח	...
10 " lenis faucalis	’h	...	....	...	....	...	ع	ع	ע	...
11 " asper fricatus	...	‘*h*	....	...	....	...	خ	خ	ח	...
12 " lenis fricatus	...	’*h*	....	...	....	...	...	...	...	...
Gutturales modificatae (palatales, &c.)										
13 Tenuis	...	*k*	....	च	𐬗	[illegible]	چ	...	...	*k*
14 " aspirata	...	*kh*	....	छ	....	...	...	...	...	*kh*
15 Media	...	*g*	....	ज	𐬘	[illegible]	ج	ج	...	...
16 " aspirata	...	*gh*	....	झ	....	...	غ	غ	...	...
17 " Nasalis	...	*ñ*	....	ञ	....	...	...	...	...	...

CONSONANTS (*continued*).	MISSIONARY ALPHABET. I Class.	II Class.	III Class.	Sanskrit.	Zend.	Pehlevi.	Persian.	Arabic.	Hebrew.	Chinese.
18 Semivocalis	y	. . .	. . . .	य	[illegible] [illegible] [illegible] } init.	[illegible]	ي	ي	י	y
19 Spiritus asper	. . .	(ẏ)	. . . .	. . .	. . . .	. . .	. . .	. . .	. . .	. . .
20 ,, lenis	. . .	(ẏ̓)	. . . .	. . .	. . . .	. . .	. . .	. . .	. . .	. . .
21 ,, asper assibilatus . .	. . .	*ś*	. . . .	श	[illegible]	[illegible]	ش	ش	. . .	. . .
22 ,, lenis assibilatus . .	. . .	*ź*	. . . .	. . .	[illegible]	[illegible]	ژ	. . .	. . .	*ź*
Dentales.										
23 Tenuis	t	. . .	. . . .	त	[illegible]	[illegible]	ت	ت	תּ	t
24 ,, aspirata	th	. . .	. . . .	थ	[illegible]	. . .	. . .	. . .	ת	th
25 ,, assibilata	. . .	. . .	TH	. . .	. . . .	. . .	ث	ث	. . .	. . .
26 Media	d	. . .	. . . .	द	[illegible]	[illegible]	د	د	דּ	. . .
27 ,, aspirata	dh	. . .	. . . .	ध	[illegible]	. . .	. . .	. . .	ד	. . .
28 ,, assibilata	. . .	. . .	DH	. . .	. . . .	. . .	ذ	ذ	. . .	. . .
29 Nasalis	n	. . .	. . . .	न	[illegible]	[illegible]	ن	ن	נ	n
30 Semivocalis	l	. . .	. . . .	ल	. . . .	[illegible]	ل	ل	ל	l
31 ,, mollis 1	. . .	*l*	. . . .	ळ	. . . .	. . .	. . .	. . .	. . .	. . .
32 ,, mollis 2	. . .	. . .	L	. . .	. . . .	. . .	. . .	. . .	. . .	. . .
33 Spiritus asper 1	s	. . .	. . . .	स	[illegible]	[illegible]	س(ث)	س	שׂ	s
34 ,, asper 2	. . .	. . .	s (ʃ)	. . .	. . . .	. . .	. . .	. . .	ס	. . .
35 ,, lenis	z	. . .	. . . .	. . .	[illegible]	[illegible]	ز (ذ)	ز	ז	z
36 ,, asperrimus 1	. .	. . .	z (ʒ)	. . .	. . . .	. . .	ص	ص	צ	ʒ, ʒh
37 ,, asperrimus 2	. . .	. . .	ẓ (ʒ)	. . .	. . . .	. . .	ض	. . .	. . .	. . .

TRANSLITERATION OF ORIENTAL ALPHABETS ADOPTED FOR THE TRANSLATIONS OF THE SACRED BOOKS OF THE EAST.

CONSONANTS.	MISSIONARY ALPHABET. I Class.	II Class.	III Class.	Sanskrit.	Zend.	Pehlevi.	Persian.	Arabic.	Hebrew.	Chinese.
Gutturales.										
1 Tenuis	k	...	....	क	𐬐	[Pehlevi character]	ک	ک	כּ	k
2 „ aspirata	kh	...	....	ख	𐬑	[Pehlevi character]	...	...	כ	kh
3 Media	g	...	....	ग	𐬔	[Pehlevi character]	گ	...	גּ	...
4 „ aspirata	gh	...	....	घ	𐬖	[Pehlevi character]	...	...	ג	...
5 Gutturo-labialis	q	...	....	...	....	...	ق	ق	ק	...
6 Nasalis	ṅ (ng)	...	....	ङ	𐬧 (ng), 𐬣 (N)	...	...	...	...	...
7 Spiritus asper	h	...	....	ह	𐬵 (𐬓 *hv*)	[Pehlevi character]	ه	ه	ה	h, hs
8 „ lenis	’	...	....	...	....	...	ا	ا	א	...
9 „ asper faucalis	‘h	...	....	...	....	...	ح	ح	ח	...
10 „ lenis faucalis	’h	...	....	...	....	...	ع	ع	ע	...
11 „ asper fricatus	...	‘*h*	....	...	....	...	خ	خ	ח	...
12 „ lenis fricatus	...	’*h*	....	...	....	...	...	...	...	...
Gutturales modificatae (palatales, &c.)										
13 Tenuis	...	*k*	....	च	𐬗	[Pehlevi character]	چ	...	...	*k*
14 „ aspirata	...	*kh*	....	छ	....	...	...	...	...	*kh*
15 Media	...	*g*	....	ज	𐬘	[Pehlevi character]	ج	ج	...	...
16 „ aspirata	...	*gh*	....	झ	....	...	غ	غ	...	...
17 „ Nasalis	...	*ñ*	....	ञ	....	...	...	...	...	...

CONSONANTS (*continued*).	MISSIONARY ALPHABET. I Class.	II Class.	III Class.	Sanskrit.	Zend.	Pehlevi.	Persian.	Arabic.	Hebrew.	Chinese.
18 Semivocalis	y	. . .	. . . .	य	𐬫, 𐬌𐬌 } init.	[illegible]	ي	ي	י	y
19 Spiritus asper	. . .	(y̔)	. . . .	. . .	. . . .	. . .	. . .	. . .	. . .	. . .
20 „ lenis	. . .	(y̓)	. . . .	. . .	. . . .	. . .	. . .	. . .	. . .	. . .
21 „ asper assibilatus . .	. . .	*s*	. . . .	श	𐬱	[illegible]	ش	ش	. . .	. . .
22 „ lenis assibilatus . .	. . .	*z*	. . . .	. . .	𐬲	[illegible]	ژ	. . .	. . .	*z*
Dentales.										
23 Tenuis	t	. . .	. . . .	त	𐬙	[illegible]	ت	ت	תּ	t
24 „ aspirata	th	. . .	. . . .	थ	𐬚	. . .	. . .	. . .	ת	th
25 „ assibilata	. . .	. . .	TH	. . .	. . . .	. . .	ث	ث	. . .	. . .
26 Media	d	. . .	. . . .	द	𐬛	[illegible]	د	د	דּ	. . .
27 „ aspirata	dh	. . .	. . . .	ध	𐬜	. . .	. . .	. . .	ד	. . .
28 „ assibilata	. . .	. . .	DH	. . .	. . . .	. . .	ذ	ذ	. . .	. . .
29 Nasalis	n	. . .	. . . .	न	𐬥	[illegible]	ن	ن	נ	n
30 Semivocalis	l	. . .	. . . .	ल	. . . .	[illegible]	ل	ل	ל	l
31 „ mollis 1	. . .	*l*	. . . .	ळ	. . . .	. . .	. . .	. . .	. . .	. . .
32 „ mollis 2	. . .	. . .	L	. . .	. . . .	. . .	. . .	. . .	. . .	. . .
33 Spiritus asper 1	s	. . .	. . . .	स	𐬯	[illegible]	س (ث)	س	שׂ	s
34 „ asper 2	. . .	. . .	s (ʃ)	. . .	. . . .	. . .	. . .	. . .	ס	. . .
35 „ lenis	z	. . .	. . . .	. . .	𐬰	[illegible]	ز (ذ)	ز	ז	z
36 „ asperrimus 1	. .	. . .	z (ʒ)	. . .	. . . .	. . .	ص	ص	צ	ʒ, ʒh
37 „ asperrimus 2	. . .	. . .	ẓ (ʒ̣)	. . .	. . . .	. . .	ض	. . .	. . .	. . .

Dentales modificatae (linguales, &c.)										
38 Tenuis	...	*t*	...	ट	...	...	ط	ط	ט	...
39 „ aspirata	...	*th*	...	ठ	...	...	ظ	ظ	...	...
40 Media	...	*d*	...	ड	[illegible]	[illegible]	...	...	...	...
41 „ aspirata	...	*dh*	...	ढ	...	...	...	ض	...	...
42 Nasalis	...	*n*	...	ण	[illegible]	...	...	...	...	...
43 Semivocalis	r	...	...	र	[illegible]	[illegible]	ر	ر	ר	...
44 „ fricata	...	*r*	...	...	...	...	...	...	...	*r*
45 „ diacritica	...	...	R	...	...	...	...	...	...	...
46 Spiritus asper	sh	...	...	ष	[illegible]	[illegible]	...	...	...	sh
47 „ lenis	zh	...	...	...	...	...	...	...	...	...
Labiales.										
48 Tenuis	p	...	...	प	[illegible]	[illegible]	پ	...	פּ	p
49 „ aspirata	ph	...	...	फ	...	...	...	...	פ	ph
50 Media	b	...	...	ब	[illegible]	[illegible]	ب	ب	בּ	...
51 „ aspirata	bh	...	...	भ	...	...	...	...	ב	...
52 Tenuissima	...	*p*	...	...	...	...	...	...	...	...
53 Nasalis	m	...	...	म	[illegible]	[illegible]	م	م	מ	m
54 Semivocalis	w	...	...	...	[illegible]	...	...	...	...	w
55 „ aspirata	hw	...	...	...	...	...	...	...	...	...
56 Spiritus asper	f	...	...	...	[illegible]	[illegible]	ف	ف	...	f
57 „ lenis	v	...	...	व	»	[illegible]	و	و	ו	...
58 Anusvâra	...	*m*	...	अं	[illegible] ã	...	...	...	...	...
59 Visarga	...	*h*	...	अः	...	...	...	...	...	...

VOWELS.	MISSIONARY ALPHABET. I Class.	II Class.	III Class.	Sanskrit.	Zend.	Pehlevi.	Persian.	Arabic.	Hebrew.	Chinese.
1 Neutralis	0	...	...	...	...	...	...	...	ֲ	ă
2 Laryngo-palatalis	ĕ	...	...	...	...	...	...	...	...	...
3 „ labialis	ŏ	...	...	...	...	𐭠 fin.	...	...	...	...
4 Gutturalis brevis	a	...	...	अ	𐬀	𐭠 init.	ـَ	ـَ	ַ	a
5 „ longa	â	(*a*)	...	आ	𐬁	𐭠	ـَا	ـَا	ָ	â
6 Palatalis brevis	i	...	...	इ	𐬌	...	ـِ	ـِ	ִ	i
7 „ longa	î	(*i*)	...	ई	𐬍	𐭩	ـِي	ـِي	ִי	î
8 Dentalis brevis	*li*	...	...	ऌ	...	...	...	...	...	...
9 „ longa	*lî*	...	...	ॡ	...	...	...	...	...	...
10 Lingualis brevis	*ri*	...	...	ऋ	...	...	...	...	...	...
11 „ longa	*rî*	...	...	ॠ	...	...	...	...	...	...
12 Labialis brevis	u	...	...	उ	𐬎	...	ـُ	ـُ	ֻ	u
13 „ longa	û	(*u*)	...	ऊ	𐬏	𐭥	ـُو	ـُو	וּ	û
14 Gutturo-palatalis brevis	e	...	...	...	𐬆(e) 𐬈(*e*)	...	...	...	ֶ	e
15 „ longa	ê (ai)	(*e*)	...	ए	𐬉, 𐬇	𐭩	...	...	ֵ	ê
16 Diphthongus gutturo-palatalis	âi	(*ai*)	...	ऐ	...	...	ـَيْ	ـَيْ	...	âi
17 „ „	ei (ĕi)	...	...	...	...	...	...	...	...	ei, êi
18 „ „	oi (ŏu)	...	...	...	...	...	...	...	...	...
19 Gutturo-labialis brevis	o	...	...	...	𐬊	...	...	...	ָ	o
20 „ longa	ô (au)	(*o*)	...	ओ	𐬋	𐭥	...	...	וֹ	...
21 Diphthongus gutturo-labialis	âu	(*au*)	...	औ	𐬆𐬎 (*au*)	...	ـَوْ	ـَوْ	...	âu
22 „ „	eu (ĕu)	...	...	...	...	...	...	...	...	...
23 „ „	ou (ŏu)	...	...	...	...	...	...	...	...	...
24 Gutturalis fracta	ä	...	...	...	...	...	...	...	...	...
25 Palatalis fracta	ï	...	...	...	...	...	...	...	...	...
26 Labialis fracta	ü	...	...	...	...	...	...	...	...	ü
27 Gutturo-labialis fracta	ö	...	...	...	...	...	...	...	...	...